a problem-solving approach

ECONOMICS

fifth edition

Elijah M. James

Dawson College and Concordia University

Prentice Hall Canada Inc., Scarborough, Ontario

DB#1580337

Dedicated to the memory of my father,
the late Newton James, and to the
memory of Darius Simon,
a philosopher and a scholar.

Canadian Cataloguing in Publication Data

James, Elijah M.
    Economics: a problem-solving approach

5th ed.
Includes index.
ISBN 0-13-083438-6

1. Economics. I. Title.

HB171.5J25 2000   330   C00-930055-5

330
.J35
2000

Prentice-Hall, Inc., Upper Saddle River, New Jersey
Prentice-Hall International (UK) Limited, London
Prentice-Hall of Australia, Pty. Limited, Sydney
Prentice-Hall Hispanoamericana, S.A., Mexico City
Prentice-Hall of India Private Limited, New Delhi
Prentice-Hall of Japan, Inc., Tokyo
Simon & Schuster Southeast Asia Private Limited, Singapore
Editora Prentice-Hall do Brasil, Ltda., Rio de Janeiro

ISBN 0-13-083438-6

Publisher: Pat Ferrier
Acquisitions Editor: Sarah Kimball
Associate Editor: Laurie Goebel
Senior Marketing Manager: Ann Byford
Copy Editor: Laurel Sparrow
Production Editor: Sarah Dann

Production Coordinator: Jane Schell
Permissions/Photo Research: Susan Wallace-Cox
Art Director: Mary Opper
Cover Design: Lisa LaPointe
Cover Image: Glenn Ryan
Page Layout: Nelson Gonzalez

1 2 3 4 5   04 03 02 01 00

Printed and bound in Canada.

Visit the Prentice Hall Canada Web site! Send us your comments, browse our catalogues, and more at **www.phcanada.com**. Or reach us through e-mail at **phcinfo_pubcanada@prenhall.com**.

CONTENTS IN BRIEF

Part V   National Income and Employment

Part VI   Money, Banking, and Stabilization Policy

Part VII Other Macroeconomic Issues

DETAILED CONTENTS

PART II   MICROECONOMICS

CHAPTER 8   THEORY OF PRODUCTION   132

CHAPTER 9   THE COSTS OF PRODUCTION   147

CHAPTER 10   THE PURELY COMPETITIVE FIRM   165

CHAPTER 11   THE THEORY OF MONOPOLY   185

CHAPTER 12   IMPERFECT COMPETITION: MONOPOLISTIC COMPETITION AND OLIGOPOLY   208

PART III   INCOME DISTRIBUTION

CHAPTER 13   THE LABOUR MARKET   230

CHAPTER 14   RENT, INTEREST, AND PROFITS   250

CHAPTER 15   INCOME DISTRIBUTION AND POVERTY   261

PART IV   CURRENT ECONOMIC PROBLEMS

CHAPTER 16   THE ECONOMICS OF ENVIRONMENTAL PROTECTION   275

CHAPTER 17   THE AGRICULTURAL SECTOR   286

CHAPTER 18   PUBLIC FINANCE   302

CHAPTER 19   INTERNATIONAL TRADE   322

CHAPTER 20   TARIFFS AND TRADE POLICY ISSUES   335

PART V   NATIONAL INCOME AND EMPLOYMENT

CHAPTER 21   AN OVERVIEW OF MACROECONOMICS   355

CHAPTER 22   NATIONAL INCOME AND PRODUCT ACCOUNTS   368

CHAPTER 23   UNEMPLOYMENT AND INFLATION   389

CHAPTER 24   AGGREGATE DEMAND AND AGGREGATE SUPPLY   408

PART VII   OTHER MACROECONOMIC ISSUES

SPECIAL FEATURES

GLOBAL PERSPECTIVE

APPLICATIONS

PREFACE

Economic times are changing, and economics textbooks should reflect these changes. Few of us teach economics the way we did 20 or even 15 years ago. Not only have the topics selected for inclusion in our courses undergone considerable change, but so has the degree of emphasis placed on various topics. Moreover, students have changed. Technology has placed certain resources at their disposal, like computers, the Internet, VCRs, and the World Wide Web. Economics textbooks should keep up-to-date with these developments.

Amidst all of these changes, the fundamental purpose of the fifth edition of *Economics: A Problem-Solving Approach* has remained the same as for the previous editions: to present introductory economics to students clearly and lucidly, so that they can understand basic economic concepts, theories, and relationships and apply these to their day-to-day lives, and be able to make sense of economic events that are happening in the world around them.

One cannot claim that the fifth edition of *Economics: A Problem-Solving Approach* is an entirely new book, but it is more than just another edition. It builds on the strengths of the fourth edition and introduces several new features. Revisions, additions, extensions, and deletions have been made in order to bring the book up to date. Some important changes have been made to the organizational structure of the book, and the author believes that these are improvements that will help students to better understand how our economic system works.

A focus of this fifth edition is "readability," which has been a hallmark of this text through all its revisions. The author has gone to great lengths and has taken great pains to ensure that students continue to find this book easy to read and understand. The fifth edition of *Economics: A Problem-Solving Approach* reflects the author's philosophy that a good introductory textbook in economics should make this abstract subject comprehensible without avoiding difficult concepts and issues. Here is a truly student-friendly textbook, designed to facilitate students' understanding of economic principles and their use of economic tools to solve real-world economic problems. This has been one of the major objectives of this book.

SUBSTANTIVE CHANGES IN THE FIFTH EDITION

Naturally, the statistics have been updated. In addition, numerous changes have been made throughout, in both the microeconomic and the macroeconomic parts of the book.

Changes to Microeconomics

1. The material in Chapters 1, 2, and 3 of the fourth edition is now contained in Chapters 1 and 3. The material covered under "Some Useful Tools" in Appendix 1A of the fourth edition has been expanded and is now contained in a new Chapter 2.

2. The appendices to Chapters 6 and 8 have been deleted.

3. Chapter 16 has been substantially rewritten and re-worked with new emphasis on pollution.

4. Chapter 17 has been expanded and now includes a discussion of the agri-food industry in Canada.

5. Chapter 20 on Tariffs now contains a more detailed discussion of NAFTA.

Changes to <u>Macroeconomics</u>

1. Chapter 24 now contains a more detailed discussion of aggregate demand and aggregate supply shifters.

2. Chapter 29 on the Foreign Sector has been eliminated and much of the material is now contained in Chapter 36 on Economic Policy in an Open Economy.

3. The material in Chapters 31 to 34 of the fourth edition has been re-arranged into three chapters (Chapters 30, 31, and 32).

4. Chapter 35 of the fourth edition has been dropped and the Rational Expectations Hypothesis is now contained in Chapter 33, with expanded treatment of the natural rate of unemployment and the NAIRU.

5. Chapter 34 on Deficits, Surpluses and the National Debt contains an expanded treatment of surpluses to reflect the Canadian reality.

SPECIAL PEDAGOGICAL AND OTHER FEATURES

1. The fifth edition of *Economics: A Problem-Solving Approach* contains a series of Web sites and Internet exercises that provide an opportunity for students to access information on economics and related topics.

2. Seven new video cases have been written for this fifth edition. They are designed to be used in conjunction with seven specially selected CBC video segments.

3. The surplus has occupied the spot once held by the deficit as a hot macroeconomic issue. It receives greater attention in this fifth edition. The public debt and unemployment continue to receive due emphasis.

4. The international economic environment and global issues continue to exert significant influence on the Canadian economy. New *Global Perspectives* have been written for this fifth edition.

5. The *Applications* feature has been retained, and new applications have been added.

6. The use of practical examples and real statistical data help to make economics come alive, as students are able to relate the theories to their own life experiences. This useful pedagogical feature is retained in this edition.

7. The fifth edition continues to engage the students by using the investigative approach and by appealing to their sense of intuition.

8. Marginal notes and definitions, the highlighting of important terms and concepts throughout the text, Chapter Summaries, and the listing of important terms at the end of each chapter are all important pedagogical devices retained in the fifth edition.

9. The Questions for Review and Discussion provide opportunities for students to test their understanding of the material, and the Problems and Exercises allow students to actually *do* economic analysis.

10. A new feature of the fifth edition is the inclusion of questions for class discussion or group work. This gives students an opportunity to actually practise economics and to discuss issues among themselves.

11. The glossary continues to be one of the most extensive glossaries of any introductory economics text.

12. As in the fourth edition, the judicious use of colour in this fifth edition enhances graphical presentations and emphasizes important points.

13. The tradition of using tabular and graphical analyses to reinforce each other in the presentation of the material continues in this edition.

14. The statistical tables in Appendix I have been updated. Students and instructors both should find this to be very useful and convenient.

TO THE INSTRUCTOR

For instructional purposes, the text is arranged so that any sequence of chapters may be followed. The following outlines are suggestions only. It is expected that instructors will adapt the text according to their own particular needs and preferences.

OUTLINE FOR A ONE-SEMESTER COURSE IN MICROECONOMICS

Chapter	Title
1.	The Nature of Economics
2.	Some Useful Tools
3.	The Economic Problem: The Problem of Scarcity
4.	Elements of Demand and Supply
5.	Elasticity
6.	The Theory of Consumer Behaviour
8.	Theory of Production
9.	The Costs of Production
10.	The Purely Competitive Firm
11.	The Theory of Monopoly
12.	Imperfect Competition: Monopolistic Competition and Oligopoly

Note: Chapters or sections of chapters may be added or deleted according to the instructor's needs. For example, given the importance of international trade to the Canadian economy, instructors may want to include material from Chapters 19 and 20.

OUTLINE FOR A ONE-SEMESTER COURSE IN MACROECONOMICS

Chapter	Title
1.	The Nature of Economics
2.	Some Useful Tools
3.	The Economic Problem: The Problem of Scarcity
4.	Elements of Demand and Supply
21.	An Overview of Macroeconomics
22.	National Income and Product Accounts
23.	Unemployment and Inflation
24.	Aggregate Demand and Aggregate Supply
25.	Equilibrium in the Product Market
26.	Changes in Income and the Multiplier
28.	Fiscal Policy
29.	Business Fluctuations
30.	Money: Its Nature and Functions
32.	Monetary Theory and Policy
33.	Inflation and Anti-Inflation Policies
34.	Deficits, Surpluses, and the National Debt
35.	Balance of Payments and Exchange rates

Note: Chapters or sections of chapters may be added or deleted according to the instructor's needs.

OUTLINE FOR A ONE-SEMESTER COURSE COVERING BOTH MICRO AND MACRO

Note: The instructor may wish to substitute certain chapters for different emphasis or to omit sections of some chapters.

SUPPLEMENTARY MATERIALS

Video segments, a study guide, an instructor's manual, a test bank, transparency masters, and a website have been prepared to accompany *Economics: A Problem-Solving Approach*, Fifth Edition.

Study Guides   A Programmed Learning Guide for each of *Microeconomics* and *Macroeconomics* takes students through a series of programs and exercises designed to enhance their understanding of economics.

Instructor's Manual   The instructor's manual is designed to help the instructor make the best possible use of his or her limited time. It outlines the objectives of each chapter, and provides answers to the questions at the end of the chapters.

Transparency Masters   These are clear and enlarged reproductions of tables, graphs, and charts presented in the text. Instructors using a projector will find these of immense value.

Test Item File   A test item file containing a wide selection of multiple-choice and true or false questions based on *Economics: A Problem-Solving Approach* has been prepared for instructors using the text. The questions have been carefully selected with economic comprehension as the central consideration.

PH Test Manager   The test item file is also available electronically in Windows.

 Videos   Seven new video segments have been selected for use with the cases in the fifth edition of the text.

Companion Website   For the fifth edition, we have added a website to our list of supplements. This site contains an online study guide as well as other valuable resources for students and instructors. Visit the site at **www.prenticehall.ca/james**.

ACKNOWLEDGEMENTS

One of the more pleasurable tasks in writing a book is that the author gets an opportunity to acknowledge the contributions of the many people who have helped to make the book a reality, and to thank them for their part in the project. So, as has been my tradition, I wish to thank the many individuals who have helped to make possible the fifth edition of *Economics: A Problem-Solving Approach*.

I am indebted to my colleagues at Dawson College, John Abbott College, Concordia University, and in colleges and universities across Canada and elsewhere. I thank them for their generosity in sharing their wisdom, experience, and insight with me. Matlub Hussain, Voyo Kovalski, and Mohammed Islam of Dawson College deserve credit for much of the improvement in the fifth edition. I owe a debt of gratitude to Dan Otchere and Alan Hochstein of Concordia University, Charles Reid, June Riley, and Cheryl Jenkins of John Abbott College, Izhar Mirza and Alaka Ganguli of Dawson College, and Sadat Kazi of Vanier College.

I acknowledge, with pleasure, the reviewers of this edition. I am appreciative of the constructive comments and suggestions made by Rene H. Blaise of Southern Alberta Institute of Technology, Tom Chambers of Canadore College, John Farrugia of Mohawk College, James Hnatchuk and John Saba of Champlain Regional College, and Peter Peters of University College of the Cariboo. Many of their suggestions have been incorporated in this fifth edition of the book. My students at Dawson College, John Abbott College, and Concordia University have again forced me to "come clear." I thank them for helping me to make the book easy to read and student-friendly.

I wish again to acknowledge the great debt that I owe to the Prentice Hall team who worked on this project. Their contributions must be registered. I thank Sarah Kimball, Acquisitions Editor; Laurie Goebel, Associate Editor; and Melanie Meharchand and Sarah Dann, Production Editors.

Ms. Constance Patricia Simon has once more demonstrated her unselfishness by sacrificing her time which was particularly scarce during the preparation of this edition. She provided expert secretarial services, and I owe her a tremendous debt of gratitude. Thanks Pat, you are wonderful. I must also thank my dear friend, Veronica Martin, for providing much-needed inspiration while I was working on the manuscript. Veronica, your contribution is much appreciated.

Finally, I must thank my children Ted and Andrea, whose support and encouragement have been forever with me, and my parents for their sacrifice and their love. In a very real sense, they started it all.

Elijah M. James

ABBREVIATIONS

AC	Average cost	LP	Liquidity preference
AD	Aggregate demand	LRAC	Long-run average cost
AE	Aggregate expenditure	M	Imports
AFL-CIO	American Federation of Labour and Congress of Industrial Organization	MC	Marginal cost
		MEI	Marginal efficiency of investment
AO	Aggregate output	M(P)P	Marginal (physical) product
A(P)P	Average (physical) product	MPC	Marginal propensity to consume
APC	Average propensity to consume	MPS	Marginal propensity to save
APS	Average propensity to save	MPW	Marginal propensity to withdraw
AR	Average revenue	MR	Marginal revenue
AS	Aggregate supply	MRP	Marginal revenue product
AFC	Average fixed cost	MTR	Marginal tax rate
ATC	Average total cost	NDI	Net domestic income
AVC	Average variable cost	NI	National income
C	Consumption (personal expenditure on consumer goods and services)	OECD	Organization for Economic Cooperation and Development
CCU	Confederation of Canadian Unions	OPEC	Organization of Petroleum Exporting Countries
CDIC	Canada Deposit Insurance Corporation		
CFL	Canadian Federation of Labour	P	Price or price level
CLC	Canadian Labour Congress	PI	Personal income
CNTU	Confederation of National Trade Unions	Q	Quantity (output)
CPI	Consumer price index	r	Rate of interest
CSD	Centrale des syndicats democratiques	S	Saving
DI	Disposable income	T	Taxes
EB	External balance	TC	Total cost
EC	European Community	TFC	Total fixed cost
G	Government purchases of goods and services	TVC	Total variable cost
		TR	Total revenue
GDP	Gross domestic product	V	Velocity of circulation (of money)
GNP	Gross national product	WHO	World Health Organization
I	Investment	X	Exports
IB	Internal balance	(X–M)	Net exports
K	Capital	Y	Income (output)

CHAPTER 1

THE NATURE OF ECONOMICS

Learning Objectives

After studying this chapter, you should be able to:

1 formulate an adequate definition of economics

2 discuss the subject matter of economics

3 discuss the importance of economics

4 explain what economists do in terms of employ-ment

5 discuss the nature of scientific inquiry

6 explain economic methodology

7 distinguish between positive and normative economics

8 explain why economists sometimes disagree

9 understand relations among variables

10 explain the meaning of economic policy

11 distinguish between microeconomics and macroeconomics

I believe economic understanding is to be gained through an understanding of the central core of economics that dominates all economics situations and issues.

Ben W. Lewis, *"Economic Understanding: Why and What."*

INTRODUCTION

The Supreme Court of Canada recently handed down its decision regarding the unity issue in Canada. This has given rise to a new round of debate over the issue of the "Quebec question." Is this a purely political issue, or does it have economic implications? What will be the impact of Quebec's secession on the economy of Canada? Does the mere threat of separation pose a problem for the Canadian economy? These are important issues.

When the fourth edition of this book was being prepared, the deficit and the debt were major economic concerns. Now, the federal government's budget has shifted from a deficit to a surplus position. At the end of 1997, the value of the Canadian dollar, in terms of the U.S. dollar, was $0.7222. By the end of August 1998, the value of the dollar had fallen to just over $0.63. Some claim that this fall in value is good for the Canadian economy, while others say that it is a disaster. Can there be elements of truth in both views?

A knowledge of economics will help us to understand many of the issues which confront us daily.

The government claims that not much can be done about the falling dollar because its decline is caused by external forces, that is, economic events in Russia and Asia. It seems as if we have been more successful in controlling inflation than in reducing unemployment. Youth unemployment is still high, and many graduates are experiencing considerable difficulty in finding suitable jobs. For many, job prospects are less than optimistic. Whereas inflation has virtually disappeared from the Canadian economy, the unemployment rate is still hovering above eight percent. Why is this so? Listen to the radio, watch television, or pick up a newspaper, and you are bound to see or hear some news relating to the economy. Indeed, economic events are all around us, reminding us of the importance of understanding economics.

There can be little doubt that economic issues occupy a key position in the political arena. Governments are frequently judged by their economic performances, and their chances of reelection are closely correlated with the effects of their economic policies. Clearly then, it is to our benefit to understand economics.

THE SUBJECT MATTER OF ECONOMICS

Consumers, businesses, the various levels of government, and all types of other organizations are always making choices. These choices determine how society uses its resources. If people choose to purchase huge quantities of personal computers and microwave ovens, society's resources will be used to produce these items. If a government chooses to upgrade its highway system and to improve the education and health of its citizens, then resources will be allocated to roads and to education and health services. How do individuals, firms, governments, and other organizations make decisions about the use of society's resources? This question is at the heart of economics.

Economics is the social science that studies how people cope with the ever-present problem of scarcity.

Economists concern themselves with the behaviour of human beings engaged in the activity of using scarce resources to satisfy their unlimited wants. As a science that studies human behaviour, economics belongs in the same category as social psychology, anthropology, sociology, and political science. For our purposes, let us adopt the following definition of economics:

Learning Objective 1: formulate a definition of economics

Economics is the social science that studies how people use scarce resources to satisfy their unlimited wants.

Social science studies aspects of behaviour of human society.

Let us examine certain aspects of this definition. First, note that we have defined economics as a **social science**. This means that it deals with certain aspects of human behaviour within a social framework. Second, the resources with which we are concerned are *scarce* or *limited*, and third, the wants that we seek to satisfy are unlimited. If society had an *unlimited* amount of all resources, and if human wants were limited, we would have a utopia, indeed. But let us return to reality. **Scarcity** of resources is a fact of life, and this is one of the facts with which society must cope.

SCARCITY AND CHOICE

Economics is the study of scarcity.

Learning Objective 2: discuss the subject matter of economics

Economics is concerned with the fact that the means or resources for satisfying human wants are limited. Most of us want more than what we currently have, and collectively, we want more than we can produce with our limited resources. The economist is interested in the use of these scarce resources in a manner that will result in the satisfaction of the most important wants. If resources were unlimited, there would be no need to use them economically. Not much practical point would exist, therefore, for studying economics. But economic problems arise out of the fact that resources are scarce or limited, while wants are unlimited. And the economist must try to find solutions for these problems. We could therefore, as an alternative, define economics as the study of how people cope with the ever-present problem of scarcity.

Because resources are both desirable and scarce, we must choose how we will allocate them among various uses. We will always have to choose between one thing and another when we do not have the means to obtain both. If you won $20 million in a lottery (good luck), and you wanted to buy a car and take a vacation in Europe, you could do both. You would not have to choose either one or the other. So too, if a society could produce all of the goods and services that each member wants, then the problem of choice would not exist. **Choice**, therefore, is a direct result of scarcity. Economics is the study of choice.

Economics is the study of choice.

PROBLEM SOLVING 1-1

Is scarcity a problem for an enormously wealthy woman who can have anything that she wants?

THE IMPORTANCE OF ECONOMICS

Learning Objective 3: discuss the importance of economics

Why should we study economics? The study of economics is important for several reasons, some of which are discussed below.

UNDERSTANDING THE ECONOMY AND SOCIETY

Economics helps us to understand society.

Understanding the operation of our economic system enables us to improve its performance and helps us to deal with many of the problems that face our country. The economy is such an important part of society that it is impossible to understand society without a basic knowledge of economics. Our relationships with one another, our environment, the manner in which our collective wealth is distributed, and the types of work we do are all related to our economic system. Our lives are shaped by the myriad economic decisions that have been made by our ancestors and that are being made today by our contemporaries. A decision to build more war planes instead of spending more money on education and health will affect us not only today, but also for a long time in the future.

The better our understanding of our economy and our society, the better the control that we are likely to have over our destiny. It has been suggested that our grandparents could have avoided the economic catastrophe of the Great Depression of the 1930s if they had had a more thorough understanding of the economic forces at work.

UNDERSTANDING WORLD AFFAIRS

Economics helps us to understand world affairs.

Rapid changes are occurring in the world. Just pick up a newspaper or turn on the radio or television and you will get an idea of the many important changes that are taking place. The Soviet Union no longer exists, the unification of Germany is a reality, there is continuing tension in the Middle East, and the face of Europe has been transformed. The European Community has moved toward a relatively high level of economic integration, and here in Canada, the possible separation of Quebec from the Canadian federation remains an issue of considerable debate and uneasiness. These issues all have economic causes or economic consequences; therefore, an understanding of economics will enhance our understanding of these and other world affairs.

BEING AN INFORMED CITIZEN

Economics helps us to be informed citizens.

As consumers, it is important for us to know how to spend our income so that we can derive maximum satisfaction from our purchases. It is also important for us to use our labour services and other resources wisely. Not only should people be wise consumers, but as citizens in a democracy, they must be able to visualize and evaluate the consequences of different courses of action in order to determine which ones are most likely to lead to improvements in economic and social well-being.

During the federal election of 1988, the dominant issue was the Canada–U.S. free trade agreement — clearly an economic issue. During the 1993 campaign, the issues were NAFTA, unemployment, and the deficit. What should be done about unemployment? What policies should be adopted to deal with the huge deficit? Should Canada pursue a policy of protectionism as a means of supporting its domestic industries? Can subsidies to farmers be justified on economic grounds? In an election, citizens are frequently asked to vote for a party on the basis of its political platform, which, to a significant degree, contains issues and intended policies that are essentially economic in nature. A knowledge of economics allows us to replace emotional judgment with reasoned analysis in the decision-making process.

THINKING LOGICALLY

Economics helps us to think logically.

One of the most important reasons for studying economics is that it develops a particular way of thinking and making decisions. Good decision-making requires a careful evaluation of the benefits (advantages) and costs (disadvantages) associated with the decision or the choice that we make. Actually, economic analysis is, to a large extent, an exercise in logic and thus helps to sharpen our common sense.

GETTING PERSONAL SATISFACTION

Economics gives personal satisfaction.

There may be a more personal, selfish reason for studying economics. Because the study of economics can be intellectually exciting and stimulating, it yields great personal satisfaction. If you happen to become a great economist, you could end up being the president or chief executive officer of a corporation, or an economic consultant to one of our levels of government, with an annual salary in the six-figure range. In the 1940s, economists worked mainly on the campuses of universities. Today, professional economists work in practically every aspect of business and government.

PROBLEM SOLVING 1-2

Economics does not teach one how to earn a living, so it does not have much practical value. Do you agree?

WHERE ECONOMISTS WORK AND WHAT THEY DO

Learning Objective 4:
explain what economists do

Economists work in many aspects of business and government. You will find economists

- working in private firms such as insurance companies, large manufacturing companies, banks, unions, service associations, telephone companies, etc.

- teaching in high schools, colleges, and universities

- working in different departments of government and government agencies

- employed as researchers in various research institutions

- working for a variety of non-profit organizations

- working for themselves as consultants

- working for international organizations and agencies such as the United Nations, the World Bank, and the International Monetary Fund.

You have a good idea of what your economics instructor does. But what other kinds of jobs do economists do? A large corporation such as General Motors or your telephone company might hire economists to estimate the demand for its products or to figure out what effects a change in price will have on its profits. A bank might employ economists to forecast interest rates or the demand for loans. The federal government or a provincial government might hire economists to determine the effects of certain taxes on the government's revenue and on the level of economic activity. Finally, a union might employ economists to study matters relating to wages and employment. Economists serve as presidents, vice-presidents, general managers, and executives of a wide variety of organizations.

THE SCIENTIFIC METHOD

Learning Objective 5:
the nature of scientific inquiry

There is a certain appeal to anything that is said to be "scientific." This is perhaps due to the fact that we are living in a scientific age. In our definition of economics, we used the term science, but is economics really a science? We shall answer this question in this section.

Before we can determine whether or not economics is a science, we must understand the meaning of science and the scientific method. Everyone knows that economics is not a science like physics or chemistry are sciences. Physicists and chemists can conduct controlled laboratory experiments, while economists and other social scientists cannot. Science refers to a particular method of inquiry: **the scientific approach** or **method** is the systematic investigation and observation of phenomena and the formulation of general laws or tendencies therefrom, after testing and verification of hypotheses. We can discuss the main elements of the scientific approach under the headings of observation and measurement, formulation of hypotheses, and verification.

Scientific investigation comprises observation and measurement, the formulation of hypotheses, and verification.

OBSERVATION AND MEASUREMENT

One of the basic tasks of scientists is to observe, measure, and record facts about what they are investigating. This is the descriptive or **empirical** aspect of science. In order to facilitate this aspect of their work, scientists use certain technical terms which have very precise meanings. The development of such a particularized vocabulary is an important step in the development of any field of scientific inquiry. Scientists must also exercise judgment in gathering information or facts relevant to the phenomenon that they are trying to explain.

Empirical: descriptive; as in observed, measured and recorded.

HYPOTHESES

The next task of scientists is to specify some relations among the variables that have been selected for investigation. Such specifications are called **hypotheses**. A hypothesis is not a statement about some fact that has been observed, but a statement about something that is observable. For example, the statement "Sixty students passed the economics examination" is not a hypothesis, but a statement about a fact that has been observed. On the other hand, the statement "If two extra review classes are given, at least sixty students will pass their economics examination" is a hypothesis. Student performance in an examination following review classes is observable. Note that the latter statement (the hypothesis) can be tested by giving (or not giving) two extra review classes and then observing the results. The statement "Review classes should be given before a final examination" is not expressed in a testable manner, because it does not express any specific relationship. A hypothesis must be stated in a testable (verifiable) manner so that it can be confirmed or disproved.

VERIFICATION

Once scientists have formulated their hypotheses, they proceed to test these hypotheses to see the extent to which they are supported by empirical evidence. Relating questions to evidence sets scientific inquiry apart from other types of inquiry.

ECONOMIC METHODOLOGY

Model: A simplified version of reality that facilitates our understanding of complex economic relations.

Learning Objective 6: how economists study the economy

We have now examined the basic components of the scientific method. Our next task is to see how economists follow the scientific approach in their attempt to explain economic phenomena. The factors involved in real-world economic events are often quite complex. The scientific economist comes to grips with these complexities by constructing models. Simply stated, a **model** or theory is an abstraction from the real world and consists of the factors that appear to pertain most to what is being studied. Details that do not pertain directly to the question that is being studied are simply stripped away in the model. The principle of stripping away irrelevant detail is often referred to as the principle of Occam's razor, named after the fourteenth-century philosopher William Occam.

Economists use models in much the same way that engineers use them. An engineer who has the job of building a bridge would, most likely, design a model before building the real thing. The model allows the engineer to study certain aspects of the bridge before it actually exists. For example, the model bridge could give information about how the actual bridge would look, how it would accommodate traffic, and what modifications might be necessary to make it safe. Similarly, economists construct and use economic models to understand how the real economy works.

The following example will help to illustrate how economists use models. People can travel from point A to point B either by air, which takes 50 minutes, or by car, which takes 4 hours. Let us assume that people are alike in terms of their preference for air travel and car travel, and that, except for the time factor, one mode of transportation is just as good as the other. What kind of people will be likely to fly, and what kind will be likely to travel by car? One of the factors that would influence a decision to travel by air or by car would be the cost involved. But here we are not talking only about the price of the plane ticket, or the price of gas and oil, and wear and tear on the car. We must consider also the cost of time. To a passenger who earns $50.00 an hour, the cost of his or her time is estimated at $50.00 an hour. To a passenger who earns $10.00 an hour, the cost of his or her time is estimated at $10.00 an hour. The greater the cost of your time, the less time you will want to spend travelling. The model predicts that the more you earn, the more likely it is that you will fly. On this basis, a decision could be made to start a plane service from A to B if there were many high-income earners travelling between points A and B.

An economic model or theory may be expressed verbally, mathematically, or graphically. Whatever form an economic model takes, it has the following components: a set of definitions, a set of assumptions, one or more hypotheses, and one or more predictions or generalizations. Let us briefly discuss each component in turn.

Definitions

Definitions, assumptions, hypotheses, and predictions are important aspects of a model.

The various terms and phrases that economists use must be clearly defined. Economists have developed an impressive number of terms and concepts that form a part of the specialized language or jargon of the discipline. As you work through this book, many of the terms and concepts that are a part of the economist's vocabulary will become familiar to you. The main purpose of the set of **definitions** is to identify the variables of the model so that measurement can be facilitated. For example, it would be extremely difficult to measure the amount of consumer spending in an economy if that variable were not clearly defined.

Definitions identify the model's variables.

Assumptions

Assumptions describe the model's operating conditions.

Assumptions are statements about the conditions under which the model operates. Basically, we usually make two types of assumptions in economic theory. One type of assumption relates to what motivates economic behaviour – for example, the objectives of consumers and producers. It is assumed that consumers try to maximize satisfaction, whereas firms try to maximize profit. Another type of assumption made in economic theory is aimed at simplifying the task of economists. For example, if economists are not currently concerned with an economy's external trade relations, they may simplify their analyses by assuming that the country does not engage in trade with the rest of the world. Abstractions of this nature are necessary because of the complexities of the real economy. An assumption of particular importance in economic theory is the idea of ***ceteris paribus***, which means *other things being equal*. By assuming that other things are equal, economists keep all other factors constant while investigating a particular relation. We shall look at this assumption more fully in a later section.

Ceteris paribus: other things being equal.

Hypotheses

We have already briefly discussed hypotheses. Recall that hypotheses specify the relations between variables. Economists have formulated a number of important hypotheses, many of which will be introduced throughout this book.

Predictions

An economic prediction is general while an economic forecast is more specific.

We formulate theories so that we can make predictions with them. Economic predictions usually take the form, "If you do this, then such and such will result." Economic prediction should not be confused with economic forecasting. Economic forecasting assigns future values to certain economic variables on the basis of known relations. An **economic prediction** is a statement about the general direction of events resulting from fulfillment of certain conditions, while an **economic forecast** gives us the specific value expected for a particular variable. The following examples help to illustrate the difference between a prediction and a forecast.

Prediction: If the rate of interest increases, the level of investment spending will fall, other things being equal.

Forecast: By the end of the year, the rate of unemployment will rise to 15%.

Economists, in attempting to explain economic events, follow the scientific procedure outlined above. They gather information, analyze it, and select what they consider to be most relevant. They formulate and test hypotheses and thus arrive at general statements or laws concerning economic phenomena. Economics, therefore, has a legitimate claim to be considered a science.

THE GOODNESS OF A MODEL

The goodness of a model depends on how well it explains and predicts reality.

When is an economic model or theory considered to be "good"? The whole purpose of an economic model is to explain some aspect of economic reality and to predict certain outcomes. A model that does this well is a good model. If model A explains and predicts economic phenomena better than model B does, then model A is judged to be better than model B. If a model fails to explain what we observe (that is, reality), then it may be rejected.

Econometricians use statistics to test economic theories.

The use of computers has enabled economists to manipulate huge amounts of data in an incredibly short time. Thus, it is relatively easy to test economic theories against observed phenomena. The branch of economics that deals with the use of statistics to test economic theories is called **econometrics**. This has become such an important branch of economics that most schools require their economics majors to take at least one course in economic statistics or econometrics.

POSITIVE AND NORMATIVE ECONOMICS

Learning Objective 7: the difference between positive and normative economics

Positive statements are statements of facts expressed in a testable (verifiable) manner.

Before we continue, we must make sure that we understand the difference between positive and normative statements. This will help us to distinguish between positive and normative economics. Economists conduct both positive and normative analyses. **Positive statements** are about *what is*. A positive statement is a statement about some fact, and is therefore conceptually verifiable. The statement that the student population of your school is 5000 is a positive statement, even if your school has only 3000 students. The point is, it is a statement about some fact – the student population. The statement can be verified (or disproved) by the simple process of counting. Note that a positive statement may be true or false. Since a positive statement relates to facts, it can be verified (or disproved) by examining the facts. A statement such as "an increase in the money supply will lead to a higher rate of inflation" is an example of a positive statement in economics.

Normative statements are value judgements about what ought to be.

On the other hand, **normative statements** are value judgements or statements of opinion about *what ought to be*. Normative statements cannot be verified by examining the facts. A statement such as "the money supply should be reduced" is a normative statement. Try to compose examples of your own to illustrate the distinction between positive statements and normative statements.

Obviously, normative statements are not scientific because they cannot be subjected to empirical testing. This does not suggest that the scientific economist is never concerned with normative issues. In fact, concern with the normative aspect of economics is a major focus for disagreement among economists. Most economists, for example, would agree on the effects of a tax on textbooks, but would likely disagree on whether a tax *should* be imposed. Value judgements, though not scientific, are therefore important. Economists should indicate, however, when they are dealing with positive statements and when they are dealing with matters of opinion.

Positive economics is the study of the state of the economy.

This discussion of positive and normative statements should help us to understand the difference between positive and normative economics. **Positive economics** deals with the behaviour of economic units and with the operation of the economic system. Positive economics attempts to explain what will happen under certain conditions, but does not explain what the economic situation ought to be. It does not seek to make any judgments about whether the result of any economic action is good or bad. The concern of positive economics is to describe the economic system as it is and how it actually works. What causes the prices of television sets to rise? What are the effects of the GST? How has the Canada-U.S. trade agreement affected employment in Canada? These types of questions fall within the subject of positive economics.

Normative economics suggests what the economy should be.

Normative economics is concerned with what the economic situation ought to be. It attempts to judge whether economic outcomes are good or bad, and to what extent they can be improved. Should the Government of Canada invest public funds in an airline company to keep it in business? Should the government sell some of its property? Should farmers be subsidized? Should the price of milk be set by government? Should there be a ceiling on the amount of profits that foreign firms are allowed to take out of Canada? Normative economics deals with answers to such questions. Note that the issues of normative economics are policy-oriented.

Obviously, normative economics often relies heavily on positive economics. Let us consider the following normative economic issue: Should Canada remain a part of the North American Free Trade Agreement? One could conceivably answer this question on the basis of emotion, but an answer based on an economic analysis of the situation would probably be preferable. What are the likely benefits of this agreement? What are the costs? Answers to these positive questions will help to answer the normative question about the trade agreement.

DISAGREEMENT AMONG ECONOMISTS

Learning Objective 8: the reasons for disagreement among economists

It is probably normal to expect economists to disagree about normative economic issues. They have different values, and they judge economic situations and events differently. When economists are asked to make judgments about some economic action, they may try to be objective, but their objectivity might be coloured by their own sense of what is right and what is wrong. One economist might argue that cigarette smoking is bad for your health, hence a heavy tax should be imposed on cigarettes in order to discourage smoking. Another economist might take the position that there are other products that are also dangerous — why single out cigarettes? The same economist might argue, moreover, that if people want to smoke cigarettes, it is their business and that the government has no right to interfere with a person's lifestyle.

It is not only on normative issues, however, that economists disagree. They also disagree over the positive, scientific aspects as well. Often, there are different explanations of how the economy operates, and it is not always clear which explanation is best. In other words, economists may disagree over the appropriate model of the economy.

Economists disagree because they have different values, and because they use different models.

One would think that it should be easy to settle the disagreement simply by confronting the theory with the data. Unfortunately, the available data might not be such as to allow definitive conclusions.

Economists may also disagree about quantities, even when they use the same model.

Economists may disagree even though they use the same economic model. They may agree over the qualitative aspects, but disagree over the quantitative aspects. Two economists might agree that a fall in interest rates will increase investment. They might disagree, however, over the magnitude of the increase, one claiming that it will rise only slightly, the other claiming that the increase will be significant. Again, this type of disagreement may be prolonged because of the lack of relevant data.

PROBLEM SOLVING 1-3

If economics is so scientific, why is there so much disagreement among economists?

VARIABLES

A variable can vary, but a constant does not vary.

We have seen that economists construct economic models to facilitate their understanding of economic phenomena. An economic model is a system of relations among economic variables. In general terms, a **variable** is anything that can assume different values under different circumstances. We call anything that does not vary a **constant**. Whether or not we consider something to be a variable or a constant depends on what we are investigating. The following are some economic variables that we shall encounter as we progress through this book: price, income, consumer spending, interest rates, demand for money, investment spending, exports, imports, taxes, and government spending.

Endogenous variable: value determined within the model.

Exogenous variable: value is predetermined.

When economists construct models to explain real world phenomena, some variables will be explained within the models, while others will be determined by factors outside the models. Those variables that are explained within a model are called **endogenous variables**. Those variables that are determined by factors outside a model are called **exogenous variables**. It is a serious mistake to assume that the exogenous variables whose values are predetermined are not important. In fact, they are extremely important. Exogenous variables affect endogenous variables.

Economists do not have a set of variables that they label endogenous and another set that they label exogenous at all times and under all circumstances. Whether a particular variable is endogenous or exogenous depends on the problem being studied. It is important to note also that we cannot determine whether or not a particular variable is endogenous or exogenous without the model.

PROBLEM SOLVING 1-4

You are constructing a model to explain consumption of goods and services in Canada. You specify that consumption depends on income and on the rate of interest. You believe, however, that changes in wealth and income distribution will have some effect on consumption. Identify the endogenous and exogenous variables.

STOCK VARIABLES AND FLOW VARIABLES

Stock variables have no time dimension. Flow variables do.

Before we proceed, we should understand the difference between **stock variables** (or stocks) and **flow variables** (or flows). A **stock** is a quantity existing *at a particular time*. A **flow**, on the other hand, is a measure of the change in a variable *per unit of time*. The number of books on the shelves of a college or university library on May 10, 1999 (that is, at a particular time) is a stock. The number of books taken out of the library each day is a flow. Note that a flow is a rate and has a time dimension (per day, per month, per year, etc.). A stock has no time dimension. Examples of economic flow variables are: income, consumption, and the interest that you earn on your savings account. Examples of economic stock variables are: the amount of equipment owned by a company, the number of dollars in circulation in Canada at 11:00 a.m. yesterday, and the amount of money in your bank account.

CAUSE-EFFECT RELATIONS

Learning Objective 9: relations among variables

Economists study economic variables to discover causes and effects. One must be careful, however, not to confuse correlation with causation. Two variables may be correlated, that is, they change together, even though a change in one does not cause a change in the other. A change could be a chance occurrence, or it could be the effect of a third variable. If it can be determined that a change in one variable causes a change in another, then we know that by changing one, the other will change. This conclusion may not hold if there is only a correlation between the variables. We must remember the age-old warning that correlation does not imply causation.

The post hoc fallacy

Post hoc, ergo propter hoc: the error in thinking that A causes B because A precedes B.

The discussion above is closely related to a common fallacy. When two events happen in sequence, one is tempted to conclude that the first event caused the second to occur. This, of course, may not be the case. This error is referred to as the **post hoc, ergo propter hoc** fallacy, which means "after this, therefore because of this." Let us assume that you began to read your economics textbook and then it began to rain. If you concluded that it rained because you started to read your textbook, then you would have fallen into the post hoc ergo propter hoc fallacy.

THE CETERIS PARIBUS ASSUMPTION

Economists concern themselves with the effects of changes in economic variables. How does a change in income affect consumption? How does a change in the price of a product affect the quantity that will be purchased? Do changes in the quantity of money affect the rate of interest? Do changes in interest rates affect other variables? Can certain policies be instituted to control certain economic variables? These are some of the questions for which the economist tries to find answers.

Suppose we are interested in finding out the effect of a fall in the price of apples on the quantity of apples that we will purchase. Obviously, factors other than the price of apples will affect the quantity that will be purchased. Some of these factors include our preferences for apples over other kinds of fruit, our incomes, and the prices of other fruit. We can hypothesize that if the price of apples falls, we will buy a greater quantity. If we observe that a fall in the price of apples is accompanied by an increase in the quantity purchased, can we conclude that the increase in quantity purchased results from the fall in price? Is it not possible that the increase in quantity purchased may result from an increase in income or some other exogenous factor?

The ceteris paribus assumption allows us to isolate the effects of changes in variables.

In order to determine how a change in one variable affects other variables, the economist must find some way of isolating the effects of other variables. In the above example, we must isolate income, preference (taste), and all other factors (except the price of apples) that may affect the quantity of apples that we will purchase. We can (almost magically) accomplish this task by making use of the ceteris paribus assumption. *Ceteris paribus*, a Latin phrase, means *other things being equal*. This assumption allows us to keep other factors constant while we examine the effects of the variable that currently interests us. Thus, we can investigate how a change in price affects the quantity purchased by assuming that income, taste, and all other factors except the price of apples remain unchanged throughout the process of investigation. We may emerge with a statement such as "If the price of a product falls, *other things being equal*, the quantity purchased will increase."

PROBLEM SOLVING 1-5

Why do economists put so much emphasis on the ceteris paribus assumption when it is well known that other things are not equal?

ECONOMIC POLICY

Learning Objective 10: *the meaning of economic policy*

A great deal of physical and human resources have been and are being devoted to the development and improvement of economic theory. These theories help us to understand how the economy functions and enable us to solve real-world economic problems. We

Economic policy is any action taken to achieve some desired economic goal.

can define **economic policy** as a course of action designed to achieve some specific economic objective. Every society usually agrees upon a number of economic objectives that it considers to be desirable. The following are among the economic objectives that most people in our society would like our policymakers to pursue: price stability; full employment; economic growth; an equitable distribution of income; economic freedom (freedom for consumers, workers, and businesses to pursue their own economic interests); economic security; and a satisfactory balance of payments equilibrium.

We should realize that some measure of conflict will occur among these goals. For example, a policy designed to reduce the rate of inflation (to achieve relative price stability) may increase the rate of unemployment. The objectives of price stability and full employment will then conflict. Similarly, the objective of an equitable distribution of income may conflict with the goal of a higher rate of economic growth. When such conflicts arise, choices must be made.

Not all of these objectives assume the same importance at any one time. Furthermore, the importance of each goal relative to other goals is likely to change from time to time. In a situation of severe unemployment, for example, it may be necessary to sacrifice another goal such as price stability. Priorities must be established, but the ranking of our priorities will change as circumstances change. For example, we are much more concerned with the environment today than we were twenty years ago, and inflation ranked higher in importance in 1975 than it does today.

MICROECONOMICS AND MACROECONOMICS

Learning Objective 11: distinguish between microeconomics and macroeconomics

Microeconomics, or price theory, deals with the behaviour of individual economic units.

Macroeconomics, or income and employment theory, concerns itself with the behaviour of economic aggregates.

The two major branches into which economics has been divided are microeconomics and macroeconomics. **Microeconomics** examines the behaviour of individual economic units and focuses on the allocation of resources. It concerns itself with what determines the composition of total output, and analyzes topics such as the behaviour of consumers and firms, the determination of relative prices, and the distribution of the economy's output among various groups. Microeconomics is sometimes called **price theory**.

Macroeconomics examines the economy as a whole rather than the individual units — the whole flock, so to speak, rather than the individual sheep comprising that flock. Macroeconomics concerns itself with the combined or aggregate behaviour of consumers and producers, and analyzes such topics as inflation, unemployment, and economic growth. Macroeconomics is sometimes called **income and employment theory**. A thorough understanding of the operation of the economic system requires knowledge of both microeconomics and macroeconomics.

CHAPTER SUMMARY

1. Economics is a social science because it is a scientific study of certain aspects of human behaviour.

2. Economics may be defined as the study of how people use scarce resources to satisfy their unlimited wants.

3. Scarcity forces us to choose. Economics is fundamentally concerned with scarcity and choice.

4. Some advantages of knowing economics are that it helps us to improve the performance of the economy and thus increases our well-being, and that it helps to sharpen our common sense.

5. Economists are employed in almost every facet of economic life. They are employed in industries, by various levels of government and different organizations, some are self-employed as economic consultants, and some teach.

6. The main elements of the scientific method are observation and measurement, the formation of hypotheses and generalizations, and testing and verification.

7. Economists employ the scientific method in describing and predicting economic phenomena. Hence, economics has a legitimate claim to be considered a science.

8. Positive economics concerns itself with explaining how an economy functions. Normative economics, on the other hand, concerns itself with opinions or value judgments about how the economy ought to function.

9. Economists disagree about normative economics because they have different values. They disagree about positive economics because they may use different models. They may also disagree over quantitative aspects.

10. A variable is anything that assumes changing values. An endogenous variable is explained within the model or theory while an exogenous variable is determined by factors outside the model.

11. What distinguishes a flow from a stock is that a flow has a time dimension while a stock does not.

12. Correlation between two variables does not establish a cause-effect relationship between them.

13. The *post hoc, ergo propter hoc* fallacy is the error of concluding that one event caused another because it preceded the other.

14. The *ceteris paribus* (other things being equal) assumption allows the investigator to study how changes in one variable affect other variables.

15. Economic policy may be defined as a course of action designed to achieve a specific objective. Economic objectives may conflict. When they do, choices must be made. The economic objectives of a society are not of equal importance or urgency at any one time. Priorities are established, and they change from time to time.

16. The two main branches into which economics is divided are microeconomics and macroeconomics. Microeconomics concerns itself with individual economic units while macroeconomics concerns itself with broad economic aggregates.

TERMS FOR REVIEW

social science (2)
scarcity (3)
choice (3
scientific method (5)
empirical (5)
hypothesis (6)
model (theory) (6)
definitions (7)
assumptions (7)
ceteris paribus (7)
economic prediction (7)
economic forecast (7)
econometrics (8)
positive statement (8)
normative statement (8)

positive economics (8)
normative economics (9)
variable (10)
constant (10)
endogenous variable (10)
exogenous variable (10)
stock variable (10)
flow variable (10)
post hoc, ergo propter hoc (11)
economic policy (12)
microeconomics (12)
price theory (12)
macroeconomics (12)
income and employment theory (12)

QUESTIONS FOR REVIEW AND DISCUSSION

1. Why do individuals, firms, and governments have to make choices? (L.O. 2)

2. Is there any relationship between choices and resource use? (L.O. 2)

3. Economics is the study of scarcity and choice. Do you consider this to be an adequate definition of economics? (L.O. 1)

4. Explain to one of your friends who is not taking economics why economics is important. (L.O. 3)

5. How can economics help you to become a better informed citizen? (L.O. 3)

6. What opportunities exist for economics graduates? (L.O. 4)

7. In what sense is economics a science? In what ways are economists different from physicists as scientists? (L.O. 5, 6)

8. What are the fundamental elements in scientific inquiry? (L.O. 5)

9. What is an economic model? Why do economists find it useful to construct models? (L.O. 6)

10. What is the difference between positive economics and normative economics? Do you agree with the statement that normative propositions have no place in scientific economics? Give reasons for your opinion. (L.O. 7)

11. Economists disagree over normative economics, but not over positive economics. Is this statement true or false? Explain. (L.O. 8)

12. Give an example of the post hoc, ergo propter hoc fallacy. (L.O. 9)

13. Give an example of an economic policy. Give reasons why such a policy might be put into effect. (L.O. 9)

14. State what the differences are between the following pairs of concepts: (L.O. 9)
    (a) stocks and flows;
    (b) endogenous variable and exogenous variable;
    (c) correlation and causation.

15. What is the difference between microeconomics and macroeconomics? Why should we study both microeconomics and macroeconomics? (L.O. 10)

PROBLEMS AND EXERCISES

1. Look through a newspaper and select three news items that are in some way related to economics and the economy. (L.O. 2, 3)
    (a) In what way are these items related to economics? (Do they have economic causes or consequences?)
    (b) Explain how a knowledge of economics might help us to understand or find solutions to issues that may have been raised in the news items.

2. Write a short dialogue in which you are trying to convince a friend of the importance of studying economics. (L.O. 3)

3. Categorize each of the following as either positive or normative statements. (L.O. 7)
    (a) An increase in price will reduce the quantity purchased.
    (b) The price of gasoline should be stabilized at its current level.
    (c) Economics is so important that it ought to be compulsory for every secondary school, college or university student.

(d) A tax imposed on cigarettes will reduce the supply of cigarettes.

(e) High interest rates tend to reduce the level of investment spending, therefore, interest rates should always be kept as low as possible.

4. Decide whether each of the following falls under the heading of positive economics or normative economics: (L.O. 7)

(a) a study of the effect of an increase in investment on the level of income;

(b) an evaluation of the outcome of a ban on the importation of alcohol to determine whether the ban is good or bad;

(c) a description of how higher interest rates affect the economy;

(d) the compilation of data with the aim of describing certain economic facts;

(e) a program designed to make people better off based on assumptions about what is in their best interest;

(f) the elimination of the deficit by the federal government because it is believed that it will make Canadians better off;

(g) a study of the effect of a reduction in the money supply on interest rates;

(h) the notion that taxing the wealthy in order to give welfare payments to the poor is unfair;

(i) a detailed study of the relationship between consumer spending and economic performance.

5. Identify which of the following are economic predictions and which are economic forecasts. (L.O. 6)

(a) If the level of income rises, people will buy more consumer goods.

(b) If the money supply increases, the rate of inflation will rise.

(c) The output of goods and services in Canada will grow by 3.2% in the year 2001.

(d) If interest rates rise, the growth rate of output will decline.

(e) By the end of the year, the unemployment rate will be 8.2%.

(f) An increase in government spending will put upward pressure on interest rates.

(g) By the year 2004, government purchases of goods and services will account for 35% of total spending.

6. List each of the following variables as stocks or flows: (L.O. 9)

(a) the number of pairs of jeans in a Zellers department store;

(b) the number of pairs of jeans sold by Zellers in one month;

(c) the number of cars produced by an automobile manufacturer in a year;

(d) the amount of office space available for rent on September 3, 1999;

(e) the amount of equipment owned by the High Tech Company;

(f) the amount deposited in your bank account each month;

(g) the unpaid balance on your student loan as of January 15, 1999;

(h) the annual interest payable on a bank loan.

7. Formulate two examples of: (L.O. 6)

(a) economic prediction;

(b) economic forecast.

8. Write up a list of five social, economic, or political problems or issues facing Canada today. For each problem or issue, discuss its economic aspects (if any). What role can economics play in helping us to understand the problem or issue, or in finding solutions? (L.O. 2,3)

9. Indicate whether each of the following falls under the category of microeconomics or macroeconomics: (L.O.11)

(a) an explanation of what causes the price of wheat to increase;

(b) an explanation of the factors that affect the total amount of spending by consumers;

(c) an explanation of how the level of investment spending affects aggregate employment;

(d) an explanation of how the price of your textbook is determined;

(e) a theory which attempts to predict changes in the average level of income and employment in an economy;

(f) a theory that leads to a prediction of the rate of growth of the economy's output of goods and services;

(g) an explanation of how a firm can maximize its profits;

(h) a theory that explains why the prices of home computers have fallen over the past few years.

Internet Site

http://economics.miningco.com

This site serves as a search engine for economics-related resources on the Internet. The site also features weekly articles on economics, and chat facilities.

INTERNET EXERCISE

1. Use the Mining Co. site listed above to find information on *Adam Smith*. He was the founder of economics as a discipline. Write a short paragraph about his theories.

2. Locate the following site:

http://macweb.acs.usm.maine.edu/economics/what.HTML

Read about economists and what they do. List three tasks performed by economists.

C H A P T E R **2**

SOME USEFUL TOOLS

Learning Objectives

After studying this chapter, you should be able to:

1 use symbols and the functional notation to express relationships among variables

2 distinguish between dependent and independent variables

3 use graphs to represent certain relationships

4 explain and calculate slopes

If mathematics is a language, then economics is one place where we use it.

E. M. James

INTRODUCTION

Economists use a number of devices to help them to understand economic relationships. The purpose of this chapter is to provide an elementary but useful introduction to some of the basic tools used by economists in attempting to understand and explain economic events. These tools help economists to express ideas clearly and precisely. You may wish to thumb through this chapter before reading it in order to determine whether or not you are already familiar with the material it contains.

The chapter begins with a brief introduction to the use of symbols and the functional notation. Next, we will see how to use graphs to illustrate certain relations. Finally, the concept of a slope is introduced and we will see how to measure the slopes of linear and non-linear curves at given points.

THE USE OF SYMBOLS AND THE FUNCTIONAL NOTATION

Learning Objective 1:
the use of symbols

Functional notation is a mathematical tool for relating one variable to another.

A function expresses a relation between variables.

Learning Objective 1:
the functional notation

Learning Objective 2:
dependent and independent variables

Economists and students of economics are constantly studying relations among economic variables. In expressing these relations, we can make use of a very convenient mathematical tool called the **functional notation**. A **function** expresses a relationship between two or more variables. Actually, it is quite easy to express relations among variables as functions. Consider the following statement: "The quantity of apples that people will buy depends on the price of apples." An alternative way of expressing this same idea is as follows: "The quantity of apples that people will buy is a function of the price of apples." Both statements mean exactly the same thing — namely, if the price of apples changes, the quantity that people will buy will change (other things being equal, of course). By using the functional notation, we can express this idea very concisely.

To do this, let us begin by using symbols. Let us use Q to denote the quantity of apples that people will buy, and P to denote the price of apples. Note that the use of these symbols has already simplified our task of expressing the relations between the variables with which we are concerned. For, instead of writing quantity, we simply write Q, and instead of writing price, we simply write P. The idea that the quantity that will be purchased depends on price can now be expressed as

$$Q = f(P)$$

and is read "Quantity depends on price" or "Quantity is a function of price."

The dependent variable is the variable to be explained.

The independent variable (or explanatory variable) is the variable that explains.

In this example, the quantity that people will buy depends upon the price. Hence, in the above function, Q is called the **dependent variable**. The variable upon which it depends is called the **independent variable** or the **explanatory variable**. The dependent variable, then, is the variable that we are trying to explain, and the independent variable is the one which provides the explanation. In economics, it is customary to modify the form of the above functional notation. Instead of using f, we replace it with the dependent variable. The above function would therefore appear as

$$Q = Q(P)$$

Sometimes it is desirable to express the idea that one variable depends on two or more other variables. For example, suppose we want to express the idea that the quantity that people will buy depends not only on price but also on their incomes. Using P for price and Q for quantity as before, and using Y to symbolize income, we can express the idea as

$$Q = Q(P,Y)$$

Note that the independent variables P and Y are separated by a comma.

PROBLEM SOLVING 2-1

Use the functional notation to express each of the following ideas:

1. **The grade (g) you obtain on a test depends on how many hours (h) you spend preparing for the test.**

2. **The higher the proportion of the population over 65 years (a), the greater the amount spent on health services (H).**

3. **Changes in the incomes of Canadians (Y) will cause changes in imports (M) from the United States.**

4. **Higher interest rates (r) and greater income (Y) will cause you to put more money in the bank (S).**

THE USE OF GRAPHS

Graphs are effective tools for showing the relation between variables.

The saying goes that a picture is worth a thousand words. The same applies to graphs. But we should consider the following modification: "A graph that is well understood is worth more than a thousand words." **Graphs** are, indeed, an effective way of showing relations among variables. We must recognize, however, that they do not really speak for themselves. Instead, they add clarity to ideas that we try to express — they actually *show* the changes that take place.

The axes intersect at the origin from which all distances are measured.

Learning Objective 3: *how to use graphs*

This section provides a general introduction to the use of graphs. Consider the diagram shown as Figure 2.1. The two lines (called axes) intersect at a 90-degree angle. The point where the two lines intersect is called the **origin**. We give this point a value of 0 and from it measure all distances. Note that the two intersecting lines divide the plane into four quadrants, numbered as shown in Figure 2.1. In quadrant II, the x is negative in value, in quadrant III, both x and y are negative, and in quadrant IV, the y is negative in value.

FIGURE 2.1

Axes, origin, quadrants, and a point on a graph.

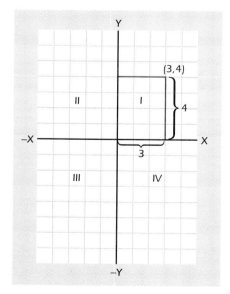

PLOTTING POINTS

Suppose we want to plot the point for the values x = 3 and y = 4, usually indicated as (3,4). First we locate the value 3 along the X-axis. Then, we move vertically up to the value 4 measured along the Y-axis. This locates the desired point (3,4). Now, consider Table 2.1, which gives values of X and Y. We can plot these values on a graph such as

Figure 2.2. Note that points will appear in quadrants II, III, and IV only when a negative value is involved.

In general, economic variables have either positive values or a value of zero. For most of our graphs, therefore, we will need only the first quadrant. Most graphs will appear without the negative parts of the axes.

TABLE 2.1	X Values	Y Values
Values of X and Y.	1	−3
	2	4
	−3	2
	4	1

FIGURE 2.2

Points plotted on a graph.

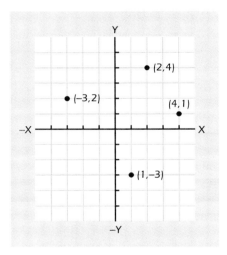

Suppose we have the information shown in Table 2.2 for the Bangalore Ice Cream Store regarding weekly ice cream sales and the number of sunny days for a six-week period.

TABLE 2.2	Week no.	Sunny days	Ice cream sales
Relationship between ice cream sales and sunny days.	1	2	$400
	2	5	900
	3	1	200
	4	3	500
	5	4	700
	6	5	800

From this table, we can see that the volume of sales increases with the number of sunny days. However, although the table does contain the information, we cannot quite see it at a glance. It would be helpful if we could display the information contained in Table 2.2 in a way that allowed us to see the relation at a glance. Figure 2.3 does this. From the graph, we can easily see that the volume of ice cream sales increases with the number of sunny days.

FIGURE 2.3

Graphic representation of the relation between ice cream sales and the number of sunny days.

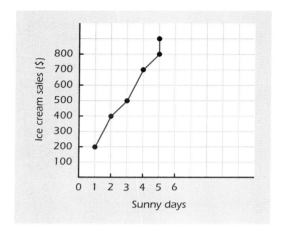

TYPICAL GRAPHS USED IN ECONOMICS

Consider the following statement: "As the rate of interest falls, the level of investment increases." Investment here refers to expenditure on plant, equipment, buildings, etc. — real capital investment. This statement deals with the relation between two variables — the rate of interest and the level of investment. We can get a very clear picture of this relation by using a graph. Note that the two variables move in opposite directions. In other words, there is an *inverse* relation between the rate of interest and the level of investment. This inverse relation is illustrated graphically by the falling curve shown in Figure 2.4. This figure shows clearly that, as the rate of interest falls from 12% to 9%, the level of investment increases from $20 million to $30 million.

FIGURE 2.4

Inverse relation between two variables.

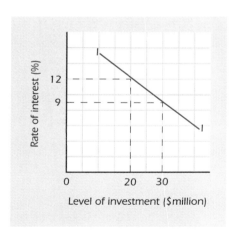

A declining curve shows an inverse relation between two variables.

Direct relation: the relation that exists between variables that increase or decrease together.

Now, let us consider a case in which two variables move in the same direction. Specifically, consider this statement: "When income increases, so does consumer spending." Again, the relation between these two variables (income and consumer spending) can be clearly illustrated on a graph. In this case, there is a **direct relation** between income and consumer spending. Figure 2.5 illustrates this relation graphically by a

FIGURE 2.5

Direct relation
between two
variables.

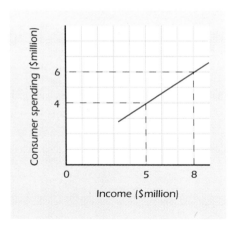

An upward rising curve
shows a direct relation
between two variables.

rising curve. As the level of income increases from $5 million to $8 million, consumer spending increases from $4 million to $6 million.

A graph might show a relationship starting at zero, rising to a maximum, and then falling to zero. Such might be the case between tax revenue and tax rates as shown in Figure 2.6.

FIGURE 2.6

Relation between tax
rate and tax revenue.

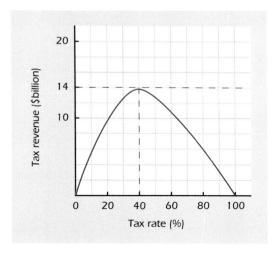

When the tax rate is zero, the government receives no tax revenue. As the tax rate increases, tax revenue rises, reaching a maximum of $14 billion at a tax rate of 40%. But as the tax rate continues to rise, it may be that the incentive to earn extra income decreases so that tax revenue falls. If the tax rate increases to 100%, no one will earn any income because any income earned will be all taxed away. The government's revenue will be zero if no one earns any income.

Economists also encounter relationships that start at a certain point, fall to a minimum, and then rise. An example of such a relationship is the cost of making photocopies shown in Figure 2.7.

FIGURE 2.7

Relation between cost per copy and number of copies.

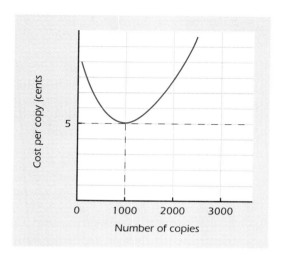

As the number of copies increases from zero, the cost per copy falls. At a volume of 1000 copies per day, the cost per copy is minimized at $0.05 per copy. But as the volume increases beyond 1000 copies per day, the cost per copy rises, due perhaps to pushing the photocopy machine beyond its most efficient operating capacity.

Quite often, it may be necessary to graph data that are unrelated. For example, there is no relation between inflation and the distance you travel per day. Such a situation is shown in Figure 2.8.

FIGURE 2.8

Graphs of unrelated data.

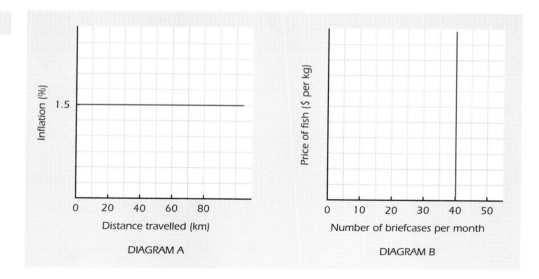

DIAGRAM A

DIAGRAM B

In Diagram A of Figure 2.8, the rate of inflation is 1.5% whether the distance travelled is 20, 40, 60 or 80 km per day. The graph is therefore a horizontal straight line. Consider now the situation shown in Diagram B. The price of fish in Canada has no effect on the number of briefcases sold in an Australian department store per month. When the price of fish changes, the sale of briefcases remains the same, namely, 40. There is no relationship between the two variables, so the graph is a vertical line.

PROBLEM SOLVING 2-2

Show the following relationship on a graph:

As a wheat farmer hires more and more workers, the output of wheat increases up to a point. But as increasingly more workers are hired, the output of wheat declines.

PROBLEM SOLVING 2-3

When interest rates are low, people tend to borrow more money from banks than when interest rates are high. Show this information on a graph.

Clearly then, the economist can make good use of graphs in presenting certain economic relations. Despite their great advantage, however, the use of graphs is limited to cases with very few variables. As the number of variables increases, our ability to graph relations among them decreases. How would you graph the idea that consumption varies with current income, the rate of interest, and consumer expectations? This is indeed a formidable, if not impossible, exercise. Models that involve relations among several variables are usually presented verbally or algebraically rather than geometrically or graphically.

THE SLOPE: CONCEPT AND MEASUREMENT

The slope is a measure of how fast a curve or line rises or falls.

In your study of economics, you will find the concept of a **slope** and its measurement of the utmost importance. Economists are interested in knowing the rates at which the curves they draw rise or fall. Measuring the slopes of these curves provides the answer. Suppose you observe or believe that as people's incomes rise, they respond by spending more money on consumer goods and services. You could show this relationship on a graph as depicted in Figure 2.9.

FIGURE 2.9

Relation between income and consumption.

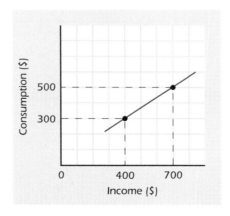

Consumption is measured along the vertical axis while income is measured along the horizontal axis. The curve in the diagram shows that as income rises, consumption also rises. The economist, however, would be also interested in knowing the degree to which

Learning Objective 4:
the concept of slope

consumers respond to changes in income. We could say, for example, that a $300 increase in income results in a $200 increase in consumption. The slope of the line gives us that information. The slope provides information on the steepness or flatness of the curve and is defined as the ratio of the vertical distance (rise) to the horizontal distance (run).

FIGURE 2.10

Slope of a straight line.

A linear curve has a constant slope.

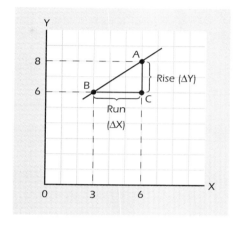

Consider Figure 2.10. Since the curve is a linear curve (that is, a straight line), it has the same slope at every point. The slope of the line in Figure 2.10 is:

$$\text{Slope} = \frac{\text{vertical distance}}{\text{horizontal distance}} = \frac{AC}{BC}$$

The slope then, is the change in the Y value over the change in the X value when Y is on the vertical axis and X is on the horizontal axis. The change in the Y value may be written as ΔY, while the change in the X value may be written as ΔX. The symbol Δ is the Greek letter *delta*, used here to mean "a change in." Thus,

$$\text{Slope} = \frac{\Delta Y}{\Delta X} = \frac{\text{rise}}{\text{run}}$$

FIGURE 2.11

Linear curves with negative and positive slopes.

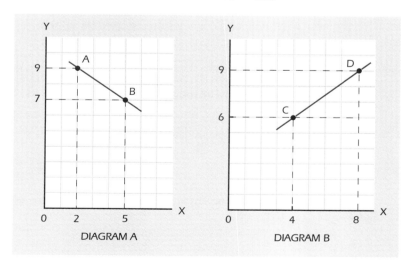

DIAGRAM A

DIAGRAM B

Let us calculate the slope of each of the lines shown in Figure 2.11. First, consider Diagram A. If we move from A to B, Y falls from 9 to 7. Hence, $\Delta Y = -2$. At the same time, X rises from 2 to 5; so $\Delta X = 3$. Therefore:

$$\text{Slope} = \frac{\Delta Y}{\Delta X} = \frac{-2}{3} = -\frac{2}{3}$$

If we move from B to A, Y rises from 7 to 9. Hence, $\Delta Y = 2$. But X falls from 5 to 2; so $\Delta X = -3$. Therefore

$$\text{Slope} = \frac{\Delta Y}{\Delta X} = \frac{2}{-3} = -\frac{2}{3}$$

A declining curve has a negative slope.

Let us now consider Diagram B. If we move from C to D, Y rises from 6 to 9. Hence, $\Delta Y = 3$. At the same time, X rises from 4 to 8; so $\Delta X = 4$. Therefore

$$\text{Slope} = \frac{\Delta Y}{\Delta X} = \frac{3}{4}$$

If we move from D to C, Y falls from 9 to 6 ($\Delta Y = -3$), while X falls from 8 to 4 ($\Delta X = -4$). Therefore

$$\text{Slope} = \frac{\Delta Y}{\Delta X} = \frac{-3}{-4} = \frac{3}{4}$$

A rising curve has a positive slope.

STRAIGHT LINES THROUGH THE ORIGIN

Figure 2.12 shows three straight lines passing through the origin. First, consider the line 0B which is a 45° line from the origin. The slope of 0B is

$$\frac{\Delta Y}{\Delta X} = \frac{3}{3} = 1$$

A 45° line through the origin has a slope equal to 1.

Now, let us consider the line 0A. Its slope is

$$\frac{\Delta Y}{\Delta X} = \frac{2}{1} = 2$$

For any line through the origin above the 45° line, its slope is greater than 1 ($\Delta Y > \Delta X$).

Finally, let us consider the line 0C. Its slope is

$$\frac{\Delta Y}{\Delta X} = \frac{1}{2}$$

For any line through the origin below the 45° line, its slope is less than 1 ($\Delta Y < \Delta X$).

FIGURE 2.12

Slopes of straight lines through the origin.

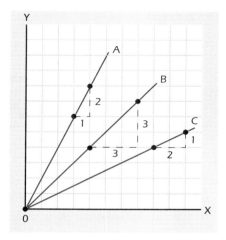

SLOPES OF NON-LINEAR CURVES

So far, we have looked at slopes of linear curves. But what if the curve is not linear? For non-linear curves, the slope is different at every point on the curve.

> **The slope of a non-linear curve at a particular point is the slope of the straight line drawn tangent to the curve at that particular point.**

Figure 2.13 shows a non-linear curve. Tangent lines are drawn at points A and B on the curve. The slope of the curve at A is the slope of the tangent line at A which is

$$\frac{\Delta Y}{\Delta X} = -\frac{2}{2} = -1$$

The slope of the curve at B is the slope of the tangent line at B, which is

$$\frac{\Delta Y}{\Delta X} = \frac{2}{1} = 2$$

FIGURE 2.13

Slope of a non-linear curve at a point.

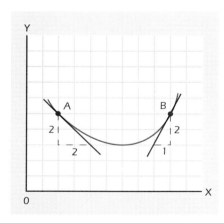

CHAPTER SUMMARY

1. If changes in A cause changes in B, then B is said to be a function of A, and is written as B = B(A).

2. By using graphs, we can depict relations between economic variables clearly and vividly, so that the relations can be seen at a glance. A rising curve shows a direct relation. A declining curve shows an inverse relation.

3. We can measure the slope of a linear curve at a point by finding the ratio of the vertical distance (rise) to the horizontal distance (run). A linear curve has a constant slope throughout.

4. A rising curve has a positive slope. A declining curve has a negative slope.

5. A 45° line through the origin has a slope of 1.

6. We can measure the slope of a non-linear curve at a point by finding the slope of the tangent line at that point. The slope varies as we move from point to point on a non-linear curve.

TERMS FOR REVIEW

functional notation (20)
function (20)
dependent variable (20)
independent (explanatory) variable
  (20)
graphs (21)

origin (21)
direct relation (23)
slope (26)
negative slope (28)
positive slope (28)
slope of a non-linear curve (29)

QUESTIONS FOR REVIEW AND DISCUSSION

1. What is the difference between: (L.O.1,2)

    (a) dependent and independent variables;

    (b) direct and inverse relations?

2. In each of the following relations, indicate the dependent and independent variables. (L.O.2)

    (a) If the price (P) of a product changes, the quantity (Q) that will be bought will also change.

    (b) Changes in the quantity (Q) that people will buy are due to changes in price (P) and income (Y).

    (c) An increase in the average income (Y) of Canadians will result in an increase in imported goods (M).

    (d) Changes in income (Y) and the rate of interest (r) will cause the level of investment (I) to change.

3. Why are graphs important in economics? (L.O.3)

4. Use the functional notation to express each of the following relations. (L.O.1)

    (a) The rate of interest (r) depends on the money supply (MS).

    (b) If the quantity produced (Q) changes, then the total cost of production (TC) will also change.

    (c) Consumer spending (C) depends on the rate of interest (r) and on the level of income (Y).

5. Explain how each of the following is measured: (L.O.4)

   (a) the slope of a linear curve;

   (b) the slope of a non-linear curve at a point.

PROBLEMS AND EXERCISES

1. Construct tables with hypothetical values to show the relations you would expect to find between: (L.O.3)

   (a) population and the number of schools;

   (b) the number of candles sold and the number of power failures in Shawinigan during a period of time;

   (c) the number of chairs and the number of desks that a carpenter can make in a given week.

2. Draw graphs to illustrate each of the relations in Question 1 above. (L.O.3)

3. Graph the relations shown in Tables 2.3 and 2.4. On the graph drawn from Table 2.3, put income on the horizontal axis and consumer spending on the vertical axis. For the graph drawn from Table 2.4, put price on the vertical axis and quantity on the horizontal axis. (L.O.3)

TABLE 2.3	Income	Expenditure on consumer goods
Relationship between income and expenditure.	40	50
	60	60
	80	70
	100	80
	120	90
	140	100

TABLE 2.4	Price of coffee	Quantity of coffee bought
Relationship between price and quantity purchased.	$7.00	15
	6.50	16
	6.00	17
	5.50	19
	5.00	21
	4.50	23
	4.00	26

4. Given that $S = S(Y)$, where S = saving, and Y = income: (L.O.1)

   (a) What is the meaning of this expression?

   (b) Which is the dependent variable?

   (c) Which is the independent variable?

5. Given that $I = I(r,E)$, where I = investment, r = rate of interest, and E = expectations: (L.O.1)

   (a) What does the expression tell you?

   (b) Identify the dependent and independent variables.

6. With price on the vertical axis and quantity on the horizontal axis: (L.O.3,4)

    (a) Plot the curve from Table 2.5.

    (b) Calculate the slope of this curve.

    (c) Compare the slope of this curve with that of a 45° line drawn through the origin.

TABLE 2.5

Relationship between price and quantity.

P	Q
10	15
20	20
30	25
40	30
50	35

7. With reference to Figure 2.14, calculate the slope of the curve at points A and B. (L.O.4)

FIGURE 2.14

Slope calculation exercise.

C H A P T E R

THE ECONOMIC PROBLEM: THE PROBLEM OF SCARCITY

Learning Objectives

After studying this chapter, you should be able to:

1 identify and classify the resources of the economy

2 discuss the incomes derived from various resources

3 establish a relationship between scarcity, choice and opportunity cost

4 explain and use the concepts of production possibility schedules and production possibility curves

5 describe economic systems and their functions

6 explain the role of government in a market economy

7 discuss the basic sectors of the economy

Every act which involves time and scarce means for the achievement of one end involves the relinquishment of their use for the achievement of another. It has an economic aspect.

Lionel Robbins, *The Nature and Significance of Economic Science*

INTRODUCTION

There are numerous economic problems (for example, unemployment, an unstable dollar, inflation, low productivity, economic instability, etc.), but the fundamental economic problem is the problem of scarcity, that is, limited resources in the face of unlimited wants. Regardless of how an economic system is organized, it has to address this fundamental economic problem.

In this chapter, we focus our attention on the economy's resources, and on how different economic systems deal with the ever-present problem of scarcity. We will also discuss the roles of government, consumers, and producers in a market economy.

THE RESOURCES OF THE ECONOMY

Learning Objective 1:
classify the economy's resources

Resources (or factors of production) are the various things that can be used to produce goods and services.

Land refers to all natural resources.

Labour refers to human effort.

Capital refers to produced means of production.

Real capital includes buildings, tools, and equipment.

Human capital includes the education, skills, and health of the labour force.

Entrepreneurship refers to organizational and innovative skills.

Take another look at our definition of economics and you will see that the efficient use of resources is of crucial importance. What exactly are these resources, and how can they be classified? **Resources** are the various things (tangible and intangible) that can be used to produce goods and services. An economy has numerous different resources (or **factors of production** as they are sometimes called). There are lakes, rivers, forests, minerals, fertile land, highways, plants and equipment, warehouses, and human labour. But these resources can all be classified into four broad categories: land, labour, capital, and entrepreneurship (entrepreneurial services).

Land refers to those resources which have been given by nature and which can be used to produce goods and services to satisfy human wants. The concept is much broader than the ordinary notion of the solid portion of the earth. Economists consider any non-human resource which is made available by nature to be land. Thus, minerals embedded in the earth, fish in the sea, oxygen in the air, the sea, rivers, and lakes — even the space within which economic activity takes place — are all classified as land. The term **natural resources** is often used as a synonym for land.

Labour refers to the physical and mental efforts that people can contribute to the production processes. It is not difficult to visualize the labour expended by a craftsperson, or a farmer in the field, or an individual engaged in the production of some manufactured good. But the services rendered by sales representatives, lawyers, teachers, doctors, musicians, and actors are also classified under the heading of labour. So next time you turn on the radio and you hear one of your favourite tunes, remember that the disc jockey is providing labour services.

Capital is any manufactured good which can be used for the production of other goods and services. Buildings, roads, plants, equipment, and tools are examples of capital goods. These are sometimes called **real capital**. It is important to note that our definition of capital differs from the everyday concept which is often equated with money. To the economist, capital refers to productive agents produced by people to be used in conjunction with other productive factors to produce goods and services. The distinction between real capital and money capital is an important one in economics. The concept of human capital as distinct from physical or non-human capital has crept into the economist's vocabulary. **Human capital** refers to education, health, and individual skills.

Entrepreneurship or entrepreneural services encompasses managerial and decision-making skills. The production of goods and services requires not only the existence of land, labour, and capital, but also that these factors be brought together and organized into production. The ability to organize land, labour, and capital into production, and to innovate is called entrepreneurship. The individual who engages in these organizational and innovative activities is called an *entrepreneur*. Innovation and the organization of land, labour, and capital into the production process with the expectation of earning a profit are entrepreneurial services that involve some element of risk. The entrepreneur therefore is a risk-taker, but the rewards for innovation and creative ability can be substantial.

This discussion of resources can be summarized as shown below. Each boxed item represents a variety of resources with common characteristics.

Land	All natural resources
Labour	Human resources
Capital	Manufactured resources
Entrepreneurship	Organizational and decision-making skills

PROBLEM SOLVING 3-1

Is a car a capital good?

FACTOR PAYMENTS

Learning Objective 2: discuss the incomes derived from various resources

The factors of production must be rewarded for the services which they provide. Economists have devised special terms for the payment received for the use of these factors of production. Table 3.1 lists groups of factors of production and the compensation associated with each group. Compensation may be in monetary form, or in the form of goods and services, or partly in money and partly in goods and services. In our economic system, payment is nearly always entirely in the form of money.

TABLE 3.1	Factors	Compensation
Factors and their compensation.	Land	Rent
	Labour	Wages and salaries
	Capital	Interest and dividends
	Entrepreneurship	Profits

Rent, wages and salaries, interest and dividends, and profits are the rewards for land, labour, capital, and entrepreneurship respectively.

Land owners receive payment for the use of their land. The term **rent** is applied for such payment. Labour is compensated by the payment of **wages and salaries**. The owners of money capital receive **interest** and the owners of real capital (shareholders) receive payments called **dividends**. Entrepreneurship is rewarded by **profits**. We should keep in mind that, in modern corporations, one aspect of the entrepreneurial function (organization and direction) is carried out by hired managers, boards of directors, and other executives who receive salaries for their services. The other aspect of the entrepreneurial function (the risk-bearing function) is performed by the owners of the corporation, who receive a share of the profits as a reward for risk-taking.

PROBLEM SOLVING 3-2

Can you think of any income the source of which is not a resource? What about government welfare payments?

SCARCITY, CHOICE AND OPPORTUNITY COST

Learning Objective 3: establish a relationship between scarcity, choice, and opportunity cost

Scarcity of resources requires a choice between wants.

Opportunity cost (or alternative cost) refers to the alternative that is sacrificed when a choice is made.

Scarcity and choice are facts of economic life. The simple truth is that there are not enough resources to enable society to produce all of the goods and services that would be required to satisfy everyone's wants. If resources were not scarce, we would satisfy all our wants and there would be no need to give up anything. Scarcity forces us to choose.

Every act of choosing requires a sacrifice. If I choose to attend a Whitney Houston concert on Saturday evening, then I am sacrificing something else that I could have done — such as watching a baseball game between the Toronto Blue Jays and the Boston Red Sox. By choosing to attend the concert, I give up the baseball game. Economists use the term **opportunity cost** or **alternative cost** to refer to alternatives or opportunities that are sacrificed.

If a city decides to build a school instead of adding a wing to a hospital, then the opportunity cost of the school is the additional hospital facilities that the city could have had instead.

PROBLEM SOLVING 3-3

1. **On the night before your final examination in economics, the Montreal Canadiens are to play against the New York Rangers for the Stanley Cup. You can either study your economics or watch the game, but you cannot do both. Use the concept of opportunity cost to decide whether you should study economics or watch the hockey game.**

2. **If Canada decided to engage in the production of anti-pollution equipment to combat acid rain, what would be the opportunity cost?**

PRODUCTION POSSIBILITIES

The economic problem of allocating resources in a situation of scarcity can be illustrated by examining the production possibility curve of an economy. Let us assume that an economy devotes all of its resources to the production of only two goods: houses and automobiles. Several possible combinations of houses and automobiles are illustrated in the **production possibility schedule** (Table 3.2).

TABLE 3.2

Production possibilities (constant cost).

Production possibility schedule: a table showing various combinations of goods that an economy can produce if it uses all of its resources.

Possibilities	Number of houses	Number of automobiles
1	0	8 000 000
2	100 000	7 000 000
3	200 000	6 000 000
4	300 000	5 000 000
5	400 000	4 000 000
6	500 000	3 000 000
7	600 000	2 000 000
8	700 000	1 000 000
9	800 000	0

If this hypothetical economy uses all of its resources to produce automobiles, it can produce a maximum of 8 000 000 automobiles and no houses (possibility 1). If it uses all of its resources to produce houses, it can produce a maximum of 800 000 houses and no automobiles (possibility 9). Between these two extreme cases, Table 3.2 shows many other possibilities. For example, the economy can produce 100 000 houses and 7 000 000 automobiles (possibility 2). Or it can produce 500 000 houses and 3 000 000 automobiles (possibility 6). Note that for every 100 000 houses, the economy sacrifices 1 000 000

Production possibility (transformation) curve: a curve showing the various combinations of commodities that can be produced if all resources are fully employed and technology is constant.

A linear production possibility curve illustrates constant opportunity cost.

automobiles. Thus the opportunity cost of 100 000 houses is 1 000 000 automobiles. That is, in order to produce one house, this economy must sacrifice 10 automobiles. In this example, the opportunity cost remains constant throughout.

The relations in Table 3.2 can also be shown on a graph known as the **production possibility curve** or the **transformation curve**. This curve (represented in Figure 3.1) shows the maximum number of houses and the maximum number of automobiles that this particular economy can produce with given technology at a particular time. Let us keep in mind that, in drawing the production possibility curve, we assume that the economy has a given amount of resources and that technology is constant. The curve in Figure 3.1 is linear (a straight line) because we assume that in this case, opportunity cost is constant. In other words, automobiles could be traded off for houses at a fixed rate.

FIGURE 3.1

Production possibility curve showing constant opportunity cost.

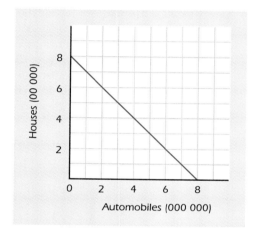

Increasing opportunity cost occurs because resources are not all equally efficient in all uses.

In the real world, however, we may seldom encounter situations of constant opportunity cost. Resources are not all equally efficient in all lines of production. Some resources will produce houses more efficiently than they will automobiles. And some will produce automobiles more efficiently than they will houses. As we continue to shift resources from the automobile industry to the housing industry, we are likely to experience increasing cost. This is so because these resources are likely to be less efficient in the housing industry. For example, it may be relatively easy at first to shift automobile workers from the automobile industry to the housing industry. As the process continues, however, it will become increasingly difficult to find automobile workers who are efficient construction workers. After all, there is a limited number of automobile workers who can work efficiently in the construction industry.

Table 3.3 is a production possibility schedule (p-p schedule for short) illustrating increasing opportunity cost. The first 100 000 houses can be obtained by giving up 1 000 000 automobiles. (The number of automobiles falls from 10 000 000 to 9 000 000.) The second 100 000 houses can be obtained by sacrificing an additional 2 000 000 automobiles. The third 100 000 houses can be obtained at an additional cost of 3 000 000 automobiles, and the fourth 100 000 houses will involve a sacrifice of 4 000 000 automobiles. Thus, each increase in the number of units of houses requires the quantities of automobiles sacrificed to increase by an increasing amount. This is the meaning of increasing opportunity cost.

	Possibilities	Number of houses	Number of automobiles	No. of automobiles given up per 100 000 houses
TABLE 3.3	1	0	10 000 000	1 000 000
	2	100 000	9 000 000	2 000 000
Production possibilities (increasing cost).	3	200 000	7 000 000	3 000 000
	4	300 000	4 000 000	4 000 000
	5	400 000	0	

A concave p-p curve illustrates increasing opportunity cost.

Figure 3.2 helps to explain this point. Note that the vertical segments CG, BR, and AP are all equal, representing equal increases in units of houses. The horizontal segments DG, CR, and BP represent the units of automobiles that must be sacrificed in order to obtain the additional units of houses. Thus, to obtain the first increase in houses (CG), the society gives up DG units of automobiles. To obtain the second increase in houses (BR), the society sacrifices CR units of automobiles. And to obtain the third increase in houses (AP), the society gives up BP units of automobiles. Note that BP > RC > DG. Thus, the opportunity cost of each additional increase in houses increases. Production possibility curves illustrating increasing opportunity cost will be concave to the origin as in Figure 3.2.

FIGURE 3.2

Production possibility curve showing increasing opportunity cost.

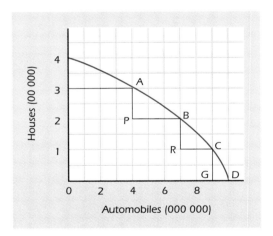

A production possibility point represents a combination of goods or services that an economy can produce.

It is important to distinguish between a **production possibility point** and a production possibility curve. A production possibility point represents a combination of goods or services that an economy can produce, whereas a production possibility curve represents all production possibility points resulting from full utilization of resources.

Let us now study the production possibility diagram shown in Figure 3.3. All points on the p-p curve such as A, B, and C represent combinations of houses and automobiles that can be produced with full employment of all available resources. A point such as U, which lies below the p-p curve, represents unemployment of resources. If the economy is operating at a point such as U, it can move to a point on the curve such as A and obtain more houses or automobiles without giving up anything else. Since the increased output associated with the move from U to A does not involve sacrificing any products, we can conclude that the opportunity cost of idle (unemployed) resources is zero.

The opportunity cost of idle resources is zero.

FIGURE 3.3

Production possibility
diagram.

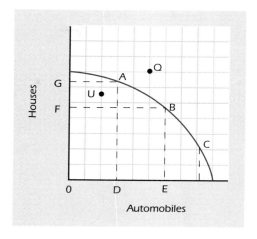

Once resources are fully employed, the output of houses can increase only if the output of automobiles decreases. A movement along the p-p curve from point B to point A, for example, implies that the production of houses increases from 0F to 0G and the production of automobiles decreases from 0E to 0D. Thus, the opportunity cost of FG houses is DE automobiles.

PROBLEM SOLVING 3-4

Antigonish Construction employs 40 previously unemployed carpenters at $80 a day. What is the opportunity cost to society of employing them for a week (5 days)?

Learning Objective 4: explain and use the concepts of production possibility schedules and curves

Refer again to Figure 3.3. Point Q is not a production possibility point because it represents a combination of houses and automobiles that is unattainable by this economy. Should technology advance or should resources increase, then the economy could produce more houses and more automobiles. This would result in a new production possibility curve lying to the right of the original curve as shown in Figure 3.4. The outward shift of the p-p curve in Figure 3.4 represents the increase in the economy's productive capac-

FIGURE 3.4

An outward shift of the production possibility curve.

Technological advance or an increase in resources will shift the production possibility curve outward.

A parallel shift in the p-p curve implies that both industries are affected equally.

Economic growth is an increase in output.

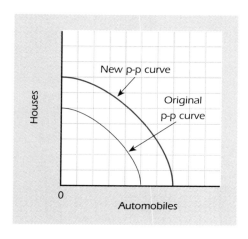

ity. Economists sometimes call this increase in productive capacity **economic growth**. Note that this new curve consists of a whole new set of production possibility points.

In Figure 3.4, the new p-p curve runs parallel to the original curve. This implies that the increase in technology or the increase in resources has affected both industries to the same extent. If the growth occurred primarily in the housing industry, the p-p curve would shift out, but in a non-parallel manner as shown in Figure 3.5A. On the other hand, if the growth occurred primarily in the automobile industry, the p-p curve would appear as indicated in Figure 3.5B.

FIGURE 3.5

Diagram A shows growth primarily in the housing industry. Diagram B shows growth primarily in the automobile industry.

A non-parallel shift in the p-p curve implies that both industries are not affected equally.

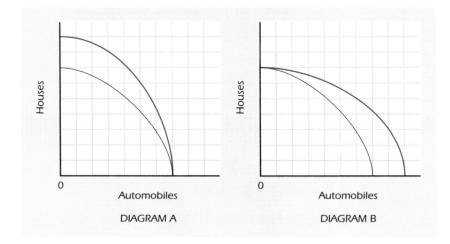

Note that the p-p curve will shift only if there is a change (increase or decrease) in the economy's resources, or if there is a change in technology. A shift in the p-p curve means that the economy's productive capacity has changed. Note also that there is a difference between an increase in actual production and an increase in the capacity to produce. For example, if existing resources that were not utilized are now used, actual production will likely increase, but there would be no increase in the economy's productive capacity, so the p-p curve would not shift. The capacity to produce was there, but it was not used.

Every economy has to decide on its level of economic activity, thus determining a point either on or below its p-p curve. Then, it has to decide on the most desirable combination of output, thus determining the specific point in relation to the curve. Finally, an economy must decide on its rate of economic growth, thus determining the rate at which its p-p curve shifts outward.

PROBLEM SOLVING 3-5
Would the employment of a group of previously unemployed computer programmers cause the p-p curve to shift?

ECONOMIC SYSTEMS

An **economic system** is a set of mechanisms — laws, institutions, and customs — by means of which a society accomplishes the task of producing goods and services to satisfy its wants. Such a system comprises a number of economic units which make decisions regarding the use of resources. We can classify these decision-making units as consumers or households, producers or firms, and government authorities. The way that choices are made about the use of resources (and the importance of each decision-making unit) depends on the type of economic system.

Although it is possible to classify economic systems in a variety of ways, we shall adopt a two-way classification: the **free enterprise system** (also known as **capitalism**), and the **socialistic system**. We must point out that there are many differences among the economies classified as free enterprise, just as there are differences among those classified as socialistic. In all free enterprise economic systems, however, most of the resources or factors of production are owned privately. In socialistic economies, by contrast, most of the factors of production are owned or controlled by the state. Economies such as those of Canada and the United States are basically free enterprise economies. The economies of Hungary and the former nations of Czechoslovakia, East Germany, and the Soviet Union, on the other hand, were basically socialistic economies. Socialistic economies are also known as centrally planned or command economies. The economies of the People's Republic of China and Cuba are two of the few remaining examples of centrally planned economies.

Free enterprise (capitalism): individual ownership and control of resources, and freedom of choice.

A socialistic system (command economy): state ownership and control of the economy's resources.

THE FREE ENTERPRISE SYSTEM

The basis of a free enterprise system is the right of private persons and private groups to own things. This principle is often referred to as the **institution of private property**. In this type of economic system, people are free to own resources and to use them in whatever way that they choose, subject to certain legal limitations designed to safeguard society. In a free enterprise economic system, individuals enjoy freedom of choice. Consumers are free, within certain legal and social constraints, to use their income to purchase the goods and services that maximize their satisfaction. They are also free to use the resources at their disposal to maximize their income. Producers also have freedom of choice. They are free to use their resources in such a way as to maximize their profits.

The institution of private property means the right of individuals to own things.

It is sometimes suggested that the freedom of choice that is characteristic of the free enterprise system results in a lack of order. This conclusion is erroneous, however. Consumers and producers in a free enterprise system will tend to act in such a manner as to promote their own self-interest. Consumers will buy the goods and services that give them the greatest satisfaction, and these are the very goods and services that will be most profitable to produce. Thus, freedom of choice and the pursuit of self-interest bring order rather than chaos into the free enterprise system. The system ensures that the goods and services that consumers want are those that are produced.

Advantages of a free enterprise system

One of the most important advantages of a free enterprise system is the freedom of choice that individuals enjoy. Because individuals and groups are free to use their resources to maximize their income, a free enterprise system provides initiative and incentive for people to pursue their economic objectives and improve their economic well-being. Under a free enterprise system, every individual has an opportunity to use his or her talents and resources for his or her own benefit.

Individuals enjoy freedom of choice under a free enterprise system.

Another major advantage of a free enterprise system is that the goods and services that consumers want are produced without any deliberate coordinated decision-making. The system works automatically and is therefore relatively efficient. Did you arrange with a bakery to supply you with bread tomorrow? The answer is most certainly no; yet you are quite confident that you will be able to obtain bread easily for breakfast tomorrow. You do not even need to know who bakes the bread. All you need to know is where you can buy it. One of the advantages of a free enterprise economic system is that it does not require a great deal of coordination for the economy to produce the goods and services that consumers want.

A free enterprise system is relatively efficient.

Weaknesses of a free enterprise system

Despite the great advantages of a free enterprise system, it does not work perfectly, and you often hear vicious attacks on the system. Indeed, some people blame almost every economic and social problem on the free enterprise system.

A free enterprise system may produce economic instability.

One of the major weaknesses of a free enterprise economic system is that it does not guarantee full employment. There are many people who genuinely want to work but are unable to find jobs. After you have completed your studies, there is a good chance that you will find a job where you can use the training and skills that you have developed, but the system does not guarantee it. Associated with the problem of unemployment is the problem of economic instability. A free enterprise economic system is susceptible to wide fluctuations in economic activity, sometimes with serious economic consequences.

A free enterprise system may not favour the production of public goods.

Another weakness of a pure free enterprise economic system is that certain goods and services may not be produced, or may be produced only in vastly inadequate quantities. A free enterprise system produces goods and services wanted by those individuals who can pay for them. Some goods and services, such as sanitation and defence, which benefit the entire community, may not be produced by private firms since it is difficult for private firms to exact a payment from all members of the community. Such goods, known as public goods, are better provided collectively through the government.

A free enterprise system may not adequately protect the environment.

Also, a free enterprise system, with its emphasis on private property, may not provide adequate protection to the environment. Resources such as rivers, lakes, and the air are common property, owned by everyone but by no one in particular. Often, no price is charged for the use of common property with the result that the environment becomes a dumping ground for all types of pollutants. This is a serious weakness of free enterprise systems.

In addition, the promotion of self-interest, a feature of a free enterprise system, may result in a very inequitable distribution of income, which may be socially unacceptable.

A free enterprise system may not distribute income equitably.

Critics of the free enterprise system often charge that under this system, the rich get richer and the poor get poorer. When this occurs, government intervention may be necessary to deal with the problem.

Finally, a free enterprise economic system does not guarantee the competition that is necessary to ensure the efficient allocation of resources by the market system. Production of certain goods may be controlled by one seller or a few sellers who may take advantage of the opportunity to exploit other members of the society.

A SOCIALISTIC SYSTEM

You must remember that socialistic economic systems are not a homogeneous group of economies. In fact, socialistic systems can take many different forms. Some, such as those of the former Soviet Union and Czechoslovakia, relied more on central planning to make decisions about the use of resources than do others. On the other hand, others (the former Yugoslavia, for example) made greater use of the market mechanism to organize production than do some other socialistic economies. The discussion that follows focuses heavily on the Soviet-type socialistic system.

Fundamental to a socialistic economic system is government or state ownership or control of the resources of the economy. Whereas a system of markets and prices guides economic activity and the use of resources in free enterprise systems, government planning directs economic activity and the use of resources in socialistic economies. The state decides what goods and services are to be produced and establishes state-owned industries to produce them. The managers of the state-owned enterprises are given production targets, and they and the workers obtain bonuses if they exceed these targets.

Whereas individual self-interest is supreme in free enterprise systems, the interests of the society as a whole supersede individual self-interest in socialistic systems. Consequently, the government in a socialistic system will employ economic resources to meet the objectives of the society as a whole as set by the state, even at the expense of individual freedom.

In a socialistic system, individuals may not have freedom of choice in determining the occupations they will enter. The government may decide that a young student must study engineering rather than medicine, depending on the number of doctors and engineers the government wants to produce. Freedom of movement is also limited in a socialistic system. Workers with special skills may be prevented from moving away from areas where such skills are needed.

Advantages of a socialistic system

A socialistic system has the great advantage that it can maintain full employment. You will recall that inability to maintain full employment was one of the weaknesses of a free enterprise system. Another advantage of a socialistic system is the relative ease with which it can shift resources from one use to another. For example, it is relatively easy for a socialistic economy to divert resources from the production of consumer goods to its space program.

A socialistic system is able to maintain full employment.

Weaknesses of a socialistic system

A major problem with a socialistic system is that individual freedom is severely limited. Individuals are not free to establish firms to produce the goods and services that consumers want, and neither are they free to pursue the occupations and professions of their own choice. Economic rewards are given at the discretion of government authorities; hence, the system does not provide much automatic incentive.

A socialistic system severely limits individual freedom.

Another weakness of a socialist system is the enormous cost of planning. Since most decisions are made by central planning rather than by the market, a significant amount of resources must be devoted to the planning process.

Finally, socialistic economic systems tend to produce a smaller variety of products than do free enterprise economies. Moreover, competition among private producers in a free enterprise system forces them to produce goods of high quality. This may not be the case in a socialistic system where producers may try to achieve their physical production targets by producing goods of poor quality.

A socialistic system may lead to production of goods of poor quality.

A TOUCH OF REALISM

A free enterprise economic system is essentially a **market economy** because, in such a system, a system of prices and markets coordinates the allocation of resources and the determination of the composition of output. By contrast, a socialistic economic system such as that used in the former U.S.S.R. is essentially a **command economy** since government dictates the use of resources. In the real world, neither total free enterprise nor total central planning has ever existed. Instead, all real-world economies have been **mixed economies** with elements of free enterprise *and* government intervention.

In a market economy, the market forces of demand and supply play a prominent role.

In a command economy, the government directs economic activity.

The economic system of the United States has been regarded as the most prominent example of a free enterprise economic system. Yet there is a certain amount of government (centralized) decision-making in the American economy. In the former Soviet Union, on the other hand, professional persons including lawyers and doctors and certain skilled craftspeople may engage in private practice and self-employment. Certain producers may sell their products on the free market, and some economic activities take place for private profit. Generally speaking though, inasmuch as all real-world economies are

In practice, all economies are mixed economies with varying degrees of government intervention.

mixed economies, the classification of economic systems on the basis of the way in which economic decisions are made remains valid.

In Canada, most economic decisions are made by households and firms acting in a complicated network of markets and prices that we call the **market mechanism**. The government, however, owns some resources and conducts a significant amount of economic activity. The Canadian economy, then, is a mixed economy. A free enterprise economic system with government intervention is often called a **mixed private enterprise economy**.

> *The market mechanism is the network of markets and prices found in most western countries.*
>
> *A mixed private enterprise economy is a free enterprise economic system with government intervention*

PROBLEM SOLVING 3-6

Of the economic systems that we have discussed, which one would you expect businesses in Canada to favour?

THE BASIC FUNCTIONS OF AN ECONOMIC SYSTEM

Learning Objective 5:
the functions of an economic system

In a market economy, questions about what, how, and for whom to produce are answered through the price system.

Any economic system, regardless of how it is organized, must deal with the fundamental economic problem of finding a way to allocate scarce resources among alternative uses. The economic system must determine what goods and services are to be produced and in what quantities, how they are to be produced, and how to distribute them among the members of the community. This fundamental economic problem is usually cast in terms of *what*, *how*, and *for whom*. Different economic systems deal with these questions in different ways. We shall examine briefly how these basic economic decisions are made in a market economy such as the Canadian economy. In a market economy, questions about what to produce, how to produce, and for whom to produce are answered through the mechanism of the **price system**.

WHAT TO PRODUCE

Firms in a free enterprise economic system engage in production because they hope to make a profit by selling the product at a price that exceeds the cost of production. It follows, then, that firms will produce what consumers want to buy. Consumers express their wants by their behaviour in the market. Firms respond by producing those goods that receive the highest number of dollar votes. Suppose the Kinski Company decides to produce a certain product called Super X, and then finds that consumers are unwilling to spend their money on that particular product. The firm will discover that the production of Super X is not profitable and will put its resources into some other venture. By their decision not to purchase Super X, consumers have communicated to the producers that they do not want Super X produced. The idea that consumers have the power to determine ultimately what is produced has been termed **consumer sovereignty**.

Consumer sovereignty means that consumers decide what to buy and hence what is produced in the economy.

Producer sovereignty means that producers decide what to produce and then convince consumers to buy it.

The concept of consumer sovereignty has come under attack from various quarters. Economist John Kenneth Galbraith, in particular, has argued that the concept of consumer sovereignty should be abandoned and replaced by the concept of **producer sovereignty**. He argues that firms produce the products that will help them to achieve their goals for the security of the organization and its growth, convenience, prestige, and profits. Then they use high-power advertising and hard selling to persuade consumers to purchase the products. In this way, the producer creates and manipulates the consumers' tastes and preferences. In this text, although we will not ignore the effect of persuasive advertising on consumers' behaviour, we will not discard the concept of consumer sovereignty.

HOW TO PRODUCE

The economic system must have a method of organizing its productive resources in order to provide the members of the community with appropriate quantities of goods and services. A mechanism must exist for shifting resources away from uses that contribute less to consumers' satisfaction and toward uses that contribute more to consumers' satisfaction.

In a free enterprise system, individual producers decide on the methods of production, but their decisions are guided by the system of prices and markets. If the goal of a producer is to earn as large a profit as possible, then that producer will use the method of production with the lowest cost; that is, the producer will use an efficient method of production. If a producer chooses an inefficient high-cost method of production, competition from more efficient producers will force that producer out of the market.

FOR WHOM TO PRODUCE

The economic system must also have some means of distributing its output of goods and services among the various members of the community. In a free enterprise economy, this task is accomplished mainly through the market system. The share of the total output that individuals receive depends mainly on their abilities to purchase goods and services. The ability of any individual to purchase goods and services depends on that individual's income, which in turn depends on the quantity and quality of human and physical resources over which that individual has control. If the market places a high value on particular resources, their owners will receive large payments for their use and will be able to obtain a large share of the total output of goods and services. Individuals who own very few resources that are poorly employed will receive low incomes and consequently, only small portions of the total output. Thus, the distribution of the economy's output in a free enterprise economic system depends largely on the distribution of income, which in turn depends on the distribution of resources among the members of the community.

PROBLEM SOLVING 3-7

In Canada at present, there are no laws forcing authors to write books; yet when you register for your courses, you are confident that there will be textbooks in the bookstores for your courses. Why?

ADDITIONAL FUNCTIONS OF AN ECONOMIC SYSTEM

Learning Objective 5: the functions of an economic system

An economic system is expected to provide economic stability, economic security, and economic growth.

In addition to the basic functions of allocation and distribution (what, how, and for whom to produce), the economic system is expected to provide economic stability, which we define as full employment without inflation. We generally consider it to be undesirable to have resources (human or physical) lying idle. Inflation, moreover, is a threat to the proper functioning of the economy and to the well-being of citizens. Later, we will discuss measures that aim at achieving full employment without inflation — an important macroeconomic issue.

The provision of economic security is another task which most modern economic systems are expected to perform. The performance of this task has found expression in programs such as unemployment insurance, old age pensions, minimum wage laws, guaranteed income, and medicare. Finally, the economic system is expected to provide for an increase in the productive capacity of the economy. Economic growth is an important objective of most nations because it determines the society's standard of living.

THE ROLE OF GOVERNMENT IN A MARKET ECONOMY

It would be a mistake for us to believe that the automatic price mechanism works perfectly. Although most economic decisions are left to private individuals acting in response to the market forces of demand and supply, the market system does not perform some tasks satisfactorily. The government therefore enters the market to assist the system in operating satisfactorily and in producing results in accord with the goals of the society.

Consideration of the weaknesses of a free enterprise system discussed above provides some guidelines as to how government intervention might improve the operation of the system. For instance, the government should ensure that conditions exist for the proper functioning of the market mechanism. One of the essentials of the market system is that individuals be free to pursue their own interests. The government should therefore enter the system to protect individual freedom.

The market mechanism functions on the basis of private ownership of property. Owners of resources need to feel secure that their properties are protected. The government must provide this security by protecting property rights. Also, individuals in a free enterprise system need to feel assured that agreements made with other individuals or groups of individuals will be honoured. The government should therefore enter the system to enforce such contracts.

There is a tendency for monopolies to develop in the market. A monopolistic situation exists when a single seller controls the supply of a product. Monopolistic elements can interfere with the proper functioning of the economic system; hence, the government must take measures to encourage competition. In some cases, however, it may be more efficient to produce certain commodities under conditions of monopoly. The government should intervene to modify and regulate such situations to prevent abuse of monopoly power.

The market economy is subject to periods of inflation and unemployment. If the rate of spending in an economy exceeds the rate of increase in the goods and services that the economy produces, then prices will tend to rise. If the rate of spending falls short of the rate of increase in the total output of goods and services of the economy, then unemployment is likely to result. Economic instability can impose severe hardships on individuals in the society. The government should therefore act to prevent such instability. The quantity of money, the rate of interest, the level of government spending, and taxation have now become important government tools to regulate spending in the economy.

The market system, if left unregulated, may distribute the total output of goods and services among the members of the society in an unsatisfactory manner. For example, individuals who own large quantities of valuable resources and who employ them where they make great contributions to the economy's output will receive large incomes, while those individuals who happen to be in less fortunate circumstances may hardly be able to afford the bare necessities of life. The government should intervene to achieve an equitable distribution of income among individuals in the society.

Finally, the market system considers only private costs and private benefits. It does not take social costs and social benefits into account. For example, a firm that freely dumps waste into the environment does not include environmental damage in its cost of production. The society bears the cost of destroyed wildlife, fish, and vegetation, and decreased aesthetic value. Now, on the benefit side, if I decide to turn on my floodlights at night, I must think that the benefit I derive compensates for the increased cost of electricity — and the market will measure these benefits in terms of greater payments for electricity. But although other people may also derive benefits from my floodlights, they do not help to pay my electricity bill and I cannot force them to pay, so the market will not take this social benefit into account. In some cases, even though a good or service may produce great social benefits, individuals acting independently may choose not to produce it because the immediate benefits to these individuals may be too small to justify the cost. When such divergencies occur between private and social benefits and costs, government intervention is desirable to attempt some reconciliation.

 PROBLEM SOLVING 3-8

Can you defend the provision of free elementary and secondary education by the government?

THE BASIC SECTORS OF THE ECONOMY

Learning Objective 7:
the basic sectors of the economy

The basic sectors of the economy are the household sector, the business sector, and the government sector.

For purposes of economic analysis, we may divide the economy into three **basic sectors**: the consumer sector (households), the business sector (producers or firms), and the government sector. Consumers enter the market in two main ways: they hire out or sell resources over which they have control, and they use the proceeds to purchase goods and services to satisfy their wants. The business sector purchases resources from consumers and other firms and uses these resources to produce goods and services to sell to other firms and consumers. The government sector engages in production and consumption. It provides goods and services through the activities of various government departments at the federal, provincial, and municipal levels, government agencies, and crown corporations. It also regulates economic activity by enacting laws that govern

 GLOBAL PERSPECTIVE

Russia's Economic Woes

Economic reform in Russia began some six or seven years ago when Gorbachev introduced capitalism into the then-Soviet economic system. Russia began the movement toward a market economy by allowing the price system to dictate the allocation of resources, and by dismantling the institutions and instruments of central planning. The Russian society was one that was unaccustomed to the workings of the "invisible hand." It is therefore understandable that the Russian people would have difficulty understanding how their well-being could be assured when no one was directly ordering the flow of resources into specific economic activities.

It did not take long for the "makeshift" market system in Russia to begin to fall apart. The International Monetary Fund hailed 1997 as a year of achievement for the Russian economy. Inflation was on the decline, there was a surplus in the balance of payments, and there was growth, though small, in the Russian economy for the first time in five years. Then came the economic woes.

In August 1998, the ruble (the Russian currency unit) tumbled and the Russian people tried to get their money out of Russian banks. The confidence that is so necessary for the proper functioning of a country's financial system was undermined. Capital flight (the swift movement of money out of the country) has become a major problem for the Russian economy. Other major problems include unpaid salaries of government workers, increasing international indebtedness, huge amounts of unpaid taxes, and a hopelessly uncompetitive industrial infrastructure.

The causes of Russia's economic woes are legion, and it would be a Herculean task to analyze them. Suffice it to say that Russia's economic woes do not necessarily reflect a failure of the market mechanism. Perhaps it does, however, teach a lesson or two about injecting capitalism into a system without first ensuring the existence of a structure that is appropriate for the operation of a free market system.

certain aspects of production and consumption, and by conducting economic policies. The government also acts as a consumer when it purchases such items as military aircraft, ships, computers, paper, and uniforms.

Note that although the foreign sector is extremely important, we do not treat it as a basic sector. It consists of consumers, producers, and government engaged in transactions with foreigners. It is thus a particular grouping of members of the basic sectors, so we treat it as a subsector.

CHAPTER SUMMARY

1. The resources of the economy may be classified as land (natural resources), labour (human resources), capital (produced means of production), and entrepreneur-ship (managerial and organizational skills, decision making, risk-taking). The payments for these resources are rent, wages and salaries, interest and dividends, and profits.

2. Because of scarcity, society has to choose. When we choose, we sacrifice something. Opportunity cost or alternative cost refers to the opportunity or alternative that is sacrificed or given up when a choice is made.

3. The production possibility curve or transformation curve shows the maximum output of two goods (or classes of goods) that an economy can produce if it uses all of its resources. In drawing the curve, we assume that technology is constant.

4. A straight line (linear) production possibility curve implies constant opportunity cost, while a concave production possibility curve implies increasing opportunity cost.

5. The production possibility curve will shift only if the economy's productive capacity changes. This could be caused only by a change in resources or a change in technology.

6. The economic system is a set of laws, institutions, and customs through which a society accomplishes the task of producing and distributing goods and services to satisfy its wants.

7. Economic systems may be classified broadly into two categories: free enterprise systems, and socialistic systems or command economies.

8. The foundation of a free enterprise system is the principle of the institution of private property. This means that it is the right of private individuals to own things.

9. Advantages of the free enterprise system include individual freedom of choice, low cost of operation, and the ability of the system to produce what consumers want. Weaknesses of this system include its inability to guarantee full enployment, lack of incentive to produce public goods, inadequate protection of the environment, and an inequitable distribution of income.

10. Government or state ownership or control of the resources of the economy is fundamental to command economies. Central planning directs economic activity and the use of resources.

11. Advantages of command economies include their ability to maintain full employment and to divert resources from one use to another. Weaknesses of these economies include limited individual freedom, high cost of planning economic activity, a limited variety of products, and a tendency to produce goods of poor quality.

12. In practice, all economies are mixed economies with a greater or lesser degree of government intervention in directing and controlling economic activities.

13. Every economic system must deal with the basic problem of deciding what to produce, how to produce, and for whom to produce. In addition, an economic system is expected to provide economic stability, economic security, and economic growth.

14. The role of government in a market economy is to ensure that the system operates in a satisfactory manner and that it gives results that are in accordance with the objectives of the society.

15. The economy may be divided into three basic sectors: the household sector, the business sector, and the government sector.

TERMS FOR REVIEW

resources (factors of production) (34)
land (natural resources) (34)
labour (human resources) (34)
capital (34)
real capital (34)
human capital (34)
entrepreneurship (34)
rent (35)
wages and salaries (35)
interest (35)
dividents (35)
profits (35)
scarcity and choice (36)
opportunity cost (alternative cost) (36)
production possibility schedule (36)
production possibility
   (transformation) curve (37)
production possibility point (38)

economic growth (40)
economic system (40)
free enterprise system (capitalism) (41)
socialistic system (command
   economy) (41)
institution of private property (41)
market economy (43)
command economy (43)
mixed economy (43)
market mechanism (44)
mixed private enterprise economy (44)
price system (44)
consumer sovereignty (44)
producer sovereignty (44)
household sector (47)
business sector (47)
government sector (47)

QUESTIONS FOR REVIEW AND DISCUSSION

1. The fundamental economic problem is scarcity of resources. What are these resources and how can they be classified? (L.O.1)

2. Give two examples each of land, labour, capital, and entrepreneurship. (L.O.1)

3. "The income derived from capital is profit because firms use money and machines to make profits." Is this statement true or false? Explain. (L.O.2)

4. Make a connection between scarcity, choice and opportunity cost. (L.O.3)

5. What is opportunity cost? Give two examples to demonstrate your understanding of opportunity cost. (L.O.3)

6. Distinguish between a production possibility point and a production possibility curve. (L.O.4)

7. Will a fall in prices shift an economy's production possibility curve? Why or why not? (L.O.4)

8. Give three examples of events that would cause Canada's p-p curve to shift to the right. (L.O.4)

9. Discuss the main features of: (L.O.5)

   (a) a free enterprise economic system;

   (b) a command economy.

10. What are the main advantages and weaknesses of a free enterprise economic system? (L.O.5)

11. What are the main advantages and disadvantages of a command economy? (L.O.5)

12. Discuss the role of prices in a free enterprise economic system. (L.O.5)

13. Discuss the role of government in a market economy. Do you think that our federal government should play a more active role in our economy? Why or why not? (L.O.6)

14. Explain how a free enterprise economic system decides what to produce, how to produce, and for whom to produce. (L.O.5)

PROBLEMS AND EXERCISES

1. Indicate whether each of the following is land (T), labour (L), capital (K), or entrepreneurial services (entrepreneurship) (Es): (L.O.1)

   (a) a personal computer in the office of a travel agency;

   (b) oil deposits off the coast of Newfoundland;

   (c) a camping ground in Parc Gatineau, Quebec;

   (d) flour bought by Good Dough Bakers from Fine Flour Mill;

   (e) the services rendered by the operator of Jacob's Corner Grocery Store;

   (f) the work performed by the cashiers in the Low Price supermarket;

   (g) Snipe Lake, Alberta;

   (h) the work done by a construction worker;

   (i) anti-pollution equipment bought by Lambertus Pharmaceuticals in North Bay, Ontario;

   (j) the work performed in establishing a large chain such as Holiday Inn.

2. Indicate whether each of the following types of income is rent (R), wages and salaries (W), interest and dividend (D), or profit (P): (L.O.2)

   (a) money paid to your economics professor for his or her services;

   (b) money you receive from your part-time job;

   (c) the annual payments made by Bell to its shareholders;

   (d) the money paid to the owner of a piece of land used as a parking lot;

   (e) the net amount received by the operator of the U-Gain Retail Outlet;

   (f) the money paid to the mayor of your city for his or her services;

   (g) the money charged by the owner of Piccolo Pond for fishing privileges.

3. Makeba Electronics produces radios and TV sets. The company finds that on any given day, it can produce any of the combinations of radios and TV sets shown in Table 3.4. (L.O.4)

TABLE 3.4	Radios	TV sets
Production for	20	0
Makeba Electronics.	16	1
	12	2
	8	3
	4	4
	0	5

(a) Using this information, draw the production possibility curve for Makeba Electronics.

(b) Why is the production possibility curve for Makeba Electronics a straight line?

(c) What is the opportunity cost of a TV set in terms of radios?

4. During periods of high unemployment when it is difficult to find jobs, enrollment in colleges and universities usually increases. Use the concept of opportunity cost to explain this phenomenon. (L.O.3)

5. Show the effect of each of the following events on a country's production possibility curve. Put oil production (in barrels) on the X-axis and all other goods on the Y-axis. (L.O.4)

(a) the discovery of new oil fields;

(b) an increase in the rate of extraction of oil from existing oil fields;

(c) technological advances in the extraction of oil;

(d) a fall in unemployment due to the hiring of more workers by all firms;

(e) an increase in the number of refugees coming to Canada and being unable to find jobs;

(f) an increase in the number of refugees coming to Canada and finding jobs.

6. The Nu-Trend Office Supply Company observed that by allocating its fixed production budget between word processors and electronic calculators, it can produce per day any of the combinations of calculators and word processors shown in Table 3.5. (L.O.4)

TABLE 3.5	Number of word processors	Number of calculators
Production for	0	15
Nu-Trend Office	1	14
Supply Company.	2	12
	3	9
	4	5
	5	0

(a) Plot the production possibility curve for Nu-Trend.

(b) What is the opportunity cost of:

　(i)　the first word processor;

　(ii)　the second word processor;

         (iii)   the first two word processors;

         (iv)   the third word processor;

         (v)   the first three word processors?

    (c) What do you notice about the opportunity cost of word processors as more and more of them are produced?

    (d) What is the shape of the production possibility curve plotted in part (a)?

7. Referring to Nu-Trend in Question 6, suppose the company receives an increase in its production budget so that it can now produce more word processors and more calculators. (L.O.4)

    (a) Show on a graph what the new production possibility curve might look like.

    (b) If the firm dismisses some of its employees, how will the production possibility curve be affected?

    (c) What will happen to the production possibility curve if employees are shifted from the word processor section to the calculator section?

8. Under the free enterprise system, individuals enjoy freedom of choice. Does this mean that economics professors can choose not to show up for their classes any time they do not feel like teaching? (L.O.5)

9. Make a case in support of (L.O.5)

    (a) consumer sovereignty;

    (b) producer sovereignty.

10. Take a sheet of paper and draw a vertical line down the middle. On the left side, list the strengths of the market system, and on the right side, list the weaknesses. (L.O.1)

11. Repeat Exercise 10, but for a planned economy. (L.O.1)

12. (a) Compile a list of all costs involved in attending college or university for one year, then add the cost of all items to arrive at the *total cost* of attending college or university. Where costs differ among individuals, use an average. You may, for example, begin with the cost of textbooks and supplies as follows:

Items	Cost for one year
Textbooks	$_____
School supplies (pens, notebooks, etc)	$_____

    (b) Having determined the total cost of attending college or university, what should be your attitude toward college or university? (How will the information affect your behaviour?)

Internet Site

http://www.imf.org
This site is the home page of the International Monetary Fund.

INTERNET EXERCISE

1. Go to the IMF home page listed above.
2. Click on *Site Map*.
3. Click on *What is the IMF?*
4. Click on *Recent Activities?*
5. Besides Russia, in what areas of the world has the IMF been active during the 1990s?

CHAPTER 4

ELEMENTS OF DEMAND AND SUPPLY

Learning Objectives

After studying this chapter, you should be able to:

1 define demand

2 distinguish between demand and quantity demanded

3 identify the factors affecting quantity demanded

4 define supply

5 distinguish between supply and quantity supplied

6 identify the factors affecting quantity supplied

7 explain market price determination

8 use demand-supply analysis to solve simple economic problems

When demand and supply are in stable equilibrium, if any accident should move the scale of production from its equilibrium position, there will be instantly brought into play forces tending to push it back to that position; just as, if a stone hanging by a string is displaced from its equilibrium position, the force of gravity will at once tend to bring it back to its equilibrium position.

Alfred Marshall, *Principles of Economics*

INTRODUCTION

The term *demand and supply* has been used so extensively both by economists and non-economists in relation to economic matters that the term has almost become synonymous with economics. How often have you heard this statement: "It's all economics, you know — demand and supply." As someone once remarked, if the only requirement for understanding economics was the ability to repeat the phrase *demand and supply,* one could successfully teach economics to a parrot. Although economics cannot be summed up in the term *demand and supply,* a good knowledge of these two important economic concepts will enable us to understand a great deal about the operation of our economic system. Of course, economics consists of much more than just simple demand and supply, but a thorough understanding of these terms and the way that they work is absolutely essential if we are to understand many economic issues and make wise economic decisions. In this chapter, we shall study the elements of demand and supply, and how these market forces work to determine the price of a good or service. We shall also consider some applications of demand-supply analysis.

The explanation of how demand and supply work to determine the price of a good or service is presented as a model. This model assumes a free enterprise system in which economic decisions are made through the market mechanism. In this model, there is no intervention to prevent the free play of the market forces of demand and supply. It is important to note also that in this discussion, we are considering the total or market demand and supply for a particular product as opposed to a household's demand or a firm's (seller's) supply. The market consists of all buyers and all sellers of the product.

THE NATURE OF DEMAND

Learning Objective 1:
define demand

Demand: the various quantities that buyers are willing and able to buy at various prices during a period of time.

One of my economics professors once said to me, "Demand is not what you think it is." He was right. Many people use the term *demand* to mean many different things. To the economist, however, demand has a very specific meaning. **Demand** refers to the various quantities of a good or service that people will be willing and able to purchase at various prices during a period of time. It is important to note that demand refers not only to the desire for a good or service, but also to the ability to purchase the good or service. Both ingredients must be present for effective demand. It is important to note also that demand does not refer to the specific quantity that will be purchased at some particular price, but rather to a series of quantities and their associated prices.

Suppose we have information on the various quantities of apples that people will be willing and able to buy at various prices. The information may be set out in a table such as Table 4.1.

TABLE 4.1	Price of apples ($)	Quantity demanded per week (000)
Hypothetical demand schedule for apples.	0.50	100
	0.45	110
	0.40	120
	0.35	130
	0.30	140
	0.25	150
	0.20	160
	0.15	170
	0.10	180
	0.05	190

Demand schedule:
a tabular representation of
demand.

A table containing this type of information is called a **demand schedule** and may be defined as a table that shows various quantities of a good or service that people will buy at various possible prices during some specified period. Note the importance of the time period. For example, to say that the quantity of apples demanded at a price of $0.35 is 130 000 is somewhat unclear. To say that the quantity of apples demanded at a price of $0.35 is 130 000 a week is more precise. Buying 130 000 apples at $0.35 each during a week is certainly not the same as buying the same quantity at the same price during a year. The quantities demanded at various prices must have some time dimension.

THE LAW OF DEMAND

The inverse relation
between price and quantity
demanded is called the law
of demand.

You will notice from Table 4.1 that as the price of apples falls, a greater quantity is demanded. This fundamental characteristic of demand is called the **law of demand**, and may be stated as follows:

> **As the price of a product falls, other things being equal, the quantity demanded increases; or alternatively, as the price of a product rises, other things being equal, the quantity demanded decreases.**

In other words, there is an inverse relation between the price of a product and the quantity demanded. Note that the law of demand assumes that all things other than price remain constant.

Let us examine the reasons for this inverse relation between price and quantity demanded. Why do people buy more as the price falls? First, as the price of apples falls, a greater number of buyers will be able to afford to buy apples. In other words, the size of the market increases, thus the quantity of apples demanded increases. We can refer to this effect as the **market size effect**. Second, those people who were buying apples

The market size effect:
demand increases when
the market size increases.

before the increase in price can afford to buy more apples now that the price has fallen. In other words, a fall in price increases the buyers' purchasing power or real income, so the quantity demanded increases. This increase in quantity demanded resulting from an increase in the buyers' purchasing power or real income is often referred to as the **income effect**. Third, when the price of apples falls, some people will switch from

The income effect:
demand increases as
incomes increase.

other goods (perhaps grapes or oranges) that they were previously purchasing but that have now become relatively more expensive. That is, some people will substitute the cheaper apples for some other fruit. This change in quantity demanded resulting from sub-stituting one good for another is often referred to as the **substitution effect**. For all of

The substitution effect:
demand changes as one
good is substituted for
another.

these reasons then, we might reasonably expect buyers to purchase a greater quantity of a product as its price falls, or alternatively, to buy less as the price rises.

THE DEMAND CURVE

The advantage of graphical representation of information is well known: a graph enables us to see much more clearly than a table the relation between two variables. The relation between the price of apples and the quantity demanded shown in Table 4.1 may be presented in the form of a graph. It has become common practice in economics to mea-sure price on the vertical axis and quantity demanded per unit of time on the horizon-tal axis. Let us see what happens if we plot the information in Table 4.1 on a graph. The result is Figure 4.1, which is called a **demand curve** and which we can define as follows:

Demand curve:
a graphical representation
of demand.

> **The demand curve is a graph showing the various quantities of a good or service that people will be willing and able to buy at various possible prices.**

Note that because of the inverse relationship between price and quantity demanded (the law of demand), the demand curve slopes downward and to the right as shown by DD in Figure 4.1.

FIGURE 4.1

Demand curve for apples.

Learning Objective 2:
distinguish between demand and quantity demanded

Let us examine the demand schedule and the demand curve. At a price of $0.20, people are willing and able to buy 160 000 apples per week. This is represented by a point (point G) on the demand curve. It would be wrong to say that at a price of $0.20, the demand is 160 000. The correct way to put it is that at a price of $0.20, the *quantity demanded* (not the demand) is 160 000. In other words, the entire demand curve represents demand while a point on the demand curve represents quantity demanded at some specific price.

You will notice that the demand curve in Figure 4.1 and the demand schedule of Table 4.1 express a linear relationship between the price and the quantity demanded. It must be pointed out, however, that there is no suggestion here that demand curves (or demand schedules) are always linear. We use a linear relationship for convenience only.

 PROBLEM SOLVING 4-1

Roisin Ferin, who sells roses on Confederation Square, wants to sell her entire stock by the end of the day. She begins by charging $5 a bouquet. As the day advances, she notices that her roses are moving very slowly. It seems that she will sell only half of her stock by the end of the day. What should Roisin do to rectify the situation?

FACTORS AFFECTING DEMAND

Learning Objective 3:
identify the factors affecting quantity demanded

We have seen that the price of a product affects the *quantity demanded* of that product. What are the factors that affect the *demand* for a product? Income, prices of related goods, tastes and preferences, expectations, and population: all are likely to affect the demand for a product. Since these are factors other than the price of the product under consideration, we sometimes refer to them as *non-price determinants*. Note that if we are referring to the price of another product as a determinant of demand, we still list it as a non-price determinant. Let us see how each of these non-price determinants can affect the demand for a product.

INCOME

If their incomes increase, consumers will tend to buy more goods and services than they did before the increase in income. Let us assume that the Kurtz family was buying three kilograms of steak each week. If their income increases, the Kurtzes may find that they can now afford to purchase five kilograms of steak per week without buying less of anything else. At the same time, the Marlowe family, may be unable to buy steaks because of a low family income. If their income increases, they may decide to enter the steak market. As income increases, then, it seems likely that more of a given product will be purchased at any given price. This is the case for most goods and services; hence, economists refer to goods whose quantity demanded varies directly with income as **normal goods**.

Although most commodities are normal goods, there are cases when consumers may not buy more as their incomes rise. Instead, they may buy less. Let us consider regular ground beef. At a certain price of ground beef, and at a given level of income, people will buy a certain amount per week. If these people's incomes increase, they may actually reduce their purchases of regular ground beef and buy steaks or lean ground beef instead. Thus, as income rises, people may buy less, not more, regular ground beef. The same may be true of potatoes, and drink mixes such as Kool-aid. Economists refer to such goods as **inferior goods**.

It is more accurate to think of the terms *normal* and *inferior* as descriptions of consumers' behaviour or reaction to a change in income rather than as descriptions of the goods per se.

PRICES OF RELATED GOODS

Goods and services may be related to each other in two main ways: they may be substitutes or they may be complements. One good is said to be a **substitute** for a second good if it can be used in place of the second good. Examples of goods that are substitutes for each other are: lemons and limes, sugar and honey, butter and margarine, and tea and coffee. Two goods are said to be **complements** if one is used in conjunction with the other. Complementary goods are demanded jointly. Examples of complementary goods are: automobiles and gasoline, stereo sets and audio tapes, word processors and floppy disks, and cameras and films.

Think about substitutable goods. If the price of limes were to increase, consumers would tend to switch to a substitute (lemons, for example). Hence, the demand for lemons would increase. In general, if the price of a substitutable commodity increases, consumers will tend to increase their purchases of the substitute in question.

Now, let us consider the case of complementary goods. As noted above, these are goods that are used together. If the price of word processors falls, people will buy more word processors and, as a consequence, the demand for floppy disks will also tend to increase. In general, if the price of a complement falls, consumers will tend to increase their purchases of the commodity in question.

We should note, in passing, that not all goods are related. Some goods are neither substitute goods nor complementary goods. For example, we would not expect any relationship between cars and milk, radios and picture frames, computers and apple juice, or telephones and microwave ovens. Goods such as those just listed, which are not at all related, are said to be **independent goods**. If the price of radios falls, for example, we can hardly expect it to have any effect on the demand for picture frames.

TASTES AND PREFERENCES

Tastes and preferences affect demand.

The quantity of a commodity that people will buy will be affected by their tastes and preferences. If tastes in Manitoba change from meat to vegetable diets, then it is obvious that more vegetables and less meat will be demanded there. Companies spend millions of dollars in advertising in an attempt to influence consumers' tastes in favour of their products. By so doing, they are trying to increase the demand for their products.

EXPECTATIONS

Expectations affect demand.

The expectations of consumers regarding prices in the future will affect present purchases of goods and services. If consumers expect the price of a product to increase in the future, they are likely to increase their purchases now to stock up on the product and thus postpone paying the ensuing higher price for as long as possible. Conversely, if the price is expected to fall in the future, consumers will attempt to delay their purchases now in order to take advantage of the lower future price.

The expectations of consumers about future changes in income will also affect present purchases of goods and services. If people expect substantial raises in their salaries sometime in the near future, they are likely to buy more goods and services even before the increase in income materializes. If people expect decreases in income (resulting from loss of employment, for example), they are likely to buy fewer goods and services. A good example of how expected future income affects present purchases of goods and services is provided by students of law and medicine in their final year of law school or medical school. Such students usually adopt higher standards of living than individuals with similar current incomes who entertain no hope of substantial increases in their future incomes.

POPULATION

The number of buyers in the market affects the quantity that people will purchase at each and every price.

The quantity of a commodity that people will buy depends on the number of buyers in the market for that particular commodity. Other things being equal, we would expect the quantity of oranges that people will buy in Toronto, Ontario, to be significantly higher than the quantity that people will buy in Corner Brook, Newfoundland, since the population of Toronto is so much greater than that of Corner Brook. If population increases, we expect the demand for most goods and services to increase as a consequence.

PROBLEM SOLVING 4-2

1. **Petit Prince Bookstore sells crayons and colouring books. Guernica Art Supplies has just offered it a large quantity of crayons at a fraction of the regular cost. How might the bookstore use its inexpensive crayons to boost its sales of colouring books?**

2. **Sometimes when the price of gold rises, we notice that people buy more, not less. Is this a refutation of the law of demand?**

A CHANGE IN DEMAND VERSUS A CHANGE IN QUANTITY DEMANDED

Learning Objective 2: *distinguish between demand and quantity demanded*

The distinction between a change in demand and a change in quantity demanded is an important one, and we should avoid confusing these concepts. When we speak of demand, we refer to the entire demand curve or schedule. It follows then, that if demand changes, the entire curve will shift. Suppose the demand for apples in Pointe Claire was as shown in the first two columns of Table 4.2, but that now there is an increase in demand for apples (perhaps research by a team of doctors has revealed that a sufficiently large intake of apples over a certain period of time will protect the body from a wide variety of illnesses). As a consequence of this announcement, we will obtain a new demand schedule showing that a greater quantity of apples will be purchased *at each price*. The new quantities are shown in the right hand column of Table 4.2.

	Price of apples ($)	Original quantity demanded per week (000)	New quantity demanded per week (000)
TABLE 4.2	0.50	100	130
Demand schedule	0.45	110	140
showing an increase	0.40	120	150
in demand.	0.35	130	160
	0.30	140	170
	0.25	150	180
	0.20	160	190
	0.15	170	200
	0.10	180	210
	0.05	190	220

We can plot these two demand curves on the same graph to illustrate the shift in demand brought about by the announcement. Figure 4.2 shows this. DD is the original demand curve; D_1D_1 is the new demand curve. The increase in demand is shown by shifting the entire demand curve to the right. The location of the curve has now changed. Note that at *any given price*, a greater quantity is purchased. A decrease in demand would mean that at *any given price* a smaller quantity would be purchased, and this would be represented by a leftward shift in the demand curve as shown in Figure 4.3.

A change in quantity demanded refers to the change in the quantity that would be bought as a result of a change in price. Let us examine the demand curve shown in Figure 4.4. At a price of $2, the quantity demanded is 48 000 per week. If the price falls

FIGURE 4.2

Increase in demand.

An increase in demand is shown by a shift in the demand curve to the right.

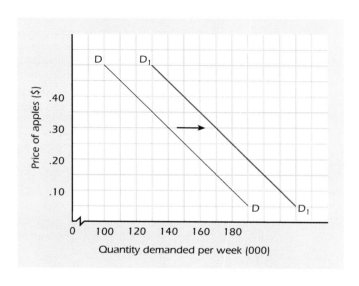

FIGURE 4.3

Decrease in demand.

A decrease in demand is
shown by a leftward shift in
the demand curve.

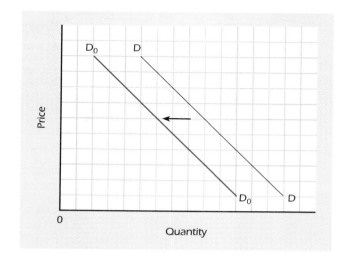

FIGURE 4.4

A change in quantity
demanded.

A change in quantity
demanded caused by a
change in price is shown
by a movement along the
demand curve.

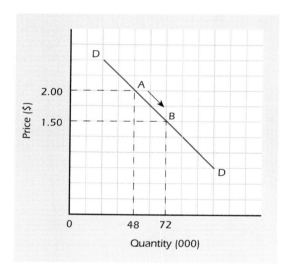

to $1.50, a quantity of 72 000 units per week will be demanded. This change in quantity demanded is represented by a movement along the same demand curve from point A to point B in Figure 4.4.

A change in the price of the commodity under consideration will not cause a change in demand, it will cause a change in quantity demanded. Only a change in a non-price determinant can cause a change in the demand for that commodity. Factors such as a change in income, a change in taste, a change in population, a change in the price of a related good, or a change in expectations will cause a change in demand — that is, cause the entire demand curve to shift.

A change in a non-price determinant causes the demand curve to shift.

Table 4.3 presents a convenient reference list of the major factors that cause the demand curve to shift. These non-price determinants are often referred to as **demand shifters.**

TABLE 4.3	Demand shifters	Illustrative examples
Demand shifters: non-price determinants that change the location of the demand curve.	1. A change in income	An increase in income increases purchasing power. The demand for most goods (normal goods) will increase, but the demand for inferior goods (used tires, for example) will decrease.
	2. A change in the prices of related goods	An increase in the price of Coke will increase the demand for Pepsi because they are substitute goods. A decrease in the price of personal computers will increase the demand for floppy disks because they are complementary goods.
	3. A change in tastes and preferences	A successful advertising campaign for eggs increases the demand for eggs because it changes buyers' tastes in favour of eggs. (Get cracking!)
	4. A change in expectations	The announcement of the imposition of a tax on video cassettes produces expectations of higher future prices and thus increases the current demand for video cassettes.
	5. A change in population	An increase in the number of immigrants into Canada increases the demand for furniture.

PROBLEM SOLVING 4-3

In January, the number of typewriters bought in Jonquière was 600. In February, the quantity bought was 750, and in March, the quantity had grown to 875. Vinud Anwar, an investor seeing these figures, decided that the demand for typewriters in Jonquière was increasing and that it was a good idea to open a store to sell typewriters. What mistake might Vinud be making?

THE NATURE OF SUPPLY

Learning Objective 4:
define supply

Supply: the various quantities that sellers are willing to offer for sale at various possible prices during a period of time.

Supply schedule: a tabular presentation of supply.

A market consists of both buyers and sellers. In order to understand market behaviour, we must consider both buyers and sellers. We have looked at the demand side (the buyers' side) of the market for a product. Let us now look at the supply side (the sellers' side) of the market. **Supply** refers to the various quantities of a good or service that sellers will be willing and able to offer for sale at various prices during a period of time. As in the case of demand, supply refers not to a specific quantity that will be sold at some particular price, but to a series of quantities and a range of associated prices.

Suppose we have information on the various quantities of apples that sellers are willing and able to offer for sale at various prices. We may set this information out in a table such as Table 4.4.

A table such as Table 4.4 is called a **supply schedule** and may be defined as a table that shows various quantities of a good or service that sellers are willing and able to offer for sale at various possible prices during some specified period.

	Price of apples ($)	Quantity supplied per week (000)
TABLE 4.4		
Hypothetical supply schedule for apples.	0.05	40
	0.10	60
	0.15	80
	0.20	100
	0.25	120
	0.30	140
	0.35	160
	0.40	180
	0.45	200
	0.50	220

THE LAW OF SUPPLY

The direct relation between price and quantity supplied is called the law of supply.

Table 4.4 shows that as the price of apples rises, a greater quantity is offered for sale. As the price falls, a smaller quantity is offered for sale. This fundamental relationship between price and quantity offered for sale is called the **law of supply**, and may be stated as follows:

> **As the price of a product falls, other things being equal, the quantity offered for sale decreases; or alternatively, as the price of a product rises, other things being equal, the quantity supplied increases.**

There is therefore a direct relationship between the price of a product and the quantity supplied.

Why is there a direct relationship between price and quantity supplied? The main reason is that higher prices serve as an incentive for sellers to offer a greater quantity for sale. The suggestion is that sellers (or producers) can be induced by higher prices to produce and offer for sale a greater quantity of goods. Moreover, increases in price may entice new suppliers into the market.

The following example will help to explain how sellers respond to an increase in price. Suppose farmers have a certain amount of land on which they produce wheat and corn. If the price of wheat increases, farmers will find it profitable to shift land out of corn production and into wheat production. Also, it is conceivable that some farmers who were not previously producing wheat will now become wheat farmers. Hence the output of wheat increases.

THE SUPPLY CURVE

Supply curve: a graphical representation of supply.

It is advantageous to present the information contained in Table 4.4 graphically as we did in the case of demand. Plotting the data in Table 4.4 on a graph results in Figure 4.5, which is called a **supply curve** and which we can define as follows:

> **The supply curve is a graph showing the various quantities of a good or service that sellers are willing and able to offer for sale at various possible prices.**

Learning Objective 5:
distinguish between supply and quantity supplied

Note that because of the direct relationship between price and quantity supplied (price and quantity supplied move in the same direction), the supply curve slopes upward as shown by SS in Figure 4.5.

FIGURE 4.5

Supply curve for apples.

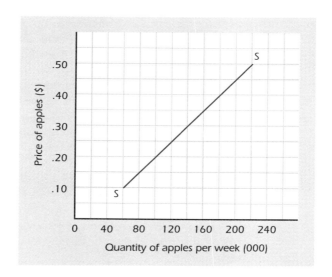

Note again that the entire supply curve represents supply while a point on the supply curve represents quantity supplied at some specific price. Also, as in the case of demand, we have assumed a linear relationship between price and quantity supplied for convenience only. There is no suggestion that supply curves are always linear.

FACTORS AFFECTING SUPPLY

Learning Objective 6: identify the factors affecting quantity supplied

You have seen that the quantity of a good or service that sellers are willing and able to offer for sale depends on the price of the good or service. In other words, the price of a product affects the *quantity supplied*. Non-price factors, such as the number of producers (sellers), the prices of related products, technology, expectations, and input prices, are likely to affect the *supply* of a product. Let us see how each of these non-price determinants is likely to affect supply.

THE NUMBER OF PRODUCERS

The number of sellers affects quantity supplied at each and every price.

The number of sellers in the market will obviously have some effect on total market supply. This is so because the market supply of a good or service is the sum of the quantities offered for sale by all of the individual sellers in the market. We can expect market supply to increase as the number of sellers increases, and to decrease as the number of sellers decreases. If, however, the average output of producers increases significantly, the total market supply can increase even if the number of producers decreases.

PRICES OF RELATED PRODUCTS

Production substitutes and production complements affect supply.

Substitutes in production are alternatives to each other.

Complements in production, or joint products, are produced together. One may be a byproduct of the other.

You will recall our discussion of substitutes and complements on the demand side. A similar situation exists on the supply side. Goods can be substitutes or complements in production. Goods are **substitutes in production** (or production substitutes) if they are produced as alternatives to each other. Examples of substitutes in production are lettuce and tomatoes (a farmer can produce one or the other on the same piece of land), and leather bags and belts (both can be produced with the same type of resources). Goods are **complements in production** (or production complements) if they are produced together; the production of one implies the production of the other. Complements in production are also called **joint products**. Beef and hides are a classic example of goods that are complements in production.

Consider the case of substitutes in production. If the price of lettuce increases, the supply of tomatoes will decrease as producers shift from tomato production to lettuce production. In general, if the price of a substitutable product increases, sellers will tend to reduce the supply of the substitute in question.

Now consider complements in production. As noted above, these are joint products. If the price of beef rises, the quantity of beef supplied will rise, but so will the quantity of hides as more cattle are slaughtered. In general, if the price of a complement in production falls, the supply of the good in question will also fall.

TECHNOLOGY

Technology affects quantity supplied at each and every price.

Producers use inputs (factors of production) to produce goods and services. An increase in technology makes existing factors (inputs) more productive, and introduces new types of inputs that are more efficient than older types. Hence, an increase in technology causes an increase in supply. Of course, the decision to adopt new technology is based on cost considerations. If the new technology does not reduce cost, producers are unlikely to adopt it.

EXPECTATIONS

Expectations affect quantity supplied at each and every price.

If producers expect prices to rise in the future, they might begin now to expand their productive capacity and thus increase their present output levels. This is particularly so in the case of products that cannot be stored easily. However, it is entirely possible that expectations of higher future prices may lead producers into building up stocks now so that they will have a larger quantity to sell at the future higher prices. Such action will, of course, reduce current supply. Therefore, generalizations should not be made about the effect of expected price changes on supply.

PRICES OF INPUTS

Prices of inputs (production costs) affect quantity supplied at each and every price.

An increase in production costs will result in a reduction in the supply of a product. Payment for factor inputs represents a significant part of production costs. The higher the prices of these inputs, the greater the costs of production will be, and hence the less will be the supply. A reduction in input prices will, of course, cause the supply to increase.

PROBLEM SOLVING 4-4

How will an increase in wages in the shoe industry affect the supply of shoes?

A CHANGE IN SUPPLY VERSUS A CHANGE IN QUANTITY SUPPLIED

You will recall the distinction made earlier between a change in demand and a change in quantity demanded. A similar distinction must be made between a change in supply and a change in quantity supplied. When we speak of supply, we refer to the entire supply curve or schedule. It follows then, that if supply changes, the entire curve will shift. Suppose the supply of apples in Pointe Claire was as shown in the first two columns of Table 4.5, but that now there is an increase in the supply of apples because of technological advances in apple production. We will obtain a new supply schedule showing that a greater quantity of apples will be supplied at each price. The new quantities supplied are shown in the right column of Table 4.5.

A change in supply is shown by a shift in the entire supply curve.

TABLE 4.5

An increase in supply.

Price of apples ($)	Original quantity supplied (000)	New quantity supplied (000)
0.05	40	80
0.10	60	100
0.15	80	120
0.20	100	140
0.25	120	160
0.30	140	180
0.35	160	200
0.40	180	220
0.45	200	240
0.50	220	260

Let us plot these two supply curves on the same graph to illustrate the shift in supply brought about by the increase in technology. The result is Figure 4.6.

SS is the original supply curve; S_1S_1 is the new supply curve. The increase in supply is shown by shifting the entire supply curve to the right. The location of the curve has now changed. Notice that *at any given price*, a greater quantity is supplied. A decrease in supply would mean that *at any given price*, a smaller quantity would be supplied, and would be represented by a leftward shift in the supply curve as shown in Figure 4.7.

FIGURE 4.6

An increase in supply.

An increase in supply is represented by a shift of the supply curve to the right or down.

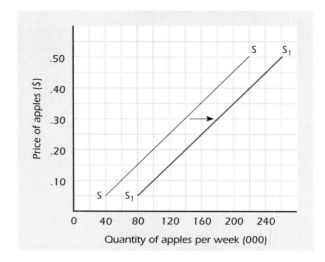

FIGURE 4.7

A decrease in supply.

A decrease in supply is shown by a shift of the supply curve upward or to the left.

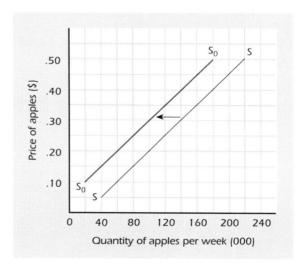

A change in quantity supplied refers to the change in quantity that would be offered for sale as a result of a change in price. Let us examine the supply curve in Figure 4.8. At a price of $3, the quantity supplied is 12 000 per week. If the price rises to $4, a quantity of 20 000 units per week will be supplied. This change in quantity supplied is represented by a movement along the same supply curve from point C to point D in Figure 4.8.

Learning Objective 5: distinguish between supply and quantity supplied

A change in a non-price determinant causes the supply curve to shift.

A change in the price of the commodity under consideration will not cause a change in supply; it will cause a change in quantity supplied. Only a change in a non-price determinant can cause a change in the supply of that commodity. Factors such as a change in the number of producers, a change in the price of a related good, a change in technology, a change in expectations, or a change in input prices will cause a change in supply — that is, they will cause the entire supply curve to shift.

The major factors that cause the supply curve to shift are conveniently collected in a reference list in Table 4.6. These non-price determinants are sometimes referred to as **supply shifters.**

FIGURE 4.8

A movement along the supply curve caused by a change in price.

TABLE 4.6

Supply shifters: non-price determinants that change the location of the supply curve.

Supply shifters	Illustrative examples
1. A change in the number of producers	An increase in the number of manufacturers of video cassette recorders (VCRs) increases the supply of VCRs. If many of the firms producing blue jeans go out of business, the supply of blue jeans falls.
2. A change in the prices of related products	An increase in the price of lettuce reduces the supply of turnips; they are production substitutes. An increase in the price of refined cane sugar increases the supply of molasses; they are joint products.
3. A change in technology	The invention of high-speed computers increases the output (supply) of computational services.
4. A change in expectations	Suppliers expect an increase in the price of coffee so they reduce present supplies with the intention of selling at the higher price in the future.
5. A change in the price of inputs	A substantial increase in the price of steel reduces the supply of chairs with steel frames.

DETERMINATION OF EQUILIBRIUM PRICE

Learning Objective 7: explain market price determination

So far in this chapter, we have looked at demand and supply separately. It is now time to bring them together to see how market forces determine the price of a product. To help with the explanation, Table 4.7 reproduces the hypothetical demand and supply schedules shown in Tables 4.1 and 4.4 respectively.

TABLE 4.7

Hypothetical demand and supply schedules for apples.

Price of apples ($)	Quantity demanded (000)	Quantity supplied (000)
0.50	100	220
0.45	110	200
0.40	120	180
0.35	130	160
0.30	140	140
0.25	150	120
0.20	160	100
0.15	170	80
0.10	180	60
0.05	190	40

Let us first consider the situation when the price is $0.15. At this price, buyers are willing and able to purchase 170 000 apples a week, but sellers are willing and able to offer only 80 000 for sale. There will therefore be a shortage of 90 000 apples. At a price of $0.45, buyers are willing and able to purchase only 110 000 apples a week while sellers are willing to offer 200 000 apples. There will therefore be a surplus of 90 000 apples on the market. Let us now consider a price of $0.30. At this price, buyers are willing to purchase 140 000 apples a week, and sellers are willing to offer 140 000 apples for sale. At this price, there is neither a surplus nor a shortage.

At any price other than $0.30, market forces are set in motion to raise or lower the price. Consider a price of $0.40. At this price, as the supply schedule shows, sellers are willing to put 180 000 apples on the market, but buyers are willing to take only 120 000. A **surplus** or **excess quantity supplied** of apples will result. Sellers will then attempt to dispose of this surplus by lowering the price. As the price falls, a greater quantity will be demanded. The price will settle at $0.30 because, at this price, the market will be cleared.

If, on the other hand, the price happens to be $0.20, buyers will be willing to purchase 160 000 apples a week, but sellers will be willing to offer only 100 000. Pricing the apples at $0.20 will result in a **shortage** or **excess quantity demanded**. Unhappy with the shortage and wanting more apples, customers will bid up the price. Sellers, then, will offer a greater quantity at the higher prices. The price will again settle at $0.30 because, at this price, the quantity demanded equals exactly the quantity supplied. Note that the price of $0.30 is the only price that will prevail in the market. There will be no tendency for this price to change. Such a price is referred to as the **equilibrium price**, and the quantity traded (exchanged) at this price is called the **equilibrium quantity**. The market for a product is said to be in equilibrium when the quantity of the product demanded equals the quantity supplied at a specific price.

The market equilibrium condition is illustrated graphically in Diagram A of Figure 4.9. The demand curve DD and the supply curve SS are drawn from the schedules in Table 4.7.

The two curves intersect at E to give an equilibrium price of $0.30, and an equilibrium quantity of 140 000. At a price of $0.40, the quantity demanded is 120 000 and the quantity supplied is 180 000. The surplus of 60 000 is indicated on Diagram B. This surplus causes the price to fall back to the equilibrium level of $0.30. At a price of $0.25, the quantity demanded is 150 000 but the quantity supplied is 120 000. The shortage of 30 000 is indicated on the Diagram C. This shortage causes the price to rise to its equilibrium level of $0.30.

A surplus occurs when quantity supplied exceeds quantity demanded at a given price.

A shortage occurs when quantity demanded exceeds quantity supplied at a given price.

The equilibrium price is that price which equates quantity demanded and quantity supplied, and the quantity traded at this price is the equilibrium quantity.

Learning Objective 7: explain market price determination

EFFECT OF A CHANGE IN DEMAND

Suppose there is an increase in the demand for apples because people have come to believe that an apple a day keeps the doctor away. What effect will such a change have on equilibrium price and quantity? Let us analyze this situation with the help of Figure 4.10.

The original demand and supply curves in this figure are DD and SS, respectively; the initial equilibrium price and quantity are $0.30 and 140 000, respectively. An increase in demand is shown by a shift in the demand curve from DD to D_1D_1. With this new higher demand, and with the initial price of $0.30, there is excess quantity demanded of 30 000 apples. This shortage will cause the price of apples to be bid up. The market establishes a new equilibrium price of $0.35 and a new equilibrium quantity of 160 000 units. The result may be stated by the following proposition:

An increase in demand increases both price and quantity. A decrease in demand reduces both price and quantity.

FIGURE 4.9

Equilibrium price and quantity.

The intersection of the demand and supply curves determines the equilibrium price and quantity.

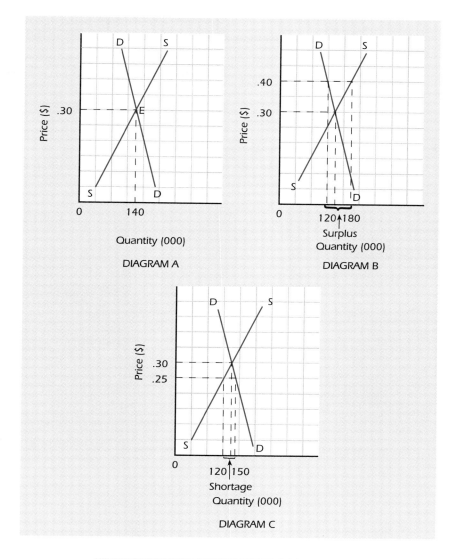

DIAGRAM A

DIAGRAM B

DIAGRAM C

FIGURE 4.10

Effect of an increase in demand.

An increase in demand results in a higher price and a greater quantity.

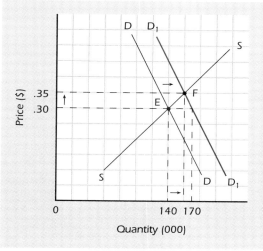

An increase in demand, other things being equal, will cause the price of the product to increase and the quantity traded to increase.

Note that although there is an increase in quantity bought and sold, there is no increase in supply; the location of the supply curve remains the same. There is, however, a movement along the supply curve from point E to point F. The effect of a decrease in demand is left as an exercise for you to work out.

EFFECT OF A CHANGE IN SUPPLY

Now suppose the supply of coffee falls because of an increase in the prices of resources used to produce coffee. Let us analyze this situation with the help of Figure 4.11.

FIGURE 4.11

Effect of a decrease in supply.

A decrease in supply results in a higher price and a smaller quantity.

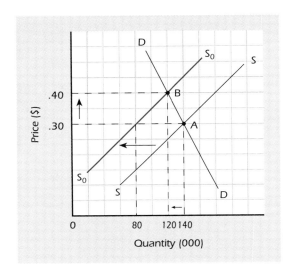

An increase in supply reduces the price and increases the quantity. A fall in supply raises the price and reduces the quantity.

The initial demand and supply curves are DD and SS respectively. A decrease in supply is shown by an upward (leftward) shift of the supply curve from SS to S_0S_0. At the initial price of $0.30, the new quantity supplied is only 80 000 cups of coffee. There is therefore a shortage (excess quantity demanded) of 60 000 cups. Competition among buyers for coffee will cause the price to be bid up. The market establishes a new equilibrium price of $0.40, and a new equilibrium quantity of 120 000 cups. We may now state the following proposition:

A decrease in supply, other things being equal, will cause the price of the product to increase and the quantity traded to decrease.

Note again that although the quantity demanded has fallen, there is no fall in demand; the location of the demand curve has not changed. Instead, there has been a movement along the demand curve from point A to point B. The effect of an increase in supply is left as an exercise for you to work out.

PROBLEM SOLVING 4-5

When the price of gold rises considerably, the price of silver also tends to rise. How might this occurrence be explained?

SOME APPLICATIONS OF DEMAND AND SUPPLY ANALYSIS

Learning Objective 8:
use demand-supply analysis to solve simple economic problems

Simple demand and supply analysis can help to clarify our thinking on a number of important economic issues. In this section, we will apply the demand and supply analysis developed in this chapter to some economic issues. In an economy such as the Canadian economy, the government often intervenes in the market system to produce results other than those that would be given by the market. You will see how demand and supply analysis can help us to understand the effects of such interventions.

THE EFFECT OF PRICE FLOORS

Price floor: a point beyond which price is not allowed to fall. A price floor is effective only if set above the equilibrium price.

The federal government has attempted to improve the condition of egg producers in Canada by preventing the price of eggs from falling below a certain level. The minimum level to which the price is allowed to fall is called a **price floor**. If the minimum price is set below the market equilibrium price, then the market price will prevail, and the minimum price will have no effect. If, however, the minimum price is set above the equilibrium price, it is the minimum price that will prevail, and, as you will see shortly, it will have some effect. Figure 4.12 will help us to analyze the effect of setting a price floor.

FIGURE 4.12

Effect of a price floor.

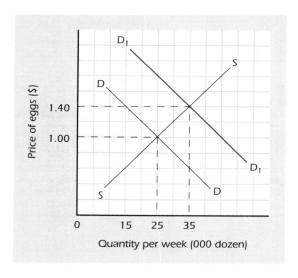

The demand and supply curves are shown by DD and SS respectively. The equilibrium price of eggs determined by the market is $1.00 a dozen. If the government sets a minimum price of $1.40 a dozen, buyers are willing to purchase only 15 000 dozen a week at that price, while producers are willing to offer 35 000 dozen for sale. A surplus of 20 000 dozen eggs results. The government will have to enter the market and purchase the surplus, thus shifting the demand curve upward to D_1D_1. The total amount received by the egg producers will be ($1.40 × 35 000) = $49 000. The government will incur a cost of ($1.40 × 20 000) = $28 000.

THE EFFECT OF PRICE CEILINGS

Learning Objective 8:
use demand-supply analysis to solve simple economic problems

In an attempt to protect the interest of consumers, a government may pass legislation forbidding the sale of a product above a certain price. For example, many cities set a limit on the prices that landlords may charge for apartment rentals (i.e., they impose rent

Price ceiling: a point beyond which a price is not allowed to rise. A price ceiling is effective only if the ceiling is set below the equilibrium price.

Black market: a market in which products are sold illegally above the price prescribed by law.

control). Such control is often referred to as a **price ceiling**. Obviously, if the maximum price permissible is above the equilibrium price, then the law will be ineffective, since there will be no conflict between the market equilibrium price and the maximum price prescribed by law.

Suppose, however, that the maximum price permissible is set below the equilibrium price. Figure 4.13 illustrates the effect that setting a price ceiling would have in this case. The demand curve is DD, the supply curve is SS, and the equilibrium price is $500 per month. Assume that a price ceiling of $400 a month is established by the government; landlords may not charge more than $400 a month for their apartments. At this price, landlords are willing to offer only 40 000 units for rent, while tenants are willing to rent 60 000 units. A shortage of 20 000 units results, and this produces a tendency for the rent to rise above the legal maximum. When a shortage exists, some form of rationing must be instituted, if not by the government, then by the market. Quite often, a **black market**, in which the product is sold at a price above that prescribed by law, is the result of maximum price legislation.

FIGURE 4.13

Effect of a price ceiling.

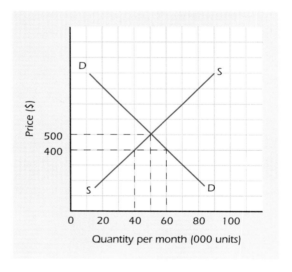

THE EFFECT OF EXCISE TAXES

An excise tax will increase the price of the commodity upon which it is imposed, and reduce the quantity bought.

Learning Objective 8: use demand-supply analysis to solve simple economic problems

THE EFFECT OF EXCISE TAXES

An **excise tax** is a tax imposed on a domestically produced good. It is actually a type of sales tax. Suppose a specific tax of $4.00 is imposed on each bottle of wine sold in Canada. We can analyze the effect of such a tax with the help of Figure 4.14. The demand and supply curves before the imposition of the tax are shown by DD and SS, and the equilibrium price is $10.00. The imposition of the tax causes production costs to rise by $4.00 per bottle, and thus reduces supply. This reduction is shown by an upward shift of the supply curve from SS to S_0S_0. The supply curve shifts up by the amount of the tax, so the vertical distance between SS and S_0S_0 represents the tax. Note that the new equilibrium price is not $14.00 but $12.25. The increase in price is less than the tax. This is because at the higher price, the quantity demanded is lower. The quantity traded falls from 10 000 bottles of wine to 9000 bottles. The government's revenue from the tax is ($4.00 × 9000) = $36 000.00 The consumer's share of the tax is $2.25 while the producer's share is $1.75 per bottle.

FIGURE 4.14

Effect of an excise tax.

An excise tax reduces
supply and increases price

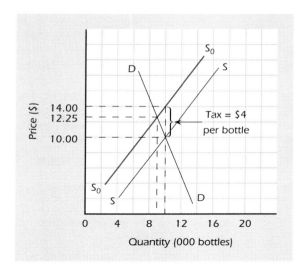

A SPECIAL APPLICATION

In January 1998, much of Quebec and Eastern Ontario was caught in the grip of an ice storm that saw vast regions literally in the dark, and hundreds of thousands of residents in the cold for a considerable period of time, as trees fell and electrical lines were broken. Economic activity as we know it came to a halt. The demand for candles skyrocketed, as did the demand for firewood, flashlights, and batteries. Naturally, the prices of these commodities rose as quantities dwindled, and, in some cases, disappeared. Some suppliers were accused of price gouging, and talks of investigations into price hikes became quite common.

GLOBAL   PERSPECTIVE

Demand and Supply Globally Contemplated

Demand and supply analysis can be used to explain the prices of certain commodities that are traded on the world market. In this capsule, we will see how decisions made in a few countries can affect the world price of a specific commodity.

A group of 13 countries, most of which are in the Middle East, accounts for a significant amount of the world's supply of oil. In 1973, this group of countries, known as the Organization of Petroleum Exporting Countries (OPEC), decided to embark on an oil embargo. The supply of oil to the West was greatly curtailed, and consequently, the price of oil rose dramatically. This rapid increase in the price of oil caused the demand for other forms of energy to increase, and led to an increase in the prices of substitutes such as electricity. Thus we see that the laws of supply and demand apply even across international boundaries.

In the winter of 1997-98, the price of crude oil plunged to its lowest level in about nine years. In an attempt to boost sagging oil prices in the early months of 1998, OPEC promised to reduce oil production. At about the same time, Norway, the world's second largest oil exporter after Saudi Arabia (but not a member of OPEC), said that it would cut its output of oil. With Norway's help, the total supply of oil on the world market would fall significantly. With no appreciable change in demand, the demand-supply model would predict an increase in the world price of oil. The predicted price increase did, in fact, occur.

An analysis of the situation is quite simple, using the tools of demand and supply. An increase in demand followed by a fall in market supply was the fundamental cause of the price increase. Suppliers saw an opportunity and seized it. The market rationed the limited supplies and, as prices rose, there was an incentive to quickly replenish stocks. Many people complained that to increase prices was heartless and cruel, since most people were already in desperate situations. But the profit motive gave suppliers an incentive to offer commodities that were in greater demand. When quantities supplied were increased and there were no further increases in demand, prices decreased.

CHAPTER SUMMARY

1. Demand refers to the various quantities of a good or service that buyers are willing and able to purchase at various possible prices during a period of time. A demand schedule is a tabular presentation of demand, whereas a demand curve is a graphical presentation of demand.

2. The law of demand states that, other things being equal, a decrease in price will cause quantity demanded to increase, and an increase in price will cause quantity demanded to fall.

3. Non-price determinants of quantity demanded include the incomes of consumers, prices of substitutes and complements, tastes, expectations, and population.

4. A change in the price of a product will cause quantity demanded to change, and is illustrated by a movement along the demand curve. A change in a non-price determinant will cause demand to change — this is illustrated by a shift in the entire demand curve.

5. Supply refers to the various quantities of a good or service that sellers (or producers) are willing and able to offer for sale at various possible prices during a period of time.

6. The law of supply is the hypothesis that, other things being equal, an increase in the price of a product will cause quantity offered for sale to increase.

7. Non-price determinants of quantity supplied include the number of sellers in the market, prices of production substitutes and production complements, expectations, technology, and the prices of factor inputs.

8. Equilibrium price is the price at which quantity demanded equals quantity supplied. This is shown graphically by the intersection of the demand curve and the supply curve.

9. A shortage exists when, at a certain price, quantity demanded exceeds quantity supplied. If a shortage exists, economic forces will be set in motion to move the price toward the equilibrium level. A surplus exists when, at a certain price, quantity supplied exceeds quantity demanded. In a surplus situation, economic forces will be set in motion to move the price toward the equilibrium level.

10. A change in demand, other things being equal, will cause price and quantity to change in the same direction as the change in demand. A change in supply will cause price to change in the opposite direction — and quantity to change in the same direction — as the change in supply.

11. A price floor is a minimum price established for a product, while a price ceiling is a maximum price established for a product. Price ceilings usually result in black markets where products are sold at prices above the legal maximum price.

12. An excise tax of a specific amount levied on a product will reduce the supply and increase the price of the product. The quantity demanded will fall.

TERMS FOR REVIEW

demand (55)
demand schedule (56)
law of demand (56)
market size effect (56)
income effect (56)
substitution effect (56)
demand curve (56)
normal goods (58)
inferior goods (58)
substitute & complementary goods (58)
independent goods (58)
demand shifters (61)
supply (62)
supply schedule (62)
law of supply (63)

supply curve (63)
substitutes in production (64)
complements in production
  (joint products) (64)
supply shifters (66)
surplus (excess quantity supplied) (68)
shortage (excess quantity
  demanded) (68)
equilibrium price (68)
equilibrium quantity (68)
price floor (71)
price ceiling (72)
black market (72)
excise tax (72)

QUESTIONS FOR REVIEW AND DISCUSSION

1. Is there a difference between demand and want? Explain. (L.O.1)

2. Use diagrams to illustrate the difference between demand and quantity demanded. (L.O.2)

3. Explain why you would expect the demand curve for home movies to be downward sloping from left to right. (L.O.1,2)

4. What are the factors likely to affect the quantity of restaurant meals bought by Edmonton families in any given month? (L.O.3)

5. "A fall in the price of television sets will result in an increase in the quantity demanded. This increase in demand resulting from the fall in price will send the price up again." Can you detect any error in this statement? If so, name it and explain. (L.O.2)

6. Which side of the market for the specified good or service will be affected by the events shown in Table 4.8? (L.O.3,6)

TABLE 4.8	Event	Good or service
Events and commodities.	(a) A fall in the price of gasoline	Cars
	(b) A sharp increase in fares for public transportation	Gasoline
	(c) An improvement in road construction technology	Roads
	(d) An increase in enrollment in colleges and universities	Textbooks

7. What is the difference between substitutes and complements in consumption? What effect will an increase in the price of coffee have on the market for tea? (L.O.3,8)

8. Explain why a surplus of a particular product will likely reduce the price of the product. (L.O.7,8)

9. Define each of the following terms: (General)

   (a) inferior good;

   (b) joint products;

   (c) price floor;

   (d) price ceiling;

(e) black market;

(f) excise tax.

PROBLEMS AND EXERCISES

1. Construct a hypothetical demand schedule for pizza in Canada. Show how this schedule will be affected by a rapid movement of Canadians to the United States. (L.O.1,3)

2. Plot a graph of the data contained in your schedule for Question 1, then show how the movement of Canadians to the United States will affect the demand curve. (L.O.1,3)

3. Use diagrams to illustrate each of the following: (L.O.3)

    (a) the effect of an increase in the price of apple juice on the demand for orange juice;

    (b) the effect of an increase in incomes on the demand for airline tickets;

    (c) the effect of an increase in the price of steel on the demand for chairs with steel frames;

    (d) the effect of a fall in the price of home computers on the demand for home computers.

4. Use a demand and supply diagram to show the effect of the following events on the shoe market: (L.O.8)

    (a) a decision by a provincial government to eliminate the sales tax on shoes;

    (b) an announcement that the price of shoes will increase by at least 25% within the next month;

    (c) the immigration into Canada of a large number of refugees;

    (d) the invention of a machine that greatly reduces the cost of manufacturing shoes.

5. College students have a choice of living in residence at college or living in private accommodation. The demand for college residence accommodation (rooms) is shown in Table 4.9. The college has 1100 places available at $20 per place per week and cannot build more accommodation. (L.O.8)

TABLE 4.9	Price per week ($)	Number of students per week
Demand for college accommodation.	30	300
	28	420
	26	500
	24	580
	22	650
	21	800
	20	1 200
	19	1 600
	18	2 000

(a) What problem results from the college's current pricing policy?

(b) How might the college solve this problem?

(c) Give a rough estimate of a price that would clear the market.

(d) Suppose that prices for private accommodation and transportation fares increase, while the price of college rooms remains unchanged. How will these price increases affect the demand for college accommodation?

6. In an attempt to deal with the problem of high residential rents, many cities have introduced rent controls. What is the effect of rent controls? (L.O.8)

7. The government imposes a tax of $10 on each pair of shoes sold, regardless of price. What effect will this tax have on the sales of more expensive shoes relative to the sales of cheaper shoes? Does this effect violate the law of demand? (L.O.8)

8. It is sometimes argued that minimum wage legislation creates unemployment. Use demand and supply analysis to show how this might be possible. (L.O.8)

9. The demand for and supply of video cassette tapes are given in Table 4.10. (L.O.7,8)

(a) On a graph, plot the demand and supply curves for video cassette tapes.

(b) What are the equilibrium price and quantity?

(c) Suppose that the government imposes a tax of $1 on each video cassette produced and sold in Canada. Fill in the column showing quantity supplied after the tax. (Hint: At a price of $8, the quantity supplied before the tax was 36 000. With the tax, this quantity will be supplied only at a price of $9).

(d) On your graph, plot the new supply curve after the imposition of the tax.

(e) What are the new equilibrium price and quantity?

TABLE 4.10	**Price ($)**	**Quantity demanded (000)**	**Quantity supplied (000)**	**Quantity supplied after tax (000)**
Demand and supply for video cassette tapes.	9.00	20	44	36
	8.50	24	40	
	8.00	28	36	
	7.50	32	32	
	7.00	36	28	
	6.50	40	24	
	6.00	44	20	

(f) How much of the $1 tax is passed on to the consumers in the form of an increase in price, and how much is paid by the producers?

(g) How much revenue does the tax produce for the government?

10. Assume that a technological breakthrough allows the production of three times as much electricity from given resources. Use the demand-supply model to predict how this will affect the equilibrium price and quantity in the market for electricity and the market for oil for heating purposes. Use diagrams to illustrate your answer. (L.O.8)

11. The tuition at Private College (a fictitious college) in 1985 was $5000 per year and in that year, the college enrolled 6000 students. Ten years later, in 1995, when the tuition had risen to $8000 per year, the college enrolled 7000 students. This information was brought to the attention of students in an introductory economics class. Clearly, when the price (tuition fee) rose, the quantity of students increased. The students therefore immediately concluded that this was an excellent example of an upward sloping demand curve for places at Private College. Were the students correct? Explain.

MATHEMATICAL APPENDIX

INTRODUCTION

The main purpose of this mathematical appendix is to provide you with another type of tool that can be used to analyze demand, supply, and market price determination. No mathematics beyond elementary algebra is used. The actual mathematics used in economic analysis is much more complex and sophisticated than the elementary algebra used here, but even this rudimentary presentation will give you a bit of the flavour of a mathematical approach to economic analysis.

THE DEMAND FUNCTION

The demand function for a commodity can be expressed as

$$Q_d = Q(P,Y,Pr,T,Ex,Po) \tag{1}$$

where Q_d = quantity demanded
   P = price of the commodity
   Y = income
   Pr = prices of related goods
   T = taste
   Ex = expectations
   Po = population

The effect of each of the independent variables on quantity demanded has been discussed earlier in this chapter.

Let us assume that income, the prices of related goods, tastes, expectations, and population are constant. The demand function now becomes a relation between price and quantity demanded and may be expressed as the demand function:

$$Q_d = Q(P) \tag{2}$$

The independent variables in equation (1) that have been assumed constant are called *shift parameters*; if they change, they cause the demand curve to shift. According to the law of demand, the relation between price and quantity demanded is an inverse one. If we assume a linear relationship between price and quantity demanded, then we can express the demand function as

$$Q_d = a - bP, a > 0, b > 0 \tag{3}$$

The value of *a* represents the quantity demanded at a price of zero, and −*b* represents the slope of the demand function, which is appropriately negative since the demand curve is downward sloping. A demand function, for example, could take the form of an equation such as

$$Q_d = 100 - 50P \tag{4}$$

THE SUPPLY FUNCTION

The supply function for a commodity can be expressed as:

$$Q_s = Q(P,N,Pr,Te,Ex,Pi) \tag{5}$$

where Q_s = quantity supplied
   P = the price of the commodity
   N = number of sellers
   Pr = prices of related goods
   Te = technology
   Ex = expectations
   Pi = input prices

If we assume that the number of sellers, the prices of related goods, technology, expectations, and the prices of inputs are constant, then the supply function can be expressed as

$$Q_s = Q(P) \tag{6}$$

There is a direct relation between price and quantity supplied. As in the case of the demand function, let us assume a linear relationship between price and quantity supplied. We can express the supply function as

$$Q_s = c + dP, \; d > 0 \tag{7}$$

where c is a constant and d is the slope of the supply function. The positive slope means that the supply curve is upward sloping. A supply function could be of the form

$$Q_s = -60 + 20P \tag{8}$$

Assuming that the price is expressed in dollars, the negative sign here means that unless the price is above \$3, sellers will not offer the product for sale.

MARKET EQUILIBRIUM

To determine equilibrium price and quantity, we must bring the demand and supply functions together in a model of price determination. The demand and supply equations give us two equations in three unknowns (Q_d, Q_s, and P). We know that equilibrium occurs when the price is such that there is neither a shortage nor a surplus in the market, hence

$$Q_d = Q_s \tag{9}$$

This equation completes the model and allows us to obtain a unique solution. The complete model is

$$Q_d = a - bP \tag{10}$$

$$Q_s = c + dP \tag{11}$$

$$Q_d = Q_s \tag{12}$$

By solving this system of equations for P and Q, we will obtain the market equilibrium price and quantity.

EXAMPLE 4-1

Consider the following demand and supply equations:

$$Q_d = 50 - 4P$$
$$Q_s = -10 + 8P$$

Since in equilibrium $Q_d = Q_s$, we know that

$$50 - 4P = -10 + 8P$$

Therefore $12P = 60$, so $P = 5$

By substituting this value of P in either the demand or the supply equation, we obtain $Q = 30$. Hence, the equilibrium price is 5 and the equilibrium quantity is 30.

EXERCISES

1. Solve each of the following equations to determine the equilibrium price and the equilibrium quantity:

   (a) $Q_d = 32 - 3P$
       $Q_s = -12 + 8P$

   (b) $Q_d = 60 - 3P$
       $Q_s = -40 + 7P$

   (c) $Q_d = 900 - 20P$
       $Q_s = -100 + 30P$

2. You are given the following demand and supply equations:

   $$Q_d = 130 - 3P$$
   $$Q_s = -20 + 12P$$

   (a) Complete the following demand and supply schedules.

Price	Quantity demanded	Quantity supplied
5		
10		
15		
20		

   (b) What are the equilibrium price and quantity?

   (c) Solve the demand and supply equations for P and Q and compare your answer with the answer obtained in part (b).

3. The demand and supply equations are

   $$Q_d = 28 - 2P$$
   $$Q_s = 5P$$

   (a) What are the equilibrium price and quantity?

(b) Set up demand and supply schedules based on these equations for prices: $7, $6, $5, $4, $3, $2, $1.

(c) Use your demand and supply schedules to plot the demand and supply curves.

4. The market demand and supply curves are given by the following equations:

$$Q_d = 18 - 2P$$
$$Q_s = 3 + 5P$$

(a) By selecting prices ranging from $1 to $6, plot the demand and supply curves.

(b) Solve the equations for the equilibrium price and the equilibrium quantity.

Ice Storm Effects

Background

In early January 1998, a massive ice storm struck eastern Ontario and southern Quebec. The freezing rain persisted for several days causing what has been titled *The Ice Storm of the Century*. Electrical power lines were broken by the sheer weight of the ice, or by falling ice-entombed trees. Candles, flashlights, and (for those who could get them) generators were people's best friends. Millions of people were without light and heat for hours, days and weeks. Without electricity, farmers were unable to milk their cows. It is safe to assume that eastern Ontario and Quebec will not soon forget the ice storm of 1998.

Many sectors of the economy were affected, and supplies of numerous products were drastically reduced. With much of economic activity at a virtual halt, shortages emerged in many markets. The market response to shortages is higher prices. Some suppliers seemed to have "helped the market along" by engaging in a practice that has been labelled "price extortion" — jacking up prices far beyond what may be considered to be reasonable under the circumstances.

While many products were in short supply, merchants in the areas affected by the ice storm suffered a big slump in sales — the direct result of a lull in economic activity. In Quebec, retailers suffered a 5% drop in sales in January 1998. The direct cost of the damage caused by the ice storm is estimated at $2 billion (some analysts offer significantly higher estimates).

Farmers Took A Big Hit

The results of the ice storm were also felt in the labour market. Thousands of people suffered temporary unemployment as the pulse of economic activity slowed down. In Quebec alone, the number of unemployed people increased by 30 000. Much of this could be attributed to the ice storm.

Ontario and Quebec farmers were hit hard by the ice storm. With no electricity to cool the milk, dairy farmers had to dump as much as 30 000 L of milk over a one-week period. That loss was onerous. Fortunately, financial assistance was available from the federal government to help defray "eligible" costs. The following costs were among those eligible for reimbursement:

- milk that had to be dumped during the ice storm;
- rental of electrical generators;
- animals that died as a result of the storm;
- repair of assets damaged by the ice storm, and loss of inventories because of power outages.

A great deal of farm equipment was damaged by the ice storm. This had an adverse effect on farm output, at least in the short term. Animal feed also was in short supply, and there was the expected increase in demand for imported animal feed and farm equipment. Clearly, the effects of the ice storm were widespread.

QUESTIONS

1. What are the main points of this case?

2. Identify demand and supply elements in this case and indicate what changes could be expected from the interplay of these market forces.

3. What are some of the costs of the 1998 ice storm? (Consider both direct and indirect costs).

4. Most economists expected an increase in economic activity *after* the ice storm. Explain why this might be a reasonable expectation.

Video Resource: "Farmers," *National Magazine* (January 1998)

5

ELASTICITY

Learning Objectives

After studying this chapter, you should be able to:

1 understand the concept of elasticity

2 interpret the elasticity coefficient

3 explain the relationship between elasticity of demand and total revenue

4 identify the factors that affect price elasticity of demand

5 discuss cross elasticity and income elasticity

6 understand elasticity of supply

7 identify the determinants of price elasticity of supply

8 understand the uses of the elasticity concept

The elasticity (or responsiveness) of demand in a market is great or small as the amount demanded increases much or little for a given fall in price, and diminishes for a given rise in price.

Alfred Marshall, *Principles of Economics*

INTRODUCTION

Elasticity: a measure of responsiveness.

The concept of **elasticity** is an important aspect of the demand-supply analysis presented in Chapter 4. We know that, other things being equal, a fall in the price of a product causes the quantity demanded to increase. But does quantity increase by just a little or by much? What effect does an increase or decrease in price have on a seller's total revenue? The answers to these questions depend on the price elasticity of demand for the product. This chapter will introduce you to the very important economic concept of elasticity. You will study various types of elasticity, how to measure them, and how to interpret the measurements. We will also consider some applications of the elasticity concept.

THE MEANING OF ELASTICITY OF DEMAND

Learning Objective 1: understand the concept of elasticity

Price elasticity of demand measures the change in quantity demanded resulting from a change in price.

Elasticity of demand is a measure of the degree to which quantity demanded responds to changes in one of the variables that can affect quantity demanded. For some goods and services, a small change in price greatly affects quantity demanded. For others, a small change in price has no appreciable effect on quantity demanded. **Price elasticity of demand** measures the percentage change in quantity demanded as a result of a small change in price. We often refer to this concept as *own price elasticity of demand* to distinguish it from cases where changes in the prices of other goods (substitutes and complements) affect the demand for a good.

THE POINT ELASTICITY FORMULA
Own price elasticity is often expressed by the formula

$$E_d = \frac{\% \text{ change in quantity demanded}}{\% \text{ change in price}}$$

or, alternatively, as

$$E_d = \frac{\text{change in quantity demanded}}{\text{original quantity}} \div \frac{\text{change in price}}{\text{original price}}$$

where E_d denotes own price elasticity of demand.

The symbol Δ (delta) is commonly used in economics. The sign means *a change in*. We can write the above expression for own price elasticity of demand as

$$E_d = \frac{\Delta Q}{Q} \div \frac{\Delta P}{P}$$

The coefficient of elasticity is used to measure the degree of elasticity or inelasticity.

where E_d represents elasticity, Q represents quantity, and P represents price. This formula is sometimes called the *point elasticity of demand* formula because it measures elasticity at a point on the demand curve. The value obtained for E_d is just a number like 2 or 5 or $\frac{1}{2}$ and is referred to as the **coefficient of elasticity**.

Recall that an increase in price causes quantity demanded to decrease, and that a decrease in price causes quantity demanded to increase. Since price and quantity demanded move in opposite directions, E_d always has a negative value. It is common practice in economics to discard the negative sign and express elasticity of demand as a positive number. In other words, we take the absolute value of E_d. The following example illustrates how the formula may be used to calculate own price elasticity of demand.

EXAMPLE 5-1

If a reduction in the price of a product from $10 to $8 causes quantity demanded to increase from 1200 units to 1800 units, what is the coefficient of elasticity of demand?

Solution: The formula for E_d is given by

$$E_d = \frac{\Delta Q}{Q} \div \frac{\Delta P}{P}$$

The change in quantity $(\Delta Q) = (1800 - 1200) = 600$. The original quantity was 1200, i.e., $Q = 1200$. The change in price $(\Delta P) = (\$8 - \$10) = -\$2$. The original price was $10. By substituting, we obtain

$$E_d = \frac{600}{1200} \div \frac{-2}{10}$$

$$= \frac{600}{1200} \times \frac{10}{-2} = \frac{-5}{2} = -2.5$$

Discarding the negative sign, we obtain

$$E_d = 2.5$$

The use of this formula may lead to confusion since different values can be obtained for the coefficient of elasticity depending on whether the price increases or decreases. In the above example, we considered a price decrease. Now consider a price increase in the following example. Note that in both examples, the prices and quantities used are identical.

EXAMPLE 5-2

If an increase in the price of a product from $8 to $10 causes quantity demanded to decrease from 1800 units to 1200 units, what is the coefficient of elasticity of demand?

Solution:

$$E_d = \frac{\Delta Q}{Q} \div \frac{\Delta P}{P}$$
$$\Delta Q = (1200 - 1800) = -600$$
$$Q = 1800$$
$$\Delta P = (10 - 8) = 2$$
$$P = 8$$

By substituting, we obtain

$$E_d = \frac{-600}{1800} \div \frac{2}{8}$$

$$= \frac{-600}{1800} \times \frac{8}{2} = -1.3$$

Again, discarding the negative sign, we obtain

$$E_d = 1.3$$

For a price decrease, we obtain an elasticity measure of 2.5. For a price increase, we obtain an elasticity measure of 1.3. This is because we are measuring elasticity at different points on the demand curve. To remedy this situation, economists refined the above formula so that the same value is obtained regardless of the direction of the price change. Let us now turn to that refined formula.

THE ARC ELASTICITY FORMULA

By taking the average of the two prices and the average of the two quantities, we obtain the following formula for the price elasticity of demand:

$$E_d = \frac{\dfrac{Q_0 - Q_1}{Q_0 + Q_1}}{2} \div \frac{\dfrac{P_0 - P_1}{P_0 + P_1}}{2}$$

$$= \frac{Q_0 - Q_1}{Q_0 + Q_1} \div \frac{P_0 - P_1}{P_0 + P_1}$$

The average formula measures elasticity between two points on the demand curve.

where Q_0 = original quantity demanded, P_0 = original price, Q_1 = new quantity demanded, P_1 = new price. This new formula is called the *average elasticity of demand* formula, or the *arc elasticity of demand* formula because it measures E_d between two points on the demand curve. We would like to obtain a measure of elasticity of demand that is the same regardless of the direction in which we move. The arc elasticity formula provides us with that measure. By using this formula, we obtain the same value whether there is a price increase or a price decrease. Let us confirm this assertion by calculating the price elasticity of demand for the price and quantity changes in Example 5-2.

$$E_d = \frac{Q_0 - Q_1}{Q_0 + Q_1} \div \frac{P_0 - P_1}{P_0 + P_1}$$

$$Q_0 - Q_1 = 1800 - 1200 = 600$$

$$Q_0 + Q_1 = 1800 + 1200 = 3000$$

$$P_0 - P_1 = 8 - 10 = -2$$

$$P_0 + P_1 = 8 + 10 = 18$$

$$E_d = \frac{600}{3000} \div \frac{-2}{18} = -1.8$$

The price elasticity of demand is therefore 1.8. Now, see if you can verify that the value for the coefficient of elasticity will remain the same for a price fall from $10 to $8. Note that the value (1.8) obtained for the elasticity coefficient when we use the average formula is about the average of the values obtained for the elasticity coefficients (2.5 and 1.3) in Examples 5-1 and 5-2 above. This is to be expected, since the average formula takes the average of the quantities and the average of the prices.

> **Arc elasticity of demand treats the price and quantity as if they were midway between the initial and new prices and quantities, and then uses the point elasticity at this midpoint.**

DEGREES OF ELASTICITY OF DEMAND

A change in the price of a product may have no effect whatever on the quantity demanded. In other words, the same quantity will be bought whatever the price may be.

We can say in this case that demand is **perfectly inelastic**. The demand for a drug prescribed by a physician is probably close to perfectly inelastic.

On the other hand, a small change in price may lead to an infinitely large change in quantity demanded. In this case, we can say that demand is **perfectly elastic**. If there are 100 sellers in a fruit market all selling the same type of grapes at the same price, and one of those sellers raises his or her price, the quantity demanded from that particular seller would probably fall to almost zero. In that case, the demand for grapes from that seller is probably close to perfectly elastic. You will encounter this situation in a later chapter.

Between the two extremes of perfectly elastic and perfectly inelastic demand, there are three important cases of elasticity of demand. If a certain percentage change in price leads to a greater percentage change in quantity demanded, then demand is said to be elastic with respect to price. If a certain percentage change in price leads to an equal percentage change in quantity demanded, then demand is said to have **unit elasticity**. Finally, if a certain percentage change in price leads to a smaller percentage change in quantity demanded, then demand is said to be **inelastic**.

Applying the elasticity formula will help us to determine the degree of price elasticity of demand. The five cases are as follows:

1. If E_d is infinitely large, then demand is perfectly elastic;

2. If E_d is greater than 1 but less than infinity (that is, $1 < E_d < \infty$), then demand is elastic;

3. If E_d is equal to 1, then demand is unitary elastic;

4. If E_d is less than 1 but greater than 0 (that is, $0 < E_d < 1$), then demand is inelastic;

5. If E_d is equal to 0, then demand is perfectly inelastic.

Demand may be perfectly inelastic, inelastic, unitary elastic, or perfectly elastic.

FIGURE 5.1

Demand curves showing various degrees of elasticity.

These different degrees of elasticity of demand can be illustrated geometrically as shown in Figure 5.1. The diagrams in Figure 5.1 are intended to serve for comparative purposes only. The units in which the axes are measured will have some effect on the slopes of the demand curves. Diagram A illustrates the case of perfectly elastic demand, which is depicted by a horizontal straight line. In this case, an infinitely large amount can be sold at the going price. Diagram B illustrates the case of elastic demand. An increase in price from P to P_1 causes a more-than-proportional decrease in quantity demanded as shown by the change in quantity from Q_1 to Q. The case of unit elasticity is illustrated by Diagram C. A change in price from P to P_1 causes a proportional change in quantity demanded. Diagram D shows the case of inelastic demand. A change in price causes a less-than-proportional change in quantity demanded. Finally, Diagram E illustrates the case of perfectly inelastic demand. A change in price leaves quantity demanded unchanged at Q units.

INTERPRETING THE ELASTICITY COEFFICIENT

Learning Objective 2:
interpret the elasticity coefficient

Previously, we meticulously computed the price elasticity of demand using the average formula and obtained a value of 1.8 for the elasticity coefficient. But what does this number really mean? On the basis of what you learned in the previous section, you will quickly say that an elasticity coefficient of 1.8 means that the demand for the product is elastic; $E_d > 1$. But it tells us more than that. Let us investigate. We know that

$$E_d = \frac{\% \, \Delta Q}{\% \, \Delta P} = 1.8$$
$$\% \, \Delta Q = 1.8 \times \% \, \Delta P$$

Thus, if there is a 10% fall in price, the resulting increase in quantity demanded is

$$\% \, \Delta Q = (1.8 \times 10) = 18\%$$

If the coefficient of elasticity of demand is 1.8, then a 10% change in price causes quantity demanded to change (in the opposite direction) by 18%.

PROBLEM SOLVING 5-1

The manager of the Kyushu Uniform Boutique knows that the price elasticity of demand for uniforms at current prices is 2.8. What effect will a price increase of 15% have on the quantity of uniforms sold by the boutique?

PRICE ELASTICITY ALONG A LINEAR DEMAND CURVE

The price elasticity of demand varies along a linear demand curve.

Let us compute the price elasticity of demand at each price change shown in Table 5.1. The calculation for the first coefficient only is shown below. The other coefficients are entered in column three of Table 5.1, and plotted in Figure 5.2. Note that in Table 5.1, because price elasticity deals with changes in quantity and changes in price, the elasticity coefficients are placed in between the lines rather than on the same lines as price and quantity.

$$E_d = \frac{Q_0 - Q_1}{Q_0 + Q_1} \div \frac{P_0 - P_1}{P_0 - P_1}$$
$$= \frac{2}{10} \div \frac{1}{17} = 3.40$$

	Price ($) (1)	Quantity demanded (2)	Elasticity (3)
TABLE 5.1	9	4	
Demand schedule.			3.40
	8	6	
			2.14
	7	8	
			1.44
	6	10	
			1.00
	5	12	

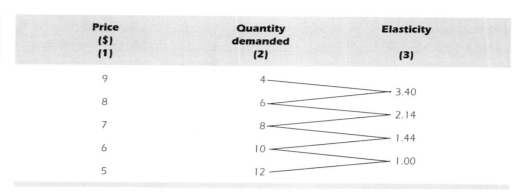

This exercise clearly demonstrates two things: first, elasticity and slope are not identical — the slope of this demand curve is 1/2 at every point on the curve (you should verify this); and second, the price elasticity of demand varies along a linear demand curve. The price elasticity of demand decreases as price falls, i.e., as we move down the demand curve.

FIGURE 5.2

Demand and elasticity.

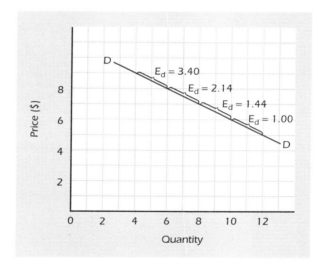

ELASTICITY OF DEMAND AND TOTAL REVENUE

If demand is elastic, price reductions result in increases in total revenue.

Learning Objective 3: explain the relationship between elasticity of demand and total revenue

Another way of looking at price elasticity of demand for a good or service is to see what happens to total revenue as the price of the good or service changes. Total revenue (TR) derived from the sale of any product is the price of the product (P) multiplied by the quantity sold (Q). That is,

$$TR = P \times Q$$

If the demand for a good or service is elastic, a fall in its price causes a more-than-proportional increase in quantity demanded. Hence, total revenue increases. Table 5.2 illustrates a case in which the demand for the product is elastic for all price ranges considered. As price falls, quantity demanded increases by a greater proportion than the fall in price, so total revenue increases.

TABLE 5.2	Price ($)	Quantity demanded	Total revenue ($)
Hypothetical demand schedule for a product with an elastic demand.	2.00	70 000	140 000
	1.90	90 000	171 000
	1.80	110 000	198 000
	1.70	130 000	221 000
	1.60	150 000	240 000
	1.50	170 000	255 000
	1.40	190 000	266 000
	1.30	210 000	273 000
	1.20	230 000	276 000

If demand is unitary elastic, a fall in price leaves total revenue unchanged.

In the case of unitary elastic demand, a fall in the price of the product causes a proportional increase in quantity demanded, leaving total revenue unchanged. Table 5.3 illustrates the case of unit elasticity of demand.

TABLE 5.3	Price ($)	Quantity demanded	Total revenue ($)
Hypothetical demand schedule for a product with unit elasticity of demand.	0.80	60 000	48 000
	0.60	80 000	48 000
	0.48	100 000	48 000
	0.40	120 000	48 000
	0.30	160 000	48 000
	0.24	200 000	48 000
	0.20	240 000	48 000
	0.16	300 000	48 000
	0.12	400 000	48 000
	0.10	480 000	48 000

If demand is inelastic, price reductions result in decreases in total revenue.

If the data in Table 5.3 were plotted on a graph, the result would be a demand curve with a constant elasticity of 1.0. Such a demand curve would be a rectangular hyperbola conforming to the equation $P \times Q = 48\ 000$, as shown in Figure 5.3. Constant elasticity demand curves are used extensively in econometric (statistical) studies of elasticity of demand.

FIGURE 5.3

Demand curve with constant elasticity.

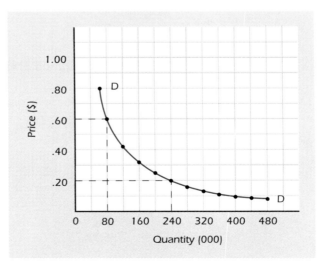

If the demand for a product is inelastic, a fall in the price of the product causes a less-than-proportional increase in quantity demanded; hence, total revenue falls as price falls. The demand schedule for a product with inelastic demand is given in Table 5.4.

TABLE 5.4

Hypothetical demand schedule for a product with inelastic demand.

Price ($)	Quantity demanded	Total revenue ($)
0.50	48 000	24 000
0.46	50 000	23 000
0.42	52 000	21 840
0.38	54 000	20 520
0.34	56 000	19 040
0.30	58 000	17 400
0.26	60 000	15 600
0.22	62 000	13 640
0.18	64 000	11 520
0.14	66 000	9 240

However, the demand for a product may be elastic in one price range and inelastic in another price range. Consider the demand schedule in Table 5.5.

TABLE 5.5

Demand and total revenue.

Price ($)	Quantity demanded	Total revenue ($)
12	10	120
10	20	200
8	30	240
6	40	240
4	50	200
2	60	120

Total revenue rises from $120 to $240 as the price falls from $12 to $8; thus demand is elastic within the price range from $12 to $8. Total revenue remains constant at $240 when price falls from $8 to $6; thus demand is unitary elastic between $8 and $6. As the price falls from $6 to $2, total revenue falls from $240 to $120; thus demand is inelastic within the price range from $6 to $2.

Figure 5.4, which is based on Table 5.5, is helpful in consolidating your understanding of the relation between elasticity of demand and total revenue. We have seen that if demand is elastic, a fall in price results in an increase in total revenue. Thus, for price decreases within the price range above $8, where the demand is elastic, total revenue rises. This is shown in Diagram B by the rising section of the total revenue curve. If demand is unitary elastic (between $8 and $6 in Diagram A), an increase or decrease in price leaves total revenue unchanged at $240. This is shown in Diagram B where $E_d = 1$. Finally, if demand is inelastic, a fall in price results in a fall in total revenue. Price reductions within the under $6 range cause total revenue to fall as shown in Diagram B by the downward-sloping section of the total revenue curve.

The relation between price elasticity of demand and total revenue is conveniently summarized in Table 5.6 for quick reference.

The demand for most products is either elastic, unitary elastic, or inelastic. The extremes of perfectly elastic and perfectly inelastic demand are rare. You will see in a later chapter, however, that, under certain conditions, the demand for the product of a seller may be perfectly elastic.

FIGURE 5.4

Relation between total revenue and elasticity of demand.

	Elasticity of demand	Direction of price change	Effect on total revenue
TABLE 5.6 Elasticity and total revenue.	inelastic	increase	increase
	inelastic	decrease	decrease
	elastic	increase	decrease
	elastic	decrease	increase
	unitary	any change	unchanged

FACTORS AFFECTING PRICE ELASTICITY OF DEMAND

Learning Objective 4: identify the factors that affect price elasticity of demand

We have seen that the demand for a commodity (good or service) may be elastic in one price range and inelastic in some other price range, as shown in Table 5.5 and Figure 5.4. It is important to note also that the demand for a commodity may be found to be elastic at a certain time and inelastic at some other time. In this section, we discuss the major factors that are likely to affect the price elasticity of demand for a product.

SUBSTITUTES

Availability of substitutes affects elasticity.

One of the most important factors likely to influence the price elasticity of demand for a good or service is whether or not substitutes are available. If a commodity has many close substitutes, its demand is likely to be elastic. This is so because, if the price of that commodity rises, buyers will switch to some of the many close substitutes available. Hence, the quantity demanded of that commodity will tend to fall significantly. Consider the case of a certain brand of coffee. If the price of that particular brand increases, consumers will buy other available brands instead. Thus, we find that the demand for products with many brands tends to be elastic. On the other hand, if there *are not* many close substitutes, quantity demanded will still tend to fall as a result of the higher price, but not by much. Consider the effect of a two-cent-per-litre increase in the price of gasoline at the pumps. There will probably be a large increase in the quantity demanded just before the increase comes into effect, but after that, we will probably observe no significant reduction in the quantity demanded as a result of the price increase.

NUMBER OF USES

The number of uses affects elasticity.

In general, the greater the number of uses a commodity has, the more elastic the demand for that commodity is likely to be. Consider a fall in the price of a commodity (eggs, for example) that has a large number of uses. As the price falls, more of it will be bought to be allocated to those different uses. On the other hand, if the commodity has only one or two uses (for example, tarragon — a plant whose leaves are used for flavouring salads), it is unlikely that a fall in its price will cause a significant increase in quantity demanded.

PERCENTAGE OF INCOME SPENT ON THE COMMODITY

The importance of the product in the budget affects elasticity.

Another factor that is likely to affect elasticity of demand is the proportion of income spent on the commodity. If only a negligible percentage of consumers' income is spent on the commodity, the demand for that commodity is likely to be inelastic. An increase in the price of such a commodity has no appreciable effect on the consumer's budget. Hence, expenditure patterns will hardly be affected. As an example of this point, consider the fraction of total income spent on matches. If the price of matches were to increase from three cents to five cents (an increase of 67%), the fall in quantity demanded is unlikely to be anywhere near 67%. As a matter of fact, the reduction in quantity demanded is likely to be minuscule. On the other hand, consider the fraction of total income spent on a television set — a relatively costly item. An increase in the price of television sets will probably result in a significant reduction in the quantity demanded. Similarly, a reduction in the price of television sets will probably result in a significant increase in the quantity demanded; many people might then consider buying a second or third set.

THE NATURE OF THE PRODUCT

The demand for necessities is likely to be inelastic.

The demand for luxuries is likely to be elastic.

Whether the product is a luxury or a necessity has some effect on its price elasticity of demand. Most people consider milk a basic necessity in the diets of children. If the price of milk increases by, say, 10%, the quantity demanded will probably not fall by that proportion. Consumers will probably sacrifice some other commodity rather than allow their children to go without milk. The demand for an item that is a basic necessity is likely to be inelastic. On the other hand, an increase in the price of a vacation package to Antigua (a small Caribbean island) is likely to cause a more-than-proportional decrease in the number bought — other things being equal, of course. In general, the demand for a luxury item is elastic. Luxury items that are also extremely expensive, however, may not quite fit into this general pattern. The demand for luxurious yachts is likely to be inelastic; the people in the market for them are so wealthy that a small increase in price is unlikely to cause any significant reduction in the quantity demanded.

TIME

The time period being considered will also have some effect on the elasticity of demand for a product. In general, the longer the time period being considered, the more elastic the demand is likely to be. This is due largely to the fact that it takes time for people to adjust to new situations. If the price of gasoline rises, people will respond by buying less gasoline, but within a short time span, they are unlikely to buy a great deal less. As time goes by, however, they are likely to use public transportation more, make more use of car pools, and ultimately purchase smaller and more fuel-efficient cars.

PROBLEM SOLVING 5-2

Based on the determinants of price elasticity of demand discussed in this section, state whether you expect demand for each of the following to be elastic or inelastic.

1. **The services of medical doctors**
2. **Toilet paper**
3. **Diamond necklaces**
4. **Telephone services**

OTHER ELASTICITY CONCEPTS

We should look at two other important demand elasticity concepts at this point: the concepts of cross elasticity of demand and income elasticity of demand.

CROSS ELASTICITY OF DEMAND

The cross elasticity of demand for a product is the relative change in the quantity demanded of that product divided by the relative change in the price of a related product.

Learning Objective 5: discuss cross elasticity and income elasticity

In Chapter 4, we noted that changes in the prices of other commodities may have some effect on the quantity of a commodity demanded. A change in the price of limes affects the quantity of lemons demanded, and a change in the price of battery-operated toys affects the quantity of batteries demanded. (Remember substitutes and complements?) **Cross elasticity of demand** measures the effect of a change in the price of a related good on the quantity demanded of the good under consideration. The cross elasticity of demand for a product A is the relative change in the quantity demanded of product A divided by the relative change in the price of product B.

Using the point formula and the notation introduced earlier in this chapter, we can express cross elasticity of demand as

$$(E_A P_B) = \frac{\Delta Q_A}{Q_A} \div \frac{\Delta P_B}{P_B}$$

Or, we may use the average formula and express cross elasticity as

$$(E_A P_B) = \frac{\Delta Q_A}{Q_{A0} + Q_{A1}} \div \frac{\Delta P_B}{P_{B0} + P_{B1}}$$

Substitutes have positive cross elasticity of demand.

Complements have negative cross elasticity of demand.

Independent goods have zero cross elasticity of demand.

where $E_A P_B$ equals cross elasticity between A and B, Q_A equals quantity of product A demanded, P_B equals price of product B, Q_{A0} and Q_{A1} are the two quantities, and P_{B0} and P_{B1} are the two prices. If A and B are substitutes, then an increase in the price of B causes an increase in the quantity of A demanded. **Substitutes** therefore show a positive cross elasticity of demand. If A and B are complementary goods, then an increase in the price of B causes a decrease in the quantity of A demanded. **Complements** therefore show a negative cross elasticity of demand. If A and B are not at all related, then a change in the price of B will have no effect on the quantity of A demanded. Therefore, independent goods show a zero cross elasticity of demand. The foregoing discussion may be summarized as follows:

1. If A and B are substitutes, then $E_A P_B > 0$;

2. If A and B are complements, then $E_A P_B < 0$;

3. If A and B are independent, then $E_A P_B = 0$.

INCOME ELASTICITY OF DEMAND

Income elasticity of demand: a measure of buyers' response to changes in income.

Other things being equal, an increase in income leads to an increase in quantity demanded if the good is normal. If the good is an inferior good, then an increase in income leads to a decrease in quantity demanded. But by how much will quantity increase or decrease? This depends on the income elasticity of demand. We may define **income elasticity of demand** as the relative change in quantity demanded divided by the relative change in income. If E_y denotes income elasticity of demand, then

$$E_y = \frac{\text{change in quantity demanded}}{\text{original quantity demanded}} \div \frac{\text{change in income}}{\text{original income}}$$

Demand for normal goods increases with an increase in income, while demand for inferior goods decreases as income increases.

You will recall that in Chapter 4, we discussed normal goods and inferior goods. For most goods, as income rises, the quantity demanded also rises. These are normal goods. The income elasticity of demand for **normal goods** will be positive. There are instances, however, when smaller quantities of certain goods are demanded as income rises. These are inferior goods. The income elasticity of demand for **inferior goods** will be negative. We may summarize the foregoing discussion as follows:

1. For normal goods (and this includes most goods), $E_y > 0$.

2. For inferior goods, $E_y < 0$.

As in the case of price elasticity of demand, either of the two formulas may be used to compute income elasticity of demand. You simply substitute income for price. It is obviously of great importance for producers to have some idea of the effect of income changes on the sale of their products. In other words, they need to know something about income elasticity of demand for their products.

PROBLEM SOLVING 5-3

1. **Farmers have been informed that the income elasticity of demand for beef is 2.2. If the price of beef is fixed, and on average, people's incomes are expected to increase by 10%, what change should beef farmers make in their production of beef?**

2. **You operate a small store that specializes in the sale of coffee. The cross elasticity of demand between coffee and tea is estimated to be 2.5. If the price of tea rises by 6%, what change should you expect in the demand for coffee?**

ELASTICITY OF SUPPLY

The concept of elasticity of supply closely parallels that of elasticity of demand. For that reason, we need not devote a great deal of time to the elasticity of supply. This, of course, in no way detracts from the importance of elasticity of supply. The degree to which quantity offered for sale responds to changes in price is known as the price elasticity of supply. **Price elasticity of supply** is the percentage change in quantity supplied divided by the percentage change in price. Using the point formula, we may express price elasticity of supply as

Price elasticity of supply measures sellers' response to changes in price.

Learning Objective 6:
understand elasticity of
supply

$$E_s = \frac{\Delta Q}{Q} \div \frac{\Delta P}{P}$$

where E_s equals price elasticity of supply, Q equals quantity supplied, and P equals price. Using the average formula, we can compute the coefficient of elasticity of supply as

$$E_s = \frac{Q_0 - Q_1}{Q_0 + Q_1} \div \frac{P_0 - P_1}{P_0 + P_1}$$

The value obtained for E_s is the *coefficient of elasticity of supply.* We say that supply is elastic if a change in price leads to a more-than-proportional change in quantity supplied. If a change in price leads to a less-than-proportional change in quantity supplied, then we say that supply is inelastic. Notice how closely the analysis parallels that of price elasticity of demand.

We can illustrate various degrees of price elasticity of supply graphically. A linear supply curve indicates an elastic supply if it cuts the vertical (price) axis. If a linear supply curve passes through the origin, supply is unitary elastic regardless of its slope. If a linear supply curve cuts the horizontal (quantity) axis, supply is inelastic. Perfectly elastic supply is depicted by a horizontal supply curve; perfectly inelastic supply by a vertical supply curve. Figure 5.5 shows supply curves with different elasticities.

FIGURE 5.5

Supply curves
showing various
degrees of elasticity.

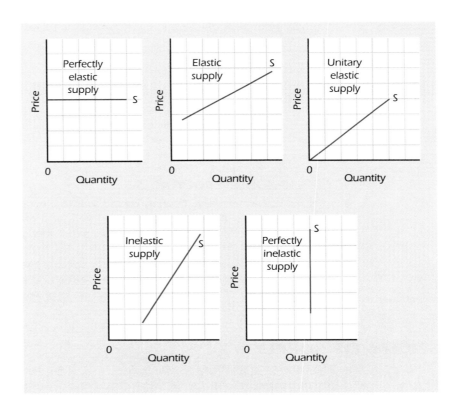

FACTORS AFFECTING PRICE ELASTICITY OF SUPPLY

TIME

The amount of time producers have to respond to changes in price is a major determinant of elasticity of supply.

Learning Objective 7: *identify the determinants of price elasticity of supply*

During the very short period (market period) an increase in price does not significantly affect the quantity offered for sale.

Reservation price: the lowest price a seller is willing to accept for a product.

Storage cost affects elasticity of supply.

The time period under consideration has a significant effect on the price elasticity of supply. If the time period is very short, then an increase in price does not significantly affect the quantity offered for sale. If a certain quantity of a commodity has already been produced and brought to market, then an increase in price does not cause a larger quantity to be offered for sale, because the quantity is fixed. We sometimes refer to this situation as the **very short period** or the **market period**. As the period under consideration becomes longer, supply tends to become more elastic. Sellers will be able to respond more easily to changes in the prices of their products. It is of interest to note that even in the very short period, sellers may withdraw their products from the market rather than sell them below certain prices. This is likely to happen in the case of goods that are not perishable and that do not have high storage costs. The price below which producers refuse to sell is referred to as a **reservation price**.

STORAGE COST

The elasticity of supply for goods that are not perishable and that can be stored at a relatively low cost tends to be greater than the elasticity of supply for perishables and goods with high storage cost. If the price of an item that can be stored cheaply falls, sellers may respond by withdrawing the item from the market and storing it. If the price of such an item rises, suppliers may be in a position to release some extra quantities from storage onto the market. These options may not be feasible in the face of high cost of storage.

PRODUCTION SUBSTITUTES AND COMPLEMENTS

Production substitutes and complements affect elasticity of supply.

If a product has a large number of substitutes in production, its supply is likely to be elastic. If the price of such a product falls, producers can shift resources into the production of any of the many substitutes. If the price of cabbage falls, producers can easily switch to lettuce or cucumbers. Because of the ease with which producers can respond to a change in the price of cabbage, its supply is elastic.

Production complements, you will recall, are goods that are produced together. When one is produced, the other is produced as a direct result. These are joint products. The supply of a relatively minor joint product is likely to be inelastic. Consider the case of beef and hides. A small increase in the price of hides is unlikely to induce farmers to butcher their cattle. Moreover, once cattle are slaughtered for beef, the hides will be sold at whatever the price may be. Therefore the supply of hides is likely to be inelastic.

PROBLEM SOLVING 5-4

The cost of producing Hollywood sunglasses is $10. Andrei Turgenev has a fixed supply of these sunglasses, which he will not sell unless he can make a profit of at least 10%. There are no storage costs and the product is durable. What will Andrei do (sell or not sell) if the market price is (a) $20, (b) $15, (c) $12, or (d) $10?

APPLICATIONS

Learning Objective 8:
understand the uses of
the elasticity concept

The concept of elasticity of demand has important applications in business decisions and in government policies. It will be helpful to refer to Table 5.6 on page 92. Suppose that farmers are contemplating an increase in the price of tomatoes in order to increase their revenues from the sale of tomatoes. The success of such a move depends on the price elasticity of demand for tomatoes. As can be seen from Table 5.6, if the demand for tomatoes is price inelastic, then a small increase in price causes total revenue to increase. If the demand for tomatoes is elastic, an increase in price causes total revenue to fall. The farmers will then fail to achieve their objective.

The following example illustrates the importance of price elasticity of demand in government tax policy. Suppose the government of Prince Edward Island wants to increase its revenue from taxation. What commodities can it tax in order to achieve this objective? Does a tax on gasoline, for example, increase tax revenues? Yes, a tax of two cents per litre produces an increase in the government's tax revenues, since the demand for gasoline seems to be inelastic at current prices. If the government increases the tax on a commodity whose demand is elastic, the resulting fall in quantity demanded will be relatively greater than the increase in the tax. This implies a fall in tax revenues.

In this section so far, we have concentrated on the price elasticity of demand. Is the price elasticity of supply also important? Certainly, we can learn a great deal about certain prices through elasticity of supply. Why, for example, are rare paintings so expensive? One answer, of course, is that there is a great demand for them. But that is only a part of the explanation. The other important aspect is that the supply of such paintings is, for all practical purposes, perfectly inelastic. A higher price will not cause another one to be produced. In such a case, the supply curve will be vertical as shown in Figure 5.6. Any increase in demand is reflected fully in an increase in price, since there can be no increase in quantity supplied to absorb or dampen the effect of the increase in demand.

FIGURE 5.6

Perfectly inelastic
supply.

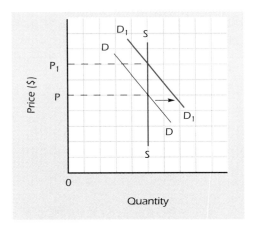

CHAPTER SUMMARY

1. Price elasticity of demand is measured by the relative change in quantity demanded divided by the relative change in price. The resulting value is the coefficient of elasticity.

2. The demand for a product may be perfectly elastic, elastic, unitary elastic, inelastic, or perfectly inelastic. Perfectly elastic demand and perfectly inelastic demand are extreme cases. The demand for most goods and services is elastic, unitary elastic, or inelastic.

GLOBAL PERSPECTIVE

Income Elasticity of Food Around the World

In developing countries where it is often a struggle to get enough food to eat, even a small increase in income is spent on food. In other words, the income elasticity of demand for food is relatively high. On the other hand, in advanced countries where it is hardly a problem to obtain food, and where people are usually consuming just about as much food as they wish, increases in income are usually spent on things other than food. In other words, the income elasticity of demand for food in advanced countries is relatively low.

India, Nigeria, and Indonesia have relatively low per capita incomes, averaging 5.6%, 6.7%, and 7.2% respectively of the U.S. per capita income, and, as can be seen from the following graph, their income elasticities of demand for food are high relative to those in Germany, Canada, and the United States.

Note: For graphical display, the income elasticity figures have been multiplied by 100. Thus, a value of 76 on the graph must be read as 0.76.

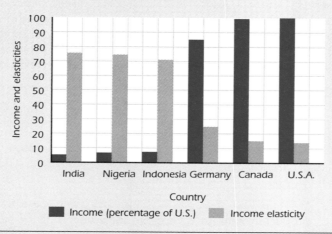

Source: Ching-Fun Cling and James Peale, Jr., "Income and Price Elasticities," in Henri Theil, ed., *Advances in Econometrics Supplement* (Greenwich, CT: JAI Press, 1989).

3. If the demand for a product is elastic, then a fall in price causes total revenue to increase. If the demand is unitary elastic, then a change in price leaves total revenue unchanged. If demand is inelastic, then a fall in price causes total revenue to fall.

4. Among the factors that affect price elasticity of demand are the availability of substitutes, the number of uses to which the commodity can be put, the proportion of income spent on the commodity, whether the commodity is a luxury or a necessity, and the time period under consideration.

5. Other important elasticity concepts are cross elasticity of demand and income elasticity of demand. Cross elasticity of demand measures the effect of a change in the price of good B on the quantity demanded of another good, A. If A and B are substitutes, their cross elasticity of demand will be positive. If they are complements, their cross elasticity of demand will be negative. If A and B are independent goods, then their cross elasticity will be zero.

6. Income elasticity of demand measures the effect of a change in income on quantity demanded. Normal goods have positive income elasticity of demand. Inferior goods have negative income elasticity of demand.

7. Price elasticity of supply measures the degree to which quantity offered for sale responds to changes in price. We measure price elasticity of supply by dividing the relative change in quantity supplied by the relative change in price.

8. Important determinants of elasticity of supply are the time being considered, storage cost, and the existence of production substitutes and production complements.

9. The elasticity concept has important applications to decisions concerning pricing and output in business and in government policy. It also helps us to understand the behaviour of certain prices.

TERMS FOR REVIEW

elasticity (84)
price elasticity of demand (84)
coefficient of elasticity (84)
perfectly inelastic (87)
perfectly elastic (87)
unit elasticity (87)
inelastic (87)
cross elasticity of demand (94)

substitutes (94)
complements (94)
income elasticity of demand (95)
normal goods (95)
inferior goods (95)
price elasticity of supply (95)
very short period (market period) (97)
reservation price (97)

QUESTIONS FOR REVIEW AND DISCUSSION

1. Under what circumstances will the own price elasticity of demand for a product be (L.O.1)

    (a) elastic

    (b) inelastic

    (c) perfectly inelastic

2. Make up a list of six products. Indicate, giving reasons, whether the demand for each product in your list is elastic or inelastic in relation to the price. (L.O.1,4)

3. Indicate the nature of the price elasticity of demand (elastic, inelastic, etc.) for each of the following commodities: (L.O.1,4)

    (a) bubble gum

    (b) beef

    (c) yachts

    (d) tea

    (e) Lloyd's electronic hand calculators

    (f) public transportation in Toronto

4. How would you interpret a value of −3.6 for the coefficient of price elasticity of demand for a product? (L.O.2)

5. Is the price elasticity of demand for a product the same as the slope of the demand curve for that product? Explain. (L.O.1)

6. What are the main determinants of price elasticity of demand? (L.O.4)

7. The government of British Columbia wants to increase its tax revenues. If lumber has a coefficient of price elasticity of demand of 2.5, while salmon has a coefficient of price elasticity of demand of 0.86, on which of these products will an increase in tax yield the larger tax revenue? (L.O.3)

8. Explain why an increase in the price of farm products may lead to larger incomes for farmers. (L.O.3)

9. Explain why a fall in the supply of farm products may lead to larger incomes for farmers. (L.O.6)

10. What are the main determinants of price elasticity of supply? (L.O.7)

11. You run a fish boat in Burgeo, Newfoundland. You have caught a certain amount of fish, which you must sell within a certain time because you have no cold-storage facilities and you do not want the fish to go bad. What is the price elasticity of supply in this situation? Would it be different if you had cold-storage facilities? (L.O.7)

12. Explain how price elasticity of supply may help us to understand the high prices of antiques. (L.O.8)

PROBLEMS AND EXERCISES

1. When the price of stopwatches falls from $15 to $12, the quantity demanded increases from 200 to 270. Compute the coefficient of price elasticity of demand for stopwatches using (L.O.1)

   (a) the point elasticity formula

   (b) the arc elasticity formula

2. Repeat Exercise 1 but with a price change from $12 to $15 and a quantity change from 270 to 200. (L.O.1)

3. Table 5.7 shows a demand schedule for good Y. (L.O.1,4)

   (a) Use the data in the first two columns to draw the demand curve for Y.

TABLE 5.7

Demand schedule for Y.

Price ($)	Quantity	Elasticity (E_d)
10	50	
8	60	
6	70	
4	80	
2	90	

   (b) Use the arc elasticity formula to compute the price elasticity coefficient at each price change, and complete the third column. (Remember that elasticity values go between the lines).

   (c) From this exercise, what have you observed about the price elasticity of demand at higher prices compared to the price elasticity of demand at lower prices?

4. (a) Construct a demand schedule for a product whose demand is perfectly inelastic within the price range $8, $7, $6, $5, $4, $3. Select your own quantities.

   (b) Graph the demand curve.

   (c) Name a good or service for which this demand is likely. (L.O.1,4)

5. Table 5.8 gives data for Fez Imports.

   (a) Complete the total revenue column. (L.O.1,3)

TABLE 5.8

Data for Fez Imports.

Price ($)	Quantity demanded	Total revenue	Elasticity coefficient
10	100		
9	120		
8	140		
7	160		
6	180		
5	200		

(b) Compute the price elasticity of demand for each price change and complete the elasticity column.

(c) Explain the relation that you observe between total revenue and price elasticity of demand.

6. When the price of X increases from $50 to $55, the quantity of Y demanded rises from 400 to 450. Use the arc elasticity formula to calculate the cross elasticity of demand between X and Y. (L.O.5)

7. When average income increases from $5000 to $8000, the quantity of automobiles demanded increases from 100 000 to 120 000. (L.O.2,5)

(a) Calculate the income elasticity of demand.

(b) What information does this elasticity coefficient give?

8. Assume that Canadian farmers face a price elasticity of demand for wheat of 0.65. How will a bad harvest that sends wheat prices up by 15% affect wheat growers? (L.O.8)

9. Show that if the demand for a product is perfectly price inelastic, then the burden (incidence) of a specific tax imposed on each unit produced (sold) will be shifted fully onto consumers. (L.O.8)

10. Show that if the supply of a product is perfectly price inelastic, then the burden (incidence) of a specific tax imposed on each unit produced (sold) will be borne entirely by the producers (sellers). (L.O.8)

11. On the basis of what you have learned in this chapter about price elasticity of demand, state whether you would expect the demand for gasoline to be elastic or inelastic. Gasoline prices have been fluctuating over a long period of time, which gives us a good opportunity to study the nature of the price elasticity of demand for gasoline in Canada. Interview local suppliers of gasoline (retail outlets) and ask them how customers respond to changes in gasoline price. Use the information that you receive to determine the nature of the price elasticity of demand for gasoline. Compare your result of this study with your expectation based on the material studied in this chapter.

CHAPTER

THE THEORY OF CONSUMER BEHAVIOUR

Learning Objectives

After studying this chapter, you should understand:

1 the concept of utility

2 the principle of utility maximization

3 the water-diamond paradox

4 the relationship between utility and demand

5 the derivation of the market demand curve

6 the concept and significance of consumer surplus

7 the idea of life-cycle saving

8 the motives for saving

The utility of articles valued for their beauty depends closely upon the expensiveness of the articles.

Thorstein Veblen, *The Theory of the Leisure Class*

INTRODUCTION

Households make three basic economic decisions. They decide how to spend their income on goods and services in the product market in order to maximize their satisfaction. They also decide how much of their income they will consume and how much they will save. Finally, they decide how to sell their resources, especially labour services, in the factor market. In this chapter, we will study the household's decision regarding how to allocate a given amount of money between various quantities of goods and services. We will also discuss the household's saving decision. A discussion of the household's behaviour in the labour market is deferred to a later chapter.

In Chapter 4, we analyzed the demand for a particular product. The total demand (or market demand) studied there is simply the sum of the demands of all the consumers in the market for that particular product. Let us now turn our attention to individual households, whose demands are added to obtain the total demand for a product.

In a very real sense, the satisfaction of wants is at the heart of economic activity. Production, consumption, and exchange are all carried out with the ultimate objective of satisfying wants. Wants are satisfied largely by the consumption of goods and services. It follows that an understanding of consumer behaviour is essential for an understanding of economic activity. This chapter will equip you with a theoretical apparatus for analyzing how a household will spend a given amount of money so that the satisfaction of the household will be maximized.

THE CONCEPT OF UTILITY

Learning Objective 1:
the concept of utility

Utility is a measure of satisfaction derived from consuming goods and services.

Util: a measure for a unit of satisfaction or utility.

Economists use the term **utility** to refer to the satisfaction derived from the consumption of goods and services. Suppose that we could actually measure satisfaction in the same way that we can measure distances or weights. Then, after a very enjoyable meal, a consumer would be able to tell us exactly how many units of satisfaction he or she obtained from that particular meal. Well, if you have not already noticed, economists are very ingenious people. They have invented a measure for a unit of satisfaction or utility, and have labelled it a **util**. The utility derived from the consumption of a good or service varies from individual to individual, and from time to time for the same individual. Although utility cannot actually be measured (you might be the one to invent a meter that can somehow be hooked up to the brain to measure the amount of satisfaction experienced), and is not subject to interpersonal comparison, the concept is nevertheless important in enabling us to understand how consumers exercise choice over the various commodities that they can buy. The concept of making decisions at the margin, which we shall develop here, will help us in other areas of economics.

Total utility is total satisfaction.

Marginal utility is extra satisfaction.

It is extremely important for us to know the difference between total utility and marginal utility. **Total utility** is the total satisfaction derived from the consumption of a good or service. For example, if you are really fond of ice cream, the more you consume per week (within reason, of course), the greater will be your total utility. **Marginal utility** is the extra or additional satisfaction derived from the consumption of additional units of a good or service. We can express marginal utility as

$$MU = \frac{\Delta TU}{\Delta Q}$$

where MU is marginal utility, TU is total utility, and Q is quantity. Table 6.1 shows hypothetical schedules of total and marginal utility for ice cream for a particular consumer for one week.

	Quantity of ice cream consumed (cones per week)	Total utility	Marginal utility
TABLE 6.1	0	0	
			40
Hypothetical utility schedules for ice cream.	1	40	
			30
	2	70	
			25
	3	95	
			20
	4	115	
			10
	5	125	
			5
	6	130	
			3
	7	133	
			1
	8	134	

The sum of all of the marginal utilities equals the total utility.

Note that the marginal utility values are placed between the lines of the total utility values. Note also that by adding all of the marginal utilities in the third column of Table 6.1, we obtain the total utility derived from all eight cones of ice cream.

FIGURE 6.1

Total utility and marginal utility.

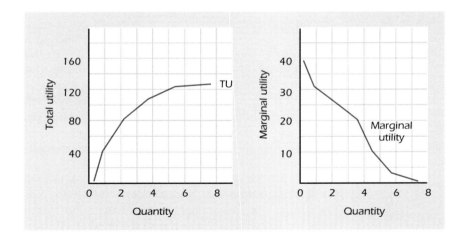

We can also illustrate total and marginal utility diagrammatically, as shown in Figure 6.1. The total utility column in Table 6.1 and the total utility graph in Figure 6.1 show that, although total utility increases as additional cones of ice cream are consumed, it does so at a decreasing rate. This phenomenon is called **the law of diminishing marginal utility** and can be stated as follows:

Marginal utility diminishes as quantity consumed increases.

> **As a consumer consumes more of a commodity, the utility or satisfaction derived from each additional unit diminishes.**

The following example will help to clarify the hypothesis. On a hot summer afternoon, you would probably really appreciate an ice cream cone. You might appreciate a second cone, though to a lesser extent than the first. You would likely enjoy a third cone even less than you enjoyed the second, and a fourth less than you enjoyed the third, and so on. Even though your total enjoyment increased, each cone of ice cream would give you less and less extra satisfaction. In other words, the marginal utility would diminish.

PROBLEM SOLVING 6-1

Assume that you have been given a case of Cherry Coke, and you must decide how much of it to consume within a given time. If, according to your subjective evaluation, the total utility derived after you have consumed the third bottle of Cherry Coke is 16 utils, and the marginal utility is positive but decreasing, should you consume more Cherry Coke?

THE CONSUMER'S PROBLEM: UTILITY MAXIMIZATION

Consumers achieve equilibrium when they maximize their satisfaction.

Learning Objective 2:
the principle of utility maximization

Let us assume that the objective of consumers is to maximize their total utility. Consumers act in such a way as to ensure that they obtain maximum satisfaction from their purchases of goods and services. When this happens, consumers have achieved their objectives, and we say that they are in equilibrium. Consumers in equilibrium have no desire to rearrange their purchases of goods and services, since any rearrangement will only result in a lower level of satisfaction.

Consider now the case of Erich Alda, a consumer who has a given amount of money to spend (budget) on two commodities, asparagus and bacon. Let us assume that Erich has spent his budget in such a way that the last dollar spent on asparagus gives more satisfaction than the last dollar spent on bacon. Let us assume, specifically, that the utility derived from the last dollar spent on asparagus is 15, while the utility derived from the last dollar spent on bacon is 10. Obviously, since an extra dollar spent on asparagus yields greater satisfaction than an extra dollar spent on bacon, Erich can increase his total satisfaction by buying more asparagus and less bacon. If the utility of the last dollar spent on bacon were greater than the utility of the last dollar spent on asparagus, then Erich could increase his satisfaction by buying more bacon and less asparagus. As long as the utility of the last dollar spent on asparagus is different from the utility of the last dollar spent on bacon, Erich can increase his total satisfaction by rearranging his purchases. It is only when the utility of the last dollar spent on each commodity is equal that the consumer will be maximizing his satisfaction.

Utility is maximized when the utility of the last dollar spent on each good is equal.

Let us return to the specific case in which the utility derived from the last dollar spent on asparagus is 15 and that derived from the last dollar spent on bacon is 10. As Erich buys more asparagus and less bacon, the marginal utility of asparagus will fall, while the marginal utility of bacon will increase (remember the hypothesis of diminishing marginal utility). If the utility of the last dollar spent on asparagus falls to 12 while the utility of the last dollar spent on bacon increases to 12, Erich will maximize his satisfaction and therefore have no desire to rearrange his purchases. When such a situation is attained, Erich will be in equilibrium. Any change from this position will result in a reduction in Erich's level of satisfaction.

So far, we have not introduced the prices of asparagus and bacon explicitly into the analysis. Erich's equilibrium position can be restated in terms of marginal utility and price. The marginal utility per dollar of asparagus is the marginal utility of asparagus divided by the price of asparagus. Similarly, the marginal utility per dollar of bacon is the marginal utility of bacon divided by the price of bacon. Thus, the condition to be met for Erich (or any other consumer) to be in equilibrium can be formulated as follows:

Learning Objective 2:
the principle of utility maximization

For a consumer purchasing two goods, A and B, to maximize satisfaction, the marginal utility of A divided by the price of A must equal the marginal utility of B divided by the price of B.

The utility maximization rule is often expressed in the following compact form:

$$\frac{MU_A}{P_A} = \frac{MU_B}{P_B}$$

Equimarginal principle: equating marginal values to maximize or minimize a variable.

where MU_A is the marginal utility of A, MU_B is the marginal utility of B, P_A is the price of A, and P_B is the price of B. This rule, known as the **equimarginal principle**, may also be expressed as

$$\frac{MU_A}{MU_B} = \frac{P_A}{P_B}$$

Expressed verbally, this formula says that the consumer will be in equilibrium (maximizing his or her satisfaction) when the ratio of the marginal utilities equals the ratio of the prices.

Of course, the consumer is usually confronted with more than just two commodities. The equilibrium condition can be extended to cover the situation of many commodities. In such a case, the equilibrium condition becomes

$$\frac{MU_A}{P_A} = \frac{MU_B}{P_B} = \frac{MU_C}{P_C} = \cdots = \frac{MU_Z}{P_Z}$$

for many goods from A to Z. The following example provides an opportunity to look at the consumer's allocation problem.

EXAMPLE 6-1

Consider the utility schedules of a consumer of two commodities, A and B, presented in Table 6.2. If the consumer, Yuki Hino, has a budget of $11 to spend on A and B, how should she allocate her funds between A and B in order to maximize her satisfaction?

TABLE 6.2

Schedule of marginal utility.

$ worth of A	MU_A	$ worth of B	MU_B
1	80	1	58
2	70	2	56
3	60	3	52
4	50	4	48
5	40	5	44
6	30	6	40
7	20	7	35
8	10	8	30
9	5	9	25
10	1	10	20

If Yuki spends the first dollar on A, she obtains 80 units of satisfaction (80 utils) but if she spends it on B, she obtains only 58 units of satisfaction. The first dollar should therefore be spent on A. The second dollar spent on A will yield 70 units of satisfaction, but if that dollar is spent on B, it will yield only 58 units of satisfaction. It should therefore be spent on A. For the same reason, the third dollar should be spent on A. Now, if the fourth dollar is spent on A, it will yield 50 units of satisfaction as compared with 58 if it is spent on B. The fourth dollar should therefore be spent on B. By similar reasoning, the fifth and sixth should be spent on B, the seventh on A, the eighth, ninth, and tenth on B, and the eleventh on A. We find that in the end, Yuki will have bought $5 worth of A and $6 worth of B. Note that this allocation accords with the principle stated earlier: that consumers will maximize their satisfaction when they allocate their incomes in such a manner that the utility of the last dollar spent on commodity A equals the utility of the last dollar spent on commodity B.

PROBLEM SOLVING 6-2

Referring to the data in Table 6.2, suppose that Yuki's spending money (budget) increases to $14. How will she rearrange her purchases in order to maximize her satisfaction?

THE WATER-DIAMOND PARADOX: THE PARADOX OF VALUE

Learning Objective 3:
the water-diamond paradox

Diamonds are more expensive than water not because they are more useful but because the marginal utility of diamonds is high relative to the marginal utility of water.

The **water-diamond paradox** or the **paradox of value** plagued numerous classical economists including Adam Smith (1723–1790), the man considered to be the father of economics as a discipline. The paradox lies in the question, "Why is water so much cheaper than diamonds when water is so much more useful than diamonds?" One solution is that diamonds are relatively scarce while water is relatively abundant. In price determination, marginal utility — not total utility — is the relevant concept. Water is useful but its marginal utility is low, while the marginal utility of diamonds is high. And since price is proportional to marginal utility, the price of diamonds is higher than the price of water.

THE CONSUMER'S DEMAND CURVE

The analysis presented above can be used to determine how a change in the price of a commodity affects the quantity demanded. Let us assume again that there are two goods, A and B, that the consumer can buy. If the price of A falls, then the marginal utility per dollar of A

$$\frac{MU_A}{P_A}$$

Learning Objective 4:
the relationship between utility and demand

increases. This being the case, the consumer will buy more of A. The following example helps us to illustrate the point. Let us assume that the price of A is $10 and that the marginal utility of A is 40 when the consumer is in equilibrium. The marginal utility per dollar of A is

$$\frac{40}{10} = 4$$

Since the consumer is in equilibrium, we know that the marginal utility per dollar of A equals the marginal utility per dollar of B — that is,

$$\frac{MU_A}{P_A} = \frac{40}{10} = \frac{MU_B}{P_B} = 4$$

Now, if the price of A falls to $8, then

$$\frac{MU_A}{P_A} = \frac{40}{8} = 5$$

which is now greater than

$$\frac{MU_B}{P_B}$$

To restore equilibrium, the consumer purchases more of A and less of B so that the MU_A falls while the MU_B rises until

$$\frac{MU_A}{P_A}$$

again equals

$$\frac{MU_B}{P_B}$$

A fall in the price of A, therefore, causes the quantity of A that the consumer will buy to increase. In other words, the consumer's demand curve slopes downward from left to right.

We can use an alternative approach to demonstrate the relation between marginal utility and the consumer's demand curve. Consider the demand curve in Figure 6.2 for your favourite consumer, you, for oranges per month. We can interpret this demand curve as follows: For a quantity of three bags of oranges, the maximum price you are willing to pay is $18. If the price were higher than $6 per bag, you would not buy the third bag of oranges.

FIGURE 6.2

Demand curve for oranges.

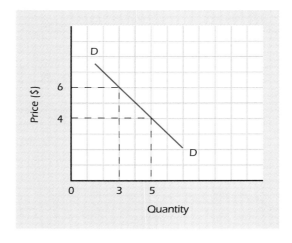

Why are you not willing to pay more than $6 for the third bag of oranges? The answer is that according to your subjective evaluation of the extra satisfaction derived from the third bag (i.e., its marginal utility), it is worth just $6 but no more. Likewise, you will not buy the fifth bag for a price exceeding $4 because that is your subjective evaluation of the marginal utility derived from the fifth bag. As we noted earlier in this chapter, the more oranges that you consume per month, the less satisfaction that you derive from each additional orange, and hence, the less you are willing to pay for extra bags of oranges. This approach clearly brings out the relation between marginal utility and demand.

Consumer demand reflects marginal utility.

MARKET DEMAND

Once we obtain a demand curve for each consumer of a particular product, we simply add these individual demand curves to obtain the market demand curve discussed in Chapter 4. Let us assume, for the sake of simplicity, that there are only three consumers, Maria Gabor, Emil Torecky, and Joan Day, in the market for a particular product. The individual demand schedules for these three consumers are given in Table 6.3, along with the market demand.

TABLE 6.3

Individual demand schedules.

	Maria's demand		Emil's demand		Joan's demand		Market demand	
	P	**Q**	**P**	**Q**	**P**	**Q**	**P**	**Q**
	8	2	8	0	8	3	8	5
	6	3	6	2	6	5	6	10
	4	4	4	4	4	7	4	15

At a price of $8, Maria will buy two units a week, Emil will buy none, and Joan will buy three units a week. Notice that at a price of $8, Emil is effectively out of the market. The total quantity demanded at $8 is therefore five units. This is shown in the market demand schedule. At a price of $6, Maria will buy three units a week, Emil will now enter the market and buy two units, while Joan will buy five units. The total quantity demanded at a price of $6 is thus 10 units, as shown in the market demand schedule. At a price of $4, Maria will buy four units, Emil will buy four, and Joan will buy seven; so together, they will buy a total of 15 units at a price of $4. You have seen, then, that the market demand is the sum of the demands of the individual consumers in the market.

Learning Objective 5:
the derivation of the market demand curve

The market demand curve is the horizontal summation of the individual demand curve.

Can we derive the market demand curve from the individual demand curves? Let us investigate. Figure 6.3 shows the demand curves for Maria, Emil, and Joan. At a price of $8, the total quantity demanded by all three consumers is five units. This combination of price and quantity gives one point on the market demand curve. At a price of $6, the total quantity demanded by all three consumers is 10 units a week. This combination of price and quantity gives another point on the market demand curve. The third point on the demand curve is obtained in a similar manner. Thus, we can conclude that the market demand curve is the horizontal summation of the individual demand curves.

CONSUMER SURPLUS

Learning Objective 6:
the concept and significance of consumer surplus

Consumer surplus is the difference between what consumers are willing to pay and what they actually pay.

We can now look at a useful economic concept called **consumer surplus**. Suppose apples are sold at $0.50 per kilogram. Quite possibly, consumers might be willing to pay $3 for the first kilogram, but they pay only $0.50 because this is the market price. They might possibly be willing to pay $2 for the second kilogram, but they still pay only $0.50. For the third kilogram, they might be willing to pay $1.20, but again, they pay only $0.50. They might be willing to pay $0.60 for the fourth kilogram, but once more they pay only $0.50. Table 6.4 shows the relevant data.

The consumer surplus is the difference between the amount that a consumer would have paid for a product and the amount that he or she actually paid.

Consumer surplus can also be shown on a graph. Consider Figure 6.4. The equilibrium price and the equilibrium quantity established by the market for this good or service are $0.50 and 5 kg respectively. Many buyers would have been willing to pay a higher price than $0.50 to obtain this commodity. But because they have to pay only $0.50, they actually receive a surplus or gain, which is referred to as consumer surplus.

FIGURE 6.3

Derivation of the
market demand
curve.

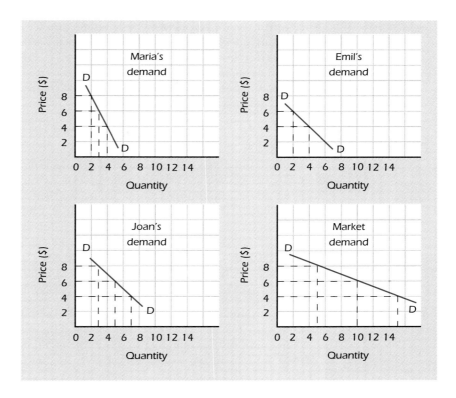

TABLE 6.4

Illustration of
consumer surplus.

Apples (kg)	Total amount the consumer would have paid	Total amount actually paid	Consumer surplus
1	$3.00	$0.50	$2.50
2	5.00	1.00	4.00
3	6.20	1.50	4.70
4	6.80	2.00	4.80

FIGURE 6.4

Consumer surplus.

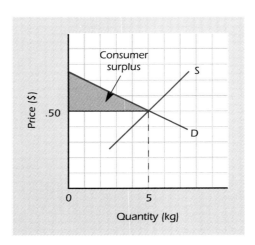

Consumers often derive a greater amount of satisfaction from a good than is suggested by the price of the good.

Each consumer's surplus differs depending on the price that he or she is willing to pay. And this price, as you have seen, depends on the consumer's evaluation of the utility derived from the product. The shaded area in Figure 6.4 measures total consumer surplus. The economic significance of the concept of consumer surplus is that consumers often derive a greater amount of satisfaction or utility from a good or service than is suggested by the price of the good.

THE SAVING DECISION

The total amount of savings in Canada is the result of the savings of individual households who decide to put aside a certain part of their income. People save for a variety of reasons: to be able to leave an inheritance to their children or grandchildren, to pay for their children's education, to purchase a car or a house, to take a cruise on a luxury ship, or to live well in retirement. These motives for saving will be discussed in greater detail.

MOTIVES FOR SAVING

The life-cycle motive for saving

Learning Objective 7:
the idea of life-cycle saving

Life-cycle saving is long-term saving, often for retirement.

Life-cycle saving refers to the idea that people will organize their consumption, and hence their saving, in such a way that they will be able to maintain an adequate level of consumption during retirement. The name of Franco Modigliani, a Nobel laureate at Massachusetts Institute of Technology (MIT), is most often associated with this concept.

Figure 6.5 illustrates the idea of life-cycle saving. We assume that this individual, Sally, obtains her first job at age 20, retires at age 65, and expects to live until she is 90. (Secretly, she thinks that she will live to be 100). As the graph shows, Sally's savings are zero before age 20. Thereafter, her savings increase until she reaches the age of 65. After age 65 she is in retirement so she has no income, except perhaps for interest earned on her savings. She then begins to use her savings to finance her consumption. At age 90, she has little or no savings left.

FIGURE 6.5

Life-cycle savings.

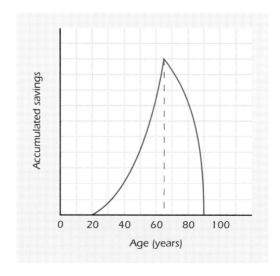

The precautionary motive for saving

Learning Objective 8:
the motives for saving

Life is filled with uncertainties, risks, and unexpected events, many of which require funds. People are able to buy insurance against some of these events — car insurance, fire insurance, etc. But there are other risks against which they may not be able to purchase insurance. For example, a writer may not be able to buy insurance against the risk of a significant decline in demand for her book. Thus, people save for unexpected events. Such savings are referred to as **precautionary savings**. The amount of precautionary savings that people undertake depends on the ease of contracting loans, and the availability of insurance against risks.

Precautionary saving is for unexpected events.

The inheritance motive

To many people, the prospect of leaving an inheritance or bequest to their children and/or grandchildren is a matter of some importance. Such people are quite willing to sacrifice current consumption so that their children and grandchildren can enjoy higher levels of consumption. This motive for saving is called the **bequest** or **inheritance motive**. Experience seems to support the existence of a bequest motive for saving since many people are known to leave considerable amounts of money for their children and grandchildren. The fact that many people do not leave substantial amounts for their children and grandchildren may be due to lack of ability rather than to the absence of a bequest motive.

Inheritance saving is for one's heirs.

Target saving

Saving for specific purposes is often referred to as **target saving**. A student who has a part-time job may save toward the purchase of a stereo system or a computer. A couple may save toward the downpayment on a car or a house. Many people believe that it is important for their children to get a college or university education, so they save for that specific purpose. In Canada, students can obtain Canada or Quebec student loans and grants. This has reduced the burden of saving for parents to educate their children.

Target saving is for a specific purpose, such as the purchase of a car or house.

SAVING AND INCOME

The amount that people are able to save depends on the level of their disposable income. (Disposable income is income left after income taxes are deducted). People with high disposable incomes will tend to spend more on consumption, and they are likely also to save more than people with low disposable incomes. Because saving varies directly with the level of disposable income, an increase in income taxes will reduce disposable income and hence saving. Conversely, a reduction in income taxes will tend to increase household saving.

SAVING AND THE RATE OF INTEREST

The rate of interest exerts considerable influence on a household's decision to save. Higher interest rates encourage saving, while lower interest rates discourage saving. When interest rates are high, households will find it attractive to postpone consumption. But high interest rates also mean bigger interest earnings on savings, so people with savings feel better off when interest rates are high. This may lead to greater current consumption. Therefore, higher interest rates are likely to cause households to consume more both now and in the future.

GLOBAL PERSPECTIVE

Trade and Global Maximization of Satisfaction

In our discussion of consumer behaviour, we have shown how, given their income and the prices of goods and services, consumers within a given economy seek to maximize their satisfaction by purchasing goods and services freely. In the same way, nations could maximize their economic well-being if they could freely exchange goods and services among themselves.

International trade is one means whereby consumers all over the globe can attempt to maximize their satisfaction. Canadians need coffee, tea, cane sugar, British-made cars, oranges, pineapple and countless other items that either we do not have or that we could produce only by diverting scarce resources from more efficient to less efficient uses. We also benefit from trade because competition from other countries forces us to use cost-saving technology in our domestic industries. Through international trade, people of all nations are able to enjoy a greater variety of goods.

In this chapter, we also discussed households' savings decisions. The greater the return on your saving, other things being equal, the better off you will be. The ability to move funds across international borders also helps global consumers to maximize their satisfaction. Consider two countries: Canada and the United States. Let's assume that a shortage of capital in Canada results in a rate of interest of 12%, while the United States has plenty of capital, reflected in a U.S. rate of interest of 4%. If American citizens can invest their savings in Canada, they will earn a return of 12% compared to 4% if they invest in the United States. This transfer of funds benefits the citizens of both countries. Americans earn considerably more on their savings, whereas Canadians acquire more capital, enabling them to save less and increase their current consumption.

Among the major objectives of free trade agreements among countries and trade agreements under the General Agreement on Tariffs and Trade (GATT) and its new replacement, the World Trade Organization (WTO), are the mutual benefits to be derived from international trade and freer access to international capital. International trade and the free flow of capital between countries allow the global economy to use its scarce resources efficiently and thus maximize satisfaction globally.

CHAPTER SUMMARY

1. Utility refers to the amount of satisfaction derived from the consumption of goods and services. Utility is not measurable, and one person's utility cannot be meaningfully compared with that of another.

2. Total utility is the total amount of satisfaction derived from consuming goods and services. Marginal utility is the additional satisfaction derived from consuming additional units of goods and services. We can obtain total utility by adding all of the marginal utilities derived from each additional unit.

3. The law of diminishing marginal utility states that, as a consumer consumes more of a commodity, the utility or satisfaction derived from each additional unit diminishes.

4. We assume that the objective of consumers is to maximize their satisfaction. They do this by equating the marginal utilities of a dollar's worth of each of the commodities on which they spend their incomes. In this position, consumers are said to be in equilibrium.

5. We can derive the consumer's demand curve from utility analysis. The consumer's demand curve reflects marginal utility.

6. The market demand curve for a particular commodity is the sum of the demand curves of the consumers in the market for that commodity.

7. The consumer's surplus is the difference between what the consumers are willing to pay and what they actually pay. The existence of consumer's surplus suggests that consumers derive more satisfaction from a good than is suggested by the price.

8. The idea of life-cycle saving is that people will save in order to be able to maintain a certain level of consumption during retirement.

9. People also save in order to provide for unforeseen contingencies, to leave an inheritance to their children or grandchildren, or to finance some specific consumption.

10. The level of disposable income and the rate of interest are likely to affect households' saving decisions.

TERMS FOR REVIEW

utility (104)
util (104)
total utility (104)
marginal utility (104)
law of diminishing marginal utility (105)
equimarginal principle (107)

water-diamond paradox (paradox of value) (108)
consumer surplus (110)
life-cycle saving (112)
precautionary saving (113)
inheritance (bequest) saving (113)
target saving (113)

QUESTIONS FOR REVIEW AND DISCUSSION

1. Give an example to show that you understand the difference between total utility and marginal utility. (L.O.1)

2. Do you think that the utility analysis of consumer behaviour is important even though utility cannot be measured? Why or why not? (General)

3. State the law of diminishing marginal utility. Do you think that this law applies to all goods and services? (L.O.1)

4. Demonstrate your understanding of the conditions that must exist for a consumer to be in equilibrium. (L.O.2)

5. Explain the relation between marginal utility and consumer demand. (L.O.4)

6. What is the relation between the individual demand curve and the market demand curve? (L.O.5)

7. Outline briefly the procedure for deriving the market demand curve from the individual consumers' demand curves. (L.O.4)

8. Explain the water-diamond paradox. (L.O.3)

9. In a few sentences, explain consumer surplus. (L.O.6)

10. What is the economic implication of consumer surplus? (L.O.6)

11. Discuss some reasons why households might save. (L.O.7,8)

PROBLEMS AND EXERCISES

1. Given the information in Table 6.2, how should Yuki Hino allocate a budget of $17 between commodities A and B in order to maximize her satisfaction? (L.O.2)

2. Given the data shown in Table 6.5 on the utilities of A and B, and given that the price of A is $2 and the price of B is $3: (L.O.2)

	Quantity of A	MU$_A$	$\dfrac{MU_A}{P_A}$	Quantity of B	MU$_B$	$\dfrac{MU_B}{P_B}$
TABLE 6.5	1	16		1	21	
Utilities of A and B.	2	18		2	24	
	3	16		3	18	
	4	14		4	15	
	5	10		5	12	
	6	6		6	6	
	7	2		7	3	

(a) Fill in the MU$_A$/P$_A$ and the MU$_B$/P$_B$ columns.

(b) How should a customer allocate a budget of $12 between A and B?

(c) What change should be made in the consumer's purchases if his or her budget increases to $22?

3. The market for salmon consists of three consumers: Sol, Luci, and Clare. Their demand schedules for salmon are given in Table 6.6.

	Sol's demand		Luci's demand		Clare's demand	
	P	**Q**	**P**	**Q**	**P**	**Q**
TABLE 6.6						
Demand schedules	10	8	10	6	10	5
for salmon.	8	10	8	8	8	7
	6	12	6	10	6	9

(a) Construct the market demand schedule for salmon.

(b) Draw the demand curve for each consumer and then draw the market demand curve. (L.O.5)

4. Table 6.7 shows the demand schedule for beef for Annie Lamb. Plot Annie's demand curve. If the market price of beef is $4 per kilogram, show Annie's total consumer surplus on your graph and calculate its value. (L.O.6)

	Price ($)	Quantity demanded per week (kg)
TABLE 6.7		
Annie's demand	7	0
for beef.	6	1
	5	2
	4	3
	3	4

5. How would you expect households to react to each of the following in terms of their motivation to save? (L.O.7,8)

(a) the elimination of an inheritance tax

(b) the introduction of easily available insurance for a wide range of risks

(c) more liberal loans and grants for students

(d) a marked decline in the birth rate

Internet Site

http://www.wto.org

This is the Web site for the World Trade Organization. Information about the WTO and its activities can be found here.

INTERNET EXERCISE

1. Go to the home page for the WTO.
2. Click on *About the WTO.*
3. List the four guiding elements which make up the General Agreement on Trade in Services (GATS).
4. List four services, other than banking, that fall under the jurisdiction of the GATS.

7

C H A P T E R

BUSINESS ORGANIZATION, SPECIALIZATION, AND INDUSTRIAL LOCATION

Learning Objectives

After studying this chapter, you should be able to:

1 discuss various forms of business organization

2 state the advantages and disadvantages of each form of business organization

3 discuss business financing

4 discuss advantages and disadvantages of specialization

5 account for the location of certain industries

The nature of our industrial organization does not lend itself to neat classification.

George J. Stigler, *Five Lectures on Economic Problems*

INTRODUCTION

The production of goods and services in Canada is undertaken by numerous firms operating under different forms of business organization. These firms may be classified in several ways. For example, we could classify them as small, medium or large, either on the basis of their annual sales, their share of the market, or on their number of employees. We could also classify them as domestic or foreign owned firms. Each classification would, of course, depend on the purpose for which the classification was made. In this chapter, we shall discuss the various forms of organization that a firm may take, the concept of specialization, and the location of production. Forms of business organization include the single proprietorship, the partnership, the corporation, and the cooperative. Numerous examples of each form of organization can be found all over the country. These various forms of business organization do not merely represent the financial arrangement under which the firm operates. They dictate the extent to which the owners are liable for the debts of the business, which laws will apply to its operation, the owner's role in running the business, and the type of taxes to be paid.

In this book, we will focus our attention on firms that operate for profit. You must realize, however, that there are many organizations that use resources to produce goods and services, but whose objectives do not include profit-making. Such organizations are often referred to as not-for-profit organizations and include charitable, social, religious, philanthropic, scientific, and educational institutions. These non-profit-seeking organizations also exist in the same four forms mentioned above.

THE SINGLE PROPRIETORSHIP

Single (or sole) proprietorship: a firm with a single private owner who is solely responsible for all decision-making.

Learning Objective 1: *discuss various forms of business organization*

Let us imagine a person, Cyril Khan, who believes that he can earn a handsome income by selling worms as fishing bait. He gets his supply of worms, and serves his customers from his garage. Cyril has established a single proprietorship. Or imagine a lawyer, Andrea Malozzi, who has left the firm of Briggs, Cahill, and Morin to start her own practice. She too has established a single proprietorship. **Single** (or **sole**) **proprietors** own their own businesses, finance them themselves (perhaps with the help of family), and make all of the decisions regarding the operation of their businesses. If their businesses prosper, the proprietors enjoy the profits; if their businesses fail, the proprietors suffer the losses. The single proprietorship is found mainly in small businesses such as confectioneries and farms and in certain professions such as accounting and business and economic consulting.

Advantages of the single proprietorship

The single proprietorship has certain advantages:

Learning Objective 2: *state the advantages and disadvantages of each form of business organization*

1. Single proprietors derive a certain amount of satisfaction, pride, and independence from owning their own businesses. You can sense the feeling of accomplishment when someone proudly states, "I own my own business."

2. Knowing that they can lose all of their possessions if their businesses fail, single proprietors are likely to make special efforts to run their businesses efficiently.

3. In situations demanding swift action, single proprietorships enjoy a considerable advantage over other forms of business organization, since owners do not need to consult with or seek the agreement of anyone other than themselves.

4. Single proprietors are likely to be more concerned about developing good working relations with the few employees that they may have, and with securing the

goodwill of their customers. If single proprietors are successful, the quality of their services will be high, and the effect on their revenues favourable.

5. Single proprietors may enjoy tax benefits. The earnings of single proprietors are subject to tax once only. We will see later that corporations do not enjoy this advantage.

Disadvantages of the single proprietorship

The single proprietorship has the following disadvantages:

1. Single proprietors are at a distinct disadvantage in situations requiring huge capital outlays. Not many single proprietors are in a position to raise the large sums of money required in many of today's modern businesses. Hence, we do not find many single proprietors owning large industrial plants.

2. The single proprietorship form of business organization suffers from the uncertainty about the continuation of the business in the event of the death or retirement of the owner. It must be observed, however, that some single proprietorships have been known to survive through several generations in the hands of the same family.

3. The biggest disadvantage of the single proprietorship, however, is the fact that the owners are legally responsible for all debts incurred by their businesses. Single proprietors are not protected by limited liability. This means that if their businesses fail, single proprietors are fully liable and can lose personal assets such as cars, furniture, or even homes since, in this form of business organization, there is no legal distinction between personal assets and business assets.

THE PARTNERSHIP

Suppose our hypothetical worm-seller, Cyril, is doing so well that he believes that he can rent a small building two blocks away and move the business out of his garage. Since the business has grown, it requires more money to run it. He now needs someone to share the rental cost and perhaps manage the store when he is out gathering worms. He discusses the idea (a business proposition?) with two of his friends who attended high school with him. They agree to go into business with him — thus forming a partnership. A **partnership** is a form of business organization in which two or more individuals agree to own and operate a business. The partners usually draw up an agreement (contract) outlining the amount of capital that each has invested in the business, the responsibilities of each partner, and the manner in which the profits will be divided among them. Partnerships are quite common among lawyers, doctors, business and management consultants, and small retail stores. Why do people form partnerships? The answer is that there are certain advantages in forming a partnership.

Advantages of the partnership

The following are the major advantages of the partnership:

1. The partnership has the ability to raise more capital than the single proprietorship is able to raise.

2. The partnership, like the single proprietorship, is not subject to tax. Individual partners, of course, pay taxes on their incomes, but the business itself pays no tax on its earnings.

3. Discussion is likely to take place among the partners before any important action is taken. These discussions are likely to lead to more sober decisions than those reached by single proprietors who do not need to engage in such discussions. According to the old adage, two heads are better than one.

4. The partnership may benefit from the variety of special talents and skills possessed by the partners. One may have expertise in marketing, another in management, another in accounting, etc., and all contribute to the successful operation of the business.

Disadvantages of the partnership

The partnership suffers from the following disadvantages:

1. The partnership lacks continuity. If one partner dies or if agreement cannot be reached among the partners, the partnership may have to be dissolved.

2. Although the partnership may be able to raise more capital than the single proprietorship, it is still severely limited in the amount of funds it can raise.

3. The partnership does not have limited liability. This is probably its most serious drawback. Each partner is fully liable to the extent of his or her personal possessions for any debts incurred by the business. It is possible for one partner to make a bad business decision in the name of the partnership, thus jeopardizing the financial security of the other partners, since they are severally and jointly liable.

THE LIMITED PARTNERSHIP

Learning Objective 1: discuss various forms of business organization

In a limited partnership, some partners are protected by limited liability, but at least one partner must have unlimited liability.

Learning Objective 2: state the advantages and disadvantages of each form of business organization

A modified version of the ordinary partnership, called the limited partnership, has emerged. The limited partnership reduces, to a certain extent, the problems of unlimited liability associated with the ordinary partnership. In a **limited partnership**, certain partners have limited liability. Such partners are liable only to the extent of the amount of money they have invested in the partnership, but they may legally take part neither in managing it nor in conducting any business in its name. A limited partnership requires at least one partner to assume unlimited liability. The limited partnership arrangement increases the ability of the partnership to raise funds, because some partners have limited liability. Knowing that they can lose, at worst, only their investment in the business, limited partners may be attracted to the partnership.

PROBLEM SOLVING 7-1
Why is a partnership the ideal form of business organization for a law firm, from the viewpoint of the client?

THE CORPORATION

Learning Objective 1: discuss various forms of business organization

Corporation: a form of business organization in which shareholders have limited liability.

Let us return to our hypothetical worm-seller, Cyril. Cyril's partnership is extremely successful. Customers from 30 km away have begun asking about fishing equipment. The partners of the business decide, therefore, to expand their operation. They want to open stores all over the city. And, in addition to selling worms and other types of bait, they want to stock all types of fishing equipment and books about fishing. They also plan to expand their business into neighbouring provinces, and ultimately, to have a chain of stores stretching from coast to coast.

For the moment, however, their focus is on expanding city-wide and offering fishing equipment as well as bait. This expansion requires a great deal of capital and, instead of gathering worms, as they do now, the partners plan to breed worms scientifically. To do so, they need to obtain very expensive equipment. If they could lure a few wealthy persons into the partnership, they would probably be able to afford the new equipment and larger facilities required. But it is extremely difficult to find people who are willing both to invest huge sums of money and to be fully liable for the debts of the business. Cyril and his partners can overcome this problem, however, by forming a **corporation**.

A corporation is a form of business organization in which a group of persons agree to engage in business in which they have limited liability. They obtain permission from either the federal government or from one of the provincial governments to incorporate. The corporation can raise vast amounts of money by selling shares to the public. The purchasers of these shares (the shareholders, or stockholders, as they are often called) are the owners of the business. A board of directors is elected by the shareholders, and this board hires senior executive officers. Legally, the corporation is an entity that exists apart from the shareholders. It can sue or be sued, enter into contracts, and be taxed just like an individual. Naturally, we would expect the corporation to be the dominant form of organization in large businesses. A corporation is identified by the word *Corporation*, *Incorporated* (or its abbreviation *Inc.*), or *Limited* (or its abbreviation *Ltd.*) at the end of the name of the firm. The following firms would be corporations: The ABC Corporation; Advicecon, Inc.; and Econoserve, Ltd.

In the modern corporation, the decision-making process is divorced from the risk-taking process, since the risk is borne by the shareholders, who are the owners of the business. A hired manager may not even own shares in the company. The profits of the corporation accrue to (are distributed to) the shareholders as dividends. Portions of the profits of the corporation may be retained to be reinvested in the business. These are known as **retained earnings** or *undistributed profits*.

> Retained earnings are not paid to shareholders, they are retained for reinvestment.

Advantages of the corporation

The corporation has a number of important advantages:

> **Learning Objective 2:** state the advantages and disadvantages of each form of business organization

1. It has a tremendous ability to raise huge amounts of money. The shares of the corporation can easily be transferred from one owner to another. If you hold shares in a corporation, you can sell your shares to any person who is willing to buy them. Investment in corporate stock is thus considered to be very attractive.

2. This form of business organization has the continuity that is lacking in the single proprietorship and the partnership. If a shareholder dies, the corporation continues as usual.

3. The corporation can usually afford to hire the services of experts. It can hire a staff of researchers, economists, top management personnel, accountants, lawyers, and experts in other fields. Policy decisions are, therefore, likely to be sound.

4. In a corporation, each owner (shareholder) is liable only to the extent of his or her investment in the business. That is, the owners have **limited liability**. If the company fails, each shareholder's liability is limited to the amount of money spent in buying shares in the business. This is undoubtedly the greatest advantage of the corporation.

> Shareholders have limited liability – liability only for the total of their investment.

Disadvantages of the corporation

Despite the significant advantages of the corporation, it still suffers from the following disadvantages:

1. The earnings of the corporation are taxed twice. The corporation pays a tax before its profits are distributed, and the shareholders also pay a tax on their dividends.

2. The owners of the corporation may have little or no control over its operation, and those who make the day-to-day decisions of the corporation may not have the same incentives as the owners.

3. The size of the corporation often forces a wedge between labour and management, and also destroys the close personal relationship between owner and customer that is typical of the single proprietorship.

PROBLEM SOLVING 7-2

1. The profitable partnership Hitchcock, James, and Chill Filmmakers finds that it could earn even larger profits if it expanded its operation. Potential partners are unwilling to join the partnership because of unlimited liability. What course of action might the firm take to overcome this difficulty?

2. If a government is primarily interested in increasing its tax revenue, should it favour the formation of corporations?

THE COOPERATIVE

Learning Objective 1:
discuss various forms of business organization

A **cooperative** is a form of business organization that is owned, financed, and controlled by its member-patrons, who share the risks and benefits in proportion to their patronage. A cooperative is established to reap the benefits of large-scale selling and buying. It is similar to a corporation in many respects. In fact, it is a modified version of the corporation. A cooperative raises funds by selling shares, and its shareholders enjoy the advantage of limited liability.

Cooperative: a form of business organization in which members provide the capital, and in which dividends are distributed according to patronage.

Unlike the corporation though, in which a shareholder is entitled to one vote for each share he or she owns, each member of the cooperative has only one vote no matter how many shares he or she controls. Hence, a true cooperative exhibits democratic control. Also, dividends are distributed not in proportion to the number of shares held, as in the case of a corporation, but in proportion to the amount of business that each member conducts with the cooperative.

TYPES OF COOPERATIVES

Cooperatives may be classified in a variety of ways depending on the main objectives of the cooperatives. Thus there are consumer cooperatives, producer cooperatives, purchasing cooperatives, and marketing cooperatives. Each of these types will be briefly discussed.

A *consumer cooperative* is formed by a group of consumers who join together to operate a business that provides consumer goods and services. Since dividends are distributed among the members in proportion to the volume of business that each member does with the cooperative (i.e., according to patronage), the members find it advantageous to do as much business as possible with the cooperative.

A *producer cooperative* is formed by a group of producers who believe that by banding together they can better serve their interests. A group of dairy farmers or fruit growers, for example, may form a cooperative for the purpose of increasing efficiency through joint action.

Purchasing cooperatives and *marketing cooperatives* are formed to take advantage of large-scale purchasing and marketing. The main objective of a purchasing cooperative is to buy on a large scale and obtain the benefits of lower costs. Similarly, marketing cooperatives can sell on a large scale and thus increase their profits.

Advantages of the cooperative

Learning Objective 2:
state the advantages and disadvantages of each form of business organization

1. The cooperative can take advantage of the benefits of large-scale operation. For example, a consumer cooperative can obtain its supplies more cheaply by buying in large quantities, and thus take advantage of quantity discounts. A producer cooperative can establish and operate a distribution system for its products more cheaply than if each producer did his or her own marketing.

2. The managers and customers of a cooperative are likely to work together towards the success of the business.

Disadvantages of the cooperative

1. The cooperative may fail to look beyond its own membership for expert management.

2. The cooperative may be limited by its inability to raise huge amounts of capital. This may be the case for two main reasons. First, only those individuals who intend to conduct a large volume of business with the cooperative are likely to purchase its shares. Second, its members are unlikely to contribute additional funds since dividends are distributed not in proportion to funds invested but by patronage.

3. The democratic control that is a feature of cooperatives may limit decision-making severely. The membership may not be sufficiently informed to vote intelligently on certain major policy issues.

PROBLEM SOLVING 7-3

You have come up with an idea for a good or service that you believe will be successful on the market, and you would like to experiment with this idea. It does not require a great deal of money to get it started. What form of business organization would you choose to establish your business?

BUSINESS FINANCING

Learning Objective 3:
discuss business financing

It would be helpful for you, as a student of economics, to have at least a general idea of business financing. This section provides that general knowledge. The method of financing available to a business enterprise depends on the specific form of business organization of the enterprise.

You have already learned that a single proprietorship is financed by the resources of its owner. The owner may raise the capital by borrowing from a financial institution, such as a bank, or from family members. In any case, the financial burden rests squarely on the shoulders of the owner. The partnership is financed in a similar fashion, except that the burden is shared among all of the partners. Once the firm becomes a going concern and begins to earn profits, funds for expansion and new investment may come from those profits.

A corporation may finance its operations internally from retained earnings, or externally by debt financing or equity financing.

Unlike the single proprietorship and the partnership, the corporation has a number of options that it may use to raise capital. First, it may rely on internal financing; that is, the firm may decide not to distribute all profits after taxes to its shareholders, but to retain a certain amount for investment. Retained earnings provide the main source of funds for total investment.

Financing through bond issue

A bond is a certificate stating that a corporation or the government owes you a certain amount of money at a specific time.

Second, the corporation may raise capital by issuing bonds. A **bond** is a certificate printed on fancy paper that is issued by a government or a corporation, promising to pay a certain amount of money as interest payment periodically (annually or semi-annually, for example) until the bond matures. The issuer of the bond (the borrower) promises to pay whoever owns it (the lender) the full amount of its face value when the bond becomes due, that is, when it matures. If you buy a $1000 bond from a corporation that promises to pay $100 every year for a period of five years, the corporation is actually borrowing $1000 from you. You will earn $100 every year for five years; and you will receive the principal of $1000 at the end of the five-year period on the maturity date of the bond.

What happens, you may well ask, if the corporation expected to earn an annual return averaging 15% but actually earns only 8%? Is it still obliged to pay you the amounts promised by the bond? The answer is yes. Your payments are not conditional upon the corporation's earnings. Failure on the part of the corporation to meet the terms specified by the bond constitutes a default of obligations and exposes the corporation to legal proceedings and the consequences prescribed by law.

Financing through bank credit

Third, a corporation may negotiate a loan with a bank or other financial institution. The corporation and the lending institution negotiate the terms of the loan. Whereas a bond is usually for a long period of time, bank credit is usually short-term — up to three years, and frequently maturing within a year. The rate of interest that the corporation pays depends largely on the lending institution's evaluation of the degree of risk associated with the corporation. The rate of interest that banks charge their most credit-worthy corporate borrowers is called the **prime rate**.

The prime rate is the interest rate charged to a financial institution's best customers.

Financing through shares

Fourth, a corporation may issue shares. When you buy shares in a company, you are actually buying part ownership in the corporation. As a part owner, you are entitled to a share of the profits, but you must also suffer any losses that may occur.

The capital raised by issuing bonds and by using bank credit is referred to as **debt capital**. The capital obtained from selling shares is called **equity capital**.

Debt capital is acquired by issuing bonds or obtaining bank loans; equity capital is acquired from selling shares in the corporation.

SPECIALIZATION

The corporation makes large-scale production possible, and one of the reasons for efficiency in large-scale operations is the ability to take advantage of specialization. There are two main forms of specialization: specialization by occupation and specialization by task.

Specialization may involve concentration on a particular occupation or task.

Specialization by occupation occurs when an individual specializes in a particular trade, occupation, or profession, instead of engaging in a number of separate occupations (generalizing). Occupational specialization is visible in the fact that some individuals are plumbers, some are farmers, some are college professors, some are sculptors, and some are doctors.

Specialization by task occurs when the production of a certain good is divided into a number of different tasks, and each worker performs one of these tasks. Adam Smith's description of the process of pin-making is such a vivid account of the process of specialization by task that we should look at the entire passage:

> One man draws out the wire, another straightens it, a third cuts it, a fourth grinds it at the top for receiving the head; to make the head requires two or three distinct operations; to put it on, is a peculiar business, to whiten the pins is another; it is even a trade by itself to put them into the paper; and the important business of making a pin is, in this manner, divided into about eighteen distinct operations, which, in some manufactories, are performed by distinct hands, though in others the same man will sometimes perform two or three of them.*

The assembly-line production method of the automobile industry is another classic example of specialization by task.

---

*Adam Smith, *The Wealth of Nations* (New York: The Modern Library, 1937), pp. 4–5

Advantages of specialization

The advantages of specialization are numerous. Consider two people, Simon Peter and Diana Nimrod. Simon fishes well, but hunts poorly. Diana hunts well, but fishes poorly.

1. Obviously, the combined output of both people will be larger if Simon concentrates (i.e., specializes) on fishing and Diana on hunting than if both fish and hunt individually. In general, specialization allows people to choose the jobs for which they are best suited.

2. Specialization saves time. It takes a great amount of time for a worker to acquire the skills for a new job even if that worker is exceptionally clever. It also takes a certain amount of time to change from one set of tools to another. Changeover time is eliminated by specialization.

3. Specialization maximizes the use of machines. Without specialization, tools and equipment would lie idle for considerable lengths of time. For example, if Diana Nimrod and Simon Peter do not specialize, then we would find that when Diana is hunting, her fishing tools would be idle, and when she is fishing, her hunting tools would be idle. The same would be true of Simon. It does not make good economic sense for each farmer, for example, to have his or her own flour mill, which would be idle for long periods, when milling can be concentrated in the hands of millers.

4. The repeated performance of a certain task causes performers to develop skills to increase their efficiency. Also, their general knowledge of their jobs is likely to increase with the length of time spent at the job.

Disadvantages of specialization

There can be little doubt that specialization has contributed significantly to increases in productivity. There are, however, some disadvantages associated with it:

1. Specialization restricts the sphere of competence of workers. Workers develop the skills necessary for the performance of their particular tasks or jobs, but have no competence in other areas.

2. Workers who are performing the same tasks day after day become bored. There is little scope for creativity, since after a while, jobs lose their challenge. Complaints from assembly-line workers that they are hardly more than machines are common.

3. Specialization implies a certain degree of interdependence. In the case of Diana Nimrod and Simon Peter, once they specialize, Diana must depend on Simon for fish while Simon must depend on Diana for venison. Thus, each will lose a certain amount of independence.

These disadvantages notwithstanding, we expect specialization to remain a permanent feature of industrial production.

INDUSTRIAL LOCATION

Up to this point, you have studied the various forms of business organization, the advantages and disadvantages of each type, the methods of financing available, and specialization in production. What we haven't yet considered, though, is that a businessperson might choose an appropriate form of business organization for a business enterprise, and the enterprise might be adequately financed, yet it still might fail to prosper if the location is inappropriate. The location of a business enterprise is of the utmost importance to the success of the operation. You should consider the understanding of industrial location an important aspect of your study of economics.

In the final analysis, the decision regarding industrial location will be guided primarily by cost considerations. In the production process, three distinct cost elements can be identified: the cost of obtaining raw material, the cost of manufacturing the product, and the cost of distributing the product to its users. These cost elements play an important part in determining where particular industries will be located. In the following sections, we will look at some of the factors that affect the location of particular industries.

DETERMINATION OF INDUSTRIAL LOCATION

The source of raw materials; availability of water, fuel, power, etc.; transportation; labour supply; population; and the political setting affect industrial location.

Many industries tend to be located near the source of raw materials used in the production process. This is particularly true in cases where the manufacturing process results in a substantial loss of weight between the raw materials and the finished products. Thus, we find sawmills in close proximity to timber, and fish canneries near the ocean.

Some industries require large supplies of water, fuel, or power. Such industries tend to be located where these supplies can be obtained at low cost. It is unlikely that a paper mill that requires a large supply of water for its operation will be located at a site where the water supply is inadequate. It is equally unlikely that a site with poor water supply will be chosen as the location for a brewery. The availability of fuel and electric power is also a crucial determinant of the location of many manufacturing industries.

Raw materials needed for production often have to be transported to the manufacturing site, and the outputs of the various industries certainly have to be transported to their users. It follows then that transportation plays an important role in determining the location of many industries. The existence of good roads, railways, water routes, and air service all feature prominently in the choice of the location for a plant.

The availability of labour is another important determinant of the location of some industries. Industries that require large amounts of labour tend to be located where labour is cheap and plentiful. In some cases, special skills may be required by the industry. If these skills are readily available in a certain area, the industry will tend to move into that area.

Certain industries tend to be located near the major markets for their products. Banks, bakeries, barber shops, and beauty salons are usually located close to their customers. Also of importance in determining the location of industries is the government's attitude toward industries. A heavy tax burden, for example, may discourage the establishment of some industries in certain areas, whereas a lenient tax structure may encourage their establishment.

A favourable political climate will tend to attract industries provided that other favourable factors exist. On the other hand, political uncertainty, fear of government takeover of certain businesses, and unwieldly tax burdens are likely to discourage the establishment of industries, and to encourage existing industries to relocate to areas where political conditions are more favourable.

PROBLEM SOLVING 7-4

In an attempt to reduce poverty, the Province of Esperanza sets its minimum wage well above that of any other province. Will this have any effect on industrial location?

CHAPTER SUMMARY

1. The single proprietorship, the partnership, and the corporation are the major forms of business organization. Single proprietors own and manage their businesses, enjoy the profits, and bear the losses. Single proprietors are fully liable for all debts incurred by their businesses and may lose all of their personal possessions if their businesses fail.

2. A partnership is a form of business organization in which two or more people own and operate a business. The partnership, like the sole proprietorship, has unlimited liability. In a limited partnership, however, some partners enjoy limited liability.

3. A corporation is a form of business organization in which a group of people (shareholders) agree to engage in business. The shareholders enjoy limited liability and the corporation is considered in law to be an entity apart from its owners.

4. A cooperative is a business owned by its members, who have only one vote each. The dividends of a cooperative are paid out to members in proportion to the amount of business that each one does with the cooperative. Cooperatives are classified as consumer cooperatives and producer cooperatives. They are also classified as purchasing cooperatives and marketing cooperatives.

5. Single proprietorships and partnerships are financed by funds that their owners are able to raise, or out of any profits that the business may make.

6. A corporation may be financed out of retained earnings, through bond issue, through bank credit, or through issuing shares. Financing through bonds or bank credit is called debt financing, while financing through issuing shares is called equity financing.

7. Specialization takes two main forms: specialization by occupation and specialization by task. Specialization has advantages and disadvantages, but the advantages generally far outweigh the disadvantages.

8. Some of the factors likely to affect the location of industries are: the proximity to raw materials; the availability of water, fuel, and power; transportation; labour availability; the market; and political factors.

GLOBAL PERSPECTIVE

Beer Brewing —On the Move Globally

Labatt and Molson are Canadian beers, Heineken is Dutch, and Coors, Budweiser, and Miller are American. Of course, through international trade, Canadians have been able to obtain beers brewed in other countries. If there is a very limited demand for Coors in Canada, it would not be cost efficient to establish a plant in Canada to brew Coors beer for a small market. Instead, it would make more sense for Canadians to simply import Coors from the United States.

Over the past thirty years or so, however, the beer brewing industry has become increasingly globalized, mainly because of increases in world demand for different types of beer. The main component of beer is water. The theory of industrial location suggests that if an industry uses large amounts of water, it makes good economic sense to set up the industry close to a good source of water supply. In the case of beer, this will significantly reduce shipping cost. Consequently, beer producers have entered into licencing agreements to brew each other's beer. For example, Molson produces Coors in Canada and Labatt produces Budweiser in Canada. Carlsberg, a Danish beer, is brewed in Canada by Labatt. Asahi, a Japanese company, brews Molson in Japan. Beer brewing is certainly on the move — globally.

TERMS FOR REVIEW

single (or sole) proprietorship (119)
partnership (120)
limited partnership (121)
corporation (121)
retained earnings (122)
limited liability (122)
cooperative (123)

bond (124)
prime rate (125)
debt capital (125)
equity capital (125)
specialization (by occupation,
    by task) (125)

QUESTIONS FOR REVIEW AND DISCUSSION

1. Small, single-owner firms enjoy certain economic advantages. What are these advantages? Mention some industries in which you would expect small, single-owner firms to flourish. (L.O.1,2)

2. What are the major advantages and disadvantages of the single proprietorship? (L.O.2)

3. What are the advantages and disadvantages of the partnership? (L.O.2)

4. What considerations might cause a group of people to form a partnership? (L.O.1,2)

5. What is a limited partnership? What are its advantages? (L.O.1,2)

6. Discuss the advantages and disadvantages of the corporation. (L.O.2)

7. What methods are available to a corporation for raising capital? Briefly discuss each method. (L.O.3)

8. What is the difference between: debt capital and equity capital? (L.O.3)

9. What are the advantages and disadvantages of the cooperative? (L.O.2)

10. What is the difference between: (L.O.1)

   (a) a consumer cooperative and a producer cooperative?

   (b) a purchasing cooperative and a marketing cooperative?

11. What is the difference between specialization by occupation and specialization by task? (General)

12. Name some advantages and disadvantages of specialization. (General)

13. "The political climate is an important determinant of industrial location." Discuss this statement. (L.O.5)

14. What are the major determinants of industrial location? (L.O.5)

PROBLEMS AND EXERCISES

1. What type of business organization would you consider most suitable for each of the following types of businesses? Give reasons for your choice. (L.O.1)

   (a) a corner newspaper stand

   (b) a small confectionery shop

   (c) a firm producing men's clothes on a large scale

   (d) a small accounting firm

   (e) a hotel chain

   (f) a firm producing computers for the world market

2. You currently earn $75 000 per year. You own shares in Bell Canada. Would you prefer to receive annual dividends from Bell or would you prefer those earnings to be reinvested by Bell? (General)

3. What form of business organization is implied by each of the following situations? (L.O.1)

   (a) You invest $50 000 of your money to start a business and hire three people to work for you.

   (b) You and your old college buddy invest $50 000 each to start a business, with an agreement that you will divide the profits equally among you. You and your buddy manage the business and hire ten people to work for you.

   (c) You invest $50 000 of your money and borrow $20 000 from your friend to start a business. You manage the business and hire your friend and five other people as your employees.

   (d) You discuss a business idea with four of your friends. They like your idea, so you and your four friends apply for and obtain a charter from the federal government for your business. To raise the capital, you sell 500 shares at $200 per share. You manage the business and hire ten people to work for you.

   (e) You believe that prices at the college bookstore are too high so you call a meeting of the student body. At the meeting, you agree to form an association consisting of members of the student body who pay $50 each to join the association. With the proceeds, you establish The Student Bookstore to sell books to the student members. You employ members of the association to run the bookstore. (L.O.1)

4. A business enterprise can raise capital by equity financing or by debt financing. For each of the following, use D to indicate debt financing and E to indicate equity financing. (L.O.3)

   (a) The firm issues 1000 shares at $50 a share.

   (b) The firm sells $2 000 000 worth of bonds with a ten-year maturity date.

   (c) The firm borrows $50 000 from a bank and uses its building as collateral.

   (d) The owner of the firm borrows $10 000 from a friend and agrees to pay 10% interest on the loan.

5. Outline how you would go about establishing a department store on the principle of a cooperative. How would you convince people to join the cooperative? (L.O.1,2)

6. Choose four industries in your area or province and suggest explanations for the location of each. (L.O.5)

7. Talk with two or three members of your class about a business venture. The discussion should lead to a determination of a business enterprise that your group could establish. Write down the details of the venture:

   (a) name of business;

   (b) product or service to be offered;

   (c) your main customers;

   (d) location;

   (e) capital required;

   (f) who will manage it;

   Draw up a partnership agreement for the business venture.

Internet Site

http://www.strategis.ic.gc.ca
This is the Web site for Industry Canada. It contains all kinds of valuable information on and for businesses in Canada.

INTERNET EXERCISE

1. Go to the Industry Canada Web site.
2. List four ways a small-business owner could use this site.
3. List four types of information that a consumer could get from this site.

CHAPTER 8

THEORY OF PRODUCTION

Learning Objectives

After studying this chapter, you will be familiar with:

1 the objectives of the firm

2 economic efficiency and technological efficiency

3 production runs or periods

4 the production function

5 total, marginal, and average product

6 the law of diminishing returns

7 efficiency in the use of inputs

8 the principle of substitution

That roundabout methods lead to greater results than direct methods is one of the most important and fundamental propositions in the whole theory of production.

Eugen von Bohm-Bawerk, *Positive Theory of Capital*

INTRODUCTION

A firm is the unit that transforms inputs into outputs.

It is via the production process that resources are converted into consumer and producer goods and services. It is worth noting that production is not limited to manufacturing. It includes other activities such as providing consulting services, transportation, and banking services. A warehouse operator who stores goods so that they can be available for distribution when needed is involved in production, just as is the car manufacturer who uses labour, machines, and materials to produce automobiles.

The **firm** may be defined as the business enterprise involved in producing goods and services. The goods and services produced may be consumer goods and services such as microwave ovens and banking services, or they may be inputs such as steel and bricks to be used by other firms. The firm may be organized as a sole proprietorship, a partnership, a corporation, or a cooperative. Although some firms produce more than one product, we assume here that the firm produces only one type of product such as computer software or photo albums. In this chapter, you will study the principles of production. The firm buys factors of production (inputs) and through the production process, transforms these inputs into outputs for sale to other firms and to consumers. In Chapter 6, we noted that the entity that makes decisions about consumption is the consumer or household. In the case of the firm, the decision-maker may be the **entrepreneur** (sole owner) or a hired manager. Technically, it is the owner who has final responsibility for actions taken by the firm, for the owners are the risk-takers.

An entrepreneur organizes factors of production to produce a good or service.

THE OBJECTIVES OF THE FIRM

Learning Objective 1: the objectives of the firm

In economic theory, it is assumed that the firm seeks to maximize its profits.

In order to analyze the firm's behaviour and to predict what course of action it will take under various circumstances, we must pinpoint its goal. In economic theory, we assume that the firm seeks to maximize its profits. The firm's profits may be defined as the difference between its revenues (that is, its receipts from the sale of its products) and its costs. Symbolically,

$$\pi = TR - TC$$

where π is profit, TR is total revenue, and TC is total cost.

Other objectives that a firm may pursue are sales maximization, public image, and the welfare of consumers.

The assumption of profit maximization has come under attack from economists and non-economists alike. Critics of the profit maximizing assumption claim that firms pursue objectives other than profit maximization. These critics do agree that a certain profit level must be achieved to provide earnings for the firm's owners. Once this level is reached, however, they feel that the firm pursues other objectives including maximizing sales, public image, and the satisfaction and general welfare of consumers. It has also been suggested that these other objectives are merely avenues through which the firm may maximize profits in the long run. Despite the criticisms of the profit maximizing assumption, we will take this assumption to be correct. The profit maximizing assumption has enabled economists to analyze and predict the behaviour of firms with a great degree of success.

PROBLEM SOLVING 8-1

If the only objective of a firm is to maximize its profits, will it discriminate against workers on the basis of sex or race in its hiring practices?

ECONOMIC EFFICIENCY VERSUS TECHNOLOGICAL EFFICIENCY

Learning Objective 2:
economic efficiency and
technological efficiency

*The method that is techni-
cally most efficient is the
one that uses the fewest
inputs.*

One of the basic decisions that the firm has to make pertains to the method of production. Usually, there are several ways of combining the factors of production in order to
produce a given output. The method that uses the least inputs is said to be the most technically efficient. The concept of **technical** or **technological efficiency** is illustrated
by Table 8.1. Suppose A, B, and C are three methods by which 10 000 shirts per week
can be produced. Method B uses more labour and more capital than method A and
method C do. Method B is therefore technically least efficient.

TABLE 8.1	Method	Capital	Labour	Output per week (shirts)
Technological efficiency.	A	100	500	10 000
	B	180	900	10 000
	C	50	800	10 000

*The method that is
economically most
efficient is the one
with the lowest cost.*

But what of methods A and C? Method A uses more capital than method C does but,
at the same time, uses less labour than method C does. Both methods are technically efficient. How does the firm choose between methods A and C? The firm could choose
the method that has the lower cost — that is, the method that is **economically more
efficient**. In order to determine whether A or C has the lower cost, we must know the
prices of the factors of production — in this case, the prices of capital and labour.

Suppose the prices of capital and labour are $40 and $5 respectively. We can compute the cost associated with each method as follows:

$$C_a = (100 \times \$40) + (500 \times \$5) = \$6500$$

$$C_c = (50 \times \$40) + (800 \times \$5) = \$6000$$

where C_a is the cost associated with method A, and C_c is the cost associated with method
C. Given the above prices, method C is economically more efficient than method A.

Now suppose the prices were $20 for capital and $10 for labour. The cost associated
with each method would be as follows:

$$C_a = (100 \times \$20) + (500 \times \$10) = \$7000$$

$$C_c = (50 \times \$20) + (800 \times \$10) = \$9000$$

In this case, method A would be economically more efficient than method C. Note
also that a method that is technically inefficient is also economically inefficient. To
choose the economically most efficient method is to choose from among technically
efficient methods the one with the lowest cost.

ECONOMIC EFFICIENCY RATIOS

We can easily determine the most economically efficient method when the output produced by all methods is the same, as in the previous example. In that case, we need only
compare costs. If, however, we are confronted with different costs for different output
levels, then the problem of deciding on the most economically efficient method becomes
a bit more difficult. In what follows, we assume that the demand for the product is
given.

*Economic efficiency ratio:
the ratio of the value of the
output to the cost of the
inputs.*

To choose the most economically efficient method in situations involving different
costs and different output levels, we can use the concept of the **economic efficiency
ratio**, which is defined as follows:

$$EER = \frac{\text{value of output}}{\text{cost of input}}$$

where EER represents the economic efficiency ratio. The higher the economic efficiency ratio, the more efficient the method.

Now, consider Table 8.2. Let us assume that the prices of capital and labour are given as $20 and $10 respectively. The values of the inputs, using methods A and C, have already been calculated as $7000 and $9000 respectively.

TABLE 8.2	Method	Capital	Labour	Output per week (shirts)
Production methods with varying output levels.	A	100	500	10 000
	C	50	800	11 000

If we assume that the price of a shirt is $5, then the value of the output from method A is $50 000 (10 000 × $5). The value of the output from method C is $55 000 (11 000 × $5).

$$EER \text{ (method A)} = \frac{50\ 000}{7000} = 7.1$$

$$EER \text{ (method C)} = \frac{55\ 000}{9000} = 6.1$$

Since method A has a higher economic efficiency ratio, it is economically more efficient than method C. In method A, for every $1 of input, the firm receives $7.10 in output. In method C, for every $1 of input, the firm receives $6.10 in output.

PROBLEM SOLVING 8-2

You are contemplating going into business to produce pen-holders. You are faced with the methods of producing pen-holders shown in Table 8.3. The prices of capital and labour are $5 and $6 respectively, and the market price of pen-holders is $10. Which method should you choose?

TABLE 8.3	Method	Capital	Labour	Output
Production methods for pen-holders.	1	10	6	24
	2	15	2	25

PRODUCTION RUNS OR PERIODS

Learning Objective 3: production runs or periods

Quantities of fixed production factors cannot be varied quickly, quantities of variable factors are more easily adjusted.

In the short run, the firm has at least one fixed factor.

The firm's decisions about the efficient use of existing equipment and the expansion or contraction of its scale of operation can be grouped into short-run and long-run decisions respectively. In order to define the short run and the long run, it is necessary to examine the nature of the firm's inputs. These inputs or productive factors are classified into fixed and variable factors. **Fixed factors** are those whose quantities cannot be varied within the period under consideration. Those productive factors whose quantities can be varied are called **variable factors**. A firm's fixed factors may be its land and its capital equipment. Its variable factors may be labour and raw materials.

The **short run** is defined as a situation in which the firm has at least one fixed factor of production. The short run is such that the firm does not have sufficient time to vary

In the long run, the firm
has only variable factors.

all of its inputs. The **long run** is a situation in which the firm is able to vary all of its factor inputs. There are no fixed productive factors in the long run. As an example, consider the following case. You are operating a small photocopy business with two photocopy machines in a rented space near your college or university. After three years, you decide to get out of the photocopy business and move on to some more lucrative pursuit. Your lease on the space has just expired but you have two photocopy machines, which you cannot get rid of for three weeks. Since it will take you three weeks to get out of the business, then the short run for you would be any time within three weeks. After three weeks, you are able to vary all your inputs — in this case getting rid of your machines — so your long-run situation would be any time after three weeks. The definitions of the short run and the long run and the example just given make it quite clear that these time horizons (the short run and the long run) do not correspond to any definite periods of calendar time. In some industries, the short run may be quite long, while in others, the long run may be quite short. For example, the long run may be only a few hours for a shoe shine business, but it may be several years for a business such as a public utility.

THE PRODUCTION FUNCTION

The production function is
a technically determined
relationship between inputs
and output.

Learning Objective 4:
the production function

Economists use the term **production function** to refer to the relation between the firm's inputs and its output of goods and services. To simplify the analysis, we shall discuss a production scenario in which there are only two factors of production: labour and land. Furthermore, we shall assume that land is a fixed factor while labour is a variable factor, and that all workers are equally efficient. This technical or engineering relation between the firm's inputs and its output may be expressed as follows:

$$Q = Q(L,\overline{T})$$

where Q represents output, L represents the quantity of labour, and T represents the fixed quantity of land. The bar over the T indicates that T is fixed. Since there is a fixed factor, this production function is a short-run production function. Table 8.4 shows how output varies as units of labour are added to a fixed quantity of land.

TOTAL, MARGINAL, AND AVERAGE PRODUCT

TOTAL PRODUCT

Total product: total output
per period of time.

Learning Objective 5:
total, marginal, and
average product

Total product (TP) refers to the total output of the firm per period of time. Column two of Table 8.4 shows how output changes with variations in the quantity of the variable factor (labour in this case). Note that as the number of units of the variable factor increases, total product increases, reaches a maximum of 144 units when eight or nine units of labour (workers) are hired, and then declines as more workers are hired.

If all workers are assumed to be equally efficient, you would expect that each additional worker would contribute equally to total output. In the example in Table 8.4, the first worker hired added 15 units of output per week. You would probably expect the second worker to add another 15 units per week, but instead, that worker added 19 units. Why? One worker alone cannot take advantage of specialization and the division of labour. But when the second worker is hired, there can be some specialization and division of labour that result in increased productivity.

TABLE 8.4	Units of variable factor (per week)	Total product (units per wk.)	Marginal product (units per wk.)	Average product (units per wk.)
Relation between inputs and output (hypothetical data).	0	0		
			15	
	1	15		15
			19	
	2	34		17
			23	
	3	57		19
			31	
	4	88		22
			22	
	5	110		22
			16	
	6	126		21
			14	
	7	140		20
			4	
	8	144		18
			0	
	9	144		16
			−4	
	10	140		14
			−19	
	11	121		11
			−25	
	12	96		8

MARGINAL PRODUCT

Marginal product of a variable factor is the extra output obtained by using one more unit of the variable factor.

Marginal product (MP) is the change in total product resulting from using an additional unit of the variable factor. We can express marginal product as follows:

$$MP = \frac{\Delta Q}{\Delta L}$$

where L is the quantity of labour, and Q is the total product or output. Table 8.4 shows that the first unit of labour causes output to increase by 15 units. Thus the marginal product is 15. Another unit of labour increases total output from 15 units to 34 units, thus the marginal product at that point is 19. Values of the marginal product are given in column three of Table 8.4. Note that the values of the marginal product are placed in between the lines on which the total product values are placed. Special attention will be paid to the behaviour of marginal product as the quantity of the variable input is increased.

AVERAGE PRODUCT

Average product is the output per unit of the variable factor.

Average product (AP) is total product divided by the number of units of the variable factor. That is, average product is simply the total output per unit of the variable factor. We can express average product symbolically as

$$AP = \frac{Q}{L}$$

Values of the average product are calculated and recorded in column four of Table 8.4. Note that the average product rises, reaches a maximum at 22 units of output when four or five workers are hired, and then diminishes as more workers are hired.

The relation between total, average, and marginal products can also be illustrated graphically, as shown in Figure 8.1. Part A shows the total product curve while part B shows the average and marginal product curves. The two diagrams are lined up in order to emphasize the relation between the three curves. The relation between marginal product and total product, and that between marginal product and average product are set out below.

FIGURE 8.1

Total, average, and marginal products.

RELATIONS BETWEEN MARGINAL PRODUCT AND TOTAL PRODUCT

1. When the marginal product is rising, the total product increases at an increasing rate. In Part B of Figure 8.1, the marginal product rises to point P, and the total product shown in Part A increases at an increasing rate to point R.

2. When the marginal product is positive, the total product is increasing. This is necessarily so since the marginal product is the change in total product as an additional unit of the variable factor is employed. If this number is positive, then the total product must increase. In Table 8.4 and Figure 8.1, the marginal product is positive up to the point when the eighth worker is hired; hence, total product increases up to that point. Note, however, that when the marginal product is positive but declining

(between points P and T in Part B), total product increases at a diminishing rate (between points R and S in Part A).

3. When the marginal product is negative, the total product falls. This is necessarily so since a negative number is being added to the total product; that is, some quantity is being taken away from the total product. In Table 8.4 and Figure 8.1, total product begins to decline after the employment of the ninth unit of labour. At that point, the marginal product is negative.

4. When the marginal product is zero, the total product ceases to rise, but does not fall either. It has reached its maximum. In Table 8.4 and Figure 8.1, this occurs at an output of 144 units when nine units of labour are used.

RELATIONS BETWEEN MARGINAL PRODUCT AND AVERAGE PRODUCT

To help you to understand and remember the relationship between marginal product and average product, think of the marginal product as a magnet that pulls the average product to it.

1. When marginal product is greater than average product, average product will rise. In Table 8.4 and Figure 8.1, this is the case until the addition (employment) of four workers. Note that when the marginal product curve is above the average product curve, it pulls the average product curve up. To illustrate this relation further, let us consider a case to which you can easily relate. If, in a class of 30 economics students, the average mark on an economics examination is 69%, and a new student enters the class and gets a mark of 77%, the new mark (the marginal mark), being higher than the class average, will pull up the class average. As another example, suppose your final grade is based on four examinations written during the term. You have written three examinations and your average is 70%. Your mark on the fourth examination will be the marginal mark of the fourth examination. If your mark on the fourth examination is better than 70%, your average will increase. In the same way, a marginal product curve that is higher than the average product curve pulls up the average product curve.

2. When marginal product is less than average product, average product will fall. This can be seen in Table 8.4 and Figure 8.1 after the employment of the fifth worker. Note that in Figure 8.1, when the marginal product curve is below the average product curve, the average product curve falls. Can you explain why? Consider what would happen to your average grade if the mark of your fourth examination was under 70%.

3. When marginal product is equal to average product, average product is at its maximum. The marginal product curve shown in Figure 8.1 cuts the average product at the maximum point on the average product curve. In Table 8.4, this occurs when the average product is 22 units and between four and five units of labour are employed.

THE LAW OF DIMINISHING RETURNS

As increasing amounts of a variable factor are added to a fixed factor, a point will be reached where the marginal product diminishes.

Learning Objective 6: the law of diminishing returns

Our observation of the short-run behaviour of total product as units of a variable factor are added to a fixed factor has given rise to a famous hypothesis in economics that has been called the **law of diminishing returns**. This law may be stated as follows:

As additional quantities of a variable factor are added to a given quantity of fixed factors, after a point the marginal product will diminish.

The point of diminishing marginal productivity occurs at the level of output at which the marginal product is at a maximum. In Figure 8.1, it occurs at point P. This means that after that point, the increase in output will diminish. The point of diminishing average productivity occurs at the level of output at which the average product is maximal. Maximum average product occurs when average product is 22 units in Table 8.4, and at point Q in Figure 8.1.

Observe that the law of diminishing returns states what will happen to physical returns rather than what will happen to monetary returns. In other words, the law deals with a physical rather than a monetary phenomenon. The existence of the law of diminishing returns presents a constant challenge to humankind to find more efficient ways of production.

A P P L I C A T I O N

The Effectiveness of Advertising

The principle of diminishing marginal returns has numerous applications, one of which will be considered in this section. Let us consider an advertising message — a commercial — prepared for radio. If the same message is heard repeatedly, it may be effective, but after a while, its impact may diminish, i.e., diminishing returns may set in. To counteract this, advertisers and sponsors tend to use different versions of the script and vary the voice or voices used to convey the message. By so doing, they may actually increase the effectiveness of the advertising message.

EFFICIENCY IN THE USE OF INPUTS

Earlier in this chapter, we used cost to define economic efficiency. The most economically efficient method is the one with the lowest cost for a given output level. In this section, we will discuss the firm's choice of inputs. The problem faced by the firm is similar in many ways to the problem faced by the consumer in deciding how to allocate a given amount of money among various commodities.

Learning Objective 7: efficiency in the use of inputs

To simplify our analysis, let us assume that the firm purchases only two factors of production: labour and capital. The firm's objective is to maximize its profits. It will therefore seek to produce any given level of output at the lowest possible cost. To minimize cost, the following condition must be satisfied:

$$\frac{MP_K}{P_K} = \frac{MP_L}{P_L}$$

where MP_K is the marginal product of capital, that is, the extra output obtained by using an additional unit of capital; MP_L is the marginal product of labour, that is, the extra output obtained by using an additional unit of labour; P_K is the price of capital; and P_L is the price of labour.

Compare the above condition with the condition for utility maximization discussed in Chapter 6. Obviously, if the last dollar spent on capital, that is

$$\frac{MP_K}{P_K}$$

causes output to increase by 15 units, and the last dollar spent on labour, that is

$$\frac{MP_L}{P_L}$$

causes output to increase by only six units, then it would benefit the firm to purchase more capital and less labour, provided that labour and capital are substitutable. On the other hand, if the last dollar spent on capital causes output to increase by a lesser amount than the increase in output resulting from an extra dollar spent on labour, that is, if

$$\frac{MP_K}{P_K} < \frac{MP_L}{P_L}$$

then the firm would benefit by purchasing more labour and less capital. It follows that the firm will be in the best position (minimizing its costs) when

$$\frac{MP_K}{P_K} = \frac{MP_L}{P_L}$$

We can also express this cost-minimizing condition as

$$\frac{MP_K}{MP_L} = \frac{P_K}{P_L}$$

In other words, the optimum input mix for the firm occurs when the ratio of the marginal product of capital to the marginal product of labour equals the ratio of the price of capital to the price of labour. This is another example of the equimarginal principle introduced earlier in this text.

The least-cost combination of inputs is achieved when the ratio of the marginal products equals the ratio of input prices.

THE PRINCIPLE OF SUBSTITUTION

Learning Objective 8: *the principle of substitution*

To minimize cost the firm will tend to use more of the cheaper factor and less of the more expensive factor.

If capital is cheap relative to labour, and the two are substitutable, the firm will tend to use more capital and less labour. But if labour is cheap relative to capital, then the firm will tend to use more labour and less capital. This tendency for the firm to substitute the cheap factor for the more expensive factor is known as the **principle of substitution** and may be stated as follows:

If two factors of production are substitutable and the price of one rises relative to the price of the other, the firm will tend to use less of the more expensive factor, substituting the less expensive factor for it.

The principle of substitution relates to the cost-minimizing condition of the firm:

$$\frac{MP_K}{P_K} = \frac{MP_L}{P_L}$$

If the price of capital (P_K) falls, then

$$\frac{MP_K}{P_K} > \frac{MP_L}{P_L}$$

In order to maintain the cost-minimizing condition, the firm will use more capital. This then causes MP_K to fall and MP_L to rise, thus restoring equality between the two ratios. It should be noted that in the short run, the firm may not be able to substitute one factor for another, or may be able to do so only to a limited extent. In the long run, substitution of factor inputs is less difficult.

GLOBAL   PERSPECTIVE

Productivity Among the Major Industrial Countries

A common and useful method of measuring productivity is output per worker. It is informative to know how labour productivity has changed in Canada over time, and how the Canadian experience compares with those of other countries. This capsule and the following table give us a global perspective of labour productivity.

Labour productivity among the major industrial countries, 1980-89 and 1990-99

1980-89		1990-99	
Country	Annual percent change	Country	Annual percent change
France	4.1	Germany	4.6
Italy	4.0	France	4.0
United Kingdom	3.9	U.S.A.	3.0
Japan	3.0	Italy	2.7
U.S.A.	2.8	United Kingdom	2.4
Germany	2.6	Canada	1.7
Canada	1.7	Japan	1.5

Source: International Monetary Fund, *World Economic Outlook*, May 1998: 158.

Between 1980 and 1989, the average annual change in labour productivity in Canada was 1.7%. Of all the major industrial countries (the so-called G-7 countries), Canada had the unenviable position of last place in terms of changes in labour productivity. It is important to understand that here we are talking about *changes* in productivity rather than *levels* of productivity. France had the highest annual average change (4.1%) during that period.

For the period 1990-99, Germany took sole possession of first place with an average annual change in labour productivity of 4.6%, while Canada, still with 1.7%, was second to last. Germany was second to last in the 1980-89 period with 2.6%. Japan fell from fourth place in the 1980-89 period (3.0%) to last place with 1.5% in the 1990-99 period. The United States jumped from fifth place in the 1980-89 period with 2.8% to third place in the 1990-99 period with 3.0%.

CHAPTER SUMMARY

1. The firm buys factor inputs and transforms them into output. The decision-maker for the firm is the entrepreneur, and the objective of the firm is to maximize its profits.

2. Technological efficiency refers to the use of inputs in physical terms, while economic efficiency refers to the use of inputs in terms of cost.

3. The method that is technologically most efficient is the one that uses the fewest inputs. The method that is economically most efficient is the one with the lowest cost.

4. The short run defines a situation in which the firm is unable to vary all its factor inputs. The long run is a situation in which the firm can vary all its inputs. These terms do not equate with any particular periods of calendar time.

5. The relation between a firm's inputs and its output of goods and services is called the production function.

6. The average product of a variable factor is total product divided by the quantity of the variable factor.

7. The marginal product of a variable factor is the change in total output or product resulting from using one more unit of the variable factor.

8. The law of diminishing returns states that, as additional quantities of a variable factor are added to a given quantity of fixed factors, the marginal product will diminish after a point. This law is a short-run phenomenon. It deals with the behaviour of physical output rather than monetary returns.

9. We can obtain the least-cost combination of inputs by equating the ratio of the marginal product of the factors to the ratio of their prices.

10. The principle of substitution states that if the price of a factor of production rises relative to the price of another factor, the firm will tend to substitute the less expensive factor for the more expensive factor.

TERMS FOR REVIEW

firm (133)
entrepreneur (133)
technical (technological)
  efficiency (134)
economic efficiency (134)
economic efficiency ratio (134)
fixed factors (135)
variable factors (135)

short run (135)
long run (136)
production function (136)
total product (136)
marginal product (137)
average product (137)
law of diminishing returns (139)
principle of substitution (141)

QUESTIONS FOR REVIEW AND DISCUSSION

1. Which of the following would you consider to be a firm and why? (General)
   (a) a Manitoba farmer
   (b) the Tizoc Driving School
   (c) a small private radio station
   (d) a college teachers' union

2. Economic theory assumes that the objective of the firm is to maximize its profits. How are profits calculated? What criticisms have been made about the profit-maximizing assumption? (L.O.1)

3. What other objectives besides profit maximization might firms pursue? (L.O.1)

4. What is the difference between technological efficiency and economic efficiency? (L.O.2)

5. What is the difference between:
   (a) the long run and the short run?
   (b) fixed factors and variable factors?
   Give examples of fixed factors and variable factors. (L.O.3)

6. What is meant by a short-run production function? (L.O.4)

7. Describe the behaviour of total product when marginal product is: (L.O.5)
   (a) positive;
   (b) negative;
   (c) positive but falling.

8. Describe the behaviour of average product when marginal product is: (L.O.5)

   (a) greater than average product;

   (b) equal to average product;

   (c) less than average product;

   (d) falling.

9. "Diminishing returns may be in operation even when total product is rising." Explain. (L.O.6)

10. Explain the law of diminishing returns. How does this law pertain to rapid population growth? (L.O.6)

11. Explain how a firm decides on its use of inputs in order to minimize cost. (L.O.7)

12. What is the principle of substitution? What is the relation between the cost-minimizing condition and the principle of substitution? (L.O.7,8)

PROBLEMS AND EXERCISES

1. Table 8.5 shows units of labour and capital required to produce 100 units of output. (L.O.2)

TABLE 8.5

Combinations of labour and capital required for 100 units of output.

Combination	Labour	Capital	Output
A	8	15	100
B	9	20	100
C	6	20	100

   (a) Which of these methods is technically inefficient and why?

   (b) If labour costs $3 per unit and capital $5 per unit, which method is economically most efficient?

   (c) If the price of labour doubles while the price of capital remains the same, which method will be economically most efficient?

2. Referring to the problem on page 135, if the price of capital changes to $6 and the price of labour changes to $5, which method would you choose? (L.O.2)

3. (a) Given the production schedule in Table 8.6, compute the marginal products of the variable factor.

   (b) Does this production schedule depict diminishing returns? (L.O.5,6)

TABLE 8.6

Production data.

Units of fixed factor	Units of variable factor	Total product
20	0	0
20	1	25
20	2	45
20	3	60
20	4	70
20	5	75

4. The Zodiac Production Company has the production schedule shown in Table 8.7. (L.O.5,6)

TABLE 8.7	Capital	Labour	Output
Production data for Zodiac Production Company.	30	0	0
	30	1	10
	30	2	30
	30	3	45
	30	4	55
	30	5	63
	30	6	68
	30	7	68
	30	8	63
	30	9	58

(a) Does the production schedule for Zodiac depict diminishing returns?

(b) Compute average and marginal product schedules for labour.

(c) On a graph, plot the total product curve.

(d) On another graph, just below the total product curve (as in Figure 8.1), plot the marginal and average product curves.

5. A firm uses two variable inputs, labour and capital, to produce its output. The price of labour is $2 per hour and the price of capital is $5 per hour. The production schedules for the firm are set out in Table 8.8. (L.O.5,7)

	Labour				Capital		
TABLE 8.8	Quantity per hr.	TP per hr.	MP_L per hr.		Quantity per hr.	TP per hr.	MP_K per hr.
Production data.	0	0			0	0	
	1	20			1	25	
	2	30			2	40	
	3	38			3	50	
	4	43			4	55	
	5	45			5	55	
	6	45			6	50	

(a) Complete the table by filling in the marginal product of labour and the marginal product of capital columns.

(b) If the firm wants to spend $9 per hour on labour and capital, how much of each should it purchase?

(c) How should the firm allocate a total cost of $30 between labour and capital in order to minimize production cost?

6. Table 8.9 shows variations in output as units of a variable factor are added to a fixed factor. (L.O.5)

TABLE 8.9	Units of variable factor	Total product	Marginal product	Average product
	0	0		
	1	12		
	2	30		
	3	51		
	4	68		
	5	80		
	6	84		
	7	84		
	8	80		
	9	72		

Production data.

(a) Complete the table by filling in the marginal and average product columns.

(b) Use graph paper and plot the marginal and average product curves on the same diagram.

(c) Locate the maximum point on the average product curve and label it M. Compare the values of the average product and the marginal product at that point.

7. Visit a local manufacturing plant and observe the production process in the plant. Describe the product or service that is produced (the output) and then write an account of the production process, including a statement of the inputs (factors of production) used in the process. Identify both fixed and variable factors. State whether the technology used is labour intensive or capital intensive, and try to find out whether the production technology has changed over the past ten years.

Internet Site

http://www.statcan.ca
The Statistics Canada site contains useful data on virtually all aspects of the Canadian economy and society.

INTERNET EXERCISE

1. Go to the Statistics Canada Web site.

2. Click on *Canadian Statistics*.

3. Click on the *Economy in Detail*.

4. Click on *Manufacturing and Construction, Employment*.

5. List three industries that had fewer employees in 1997 than in 1993.

6. List three industries that had more employees in 1997 than in 1993.

7. What year saw the biggest increase in the number of employees in all industries?

9

THE COSTS OF PRODUCTION

Learning Objectives

After studying this chapter, you should be able to:

1 analyze costs in the short run

2 describe the relations between marginal cost and marginal product, and between average variable cost and average product

3 analyze costs in the long run

4 understand returns to scale

5 understand economies of scope

In calculating the expenses of production of a commodity, we must take account of the fact that changes in the amounts produced are likely, even when there is no new invention, to be accompanied by changes in the relative quantities of its several factors of production.

Alfred Marshall, *Principles of Economics*

INTRODUCTION

In Chapter 8, you studied how a firm decides on the various quantities of inputs to purchase in order to produce a certain volume of output. The relationship between the firm's inputs and its output is one aspect of the information that the firm needs in order to decide on the optimum level of output. The other aspect needed is information on the relationship between costs and output. When a firm increases its output, it uses more resources (labour, space, material, etc.), and it thus incurs greater costs. It follows that the benefits from increases in production must outweigh the additional costs of greater production in order for firms to have an incentive to increase output. This chapter examines the relation between a firm's costs of production and its volume of output. This relation is often referred to as the firm's **cost function**, which may be expressed as

The cost function is a relation between cost and output.

$$C = C(Q)$$

where C represents cost and Q represents output. The firm incurs costs by engaging in production. There is therefore a close relationship between production and cost. This chapter highlights that close relationship.

THE FIRM'S COSTS

Cost may be defined as payments for the factors of production that the firm uses to produce goods and services. These payments include wages and salaries, rent for land and buildings, expenditures for raw materials, fuel and electricity, and taxes. Costs of this nature are called **explicit costs**. In addition to these direct business outlays, the firm may use its own resources. In this case, a cost is incurred although no direct payment is made to anyone outside the firm. Such costs are known as **implicit costs** or *imputed costs*, and must be taken into account when calculating the firm's costs.

An explicit cost is a direct outlay. An implicit cost is an opportunity cost where no direct payment is made to anyone outside the firm.

An example of an implicit cost is provided by the case of Cyril, the worm-seller who served his customers from his garage. Cyril incurred a cost by using his garage as a store. This cost can be estimated by invoking the concept of opportunity cost. In this case, the opportunity cost would be the best possible alternative use to which Cyril could put his garage. Suppose a man chooses to work on his farm instead of accepting paid employment elsewhere at a salary of $15 000 per year. The implicit cost of working on his farm is $15 000.

To further illustrate the concept of implicit cost, suppose that Peter Bright invests $100 000 of his own money to start the Bright Look Company. The money is used to purchase machines. Suppose Peter could have earned 8% interest annually by leaving his money in the bank. Then at the end of the year, Peter should include $8 000 (i.e., 8% of $100 000) as a part of his costs (implicit cost of capital). Moreover, during the year, Peter's machines would have suffered a certain amount of wear and tear through use. This **depreciation** or loss of value of the machines also represents an implicit cost and should be considered as a part of the cost of capital.

Depreciation is the loss in value of capital stock over time.

Business managers and accountants tend to focus on explicit costs. Economists believe, however, that decisions should be based on considerations of total cost, both explicit and implicit.

PROBLEM SOLVING 9-1

You decide to go into house painting for the summer months. You spend $50 to place an advertisement in the local newspaper. You use your own car to transport your tools. You spend $550 for paint, brushes, rollers, etc. At the end of the summer, your total receipts from your painting business amount to $2000. Did you make a profit?

COSTS IN THE SHORT RUN

In the short run, the firm has both fixed costs and variable costs.

Learning Objective 1: analyze costs in the short run

Some costs incurred by the firm affect its decisions in the short run while others do not. For example, the decision to increase output by a few extra units may require only that the firm hires more workers and uses more raw materials without adding to its existing stock of machines. For this reason, a distinction is made between these two types of costs. The firm's total cost (TC) consists of total fixed costs (TFC) and total variable costs (TVC):

$$TC = TFC + TVC$$

Fixed (overhead) costs do not vary with output.

Fixed costs are those costs that do not change as output changes. These costs remain the same whether the firm produces a little or a lot. They are incurred even if the firm temporarily suspends its operation. Examples of fixed costs are insurance costs, interest payments on borrowed money, certain taxes (property taxes, for example), rental payment on factory building, and management salaries. In common business language, fixed costs are referred to as **overhead costs**. Fixed costs apply only to the short run because fixed factors of production exist only in the short run.

Variable costs depend on the volume of output.

Variable costs are those costs that change with the volume of output. Examples of variable costs are payments for raw materials, labour costs, fuel, and depreciation associated with production. In other words, variable costs are the operating costs of production. Variable costs are incurred both in the short run and in the long run.

AVERAGE COST

Average cost or average total cost (ATC) is the sum of average fixed cost and average variable cost.

For many purposes, it is important to know the firm's average cost; that is, cost per unit of output. **Average cost** (AC) or **average total cost** (ATC) is total cost divided by the number of units produced. Thus, if Q represents the quantity of output produced, we can define average total cost as follows:

$$ATC = \frac{TC}{Q}$$

Average total cost (also called unit cost) consists of average fixed cost (AFC) and average variable cost (AVC):

$$ATC = AFC + AVC$$

Average fixed cost (AFC) is total fixed cost divided by the number of units produced.

Average fixed cost (AFC) is total fixed cost divided by the number of units produced. Symbolically,

$$AFC = \frac{TFC}{Q}$$

Average variable cost (AVC) is total variable cost divided by the number of units produced.

Average variable cost (AVC) is total variable cost divided by the number of units produced. That is,

$$AVC = \frac{TVC}{Q}$$

Note that we can obtain average total cost by dividing each component of total cost by quantity, as follows:

$$TC = TFC + TVC$$

$$ATC = \frac{TC}{Q} = \frac{TFC}{Q} + \frac{TVC}{Q}$$

$$ATC = AFC + AVC$$

MARGINAL COST

Marginal cost or incremental cost is the extra cost incurred in increasing output by one additional unit.

Another cost concept that we shall use quite frequently is marginal cost (MC). **Marginal cost** is the extra or additional cost incurred by producing an additional unit of output. Accountants and business executives often use the term **incremental cost** when referring to marginal cost. Symbolically,

$$MC = \frac{\Delta TC}{\Delta Q}$$

The marginal cost concept is similar to the marginal utility concept discussed in Chapter 6 and the marginal product concept discussed in Chapter 8. For example, if the total cost of producing nine units of output is $200, and the total cost of producing 10 units is $220, then the marginal cost of increasing output by 10 units (that is, the extra cost of producing one more unit) is $20. The various cost concepts are summarized below, and the relation between them is illustrated in Table 9.1.

SUMMARY OF COST CONCEPTS

Learning Objective 1:
analyze costs in the short run

TC   = total cost
ATC = average total cost
TFC = total fixed cost
TVC = total variable cost
AFC = average fixed cost
AVC = average variable cost
MC   = marginal cost

TC = TFC + TVC

$$ATC = \frac{TC}{Q} = \frac{TFC}{Q} + \frac{TVC}{Q}$$

ATC = AFC + AVC

$$MC = \frac{\Delta TC}{\Delta Q}$$

The various levels of output produced per period of time are given in column one of Table 9.1. Column two shows the firm's total fixed cost. This amount ($200 in the example) remains unchanged for any level of output. Note that even when the firm produces no output at all (Q = 0), it still has to pay for its fixed factor inputs. Total variable cost is given in column three. Total variable cost rises continuously as output expands: from $400 for the first unit to $15 000 for 12 units of output. In order to produce a greater quantity of output, the firm must use more of its variable inputs (more labour, more raw materials, etc.) so its total variable cost increases. Column four shows total cost, which is obtained by adding total fixed cost and total variable cost. Total cost rises continuously because total variable cost rises continuously with increasing output.

The total cost curve is the sum of the total variable cost and total fixed cost curves.

Figure 9.1 shows total cost, total fixed cost, and total variable cost curves. The total fixed cost curve (TFC) is a horizontal straight line, indicating that total fixed cost is constant at $200 for any level of output. The total variable cost (TVC) curve rises continuously with increasing output. The total cost (TC) curve is obtained by adding the total fixed cost curve to the total variable cost curve. Since the total fixed cost curve is a horizontal straight line, the total cost curve will have the same shape as the total variable cost curve but will lie above the total variable cost curve. The vertical distance between the TC curve and the TVC curve at any level of output is the TFC.

Column five of Table 9.1 shows the average fixed cost of the firm, which is obtained by dividing column two by column one. Average variable cost is given in column six and is obtained by dividing column three by column one. Column seven, the average total cost column, is obtained by adding average fixed cost to average variable cost. Alternatively, column seven may be obtained by dividing column four by column one. Column eight gives marginal cost, which can be obtained from column three or from column four. Can you see why?

TABLE 9.1

Hypothetical cost data for a firm.

Quantity of output (units) (1)	TFC ($) (2)	TVC ($) (3)	TC ($) (4)	AFC ($ per unit) (5)	AVC ($ per unit) (6)	ATC ($ per unit) (7)	MC ($ per unit) (8)
0	200	0	200	—	—	—	
							400
1	200	400	600	200.00	400.00	600.00	
							200
2	200	600	800	100.00	300.00	400.00	
							100
3	200	700	900	66.67	233.33	300.00	
							100
4	200	800	1 000	50.00	200.00	250.00	
							300
5	200	1 100	1 300	40.00	220.00	260.00	
							400
6	200	1 500	1 700	33.33	250.00	283.33	
							700
7	200	2 200	2 400	28.57	314.28	342.85	
							800
8	200	3 000	3 200	25.00	375.00	400.00	
							1 000
9	200	4 000	4 200	22.22	444.44	466.66	
							2 000
10	200	6 000	6 200	20.00	600.00	620.00	
							4 000
11	200	10 000	10 200	18.18	909.09	927.27	
							5 000
12	200	15 000	15 200	16.67	1 250.00	1 266.67	

FIGURE 9.1

Total cost curves.

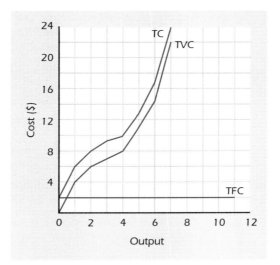

Figure 9.2 shows the relation between average fixed cost (AFC), average variable cost (AVC), average total cost (ATC), and marginal cost. The average fixed cost curve declines continuously as output expands. This is so because as output expands, the fixed cost is spread over more and more units of output. The average variable cost curve first declines, reaches a minimum at point K, and then rises. The average total cost curve also declines

FIGURE 9.2

Average and marginal
cost curves.

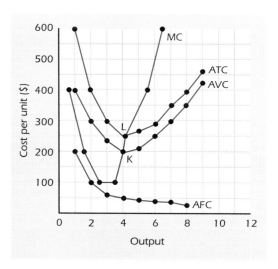

The marginal cost curve
cuts the average variable
cost curve and the average
total cost curve at their
minimum points.

at first, reaches a minimum at point L, and then rises thereafter. The marginal cost curve falls and then rises as output increases.

Note that the rising marginal cost curve cuts the average variable cost curve and the average total cost curve at their minimum points. It is easy to see why this is so: If the marginal cost is less than the average cost, the average cost will fall. If the marginal cost is greater than the average, the average cost will rise. When the marginal cost equals the average cost (at the point of intersection), the average cost ceases to fall and is about to rise. The average cost must therefore have reached its lowest point at its intersection with the marginal cost. Note also that the average variable cost reaches its minimum point at a lower level of output than the average total cost does. This is so because of the effect of the falling AFC, which is added to AVC to obtain ATC.

The relations between marginal cost and average cost are conveniently summarized below. Remember the magnetic effect of the marginal on the average — the marginal pulls the average to it like a magnet.

RELATIONS BETWEEN MC AND AVC

1. When MC < AVC, AVC will fall (the marginal pulls the average down). This occurs over the range of output from zero to four units in the example in Figure 9.2.

2. When MC > AVC, AVC will rise (the marginal pulls the average up). This occurs over the range of output from five units and above.

3. When MC = AVC, AVC will neither rise nor fall; it will be at its minimum. This occurs somewhere between the fourth and fifth units of output.

RELATIONS BETWEEN MC AND ATC

1. When MC < ATC, ATC will fall.

2. When MC > ATC, ATC will rise.

3. When MC = ATC, ATC will be at its minimum.

RELATIONS BETWEEN MC AND MP, AND BETWEEN AVC AND AP

Learning Objective 2: describe the relations between marginal cost and marginal product, and between average variable cost and average product

By this time, you might have concluded intuitively that a relation exists between marginal product and marginal cost. Let us explore this relation. In Table 9.2, we present hypothetical cost and product data. Let us assume that each additional unit of the variable factor (for example, each worker, if the variable factor is labour) is hired at a constant price of $5 per unit of time. The marginal cost per unit of extra output is simply the extra cost ($5) divided by the extra output (marginal product) contributed by the worker. Thus, provided that the marginal product of each additional worker is rising, the marginal cost of each additional unit will fall.

TABLE 9.2

Hypothetical cost and product data.

Quantity of varia- ble factor (workers)	Total product (units per week)	Marginal product (units)	Average product (units)	Marginal cost per unit of ex- tra output	AVC per unit of extra output
0	0		—		—
		5		1.00	
1	5		5		1.0
		7		0.71	
2	12		6		0.83
		9		0.56	
3	21		7		0.71
		7		0.71	
4	28		7		0.71
		6		0.83	
5	34		6.8		0.74
		4		1.25	
6	38		6.3		0.79
		2		2.50	
7	40		5.7		0.88

In Table 9.2, the marginal product of the first worker is five, but the extra cost of hiring this worker is $5, so the marginal cost per unit of extra output is $5/5 = $1. The marginal product of the second worker is seven, but the extra cost of hiring that worker is again $5, so the marginal cost per unit of extra output is $5/7 = $0.71. The other marginal cost values are obtained in a similar manner.

Note, however, that after the third worker is hired, diminishing returns set in. Since the marginal product is now falling, the marginal cost rises.

> **Given the price of a variable factor, increasing marginal product (increasing returns) implies decreasing marginal cost; and diminishing marginal product (diminishing returns) implies increasing marginal cost.**

These relations are illustrated graphically in Figure 9.3. Similar relations that exist between the average product and the average variable cost are also shown in Figure 9.3.

SUMMARY OF RELATIONS

The marginal cost and average variable cost curves are mirror reflections of the marginal product and average product curves.

The following six points provide a convenient summary of the relations discussed in this section.

1. When marginal product rises, marginal cost falls.

2. When marginal product falls, marginal cost rises.

FIGURE 9.3

Relations between marginal product and marginal cost, and average product and average variable cost.

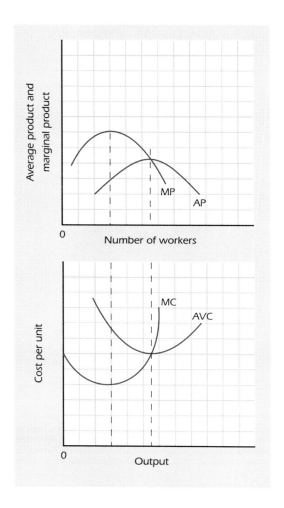

3. When marginal product is at its maximum, marginal cost is at its minimum.

4. When average product rises, average variable cost falls.

5. When average product falls, average variable cost rises.

6. When average product is at its maximum, average variable cost is at its minimum.

COSTS IN THE LONG RUN

Learning Objective 3:
analyze costs in the long run

In the long run, all the firm's inputs are variable, therefore all its costs are variable.

Up to this point in our analysis, we have concentrated on the situation in which the firm had at least one fixed factor of production; our analysis dealt with a firm in the short run. We now turn our attention to the situation where the firm is able to vary all of its factor inputs; our analysis now turns to the firm in the long run.

In the long run, all of the firm's factors of production can be varied. In this situation, the firm has no fixed factors of production, and hence no fixed costs. The firm is in a position to be able to make any adjustment to the size of its plant and to its scale of operation that it deems necessary. The profit-maximizing firm will, of course, choose the minimum cost for each level of output.

FIGURE 9.4

Short-run cost curves of three plants.

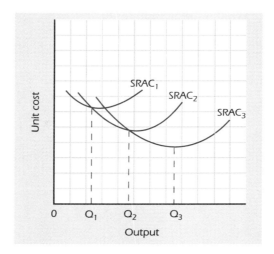

The firm will choose the plant size that minimizes cost for any desired output level.

To illustrate how the firm chooses in the long run, let us assume that the firm has three plants of different sizes. Figure 9.4 shows the short-run average cost curves of the three plants, and allows us to compare the average cost of producing any given level of output in each of the three plants. $SRAC_1$ is the short-run average cost curve for plant 1, $SRAC_2$ is the short-run average cost curve for plant 2, and $SRAC_3$ is the short-run average cost curve for plant 3. If the firm contemplates an output of less than Q_1 units, it will choose plant 1. This is so because plant 1 has the lowest average cost at that output level. If the firm contemplates an output between Q_1 and Q_2, it will choose plant 2. For an output level greater than Q_2, the firm will choose plant 3, which evidently has the lowest average cost at that level of output.

For any desired level of output then, the firm will choose the plant size for which the average cost is lowest. In Figure 9.4, we have assumed that the firm has only three plant sizes from which to choose. Let us assume instead, that the firm has an infinite number of plants of different sizes from which to choose. Figure 9.5 illustrates this situation.

FIGURE 9.5

Derivation of the long-run average cost curve.

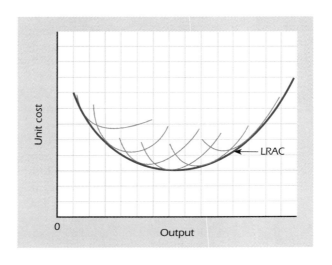

Here, several short-run cost curves appear. The firm's long-run average cost (LRAC) curve is tangent to the infinite number of short-run average cost curves. For this reason, the LRAC curve is sometimes called the **envelope curve** — geometrically, the LRAC curve envelops the SRAC curves.

Note that when the LRAC curve is falling, the points of tangency lie to the left of the minimum points of the SRAC curves. When the LRAC curve is rising, the points of tangency lie to the right of the minimum points of the SRAC curves. A firm's long-run average cost is the lowest cost per unit at which the firm can produce a given level of output in a situation where the firm can vary all its factors. Figure 9.6 shows a long-run average cost curve without the associated short-run average cost curves.

> An envelope curve is a firm's long-range average cost curve.
>
> Long-run average cost: the lowest cost per unit at which a firm can produce a given level of output when it can vary all its inputs.

FIGURE 9.6

Long-run average cost curve.

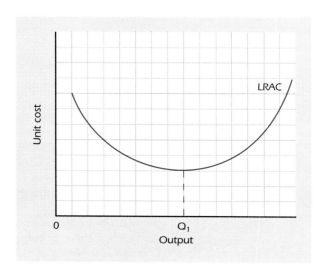

RETURNS TO SCALE

You will recall that in Chapter 8 you studied how a firm's total output will respond when increasing quantities of a variable input are added to a fixed input. There, we discussed the law or principle of diminishing returns. In this section, we shall discuss how a firm's total output responds to changes in all its inputs. You will now study the following cases: increasing returns to scale, constant returns to scale, and decreasing returns to scale.

INCREASING RETURNS TO SCALE

> **Learning Objective 4:** understand returns to scale
>
> Increasing returns to scale: a more-than-proportional increase in output resulting from an increase in all inputs.

If a firm increases all of its factors of production by some proportion (that is, its entire scale of operation) and as a result, increases its output proportionately more than it increases its factors of production, we say that the firm operates under conditions of **increasing returns to scale**. If we assume that factor (input) prices remain unchanged, increasing returns to scale imply that unit cost is falling.

The relation between increasing returns to scale and unit long-run cost can be illustrated as follows. For simplicity, let us assume that the firm uses only two factors of production: labour (L) and capital (K). Let us assume further that the price of labour is $2 per unit of time, the price of capital is $1 per unit of time, and the firm uses three units of labour and two units of capital to produce one unit of output. In this case, when the firm doubles all its inputs, its output more than doubles. In fact, its output triples. This is precisely the meaning of increasing returns to scale. Production and cost information are shown in Table 9.3. Note that long-run average cost falls from $8 to $5.33.

TABLE 9.3

Production, cost, and increasing returns to scale.

| Inputs | | Output | Total Cost | Long-run average |
L	K	(units)	($)	cost ($)
3	2	1	8	8/1 = 8
6	4	3	16	16/3 = 5.33

Economies of scale: the decline of average cost as the firm's scale of operation expands.

As a consequence of this relation, the terms *increasing returns to scale* and *decreasing costs* are often used synonymously. Figure 9.7 shows decreasing costs or increasing returns to scale as the downward-sloping section of the long-run average cost curve. The firm enjoys increasing returns to scale over the range of output from 0 to Q_1. We say that a firm operating under conditions of decreasing cost enjoys **economies of scale**.

FIGURE 9.7

Long-run average cost curve showing returns to scale.

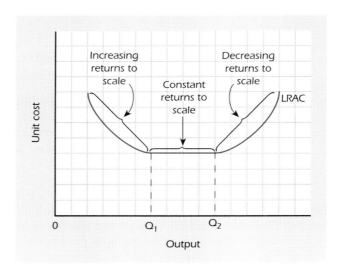

CONSTANT RETURNS TO SCALE

Constant returns to scale: a proportional increase in output resulting from an increase in all inputs.

A firm operates under **constant returns to scale** if an increase in all of its inputs results in a proportional increase in output. Constant returns to scale imply that unit long-run cost remains unchanged as output increases. Consider the information given in Table 9.4. In this case, as the firm doubles its inputs, its output also doubles. Note that long-run average cost remains unchanged at $8. Figure 9.7 illustrates the case of constant returns to scale. The firm operates under constant returns to scale over the range of output from Q_1 to Q_2.

The level of output at Q_1 has some significance. At this level of output, increasing returns to scale are exhausted and constant returns to scale begin. At a level of output less than Q_1, the firm is not taking full advantage of economies of scale, and there are no economies of scale to be gained at any level of output beyond Q_1. The level of output at which economies of scale end and constant returns to scale begin (Q_1 in Figure 9.7) is referred to as the firm's **minimum efficient scale**.

Minimum efficient scale: the level of output at which economies of scale end.

TABLE 9.4	Inputs		Output (units)	Total Cost ($)	Long-run average cost ($)
	L	**K**			
Production, cost, and constant returns to scale.	3	2	1	8	8/1 = 8
	6	4	2	16	16/2 = 8

DECREASING RETURNS TO SCALE

Decreasing returns to scale: a less-than-proportional increase in output resulting from an increase in all inputs.

If an increase in all of the firm's inputs results in a less-than-proportional increase in the firm's output, then the firm is experiencing **decreasing returns to scale**. Decreasing returns to scale imply increasing long-run average cost. This situation is illustrated in Table 9.5.

TABLE 9.5	Inputs		Output (units)	Total Cost ($)	Long-run average cost ($)
	L	**K**			
Production, cost, and decreasing returns to scale.	3	2	1	8	8/1 = 8
	6	4	1.5	16	16/1.5 = 10.67

Diseconomies of scale: a situation in which long-run costs rise as output increases.

In this case, when the firm doubles its inputs, the resulting output is less than double. Note also that long-run average cost is illustrated graphically in Figure 9.7 by the rising portion of the long-run average cost (LRAC) curve. The firm faces increasing costs over the range of output beyond Q_2. At any point beyond Q_2, **diseconomies of scale** are said to be in effect.

REASONS FOR INCREASING AND DECREASING RETURNS TO SCALE

Increasing returns to scale may result from specialization, large volume purchasing, and the greater efficiency of larger plants.

Constant returns to scale would seem to be the normal condition to expect. If one plant can produce 500 units of output per day, then two plants of the same type should produce 1000 units per day. In fact, many firms do experience constant returns to scale over certain ranges of output.

Decreasing returns to scale are due largely to management inefficiency.

But why do increasing returns to scale and decreasing returns to scale occur? Increasing returns to scale may result from specialization, which may not be practical in a small-scale operation. Also, decreasing cost may result from the firm's ability to purchase inputs in large quantities and thus take advantage of quantity discounts for which smaller orders may not qualify. For these reasons, larger plants tend to be more efficient than smaller ones (at least up to a point), so the firm may enjoy decreasing costs as it expands its operation. The reason generally given for increasing costs is inefficiency in management. As the size of the operation grows, management becomes more complex and the decision-making process becomes ensnared in red tape.

ECONOMIES OF SCOPE

In our discussion of the costs of production up to this point, we have assumed that the firm produces only one product or service. In fact, many firms produce more than one product. One firm may produce radios, televisions, VCRs, and other electronic goods. The

Learning Objective 5:
understand economies
of scope

*Economies of scope exist
when the costs of produc-
tion are less for producing
different goods together
than they would be if produced separately.*

production of audio tapes might affect the cost of producing videotapes since there might be some common elements in the production of both.

When the costs of production fall by producing a set of different goods together rather than separately, **economies of scope** are said to exist. This explains why we find certain firms producing several different but closely related products at the same time. We should not at all be surprised to find the same firm producing refrigerators, washers, dryers, air-conditioning units, dishwashers, ovens, and even vacuum cleaners.

A P P L I C A T I O N

Two Ways to Reduce Unit Cost

Knowledge of the behaviour of cost can help a firm to reduce unit cost. If increasing returns to scale exist, then the firm may reduce unit cost by increasing output. That is, it may take advantage of economies of scale. But it may also be able to lower its long-run average cost curve. For example, as the workers gain experience and learn to perform their respective functions with greater proficiency, the average cost curve will shift downward. This is one of the great benefits of training, and it explains why firms are willing to spend hundreds of thousands of dollars in providing training for their employees.

G L O B A L   P E R S P E C T I V E

Unit Labour Cost: An International Comparison

In this chapter, emphasis was placed on the costs of production. For most industries, the cost of labour constitutes the biggest cost. Rapidly rising labour cost has been known to present severe problems for many firms, and many companies have been influenced by labour costs when making decisions about the location of their plants.

This capsule compares unit labour costs in manufacturing in seven industrial countries. The average annual change between 1990 and 1999 is used as the index for comparison. Over the period under consideration, unit labour costs grew fastest in the U.K., among the seven countries selected (see the accompanying table). The values for Germany and France were negative. The average annual growth rate of unit labour cost in Canada over the 1990-99 period was 0.8%. In Italy it was relatively high at 2.6%.

Unit labour cost	
Country	**Unit Labour Cost (%)**
Canada	0.8
United States	0.7
Japan	1.4
Germany	–0.7
France	–0.3
Italy	2.6
United Kingdom	3.1

Source: International Monetary Fund, *World Economic Outlook*, May 1998. Washington, D.C., 1998: 158.

CHAPTER SUMMARY

1. The firm incurs costs by purchasing and using factors of production to produce its output of goods and services.

2. The cost function is the relation between cost and the quantity of output produced.

3. Explicit costs are those costs for which direct payment is made for factor inputs. Implicit costs or imputed costs are those costs for which no direct payment is made since the resources are already owned by the firm.

4. The firm's total cost in the short run consists of fixed costs and variable costs. Fixed costs are those costs incurred even if the firm suspends its operation temporarily. Variable costs are the costs that change with the level of output.

5. Average total cost is total cost divided by the number of units produced. Average fixed cost is total fixed cost divided by the number of units produced. Average variable cost is total variable cost divided by the number of units produced. Average total cost is the sum of average fixed cost and average variable cost.

6. Marginal cost or incremental cost is the extra cost incurred by producing an extra unit of output.

7. Total fixed cost does not vary with the volume of output produced. Total cost and total variable cost rise as the volume of output increases.

8. Average fixed cost declines continuously; average variable cost and average total cost first decline, reach a minimum, and then rise. Marginal cost cuts average variable cost and average total cost at their minimum points.

9. Increasing marginal product implies decreasing marginal cost, and diminishing marginal product implies increasing marginal cost. Similar relations exist between average product and average variable cost.

10. In the long run, the firm has only variable costs since it has no fixed inputs.

11. The long-run average cost is the lowest unit cost at which the firm can produce a given level of output in a situation where the firm is able to vary all its inputs.

12. Increasing returns to scale (also known as decreasing costs) exist when an increase in all the inputs leads to a more-than-proportional increase in output. Increasing returns to scale are illustrated by the downward sloping portion of the long-run average cost curve.

13. Constant returns to scale exist when an increase in all the inputs results in a proportional increase in output. Constant returns to scale are illustrated by the flat (horizontal) portion of the long-run average cost curve.

14. The minimum efficient scale for a firm occurs at the level of output at which economies of scale are exhausted and constant returns to scale begin.

15. Decreasing returns to scale (also referred to as increasing costs) exist when an increase in all the inputs leads to a less-than-proportional increase in output. Decreasing returns to scale are illustrated by the upward-sloping portion of the long-run average cost curve.

16. Economies of scope refer to the gain in economic efficiency that results from producing different products together rather than separately.

TERMS FOR REVIEW

cost function (148)

explicit costs (148)

implicit costs (148)

depreciation (148)

fixed (overhead) costs (149)

variable costs (149)

average cost (149)

average total cost (ATC) (149)

average fixed cost (AFC) (149)

average variable cost (AVC) (149)

marginal (incremental) cost (150)

envelope curve (156)

increasing returns to scale (156)

economies of scale (157)

constant returns to scale (157)

minimum efficient scale (157)

decreasing returns to scale (158)

diseconomies of scale (158)

economies of scope (159)

QUESTIONS FOR REVIEW AND DISCUSSION

1. What do economists mean by the term *cost function?* (General)

2. Distinguish between explicit costs and implicit costs. (General)

3. What is the difference between fixed costs and variable costs? Give an example of a cost that is likely to be fixed and one that is variable. (L.O.1)

4. Your family plans to open a gas station along the Trans-Canada Highway. Make a list of possible cost items for the operation of this business, then state which ones are fixed and which ones are variable. (L.O.1)

5. What is the relation between (L.O.1)

   (a) marginal cost and average cost?

   (b) marginal cost and total cost?

6. Explain why the average fixed cost curve declines continuously. (L.O.2)

7. State the relation between (L.O.2)

   (a) marginal product and marginal cost.

   (b) average product and average variable cost.

8. Explain each of the following terms: (L.O.3)

   (a) increasing returns to scale;

   (b) constant returns to scale;

   (c) minimum efficient scale;

   (d) decreasing returns to scale.

9. What is the difference between diminishing returns and decreasing returns to scale? (L.O.3)

10. What reasons can you give for the existence of decreasing costs? (L.O.3)

11. Distinguish between economies of scale and economies of scope. (L.O.4,5)

PROBLEMS AND EXERCISES

1. Table 9.6 shows cost data for a firm. (L.O.1)

TABLE 9.6	Q	TFC	TVC	TC	AFC	AVC	ATC	MC
Cost data for a firm.	1	100	25					
	2	100	40					
	3	100	48					
	4	100	60					
	5	100	80					
	6	100	108					
	7	100	140					
	8	100	192					
	9	100	270					
	10	100	380					
	11	100	550					
	12	100	780					

(a) Complete the table by filling in the remaining five columns.

(b) On graph paper, plot curves for the average fixed cost, the average variable cost, the average total cost, and the marginal cost.

(c) At what levels of output does the marginal cost curve cut the average variable cost curve and the average total cost curve? Compare these levels with the output levels at which the average variable cost curve and the average total cost curve reach a minimum.

2. You are given the data contained in Table 9.7 for Providex Ltd. (L.O.1)

TABLE 9.7	Output	AFC ($)	AVC ($)
Cost data for Providex, Ltd.	0	—	—
	1	20.00	30.00
	2	10.00	28.00
	3	6.67	27.00
	4	5.00	26.00
	5	4.00	24.00
	6	3.33	23.00
	7	2.86	24.00
	8	2.50	26.00
	9	2.22	29.00
	10	2.00	32.00

Calculate each of the following at each level of output.

(a) TFC

(b) TVC

(c) MC

3. Use your answer from Question 2 above to graph the TFC, TVC, and TC curves for Providex. (L.O.1)

4. A firm has total fixed costs amounting to $400. Draw the firm's average fixed cost curve for output ranging from one unit to eight units. (L.O.1)

5. The cost data in Table 9.8 are for the Excelcom Corporation. (L.O.1)

	Output	TC	MC	TVC	ATC	AVC
TABLE 9.8	0	60				
	1	65				
Cost data for Excelcom	2	70				
Corporation.	3	75				
	4	80				
	5	85				
	6	96				
	7	112				
	8	136				
	9	162				
	10	190				

(a) Compute MC, TVC, ATC, and AVC and fill in the appropriate columns.

(b) Compute AFC values for Excelcom.

(c) Graph Excelcom's AFC, AVC, ATC, and MC curves all on the same diagram.

6. A textbook publisher finds that at an output of 10 000 books, its average fixed cost (per book) is $5. What will the firm's average fixed cost be if it increases its output to 15 000 books? (L.O.1)

7. The Unipro Company uses labour as its only variable input. Table 9.9 shows production data for Unipro. The wage rate is $5 per hour. (L.O.1)

	Number of workers	Total product units
TABLE 9.9	0	0
	1	15
Production data for	2	25
Unipro.	3	33
	4	38
	5	42
	6	44

(a) Compute total variable cost for the range of output indicated.

(b) Compute Unipro's AVC for each level of output indicated.

(c) Plot Unipro's AVC curve.

8. Table 9.10 shows short-run cost schedules for the production of T-shirts, using three different plant sizes. (L.O.1,3)

	Plant 1		Plant 2		Plant 3	
TABLE 9.10	Q	AC	Q	AC	Q	AC
	10	20	10	30	10	35
Short-run cost	20	18	20	25	20	32
schedules for the	30	17	30	16	30	23
production of T-shirts.	40	19	40	13	40	16
	50	25	50	12	50	13
	60	40	60	18	60	10
	70	65	70	27	70	15
	80	102	80	46	80	25
	90	150	90	78	90	45

(a) For what output range should the firm use plant 1?

(b) For what output range should the firm use plant 2?

(c) For what output range should the firm use plant 3?

(d) On the basis of the information given in Table 9.10, complete a table of the firm's long-run cost schedule for Q from 10 to 90 in increments of 10.

9. How would economic efficiency be affected if General Electric (a company that produces a wide variety of products) were broken up into a number of companies, each producing only one product? Explain your answer. (L.O.4,5)

10. A hypothetical small firm manufactures plastic clips used largely in the furniture industry. The firm employs 10 workers and pays rent of $12 000 annually for its facilities. The owner-manager is concerned about the rising costs of production. Make up a list of possible causes of the increase in cost and recommend steps that may be taken to reduce cost in this firm.

THE PURELY COMPETITIVE FIRM

Learning Objectives

After studying this chapter, you will be familar with:

1 market structures

2 short-run output decisions in a purely competitive firm

3 the purely competitive firm's short-run supply curve

4 the short-run industry supply curve

5 long-run equilibrium and adjustment

6 the importance of the purely competitive model

Monopoly, besides, is a great enemy to good management, which can never be universally established but in consequence of that free and universal competition which forces everybody to have recourse to it for the sake of self-defence.

Adam Smith, *Wealth of Nations*

INTRODUCTION

In Chapter 8, you studied the aspects of the firm's behaviour that deal with its choice of inputs, and in Chapter 9, you studied how the firm's production costs are related to its volume of output. These are all aspects of supply. In this chapter, you will study yet another aspect of supply — supply under perfect competition. The aspect of supply that we will now study deals with the firm's pricing and output decisions under specific market conditions. The firm's pricing and output decisions depend, to a great extent, on the characteristics of the market within which the firm operates. This chapter focuses mainly on the behaviour of a firm in a purely competitive industry.

MARKET STRUCTURES

Learning Objective 1:
market structures

Market structures, such as pure competition and monopoly, affect pricing and output decisions.

An industry is a group of firms producing similar products.

The term **market structures** refers to certain market characteristics that influence the firm's pricing and output behaviour. These market characteristics define, in part, the environment within which the firm operates. In discussing market structures, you will find the concept of the industry quite useful. An **industry** is defined as a group of firms producing similar products. A firm that is the only one in an industry will most likely behave quite differently from a firm that is just one among many in the industry.

Different markets have different characteristics, but economists have managed to group these characteristics into four broad categories of market structures. These market structures are:

1. pure or perfect competition
2. monopoly
3. monopolistic competition
4. oligopoly

Imperfect competition includes monopolistic competition and oligopoly.

As you will see shortly, pure competition and monopoly are at opposite ends on a continuum of market structures (see Table 10.1). Between these polar opposites are monopolistic competition and oligopoly, which, together with monopoly, are frequently referred to by economists as **imperfect competition**. We shall deal with each of these market structures in turn.

PURE COMPETITION

Pure (perfect, atomistic) competition is a market structure characterized by a large number of firms, homogeneous products and freedom of entry and exit.

A price taker is a firm that, by itself, cannot affect the market price of its product.

The market structure termed **pure competition** or **perfect competition** is defined by the following characteristics:

1. The market consists of a large number of firms — so many of them that no single firm has any control over the price of its product. The purely competitive firm is therefore a **price-taker**. Each firm produces such a small fraction of the total output of the product that output will not be noticeably affected by one firm producing and selling as much as it can or by ceasing production. Because each firm represents such a tiny fraction of the industry, the term **atomistic competition** is sometimes used to define pure competition.

   Farming, the stock market, and international money markets are usually cited as good examples of perfect competition. It is not easy to find many other good examples of purely competitive markets in the real world. Even in the case of agriculture, government programs influence the price at which the farmers sell their products. Pure competition, therefore, does not really exist in these markets.

2. The products of the firms are homogeneous or standardized. Because the products are identical, buyers have no preference for purchasing from one firm rather than from another.

3. There is freedom of entry into and exit from the industry. There are no entry or exit barriers, so resources are perfectly mobile in and out of the market.

4. Buyers know the price charged by each firm. If one firm attempts to charge a price higher than the market price, it will lose all of its customers.

Note: When a distinction is made between pure competition and perfect competition, the distinguishing feature is that in perfect competition, consumers have perfect knowledge regarding the prices charged by the firms in the market. In our analysis, we will make no distinction between pure competition and perfect competition; the two terms may be used interchangeably.

It is important to note that in order for competition to exist in a market, only two features are essential. These are: numerous sellers (firms), and freedom of entry and exit. The conditions for the existence of pure competition are therefore more restrictive in scope than the conditions for competition.

MONOPOLY

A monopolized market or monopoly is an industry with a single firm producing a product that has no close substitutes.

In contrast to a purely competitive market, a **monopolized market** is one that is dominated by a single firm. A **monopoly** exists when there is one firm in an industry producing a good or service that has no close substitutes. The firm in monopoly has significant control over the price that it charges for its product. The entry of other firms into the industry is precluded by a variety of barriers. Ontario Hydro, Hydro-Québec, and Bell Canada (to some degree) are examples of monopolies.

MONOPOLISTIC COMPETITION

Monopolistic competition exists when there is a large number of firms selling differentiated products.

Monopolistic competition is a market structure consisting of a large number of firms, each selling a differentiated product and exerting some slight influence on the market price. Price differences are likely to be small among products sold by firms in monopolistic competition because, although consumers acknowledge differences among the products, they perceive these differences as minor. For example, many different stores sell clothing, and we do observe differences in price as we move from one store to the next. Not very often, however, do we observe startling differences in the prices of suits of similar quality.

OLIGOPOLY

Oligopoly exists when there are few interdependent firms in the industry.

Oligopoly is a market structure in which there are only a few sellers. Since each firm in this situation usually produces a substantial portion of the total output of the industry to which it belongs, it will take account of the policies and strategies adopted by its rivals. A firm in an oligopoly situation has considerable influence on the price of its product. If the firms happen to agree to act as a group to control price and output, their influence increases substantially. Examples of oligopolistic firms are those in the automobile industry, the brewing industry, and the tobacco industry. The four largest firms in each of these industries produce over 90% of the total output of these industries. Table 10.1 illustrates the spectrum of market structures with their major characteristics.

We shall analyze the behaviour of the purely competitive firm in the remaining sections of this chapter. Pure competition is one of the best known and most widely used models in economics. It is also one of the most widely criticized. The following two chapters will discuss the behaviour of firms in the other market structures. In Chapter 4, we saw how the price of a product is determined in a purely competitive market. We shall now study in some detail the behaviour of a purely competitive firm seeking to maximize its profits.

TABLE 10.1	Pure competition	Monopolistic competition	Oligopoly	Monopoly
Market structures and their characteristics.	Large number of firms	Large number of firms	Few firms	Only one firm
	Identical products	Differentiated products	Similar or differentiated products	Product has no close substitutes
	No barriers to entry and exit	Freedom of entry and exit	Some barriers to entry	Effective barriers to entry
	No control over market price	Small control over market price	Substantial control over price	Significant control over price

PROBLEM SOLVING 10-1

Can you expect a single firm in a purely competitive industry to advertise its product?

THE SHORT-RUN OUTPUT DECISION IN A PURELY COMPETITIVE FIRM

A purely competitive firm must decide on the level of output that will maximize its profits.

Recall that a purely competitive firm has no control over the price at which it sells its output. Since the firm in pure competition must accept the market price as a given, such a firm must determine only what level of output to produce in order to maximize its profits. Actually, there are two ways in which a firm can determine the level of output that will earn maximum profits: the total cost/total revenue method and the marginal method. These two methods will be discussed in turn.

THE TOTAL COST/TOTAL REVENUE APPROACH TO PROFIT MAXIMIZATION

Learning Objective 2: short-run output decisions in a purely competitive firm

Profit is the difference between total revenue and total cost. If TR > TC, then $\pi > 0$; if TR = TC, then $\pi = 0$; and if TR < TC, then $\pi < 0$. To maximize its profits, the firm can choose that level of output at which the difference between total revenue and total cost is greatest. The procedure for calculating maximum profit is outlined in Table 10.2.

Column one of Table 10.2 shows various levels of output. The price of the product is $10, as shown in column two. Total revenue in column three is obtained by multiplying price by quantity of output. Column four gives total cost, and column five, the total profit column, is obtained by subtracting column four from column three. As we can see from the table, total profit is at a maximum when the firm produces an output level of seven or eight units.

We can also illustrate the total cost/total revenue approach to profit maximization diagrammatically. Figure 10.1 plots the cost and revenue data shown in Table 10.2. The firm's total revenue (TR) is represented by a straight line through the origin. If there is no output, there will be no revenue. As output expands, total revenue rises in proportion to the increase in output — given a fixed price. Total cost rises as output expands. The profit-maximizing output appears where the difference between total revenue and total cost (TC) is greatest.

	Output (units) (1)	Price ($) (2)	Total revenue ($) (3)	Total cost ($) (4)	Profit ($) (5)
TABLE 10.2	1	10	10	30	−20
	2	10	20	35	−15
Hypothetical revenue,	3	10	30	39	−9
cost, and profit	4	10	40	41	−1
data for a purely	5	10	50	44	6
competitive firm.	6	10	60	49	11
	7	10	70	56	14
	8	10	80	66	14
	9	10	90	80	10
	10	10	100	95	5

FIGURE 10.1

Total revenue and total cost.

THE MARGINAL APPROACH TO PROFIT MAXIMIZATION

Learning Objective 2: short-run output decisions in a purely competitive firm

Remember that marginal cost is the extra or additional cost incurred in producing one more unit of output. **Marginal revenue** is the extra revenue obtained from selling an additional unit of output. Marginal revenue and marginal cost are calculated in columns six and seven of Table 10.3.

Marginal revenue is the additional revenue received from selling one more unit of output.

If the cost of producing an additional unit of output is less than the revenue obtained from that unit, then it will pay the firm to produce that additional unit. In other words, as long as the marginal cost is less than the marginal revenue, the firm will expand its output. If, however, the cost of producing an additional unit of output is greater than the revenue obtained from that unit, then the firm will not produce the additional unit. To do so would reduce the firm's profits. In other words, as long as marginal cost exceeds marginal revenue, the firm will reduce its output. It follows that, when its marginal revenue equals its marginal cost, the firm will be in the best profit position.

The firm maximizes profits when it produces a level of output that equates its marginal revenue and its marginal cost.

This profit-maximizing condition is illustrated in Figure 10.2. At a level of output of nine units, the marginal cost exceeds the marginal revenue. Hence, the firm will reduce its output. At a level of output of three units, marginal revenue exceeds marginal cost. Hence, the firm will increase its output. At an output level between seven and eight units, the firm cannot increase its profits by changing its output. Hence, an output between

TABLE 10.3	Quantity (units) (1)	Price ($) (2)	Total revenue ($) (3)	Total cost ($) (4)	Profit ($) (5)	Marginal revenue ($) (6)	Marginal cost ($) (7)
Hypothetical revenue, cost, and profit data for a purely competitive firm.	1	10	10	30	−20		
						10	5
	2	10	20	35	−15		
						10	4
	3	10	30	39	−9		
						10	2
	4	10	40	41	−1		
						10	3
	5	10	50	44	6		
						10	5
	6	10	60	49	11		
						10	7
	7	10	70	56	14		
						10	10
	8	10	80	66	14		
						10	14
	9	10	90	80	10		
						10	15
	10	10	100	95	5		

FIGURE 10.2

Marginal revenue and marginal cost.

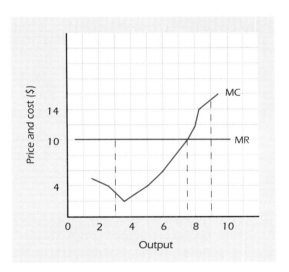

seven and eight units is the output level that maximizes the firm's profits. Note that the profit-maximizing level of output occurs where the rising marginal cost curve cuts the marginal revenue curve.

You may ask, "Why increase output to the point where MR = MC? Why not stop at some level of output just before seven units where MR > MC?" The reason for trying to operate where MR = MC may become much clearer if you think of the difference between MR and MC as extra profits. As long as MR > MC, the firm will earn extra profits by increasing its output. When there are no more extra profits to be made (i.e., when MR = MC), the firm will be in a profit-maximizing position.

PROBLEM SOLVING 10-2

Many people who manage firms know nothing about marginal revenue and marginal cost. Does this mean that they can never maximize their profits?

PRICE, AR, AND MR IN PURE COMPETITION

The demand curve for a purely competitive firm is perfectly elastic.

The relation between price, average revenue, and marginal revenue in a purely competitive market structure is something we should understand. Recall that a purely competitive firm is a price-taker. The price at which it sells its output is given. Since variations in the output of a purely competitive firm will have no appreciable effect on the market price of the product, the purely competitive firm faces a perfectly elastic demand curve. This kind of curve appears on a graph as a horizontal straight line (see Figure 10.3).

FIGURE 10.3

Average revenue and marginal revenue in pure competition.

The demand curve for a purely competitive firm coincides with its average and marginal revenue curves.

Average revenue is total revenue divided by number of units sold.

Average revenue and price are identical.

Average revenue (AR) is simply total revenue divided by the number of units sold. But this is exactly the same as price. The following simple algebraic exercise demonstrates that average revenue and price are identical.

$$TR = P \times Q$$

$$AR = \frac{TR}{Q} = \frac{P \times Q}{Q} = P$$

Therefore AR = P.

Note that in Table 10.3, marginal revenue remains constant and equals price or average revenue. This relation holds only in a situation of pure competition, where the price is given. The profit-maximizing condition for a purely competitive firm is often stated as:

$$MR = MC = P$$

We shall see later that pure competition is the only market structure in which profits are maximized when marginal cost equals price.

THE COMPETITIVE FIRM'S PROFIT LEVEL: THE SHORT RUN

The firm earns a profit provided that the price is above its ATC. It incurs a loss if the price is below its ATC.

The purely competitive firm maximizes its profits and will therefore be in equilibrium when it produces at an output level at which marginal cost equals price. But how large or how small are these profits? A quick look at Figure 10.4 will reveal whether or not the firm is earning a profit. For this purpose, you must remember that a firm's total profit is the difference between TR and TC. We can therefore determine the firm's profit per unit of output by dividing its total profit by the number of units produced and sold.

$$\text{Profit per unit} = \frac{\text{TR} - \text{TC}}{\text{Q}}$$

$$= \text{AR} - \text{ATC}$$

$$= \text{P} - \text{ATC}$$

FIGURE 10.4

The competitive firm's profit level.

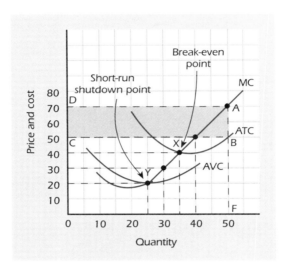

By comparing price and average total cost, we can easily determine whether or not the firm is earning a profit.

$$\text{If P} > \text{ATC, then } \pi > 0;$$

$$\text{If P} = \text{ATC, then } \pi = 0;$$

$$\text{If P} < \text{ATC, then } \pi < 0.$$

In Figure 10.4, if the price of the product is $70, the profit-maximizing firm will produce an output of 50 units where MR = P = MC. At this level of output, ATC = $50, so the firm makes a profit of $70 – $50 = $20 on each unit of output. At a price lower than $70, the firm's profit is reduced. In fact, it is possible for the price to be so low that the firm earns no profit at all and may even incur a loss. At a price of $30, for example, the firm does not cover its ATC (the price is below ATC); hence, the firm incurs losses.

We can also use Figure 10.4 to determine the firm's total revenue, total cost, and total profit at various price-output combinations. Let us assume that the price of the product is $70. The firm seeking to maximize its profits will produce 50 units of output. The firm will receive a total revenue of $70 × 50 = $3500. This total revenue is illustrated by the rectangle 0DAF. The total cost (ATC × Q) of producing an output of 50 units is $50 × 50 = $2500, and is illustrated by the rectangle 0CBF. The firm's total profit is the difference between its total revenue (0DAF) and its total cost (0CBF). This is shown by the area of the shaded rectangle ABCD, which is 20 × 50 = $1000.

THE SHORT-RUN SUPPLY CURVE OF THE PURELY COMPETITIVE FIRM

Learning Objective 3:
the purely competitive firm's short-run supply curve

At the break-even point, total revenue equals total cost, and profits are zero.

The break-even level of output is that output level at which the firm's total cost is just equal to its total revenue.

The foregoing analysis provides a method of determining the short-run supply curve of the purely competitive firm. The firm is doing the best it can in the short run provided that it produces an output at which MR = MC. Figure 10.4 shows that at a price of $70, the firm earns a profit. In fact, the firm earns a profit if the price is anywhere above $40. At a price of $40, the firm makes neither a profit nor a loss; it just breaks even. The price equals its average total cost (or its total revenue equals its total cost). This point is sometimes called the **break-even point**. In Figure 10.4, point X is the break-even point and the output of 35 units is the **break-even level of output**. If the price falls below $40, the firm incurs losses. At a price of $30, for example, the firm is doing its best in the short run when it produces an output of 30 units (MR = MC), yet it is incurring losses. Any different level of output will merely increase the firm's losses. A firm in such a situation is said to be *minimizing its losses*.

If price falls below AVC in the short run, the short-run shutdown point has been reached and the firm should close its plant.

Since the firm incurs losses when the price falls below $40, is it not better for the firm to cease operation? The answer is no. As long as the firm covers its average variable cost in the short run, it should continue to operate. If it suspends its operation, it still has its fixed costs; whereas if it continues to operate, its losses will be less than its total fixed costs. When the price falls below $20, the firm does not cover its variable costs and should therefore shut down. This point is called the **short-run shutdown point**. In Figure 10.4, point Y is the short-run shutdown point. Points along the marginal cost curve show the various quantities that the firm will supply at various prices. Note, however, that no output will be supplied at prices below $20. The various quantities supplied at various prices are shown in Table 10.4.

TABLE 10.4

The short-run supply schedule for a competitive firm.

Price ($)	Quantity supplied
70	50
60	45
50	40
40	35
30	30
20	25
Less than 20	0

The short-run supply curve is that portion of the MC curve that lies above the AVC curve.

This, of course, is the short-run supply schedule for a purely competitive firm. It corresponds with the marginal cost (MC) curve above the average variable cost (AVC) curve in Figure 10.4. Thus, the **short-run supply curve** of the purely competitive firm seeking to maximize its profits is the section of its marginal cost curve that lies above its average variable cost curve.

Let us return for a moment to Figure 10.4. We said that in the short run, if the price of the product is between $20 and $40, the firm should continue to operate even though it is incurring losses. When does a firm operating in that position go out of business? A firm will not continue to incur losses forever. In the long run, the firm has no fixed factors. In the long run therefore, a firm that is incurring losses will leave the industry. We will study the firm's adjustment to the long run later in this chapter.

PROBLEM SOLVING 10-3

"Any firm operating at a loss would be better off closing down." Do you agree?

THE SHORT-RUN INDUSTRY SUPPLY CURVE

You know that a purely competitive industry consists of a large number of firms. However, in order to illustrate geometrically the derivation of the short-run industry supply curve, we will assume that there are only three firms, A, B, and C, in an industry, D. Table 10.5 shows the various quantities supplied by each firm at each possible price.

	Price ($)	Output firm A	Output firm B	Output firm C	Output industry D
TABLE 10.5					
Derivation of short-run industry supply.	3	2 000	3 000	2 000	7 000
	6	3 000	5 000	4 000	12 000
	9	4 000	7 000	6 000	17 000
	12	5 000	9 000	8 000	22 000
	15	6 000	11 000	10 000	27 000
	18	7 000	13 000	12 000	32 000
	21	8 000	15 000	14 000	37 000
	24	9 000	17 000	16 000	42 000

Learning Objective 4:
the short-run industry supply curve

The industry supply curve is derived from the horizontal summation of the supply curves of the individual firms. This is shown in Figure 10.5. At a price of $3, firms A and C supply 2000 units each and firm B supplies 3000 units.

The total quantity supplied by the industry at a price of $3 is:

$$2000 + 3000 + 2000 = 7000$$

This gives us point E on the industry supply curve. At a price of $6, firm A supplies 3000 units, firm B supplies 5000 units, and firm C supplies 4000 units. The total quantity supplied by the industry at a price of $6 is:

The short-run industry supply curve is derived by adding horizontally the supply curves of all the firms in the industry.

$$3000 + 5000 + 4000 = 12\ 000$$

This gives point E_1 on the industry supply curve. In a similar manner, we can plot the other points on the industry supply curve as shown in Figure 10.5.

FIGURE 10.5

Derivation of the industry supply curve.

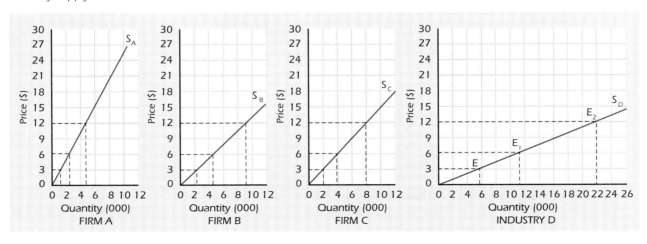

LONG-RUN EQUILIBRIUM

Learning Objective 5:
long-run equilibrium and adjustment

In a purely competitive market structure, firms are free to enter or to leave the industry: there are no barriers to entry or exit. If the firms in the industry earn profits in the short run, other firms will enter the industry. The entry of these new firms will increase total industry supply and, assuming no change in demand occurs, the price will tend to fall. New firms will tend to enter the industry provided that there are positive profits to be made. If firms in the industry are suffering losses, they will not remain in the industry in the long run. The exit of firms from the industry will cause total supply to fall and the price of the product will tend to rise.

A purely competitive firm in long-run equilibrium earns zero economic profits, called normal profits.

Movement of firms into and out of the industry will cease when each firm in the industry is earning zero profits — sometimes referred to as **normal profits**. You may wonder why a firm would stay in an industry if it were making zero profits, but the matter is easily clarified if we remind ourselves that profits are defined as total revenue minus total cost, and that total cost includes opportunity cost (that is, what the resources could earn in their best alternative uses). When a firm earns zero profits, it earns a return just equal to what the inputs could have earned if they were employed in their best alternative use.

The firm's long-run equilibrium position can be illustrated diagrammatically. If the price of the product is $15, as determined by the demand and supply curves for the industry shown in Figure 10.6, the firm will earn positive economic profits. New firms will enter the industry. As this happens, the industry supply curve shifts to the right, say, to S_1. This causes the price to fall to $6. At this price, firms will incur losses and therefore leave the industry. This exit of firms from the industry causes the industry supply curve to shift to the left (from $S_1 S_1$ to $S_0 S_0$ in Figure 10.6) resulting in an increase in price from $6 to $10. At this price, each firm earns zero profits. Note that this price equals average cost, and that the firm is in equilibrium, since marginal revenue equals marginal cost.

FIGURE 10.6

Long-run equilibrium of the purely competitive firm.

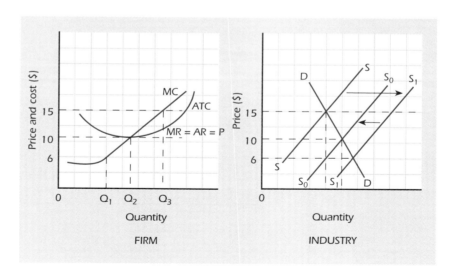

FIRM

INDUSTRY

In long-run equilibrium in pure competition, price equals minimum average cost.

Note further that in equilibrium, price equals marginal cost; but marginal cost passes through the minimum point of the average cost curve, so the price equals minimum average cost. This is important. The firm is in long-run equilibrium when

$$MR = MC = AC = P$$

MR equals MC and AR equals AC when an industry is at long-run industry equilibrium.

When each firm in the industry is in long-run equilibrium, and when there is no incentive for firms to enter or leave the industry, the output of the industry will remain steady — the industry supply curve will not shift. In this case, we say that the industry is in long-run equilibrium. Long-run **industry equilibrium** exists when both marginal revenue equals marginal cost and average cost equals average revenue.

LONG-RUN INDUSTRY ADJUSTMENT

Learning Objective 5: long-run equilibrium and adjustment

The long-run supply curve shows all of the goods that an industry will supply in long-run equilibrium.

In the previous section, we assumed implicitly that the industry operates under constant cost. In this section, we explicitly analyze constant-cost and increasing-cost industries. There is some controversy as to whether an industry can have decreasing cost. However, we will not pursue this issue. Regardless, the long-run industry supply curve is extremely important in our analysis. The **long-run supply curve** of a purely competitive industry shows the various quantities of a good that all the firms in the industry will be willing to supply at various prices when the industry is in long-run equilibrium.

CONSTANT-COST INDUSTRIES

In a constant-cost industry, costs remain unchanged as the industry expands.

A **constant-cost industry** is one in which the prices of the factors of production, and hence the costs of production, remain constant as the industry's output expands by the entry of new firms into the industry. When the industry is in long-run equilibrium, the price equals minimum long-run average cost. In a constant-cost industry, the expansion of industry output by the entry of new firms has no effect on cost. The entry and exit of firms cause total output to change, but the price of the product always returns to the point where it is equal to the minimum average total cost. Thus, in the long run, the industry supplies various quantities at a constant price. This means that:

the long-run supply curve of a constant-cost industry is horizontal (perfectly elastic) at the minimum average total cost.

FIGURE 10.7

Constant-cost industry adjustment.

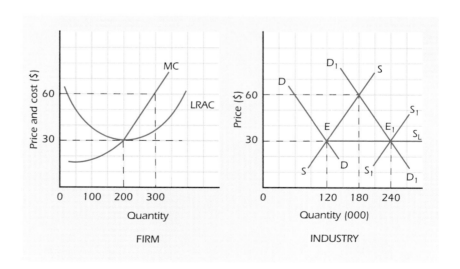

Let us continue our analysis with the help of Figure 10.7, which shows a firm and an industry, both in equilibrium. The firm shown in the diagram is typical of all of the firms in the industry. It produces 200 units of output, and the price of the product is $30.

The industry demand curve is DD, the supply curve is SS, and the quantity produced by the industry is 120 000 units.

Let us assume now that the demand for the product increases from DD to D_1D_1 as shown in Figure 10.7. This causes the price to rise from $30 to $60. This price is now above average cost, so the firms now earn positive economic profits. At a price of $60, the typical or representative firm increases its output to 300 units. The output of the industry increases along SS from 120 000 units to 180 000 units. Because profits are being earned in this industry, it attracts new firms. The entry of these new firms shifts the supply curve from SS to S_1S_1, and forces the price back to $30. With the price now back at $30, the initial firms reduce their output along their marginal cost curves. Each firm in the industry now produces 200 units, but because there are now more firms, the industry output increases to 240 000 units. Profits are again zero; and there is no movement of firms into or out of the industry. We started with an initial price of $30 and a total quantity of 120 000 units. We end up with a price of $30 and a total quantity supplied of 240 000 units. By joining points E and E_1, we obtain the long-run supply curve (S_L) of the industry.

INCREASING-COST INDUSTRIES

An **increasing-cost industry** is one in which the prices of the factors of production, and hence production costs, increase as the industry's output expands by the entry of new firms into the industry. Although many industries seem to have constant cost in the long run, it is reasonable to expect that as an industry expands, the increase in demand for scarce factors of production will raise the prices of inputs, and thus increase production costs.

Figure 10.8 will be helpful in our analysis. The firm and the industry are in equilibrium at a price of $30. The typical firm produces 100 units of output. DD and SS are the initial demand and supply curves of the industry, and the total output of the industry is 50 000 units.

FIGURE 10.8

Increasing-cost industry adjustment.

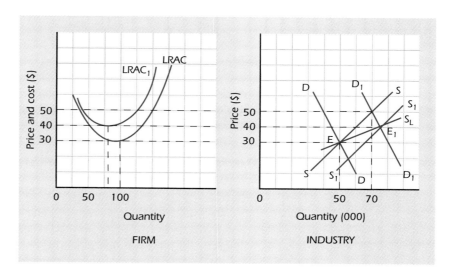

FIRM   INDUSTRY

Suppose that the demand for the output of the industry increases from DD to D_1D_1. This causes the price to rise from $30 to $50. The existing firms increase their output, moving along their marginal cost curves (not shown), and the industry output increases along SS from 50 000 to 70 000 units. New firms enter the industry, thus causing the supply curve to shift from SS to S_1S_1, but the cost rises, as shown by the shift of the long-run average cost curve from LRAC to $LRAC_1$. Therefore, the increase in supply resulting from the entry of new firms does not force the price back to its initial level of $30, but only to $40. We obtain the long-run supply curve (S_L) of the industry by joining points E and E_1. This analysis shows that:

the long-run supply curve of an increasing-cost industry has a positive slope.

THE IMPORTANCE OF THE PURELY COMPETITIVE MODEL

Learning Objective 6:
the importance of the purely competitive model

We saw earlier in this chapter that real-world examples of pure competition are not easy to find. Why then do economists spend so much time analyzing behaviour in this type of market structure? It is easier to understand the issue if you view pure competition as a model. Let us remind ourselves first that the competitive solution occurs where price equals marginal cost. This **marginal cost pricing** (a characteristic feature of pure competition) implies that the firm sells its product at a price just equal to the opportunity cost. Let us also remind ourselves that long-run competitive equilibrium occurs where price equals minimum average cost. Hence, resources are efficiently employed in the purely competitive model.

The marginal cost pricing strategy sets price equal to marginal cost.

The purely competitive model serves as an ideal by which other market structures may be judged.

The purely competitive model serves as an ideal situation by which we can measure other market structures. We can, in fact, consider it a kind of measuring rod. Moreover, many of the predictions of the purely competitive model hold true even in situations where pure competition does not prevail.

PARETO EFFICIENCY

One of the objectives of economic science is to allocate resources efficiently. How do we know if resources are allocated efficiently? One way is to test for **Pareto optimality** or **efficiency**. Pareto optimality (named after the Italian-born economist Vilfredo Pareto) states that efficiency exists if it is impossible to rearrange inputs and outputs so as to make someone better off without making anyone else worse off. Stated slightly differently, if it is possible to make someone better off without making someone else worse off, the economy is not operating at maximum efficiency.

Pareto optimality (efficiency) exists when it is impossible to make someone better off without at the same time making someone else worse off.

The following conditions are necessary to the existence of Pareto optimality:

1. Each consumer must have the opportunity to maximize his or her own satisfaction.
2. For each consumer, the ratio of the marginal utilities of any two goods must be the same. This means essentially that all consumers must pay the same price for each good.
3. Each firm must produce an output level at which marginal cost equals price.
4. The production of each good must be at the lowest possible cost.
5. Each factor of production must be employed in its most efficient use.
6. Each household must have the opportunity to supply as many factor services as it chooses.
7. People must be free to enter whatever occupation they choose.

If all markets are purely competitive, Pareto optimality will be realized.

It can be shown that if pure competition exists in all markets, all of the above conditions will prevail and Pareto efficiency will be attained. We can conclude then, that there is some basis for the popular notion that competition is good.

GLOBAL PERSPECTIVE

Global Competition

Competition among firms in an industry in one country may have nothing to do with competition among the firms in the same industry in another country. For example, competition among small retail stores in Canada is virtually independent of competition among similar retail stores in Britain. In many cases, however, a firm's competitive position is truly global rather than national or domestic. In this capsule, we will take a quick glance at global competition.

Global competition refers to competition among firms in many different countries. Manufacturers of tires, television sets, and automobiles, for example, sell their products internationally. Such firms face global competition. A Canadian firm that might have great monopoly power at home might find itself with little or no market strength as a global competitor. Telecommunications equipment is one of the areas in which Canadian firms are believed to have acquired some competitive advantage on the global market. The behaviour of such firms in the domestic market will be different from their behaviour in the global market. The pricing and output decisions of such firms will tend to reflect the competitive environment in which they operate.

In an effort to increase their strengths in the global market, many firms have adopted a strategy of global alliance. Examples of such alliances are: GM and Toyota; Boeing, Kawasaki, and Fuji; and alliances among firms in the aerospace industry in Britain, France, Germany, and Spain. An alliance between American Airlines and Canadian Airlines has been approved by the National Transportation Agency, and other alliances between Canadian and American airline companies are quite possible.

CHAPTER SUMMARY

1. Economists have grouped different market structures into four categories. These categories are: pure competition, monopoly, monopolistic competition, and oligopoly.

2. Pure or perfect competition and monopoly are at opposites ends of a continuum of market structures. Monopoly, monopolistic competition, and oligopoly are usually referred to collectively as market structures of imperfect competition.

3. In a purely competitive market, there are many firms selling a homogeneous product. The sellers are so numerous that no single firm has any noticeable effect on the price of the product. Each seller (firm) is a price-taker. In this type of market structure, firms are free to enter or to leave the industry. Pure competition is also called atomistic competition.

4. A market is said to be monopolized when it is dominated by a single firm. In a pure monopoly, there is only one firm in the industry. This firm (the monopolistic firm) produces a product that has no close substitutes. The monopolist has a great deal of control over the price of its product.

5. In a market characterized by monopolistic competition there are many firms, each selling a differentiated product. Each firm has a small amount of influence on the price of the product.

6. An oligopoly is a market structure in which there are only a few sellers. In this market situation, each firm has substantial influence over the price of the product, and each firm is likely to be affected by the behaviour of the other firms in the industry.

7. A firm's profit is the difference between its total revenue and its total cost. The firm maximizes its profits by producing that output at which the difference between total revenue and total cost is greatest, or by producing an output level at which marginal revenue equals marginal cost.

8. The purely competitive firm faces a perfectly elastic (horizontal) demand curve. Its average revenue curve is the same as its marginal revenue curve.

9. A firm in pure competition earns positive short-run profits provided that the price at which it sells its product is above its average total cost. When the price just equals average total cost, the firm is in a break-even position.

10. If the firm is covering its variable costs but not its total costs, and if it produces an output level at which marginal revenue equals marginal cost, we say that it is minimizing its losses. The firm is better off doing this in the short run than closing down. The short-run shutdown point is the point at which the firm is just barely covering its variable cost with nothing left over.

11. The competitive firm's short-run supply curve is the portion of its marginal cost curve that lies above its average variable cost curve. We can obtain the short-run industry supply curve by adding horizontally the supply curves of the firms in that industry.

12. At long-run equilibrium, the purely competitive firm earns zero profits. The long-run equilibrium position may be stated as "marginal revenue equals marginal cost equals average cost equals price." The industry is in equilibrium when each firm is in equilibrium and when there is no entry or exit of firms into or out of the industry.

13. The long-run supply curve of a purely competitive industry shows the various quantities of the product that the firms in the industry will supply at various prices in long-run equilibrium.

14. A constant-cost industry is one in which the cost of production remains unchanged as the industry expands by the addition of new firms. Constant-cost industries have horizontal long-run supply curves.

15. An increasing-cost industry is one in which production costs rise as the industry expands by the addition of new firms. Increasing-cost industries have upward sloping long-run supply curves.

16. Although examples of pure competition may be hard to find in the real world, the purely competitive model is useful as an ideal situation by which we may evaluate other types of market structures.

17. Pareto optimality exists when one person cannot be made better off without making someone else worse off.

18. If all markets are purely competitive, Pareto optimality will be realized.

TERMS FOR REVIEW

market structures (166)
industry (166)
imperfect competition (166)
pure (perfect, atomistic)
 competition (166)
price-taker (166)
monopolized market (167)
monopoly (167)
monopolistic competition (167)
oligopoly (167)
marginal revenue (169)
average revenue (171)

break-even point (173)
break-even level of output (173)
short-run shutdown point (173)
short-run supply curve (173)
normal profits (175)
industry equilibrium (176)
long-run supply curve (176)
constant-cost industry (176)
increasing-cost industry (177)
marginal cost pricing (178)
Pareto optimality (efficiency) (178)

QUESTIONS FOR REVIEW AND DISCUSSION

1. What are the characteristics of each of the following market structures? (L.O.1)
   (a) pure competition
   (b) monopoly
   (c) monopolistic competition
   (d) oligopoly

2. Why would you expect a single price to prevail in a purely competitive market? (L.O.1)

3. "The purely competitive firm is a price-taker and a quantity-adjuster." Explain. (L.O.1)

4. Distinguish between competition and perfect competition. (L.O.1)

5. Why are marginal revenue and price identical for a firm in pure competition? (L.O.1,2)

6. Show that a firm will maximize its profits when it produces a level of output at which marginal revenue equals marginal cost. (L.O.2)

7. Explain how to derive the short-run supply curve for a firm trying to maximize its profits in pure competition. (L.O.3)

8. Explain the process of deriving the industry's short-run supply curve. (L.O.4)

9. Explain how a firm could be in equilibrium in the short run when it is incurring losses. (L.O.2)

10. "The objective of the firm is to maximize its profits. If this objective is achieved, the firm is in equilibrium. The firm cannot therefore be in equilibrium if it is not making a profit." Discuss this statement. (L.O.2)

11. Describe the process by which a purely competitive industry reaches long-run equilibrium. (L.O.5)

12. "The purely competitive model is completely useless in a world where pure competition rarely exists." Discuss. (General)

13. How useful is the economic model of perfect competition? (General)

14. What is Pareto optimality? Mention at least four conditions that are necessary for the existence of Pareto optimality. (General)

15. Is there any relation between pure competition and Pareto optimality? Explain. (General)

PROBLEMS AND EXERCISES

1. The demand schedule facing a firm is shown below in columns 1 and 2 of Table 10.6. (General)

TABLE 10.6

Demand and revenue data.

Price (1)	Quantity (2)	TR (3)	AR (4)	MR (5)
$5	1			
5	2			
5	3			
5	4			
5	5			
5	6			

(a) Compute total revenue, average revenue, and marginal revenue, and complete the table.

(b) Plot average revenue and marginal revenue on a graph.

(c) On the same graph, plot the demand curve.

(d) What do you notice about the demand curve and the average revenue curve?

2. The Wisepro Manufacturing Company has the cost data shown in Table 10.7. The market price of the product is $5. (L.O.2)

TABLE 10.7

Cost data for Wisepro.

Quantity (units)	Total cost ($)
0	10
1	14
2	17
3	19
4	20
5	21
6	23
7	26
8	30
9	35
10	44

(a) What is Wisepro's total revenue at each level of output?

(b) Calculate Wisepro's total profit or loss at each level of output.

(c) At what level of output does Wisepro earn maximum profits?

(d) Graph the total revenue and the total cost curves for Wisepro and indicate the maximum total profit.

3. Referring to Table 10.7, and given that the price of the product is $5: (L.O.3)

(a) compute the firm's marginal cost and marginal revenue at each level of output;

(b) graph the firm's marginal cost and marginal revenue curves;

(c) from your graph, determine the firm's optimal (best) output level.

4. Table 10.8 refers to a purely competitive firm whose objective is to maximize its profits. (L.O.2,3)

TABLE 10.8

Cost and revenue data for a firm.

Q	TFC	TVC	TC	AFC	AVC	ATC	MC	MR	TR
0	100	0	100						0
1	100	25							100
2	100	35							200
3	100	50							300
4	100	100							400
5	100	180							500
6	100	340							600
7	100	560							700

(a) Determine the price of the product.

(b) Complete the table.

(c) If the price were $80, should the firm continue to operate? Why or why not?

(d) If the price were to fall to $40, should the firm continue to operate? Why or why not?

(e) What is the minimum price this firm must receive in order for it to continue to operate in the short run?

5. Referring to Table 10.8, draw the firm's short-run supply curve. (L.O.3)

6. You find that you are operating your small grocery store at a loss but are covering your variable costs. Should you continue to operate in the short run? Explain. (L.O.2)

7. The information in Table 10.9 is provided for the Best Hits Recording Company, which is a purely competitive firm. The price of its product is $20. (L.O.2)

TABLE 10.9

Cost data for Best Hits Recording Company.

Q (units)	TR ($)	MR ($)	TC ($)	MC ($)	Profits ($)
1			30		
2			40		
3			48		
4			58		
5			70		
6			90		
7			120		
8			160		

(a) Complete the table and determine what level of output the firm should produce in order to maximize its profits.

(b) On graph paper, draw the total revenue and total cost curves. At what level of output is the difference between total revenue and total cost greatest?

(c) On graph paper, draw the marginal revenue and marginal cost curves. At what level of output do these curves intersect?

8. Referring to Figure 10.9, describe the firm's position in terms of profitability for each marginal revenue curve shown. (L.O.2)

FIGURE 10.9

ATC, AVC, MC, and MR curves.

9. Figure 10.10 is for a purely competitive firm that is a profit-maximizer. The price of the product is $50. (L.O.2)

FIGURE 10.10

Price and cost for a purely competitive firm.

(a) What is the maximum profit this firm can make on all units produced?

(b) At this profit level, what is the firm's total revenue?

(c) What is the firm's total cost at the profit-maximizing level of output?

10. "Introductory economics textbooks are very much alike." Go to the library and pick out a few modern textbooks on introductory economics. Look through the textbooks and see if your research supports the above assertion. Using your knowledge of a competitive industry, explain why introductory economics textbooks are so much alike.

11
C H A P T E R

THE THEORY OF MONOPOLY

Learning Objectives

After studying this chapter, you should be able to:

1 discuss barriers to entry

2 describe the demand curve for a firm in monopoly

3 describe the marginal revenue of a monopolist

4 discuss the profit level of the monopolist

5 understand the relation between elasticity and marginal revenue

6 compare monopoly with pure competition

7 understand monopoly regulation

8 discuss price discrimination

The price of monopoly is upon every occasion the highest which can be got.

Adam Smith, *Wealth of Nations*

INTRODUCTION

In the previous chapter, we examined the determination of price and output under pure competition. In this chapter, we shall look at the opposite extreme and examine price and output determination under monopoly. The pure monopolist is the sole producer of a product that has no close substitutes. The firm and the industry are identical. Although this definition seems simple and straightforward enough, it raises some important issues. First, the notion of close substitutes is subjective and arbitrary. While most people may agree that coffee and tea are close substitutes, they may not agree so readily on electricity and oil. Electricity and oil may be considered close substitutes for heating purposes, but very poor substitutes, or not substitutes at all, for lighting purposes. Second (and this is related to the first), the definition of monopoly and the product that is monopolized are inseparable.

A definition of monopoly should indicate the market that is monopolized.

Just as it is difficult to find examples of pure competition in the real world, so too is it difficult to find examples of pure monopoly. The term **monopoly** often conjures up an image of a large firm that mercilessly takes advantage of consumers, controls price and output, and earns unconscionably large profits. But not all monopolies deserve this "bad guy" image. Public utilities are often monopolies. You may be able to think of some local monopolies in your area: the local public transit system or the water supply system, for example.

BARRIERS TO ENTRY

Monopolies exist because of certain barriers that block the entry of potential competitors.

For a monopoly to exist, there must be circumstances that restrict the entry of other firms into the particular monopolized industry. These prohibitive factors or circumstances are called **barriers to entry**. Let us look at some of these barriers.

Learning Objective 1:
discuss barriers to entry

BARRIERS CREATED BY THE GOVERNMENT

You are a very enterprising economics student and you have come up with an idea that you believe will earn you a great deal of money. You and your friends are going to pick up letters, mainly from businesses, and deliver them to their destination anywhere within a radius of 30 km from the downtown core. You know you can do this at a cost significantly below what the post office charges and still make a very good profit.

Patents and franchises are barriers to entry.

Hold it! You can't do it. The government won't let you. It's illegal, so you will have to dream up some other scheme for making your million dollars. The government prevents other firms from entering certain industries and competing with the existing firms. This type of legal barrier is quite common and quite effective in maintaining monopolies. A patent is one of the legal devices used to maintain monopolies. A **patent** is an exclusive right that the government grants to a producer to produce a product. During the term of the patent (a period of 17 years), the producer is protected against potential competitors. Patents can often be circumvented, however, for although other firms are not allowed to produce an identical product, they can produce a product that is quite similar. The government grants approximately 21 000 new patents each year.

Ownership or control of an essential input can be an effective barrier to entry into a monopolized market.

A government may also grant an exclusive **franchise** to a producer to operate a business or provide a service in a certain area. The granting of a franchise means that no other producer may legally operate an identical business or provide an identical service in the same area. You should not interpret the foregoing to mean that only governments can grant franchises. Private concerns may also grant franchises. If you obtain a franchise from McDonald's, you are protected against competition from any other McDonald's restaurant, since another one will not be established within the boundaries of your business area.

You will enjoy a monopoly on McDonald's hamburgers, but you will face competition from Harvey's, Wendy's, Burger King, and other restaurants.

BARRIERS CREATED BY OWNERSHIP OR CONTROL OF ESSENTIAL RAW MATERIALS

If a particular firm owns a certain raw material essential to the production of a certain product, and if the firm does not allow any other firm to use that essential material, then obviously a monopoly situation will develop. For example, bauxite is a necessary ingredient in the production of aluminum. If one company owns or controls all sources of bauxite in the country, and if the import of bauxite or aluminum is strictly forbidden by law, then that company will have a monopoly in the domestic market for aluminum. One South African company has a virtual monopoly on the world's diamond market since it owns or controls most of the world's diamond mines.

BARRIERS CREATED BY ECONOMIES OF SCALE

Substantial economies of scale may effectively block the entry of new firms into an industry.

Because of substantial economies of scale, one firm may be able to supply the entire market more cheaply than two or more firms. Often, the cost of establishing an efficient plant in this case is enormous, and the minimum average cost will be covered only at a level of output large enough to supply the entire market. If there are two or more firms in this type of industry, the average cost will be quite high. This is so because these firms divide among them the total market supply. Consider how much it would cost to start up a telephone company to provide telephone service to people in a certain area. Now compare that cost with the cost to an existing telephone company of providing the same service to those people. The market situation in which a single firm is likely to be more efficient than two or more firms is often referred to as **natural monopoly**. Examples of natural monopolies are telephone companies, gas companies, and electrical power companies like Hydro-Québec and Ontario Hydro.

In a natural monopoly, a single firm is more efficient than two or more firms.

THE DEMAND CURVE FOR A FIRM IN MONOPOLY

The monopolistic firm's demand curve is identical to the total demand curve for its product.

In Chapter 4, we noted that the market demand curve slopes downward from left to right. Since the monopolistic firm is the only firm in the industry, the demand curve of the monopolistic firm is exactly the same as the industry or market demand curve. If the monopolistic firm wishes to sell a larger quantity, it can do so by lowering the price of its product. If it increases the price of its product, the quantity that it can sell will decrease.

Learning Objective 2: describe the demand curve for a firm in monopoly

The monopolist cannot control both price and output at the same time.

Figure 11.1 shows a hypothetical demand curve for a monopolistic firm. At a price of $8, the monopolistic firm can sell 120 units. When the price is $4, it can sell 240 units. Note that the monopolistic firm is not a price-taker: it does have significant control over the price it charges for its product. However, it cannot completely control both price and quantity. If the monopolist has the demand curve shown in Figure 11.1, it cannot, for example, charge a price of $8 and sell more than 120 units. Once it sets the price, the quantity that it can sell at that price is determined by the demand curve. The monopolistic firm must operate within the constraint imposed on it by its demand curve. The fact that the demand curve facing the monopolistic firm slopes downward tells us that the demand for its product is not perfectly inelastic.

PROBLEM SOLVING 11-1

A monopolistic firm is in an enviable position because it can charge any price it wishes and sell as much as it pleases at that price. Is this a true statement?

FIGURE 11.1

A monopolistic firm's demand curve.

The monopolist faces a downward-sloping demand curve.

THE MARGINAL REVENUE OF THE MONOPOLIST

Learning Objective 3: describe the marginal revenue of a monopolist

Recall that, under pure competition, demand (or average revenue) and marginal revenue are identical. Under monopoly however, this is not the case. It becomes necessary then, to distinguish between demand or average revenue and marginal revenue. Marginal revenue is crucial in deciding whether or not the firm should produce a little more or a little less in order to maximize its profits. A declining average revenue implies a declining marginal revenue. (Remember the magnetic effect of the marginal on the average). Moreover, the marginal revenue will fall at a faster rate than the average revenue. This must be the case since, in order to sell a larger volume of output, the monopolistic firm receives a lower price on those units it could have sold at a higher price had it not chosen to increase its output. Table 11.1 helps to illustrate this idea.

Table 11.1 shows that the monopolistic firm can sell one unit of output if the price is $10. The firm can sell two units only if it charges a price of $9. Total revenue is now $18 — an increase of $8 due to the sale of the additional unit. In other words, marginal revenue is now $8. The firm could have sold the first unit for $9, thus losing $1 of the selling price on that unit. Similarly, the firm can sell three units only if the price is $8. Total

TABLE 11.1

Hypothetical demand and marginal revenue for a monopolist.

P ($)	Q (units)	TR ($)	MR ($)
10	1	10	
9	2	18	8
8	3	24	6
7	4	28	4
6	5	30	2
5	6	30	0
4	7	28	-2
3	8	24	-4

The marginal revenue of the monopolistic firm is less than its average revenue.

revenue is now $24 and marginal revenue $6. The firm could also have sold the first two units for $9 each, thus losing $1 of the selling price on each of the first two units. This exercise shows that:

for a monopoly, marginal revenue is less than average revenue, and falls at a faster rate than average revenue.

Notice that price and average revenue are identical — a relation you learned in the previous chapter. Figure 11.2 shows the relation between average revenue and marginal revenue.

FIGURE 11.2

Average revenue and marginal revenue of a monopolist.

When the average revenue curve slopes downward, the marginal revenue curve slopes downward also, but more steeply than the average revenue curve.

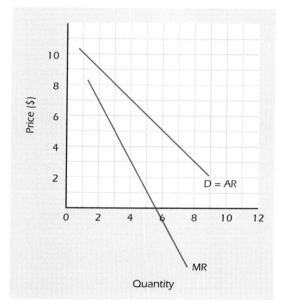

Note that if both the demand and marginal revenue curves are linear and downward sloping, then the marginal revenue curve will bisect any horizontal line between the vertical axis and the demand curve. In Figure 11.3, the marginal revenue curve bisects 0Q and HK.

FIGURE 11.3

Relation between linear demand and marginal revenue curves.

The marginal revenue curve lies halfway between the demand curve and the vertical axis at all points.

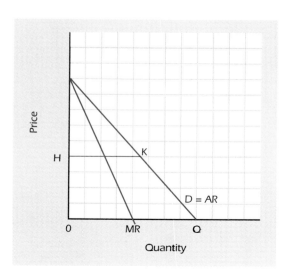

We have seen that the concept of marginal revenue is important in determining the output level at which the firm maximizes its profits. (Recall the MR = MC condition discussed in the previous chapter). Let us now determine the equilibrium position of a monopolistic firm.

EQUILIBRIUM UNDER MONOPOLY

The monopolist must decide how much to produce and what price to charge in order to maximize profits.

The firm in pure competition is a price-taker and a quantity adjuster. That is, the purely competitive firm accepts the price determined by the market for the product, and then decides on the level of output that will maximize its profits. For a monopolistic firm, the price of the product is not given. The monopolistic firm, therefore, faces two problems in terms of its profit maximization objective: the problem of deciding what price to charge for its product and the problem of deciding what level of output to produce. Once it sets the price, the maximum amount that it can sell at that price is determined by its demand curve.

The monopolistic firm maximizes its profits when its marginal cost equals its marginal revenue.

We can reasonably assume that the monopolistic firm faces a cost situation similar to that faced by a firm in any other type of market structure. Table 11.2 contains hypothetical cost and revenue figures for a firm in a monopoly situation. Profits are maximized at a level of output of four units, where the difference between total revenue ($28) and total cost ($21) is greatest at $7, and the price $7. Alternatively, using the marginal-revenue-equals-marginal-cost condition, we arrive at the same conclusion that the monopolistic firm maximizes its profits by producing four units and selling at a price of $7.

Figure 11.4 illustrates graphically the relations between the data shown in Table 11.2. In this figure, MR = MC at a level of output of four units. If the monopolistic firm charges a price of $7, it will maximize its profits. The maximum profit is shown on Diagram A as the greatest distance between TR and TC, and as the shaded area in Diagram B.

A monopolist may deliberately earn less than maximum profits.

We have determined the price-output combination that maximizes the profits of the monopolistic firm. Given the conditions of demand and cost, any other price-output combination results in lower profits for the monopolist. But whether or not the monopolist will choose to charge that particular price at which profit is greatest is another

TABLE 11.2

Hypothetical cost and revenue data for a monopolist.

Price ($)	Quantity (units)	Total cost ($)	Marginal cost ($)	Total revenue ($)	Marginal revenue ($)	Profits ($)
11	0	10		0		−10
			2		10	
10	1	12		10		−2
			3		8	
9	2	15		18		3
			2		6	
8	3	17		24		7
			4		4	
7	4	21		28		7
			5		2	
6	5	26		30		4
			7		0	
5	6	33		30		−3
			10		−2	
4	7	43		28		−15
			17		−4	
3	8	60		24		−36

FIGURE 11.4

Profit maximization for a monopolist.

DIAGRAM A

DIAGRAM B

question. For several reasons, the monopolist may decide against earning maximum profits. First, extremely high profits provide incentive for other firms to attempt to break through the barriers and end the monopoly. Second, social conscience may prevent those who make the decisions in the monopolistic firm from undertaking measures necessary to maximize profits. Public opinion may enter into such a decision. In this case, the firm may decide to earn a satisfactory profit instead of trying to earn maximum profits. Third, the monopolist may want to avoid provoking the government to regulate its price and other profit factors.

The firm shown in Figure 11.4 is earning positive economic profits (its price is above its average total cost). This situation could continue even in the long run since there are barriers that effectively block the entry of new firms into this industry. If potential firms are able to surmount the entry barriers and compete with the monopoly, the monopoly will be destroyed and the positive economic profits will dwindle away in the long run.

PROBLEM SOLVING 11-2

Can a monopolistic firm always succeed in increasing its profits by raising its price?

THE MONOPOLIST'S PROFIT LEVEL

Even a monopolist may suffer losses.

Learning Objective 4: discuss the profit level of the monopolist

A commonly held misconception is that monopolistic firms always make huge profits. In fact, while some monopolies make large profits, others incur losses. In some cases, excessively high production costs result in losses to the firm. Such a situation is illustrated in Figure 11.5. At an output level of Q_1, this monopolistic firm is doing the best it can under the existing circumstances. Nevertheless, the firm is suffering losses because the price, P, is below average total cost. The price is, however, above the firm's average variable cost. The firm, then, will likely continue to operate in the short run in order to minimize its losses. These losses are shown as the shaded area in Figure 11.5. In the long run, however, the firm will likely shift its resources into more profitable uses.

The firm may try to improve its profit position by increasing its total revenue. It would be possible to increase total revenue if the firm could raise its price without reducing quantity demanded. Quite often, this is easier said than done. The firm's demand curve would have to shift to the right. Advertising is one means of trying to shift the firm's demand curve to the right.

FIGURE 11.5

A monopolist incurring losses.

Marginal revenue and marginal cost may be equal at a price below average cost.

APPLICATION

Research and Development

We have seen that not all monopolies make huge profits. However, if firms in an industry perceive that it is profitable to become a monopolist, they will vie for monopoly position. One way of winning the race to become a monopoly is through research and development (R&D) that will enable a firm to be the first to introduce a product on the market. Pharmaceutical companies spend hundreds of thousands of dollars on R&D. A question well worth asking is, why do firms spend so much money on R&D?

Let's assume that a pharmaceutical company estimates that there is a very high demand for a drug that increases intelligence. The first company that produces such a drug and obtains government approval to market it will enjoy monopoly power. The winning firm will be able to sell the product at a monopoly price and earn enormous profits for the duration of the time that it has the sole right to market that drug. Although the firm that wins the race earns impressive profits, we must note that the losers also spend a great deal on R&D even though they do not produce and market the drug.

THE INEFFICIENT MONOPOLIST

Inefficiency will reduce the monopolist's profits.

X-inefficiency is the failure to use resources in their most economically efficient way.

A monopolistic firm that adopts the attitude that customers have no alternative but to buy the product from that firm may not feel the need to control cost adequately. Such inefficiency can destroy the profit potential of the monopoly. The term **X-inefficiency** is used to describe the situation in which the firm does not produce its output at the lowest possible cost. X-inefficiency may result from keeping on unproductive workers out of loyalty, putting unproductive relatives and friends on the payroll, or padding executives' expense accounts.

Figure 11.6 illustrates the effect of X-inefficiency on the profit level of the monopolistic firm. Diagram A shows an efficient monopolist, while Diagram B shows an inefficiently run monopolistic firm. The demand and marginal revenue curves of both firms are identical. The efficient monopolist produces its output at an average total cost of C_1. Note that the average total cost (ATC_1) of the inefficient monopolist is higher than that (ATC) of the efficient monopolist. This illustrates X-inefficiency. The smaller profit earned by the inefficient monopolist is due to X-inefficiency.

FIGURE 11.6

The effect of X-inefficiency.

X-inefficiency raises the costs of the monopolistic firm and reduces its profits.

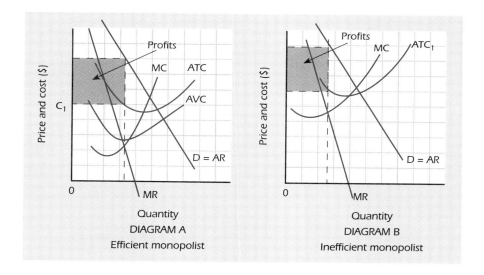

DIAGRAM A
Efficient monopolist

DIAGRAM B
Inefficient monopolist

ELASTICITY, TOTAL REVENUE, AND MARGINAL REVENUE

Remember that if the demand for a product is elastic, a reduction in price will cause total revenue to increase. But total revenue can increase only if marginal revenue is positive. It follows, therefore, that if marginal revenue is positive, the demand for the product in that range must be elastic.

When the price elasticity of demand is unitary, a reduction in the price of the product will not change total revenue. If total revenue is stable, then marginal revenue must be zero. Therefore, it follows that when marginal revenue is zero, the elasticity of demand for the product at that price must be one.

Learning Objective 5:
understand the relation between elasticity and marginal revenue

An inelastic demand implies that a reduction in price will cause total revenue to fall. But total revenue can fall only if marginal revenue is negative. Hence, when marginal revenue is negative, the demand for the product must be inelastic. Table 11.3 shows the relation between demand, total revenue, and marginal revenue for a monopolist.

	Q (units)	P ($)	TR ($)	MR ($)
TABLE 11.3	0	10.50	0	
Demand, total rev-				10
enue, and marginal	1	10.00	10	
revenue for a monopo-				9
list.	2	9.50	19	
				8
	3	9.00	27	
				7
	4	8.50	34	
				6
	5	8.00	40	
				5
	6	7.50	45	
				4
	7	7.00	49	
				3
	8	6.50	52	
				2
	9	6.00	54	
				1
	10	5.50	55	
				0
	11	5.00	55	
				−1
	12	4.50	54	
				−2
	13	4.00	52	
				−3
	14	3.50	49	
				−4
	15	3.00	45	
				−5
	16	2.50	40	
				−6
	17	2.00	34	
				−7
	18	1.50	27	
				−8
	19	1.00	19	
				−9
	20	0.50	10	

The relationship is illustrated graphically in Figure 11.7. At an output level less than Q_1, the marginal revenue is positive, the total revenue is rising, and the demand for the product is elastic in that range. At an output level of Q_1, marginal revenue equals 0, total revenue is at its maximum, and demand is unitary elastic at a price of P. At an output level greater than Q_1, marginal revenue is negative, total revenue is falling, and the demand is inelastic at any price below P.

The monopolistic firm incurs additional costs as it increases its output — that is, its marginal cost is positive. This implies that marginal revenue and marginal cost will intersect at some positive value. But if marginal revenue is positive, the demand is elastic. This leads to the following proposition:

A profit-maximizing monopolistic firm will operate only within that range where the demand for its product is elastic.

FIGURE 11.7

Relation between demand, total revenue, marginal revenue, and elasticity.

PROBLEM SOLVING 11-3

Demonstrate that if marginal cost is zero, the monopolistic firm will maximize its profits by producing at that point where the price elasticity of demand is one.

MONOPOLY VERSUS PURE COMPETITION

Learning Objective 6:
compare monopoly with pure competition

Allocative efficiency exists when resources are optimally allocated. This occurs when price equals marginal cost.

In the previous chapter, we noted that the model of pure competition served as a convenient reference for the evaluation of other market structures. It is a useful exercise to compare the price and output behaviours of a purely competitive industry with those of a monopoly.

First, in a purely competitive market, each firm charges a price that just equals its marginal cost. Economists refer to this situation as **allocative efficiency**. In pure competition, resources are allocated efficiently. In a monopoly, on the other hand, the price is above marginal cost. Therefore, resources are not allocated efficiently. This situation is illustrated graphically in Figure 11.8. We assume that the cost curves are the same in both market structures. AR represents the demand or average revenue of the monopolist, which is the same as the industry demand curve. For convenience, we show the position of one of the firms in the competitive industry. The subscript F indicates that the reference is to the firm. To maximize profits, the monopolist produces an output of Q_m and charges a price of P_m, thus equating marginal revenue and marginal cost. The purely competitive price will be P_c, which equals marginal cost. Note that P_m is greater than marginal cost.

FIGURE 11.8

Monopoly vs. competition.

The monopolist charges a price that is higher than MC.

Compared with pure competition, the monopoly output is less, and unit cost is higher.

Second, the purely competitive output is produced at a minimum unit cost. This is not the case under monopoly. The monopolist produces its output at a higher unit cost. Figure 11.8 shows that the profit-maximizing monopolist produces at point A on the average cost curve. In the long run, however, production in a purely competitive industry takes place at point B, the minimum point on the average cost curve.

Third, other things being equal, the monopolist produces less output than the competitive industry does. As illustrated in Figure 11.8, the monopolist produces an output of Q_m while the competitive industry produces an output of Q_c. This suggests that employment will be greater in the competitive industry than in the monopolistic firm. The monopolist charges a higher price and supplies a smaller quantity than the purely competitive industry does.

A monopolist may earn positive profits even in the long run.

Finally, if the monopolistic firm's price is greater than its average cost, it will earn positive profits. If the firms in a purely competitive industry earn positive profits in the short run, other firms will enter the industry and compete until profits settle down at zero in the long run. In the case of the monopolist, however, positive profits may remain because of barriers preventing other firms from entering the industry.

PROBLEM SOLVING 11-4

How does the existence of economies of scale affect the general conclusion that pure competition results in a lower price for the consumer and a larger quantity of output than monopoly does?

THE REGULATED MONOPOLY

Learning Objective 7:
understand monopoly regulation

A firm exhibiting monopoly power (market power) can control either output or price, but not both.

Regulated monopolies are controlled by government legislation.

The analysis presented in the previous section suggests that monopolies have certain social consequences that are less desirable than those associated with pure competition. Compared with pure competition, for example, the monopolist produces a smaller output at a higher unit cost and sells at a higher price, other things being equal. This ability to exert control over price and output is called **monopoly power** or **market power**. The misallocation of resources associated with monopolies has no parallel in the purely competitive market structure. The prices charged by many natural monopolies are determined by government regulatory agencies. Let us now turn our attention to the ways in which a government or its regulatory agencies may **regulate monopolies**, and the consequences of such regulation.

MARGINAL-COST PRICING

One of the things we noted about a firm in a monopoly situation is that it will operate at a point where price is greater than marginal cost. From a social point of view, resources are optimally allocated when price equals marginal cost. Let us examine the consequences of a regulatory body setting the monopolist's price at a level equal to its marginal cost. Figure 11.9 will help to clarify the effects of monopoly regulation.

FIGURE 11.9

Monopoly regulation.

Regulation may force a monopolist to equate price and marginal cost, or to equate price and average cost, or to produce that output at which average cost is at its minimum.

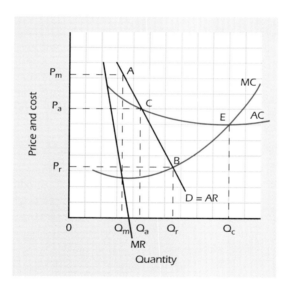

The diagram illustrates a natural monopoly. Note that because of huge fixed costs, the average revenue curve cuts the average cost curve while the latter is still falling. The unregulated monopolist, who is a profit-maximizer, produces an output of Q_m and sells at a price of P_m since, at this point, marginal revenue equals marginal cost (position A in Figure 11.9). A regulation that sets price equal to marginal cost will cause the monopolist to produce an output of Q_r at a price of P_r (position B). By setting a price of P_r, the regulatory agency prevents the monopolist from restricting output in order to exact a higher price. *Marginal-cost pricing regulation* does not necessarily result in losses for the monopolist, but it sometimes does. The firm depicted in Figure 11.9 incurs a loss by operating where price equals marginal cost. Since no firm wants to continue to incur losses indefinitely, this firm will have to take measures to survive, or leave the industry. If the monopoly is considered to be essential, the government may decide to take over its operation and endure the losses resulting from marginal-cost pricing, or it could subsidize the monopoly. But the notion of a government subsidizing a private monopoly is likely to incite public indignation.

AVERAGE-COST PRICING

If the regulatory agency considers marginal-cost pricing to be inappropriate, it may consider average-cost pricing as an alternative. *Average-cost pricing regulation* sets the price of the product equal to the average cost (position C in Figure 11.9). The monopolist will produce an output of Q_a at a price of P_a. This alternative eliminates any monopoly profits that the monopolist may otherwise have made. Average-cost pricing accords with the idea of a fair return on the owners' resources. Note that average-cost pricing results in a level of output that, though greater than the unregulated monopoly output, is still less than the socially optimum output of Q_r, where price equals marginal cost.

MINIMUM AVERAGE-COST PRICING

Finally, the regulatory agency may choose to have the monopolist operate at the lowest point on the average cost curve (point E in Figure 11.9). If the average cost curve declines over a large range of output as in Figure 11.9, this minimum point could occur at a level of output too large for the market served by the monopolist.

In order to operate at the minimum point on the average cost curve, this monopolist would have to produce a level of output of Q_c — clearly more than the firm would be able to sell at any price. The alternative chosen by the regulatory body ultimately depends on its objective. In any case, the regulated monopoly produces a larger output and sells at a lower price than if the monopoly were not regulated.

THE DISCRIMINATING MONOPOLIST

Up to this point in our analysis, we have assumed implicitly that the monopolist charges all of its customers the same price. In certain circumstances, the monopolist may find it profitable to charge different prices to different buyers for the same good or service. This practice is called **price discrimination**, defined as the practice of selling a product to different buyers or groups of buyers at different prices for reasons unrelated to cost differences.

Learning Objective 8: discuss price discrimination

Bell Canada, for example, charges commercial users of its telephone service one price and residential users a different price. Many suppliers of electricity also have different rates for commercial and residential users. Similarly, lawyers may charge a wealthy client more than they charge a poor one for a similar case; or a company may sell goods in a foreign market at a lower price than it charges in the domestic market.

To practice price discrimination, the monopolist must be able to group buyers into different classes on some basis, and prevent arbitrage dealings.

Arbitrage transactions occur when product is bought in a low-price market for resale in a high-price market.

For price discrimination to be possible, two conditions must be satisfied. First, the monopolistic firm must be able to group the buyers of its product into different classes such as rich and poor, adults and children, or residential and commercial. Second, the monopolist must be able to maintain a separation between the markets in which the product is sold so that buyers will not be able to engage in **arbitrage transactions** (buying in one market and selling in another, thereby making a profit by the price differential in the two markets). Those who buy in the market with the lower price must not be able to sell in the market with the higher price. If the monopolist cannot separate the markets in this way, the price will tend to rise in the cheaper market and fall in the more expensive market until the price differential is eliminated. The two conditions stated above are necessary for price discrimination to exist. They do not, however, ensure the profitability of price discrimination. Price discrimination will be profitable only if the price elasticity of demand is different in each market in which the monopolist sells its product.

Price discrimination will be profitable only if the price elasticity of demand in each market is different.

The following example illustrates why price discrimination is profitable. Suppose there are only two groups of people — students and professors — buying a certain product. Suppose also that students are willing to pay $10 per unit while the professors are willing to pay only $6. Obviously, the monopolistic firm can increase its profits by charging a price of $10 to the students and a price of $6 to the professors. By not charging a single price of $6, the monopolist has succeeded in preventing the students from paying only $6 when they would be willing to pay $10. If, on the other hand, the monopolist charges a single price of $10, the professors will not purchase any of the product. We can use the concept of consumer's surplus discussed in Chapter 6 to illustrate why the monopolist benefits from price discrimination. By charging each consumer the maximum amount that he or she is willing to pay, the monopolist captures the entire amount of the consumers' surplus.

THE DISTRIBUTION OF OUTPUT BETWEEN THE MARKETS

We now turn our attention to the decision faced by the discriminating monopoly. The discriminating monopoly must decide how much to sell in each market and at what price. We can analyze the behaviour of the discriminating monopoly with the help of Figure 11.10. Diagrams A and B show the demand and marginal revenue curves in two markets, A and B. Here we assume, for simplicity, that the marginal cost is constant in each market at 0C. In order to maximize profits, the monopolistic firm will sell, in each market, an amount such that marginal revenue equals marginal cost. The firm will therefore sell Q_a units in market A and Q_b units in market B. The price in market A will be P_a, while the price in market B will be P_b. Note that the higher price occurs in the market with the less elastic demand.

FIGURE 11.10

The distribution of output by a discriminating monopolist.

To maximize profits, the discriminating monopolist will allocate output in the various markets in such a way that marginal revenue equals marginal cost in each of the markets.

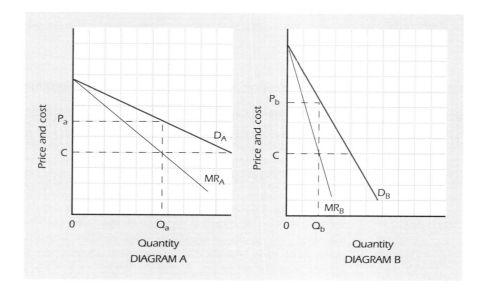

DIAGRAM A

DIAGRAM B

THE EFFECTS OF PRICE DISCRIMINATION

We have seen that by engaging in price discrimination, the monopolistic firm can increase its profits. Let us now compare the output of a discriminating monopoly with that of a non-discriminating monopoly. Figure 11.11 illustrates that a non-discriminating monopoly will produce an output of Q_1, where marginal revenue equals marginal cost. If it engages in complete price discrimination, selling each unit at the maximum price that a consumer is willing to pay, its demand curve will, in effect, become its marginal revenue curve. The discriminating monopoly will equate marginal revenue and marginal cost and thus produce an output of Q_2 units. It is unlikely that the monopolist will be able to practise complete price discrimination, because this would require the firm to know exactly the maximum price that each buyer is willing to pay. However, we can conclude that a discriminating monopoly will produce a greater output than a non-discriminating monopoly.

FIGURE 11.11

Discriminating and non-discriminating monopolists.

Price discrimination allows the monopolist to produce a greater output than would be the case without price discrimination.

IS PRICE DISCRIMINATION BAD?

There can be little doubt that many of those who pay the higher prices under price discrimination consider the practice to be unfair. It is also clear that price discrimination is beneficial to the monopolists who practise it. Let us now proceed beyond these obvious facts and delve more deeply into the pros and cons of price discrimination.

The pros

Many goods and services might not be produced if the monopolist were not able to practise price discrimination.

On the positive side, we may note that many goods and services might not be produced at all if the monopolist were not to engage in price discrimination. For example, physicians in small remote communities may find it worthwhile to keep their practices in those communities only if they can charge their wealthy clients a higher price than they can their poorer clients. Similarly, price discrimination in airfares makes it possible for many parents to take their children on vacation. Price discrimination along these lines seems to be desirable and therefore should not be condemned.

The cons

On the negative side, the practice of price discrimination may be carried to the point where the price falls below marginal cost. For example, price discrimination in electricity rates could result in such low rates to residential users that they end up wasting electricity. When price is allowed to fall below marginal cost, a misallocation of resources results. The amount of resources that would flow into the industry is above the social optimum. As another example, consider the case of a public transit system. Price discrimination is usually practised in favour of children and the elderly. If price discrimination is carried too far in this case, taxpayers may have to subsidize the transit system. Resources that could be better allocated elsewhere would be diverted into this industry.

APPLICATIONS

The analytical tools that we have introduced in this chapter can help us to organize our thoughts properly on certain issues relating to decisions in a monopolistic situation. In this section, we shall study the effects of taxes on monopolistic behaviour. First, we shall study the effect of an excise tax. (You will recall that an excise tax is a tax imposed on a particular commodity that is domestically produced.) We shall then study the effect of a tax on the profits of the monopolist.

THE EFFECT OF AN EXCISE TAX

Let us assume that a monopolist has to pay an excise tax on each unit of a product that it sells. Will the monopolist raise the price by the amount of the tax? Many people would answer yes to this question, but let us analyze the situation with the help of Figure 11.12. We assume, for simplicity, that the demand and marginal revenue curves are linear, and that the monopolist has constant marginal cost. AR and MR are, as usual, average revenue and marginal revenue and MC is marginal cost before the imposition of the tax. According to Figure 11.12, the monopolist produces a quantity of Q and charges a price of P in order to maximize profits. After the tax is imposed, the marginal cost curve shifts up by the amount of the tax, to MC_t. The firm now produces an output of

FIGURE 11.12

The effect of an excise tax.

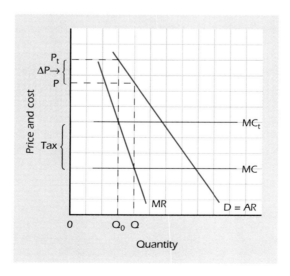

Q_0 and charges a price of P_t. The increase in price from P to P_t is less than the tax (the distance between MC and MC_t). We can therefore draw the following conclusion:

If an excise tax is imposed on each unit of a commodity sold by a monopolist, the price will rise, but by an amount less than the tax.

THE EFFECT OF A TAX ON PROFITS

In Canada, as in many other countries, firms are required to pay taxes on their profits. Let us assume that a monopolist has to pay 30% of its profits in taxes. Should it raise its price by 30% in order to shift the burden of the tax on to its customers? Let us investigate. Let us assume that the monopolist is maximizing its profits by equating its marginal revenue and its marginal cost. If it raises its price, its profits will fall. It makes more sense to pay the tax out of the maximum profits than out of reduced profits that would result from an increase in price.

The data in Table 11.4 illustrate this point. Clearly, the price that maximizes profits before taxes is $5. After taxes, the price that maximizes profits is still $5.

TABLE 11.4	Price	Profits before tax	30% tax	Profits after tax
Profits before and after tax.	$6	$10 000	$3 000	$ 7 000
	5	15 000	4 500	10 500
	4	9 500	2 850	6 650

GLOBAL PERSPECTIVE

De Beers and Diamonds

The De Beers Company of South Africa provides a famous example of a monopoly over a commodity — diamonds. De Beers has exercised control over the world production of diamonds for many years, either through ownership of diamond mines or by entering into marketing agreements with other mine owners. De Beers Consolidated Mines has interests in 19 diamond mines in Africa, and through its cartel, the Central Selling Organization (CSO), it wields tremendous control over much of the world's diamond production.

But the power of the cartel has been challenged by diamond producers in Angola, Australia, Canada, and Russia. Moreover, monopoly pricing practices by De Beers have made the production of diamond substitutes attractive. In the past, it was relatively easy even for a nonprofessional in the field to distinguish a real diamond from a synthetic diamond, so the synthetic product was not really considered a close substitute for the real product. However, technological advances in the production of synthetic diamonds have made them so close in appearance to real diamonds that it is now extremely difficult for most purchasers of diamonds to distinguish between real and synthetic. The production of close substitutes for diamonds has weakened the monopoly position of De Beers in the world market for diamonds.

CHAPTER SUMMARY

1. In a monopoly situation, only one firm sells a product that has no close substitutes. Since substitutes can be found for most products, examples of pure monopoly are hard to find in the real world.

2. Monopolies exist because of barriers to entry into a market. Such barriers include legal barriers such as patent rights, ownership of essential raw materials, and economies of scale.

3. Since the monopolistic firm is the only firm in the industry, its demand curve is identical to the industry demand curve and slopes downward from left to right.

4. Because the demand curve of the monopolistic firm slopes downward, the marginal revenue curve must also slope downward. Also marginal revenue will be less than demand or average revenue in the case of a monopoly.

5. The monopolist maximizes profits at a level of output at which marginal revenue equals marginal cost. However, the monopolist's price will exceed marginal cost. Fear of government regulation, fear of the entry of other firms into the market, and a desire not to incite public outcry are some of the factors that may prevent a monopolist from seeking maximum profits.

6. When marginal revenue is positive, demand is elastic. When marginal revenue is zero, demand is unitary elastic; and when marginal revenue is negative, demand is inelastic. The profit-maximizing monopolist will never operate at an output level at which demand is inelastic.

7. Compared with purely competitive firms, the monopolist produces a smaller output and sells at a higher price. Also, the monopolist may earn positive economic profits in the long run. Any positive profits that a competitive firm may earn in the short run will disappear in the long run due to competition.

8. Because of certain socially undesirable consequences of monopolization, the government may regulate certain monopolies. The regulated monopoly usually produces a greater output and sells at a lower price than would be the case if the monopoly were unregulated.

9. Price discrimination is the practice of charging different prices among different buyers for the same product or service. Price discrimination is possible only if the buyers can be grouped into different classes and if the monopolist can prevent purchases in one market for resale in another.

10. Price discrimination is possible only if the price elasticity of demand in each market is different. The discriminating monopolist tries to capture the consumers' surplus.

11. The discriminating monopolist will produce an output at which marginal revenue equals marginal cost, and will distribute this output among the markets in such a way that marginal revenue equals marginal cost in each market.

12. The discriminating monopolist produces a greater output and sells at a lower price than a non-discriminating monopolist.

13. Price discrimination may result in the wasteful use of the product, but, on the other hand, it may make certain goods and services available to consumers, which might not be possible in the absence of price discrimination.

TERMS FOR REVIEW

monopoly (186)
barriers to entry (186)
patent (186)
franchise (186)
natural monopoly (187)
X-inefficiency (193)

allocative efficiency (195)
monopoly power (market power) (197)
regulated monopoly (197)
price discrimination (198)
arbitrage transactions (198)

QUESTIONS FOR REVIEW AND DISCUSSION

1. What difficulty is involved in defining a monopoly? (General)

2. Name and discuss factors that give rise to monopolies. (L.O.1)

3. Explain why a monopolist faces a downward-sloping demand curve. (L.O.2)

4. Give examples of monopolies in your area and explain why they are monopolies. (L.O.2)

5. Do monopolies always earn large positive economic profits? Explain. (L.O.4)

6. Explain why a monopolistic firm seeking to maximize its profits will not operate at a level of output and price range at which the demand for its product is inelastic. (L.O.5)

7. What considerations may lead a monopolist to seek less than maximum profits? (General)

8. "A profit-maximizing monopolist will always charge the highest possible price for its product." Discuss. (General)

9. By examining pricing and output decisions under monopoly, explain how monopolies affect the allocation of resources. (L.O.6)

10. Explain the term monopoly power. What actions might a government take to prevent the abuse of monopoly power? (L.O.7)

11. What problem may result from marginal-cost pricing regulation of a monopoly? (L.O.7)

12. From a social point of view, what advantages does pure competition have over monopoly? (L.O.6)

13. What is price discrimination? What circumstances encourage a monopolist to practise price discrimination? (L.O.8)

14. When is price discrimination possible? When is it profitable? (L.O.8)

15. Explain how a discriminating monopolist allocates output between two markets with different price elasticities of demand in order to maximize profits. (L.O.8)

16. What are the economic effects of price discrimination? (L.O.8)

17. Do you think that we should always condemn price discrimination? (L.O.8)

18. What are the pros and cons of price discrimination? (L.O.8)

PROBLEMS AND EXERCISES

1. Table 11. 5 shows the demand schedule for Clockwise Ltd., a monopolistic firm. (L.O.2,3)

   (a) Compute the marginal revenue for Clockwise at each level of output.

   (b) On a graph, plot the average revenue and the marginal revenue curves for Clockwise.

TABLE 11.5	Quantity	Price
Demand schedule for Clockwise.	1	$20.00
	2	17.50
	3	15.00
	4	12.50
	5	10.00
	6	7.50

2. Figure 11.13 represents Power Plus, a monopolistic firm. (L.O.4)

FIGURE 11.13

Revenue and cost curves for Power Plus.

(a) What output should Power Plus produce in order to maximize its profits?
(b) What price should it charge?
(c) What is the maximum total profit that this firm can earn?
(d) What is the firm's total revenue at the profit-maximizing output?
(e) What is the firm's total cost when it is maximizing its profits?

3. The data presented in Table 11.6 are for the Isotemp Corporation, which is a monopoly. (L.O.3,4)

   (a) Construct a table showing Isotemp's marginal cost and marginal revenue.

   (b) Plot Isotemp's marginal revenue and marginal cost curves.

   (c) What level of output should Isotemp produce so as to maximize profits?

   (d) At what price will this output sell?

TABLE 11.6

Isotemp's cost and revenue.

Quantity	Total cost ($)	Total revenue ($)
0	10	0
5	15	15.00
10	21	27.50
15	28	37.50
20	36	45.00
25	45	50.00
30	55	52.50
35	66	52.50

4. Figure 11.14 shows the revenue curves for the Safe-T Transport Company (a monopoly). The cost of transporting an additional passenger from point A to point B is practically zero. (L.O.4)

   (a) What price should this firm charge in order to maximize its profits?

   (b) What level of output should it produce?

FIGURE 11.14

Cost and revenue for Safe-T Transport.

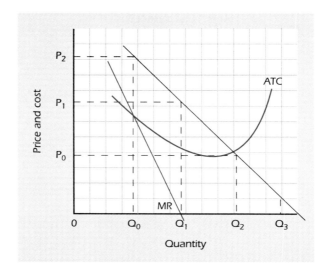

5. Show that if marginal cost is zero, the monopolistic firm maximizes its profits by producing at the point where the price elasticity of demand is 1. (L.O.5)

6. Table 11.7 contains data for a monopolistic firm called Monopole. (L.O.3,4)

TABLE 11.7

Price and cost data for Monopole.

P	Q	TR	MR	TC	MC	Total profit
$900	0			$ 400		
800	1			500		
700	2			550		
600	3			650		
500	4			850		
400	5			1 150		
300	6			1 430		
200	7			1 800		

(a) Complete the table.

(b) What output should Monopole produce in order to maximize its profits?

(c) What price will Monopole charge?

(d) What will Monopole's total profit be at this price?

7. Use the data in Table 11.7 to draw the demand and marginal revenue curves for Monopole. What do you notice about the relation between demand and marginal revenue? (L.O.2,3)

8. Figure 11.15 shows the average revenue and marginal cost curves for a monopolist called Unifirm. (L.O.3,4)

(a) Draw in the marginal revenue curve.

(b) What price will maximize Unifirm's profit?

(c) What output should the firm produce?

FIGURE 11.15

Unifirm's MC and AR curves.

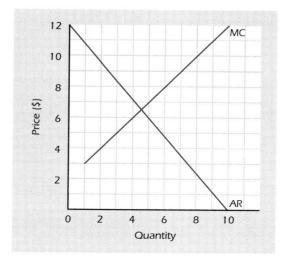

9. A monopolistic firm, Coverall Ltd., produces a particular type of garment. Coverall has to pay a tax of 40% of its profits. Should Coverall raise its price and thus try to pass the tax on to its customers? (L.O.4)

10. To a large extent, Bell Canada enjoys a monopoly in the sale of telephone service. If the federal government imposes a tax of $2 on each unit of telephone line installed by Bell, will Bell increase the price of each unit by $2? (L.O.4)

 11. Municipal governments have a monopoly on garbage collection and disposal, and people pay for this service through their taxes. Discuss the pros and cons of breaking up the government's monopoly and permitting private contractors to enter the garbage collection business, selling their services privately to households and firms.

Internet Site

http://www.bayer.ca

This site is the home page for Bayer Inc.-Canada. This company is heavily involved in the research and development of pharmaceutical and other products worldwide.

INTERNET EXERCISE

1. Go to the Bayer site listed above.
2. Click on *Bayer Facts.*
3. Click on *Bayer and Innovations.*
4. List five breakthrough products developed by Bayer.
5. In one short paragraph, outline Bayer's attitude to R&D.
6. Click on *Bayer and Its Products.*
7. Click on one room of the house, and list all of the Bayer products found there.

CHAPTER 12

IMPERFECT COMPETITION: MONOPOLISTIC COMPETITION AND OLIGOPOLY

Learning Objectives

After studying this chapter, you should:

1 understand the concept of monopolistic competition

2 be familiar with demand and marginal revenue of the firm in monopolistic competition

3 understand short-run equilibrium in monopolistic competition

4 know the conditions for long-run equilibrium in monopolistic competition

5 know the differences and similarities between monopolistic competition and pure competition

6 understand the effects of advertising

7 understand the behaviour of firms in oligopoly

8 understand oligopolistic pricing and output

9 be familiar with the kinked demand curve model

10 understand alternative pricing strategies

11 understand cartels and other forms of collusion

12 know the theory of contestable markets

Each firm in any sector of the system in which monopolistic competition prevails offers products that differ in some way from the products of every other firm in the sector, and thus supplies a special market of its own.

Joseph A. Schumpeter, *Business Cycles*

INTRODUCTION

Imperfect competition is neither monopolistic nor pure competition.

In this chapter, we shall concern ourselves mainly with the pricing and output decisions of firms in monopolistic competition and oligopoly markets. Economists often use the term **imperfect competition** to refer to a market structure that is neither purely competitive nor purely monopolistic. Hence, the term encompasses both monopolistic competition and oligopoly. In Canada, most firms operate in market structures that are neither purely competitive nor purely monopolistic, but lie somewhere between these two opposites. Most firms in Canada operate in monopolistically competitive or oligopolistic market structures.

MONOPOLISTIC COMPETITION

Learning Objective 1: understand the concept of monopolistic competition

As the name implies, monopolistic competition contains elements of both pure competition and monopoly. In this type of market structure, there are many firms selling similar but differentiated products. The characteristics of monopolistic competition are set out below. As these characteristics are outlined, you will recognize the similarity between this market structure and pure competition. You may find it helpful to refer to Table 10.1 on page 168 to review market structure characteristics.

1. RELATIVELY LARGE NUMBER OF FIRMS

Monopolistic competition involves a relatively large number of firms.

A monopolistically competitive market structure (monopolistic competition) consists of a relatively large number of firms. The number need not be as large as in pure competition. Although a specific number will only be arbitrary, most students still like to have an idea of what is relatively large when referring to monopolistic competition. For this purpose, a number between 30 and 100 will suffice. Because the number of firms is relatively large, each one's share of the total market, though not negligible, is relatively small — just enough to cause each firm to have a slight influence on price. Also, the number of firms is sufficiently large to make it impractical for the firms to get together to act jointly to control price and output in the market. Each firm acts independently of the others because the action of any one will have a very small (almost unnoticeable) effect on the others.

2. DIFFERENTIATED PRODUCTS

Product differentiation is characteristic of firms in monopolistic competition.

You will recall that in pure competition, the firms produce identical products. In monopolistic competition, the firms produce differentiated products. Indeed, product differentiation is a key feature of monopolistic competition. **Product differentiation** is a situation in which firms use a number of devices to distinguish their products from those of other firms in the same industry.

An important point to grasp here is that it does not matter much whether the products *are* different. What matters is whether buyers *perceive* them to be different. The true test of the existence of product differentiation is whether or not buyers prefer to purchase the item from one seller rather than from another.

Product differentiation may be achieved in many ways. First, it may be achieved through product characteristics such as distinctive designs, packaging, trademarks, colour, durability, and brand names. Some trademarks and brand names have become so popular that the product is identified by the brand name or trademark. Examples that may come to mind are Kleenex (for tissues), Band-Aid (for plastic bandage strips), Xerox (for photocopy), Scotch tape (for transparent adhesive tape), Q-tips (for cotton swabs), Vaseline (for white petroleum jelly), and Walkman (for mini stereo cassette players).

Second, product differentiation may be achieved through product image. The idea is to create a certain image of the product with the hope that it will appeal to certain buyers. For example, a product that has a conservative image will likely appeal to people who behave conservatively. A certain type of car, for example, may portray this conservative image.

Finally, product differentiation may be achieved through emphasizing certain features of the firm. These features may include convenient location, attention given to customers by the firm's employees, and the services provided along with the product. A beauty salon may provide reading material or free coffee while its clients are waiting to be served. A furniture store may offer free delivery anywhere in the city and surrounding areas. These services differentiate these firms from those that offer no such services. A car dealer may build a reputation on the basis of the service offered to its customers after they purchase a car. Product differentiation on the basis of services rendered is an attempt to compel consumers to view the product and the service offered with it as a single item. This type of product differentiation is particularly prevalent in retail outlets where it is difficult or impossible to differentiate the physical characteristics of the product. The video cassettes rented from one video outlet are identical to those of other outlets. The service, however, may vary from one outlet to another.

Monopolistic competition is prevalent in service industries. The many different beauty salons, barber shops, and restaurants operating in any large city are good examples of monopolistic competition. Other examples include bakeries, gasoline stations, shoe stores, men's and women's clothing stores, automotive garages, stationery stores, and florists.

3.   FREEDOM OF ENTRY AND EXIT

In the case of pure competition, there is freedom of entry into, and exit from, the industry. In the case of monopolistic competition, entry and exit are relatively easy. Entry may not be as easy as in pure competition because of the need to differentiate one's product in a monopolistically competitive market. Also, to break into the monopolistically competitive industry may require significant advertising, the financial burden of which may be a factor limiting entry into the market.

There is relative freedom of entry and exit in monopolistic competition.

PROBLEM SOLVING 12-1

You operate a pharmacy in your neighbourhood. Will you set your prices significantly above the prices in other pharmacies?

DEMAND AND MARGINAL REVENUE OF THE FIRM IN MONOPOLISTIC COMPETITION

Learning Objective 2: be familiar with demand and marginal revenue of the firm in monopolistic competition

The firm in monopolistic competition is one among many. However, because its product is perceived to be different from those of its competitors, the monopolistic competitor is able to exercise some control over price. If the monopolistic competitor raises its price, it will lose some of its customers. But those who strongly prefer the product in question may remain; brand loyalty will cause them to stay with their preferred brand. If the firm lowers its price, it will attract some customers from its competitors. But all buyers will not be attracted by the small reduction in price. This implies that the demand curve for the monopolistic competitor slopes downward. Because there are so many close substitutes for the product of any one firm in monopolistic competition, the demand for the product of any one firm is likely to be relatively elastic. The degree of elasticity will depend on the degree of product differentiation that the firm is able to achieve.

A downward-sloping demand curve implies a downward-sloping marginal revenue curve. The firm in monopolistic competition can sell a greater quantity only by lowering the price. Hence, each additional unit adds a smaller amount to total revenue. Demand and marginal revenue curves for a firm in monopolistic competition are shown in Figure 12.1.

FIGURE 12.1

Demand and marginal
revenue curves for a
firm in monopolistic
competition.

The average and marginal
revenue curves of a firm in
monopolistic competition
slope downwards.

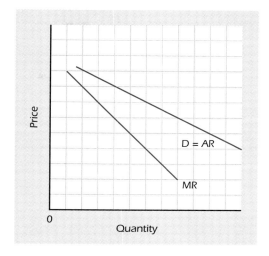

SHORT-RUN EQUILIBRIUM IN MONOPOLISTIC COMPETITION

Learning Objective 3:
understand short-run
equilibrium in monopolis-
tic competition

The individual firm in a monopolistically competitive industry must decide on the price and output combination that will maximize its profits. Profits will be maximized when marginal revenue equals marginal cost. The short-run equilibrium (profit-maximizing) position of a monopolistically competitive firm is shown in Figure 12.2. The firm shown in the diagram will earn maximum profits by producing an output of 0Q and selling at a price of 0P. The firm is earning positive economic profits since its price of 0P is greater than its unit cost of 0C. The profit is shown by the shaded rectangle in Figure 12.2.

A firm in monopolistic competition may incur losses in the short run. Figure 12.3 illustrates this situation. We assume that this firm is covering its variable costs. The firm is doing

FIGURE 12.2

Short-run equilibrium
of a firm in monopol-
istic competition.

The monopolistically
competitive firm will be in
equilibrium when its
marginal revenue equals
its marginal cost.

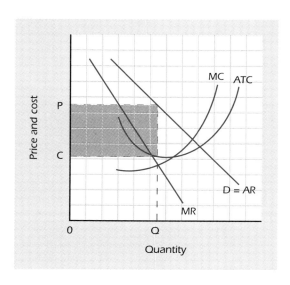

FIGURE 12.3

A monopolistically
competitive firm
incurring losses.

A firm in monopolistic
competition may incur
losses in the short run
when its marginal revenue
equals its marginal cost.

the best it can in the short run by producing an output of 0Q and charging a price of 0P.
It is, however, incurring losses because its price, 0P, is below its average total cost, 0C.
The losses are illustrated by the shaded area in Figure 12.3.

LONG-RUN EQUILIBRIUM IN MONOPOLISTIC COMPETITION

In monopolistic competition, as in pure competition, entry into and exit from the industry are easy. If the firms in the industry are earning positive economic profits, new firms
will be attracted into the industry. As this happens, the demand curve for each firm will
shift to the left, as shown in diagram A of Figure 12.4, as each firm's share of the total
industry demand falls. D is the original demand curve, representing the firm's share of
the market demand, and D_0 is the new demand curve after the adjustment to the entry
of new firms into the industry. The firm is still earning profits since its demand curve is
still above its average total cost curve.

FIGURE 12.4

Effects of the entry of
new firms.

Entry and exit in monopolistic competition change the
firm's share of the market.

Learning Objective 4:
know the conditions for
long-run equilibrium in
monopolistic competition

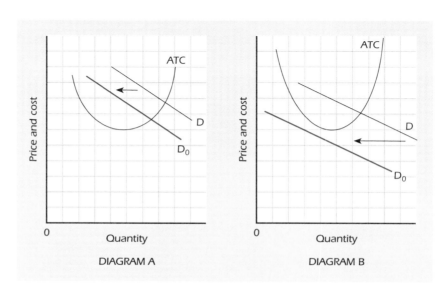

If too many firms enter the industry, the demand curve will shift below the average cost curve. The firm will then incur losses. This occurrence is shown in diagram B of Figure 12.4. Here, the demand curve has shifted from D to D_0, which is now below the average total cost curve. This drop will cause some firms to leave the industry, and as a result, the demand curve will shift back to the right.

When each firm in the industry is earning only normal profits (that is, when P = ATC), the entry and exit of firms will cease, and long-run equilibrium will be achieved. This situation is illustrated in Figure 12.5. The firm will produce an output of 0Q units at a price of 0P. Note that in long-run equilibrium, marginal revenue equals marginal cost, and price equals average cost.

FIGURE 12.5

Long-run equilibrium of a firm in monopolistic competition.

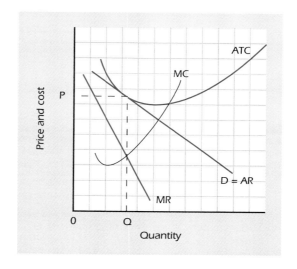

In long-run equilibrium, a firm in monopolistic competition earns only normal profits.

MONOPOLISTIC COMPETITION COMPARED WITH PURE COMPETITION

Learning Objective 5: know the differences and similarities between monopolistic competition and pure competition

A monopolistically competitive firm in long-run equilibrium will operate with excess capacity.

We can evaluate the efficiency of monopolistic competition relative to pure competition with the help of Figure 12.6. This diagram shows that, in pure competition, price equals marginal cost. In monopolistic competition, price exceeds marginal cost. This means that resources are not optimally allocated in monopolistic competition. An increase in output by the monopolistically competitive firm would benefit the society. The firm in monopolistic competition is wasteful in the sense that it does not produce at the lowest point of its average cost curve as the purely competitive firm does. The fact that the monopolistic competitor does not produce at minimum average cost implies that the firm has excess or under-utilized capacity. This concept has been termed the **excess capacity theorem**, and may be stated as follows:

> **In long-run equilibrium, a firm in monopolistic competition will operate with excess capacity. That is, it will operate at a point to the left of the minimum point on its long-run average cost curve.**

Figure 12.6 also shows that the purely competitive firm produces a greater output (Q_{pc}) than the monopolistically competitive firm does (Q_{mc}), and that the price charged by the monopolistically competitive firm (P_{mc}) is higher than the purely competitive price (P_{pc}).

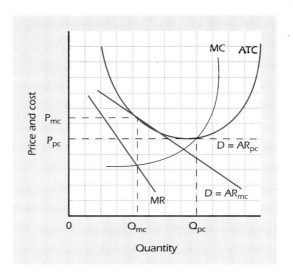

A question that is quite often asked is whether the consumer is better off under pure competition than under monopolistic competition. Under pure competition, the consumer pays a lower price, but his choice of product is limited. In a purely competitive industry, all of the firms in that industry produce identical products. In a monopolistically competitive industry, the consumer can choose from a wide variety of differentiated products. We can argue that the higher price under monopolistic competition is offset by the greater choice that the consumer enjoys. Whether or not the greater variety of products sufficiently compensates for the higher price is a normative matter and cannot be answered by economic analysis. The decision rests with the individual consumer.

ADVERTISING

A firm advertises in order to maintain or increase its share of the market.

Learning Objective 6:
understand the effects of advertising

Advertising is, in itself, a form of non-price competition. A purely competitive firm need not spend money trying to increase the amount that it can sell. It can sell as much as it can produce at the going price. But for a monopolistic competitor, advertising may result in an increase in profits. It is obvious that for advertising to be profitable, it must add more to the firm's total revenue than it does to its total cost. If advertising is successful, it will increase the demand for the firm's product and will also make it less elastic. This will increase the market power of the monopolistically competitive firm. If advertising outlay is a fixed cost, then it will not affect marginal cost. And if advertising does not significantly affect demand for the firm's product, then the price and quantity at which MR = MC will not change appreciably. In that case, advertising will simply push up the firm's total cost and hence reduce the firm's profits.

PROBLEM SOLVING 12-2
You manage a café in Port Alberni. Another café across the street has just installed an air-conditioner. What will you do?

APPLICATION

A Competitive Strategy

Firms in monopolistic competition can adopt a variety of competitive strategies. They can employ price competition, **quality competition**, or competitive advertising, in which product differentiation may be emphasized. A company that has built up a reputation for the high quality of its products may be able to keep its prices above those of its competitors. Whereas its competitors may compete on the basis of price, it may compete on the basis of quality. Historically, IBM typewriters and computers and Fisher Price toys have long been considered products of "superior value," and consequently these firms were able to charge a higher price for their products.

A competitive strategy based on superior-quality goods is likely to succeed when the market consists of buyers who are more quality-conscious than price-conscious. The model of monopolistic competition, with its product-differentiation feature, helps to explain the coexistence of higher-priced and lower-priced firms, and high-quality and lower-quality products, in the same industry.

THE PROS AND CONS OF ADVERTISING

Quality competition: competition by a firm attempting to make its products superior to the competitors'.

The issue of advertising has received a great deal of attention in economics and marketing literature. Does advertising increase or reduce prices? Is advertising wasteful? Does advertising hinder or promote competition? These issues are debatable. In this section, we shall take a quick look at the main arguments in favour of and against advertising.

The pros

Those who argue in favour of advertising make the following claims:

Advertising may create employment and income.

1. Advertising creates employment and income for people in the advertising business, and for people who work in the media. In addition, advertising increases the demand for goods and services, and since the production of goods and services requires the use of resources, including labour, it increases employment in general.

Advertising may lead to economies of scale.

2. Advertising enables firms to take advantage of economies of scale. This argument can be illustrated with the help of Figure 12.7. AC represents the firm's average cost without advertising. Suppose the quantity of the firm's product demanded without advertising is 0Q. This output will be produced at an average cost of 0C. Now, because of advertising, the firm's average cost curve shifts upward from AC to AC_a, and the quantity demanded now grows from 0Q to $0Q_1$. But the average cost of producing this greater output has fallen from 0C to $0C_0$. Here, the benefits from economies of scale outweigh the increase in average cost resulting from advertising. Consumers benefit by obtaining the product at a lower price with advertising than without it.

Advertising gives valuable information.

3. Advertising provides consumers with valuable information that enables them to make better decisions in the market. By informing consumers about new products, new locations and new firms, advertising greatly reduces search costs to consumers.

Advertising results in product improvement and development.

4. Advertising leads to product improvement and development. When a firm advertises its product, it emphasizes some advantage of its product over the products of its competitors. A firm must therefore improve its product in order to justify its advertising claims. Moreover, the fact that its competitors are also advertising puts pressure on the firm to improve its product and its service.

FIGURE 12.7

The effect of advertising.

5. Advertising increases competition. Advertising makes it easier to successfully launch new products that are close substitutes for existing products. Thus, advertising increases the number of firms in the industry and makes it more competitive.

Advertising may make markets more competitive.

The cons

Those who argue against advertising raise the following points to support their case:

1. Advertising increases monopoly power. Firms in certain industries spend millions of dollars each year on advertising. In order to break into such industries, potential competitors must be willing to make those massive advertising outlays. This in itself may prove to be an effective barrier to new firms.

Advertising may increase monopoly power.

2. Advertising is wasteful. Resources that could be productively employed in other industries to produce goods and services to satisfy wants are wasted in advertising. Why, it is argued, use so much ink and paper in advertising, when those same resources could be used in producing educational books, which would improve the society's well-being?

Advertising may lead to a misallocation of society's resources.

3. Advertising may increase costs and prices. A good portion of advertising simply causes consumers to switch from brand to brand. The output of the industry does not increase as a result of advertising, but costs rise, the market share of each firm hardly changes at all, and consumers end up paying higher prices.

Advertising may result in higher costs and prices.

4. Advertising is mainly persuasive, not informational. Many of the advertisements on radio and television give very little useful information to consumers in terms of helping them to make rational choices. Some advertisements, it is claimed, may even give misleading or false information.

Most advertising is persuasive or competitive rather than informative.

5. Advertising imposes indirect costs on society. Unsightly billboards that mar the beauty of the landscape, tons of advertising circulars that must be disposed of, and advertisements that are in bad taste are some examples of the costs imposed on society by advertising.

Advertising forces society to incur indirect costs.

OLIGOPOLY

Learning Objective 7: understand the behaviour of firms in oligopoly

Duopoly: a market structure consisting of only two firms.

An oligopolistic industry consists of only a few firms.

Oligopolistic firms recognize their interdependence.

Entry barriers exist in oligopoly.

A differentiated oligopoly is a market with a few firms selling differentiated products.

Concentration ratios provide information about the competitive nature of an industry.

The term **oligopoly** has been applied to an industry that consists of a few firms, each producing a substantial share of the total output of that industry. This type of market structure is typical of the petroleum industry, the automobile industry, and the steel industry, to name only a few. If the industry consists of only two firms, the term **duopoly** is generally used. The main features of oligopoly are outlined below.

1. FEW FIRMS

The industry consists of only a few firms — so few that each produces a relatively large share of the total output of the industry. As in the case of monopolistic competition, any specific number given must be quite arbitrary, but one typically thinks of an oligopolistic industry as consisting of two to 15 firms.

2. INTERDEPENDENCE RECOGNIZED

As a consequence of the small number of firms in an oligopolistic industry, the actions taken by any one firm have a noticeable effect on the other firms. Acknowledging this interdependence is crucial in understanding the behaviour of firms in oligopolistic industries.

3. BARRIERS TO ENTRY

There are barriers to entry into an oligopolistic industry. These barriers often include the huge capital investment necessary to establish an oligopolistic firm, and the enormous advertising necessary to capture a worthwhile share of the market.

4. IDENTICAL OR DIFFERENTIATED PRODUCTS

Oligopolistic firms may produce identical products or they may produce differentiated products. For example, the cement produced by one firm is similar to that produced by the other firms. There is an obvious difference, however, between General Motors' compact cars and Ford's compact cars. The term **differentiated oligopoly** is used when the products of the firms in an oligopolistic market are differentiated.

CONCENTRATION RATIOS

The extent to which a market is dominated by a few firms can be determined by looking at **concentration ratios**. These ratios show the percentage of total market supply accounted for by a few of the largest firms in the industry, for example, a concentration ratio would tell you what percentage of the beer industry's business is done by only two of the largest breweries. The larger companies in highly concentrated industries usually have branches in several provinces and sell their output from coast to coast. Table 12.1 contains a list of manufacturing industries with relatively high concentration ratios.

TABLE 12.1

Industries with high concentration ratios.

Industry	
Tobacco products	Aircraft and aircraft parts
Breweries	Business and office machines
Motor vehicle manufacturing	Organic chemicals
Iron and steel mills	Publishing and printing
Electrical wire cables	Petroleum refining
Smelting and refining	Telecommunications material

Source: Statistics Canada, *Canada Yearbook, 1988*. (Latest data available).

OLIGOPOLISTIC PRICING AND OUTPUT

Learning Objective 8:
understand oligopolistic pricing and output

The oligopolistic firm produces a substantial portion of the total industry output and therefore has some control over the price of its product. Product differentiation by the oligopolistic firm may also increase its market power. The demand curve for the oligopolistic firm therefore slopes downward. Like firms in other market situations, the oligopolistic firm is assumed to be a profit-maximizer. The oligopolistic firm will therefore produce an output at which marginal revenue equals marginal cost. In Figure 12.8, the profit-maximizing output is 0Q, and the price charged is 0P.

FIGURE 12.8

Price and output in an oligopolistic firm.

The profit-maximizing oligopolist firm equates its marginal revenue and its marginal cost.

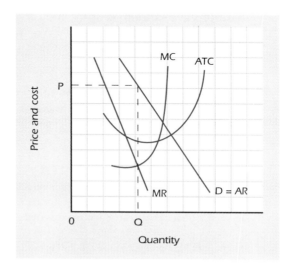

An increase in the cost of production will normally lead a firm to increase the price of its product. If an oligopolistic firm increases its price, however, some buyers will probably switch to substitutes offered by other firms. Such crossover may result in an increase in the prices of the substitutes.

PROBLEM SOLVING 12-3

Suppose that you are the manager of a grocery store, and there are only two other grocery stores in the area. Suppose also that you and your competitors are earning satisfactory profits but you know that you could increase your profits if you could increase your sales. Would you cut your prices in order to woo customers away from your competitors?

THE KINKED DEMAND CURVE

It has been observed that prices tend to remain relatively stable in oligopoly markets. One explanation for this relative price stability is that firms in oligopolistic industries realize that a price cut by one firm will cause other firms to retaliate by cutting their prices also. Instead of engaging in a price war, which will hurt every firm, each firm tacitly agrees to live and let live by sharing the market — and the profits. This, of course, is a result of the strong interdependence of firms in oligopoly markets, which is absent in other market structures.

The kinked demand curve explains price rigidity.

The model of the **kinked demand curve,** advanced independently but almost simultaneously in 1939 by Paul Sweezy in the United States and by R. Hall and C. Hitch in

Learning Objective 9:
be familiar with the
kinked demand curve
model

Britain, explains price rigidity in oligopolistic industries. The theory is based on two basic assumptions about firms' reactions to price changes by their rivals. The assumptions are:

1. a price increase by one firm will not be matched by similar increases in other firms;

2. a reduction in price by one firm will be matched by similar reductions in other firms.

Oligopolistic firms are assumed to behave in this manner in order to keep their customers or to capture a larger share of the market. If, for example, Coke increases the price of its cola, we can assume that Pepsi, in order to attract customers from Coke, will leave its price unchanged. But if Coke reduces its price, it is assumed that Pepsi will follow suit in order not to lose customers to Coke.

This situation is illustrated in Figure 12.9. Consider an oligopolist selling a product at price P. If the firm raises its price above P, its rivals, by assumption, will not raise their prices. Thus, the quantity of the firm's product demanded can be expected to fall significantly as buyers switch to the firm's rivals. This implies that the demand curve is relatively elastic at prices above P.

If the oligopolist lowers its price from P, its rivals will, by assumption, follow its lead and lower their prices in order not to lose their customers. Thus, the quantity of the firm's product demand as a result of lowering its price will not increase significantly. There is no price incentive for buyers to switch from the firm's rivals. This implies that the demand curve is relatively inelastic at prices below P. The demand curve is relatively elastic at prices above P and relatively inelastic at prices below P.

Thus, the demand curve has a kink at point A in Figure 12.9. The marginal revenue curve associated with such a demand curve is also illustrated. Note that the marginal revenue curve has a discontinuous section.

Figure 12.9 shows that if the marginal revenue and the marginal cost curves intersect within the range of the vertical section of the marginal revenue curve, an appreciable shift in the marginal cost curve will have no effect on the profit-maximizing price and output for the firm. For example, an increase in the marginal cost from MC_1 to MC_2 leaves price and output unchanged at 0P and 0Q respectively. Changes in cost will affect price and output only when they are very substantial.

FIGURE 12.9

The kinked demand
curve.

An appreciable increase in
cost leaves the price
unchanged.

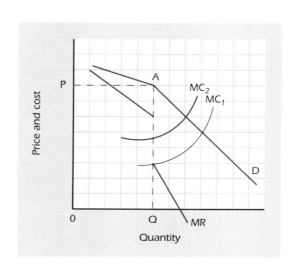

The model of the kinked demand curve explains how a kink occurs in the demand curve, but it does not explain where. Once the price is known, we can use the model to explain price rigidity, but it does not tell us anything about the determination or the establishment of the rigid price in the first place. To conclude, the model of the kinked demand curve is one explanation of relative price rigidity in oligopolistic markets, but it is not the only explanation, and it cannot be regarded as a general theory of price and output determination in oligopoly markets.

OTHER EXPLANATIONS OF STICKY PRICES

The kinked demand curve model does a good job of explaining "sticky" (inflexible) prices. In this section, we examine two other explanations of sticky prices that have been advanced. These are long-term contracts and small menu costs.

LONG-TERM CONTRACTS

Many firms enter into long-term agreements with their suppliers to provide inputs at pre-arranged prices. Many companies also enter into contracts to provide retail outlets with a certain amount of output at some pre-determined price. Such arrangements obviously contribute to price rigidity as they prevent prices from responding to short-run changes in demand and supply.

SMALL MENU COSTS

Menu costs are those costs incurred when changing prices.

There are costs involved in changing prices. The firm that is changing its prices has to pay employees to remove old price tags and replace them with new ones. New catalogues and price lists may have to be printed and distributed to customers. Such costs are referred to as **menu costs**. The existence of these menu costs may cause a firm to be hesitant to change its prices.

OTHER MODELS OF OLIGOPOLISTIC BEHAVIOUR

LIMIT OR PREDATORY PRICING

Predatory (limit) pricing serves as an effective barrier to the entry of new firms into a market.

Learning Objective 10: understand alternative pricing

In cases where significant economies of scale exist and initial capital outlays are high, the firms in an oligopoly situation may deliberately set the prices so low that it would be impossible for new firms to enter the industry and make a profit. This pricing strategy is known as **limit pricing** or **predatory pricing** and may be formally defined as the practice of setting the price of a product so low that it precludes the possibility of potential firms entering the industry and making a profit.

Figure 12.10 illustrates how predatory pricing works. The profit-maximizing price shown in diagram A is P_e. If the existing firms set a price of P_L, they still earn a profit at this low price because they control such a large share of the market. When the existing firms charge a price of P_L, the share of the market that can be captured by any potential competitor is represented by the demand curve D_N in diagram B of Figure 12.10. This price is too low for any new firm to make a profit. At any level of output, the new firm's demand curve lies below its average cost curve AC_N. The potential firm's share of the market, therefore, will be too small for profitable operation.

FIGURE 12.10

Predatory pricing.

Low industry price and small market share for potential entrants prevent entry.

DIAGRAM A   DIAGRAM B

PRICE LEADERSHIP

Price leadership means that one firm in an industry sets prices and the other firms adopt those prices.

The firms in an oligopolistic industry may refrain from engaging in price competition and, consequently, a situation of price leadership may emerge. **Price leadership** is a situation in which a single firm in an industry sets the price of its product, and the other firms follow the price set by the leader. Two types of price leadership exist: dominant price leadership and barometric price leadership. *Dominant price leadership* exists when the industry consists of a single large firm that dominates the industry, and a few smaller firms. Price changes are initiated by the dominant firm, and the smaller firms simply follow the leader.

In a situation of *barometric price leadership*, the industry may not be dominated by any single firm. Any firm may be the leader, or the leadership role may rotate in a rather orderly manner. Changes in demand and cost conditions in the industry may cause one firm to initiate a price change that is followed by the other firms in the industry.

Price leadership allows an orderly change from one price to another, but it may not benefit all firms equally.

Although price leadership may prevent the dangerous problem of a price war, in which all of the firms lose, the arrangement is unlikely to benefit all firms equally. As you know, a firm maximizes its profits by setting a price at which its marginal revenue equals its marginal cost. Since all of the firms in the industry are unlikely to have the same cost, it follows that if the leader sets a price that will maximize its profits, that single price will not benefit all firms equally. To reduce the risk of a price war, the price leader must take the situation of its followers into consideration when initiating price changes for the industry.

COST-PLUS PRICING

Many oligopolistic firms determine their prices by adding a mark-up to their average cost.

It is believed that many firms in oligopoly markets determine the prices of their products by adopting a method of pricing known as **cost-plus pricing** or **mark-up pricing**. The idea of cost-plus pricing is very simple. The firm simply adds a certain percentage mark-up to its average cost and thus determines its price. Thus, if the firm's average cost is $12, say, it may choose a mark-up of 25% and set its price at $15.

The advantage of this method of price determination is that it is easy to calculate and easy to understand. But it does have some problems. First, if the firm is trying to maximize its profits, how does it know that a mark-up of 25% rather than a mark up of 20% or 30% will equate its marginal revenue and its marginal cost? Second, the cost-plus method is practical only if the firm knows exactly how much it can sell at various prices. If it puts its mark-up at 25%, it may find that it can sell only 70% of its output at that price. It may then be forced to lower its mark-up.

CARTELS

Learning Objective 11: understand cartels and other forms of collusion

Collusion occurs when firms agree not to compete among each other.

A gentlemen's agreement is not put down on paper, and is usually concluded simply with a handshake.

Cartels engage in market sharing and price fixing.

It is certainly not uncommon for oligopolistic firms to act in unison to control the market for a particular product. Such **collusion** is often illegal in Canada. Nevertheless, firms still seem to get together informally and enter into so-called **gentlemen's agreements** to control price and output. Tacit agreement among firms is more likely to occur when the industry consists of only two or three firms.

The best-known form of collusion among firms in oligopoly is probably a **cartel**, defined as a group of independent producers who have entered into a formal agreement to control price and output in a particular industry.

In many international markets, agreements to control prices and output are legal. Therefore, many cartels operate in international markets. Cartels are quite common in markets for natural resources. The International Bauxite Association, the Organization of Petroleum Exporting Countries (OPEC), and the International Association of Airlines are examples of cartels.

Cartels may be *perfect* or *imperfect*. In a perfect cartel, all decisions regarding price and output are surrendered to a central decision-making body, and the profits distributed to each firm according to the terms of the cartel agreement. In an imperfect cartel, each firm reserves some decision-making powers, and may be allowed to keep whatever profits it may earn. This is the type of cartel likely to be found in practice.

Cartels face a variety of problems. However, we shall focus our attention on three common problems that plague cartels. First, individual independent firms are unlikely to be willing to surrender their decision-making powers to the central body. Second, there is a strong temptation for each firm in the cartel to cheat and produce more than its quota at the prospect of earning greater profits. Whether other cartel members cheat or not, there is a strong profit incentive for any individual firm to cheat. Here the firm's individual interest supersedes the interest of the cartel. The cartel may have to resort to industrial surveillance (spying) because of the enormous incentive to cheat. Third, there is the problem of the entry of new firms into the industry. If a new firm enters the cartel, and there is no increase in the total demand for the industry's product, the optimum output for the cartel remains unchanged, but the given profits of the group must now be shared among a greater number of members. If the new firm enters the industry but is not admitted into the cartel, then the survival of the cartel is threatened.

Cheating among cartel members is one of the most serious problems of a cartel.

PRICING AND OUTPUT POLICIES IN CARTELS

Joint profit maximization

If the cartel decides to maximize joint profits, it chooses a price-output combination that equates marginal revenue with marginal cost. In other words, the cartel behaves exactly like a monopolist producing its output in different plants.

Once the cartel decides on its price-output combination, it faces the further problem of allocating output and profits among cartel members. The allocation of output may be done in any of several ways, including the assignment of exclusive territories and the establishment of output quotas for members. The output quota approach is followed by OPEC — perhaps the best-known cartel.

EVALUATION OF OLIGOPOLY

Like monopoly, oligopoly has certain undesirable social consequences. Barriers to the entry of new firms into the industry may result in a price that exceeds average total cost in most oligopolistic firms. Thus, oligopolistic firms are likely to earn excess profits. Also, the price established in an oligopolistic market is likely to be above marginal cost. This imbalance between price and marginal cost implies a misallocation of resources. Furthermore, oligopolistic firms spend huge amounts of money on advertising in an attempt to maintain or increase their share of the market. Many people consider this enormous advertising outlay to be wasteful.

Under workable competition, an industry is competitive enough to maintain output and keep profits at reasonable levels.

Despite its disadvantages, oligopoly is not always socially undesirable. If there is **workable competition** — that is, if there is sufficient competition in the industry to ensure that output is not unduly restricted and that profits are not excessively high — oligopoly may not be totally undesirable. We can even argue that economies of scale under oligopoly may lead to lower cost and hence lower prices in oligopolistic firms.

Moreover, many firms in oligopoly do undertake a significant amount of research and development (R&D). New and important products are developed, new techniques are introduced — often with significant benefits to society.

A large percentage of the goods and services produced in the Canadian economy are produced by oligopolistic firms. It is obvious, therefore, that an understanding of the theories that attempt to explain the behaviour of firms in oligopolistic markets contributes to our understanding of the Canadian economy.

CONTESTABLE MARKETS

Learning Objective 12: know the theory of contestable markets

In discussing market structures, we have concentrated on the number of firms in the industry and the conditions for entry into the industry. In some cases, however, the number of sellers might not provide a proper indication of how the firms in the industry will behave.

Let us assume that Jane Justice is the only lawyer in town, and she also serves the neighbouring communities. There is not another lawyer in the area. Jane Justice is a monopoly. She will charge a price that equates marginal revenue and marginal cost. She may even be able to practice price discrimination and thus increase her profits.

Consider now the case of John Janitorial Services, a firm that specializes in cleaning services. Like Jane Justice, John Janitorial is a monopoly. However, the pricing behaviour of the two firms will likely be quite different. Whereas Jane Justice may set a price that results in positive economic profits, John Janitorial Services may behave like a pure competitor and deliberately earn only normal profit (zero economic profit).

Entry into a contestable market is easy and no firm can exercise monopoly power.

Why do these two firms adopt different pricing strategies? Entry into Jane Justice's market requires legal training and passing certain special examinations. Thus, her market is not easily contestable. On the other hand, it is relatively easy to enter John Janitorial's industry. His is a **contestable market**. A market with one or a few sellers is said to be contestable if entry into the industry is easy so that the threat of entry of potential competitors prevents the existing firms from exercising any monopoly power.

The concept of contestable markets suggests that looking at the number of firms in an industry is not enough to determine the extent of market power. The ease of entering the industry, and thus potential competitors, must also be considered.

GLOBAL PERSPECTIVE

Russian Caviar

Caviar is a seafood delicacy from a fish (the sturgeon) found primarily in the Caspian Sea. The supply of so-called *fine Soviet caviar* to Western countries was, for many years, controlled by a Soviet state cartel. This cartel limited the supply of caviar to the West to only about 7% of the annual production of approximately 2000 tonnes, and was thus able to command a relatively high export price.

With the collapse of the former Soviet Union, each independent state (Russia, Kazakhstan, Azerbaijan, and Turkmenistan) along with Iran that borders the Caspian Sea produces caviar for export. Concern with overfishing of sturgeon aside, the desire on the part of each independent state to earn foreign currency has resulted in an increase in the supply of caviar to the West and a significant reduction in price. In the absence of this cartel, the independent states mentioned above and individual fishermen have increased competition in the supply of caviar. The formation of a cartel can affect the world price of a commodity, but so too can the disbandment of a cartel.

CHAPTER SUMMARY

1. Monopolistic competition is a market structure characterized by a large number of firms selling a differentiated product.

2. Because of product differentiation, the monopolistically competitive firm has slight control over the price charged for the product. It can raise the price slightly without losing all of its customers and, thus, its demand curve slopes downward.

3. The firm in monopolistic competition maximizes profits when its marginal revenue equals its marginal cost. Its price exceeds marginal cost.

4. If the monopolistically competitive firm is earning positive economic profits in the short run, new firms will enter the industry and compete, and those profits will dwindle away. In long-run equilibrium, price equals average cost.

5. The excess capacity theorem states that a monopolistically competitive firm will have excess capacity in long-run equilibrium. The firm will not produce at the minimum point on the average cost curve.

6. Monopolistic competition gives consumers a relatively wide variety of products from which to choose.

7. Firms in monopolistic competition often engage in advertising in order to increase the demand for their products or to maintain their share of the market.

8. Oligopoly, a market structure involving few sellers, is typical in industries that require huge capital outlays. Duopoly refers to a situation in which there are only two firms in the industry. Because so few firms exist in this market structure, interdependence is crucial.

9. Concentration ratios show the percentage of total market supply accounted for by a few of the largest firms in the industry.

10. The oligopolistic firm exercises considerable market power. Like firms in other market structures, the oligopolistic firm maximizes profits when its marginal revenue equals its marginal cost.

11. The model of the kinked demand curve explains price rigidity in oligopolistic markets. Given the demand for the product, the price will change only when there is a substantial change in cost.

12. Predatory pricing or limit pricing may be used as a device to restrict the entry of firms into a particular market. When this happens, the price of the product is kept artificially low.

13. Price leadership, a situation in which a price charged by one firm is followed by the other firms, may develop in an oligopolistic industry. Various other forms of collusion may also result.

14. Cost-plus or mark-up pricing may be used by oligopolistic firms to establish the prices of their products.

15. A cartel is a group of firms that have formally agreed to unite for the purpose of controlling price and output in a particular industry. Cartels may be either perfect or imperfect. Perfect cartels, however, are not usually encountered in the real world.

16. Workable competition is the term applied to a situation in which there is sufficient competition in the industry to ensure that output is not unduly restricted and that the firms do not earn excessively high profits.

17. A contestable market exists when easy entry into an oligopolistic or monopolistic market forces the existing firms to deliberately earn only normal economic profits.

TERMS FOR REVIEW

imperfect competition (209)
product differentiation (209)
excess capacity theorem (213)
quality competition (215)
oligopoly (217)
duopoly (217)
differentiated oligopoly (217)
concentration ratios (217)
kinked demand curve (218)

menu costs (220)
predatory (limit) pricing (220)
price leadership (221)
cost-plus (mark-up) pricing (221)
collusion (222)
gentlemen's agreements (222)
cartel (222)
workable competition (223)
contestable market (223)

QUESTIONS FOR REVIEW AND DISCUSSION

1. What are the main features of a monopolistically competitive market? (L.O.1)

2. What do you understand by the term *product differentiation?* Name some devices used to achieve product differentiation. (L.O.1)

3. Name four industries, other than those listed in the text, that can be classified as monopolistically competitive. Give reasons for your choice. (L.O.1)

4. Explain why a firm in monopolistic competition faces a downward-sloping demand curve that is very elastic. (L.O.2)

5. With the help of an appropriate diagram, explain the profit-maximizing position of a firm in monopolistic competition. (L.O.3)

6. Explain why a monopolistically competitive firm earns only normal profits (zero economic profits) in the long run. (L.O.4)

7. How does the long-run equilibrium of a monopolistically competitive firm differ from that of a purely competitive firm? Illustrate with a diagram. Account for the difference. (L.O.4,5)

8. What arguments can you advance for and against advertising? (L.O.6)

9. Why might a firm in monopolistic competition advertise its product? (L.O.6)

10. What are the main characteristics of an oligopolistic industry? (L.O.7)

11. Why is it so difficult to develop any general theory of oligopolistic behaviour? (L.O.7,8)

12. What does the model of the kinked demand curve explain? (L.O.9)

13. Would you consider the kinked demand curve model to be an adequate model of price and output determination in oligopoly markets? Why or why not? (L.O.9)

14. The kinked demand curve model explains price rigidity in oligopoly markets. Discuss other explanations that have been offered for sticky prices.

15. What is the difference between each of the following pairs of concepts? (L.O.10,11)

    (a) dominant price leadership and barometric price leadership

    (b) cartel and gentleman's agreement

    (c) perfect cartel and imperfect cartel

    (d) collusion and workable competition

16. What is cost-plus pricing? Will it automatically lead to profit maximization? (L.O.10)

17. Explain how predatory pricing may be used as a technique to prevent potential competitors from entering an industry. (L.O.10)

18. What are some of the problems faced by cartels? (L.O.11)

19. "There is a great incentive to engage in product improvement and development when there is imperfect competition." Discuss. (General)

20. "Monopoly may be less undesirable from society's point of view than oligopoly." Discuss. (General)

PROBLEMS AND EXERCISES

1. Explain why people buy name brands of a product when in-house brands are available at lower prices. (L.O.1,2)

2. Is it possible for monopolistic competition to exist in an industry where many firms sell identical products? Explain. (L.O.1)

3. Table 12.2 shows data for Prodif, a firm in monopolistic competition. (L.O.2,3)

TABLE 12.2	P	Q	TR	MR	ATC	TC	MC	Profit
Price and cost data for Prodif.	200	1			210			
	190	2			175			
	180	3			160			
	170	4			155			
	160	5			155			
	150	6			165			
	140	7			170			
	130	8			180			

(a) Compute total revenue, marginal revenue, total cost, marginal cost, and profit for Prodif, and complete the table.

(b) How many units should Prodif sell in order to maximize profits?

(c) What should the price of each unit be?

(d) What will Prodif's total profit be?

4. Figure 12.11 represents a monopolistically competitive firm called Best-Brand Ltd. (L.O.3)

FIGURE 12.11

Cost and revenue curves for Best-Brand Ltd.

(a) What level of output should Best-Brand produce in order to maximize profits?

(b) What price should Best-Brand charge for this output?

(c) What is the maximum total profit that Best-Brand can earn?

5. Draw a demand curve for a firm in monopolistic competition, then draw another demand curve to show the effect of a successful advertising campaign on the firm's demand. Explain your diagram. (L.O.6)

6. You and your brother decide to enter a business that is monopolistically competitive. You have carefully calculated your costs, and you know the demand for your product. Your objective is to maximize your profits. Your brother, who has a degree in marketing, suggests that you take a sample of the prices being charged by your competitors, and then set your price as the average of your sample prices. Would you agree with your brother that this is the best pricing strategy? Explain. (L.O.3,10)

7. Figure 12.12 represents Oliotel, a firm in an oligopoly situation. Oliotel is a profit maximizer. (L.O.8)

(a) What output should Oliotel produce?

(b) What price should it charge?

(c) What price adjustment should Oliotel make following a $2.50 increase in marginal cost?

FIGURE 12.12

Oliotel's cost and revenue.

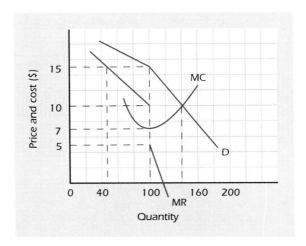

8. "Monopolists and oligopolists are both price-setters but their actions are guided by different considerations." Explain. (General)

9. Video rental stores are numerous in any Canadian city. There seems to be a good case for describing this industry as monopolistically competitive.

    a) What arguments can you advance for describing the video rental industry as monopolistically competitive?

    b) Telephone a few of these outlets to gather information on prices. Compare these prices.

    c) Visit three video rental outlets and see if you can detect any methods used to differentiate one outlet from another.

VIDEO CASE

The Newspaper Scene: A New Entrant

Background

For many years, the Globe and Mail, founded in 1844, has claimed to be Canada's only national daily newspaper. On October 27, 1998 a new Canadian publication, the National Post, billing itself as Canada's only truly national daily newspaper brought an end to the Globe and Mail's claim. Not surprisingly the Canadian newspaper market is highly concentrated. Not too many cities can support two or three daily papers. Toronto, Canada's largest city, is home to the Toronto Sun, the Toronto Star and now, the National Post, but some people doubt if even Toronto can support four daily newspapers.

The main player

The National Post will compete with existing newspapers, but its main competitor is the Globe and Mail. The man who dared to go head to head with the "Grand Old Man" (the Globe and Mail) is newspaper baron Conrad Black. Prior to October 1998, Mr. Black owned daily newspapers in all of Canada's major cities (Vancouver, Montreal, Winnipeg, Halifax) except Toronto. As of October 27, 1998, the exception no longer exists. Of 105 newspapers in Canada, Mr. Black controls 68 of them. That is power plus.

The market

Each of the newspapers mentioned above seems to appeal to a specific group of readers. For example, the Globe and Mail has traditionally been a rather conservative newspaper, appealing to the intellectuals, the business executives, the professionals, and the well-to-do, while the Toronto Star seems to cater to a more general readership. The Toronto Sun has a tabloid format and appears to cater to a younger generation of readers. By proclaiming itself to be a national newspaper, the National Post will probably compete more closely with the Globe and Mail than with the other newspapers. Clearly, the National Post will be in fierce competition for the advertising dollars of companies that advertise nationally (and locally too).

The theory

The theory of oligopoly should help us to understand the impact that the National Post will have on the behaviour of its competitors. The paper entered the market at a price below that of the Globe and Mail. Will that pricing strategy cause price-sensitive consumers to switch? Will the Globe and Mail match the lower price charged by the National Post? And what about product differentiation? Will the papers differentiate themselves by their content?

When the National Post arrived on the scene, its contents were similar in many ways to those of its major competitor. There was the colourful front page leading to the first section, followed by an *Arts and Life* section dealing with entertainment, fashion, and sports. And then there was the *Financial Post* section with business news, followed by *FP Investing* with reports on the financial markets.

The Globe and Mail is no longer that ultra conservative-looking newspaper. If its content has not changed much, its appearance certainly has. It is now a flashy paper. After the front section, there is the *Report On Business* (with colour) including the financial markets and a special *Careers* section. And how about sports coverage in the Globe and Mail? Well, it's right there in the A section — all five (more or less) pages.

As the theory predicts, the Globe and Mail has reacted — with colour, more excitement, and by apparently broadening its scope to attract women and younger readers. The possibility of a newspaper war exists, and whenever that happens in Canada, some casualty can be expected.

QUESTIONS

1. Isolate the main points in this case.

2. Do you see any danger in one man owning approximately 65% of the newspapers in Canada?

3. Do you think that an oligopoly model is appropriate for analyzing Canada's newspaper industry? Justify your answer.

4. How might the newspapers achieve product differentiation?

Video Resource: "2 × 1 Canadian," *National Magazine* (April 1998).

13

C H A P T E R

THE LABOUR MARKET

Learning Objectives

After studying this chapter, you will understand:

1 the demand for and supply of labour

2 competitive wage determination

3 predictions of the theory of wage determination

4 the effects of discrimination in the labour market

5 wage differentials

6 unions and collective bargaining

7 factors in wage negotiations

8 the effects of labour unions in the labour market

9 how unions affect resource allocation

When an attempt is made to apply to the labour market the ordinary principles of price determination — without making allowance for the type of market — the result appears at the first sight very odd.

J. R. Hicks, *The Theory of Wages*

INTRODUCTION

Up to this point, we have concentrated mainly on the product market, studying the demand for and supply of a product; households' decisions about how much of a product to buy in order to maximize satisfaction; and firms' decisions about how much to produce and what price to charge. In this chapter and the next, we concentrate on the factor market. Recall that households and firms operate in both markets. In the product market, the firms are the sellers while the households are the main buyers. In the factor market, however, the firms are the buyers while the sellers can be households or firms.

This chapter deals with labour — the most important resource used in the process of production. You will recall that the wage rate is the price of labour. We shall now study how the wage rate is determined in a competitive market structure, discuss wage differentials briefly, and take a quick look at labour unions and the collective bargaining process. In the process, you will see how the theory of wage determination applies to real-world situations.

Functional distribution of income is among the various factors of production.

In 1997, income from labour services in Canada amounted to $445 804 million or approximately 71% of total income earned from all sources. Table 13.1 shows the relative incomes from various sources, and Figure 13.1 compares the 1997 figures with the 1995 data. The distribution of income among the various factors of production is called the **functional distribution of income**.

TABLE 13.1

Sources of income and relation to total income.

Income Source	Value ($million)	% of total income
Labour income	445 804	70.7
Corporate profits before taxes	78 988	12.5
Government enterprise profits	6 707	1.1
Interest and investment income	46 187	7.3
Accrued net farm income	1 422	0.2
Unincorporated business income	52 978	8.4
Inventory valuation adjustment	−1 622	(0.2)
Net domestic income	630 464	100.0*

*Note: Percentages may not add up to 100 because of rounding.

Source: Statistics Canada, Canadian Economic Observer, July 1998 (Cat. 11-010-XBP): 3.

FIGURE 13.1

Comparison of income shares.

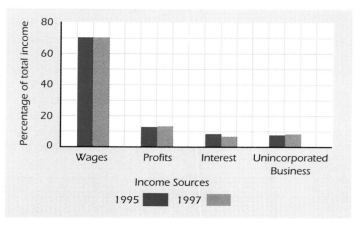

Source: Adapted from Table 13.1.

Figure 13.1 shows that the share of labour income remained constant at 70.7% from 1995 to 1997, while profits rose slightly from 13% in 1995 to 13.6% in 1997. The share of interest and investment income fell from 8.5% in 1995 to 7.3% in 1997, while unincorporated business income rose from 7.8% to 8.4%.

THE DEMAND FOR LABOUR

Learning Objective 1:
the demand for and supply of labour

A direct demand is a demand for goods and services.

The demand for labour is a derived demand.

The marginal physical product of labour is the extra output from adding one unit of labour.

The marginal revenue product is the additional revenue contributed by the last unit of a factor.

Consumers buy goods and services in the product market because they derive utility (satisfaction) directly from goods and services. The demand for goods and services is therefore a **direct demand**. In contrast, producers buy factors of production in the factor market to produce goods and services. Factor inputs do not give satisfaction directly as consumer goods and services do. The demand for factors of production (such as labour) depends on the demand for the goods and services that the factors of production are used to produce. If the demand for goods and services increases, then more factors of production are required to produce them. The demand for factors of production is therefore a **derived demand**.

In addition to firms that demand labour services to help with the production of goods and services, the various levels of government also demand labour services to offer the wide variety of services that governments provide. The government's use of labour services has some effect on the availability of workers for the private sector.

The principle of substitution (see Chapter 8) indicates that if the price of labour (the wage rate) falls, firms tend to use more labour. The following analysis helps to determine how a firm decides how many workers it will hire. We assume that the firm is in a purely competitive industry, and that it buys its inputs in a purely competitive market.

The marginal product of labour (MP_L) is the change in total output resulting from the use of one additional unit of labour. If this magnitude is expressed in physical terms, economists call it the **marginal physical product of labour** (MPP_L). The extra revenue resulting from the sale of the extra output produced by the additional unit of labour is called the **marginal revenue product** (MRP_L). The marginal revenue product, then, is simply the value of the marginal physical product (VMPP). We can calculate the value of the marginal physical product by multiplying the marginal physical product by the market price of the product. That is,

$$MRP_L = VMPP_L = MPP_L \times P$$

where P is the price of the product.

If an additional worker will contribute more to total revenue than to total cost, then it will pay the firm to hire the extra worker. Hence, if the marginal revenue product (MRP) is greater than the wage rate (W), the firm will likely employ additional units of labour. If the marginal revenue product is less than the wage rate, then the firm will likely reduce its employment of labour. It follows that the firm seeking to maximize its profits will employ labour up to the point where MRP = W. Figure 13.2 illustrates this fact.

Since marginal product declines as additional units of labour are employed (diminishing returns), the marginal revenue product curve slopes downward. The market wage rate is assumed to be 0W. If the firm were hiring $0Q_0$ units of labour at a wage rate of 0W, the marginal revenue product $0W_1$ would be greater than the wage rate, and the firm would benefit by hiring more labour. If it were hiring $0Q_1$ units of labour at a wage rate of 0W, the marginal revenue product $0W_0$ would be less than the wage rate, and the firm would benefit by hiring fewer units of labour. At a wage rate of 0W, the firm will hire 0Q units of labour since, with that amount of labour, the marginal revenue product

FIGURE 13.2

The firm's demand curve for labour.

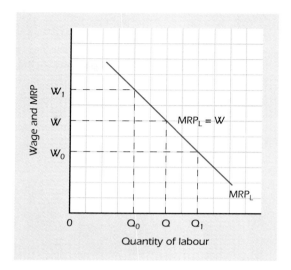

The firm employs labour up to the point where the marginal revenue product equals the wage rate.

The marginal productivity theory of wages states that labour should be employed to the point where the MRP equals the wage rate.

The marginal revenue product curve is the firm's demand curve for labour.

of labour equals the wage rate. This concept, known as the **marginal productivity theory of wages**, may be stated as follows: under purely competitive conditions, a profit-maximizing firm will hire labour up to the point where the wage rate equals the value of the marginal product of labour.

Note that if the wage rate were $0W_1$ instead of $0W$, then the firm would employ $0Q_0$ units of labour instead of $0Q$. If the wage rate were $0W_0$, then the firm would employ $0Q_1$ units of labour instead of $0Q$. As the wage rate falls, the firm employs more units of labour. The marginal revenue product curve shows the various quantities of labour that a firm will hire at various wage rates. The marginal revenue product curve, therefore, is the firm's demand curve for labour. Observe that a change in the wage rate causes a movement along, not a shift in, the firm's demand curve for labour. Factors such as changes in income, changes in tastes, and changes in market size, which affect the demand for the firm's product, will change the quantity of labour demanded by the firm at any given wage rate, and thus shift the firm's demand curve for labour. To obtain the market demand curve for labour, we add the demand curves of all the firms in the industry.

A complication arises, however, from this procedure. This is so because as the wage rate falls, the increased employment of labour by all firms in the industry is likely to increase the supply of the product. Such an increase in supply lowers the price of the product. For this reason, the market demand curve for labour will be less elastic than that derived by adding the demand curves of the individual firms. To overcome this complication, we can assume, just for analytical purposes, that the price of the product is not affected by the firm's employment of labour.

THE SUPPLY OF LABOUR

The supply curve of labour shows the number of units of labour offered at each possible wage rate. Of course, it is the households that supply labour services to the labour market. We assume that at low wage rates, only small amounts of labour are offered. Households regard both income and leisure as being desirable. As the wage rate increases, households will be more willing to sacrifice leisure and offer more labour services. We assume also that there is labour mobility between industries. One industry may attract

Learning Objective 1: the demand for and supply of labour workers by offering higher wage rates than those offered in other industries. The market supply curve of labour then slopes upward, as shown in Figure 13.3. At a wage rate of $0W_1$, the quantity of labour supplied is $0Q_1$. At the higher wage rate of $0W_2$, a larger quantity of labour ($0Q_2$) is offered for hire. You will observe here also that the change in the wage rate causes a movement along, not a shift in, the supply curve. Factors such as changes in taxes and changes in the size of the labour force will shift the supply curve of labour.

FIGURE 13.3

The supply curve of labour.

The higher the wage rate, the greater the quantity of labour offered by households.

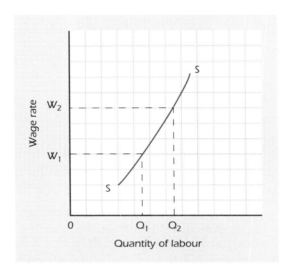

THE BACKWARD-BENDING LABOUR SUPPLY CURVE

A backward-bending labour supply curve shows the wage rates at which the number of hours worked decreases.

The labour supply curve discussed above is upward-sloping. There is, however, the possibility that the **supply curve of labour** could be negatively sloped (i.e., **backward-bending**) once the wage rate has reached a certain level. This situation is illustrated in Figure 13.4. At any wage rate up to W_1, a higher wage rate is an incentive to offer more hours of work. But at any wage rate above $0W_1$, the number of hours worked decreases

FIGURE 13.4

A backward-bending supply curve for labour.

A P P L I C A T I O N

A Question of Motivation

It is generally agreed that workers can be encouraged to work extra hours by offering them a higher wage. It is sometimes argued, however, that in many less-developed countries where workers have grown accustomed to a traditional lifestyle, their horizons are so limited that they are really not interested in earning extra income by working longer hours. This is the notion of the backward-bending supply curve of work effort in less-developed countries.

If such a supply curve of work effort does indeed exist, then higher wages will discourage rather than encourage greater effort. Thus, in order to motivate workers, incentives other than higher wages will be required. Such incentives may be provided by education aimed at changing attitudes and the way of life, and by providing opportunities for greater enjoyment of extra income. In other words, in such circumstances, it may be necessary to change the income-leisure choice.

as the wage rate increases. In this case, people prefer to choose leisure over additional income from labour services. It is suggested that some high-income-earning professionals, such as doctors and lawyers, who choose to work four days a week probably demonstrate the existence of a backward-bending supply curve for labour.

WAGE DETERMINATION IN A COMPETITIVE LABOUR MARKET

Learning Objective 2:
competitive wage determination

We can determine the equilibrium wage rate and the amount of labour employed in a competitive labour market by bringing together demand for labour and supply of labour. Figure 13.5 shows the demand curve for labour (D_L) and the supply curve for labour (S_L). At a wage rate of $0W_1$, the quantity of labour supplied exceeds the quantity demanded. This surplus of labour tends to force down the wage rate. At a wage rate of $0W_0$, the quantity of labour demanded exceeds the quantity supplied. At a wage rate of $0W$, the quantity demanded equals the quantity supplied. The labour market clears and the wage rate stabilizes. The equilibrium wage rate is $0W$, and $0Q$ units of labour are hired.

FIGURE 13.5

Equilibrium in the labour market.

The intersection of the demand and supply curves of labour determines the equilibrium wage rate.

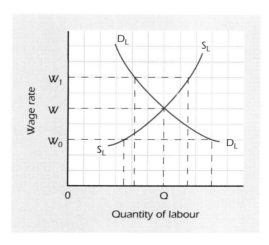

PREDICTIONS OF THE THEORY OF WAGE DETERMINATION

An increase in the demand for labour results in an increase in the wage rate.

Learning Objective 3: predictions of the theory of wage determination

How does an increase in demand for labour in a particular industry affect wages in that industry? For help in answering this question, let us look at Figure 13.6. DD is the original demand curve, SS is the original supply curve, 0W is the initial equilibrium wage rate, and 0Q is the amount of labour hired. A shift in the demand curve upward and to the right (from DD to D_1D_1) shows an increase in the demand for labour. We can see that the wage rate increases from 0W to $0W_1$, and that the amount of labour employed increases from 0Q to $0Q_1$. Hence, we can conclude that:

> **an increase in the demand for labour, other things being equal, causes a rise in the wage rate and an increase in the quantity of labour hired.**

FIGURE 13.6

Effect of an increase in the demand for labour.

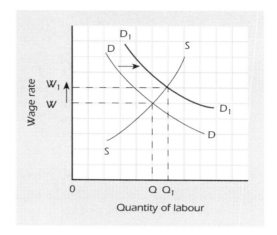

We can also easily determine the effects of a change in the supply of labour. Let us suppose that the supply of labour falls. Figure 13.7 shows such a fall as a shift in the supply curve from SS to S_0S_0. Assuming there is no change in demand for labour, the wage rate increases from 0W to $0W_1$, and the amount of labour falls from 0Q to $0Q_0$. In other words:

A reduction in the supply of labour results in an increase in the wage rate.

> **A reduction in the supply of labour, other things being equal, will cause an increase in the wage rate and a fall in the equilibrium quantity of labour.**

FIGURE 13.7

Effect of a decrease in the supply of labour.

PROBLEM SOLVING 13-1

"The institution of minimum wage laws contributes to unemployment." Can this claim be valid?

DISCRIMINATION IN THE LABOUR MARKET

Learning Objective 4:
the effects of discrimination in the labour market

Discrimination affects the labour market and imposes a cost on society. To show the effect of discrimination in the labour market, let us refer to Figure 13.8. The demand and supply curves for labour in a particular profession (teaching, engineering, etc.) are shown as DD and SS respectively. The equilibrium wage rate is W and the quantity of labour employed is 0L. The effect of discrimination is reflected in its effect on the demand curve of labour for the group discriminated against. Because of discrimination, the demand curve for the group that is the victim of discrimination shifts from DD to D_0D_0. This demand shift results in a fall in wages from W to W_0 and a decrease in the quantity of labour employed from 0L to $0L_0$. Discrimination therefore causes members of the group discriminated against to earn less and to find less employment than would be the case in the absence of discrimination.

Discrimination results in a misallocation of labour resources.

This type of discrimination is costly to society in terms of the loss of goods and services that could have been provided by the group discriminated against. By shifting the demand curve and lowering wages, discrimination causes labour resources to be misallocated. In this case, labour is not paid the value of its marginal product.

FIGURE 13.8

Effect of discrimination in the labour market.

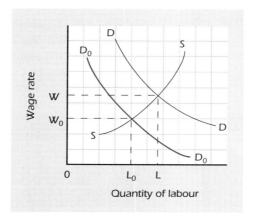

WAGE DIFFERENTIALS

Learning Objective 5:
wage differentials

There are significant differences in wage rates among occupations. In this section, we shall examine some of the reasons for these wage differentials. First, education, experience, and responsibility affect wage-earning potential. Material handlers require less training and skill than operators of complicated machines. Hence, we expect machine operators to be better paid than material handlers. A director of nursing at a large city hospital has greater responsibilities than a nursing assistant, so we expect the director to be better paid than the assistant. Quite often, responsibility is a function of experience and education; and wages are normally a function of responsibility. Of course, superior talent and ability cannot be overlooked. This accounts for the high salaries earned by superstars in sports and in entertainment. We shall return to this issue when we discuss the concept of economic rent in Chapter 14.

Second, the existence of unions in some occupations and professions may account for wage differentials. Unionized workers supposedly earn more than their non-union counterparts. It may be pointed out, however, that the evidence is not conclusive that unionized workers do in fact earn more than non-unionized workers in the same occupation.

Psychic income is the non-monetary rewards derived from a job.

Third, wage differentials may also be explained by the non-monetary benefits associated with certain occupations and professions. These benefits, referred to as **psychic income**, include such things as good working hours, pleasant working surroundings, long summer and winter vacations, and the enjoyment that some people derive from their jobs. Some employees may opt for psychic income in lieu of a higher money wage.

Finally, we should recognize that the degree of danger associated with various jobs affects wage differentials. The more hazardous the job, other things being equal, the greater the salary. For example, a nuclear medical technician will earn more than an audio-visual technician, not only because of a difference in training, but also because of a difference in the degree of danger associated with the job.

Wage differentials are due basically to differences in the relative scarcities of different types of labour.

Of course, the reasons for these wage differentials are related largely to demand and supply. For example, there is enormous demand for athletes with superior ability and the supply is small; these people therefore earn high wages. Material handling, however, can be learned fairly easily by almost anyone. In this case, there is an enormous supply of material handlers and these people therefore earn low wages. Generally, then, wage differentials are a function of demand and supply.

UNIONS AND COLLECTIVE BARGAINING

Learning Objective 6: unions and collective bargaining

Unions have played, and continue to play, an important role in the labour market. We have come to accept labour unions as quite normal in our society. But this was not always the case. The rights now enjoyed by labour unions were won only after bitter struggles. The union movement has contributed significantly to the pleasant working conditions that modern workers (unionized and non-unionized) now enjoy. For our purposes, let us define a union as an association of workers organized to promote the interests of its members in negotiations with their employers.

A craft or trade union's membership consists of workers in a single occupation.

There are different types of unions. In a **craft** or **trade union**, the membership comprises workers in a single occupation irrespective of where they work. In an **industrial union**, the membership comprises workers in a given industry. Unions have become an important institution in the modern economy.

All members of an industrial union work in a given industry.

Unions are organized at the local, national, and international levels.

Let us begin our examination of unions by looking at their structure and their organization. Unions are organized at four levels. First, there is the **local union**, to which the individual worker belongs directly. The local union holds meetings to discuss problems and to decide on courses of action. The local union also collects membership dues. Second, there is the **national union**, of which the local union is a member. The national union often does the bargaining and sets broad policy outlines. It receives a part of the dues paid to the locals. The Canadian Labour Congress (CLC), the Centrale des syndicats democratiques (CSD), and the Confederation of Canadian Unions (CCU) are examples of national unions. Third, there is the **international union**, whose membership consists of local unions in different countries. The American Federation of Labour-Congress of Industrial Organizations (AFL-CIO) is an example of an international union. Finally, there is the **federation**, which is an association of national unions. The Confédération des Syndicats Nationaux (CSN), based in Quebec, is an example of a federation of unions. Table 13.2 shows union membership in Canada by type of union and affiliation.

A federation is an association of national unions.

	Type of affiliation	Number of unions	Membership	
			Number	%
TABLE 13.2	International unions	51	1 216 725	29.9
	AFL-CIO/CLC	34	1 087 285	26.7
Union membership by	AFL-CIO/CFL	8	99 400	2.4
type and affiliation,	CLC only	2	6 830	0.2
1997.	AFL-CIO only	4	17 980	0.4
	Unaffiliated unions	3	5 230	0.1
	National unions	233	2 662 550	65.4
	CLC	55	1 575 935	38.7
	CSN	10	251 420	6.2
	CEQ*	14	109 775	2.7
	CCU	9	17 275	0.4
	CSD	2	14 330	0.4
	CFL	2	1 780	0.0†
	Unaffiliated unions	141	692 035	17.0
	Directly chartered unions	401	60 600	1.5
	CSD	390	59 500	1.5
	CLC	11	1 100	0.0†
	Independent local organizations	326	134 025	3.3
	TOTAL	1 011	4 073 900	100.0

* Centrale de l'enseignement du Quebec
† Less than 0.1 per cent

Source: Human Resources Development Canada, *Directory of Labour Organizations in Canada*, 1998: XXIII

Many of the rights for which unions have fought over the years have now been incorporated into law. In many countries, there are labour codes that define the rights and privileges of workers, and governments have enacted legislation that protects workers. Yet unions continue to be popular. The number of unions in Canada increased from 911 in 1994 to 1011 in 1997, and union membership decreased slightly from 4 077 987 to 4 073 900 (a fall of about 0.10%) during the same period.

UNION SECURITY

A union tries to secure its position by a variety of methods. These methods include the closed shop and the union shop. The concept of an open shop helps to explain how a closed shop or a union shop arrangement helps the union. An **open shop** is an arrangement whereby an employee does not necessarily have to be a union member to obtain or keep a job. On the other hand, a **closed shop** arrangement is one in which membership in a union is a prerequisite for obtaining employment. Between these two practices is the **union shop**, in which the employee may be hired even if he or she is not a union member, but must join a union within a specified period of time. It should be obvious that unions are least likely to support open shops. A union is most powerful when all of the workers at an establishment are unionized.

Another technique that a union might use to increase the job security of its members and strengthen its own position is **featherbedding**. This is the practice of enforcing and insisting on work rules and methods that may be inefficient (at least in the view of the employer), but that may keep the employee in the position. Featherbedding represents an inefficient use of labour resources, but it also protects workers who might otherwise experience great difficulty in finding another job. The issue therefore involves a trade-off between economic efficiency on the one hand and humanitarianism on the other.

In an open shop, workers do not need to belong to a union.

Closed shop and union shop arrangements increase union security.

In featherbedding, workers are given unnecessary work to keep them on the payroll.

The Rand Formula makes it compulsory for a worker to pay union dues even if he or she is not a union member.

An important development in Canadian labour practice was the introduction in 1945 of the **Rand Formula**. Of enormous support to union security, the Rand Formula was named after Mr. Justice Ivan Rand, who passed an arbitration decision in a labour dispute at the Ford Motor Company of Canada. According to that decision, Ford workers were to pay union dues whether or not they were members of the union. These dues were to be deducted from the workers' pay by the company's administrators and then handed over to the union. Canadian industries now commonly use the Rand Formula or some version of it.

 PROBLEM SOLVING 13-2

Can an employer benefit from a closed shop?

THE COLLECTIVE BARGAINING PROCESS

Employers and employees arrive at a contract (collective agreement) by collective bargaining.

Learning Objective 6:
unions and collective bargaining

A union is supposed to represent its members and protect their interests. It represents the collective voice of its members. Instead of individual employees negotiating directly with their employer, the union, representing all of its members, negotiates on their behalf. Sometimes, several different unions unite to form a common front when negotiating with an employer. This often happens with public-sector unions.

Collective bargaining is the entire process by which unions and management arrive at an agreement through negotiations on the terms of employment. The contract arrived at (the **collective agreement**) specifies the responsibilities of employers and employees concerning wages, vacation, safety on the job, non-monetary benefits such as maternity leaves and training, job security, and other issues. The wage and other conditions of work determined by the collective bargaining process depend on the relative strengths of the bargaining parties and on the skills of the negotiators. In a period of heavy unemployment, the employer tends to have greater market power. In a period of general labour shortage and rising demand for labour, the unions enjoy greater market power.

Negotiations between the union and the employer usually begin well in advance of the expiry date of the existing contract. The union makes its demands, and the employer makes its proposals. Usually, each side finds something in the other's proposal that is unacceptable. Bargaining continues with each party making proposals and counterproposals until a settlement is reached and a contract is signed.

SETTLEMENT OF DISPUTES

Labour disputes may be settled by conciliation (mediation) or by voluntary or compulsory arbitration.

It is reasonable to expect disputes between employers and employees. In cases in which a compromise cannot be reached by the two parties, there are several ways of attempting to settle such disputes. One procedure is to call in an outside neutral mediator to study the situation and suggest possible moves toward a settlement. This is the process of **conciliation** or **mediation**. There is no obligation on the part of either party to accept the conciliator's suggestions.

Another procedure used in settling labour disputes is **voluntary arbitration**. Each party to the dispute agrees to submit its case to an impartial third party and to abide by the decision of the arbitrator. A third technique used to settle labour disputes is **compulsory arbitration**. The government compels the disputing parties to submit their disputes to an arbitrator, whose decision is binding upon both parties.

STRIKES AND LOCKOUTS

A strike is a temporary work stoppage by employees; a lockout is a temporary plant closing by the employer.

As a means of obtaining its demands, a union may resort to strike action. A **strike** is a temporary work stoppage by employees, designed to force an employer to grant their demands. From the employer's side, the equivalent of a strike is a **lockout**, which is a temporary closing of the plant by an employer, designed to win a dispute.

Contrary to popular belief, strikes and lockouts occur relatively infrequently in Canada. In most years, the working time lost because of strikes and lockouts amounts to only about 0.16% of overall working time. This means that the average unionized worker in Canada strikes for only about half a day per year. This suggests that the vast majority of collective agreements are reached without resort to strikes and lockouts.

Most contract agreements are reached without resort to strikes or lockouts.

THE COSTS OF STRIKES

Strikes are costly. We are fortunate that they do not occur more frequently in this country. A proper analysis of the costs of strikes requires that these costs be grouped into at least two categories: direct costs and indirect costs.

Strikes impose costs on the parties directly involved, and on others not directly involved in the strike.

Direct costs

It is relatively easy to pinpoint the direct costs of a strike. The cost to workers is lost wages. The cost to employers is lost production, lost sales, and lost profits.

Indirect costs

A strike in one industry affects other industries and the general public. For example, a strike by truck drivers affects grocery stores and other retail outlets, since they cannot obtain supplies during the strike. This is an indirect cost. If workers in the steel industry go on strike, the auto industry may have to shut down because of a shortage of steel, which is an important input in the auto industry. In many cases, strikes cause a great deal of inconvenience to the public — as, for example, when a public transportation company goes on strike. These indirect costs often outweigh the direct costs of the strike.

PROBLEM SOLVING 13-3

Do strikes necessarily result in a reduction of total output in the economy?

FACTORS IN WAGE NEGOTIATIONS

Learning Objective 7: *factors in wage negotiations*

An escalator clause stipulates automatic wage increases to reflect price changes or cost of living changes.

Indexed wages rise with prices.

Cost of living, productivity, and profitability are important considerations in wage negotiations.

In the early stages of negotiation, both parties consider a variety of factors when drawing up their lists of proposals. In deciding on wage demands and wage offers, one factor that is likely to be particularly significant is the cost of living. Workers try to protect their purchasing power against a rising cost of living. The employer cannot easily ignore such a consideration. Unions try to protect their members' purchasing power by building escalator clauses into their contracts. An **escalator clause** is a provision in a contract specifying that wages will rise automatically to compensate for any increase in the cost of living. **Indexation** is the adjustment of wages to the rate at which prices rise. A **cost of living adjustment** (COLA) allows wages to be adjusted to the cost of living.

Another factor likely to carry some weight is productivity. Workers will naturally expect to share in any increase in their productivity. And employers are less likely to resist demands for wage increases in the face of productivity increases. By the same token, a fall in the productivity of workers is likely to result in the refusal of employers to grant anything but modest wage increases.

A third factor likely to feature significantly in wage demands and offers is the profitability of the business. If the firm has had a substantial increase in profits, the union will certainly use that fact as justification for higher wage demands. On the other hand, if the firm has undergone a period of declining profits, the employers will likely refuse to grant higher wages.

GLOBAL PERSPECTIVE

Labour Relations in Japan

You have probably heard a great deal about differences between Japanese and North American unions. This capsule takes a brief look at labour relations in Japan so that you can compare the Japanese and Canadian situations. Japanese unions operate on the concept of *enterprise unionism*, where a single union is organized within each enterprise rather than within a craft or an industry. The enterprise unions are then organized into industrial federations and central national labour organizations.

In the spring of each year, negotiations between labour and management take place in order to determine wages and other working conditions. These enterprise unions, also called company unions, work very closely with management. The attitude is one of cooperation rather than confrontation. In fact, union leadership in Japan is an extension of management since union leaders hold management positions in the companies. It is claimed that labour relations in Japan are better than they are in North America. The system seems to work well since there are very few strikes. Japanese workers know that they benefit from a profitable company.

EFFECTS OF LABOUR UNIONS IN THE LABOUR MARKET

Unions attempt to influence the wage rate by shifting the demand and supply curves for labour.

One of the objectives of a union is to secure higher wages for its members. Economic theory predicts that higher wages will result from an increase in the demand for labour. A union may therefore attempt to shift the equilibrium wage rate upward by shifting the labour demand curve to the right or by shifting the labour supply curve to the left.

INCREASING THE DEMAND FOR AND REDUCING THE SUPPLY OF LABOUR

Learning Objective 8:
the effects of labour unions in the labour market

Recall that the demand for labour is a derived demand. That is, if the demand for a certain product increases, the demand for inputs (including labour) used to produce that product also increases. This relationship suggests that one way in which unions may increase the demand for labour is to increase the demand for the products of unionized producers. This increase in the demand for labour will likely increase the wage rate.

Many unions encourage their members to purchase union-made products. The effect of this practice is illustrated in Figure 13.9. DD and SS are the initial demand and

FIGURE 13.9

Effect of increasing the demand for labour.

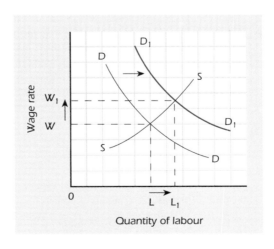

supply curves for labour. The equilibrium wage rate is W. A campaign to encourage people to buy union-made products, if successful, will increase the demand for labour. This increase in demand is shown by the new demand curve D_1D_1. Assuming that there is no change in supply, the wage rate increases to W_1, and the quantity of labour hired increases from L to L_1.

A union may shift the supply curve of labour upward and to the left by restricting the entry of newcomers into certain occupations and professions. The effect of this practice on the wage rate is illustrated in Figure 13.10. The initial demand curve in the particular occupation or profession is DD. The initial supply curve is SS. The initial wage rate is 0W. By limiting new entrants into the occupation or profession, the union shifts the supply curve from SS to S_0S_0. This has the effect of raising the wage rate from 0W to $0W_1$.

FIGURE 13.10

Effect of a decrease in the supply of labour.

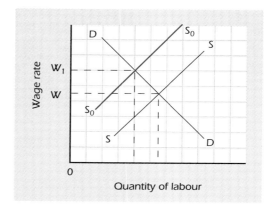

An increase in wage rates in one occupation or profession may spark demands for wage increases in other occupations and professions, leading to higher wages. This process by which wage increases in one occupation lead to wage increases in other occupations is referred to as the **wage transfer mechanism**. There is no doubt that wage rates have increased significantly in the various industries. Whether these higher wages result from union activities, however, is still a matter of considerable debate among economists. It is suspected that unions have played a role, but that other factors have also contributed.

A wage transfer mechanism adjusts wages in one occupation based on wage increases in another.

PROBLEM SOLVING 13-4

If all economists in Canada had to obtain a licence from an association called the Economics Association of Canada in order to work as economists, what would happen to the market for economists?

UNIONS AND RESOURCE ALLOCATION

Learning Objective 9: how unions affect resource allocation

Labour mobility is one requirement for market forces to allocate labour resources efficiently. Labour tends to move from low-wage occupations to high-wage occupations. The marginal productivity theory of wages discussed earlier in this chapter, moreover, asserts that high productivity is associated with high wages. It follows, then, that the movement of labour from low productivity jobs to high productivity jobs causes an increase in output.

Some critics have claimed, however, that unions restrict labour mobility and thus cause a misallocation of resources. Some have also argued that unions contribute to the

APPLICATION

Union Objective Determines Strategy

Over four million Canadians are members of unions. Many of these union members have families and close relatives, therefore the agreements that are negotiated between unions and employers affect not only a few people. It has come to be generally accepted that unions have as their mandate to secure better working conditions for their members, to obtain higher wages, and to seek greater job security.

The analysis presented here shows that a union's objective will determine its negotiating strategy. The following diagram will facilitate the analysis.

Let us assume that there are L workers in the union. If the objective of the union is to have all of its members employed, it will negotiate for a wage rate of W. The quantity of workers demanded at a wage rate of W is L, as determined by the demand curve, so all members would be employed at a wage rate of W.

If, however, the objective of the union is to maximize total wages, it would adopt a different strategy and negotiate for the employment of L_o workers where the marginal revenue is zero. Recall that total revenue is at its maximum when marginal revenue is zero. The wage rate associated with the employment of L_o workers is W_1. This latter strategy leaves some workers $(L-L_o)$ unemployed.

misallocation of labour resources by allowing promotions and job security on the basis of seniority rather than on the basis of competence. Often, a competent worker with low seniority loses his or her job, while a much less competent employee may be sheltered by seniority.

Supporters of labour unions, on the other hand, claim that the higher wages resulting from union activity actually serve as an incentive for greater productivity. Union supporters claim that discontented and disgruntled workers cannot be expected to have high productivity, but that good wages and working conditions contribute to good worker morale and productivity.

SOME UNSETTLED ISSUES

It goes without saying that unions occupy an important position in our economy and in our society. Their activities often touch our lives in significant ways. The economic, political, and social impact of unions has generated a number of debatable issues. We outline some of these issues in this closing section.

First, strikes in key industries can be crippling to the economy. This fact has led some critics to argue that strikes should be outlawed in key industries. Instead of strikes, would it not be better to settle disputes by compulsory arbitration? This is a debatable issue. Is a limitation on the right to strike an infringement on workers' rights? Should strike action by any group of workers be allowed to disrupt the lives of the majority of people?

Second, union wage demands have been blamed for inflation — rapidly rising prices. Currently, inflation is not a problem in the Canadian economy, but the Canadian economy has experienced bouts of inflation, and the effects have been costly. Should controls be imposed on wage increases? And if wages are controlled, should other prices be controlled as well?

Labour organized itself in order to achieve some monopoly power in the labour market. Organized labour has been able to win concessions from employers — concessions that would not have been possible if labour had not been organized into unions. Some people argue that unions now have too much power in the labour market while others argue just as emphatically that they do not have enough power. The debate rages on.

CHAPTER SUMMARY

1. Labour is a very important input into the production process. Income from labour accounts for approximately 71% of total income from all sources.

2. The demand for labour is a derived demand since it depends on the demand for goods and services, which labour is used to produce.

3. The marginal revenue product of labour (MRP_L) is the extra revenue obtained from selling an extra unit of output produced by an additional unit of labour. By multiplying the marginal physical product of labour (MPP_L) by the price of the product, we can obtain the marginal revenue product of labour.

4. The firm will employ labour up to the point where the marginal revenue product of labour equals the wage rate. The firm's demand curve for labour is the marginal revenue product of labour curve. We can approximate the industry demand curve for labour by adding the demand curves of all the firms in the industry.

5. The supply curve for labour slopes upward, generally. Higher wage rates serve as an incentive to increase the quantity of labour supplied. But in particular cases, the labour supply curve may be backward bending as extra income from labour causes people to work fewer hours.

6. The equilibrium wage rate is determined by the intersection of the demand and supply curves for labour. An increase in the demand for labour, other things being equal, results in an increase in the wage rate. An increase in the supply of labour results in a fall in the wage rate.

7. Differences in wages among occupations and professions are due to differences in education, skill and experience, responsibility, the existence of unions, and the degree of risk associated with the job. Psychic income also plays a role.

8. A union is an association of workers organized to promote the interests of its members in negotiations with their employers.

9. The membership of a craft or trade union consists of workers in a single occupation irrespective of where they work. The membership of an industrial union consists of workers in a particular industry.

10. Unions are organized at the local, national, international, and federation levels.

11. An open shop is an arrangement whereby an employee does not have to be a union member in order to obtain or keep a job. A closed shop requires membership in a union before employment can be obtained. A union shop allows for the hiring of workers who are not union members but who must become union members in a specified time.

12. The Rand Formula makes it compulsory for workers to pay union dues even if they are not members of the union.

13. Collective bargaining refers to the whole process whereby union and management arrive at an agreement about the terms of employment. The contract agreement deals with wages, vacation, safety, and other non-monetary matters such as job security.

14. Among the factors considered by the negotiating parties when deciding on wage demands and offers are productivity, profitability, and the cost of living.

15. An escalator clause is a provision in a contract specifying that wages will increase automatically to compensate for increases in the cost of living.

16. Unions can shift the wage rate up by increasing the demand for union-made products, and by restricting the entry of newcomers into certain occupations and professions.

17. Some critics claim that unions restrict labour mobility and thus contribute to misallocation of labour resources. Union supporters claim that union activity actually increases productivity.

TERMS FOR REVIEW

functional distribution
 of income (231)
direct demand (232)
derived demand (232)
marginal physical product
 of labour (232)
marginal revenue product (232)
marginal productivity theory
 of wages (233)
backward-bending labour
 supply curve (234)
psychic income (238)
craft or trade union (238)
industrial union (238)
local union (238)
national union (238)

international union (238)
federation (238)
closed shop, open shop, and
 union shop (239)
featherbedding (239)
Rand Formula (240)
collective bargaining (240)
collective agreement (240)
conciliation (mediation) (240)
voluntary arbitration (240)
compulsory arbitration (240)
strike (240)
lockout (241)
indexation, COLA, and escalator
 clause (241)
wage transfer mechanism (243)

QUESTIONS FOR REVIEW AND DISCUSSION

1. In what respect does the demand for an input such as labour differ from the demand for a product such as bread? (L.O.1)

2. Briefly explain the marginal productivity theory of wages. Do you think that the theory is relevant to present-day Canada? (L.O.1)

3. Explain how the wage rate is determined in a purely competitive labour market. (L.O.2)

4. Why might an increase in wages cause unemployment? (L.O.3)

5. If a provincial government sets the minimum wage in the province significantly above those in other provinces, what economic consequences (for labour) would you expect? (L.O.3)

6. You operate an apricot orchard in the Okanagan Valley. Your employees are not unionized. How would you decide on the number of employees to hire? (L.O.1,2)

7. Discuss the effect of discrimination in the labour market. (L.O.4)

8. Give some reasons for differences in wages among occupations in Canada. (L.O.5)

9. What is psychic income? How might psychic income influence a person's occupational choice? (L.O.5)

10. Give a brief account of union organization in Canada. (L.O.6)

11. How might a union secure higher wages for its members? (L.O.6,7)

12. Strikes are costly. What are some of the costs of strikes? (L.O.6,7)

13. Discuss some of the factors that union leaders and employers consider when deciding on wage demands and offers. (L.O.7)

14. "Unions cause resources to be misallocated." Do you agree with this assertion? (L.O.9)

PROBLEMS AND EXERCISES

1. Table 13.3 contains hypothetical data for a firm in pure competition. The labour market is also purely competitive, and the price of the firm's product is $2. (L.O.1)

TABLE 13.3

Wage and employment data.

Units of labour	Wage rate ($)	MPP_L	MRP_L
0	10		
		4	
1	10		
		6	
2			
		5	
3			
		4	
4			
		3	
5			
		2	
6			
		1	
7			

(a) Complete the table.

(b) On a graph, draw this firm's demand curve for labour.

(c) How many units of labour will this firm hire?

(d) Now, suppose that the wage rate falls to $6. How many units of labour will the firm hire?

2. The information in Table 13.4 is given for the Stanco Production Company, which operates in a purely competitive market. Stanco sells its product for $10, and pays its workers a wage of $50 per day. (L.O.1)

TABLE 13.4	Number of workers	Total product
Production schedule for Stanco.	0	0
	1	25
	2	35
	3	43
	4	48
	5	52
	6	52
	7	50

(a) How many workers will Stanco hire?

(b) How many workers would be hired if the wage rate were to rise to $80 per day?

3. The production schedule for the Minilite firm, which uses labour as its only variable input, is given in Table 13.5. Workers are paid $50 a day and Minilite's product sells for $5 in a purely competitive market. What is the optimum number of workers for Minilite to employ? (L.O.1,2)

TABLE 13.5	Number of workers	Total product
Minilite's production schedule.	0	0
	5	100
	10	175
	15	235
	20	285
	25	325
	30	350

4. Table 13.6 shows the demand and supply of labour. (L.O.1,2)

TABLE 13.6	Wage rate ($)	Quantity of labour demanded	Quantity of labour supplied
Demand and supply	4	11	1
	5	9	4
	6	7	7
	7	5	10
	8	3	13

(a) Draw the demand and supply curves on a graph.

(b) What is the equilibrium wage?

(c) How many workers will be hired at this wage rate?

5. Based on the information given in Question 4 above, suppose the government legislates a minimum wage rate of $7. How many units of labour will remain unemployed? (L.O.2,3)

6. With the help of diagrams, explain how each of the following will affect the labour market (ignore long-term effects): (L.O.3)

(a) an increase in the labour force due to immigration;

(b) a more optimistic economic outlook on the part of firms;

(c) an increase in the demand for Canadian goods because of the free-trade arrangement between Canada and the U.S.A;

(d) an increase in the tax rate, which reduces work incentive.

7. It is sometimes argued that labour unions, by demanding higher wages for their members, may end up hurting them. Discuss. (L.O.3)

8. Use a diagram to explain why, on average, lawyers earn more than service station attendants. (L.O.5)

 9. Many of the causes for which unions fought have now been incorporated into labour laws. Does this mean that unions have outlived their usefulness? Discuss.

Internet Site

http://labour-travail.hrdc-drhc.gc.ca/wip/othersites.html-ssi
This site takes you to several other sites dealing with labour.

INTERNET EXERCISE

1. Go to the Web site indicated above.

2. Click on *Unions* in *Canada* and then click on one of the sites that may be of interest to you.

You can learn about any of the unions listed on the site.

14

RENT, INTEREST, AND PROFITS

Learning Objectives

After studying this chapter, you will know about:

1 the meaning of rent

2 rent determination

3 rent differentials

4 interest and interest rate determination

5 profit and its economic significance

Rent is that portion of the produce of the earth which is paid to the landlord for the use of the original and indestructible powers of the soil.

David Ricardo, *Principles of Political Economy and Taxation*

INTRODUCTION

In addition to labour services, firms use land (natural resources) and capital in the production process. Government also uses these factors of production in providing services for its citizens. These factors of production, like labour, are purchased in factor markets, and the sellers of these resources receive some form of factor income. Entrepreneurial services are also traded in factor markets, and the providers of such services receive another form of factor income. Recall that rent, interest, and profits are incomes derived from land, capital, and entrepreneurial services respectively.

According to Karl Marx, a nineteenth-century German philosopher and economist, rent, profits, and interest are surplus values obtained from oppressing workers whose labour services are, Marx felt, the source of all value. The demanding of rent, interest, and profits by landlords and capitalists was nothing but the exploitation of labour. In this chapter, we shall see whether Marxist views on rents, interest, and profits are valid. In doing so, we shall also determine what purposes are served by these types of income.

About 75% of total income goes to labour in the form of wages, salaries, and supplementary labour income. The remaining 25% is allocated between land, capital, and entrepreneurial services in the form of rent, interest, and profits. It is important for the student to be clear about the sense in which these terms are used; we will discuss their meanings in the next few sections.

THE MEANING OF RENT

Rent: the return to a factor whose supply is fixed.

Learning Objective 1: *the meaning of rent*

Pure economic rent: the income earned from a factor of production whose supply is completely price inelastic.

The monthly payment made by a tenant to a landlord for an apartment is commonly called rent. You can also rent a car for a weekend. Or you can rent tools from a tool rental company. These notions of rent, however, differ from the economic concept of rent. In economics, **rent** refers to the return on a productive factor the supply of which is fixed. **Pure economic rent** is the income earned by a factor of production whose supply is completely price inelastic. Land is often used as the best example of a factor of production that generates pure economic rent because, for practical purposes, the total quantity of land available is fixed.

Let us examine briefly this notion of a fixed quantity of land. Physically, the supply of land available to society is fixed. There is just so much land available to society, and offers of higher prices will not induce a greater quantity. The fertility of land, however, can be increased or reduced. Moreover, land can undergo a variety of improvements, such as drainage of swamps. But these improvements do not actually create new land. We can view these improvements to land as increasing capital rather than creating new land. It is important to note also that the quantity of land available for one use can be increased by reducing the quantity available for some other use. For example, farm land can be converted into land for residential purposes.

RENT DETERMINATION

Learning Objective 2: *rent determination*

Let us follow the classical tradition of using land to illustrate the determination of rent. Rent is determined in the market like any other price: by demand and supply. In Figure 14.1, the demand curve D_L slopes downward. This downward slope indicates that as the rent decreases, the quantity of land demanded increases. The vertical supply curve S_L shows that the supply of land is fixed at Q_L. The demand and supply curves intersect at R to give the market-determined rental value of r_e.

FIGURE 14.1

Demand and supply
curves for land.

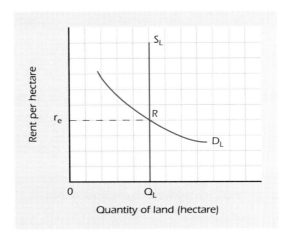

Rent is determined by the
intersection of the demand
and supply curves for land.

Because supply is fixed,
changes in rent are due to
changes in demand.

Note that changes in demand will change the rent per hectare of land. In Figure 14.2, if the demand for land is D_1, the rent per hectare will be r_1 and total economic rent will be the shaded area in the diagram ($Q_L \times r_1$). An increase in the demand for land from D_1 to D_2 will cause the rent per hectare to increase from r_1 to r_2, and the additional economic rent will be the unshaded area in Figure 14.2.

FIGURE 14.2

Effect of an increase in
demand for land.

An increase in the demand
for land causes an increase
in rent.

RENT DIFFERENTIALS

Yield per hectare, resource
content, and location affect
the demand and hence the
rental value of land.

It is clear from the foregoing analysis that differences in rent are due to differences in demand for different parcels of land. In explaining rent differentials then, we must consider the factors that affect the demand for different parcels of land.

Let us consider a piece of land intended for wheat farming somewhere in Manitoba. Obviously, the demand by potential users depends on the expected yield per hectare. The higher the yield per hectare of this particular parcel of land, the greater the demand for it will be. And the greater the demand, the higher the rent.

Learning Objective 3:
rent differentials

Resource content also affects the demand for land — and thus rent. We can expect a parcel of land rich in mineral deposits to generate a higher rental value than a parcel with no mineral deposits. We base such an expectation on the assumption that the demand for the resource-rich parcel is likely to be higher than the demand for the barren parcel.

Finally, the location of land will have some effect on its demand and hence on its rental value. Compare the rent for land in the heart of a large city such as Montreal, Toronto, or Vancouver with the rent for land in a more remote area such as Petty Harbour, Newfoundland.

PROBLEM SOLVING 14-1

The downtown area of many cities is cluttered by high-rise buildings. In outlying areas, however, high rises are few. Explain this phenomenon.

ECONOMIC RENT AND TRANSFER EARNINGS

We defined rent earlier as the income earned by a factor of production whose supply is perfectly price inelastic. Another way of understanding rent is to view it as a return to a factor of production over and above its opportunity cost. Many superstars in music, sports, and entertainment earn exceptionally high incomes, and many people openly express dissatisfaction with the huge incomes earned by these individuals. Criticism of superstar salaries, however, is actually aimed at the rent portion of their incomes.

Many salaries consist of rent and transfer earnings.

Transfer earnings is the minimum payment required to attract resources away from other uses.

What is the rent portion of the income of a hockey player who earns $450 000 annually? To answer this question, we must determine the next best employment alternative for this hockey player. In other words, what is the opportunity cost? Or what is the minimum that this hockey player must earn playing hockey to decide not to quit hockey and take up some other job? This minimum is sometimes called **transfer earnings**, which is the amount of money that a factor of production can earn in the next best employment alternative.

Let us assume that the best employment this hockey player could get outside of hockey is a job that pays $30 000 a year. Then the excess ($420 000) is the rent portion of the hockey player's income. Superstars are paid very high salaries because their employers judge their marginal revenue products to be very high. Note that resources other than land are fixed in supply only in the short run. Incomes derived from such resources are usually called **quasi rent** to distinguish them from pure economic rent.

Quasi rent is the return on a factor whose supply is fixed only in the short run.

An issue often raised in connection with the rent portion of income is the economic effect of taxing away such income. Some people argue that taxing away the rent portion of income does not affect incentives or resource use. For example, if the rent portion of a hockey player's income is taxed, that person will likely continue to be a hockey player. Hockey players are unlikely to quit hockey for other careers because their incomes as hockey players are higher than the incomes that they could earn in other occupations.

Rent may be necessary to maintain certain resources.

However, if the rent portion of income is taxed away, will individuals still push themselves to achieve that rare quality that makes them superstars? Will they still take the time and trouble to develop and maintain those talents and skills that contribute to their exceptionally high incomes? How many would continue to strive for perfection? These questions are not easy to answer. One could conclude that rents are essential because they provide incentives for certain resources to be maintained.

A TAX ON LAND

The incomes of superstars can be explained, at least partly, by their practice and hard work in order to excel at what they do. But what about landowners? Consider the owner of a piece of land in some isolated area. Population growth or a population shift could increase the demand for the land, thus raising its price twentyfold within a relatively short time. This massive economic rent on the land would be a matter of luck rather than exerted effort or diligent work. For this reason, many argue that the economic rent from land should be taxed. Such a tax, it is argued, is neutral in that it affects neither the incentives to produce nor the allocation of resources. The landowner simply pays the tax, and that's it. The incidence (burden) of the tax falls entirely on the landowner.

In practice, however, a land tax as suggested above may have some difficulties. Rarely is the payment for land limited to the land itself. It often includes payment for investment made to improve the land, and it may not be easy to separate the improvements made to the land from the land itself. Taxing the economic rent from land under such circumstances would adversely affect investment such as land clearing and drainage.

INTEREST

Interest is the payment for or the income derived from a loan.

Learning Objective 4:
interest and interest rate determination

Quite simply stated, interest is the payment for the use of money for a specified period of time. In order to purchase capital (machines, buildings, tools, etc.), many firms borrow funds and pay interest to those who lend these funds. Households also borrow money from financial institutions such as banks to purchase certain items such as cars, furniture, and appliances, and pay interest to these lenders. People lend money directly to corporations by purchasing corporate bonds, or indirectly by depositing funds in banks and other financial institutions that accept deposits. People lend money to the federal government by purchasing Canada Savings Bonds. To the lenders, interest represents income, while to the borrowers, it represents a cost. We can look at interest in a slightly different way. If I lend you $500, I am foregoing consumption that I could have had with my money. In order to induce me to forego that consumption, you must pay me something. This payment is interest.

It is important at this point to distinguish between interest and the rate of interest or interest rate. Clearly, from the discussion so far, interest is a sum of money. The amount lent or borrowed is called the principal. The rate of interest is the ratio of the interest to the principal, expressed as a percentage.

$$\text{rate of interest} = \frac{\text{interest}}{\text{principal}} \times 100$$

For example, if you borrow $500 for one year and you pay $60 interest, then the rate of interest on your loan is 12% per year. The rate of interest can be viewed as the price paid for the use of borrowed money.

Interest income depends on the amount of funds a factor owner has lent out and on the rate of interest. If I lend $1000 at an interest rate of 5% per year, my interest income will be $50 a year. If the interest rate were 10% a year, my interest income would be $100 a year. Clearly then, the rate of interest is important in determining the return on loans.

DETERMINATION OF THE RATE OF INTEREST

The rate of interest is determined by the demand for and supply of loanable funds.

Learning Objective 4:
interest and interest rate determination

Loanable funds theory of interest: the interest rate is determined by the demand for and supply of loanable funds.

The rate of interest is a price — the price of a loan. This price is determined in the market by the demand for and supply of borrowed funds or loanable funds. In Figure 14.3, the demand for loanable funds is shown by D. This demand is assumed to come from firms that want to borrow funds for investment purposes, from consumers who want to purchase certain consumer items, and from governments that want to spend more than their revenues, that is, to finance their deficits. The demand curve slopes downward, indicating that a greater amount of funds will be borrowed as the rate of interest falls. The supply of loanable funds comes from the savings of consumers, businesses, and governments in surplus positions. The demand and supply curves intersect at point A to give the equilibrium rate of interest, r, and the equilibrium quantity of loanable funds, LF. This model of interest rate determination is referred to as the **loanable funds theory of the rate of interest**.

FIGURE 14.3

Demand for and supply of loanable funds.

The intersection of the demand and supply curves for loanable funds determines the equilibrium rate of interest.

PROBLEM SOLVING 14-2

Canadians are big savers. How would interest rates be affected if Canadians were not such big savers?

INTEREST RATE DIFFERENTIALS

So far, we have talked about the rate of interest as if a single rate of interest existed for all types of credit instruments. (Credit instruments are written evidences that credit has been extended by the holder of the instrument.) In fact, interest rates vary according to the borrower and type of loan.

The risk premium is an addition to the interest rate to compensate for the risk of defaulting.

All loans carry a certain amount of risk, but the risks associated with different types of loans vary. One reason for differences in interest rates is differences in the degree of risk associated with loans. The probability of defaulting on a loan varies from borrower to borrower. Those borrowers likely to default will be charged a **risk premium**, an addition to the interest rate to compensate for the risk of defaulting. For example, the **prime lending rate** (the interest rate charged by banks to their most credit-worthy corporate customers) is lower than the rate charged to less credit-worthy borrowers. The greater the risk of default, other things being equal, the higher the risk premium will be.

The prime lending rate is the interest rate charged to the most credit-worthy customers.

A loan is paid off at maturity.

Another factor that contributes to interest rate differentials is maturity. **Maturity** is the length of time before the loan is paid off. Generally, the interest rate on a long-term loan is higher than that on a short-term loan. This conclusion is based on the assumption that people prefer to have their money now than later. In other words, people have a preference for liquidity; that is, they like to have ready access to their money. Since short-term loans are more liquid than long-term loans, lenders have to be induced to lend for longer periods by offering them higher interest rates.

A third factor that explains differences in interest rates is the stage of development of the market for the specific credit instrument. If the market for a specific credit instrument is well-developed, the transaction cost of buying or selling that instrument will be relatively low; hence the rate of interest will tend to be low. In places where financial markets are not well-developed, it is very difficult to negotiate loans, and often the very few lenders that operate in such places charge usurious interest rates.

REAL VERSUS NOMINAL INTEREST RATES

The nominal rate of interest is the real rate plus an adjustment for inflation.

Economists usually distinguish between the real rate of interest and the nominal rate of interest. The **real rate of interest** is the rate charged in the absence of inflation. The

nominal rate of interest is the rate quoted for a loan or a deposit, and includes a premium to compensate for the level of inflation. Let us illustrate the relation between the real and nominal rates of interest with the following example. Let us assume that the annual rate of inflation is 10%. This means that at the end of the year, a given sum of money will purchase only 90% of what it could purchase at the beginning of the year. If Mary Braley borrows $1000 for a year, when she repays the loan at the end of the year, the $1000 will purchase only $900. Without making any allowance for inflation, the lender would have lost 10% purchasing power over the year. An increase in prices lowers the value (purchasing power) of money. Thus, if lenders expect a rate of inflation of 10% per year, they will likely protect themselves from loss due to inflation by adding 10 percentage points to the real rate of interest. If lenders would normally have charged 7% interest in the absence of inflation, they would now charge 17% because of inflation. In the above example, the real rate is 7% while the nominal rate is 17%. The following equation expresses the relation between the nominal rate and the real rate:

$$NR = RR + e$$

where NR is the nominal rate, RR is the real rate, and e is the rate of inflation.

PROBLEM SOLVING 14-3
Is it always less costly to borrow money at a 4% interest rate than at a 17% interest rate?

PROFITS

In computing profits, economists consider all opportunity costs; accountants do not.

Learning Objective 5: profit and its economic significance

It is important for you to understand the difference between the accountant's notion of profits and the economist's concept of profits. Accounting profits refer to the excess of sales revenues from goods and services over the expenses incurred in producing the goods and services. Economic profits, on the other hand, refer to the excess of revenues from the sale of goods and services over the total cost, including opportunity cost, of producing the goods and services. The following example will help to illustrate the difference. The revenues and expenses of Joseph Seanan, the owner of a pine cabinet shop, are shown in Table 14.1. Such a statement is referred to as an **income statement**. Note that accounting profits are also referred to as **net income**.

TABLE 14.1

Revenues and expenses.

An income statement shows revenues, expenses, and net income.

Revenue:		
Sales..		$50 000
Expenses:		
Rent..	$ 2 500	
Utility	600	
Wages...	15 000	
Transportation	800	
Materials & supplies	10 000	
Miscellaneous...............................	500	
TOTAL expenses.......................		$29 400
Net Income ($50 000 – $29 400)		$20 600

Net income: revenue minus expenses.

In order to calculate economic profits, however, we would need to know not just the expenses incurred by Joseph Seanan, but also how much Joseph could have earned in the next best alternative job. In other words, what is Joseph's opportunity cost? Let us assume that Joseph's opportunity cost is $20 600. Then we would have the following situation:

Total revenue ……................ $50 000

Total cost = $29 400 + $20 600 = $50 000

Profits ($50 000 – $50 000) …. = $0

Normal profits are returns that just equal the opportunity costs of the resources.

In this case, Joseph is earning zero economic profits, or normal profits. If, however, Joseph can earn only $18 000 instead of operating his shop, then the situation would change as follows:

Total revenue ……................ $50 000

Total cost = $29 400 + $18 000 = $47 400

Profits ($50 000 – $47 400)…… = $ 2 600

He would then earn positive economic profits of $2600.

PROFIT AS A RETURN ON INNOVATION AND ENTREPRENEURIAL ABILITY

Why do people decide to own their own business enterprises rather than sell their factor services to others? One answer is the prospect of greater profits. Presumably, many people feel that they have better insight, more imagination, and are more adventurous than anyone they have worked for. If these people are indeed as innovative as they think and their innovations succeed, then they are compensated with profits. If they fail, they suffer losses.

PROFIT AS A RETURN FOR RISK-TAKING

Profits may be viewed as a return on innovation, a reward for risk-bearing, or the result of market power.

No matter how shrewd businesspeople may be, they must confront the risk involved in owning their own businesses. Profits are sometimes viewed as a reward for bearing the risks of business ownership — a sort of risk premium. In the absence of this risk premium, many people would not consider it worth their while to bear the risks associated with ownership.

PROFITS FROM MARKET POWER

We have already seen that a firm in pure competition may earn positive economic profits in the short run, but that in the long run, because of competition, such profits will dwindle away. A firm with significant market power may be able to earn positive economic profits even in the long run because of effective barriers to entry such as patent rights, economies of scale, and limit-pricing techniques.

THE ECONOMIC ROLE OF PROFITS

Profits serve as a signal for resource allocation, a motive for efficiency, and a reward for the enterprising.

Learning Objective 5:
profit and its economic significance

Basically, profits perform three economic functions:

1. they serve as a signal to resource owners;

2. they provide a motive or incentive for efficiency;

3. they reward the resourceful.

Let us now briefly examine each of these economic functions of profits.

PROFITS AS A SIGNAL TO RESOURCE OWNERS

The existence of profits in any industry or sector of the economy is a clear signal that price exceeds average cost of production, and that resources should be shifted into that industry or sector. Likewise, the existence of losses in an industry is a loud and clear signal that resources should be shifted out of that industry and put to more productive uses.

PROFITS AS A MOTIVE FOR EFFICIENCY

The desire for profits serves as an incentive for producers to cut production costs where possible. In the face of competition, high-cost firms will lose their market shares to low-cost firms. Unless high-cost firms can increase their efficiency, they will ultimately be forced out of the market.

PROFITS AS REWARD

Profits serve as a reward for the resourceful, the imaginative, the innovative, and the enterprising. The prospect of earning profits is often the driving force behind the development and maintenance of special resources and talents.

PROBLEM SOLVING 14-4
What are the economic effects of taxation of excess profits?

A P P L I C A T I O N

Understanding Income Inequality

Why is income unequally distributed in a market economy? People derive income from the resources at their disposal. Owners of labour of high quality in great demand will tend to earn high wages and salaries. Owners of prime land in great demand will receive huge payments in the form of rent. Owners of scarce capital will earn income in the form of interest and dividends, and people with entrepreneurial skills will receive profit income. Resources are unevenly distributed. Some individuals in our society, for a variety of reasons, do not own or have control over valuable resources, hence they receive relatively small incomes.

CHAPTER SUMMARY

1. About 25% of total income takes the form of rent, interest, and profits.

2. Pure economic rent is the return on a factor of production that is completely fixed in supply. The return on a factor that is fixed only in the short run, such as exceptional talent, is quasi rent.

3. Rent is determined in the market by demand and supply. Changes in demand explain changes in rent.

4. Rent differentials result mainly from differences in the demand for different parcels of land. Location is an important factor in rent differentials.

5. Rent serves as an incentive for the development and maintenance of certain types of resources.

6. Interest is income derived from loans. The loans may be made directly by the purchase of bonds or indirectly by deposits on financial institutions.

7. The demand for and supply of loanable funds determine the rate of interest. The demand for loanable funds comes from firms, consumers, and government. The supply of loanable funds comes from savers.

8. Profits may be viewed as a return on entrepreneurial ability or a reward for risk-taking.

9. Profits serve as a signal for resource movement, a motive for efficiency, and a reward for enterprise.

TERMS FOR REVIEW

rent (251)
pure economic rent (251)
transfer earnings (253)
quasi rent (253)
loanable funds theory of interest (254)
risk premium (255)

prime lending rate (255)
maturity (255)
real versus nominal rate of interest (255)
income statement (256)
net income (256)

QUESTIONS FOR REVIEW AND DISCUSSION

1. In what way does rent differ from other types of income? (L.O.1)

2. What are the main determinants of rent differentials? (L.O.3)

3. Justify the high salaries earned by superstars. (L.O.2,3)

4. Would you support a proposal to tax away the rent portion of income? Defend your position. (L.O.3)

5. Distinguish between interest and the rate of interest. (L.O.4)

6. How is the rate of interest determined in a purely competitive market for funds? (L.O.4)

7. How would an increase in government borrowing affect the rate of interest? (L.O.4)

8. Interest rates tend to be high during inflationary times. Explain why this is so. (L.O.4)

9. Why are some groups able to borrow at lower rates of interest than other groups? (L.O.4)

10. Differentiate between accounting profits and economic profits. (L.O.5)

11. Do profits perform any economic functions? (L.O.5)

PROBLEMS AND EXERCISES

1. Use diagrams to illustrate the difference in demand for a hectare of swamp land 60 km east of Blissfield, New Brunswick, and a hectare of commercial real estate in downtown Fredericton. Which piece of land would normally have the higher rental value and why? (L.O.2)

2. Buffy Fleetfoot plays lacrosse for the Winnipeg Wendigos and earns a salary of $175 000 per year. Outside of lacrosse, she could earn a maximum of $80 000 annually as the proprietor of a sporting goods store. Apart from the money, it makes no difference to Buffy whether she continues to play lacrosse or whether she assumes proprietorship of the store. What portion of Buffy's salary can be considered rent? (L.O.3)

3. Bab Rushdie earns $400 000 a year as an actor. He could have earned $60 000 at best as a consultant in the public relations department of TV Ontario. What part of his earnings is economic rent and what part is transfer earnings? (L.O.3)

4. How has the invention of television affected the rent portion of the earnings of sports and entertainment superstars? (L.O.3)

5. Your friend, Mei Ling, borrows $100 from you. Because she is your friend, you do not want to make a profit on the loan transaction. Therefore you do not charge her interest. Is this a rational decision? Explain. (L.O.4)

6. It has been said that one difference between profit and rent is that profit can be reduced by competition while rent cannot. Do you agree with this statement? Explain. (L.O.1,5)

7. Pierre Gunter is the proprietor of a photography studio. His typical monthly expenses are shown in Table 14.2. Pierre has been offered as much as $1500 per month to work for other companies. (L.O.5)

TABLE 14.2

Cost and revenue data for Pierre Gunter.

Revenue:

Sale of goods	$ 150
Sale of services	2 500
TOTAL	$2 650

Cost:

Rent	$ 200
Materials	50
Telephone	40
Utilities	30
Wages	500
Other expenses	25
TOTAL	$ 845

Compute:

(a) Pierre's monthly profit (in an accounting sense);

(b) Pierre's monthly profit (in an economic sense).

Internet Site

http://www.bmo.com
This site is the home page for the Bank of Montreal.

INTERNET EXERCISE

1. Go to the Bank of Montreal Web site.
2. Click on *Rates*.
3. List the different interest rates offered for prime, MasterCard, mortgages, RRSPs, GICs, Small Business, and Savings Accounts.

15

C H A P T E R

INCOME DISTRIBUTION AND POVERTY

Learning Objectives

After studying this chapter, you will know about:

1 the criteria for income distribution

2 the size distribution of income

3 the dimensions of poverty

4 measures to alleviate poverty

5 aspects of the welfare system

6 the negative income tax (NIT)

7 Canada's income security program

For my own part, I believe that there is social and psychological justification for significant inequalities of incomes and wealth, but not for such large disparities as exist today.

J. M. Keynes, *The General Theory*

INTRODUCTION

In the two previous chapters, we looked at various sources of income, including wages, rent, interest, and profits. Each year, Canadians earn a considerable amount of income through the use or sale of the resources at their command. This income, however, is not distributed equally among Canadians. Some Canadians earn annual incomes in excess of $250 000, while others hardly earn enough for the bare necessities of life.

This apparent unfairness in the distribution of income is among the most hotly debated economic and social issues. In this chapter, we shall discuss income distribution in Canada. We shall also discuss the problem of poverty and look at some measures to deal with this great social problem. Finally, we shall look briefly at Canada's welfare system.

CRITERIA FOR INCOME DISTRIBUTION

Learning Objective 1:
the criteria for income distribution

Most people in our society seem to agree that income and wealth should be shared in some manner that is fair. There is no general agreement, however, about what constitutes fairness or equity, or how to distribute income equitably. We shall briefly examine three views about the equitable distribution of income.

DISTRIBUTION ACCORDING TO CONTRIBUTION

Three views on the equitable distribution of income: contribution, need, and equality.

According to this view, income should be distributed according to productivity. Supporters of this view claim that it is only fair to reward people according to their contribution to total output. They see certain advantages to this approach. First, it provides incentives for greater productivity. Second, the system works automatically through the market system.

DISTRIBUTION ACCORDING TO NEED

Another view of income distribution is based on the biblical model of Christian communism:

> For there was not a needy person among them, for all who were owners of land or houses would sell them and bring the proceeds of the sales, and lay them at the apostles' feet; and they would be distributed to each, as any had need.*

This idea has found subsequent expression in the popular saying of the early French revolutionary Louis Blanc: "From each according to his ability, to each according to needs." There are, however, obvious problems with this approach. First, how are needs to be determined? This, in itself, presents an almost insuperable problem. Second, if goods are distributed according to need, is there any incentive to work?

EQUAL DISTRIBUTION TO ALL

According to this view, income should be distributed equally to all. The simplicity of this procedure is appealing. To arrive at the amount to be distributed to each, we simply divide the total income by the population. The problem with this approach to income distribution is that it fails to provide incentives for economic activity; and if there is no incentive for economic activity, the level of economic activity will fall. Such a fall is undesirable.

THE SIZE DISTRIBUTION OF INCOME

Learning Objective 2:
the size distribution of income

The size distribution of income is the distribution of income according to the income groups of the households.

The distribution of income among individuals and households is referred to as the **size distribution of income**. It is a measure that is frequently used to determine how evenly total income is distributed in a given society. If 5% of the households controlled over 90% of the total income and wealth in a society, most people would conclude that the income disparity was too large, and would probably grumble about social injustice. Is income fairly evenly distributed in Canada? Let us consult Table 15.1 for the answer. It contains data on the size distribution of income in Canada in 1996.

---

*Acts of the Apostles 4:34–35.

	Income group	Percentage of families in group	Percentage of income received	Cumulative percentage of families	Cumulative percentage of income received
TABLE 15.1	**(1)**	**(2)**	**(3)**	**(4)**	**(5)**
Distribution of families and of aggregate income of families by income groups, 1996.	Under $10 000	2.3	0.2	2.3	0.2
	$ 10 000 – 14 999	4.2	0.9	6.5	1.1
	$ 15 000 – 19 999	5.5	1.7	12.0	2.8
	$ 20 000 – 24 999	7.0	2.8	19.0	5.6
	$ 25 000 – 29 999	6.5	3.2	25.5	8.8
	$ 30 000 – 34 999	6.2	3.6	31.7	12.4
	$ 35 000 – 39 999	6.6	4.4	38.3	16.8
	$ 40 000 – 44 999	6.4	4.8	44.7	21.6
	$ 45 000 – 49 999	6.0	5.0	50.7	26.6
	$ 50 000 – 54 999	6.3	5.8	57.0	32.4
	$ 55 000 – 59 999	5.3	5.4	62.3	37.8
	$ 60 000 – 64 999	5.2	5.8	67.5	43.6
	$ 65 000 – 69 999	4.4	5.3	71.9	48.9
	$ 70 000 – 74 999	4.2	5.4	76.1	54.3
	$ 75 000 – 79 999	3.7	5.0	79.8	59.3
	$ 80 000 – 89 999	6.1	9.1	85.9	68.4
	$ 90 000 – 99 999	3.9	6.6	89.8	75.0
	$100 000 and over	10.1	25.1	100.0	100.0

Source: Statistics Canada, Income Distribution by Size in Canada, 1996 (Cat. 13-207-XPB):100.

The table shows that in 1996, 2.3% of Canadian families had incomes under $10 000 per year. On the other hand, 10.1% of Canadian families received incomes of $100 000 and over. The information in columns four and five of Table 15.1 is useful in this discussion. About 19% of families received 6% of the total income, while about 90% of the total number of families received about 75% of the total income.

THE LORENZ CURVE

The Lorenz curve is used to measure the degree of income inequality.

An important device for measuring income inequality is the **Lorenz curve**, named after a German economic statistician. The construction of a Lorenz curve is a relatively simple matter, and is illustrated in Figure 15.1. We are measuring the cumulative percent of income along the vertical axis and the cumulative percent of families along the horizontal axis. The diagonal straight line 0A in Figure 15.1 represents an equal distribution

FIGURE 15.1

A Lorenz curve.

The shaded area in the diagram shows the extent of income inequality.

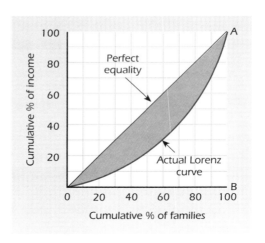

of income. If we were to plot the data contained in columns four and five on a graph, the resulting curve would resemble the actual Lorenz curve indicated in Figure 15.1. The shaded area in the diagram shows the degree of income inequality. The greater the shaded area, the greater the inequality in income distribution.

The Gini coefficient gives an even more precise measure of the extent of inequality in income distribution. The **Gini coefficient** is the area enclosed by the Lorenz curve and the line of perfect equality in income distribution (that is, the shaded area) expressed as a proportion of the area of triangle 0AB in Figure 15.1. For example, if the area of the shaded area is F and the area of the triangle is H, then the Gini coefficient is F/H. The larger the Gini coefficient, the greater the inequality in the distribution of income.

The Gini coefficient is a ratio that measures the degree of inequality in income distribution.

INCOME INEQUALITY BETWEEN THE SEXES

Even before the advent of feminism, there were cries against prejudicial treatment of women. It was claimed that income has always been distributed in favour of men. Figure 15.2 is a graphic presentation of the present-day distribution of income between males and females.

In 1996, about 15% of women but only about 8% of men had incomes under $5000 per year. At the other extreme, 23.3% of men had incomes of $45 000 or more per year, compared with only 7.6% of women. In fact, while the highest concentration of men was in the $50 000-and-over income bracket, the highest concentration of women was in the $10 000-$12 999 income group. We may note also that the average income for men in 1996 was $31 788, while the average for women was only $19 855. Hence, on average, men received more than one and a half times as much income as women did.

PROBLEM SOLVING 15-1
Should everyone in Canada receive the same income?

FIGURE 15.2

Income distribution by sex, 1996.

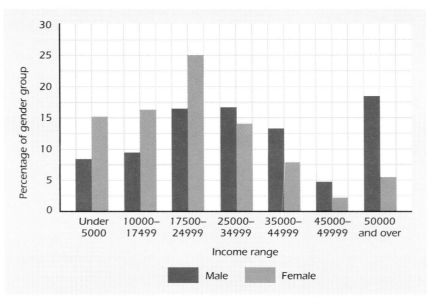

Source: Statistics Canada, *Income Distribution by Size in Canada, 1996* (Cat. 13–207-XPB): 136.

POVERTY

Canada is viewed as a wealthy country and Canadians enjoy a relatively high standard of living. These facts notwithstanding, many Canadians live in poverty. In this section, we shall attempt to define poverty and examine the incidence of poverty.

DEFINITION OF POVERTY

People are poor absolutely when their incomes are below the poverty line.

We can define poverty either in an absolute sense or in a relative sense. We say that a family is living in **absolute poverty** if its income is so low that it cannot afford the goods and services that most people in the society would consider to be just enough to enable the family to live in minimum comfort. There are obvious problems with this definition. How is minimum comfort defined? Who decides what is minimum comfort? Evidently, the amount required to achieve this minimum comfort will vary from family to family and from individual to individual. Despite these problems, it is clear that poverty is the condition of not having enough money to afford the basic needs as society views these needs.

The poverty line (low-income cut-off) is the income level below which a family cannot maintain a satisfactory standard of living.

Poverty is often discussed in terms of what has become known as the **poverty line**, an arbitrary measure of a level of income below which a family or an individual is unable to maintain a satisfactory standard of living.

Statistics Canada has established a **low-income cut-off** or *poverty line* based on the size of the area of residence and on the size of the family unit. For example, the poverty line for an unattached person living in a rural area will be much lower than the poverty line for a couple with three children living in a large urban area. This difference, of course, reflects the fact that the latter would require a larger sum of money to be able to afford the basic necessities of food, shelter, and clothing. According to this criterion, any family or unattached individual whose income is below the poverty line is considered to be living in poverty. Table 15.2 shows low income cut-offs for family units. Based on these low income cut-offs, approximately 1 207 000 families and 1 587 000 unattached individuals, totalling an estimated 5 million persons or about 17% of the Canadian population, were living below the poverty line in 1996. It is interesting to note that in 1991, the figure was 14%.

Another way of determining poverty is to consider the proportion of income spent on food, shelter, and clothing. Statistics Canada has established that families who on average spend 56.2% or more of their income on food, shelter, and clothing are considered to be in straitened circumstances.

TABLE 15.2

Low-income cut-offs of family units, 1996, in dollars.

Size of family unit	Low income cut-offs, based on population of area of residence				
	500 000 and over	**100 000– 499 999**	**30 000– 99 999**	**Less than 30 000**	**Rural areas**
1 person	17 132	14 694	14 591	13 577	11 839
2 persons	21 414	18 367	18 239	16 971	14 799
3 persons	26 633	22 844	22 684	21 107	18 406
4 persons	32 238	27 651	27 459	25 551	22 279
5 persons	36 036	30 910	30 695	28 562	24 905
6 persons	39 835	34 168	33 930	31 571	27 530
7 or more persons	43 634	37 427	37 166	34 581	30 156

Source: Statistics Canada, *Income Distribution by Size in Canada, 1996* (Cat. 13-207-XPB): 51.

A family is in **relative poverty** if its income forces it to accept a standard of living significantly below that enjoyed by other families in the society. Thus, an unattached individual with an annual income of $60 000 will be considered to be relatively poor if the majority of people in the society have annual incomes in excess of $250 000. If we define poverty in relative terms, then there is a great deal of truth in the biblical saying, "ye shall have the poor with you always." Viewed in this way, any substantial unequal distribution of income will give rise to poverty, regardless of the absolute size of the income shares.

People are poor relatively if their incomes are far below the incomes of others.

DIMENSIONS OF POVERTY

Poverty hurts the society as well as the individual.

Poverty imposes severe hardships on individuals. The poor are barred from enjoying the good things in life that many people take for granted. They are deprived of good homes and good health, and their children may be deprived of a good education. As a result, they may turn to various forms of criminal activities. Thus, not only the individual but the society also suffers as a result of poverty.

Learning Objective 3:
the dimensions of poverty

In addition to the loss of property (and possibly life) that may result from poverty, there are other economic disadvantages. Because the poor are likely to have low levels of education and skills, their productivity is likely to be low. This low productivity prevents the economy's output of goods and services from reaching its full potential. Hence, the population as a whole must accept a lower standard of living.

THE INCIDENCE OF POVERTY

The incidence of poverty refers to the chances or likelihood of being poor.

Poverty is not confined to any one region, age group, sex, or race. It is found among the young as well as the old, among rural areas as well as large urban centres, among men as well as women. The distribution of low income families and unattached individuals roughly follows the distribution of the population. Yet, in general, there are certain groups that are more likely to be poor than other groups. Below, we discuss the **incidence of poverty**, identifying groups with a high probability of being poor.

Families with many children

Families with a large number of young children have a high incidence of poverty. For example, the incidence of poverty for a family with three or more children under 16 is nearly one and a half times as high as for a family with one or two children under the age of 16.

Families in certain provinces

Certain groups have a higher incidence of poverty than others.

Families in the Atlantic provinces (particularly in Newfoundland and Nova Scotia) and Quebec are more likely to be poor than families in Ontario or B.C. This should not obscure the fact that most Canadians living in poverty are from Quebec and Ontario, the two provinces that comprise the country's largest population.

Families in rural areas

The incidence of poverty is also usually high among families in rural areas. Poverty in rural areas is usually less visible than in urban areas. For instance, the urban poor may live in run-down houses, while the rural poor may not. The prospects of finding jobs that offer high remuneration in rural areas are usually not very good, and in general, the incomes of farm operators and farm workers tend to be substantially below incomes earned by families in urban areas. Expectations of a better life in the city may attract some people (especially young adults) into the city, where they are only added to the list of the urban poor. This fact partly explains the high incidence of poverty in large urban areas.

Families headed by females

Poverty is widespread among families headed by females. A family headed by a female is over four times as likely to be poor as a family whose head is a male. Proportionally, the incidence of poverty is particularly high among families headed by single females. About 38% of all low-income families in Canada are headed by females. Fifty-eight per-cent of unattached females are poor.

Young families

The incidence of poverty is high among families whose heads are 24 years old or less. Such families are more than four times as likely to be poor as families whose heads are between 45 and 54 years old. One of the reasons for poverty among young families is that they often lack education, valuable skills, and working experience.

Elderly families

Female heads of families and unattached individuals who are over 70 years old have a high incidence of poverty. Just over 5% of all low-income families in Canada have heads who are 70 years old or older. These are mostly retired people who live on pension income.

Families headed by self-employed individuals

The incidence of poverty for families whose heads are self-employed is nearly twice as high as that for families whose heads are paid workers. About 10% of all low-income families in Canada have self-employed heads.

Families headed by individuals not in the labour force

Families whose heads are not in the labour force have a high incidence of poverty. The heads of such families are usually infirm or incapacitated, and must therefore look for ways of sustaining themselves other than employment income.

Unattached individuals

Those who are unattached, unemployed, self-employed, 70 years and older, female, or resident in the Atlantic provinces are most likely to be poor.

In general, the incidence of poverty among unattached individuals is about three times as high as that among families. The incidence of poverty is particularly high among unattached individuals who are not in the labour force, who are 70 years and older, who have low levels of education, who are self-employed, who live in the Atlantic Provinces, or who are females.

PROBLEM SOLVING 15-2

Can you account for the relatively large number of unattached individuals living below the poverty line in urban areas?

CAUSES OF POVERTY

It is impossible to identify any single cause of poverty or to attribute poverty to one major cause. The causes of poverty are numerous and no one cause can claim supremacy over the others. We can, however, discuss some of the prime causes of poverty.

Low productivity

Causes of poverty include low productivity, low eco-nomic growth, lack of resources, physical and mental disabilities, and discrimination.

One cause of poverty is low productivity. We know that in a purely competitive labour market, each worker will be paid the value of his or her marginal product. Even in an imperfect market setting, workers with high productivity tend to be paid higher wages than workers with low productivity. Workers with low productivity, then, will likely have low incomes.

THE CANADA PENSION PLAN

The Canada Pension Plan (CPP) and its counterpart in Quebec, the Quebec Pension Plan (QPP), provide benefits to people who have contributed to the plan. Contributors are eligible to receive monthly retirement pension after their 60th birthday. Almost all employed and self-employed persons between the ages of 18 and 70 who earn more than a minimum yearly level of income are covered by the CPP/QPP. The plan is funded through contributions from employees, employers and self-employed persons, and from interest from the Canada Pension Plan Fund. The CPP and QPP are indexed to the cost of living.

EMPLOYMENT INSURANCE AND WORKERS' COMPENSATION

Established in 1940, the Unemployment Insurance program was intended to insure workers against loss of income during periods of unemployment. Employees contribute a certain percentage of their income to the plan while they are employed. Once they become unemployed and they qualify for benefits under the plan, they can draw benefits. This program was replaced by the new Employment Insurance system, the stated objective of which is to encourage people to return to the job market. In fact, the system emphasizes the merits of a rapid return to work. The Employment Insurance system extends temporary income support or income benefits to about three million people.

PROBLEM SOLVING 15-3

The depressing statistics on poverty seem to conflict with everyday observations of affluence. Why?

THE NEGATIVE INCOME TAX (NIT)

Negative income tax: a scheme whereby the government pays a subsidy to low-income people to provide a guaranteed minimum income.

Most people would probably agree that families ought to be guaranteed some minimum income. They would also agree that it is desirable to provide this minimum income without at the same time destroying the incentive to work. To accomplish both, however, is easier said than done. A negative income tax is one scheme proposed to deal with this question.

Learning Objective 6: *the negative income tax (NIT)*

Under a **negative income tax** (NIT) system, an individual whose income is below a prescribed level need not pay income tax to the government: instead the government pays the individual. The amount of payment varies with the individual's income. There are many ways in which the payment by the government may vary with the individual's income. Table 15.3 illustrates one way in which an NIT program might work.

TABLE 15.3

Operation of a negative income tax.

Earned income	Government payment (a negative tax)	After-tax income
$ 0	$ 4 000	$4 000
1 000	3 500	4 500
2 000	3 000	5 000
3 000	2 500	5 500
4 000	2 000	6 000
5 000	1 500	6 500
6 000	1 000	7 000
7 000	500	7 500
8 000	0	8 000
9 000	−500	8 500
10 000	−1 000	9 000

Suppose the government decides to guarantee a minimum annual income of $4000 and that thereafter for every extra dollar earned up to say, $8000, the government subsidy will be reduced by $0.50. Thus, the government pays an individual who has earned no income for a year a subsidy — a negative income tax — of $4000. For an income of $1000, the subsidy of $4000 will be reduced by $500 ($0.50 for every dollar of income), so the individual receives a payment of $3500. If the individual earns $8000, the subsidy of $4000 is reduced by a half of that income (that is, by $4000) so no payment is received from the government. It is important to note that, under the NIT scheme, the income subsidy is reduced but not taken away entirely if the individual earns an income below $8000.

ADVANTAGES OF THE NIT

Proponents of the NIT claim for it the following advantages:

1. Under the NIT, the incentive to work is not destroyed. Under some welfare programs, the individual may be better off not working because the reduction in the subsidy may be greater than any extra income that could be earned by working. This is not the case with the NIT.

2. Individuals are left to spend their income as they see fit. They are not told how they should spend their income as is the case, for example, with subsidized housing. Thus, under the NIT, individuals have a greater freedom of choice.

3. The administration of an NIT program is relatively simple. It should require a smaller bureaucratic structure than that required for many other programs because for the most part, it would be administered by Revenue Canada personnel.

PROBLEMS WITH THE NIT

The above arguments in favour of the NIT have been countered by critics. The opponents of the NIT scheme advance the following arguments:

1. The NIT would not be less expensive than the programs now in existence, and the cost would also escalate.

2. The establishment of a national low-income cut-off is impractical. An established poverty line may be too low for Ontario but too high for Newfoundland. So it may be necessary to establish poverty lines on a regional or provincial basis.

3. The NIT is politically problematic, because many voters vehemently oppose the idea of making direct cash payments to people for staying at home and doing nothing.

CANADA'S EXPERIENCE WITH NIT

An experimental NIT program was introduced in Manitoba in the 1970s. As yet, no conclusive statement can be made about the effects of the NIT based on this experiment. However, evidence seems to suggest that less social stigma is attached to people who quit their jobs to accept an NIT than to those who quit to go on welfare as the term is traditionally understood. This implies that the NIT has an adverse effect on incentives to work. This view is supported by results from similar experiments in the United States where the NIT, aimed at encouraging people to work, seemed to have a disincentive effect on work effort.

CHAPTER SUMMARY

1. The unequal distribution of income among families and individuals is a hotly debated issue.

2. Three competing schools of thought about the equitable distribution of income

are: the productivity approach, the need approach, and the equality approach. The need and equality approaches may adversely affect work incentive.

3. The Lorenz curve is a useful graphic device for measuring and illustrating the degree of income inequality in income distribution.

4. The Gini coefficient expresses income inequality as a ratio. The larger the ratio, the greater the degree of income inequality.

5. Poverty, defined in an absolute sense, exists when families or individuals have such a low income that they cannot afford the goods and services necessary to maintain minimum comfort.

6. Poverty, defined in a relative sense, exists when a family or an individual has an income that is substantially lower than that of many other families or individuals.

7. Although poverty is not confined to any particular group, some groups are more likely to be poor than others. Groups with high incidence of poverty include families with many young children, families in the Atlantic provinces, families in rural areas, families with female heads, young families, elderly families, families with self-employed heads, families whose heads are not in the labour force, and unattached individuals.

8. Some of the causes of poverty are low productivity, low economic growth, lack of large quantities of valuable resources, physical and mental disabilities, and discrimination.

9. Suggestions to alleviate poverty include increasing the productivity of the working poor, accelerating the rate of economic growth, making laws forbidding discriminatory practices, assisting the poor, and providing employment for disabled persons in special government-operated workshops.

10. Through various income security programs, Canada offers assistance to people in difficult economic circumstances and provides income security for its citizens and legal residents.

11. A negative income tax, whereby instead of taxing people with low incomes, the government gives them subsidies, has been proposed as a means of dealing with the problem of poverty.

12. Supporters of the NIT claim that it does not destroy work incentive, that individuals are better off because they are left to decide how to spend their incomes, and that its administration is relatively simple. Arguments against the NIT are that it would be costly to operate, that it would be impractical to establish a national low-income cut-off, and that it is likely to encounter political resistance.

TERMS FOR REVIEW

size distribution of income (262)
Lorenz curve (263)
Gini coefficient (264)
absolute poverty (265)
poverty line (265)
low-income cut-off (265)

relative poverty (266)
incidence of poverty (266)
economic discrimination (employment, wage, and occupational discrimination) (268)
negative income tax (NIT) (270)

QUESTIONS FOR REVIEW AND DISCUSSION

1. What criteria have been suggested for an equitable distribution of income? (L.O.1)

2. Of the three criteria suggested for an equitable distribution of income, which do you consider to be the best? Support your choice. (L.O.1)

3. What problems could be expected from using the need approach to income distribution? (L.O.1)
4. What do you understand by the term size distribution of income ? (L.O.2)
5. What is the Lorenz curve? Is it of any practical importance? (L.O.2)
6. Write a short note on the incidence of poverty. (L.O.3)
7. What are some of the major causes of poverty? (L.O.3)
8. What are some of the measures that can be taken to alleviate poverty? (L.O.4)
9. What are the main issues in the NIT debate? (L.O.6)
10. Briefly describe the income security program. (L.O.7)

PROBLEMS AND EXERCISES

1. On the basis of Table 15.1, do you consider the size distribution of income in Canada to be unfair? Why or why not? (L.O.2)
2. On a graph, draw four Lorenz curves ranging from equal income distribution to most unequal distribution. Label the curves (L.O.2)

FIGURE 15.3

Lorenz curves.

(a) equal distribution
(b) unequal distribution
(c) more unequal distribution
(d) most unequal distribution

3. Figure 15.3 shows Lorenz curves for two countries, A and B. The numbers in the diagram are for the areas indicated. (L.O.2)
   (a) Compute the Gini coefficient for countries A and B.
   (b) What do these coefficients tell you about income distribution in A relative to B?
4. "Poverty is not a serious problem in Canada because Canada is a rich country. Moreover, we have a welfare system that relieves the hardships that the poor would otherwise suffer." Discuss. (L.O.3)
5. "Poverty is a problem that will always exist." Discuss. (L.O.3)
6. The government establishes a guaranteed annual income of $2000 and decides to reduce the income subsidy (negative tax) by 40% of each extra dollar of earned income. Complete Table 15.4. (L.O.6)

TABLE 15.4	Earned income	NIT	Total income
Negative income tax.	$ 000	$2 000	$2 000
	1 000		
	2 000		
	3 000		
	4 000		
	5 000		

7. Find out what social assistance or welfare programs are available from your provincial government and compile a list of those programs or services. (L.O.7)

VIDEO CASE

A UNION AT MCDONALD'S?

Introduction

Early Industrial-Revolution workers earned low wages for long hours of work in poor conditions. Groups of trade and craft workers tried to organize for better wages and working conditions but encountered severe problems, and union organizers experienced ugly incidents. Even the courts were unsympathetic to the labour union movement. Only in 1939 did it become illegal for employers to dismiss pro-union workers. Today, workers enjoy many advantages because of labour union activity.

A Brief Review of McDonald's

In 1948, Californian brothers Richard and Maurice McDonald opened the world's first McDonald's restaurant. In 1954, they granted exclusive U.S. franchising rights to 52-year-old salesman Ray Kroc, who in 1955 founded McDonald's Corporation.

In 1963, McDonald's was selling one million hamburgers a day. When Ray Kroc died in January 1984, McDonald's sales had reached over $10 billion, having sold over 50 billion hamburgers in 8300 restaurants across 36 countries. Over 24 500 McDonald's restaurants now exist in 114 countries. In 1997, sales totalled $33 638.3 billion.

McDonald's in Canada

On June 1, 1967, McDonald's opened in Richmond, B.C., its first non-American restaurant. In 1997, McDonald's Restaurants of Canada Limited had nearly 1000 outlets across Canada, employed more than 70 000 Canadians, and served on average two million customers daily.

The Labour Scene — The Context

McDonald's employs tens of thousands of high school and college students across Canada. McDonald's says it's a good place to work, offering employees exceptional training, specific skills, and important values like responsibility, self-esteem, punctuality and teamwork. Home Office employees enjoy educational assistance, excellent salary, life insurance, medical and dental benefits, and paid vacations and holidays. These benefits are not extended to the tens of thousands of employees who "sling burgers" at McDonald's, however. On March 5, 1997, employees of McDonald's in Montreal-suburb St. Hubert publicly complained of poor working conditions and low wages, and started a drive for unionization. The workers claimed that management made them work 30 minutes prior to their scheduled start time for free, and had them perform unsafe jobs apart from their assigned responsibilities. One employee alleged that after six years at McDonald's he was earning only $6.90/h—just $.20/h above minimum wage. Another claimed to be earning only $6.75 an hour after 15 months of employment. The powerful Teamsters union supported the unionization bid, and the organizers were optimistic that the union at McDonald's would be a reality. It did not happen. The restaurant closed its doors.

QUESTIONS

1. List the main points in this case.
2. Despite other attempts, no McDonald's restaurant in Canada has been unionized. Why do you think that management so resists unionization of McDonald's workers?
3. The St. Hubert outlet preferred to close rather than to allow unionization. What considerations might have led to that decision?
4. Find out from a McDonald's employee whether or not it is a good place to work.

16

C H A P T E R

THE ECONOMICS OF ENVIRONMENTAL PROTECTION

Learning Objectives

After studying this chapter, you should be able to:

1 discuss the main sources of market failure

2 understand the nature of economic externalities

3 discuss the concept of public good

4 evaluate the role of government in the light of market failure

5 explain how economic analysis can help to arrive at an appropriate level of pollution

6 discuss measures to deal with the problem of pollution

Nevertheless, there are responsible decisions to be made in this area, and these decisions are not reached wholly in the dark.

Kenneth E. Boulding, *Principles of Economic Policy*

INTRODUCTION

In our study of pure competition in Chapter 10, we observed that the purely competitive model resulted in the efficient allocation of resources. Under this hypothetical economic system, the economy produces what people want, and it does so efficiently, i.e., at the lowest cost. We showed that the purely competitive model achieves Pareto efficiency. We have also seen that when the assumptions of the purely competitive model are relaxed, as in the case of monopoly and imperfect competition, then the market fails to achieve efficient outcomes.

In this chapter, we study the problem of market failure, paying special attention to the economics of environmental protection. We shall also look at various responses (solutions) to market failure and examine the role of government.

SOURCES OF MARKET FAILURE

Learning Objective 1:
discuss the main sources
of market failure

Economists use the term **market failure** to refer to malfunctions in the market mechanism that lead to inefficient outcomes. In this section, we examine four main causes of market failure. Market failure may result from imperfections in the market, lack of adequate information, the existence of externalities, or the existence of public goods. We shall discuss each cause in turn.

MARKET IMPERFECTION

Market failure is the inability of the price system to achieve an efficient allocation of resources.

A market is considered to be imperfect if individual buyers and sellers have so much power in the market that they can influence the prices of inputs and outputs. This is the situation described earlier as **imperfect competition.** Market imperfections lead to a misallocation of society's resources or to their unproductive use. The freedom of entry that is characteristic of a purely competitive industry ensures that other firms will enter the industry if there are profits to be gained in that industry. Their entry will reduce the price of the product to the point where economic profits are zero. In the case of a monopoly or oligopoly, effective barriers to entry prevent firms from entering the industry. Such firms will tend to set the prices of their products in order to earn maximum profits. Such firms may deliberately restrict output in order to keep price above average total cost.

Market imperfection is a source of market failure.

Product differentiation is when firms in an industry sell similar but not identical products.

In monopolistic competition, even though there is freedom of entry and exit, the firms acquire some degree of market power through **product differentiation**. In the long run, firms in monopolistic competition earn zero economic profit, but the price of the product is above the purely competitive price, and there is underproduction of the product. Allocative efficiency does not exist in this case.

INADEQUATE INFORMATION

Inadequate information causes market failure.

In the purely competitive model, buyers and sellers are assumed to have full knowledge of the market. In making their decisions in the market, they have full knowledge of the products and prices. Lack of adequate information may cause market players to make decisions that do not maximize their profits or their satisfaction.

Quite often, households may not have the expertise to be able to judge the quality of a product. The complexity of some products requires specific knowledge on the part of buyers if they are to be able to evaluate them — knowledge that many buyers just do not possess. We may conclude, erroneously, that a stereo system or a television set with a $1500 price tag is better than one with a price tag of $1000. But the price may not always send the right signal about quality. Also, buyers often purchase items on the basis of information contained in advertisements. If the advertisement lacks truth, then buyers' decisions will be based on false advertising, resulting in inefficient outcomes.

ECONOMIC EXTERNALITIES

Economic externalities are a major source of market failure.

Learning Objective 2: understand the nature of economic externalities

Private costs are borne solely by the individuals or firms directly involved.

The existence of external costs and benefits is another source of market failure. We can discuss the concept of economic externality by first introducing the concepts of private costs and social costs. When a firm decides to produce a product, the costs considered include such items as labour and raw materials. When an individual decides to take a vacation in a foreign country, the costs considered include items such as air fare, accommodation, and entertainment. Such costs are called **private costs,** borne solely by the firms or individuals directly involved in acquiring inputs or purchasing goods and services.

Some costs, however, are not borne solely by the individuals or by the firms, but by the society as a whole. Consider the case of a chemical manufacturer who dumps wastes into a river. The river becomes polluted, the fish population in the river is destroyed, and the river can no longer be used for swimming and recreation. Moreover, property values along the riverside decrease. These are costs that have to be borne, not only by the manufacturer, but by others as well. When these costs are added to private costs, we obtain what economists call *social costs*. **Social costs** are those costs that are borne, not just by private firms and households, but by society as a whole, in terms of the total sacrifice made when resources are used.

The social cost is the total cost to society of decisions made and actions taken by individuals or firms.

PROBLEM SOLVING 16-1

We are a family living upstream of a pharmaceutical company on a certain river. Why should we, as members of society, concern ourselves with the fact that the company is using a part of the river to dispose of wastes? After all, we live upstream and the pollution is occurring downstream.

Economic externalities are costs (or benefits) that accrue to persons not directly involved in a firm's actions. An external economy is a benefit, and an external diseconomy is a cost.

Pollution is a good example of an external diseconomy.

Very often, we encounter situations in which private costs conflict with social costs. For example, a chemical manufacturer who pollutes the environment bears only a part of the cost of production: the private costs. The society as a whole bears the social costs. Such divergencies between private costs and social costs are called **economic externalities**. They are external because the firm or the individual does not take them into consideration when calculating costs. Society bears these costs in the form of a less healthy population, higher medical bills, the loss of animal life, the loss of good recreational areas, the loss of aesthetic value, and higher taxes to pay for the cleaning up of the environment.

An economic externality need not be a cost; it could also be an external benefit. For example, the development of a resort area will increase property values in that area. If the externality results in some benefit, we refer to it as an **external economy** or a **positive externality**. If it results in a cost, as in the case of pollution, we refer to it as an **external diseconomy** or a **negative externality**.

Throughout most of the 1980s, the big environmental issue was acid rain. Although the furor has died down somewhat, acid rain is still falling. Factories and power plants in the midwestern United States spew out dangerous amounts of sulphur compounds, which, when mixed with water, produce sulphuric acid. The acid then falls as acid rain in Canada and the northern United States. Acid rain is an example of a negative externality.

PUBLIC GOODS

We have seen that the unregulated market system may lead to the overproduction of some products that are harmful to society. It may also lead to the underproduction of some goods that society values, but that may not be produced by private, profit-seeking enterprise. Such goods are known as **public goods**, goods or services that bestow collective benefits on society. Once such a good or service is produced, it is generally impossible to exclude anyone from enjoying the benefits that it provides. Classic examples of public goods are police protection, public health services, national defence, and education.

The production of public goods presents a difficulty for the unregulated market mechanism. Private goods present no such difficulty. Automobile producers, for example, can earn a profit producing cars because people cannot obtain the services of these cars without purchasing them. But let us now consider the case of national defence. If a private firm were to provide this service, I would benefit from it, and so would every other person living in Canada. The firm, however, would not be in a position to enforce payment from me or from anyone else; hence, a private, profit-seeking firm is not likely to produce a public good. This explains why public goods are provided by the government and paid for collectively out of taxes.

The government may enact legislation making the consumption of certain goods mandatory. Education is a case in point. In Canada, children must attend school up to a certain age. Goods for which consumption is mandatory are referred to as **merit goods**, goods determined by the government to be good for people, regardless of how people evaluate these goods.

ENVIRONMENTAL PROTECTION

There can be no doubt that industrial nations such as Canada, the United States and Japan have made a significant amount of progress. Unfortunately, along with this progress comes a variety of problems: progress comes with a cost. In our attempt to maximize our total output of goods and services, we have seriously damaged our environment. For example, as the national output of goods and services rises, so does the national output of garbage. One of the questions that our society must answer is whether progress is worth the associated sacrifice. Since rapid economic progress is a major cause of environmental problems, should we not therefore have zero economic growth? This is exactly what some people have advocated. The fact is, however, that economic growth is essential in order that we can meet the challenges that face our economies and our societies.

Economic growth exacts a cost. Smog, water pollution, and acid rain threaten our environment. Greenhouse gases are causing global warming with potentially disastrous consequences. Our ecosystems are less productive and our health, our lifestyles, our economy and our society are all at risk because of pollution. We must protect our environment, and by doing so, we will be protecting ourselves.

THE APPROPRIATE LEVEL OF POLLUTION ABATEMENT

We have seen that pollution imposes severe costs on society. Should we not therefore eliminate pollution altogether? If the cost of eliminating pollution were zero, the answer to this question would be emphatically yes! And perhaps the question would not even be asked. But the cost of achieving a zero level of pollution would be prohibitive. Economic analysis, however, can help us to determine what amount of pollution we should allow. If society considers the level of pollution to be sufficiently serious, then society should be willing to sacrifice some goods and services in order to attain a lower level of pollution. If the benefits derived from further pollution abatement exceed the costs, then additional funds should be spent on pollution abatement. On the other hand, if the costs of additional pollution abatement exceed the benefits, then the extra costs should not be incurred.

These tradeoffs are illustrated in Figure 16.1. As more and more abatement is undertaken, the extra benefit declines. Figure 16.1 shows this decline as a downward-sloping marginal benefit curve. On the other hand, as more pollution abatement is undertaken, the extra cost increases. The upward marginal cost curve depicts this increase. At a pollution abatement level of 0C, the extra benefits (0D) are less than the costs (0F). Therefore, there is too much abatement. At an abatement level of 0A, additional benefits (0G) exceed the extra costs (0D). Hence, more pollution abatement should be undertaken. At a level of 0B, the additional costs equal the additional benefits. Hence, 0B is considered to be the appropriate level of pollution abatement. Obviously, once the appropriate level of pollution abatement is determined, the appropriate level of pollution is also determined.

FIGURE 16.1

The appropriate level of pollution abatement.

The appropriate level of pollution abatement is that level at which the marginal cost is equal to the marginal benefit.

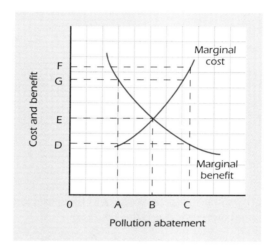

MEASURES TO DEAL WITH THE PROBLEM OF POLLUTION

There are several ways of dealing with the problem of pollution. We may discuss these under the headings of direct regulation, effluent fees, tax incentives, property rights, and moral appeal.

DIRECT REGULATION

Learning Objective 6: *discuss measures to deal with the problem of pollution*

One way of dealing with the problem of pollution is for the government to prohibit the dumping of waste in certain areas, and to prohibit the use of certain chemicals. Regulations forbidding the use of DDT and the setting and enforcement of emission standards for automobiles and certain manufacturing plants that pollute the environment are examples of direct regulation.

One problem with direct regulation is the difficulty of enforcing it. For the regulation to be effective, an effort must be made to detect the offenders; and this involves a substantial cost. The offenders, if caught, must then be prosecuted. This can also be a costly process. The detection of an offence may be quite difficult. Some polluters, therefore, may find it less expensive to continue to pollute and pay the penalty (if caught) than to install expensive anti-pollution equipment.

Another problem with direct regulation is that of determining the permissible level of pollution for each polluter. If we aim to reduce pollution levels by say, 20%, should all polluters reduce their pollution levels by 20% regardless of cost and the amount of pollution caused? Or should pollution levels be reduced by more than 20% in some plants and by less than 20% in others? The decision is not an easy one.

EFFLUENT FEES

Effluent charges (fees) are part of an attempt to force polluters to internalize their costs.

Another way of dealing with the problem of pollution is to charge the polluter a fee for polluting the environment. This charge, known as an **effluent fee**, forces polluters to consider the social costs rather than just the private costs of their activities. In other words, they are forced to internalize their costs. The fee charged would vary directly with the level of pollution caused by each polluter. This approach to the problem of pollution has strong appeal among economists because it works through the market mechanism. Polluters are left free to pursue their objectives of profit maximization (in the case of firms) or utility maximization (in the case of consumers). Effluent fees provide polluters with an economic incentive not to pollute the environment. We can expect this method, therefore, to result in lower levels of pollution. The higher the level of the effluent fee, the lower the level of pollution.

TAX INCENTIVES

Tax incentives reduce pollution.

Anti-pollution devices impose a substantial cost on those who buy them. If tax relief is given to people who incur the cost of installing anti-pollution equipment, the level of pollution is likely to decrease as more and more of these anti-pollution devices are installed. One objection to tax incentives as a method of reducing pollution is that the practice of giving tax incentives may become widespread. If tax incentives are given for anti-pollution equipment, why not for other types of investment that may be considered by some groups to be equally important? We may find ourselves in a situation where tax incentives are given for just about anything.

Another problem with tax incentives is that there is a tendency to abuse them. For example, a producer could buy some equipment, state that it is to be used for pollution abatement, claim the tax credit, and then use the equipment for some other purpose.

PROPERTY RIGHTS

The establishment of property rights reduces pollution.

One reason that polluters abuse the environment is that nobody owns the environment. No one owns the air around us, so we can dump all kinds of poisonous gases into it without paying anything. Some people have suggested that the assignment of property rights to individuals and firms may lead to a reduction in the overall level of pollution. Let us suppose that there is a lake — Lake Blythe — owned by no one, and that the Morbus plant uses the lake for waste disposal. In the absence of government regulation forbidding the dumping of waste into the lake, the Morbus plant will use Lake Blythe for waste disposal. Let us now suppose that the government offers to sell Lake Blythe or to sell exclusive rights to use it for any purpose.

If there are individuals or groups of individuals who value the purity of Lake Blythe for recreation above the value placed on it by the Morbus plant for waste disposal, then they will be willing to buy the lake and keep it free from pollution. If the value of Lake Blythe to the Morbus plant as a place for waste disposal is greater than its value to those people who want to use it for recreation, then the Morbus plant will acquire the rights to the lake and use it for waste disposal. Note that the manufacturer will buy Lake Blythe for waste disposal only if the cost is lower than the cost of any alternative way of disposing of its waste.

MORAL APPEAL

Finally, an appeal to producers and consumers may help to reduce the level of pollution. Consumers can be persuaded to use public transportation and to organize car pools rather than to drive millions of air-polluting cars into the city every day. An appeal to firms to develop cleaner methods of production can also help to win the battle against pollution.

Moral appeal is most effective where polluters are convinced that a polluted environment is against their own interests.

PROBLEM SOLVING 16-2

Would you expect an individual producer voluntarily to take social costs into account in its production decisions?

ENVIRONMENTAL ROUND-UP

In this final section of this chapter, we take a close look at our environment, focusing on air pollution, water pollution, ecosystems and habitat, and climatic change. We shall examine the threats to our health, our economy and our lifestyles, and we shall pay some attention to efforts that are being made to deal with the problem. Let us begin with air pollution.

AIR POLLUTION

Air pollution: smog due mainly to burning fuels.

The importance of clean air is obvious. Without it, our environment and our health suffer. Because of the fuels we burn in our vehicles, in our homes and in our factories, the air is polluted. Smog signals the presence of air pollution. Ontario, the southern Atlantic region, and British Columbia are susceptible to smog. Vigourous economic activity in Ontario and air pollution from the United States account for almost all of the smog in Ontario. Much of the smog in parts of New Brunswick and Nova Scotia can be attributed to air pollution from the Eastern United States, while British Columbia itself generates the major part of its smog.

How serious is air pollution? It is claimed that thousands of Canadians die prematurely each year from air pollution as ground-level ozone (the major component of smog) and other pollutants are inhaled into the lungs. Because of air pollution, over 300 000 lakes are vulnerable and over 14 000 are acidified. It is estimated that damage to the ozone layer reduces the productivity of commercial crops in Ontario by $70 million annually. The benefit of reducing smog in our major cities is evaluated at about $10 billion annually. Thanks to government action, our cars are now equipped with catalytic converters, our gasoline is cleaner, and emissions from our factories are lower.

WATER POLLUTION

Water pollution: toxic waste, chemical spills, chemical production, municipal waste and acid rain.

Canada is blessed with an abundance of fresh water. Unfortunately however, some of the waters are polluted to the extent that they are unsafe for swimming, and the fish that they contain cannot be eaten. One of the main sources of water pollution is toxic waste from industrial, agricultural, and domestic activities. Chemical spills, chemical production, municipal waste and acid rain all contribute to water pollution.

Clearly, water pollution affects both our health and our economy. Toxic substances in our water are injurious to our health and are damaging our environment. Some are carcinogenic (cancer causing), and some are harmful to reproductive and immune systems. Toxic substances are adversely affecting beluga whales in the St. Lawrence River, and acid rain is threatening 15 000 lakes in eastern Canada.

Canada has made significant progress in reducing water pollution. Lake Erie, for example, which was considered dead about 30 years ago, now sustains commercial fishing. Tougher federal and provincial regulations have significantly reduced overall emissions of certain toxic substances. Reductions of pollution in the St. Lawrence River, the Great Lakes, and the Fraser River are success stories for Canada. Through a renewed and strengthened Canadian Environmental Protection Act, more success stories can be expected.

NATURE

Our activities are putting nature to the test. Many species of birds, mammals, and other creatures are disappearing or are threatened globally. In Canada, species of wildlife are being threatened or endangered. Rapid industrial and urban development are threatening and destroying habitat. Our ecosystems are under attack and their ability to maintain environmental balance is weakened. Urban development and resource-based industries such as mining and forestry have exerted severe strains on natural habitat.

We have much to gain by protecting nature. Nature provides many health benefits through the development of new sources of food and medicine. Many drugs used to treat diseases are derived from living organisms. Many economic benefits are also derived from nature. For example, agriculture, forestry and fishing provide employment for many Canadians and make significant contributions to the total value of goods and services produced in Canada annually.

Federal, provincial and community efforts and initiatives have reduced the threats to our ecosystems. The St. Lawrence Action Plan and the Fraser River Action Plan have protected over 70 000 hectares of wildlife habitat. Ecologically sensitive land has also been protected.

GLOBAL PERSPECTIVE

Environmental Protection: A Global Problem

Not too long ago, many people regarded pollution as a local problem. The pollution of a small lake, for example, was thought to affect only those people who lived in close proximity to the lake. It became clear, however, that a polluted river affects not only those who live close to the source of the pollution, but also people who live hundreds of kilometres from the source. The realization that pollution at a particular point is often spread throughout a wide area forced many people to adopt a regional or even a national perspective when thinking about pollution. Lately, it has become increasingly evident that pollution is a global problem.

It is now known, for example, that factories in the United States emit pollutants into the Canadian environment. Hence, even if Canada introduces legislation to reduce significantly the amount of pollutants that Canadian firms dump into the environment, unless Canada's initiative is matched by similar anti-pollution efforts in the U.S.A., our environment could still be very polluted.

In a more dramatic example of global pollution, the 1986 explosion of a nuclear power plant in Chernobyl, in the former U.S.S.R., was an environmental disaster of epic proportions. Radioactive material was spread over thousands of square kilometres. A dramatic increase in cancer in parts of the former Soviet Union and radioactive contamination in animals as far away as Sweden have been linked directly to this major environmental disaster.

The Exxon-Valdez catastrophe will also go down in history as one of the world's greatest environmental disasters. In 1989, an Exxon oil tanker spilled several million litres of oil in Prince William Sound, Alaska, the aftermath of which was the widespread destruction of fisheries, wildlife, and the environment. This was a global disaster.

There are many more ongoing environmental problems. A serious issue is the depletion of the ozone layer. The use of certain chemicals and gases has been found to destroy the ozone layer, which gives us some protection from cancer-causing radiation from the sun. Also of grave concern are global warming and the destruction of the Brazilian rain forests, which could have disastrous consequences for humanity.

Clearly, environmental protection is an issue that affects us all. International cooperation is required if we are to avert further disasters of this magnitude.

CLIMATIC CHANGE

Greenhouse effect: green-house gases maintaining the earth's temperature at comfortable levels.

Climate change is a pressing environmental problem. It can affect our economy and our way of life. The **greenhouse effect** regulates the earth's temperature. Greenhouse gases keep the earth's temperature at comfortable levels. Without them, the average temperature on earth would be –18ºC, instead of the current 15ºC. Human activities seem to be increasing the amount of greenhouse gases in the atmosphere, and hence global average temperature. An increase in global temperatures results in climatic change. The major causes of climatic change are the burning of fossil fuels and deforestation.

The consequences of climatic change for Canada are new infectious diseases, pollution, increased health problems from heat stress, reduced capability to grow crops, severe droughts, flooding, more frequent forest fires, and more severe weather disturbances. Climatic change could indeed have serious consequences for our environment, our economy, and our lifestyles.

20% Club: organizations which aim to reduce local greenhouse gas emissions by 20% from 1990 levels.

How is Canada responding to climate change? In 1995, the federal, provincial and territorial governments approved a National Action Program on Climate Change (NAPCC). Through this initiative, many companies have developed action plans to reduce their greenhouse gas emissions, and many Canadian municipalities have joined the **20% Club** whose objective is to reduce local greenhouse gas emissions by 20% from 1990 levels. The various levels of government are involved in other programs to reduce greenhouse gas emissions.

CHAPTER SUMMARY

1. Market failure refers to malfunctions in the market mechanism that result in inefficient outcomes or the unproductive use of resources.
2. Sources of market failure include market imperfection, lack of information, economic externalities, and the existence of public goods.
3. Private costs are costs borne solely by the firms or individuals who incur them. Social costs are borne by the whole society.
4. Economic externalities are the divergencies between private costs and social costs. If the economic externality results in some benefit, we call it an external economy. If it results in a cost, we call it an external diseconomy.
5. Pollution causes a variety of problems. It affects our health, our economy, and our way of life. There are numerous benefits to be derived from environmental protection.
6. Since pollution abatement involves substantial costs, the appropriate level of pollution abatement is not that which reduces the level of pollution to zero, but that level at which the marginal cost of pollution abatement equals the marginal benefit.
7. Measures to deal with the problem of pollution include direct regulation, charging effluent fees, providing tax incentives, selling property rights, and moral appeal.
8. Air pollution is a serious problem. It threatens the lives of many Canadians each year as they inhale ground-level ozone into their lungs. Government action has resulted in cleaner air as harmful emissions into the atmosphere are reduced.
9. Some of our waters are quite polluted as a result of toxic substances from industrial, agricultural and domestic activities. Tougher federal and provincial regulations have made our waters cleaner and safer.

10. Habitat and our ecosystems are threatened by rapid industrial expansion, rural development, and resource-based industries such as mining and forestry. Nature provides many benefits to us so when we protect nature, we also protect ourselves.

11. The greenhouse effect regulates the earth's temperature. It would be impossible for us to live without greenhouse gases. Our activities are increasing the amount of greenhouse gases in the atmosphere and causing climate changes which have severe consequences.

12. Cooperation between the various levels of government and various programs and initiatives have resulted in improvements in our environment.

TERMS FOR REVIEW

market failure (276)
imperfect competition (276)
product differentiation (276)
private cost (277)
social cost (277)
economic externality (277)
external economy
  (positive externality) (277)

external diseconomy
  (negative externality) (277)
public goods (278)
merit goods (278)
effluent charge (fee) (280)
air pollution (281)
water pollution (281)
greenhouse effect (283)
20% Club (283)

QUESTIONS FOR REVIEW AND DISCUSSION

1. What is market failure? What are some sources of market failure? (L.O.1)

2. Distinguish between private costs and social costs. (L.O.2)

3. What are economic externalities? How is the concept of economic externality related to environmental pollution? (L.O.2)

4. What is environmental pollution? Why is it considered such a serious problem? (General)

5. "Society should aim at a zero level of pollution." Discuss. (L.O.5)

6. Briefly discuss the measures that can be taken to reduce the level of pollution. (L.O.6)

7. Do you think that tax incentives are effective in reducing the level of pollution? Why or why not? (L.O.6)

8. What regions of Canada are most susceptible to smog, and what accounts for the smog in each of those regions? (L.O.6)

9. Give some indication of the seriousness of air pollution in Canada. (L.O.6)

10. What are some of the main sources of water pollution in Canada, and what progress has Canada made in dealing with water pollution? (L.O.6)

11. "We have much to gain by protecting nature." Discuss this statement. (L.O.6)

12. What are some of the consequences of climate change? How is Canada responding to climate change? (L.O.6)

PROBLEMS AND EXERCISES

1. The Campo Steel plant is situated upstream from the Clairview Recreation Park. Clairview has to clean up the water polluted by Campo Steel. Campo Steel decides to purchase Clairview. Will Campo Steel continue to dump the same amount of pollutants into the river? Explain. (L.O.7)

2. In the summer months, many of the beaches around Montreal have to be closed because of high levels of pollution. Do you think that private ownership of those beaches would solve the problem? Explain. (L.O.6)

3. Do you agree that we can reduce pollution only by reducing population? (L.O.6)

4. Why should we expect people in Toronto to be more concerned with air pollution than people in Twillingate, Newfoundland? (General)

5. Explain what has been done in your community to reduce pollution in any of its forms or to protect the environment. (General)

 6. Visit a manufacturing concern in your community and find out what steps it has taken to reduce pollution or to protect the environment. Write up a *brief* report on your findings.

Internet Site

http://www.doe.ca/envhome.html

This "Green Lane" home page is an Environment Canada site. It contains a great deal of useful information about climate change, clean air, clean water, and other important environmental issues.

INTERNET EXERCISE

Visit the Greenpeace Web site at **http://www.greenpeace.org** and read up on some of their activities.

17

THE AGRICULTURAL SECTOR

Learning Objectives

After studying this chapter, you should know about:

1 agriculture in the Canadian economy

2 some problems of agriculture

3 policies dealing with the problems of agriculture

4 the role of government in agriculture

We have therefore a strange paradox, that labour-saving techniques in agriculture are of supreme importance to society at large but are a distinct source of embarrassment to agriculture itself.

Kenneth E. Boulding, *Economic Analysis and Agricultural Policy*

INTRODUCTION

This chapter deals with a very important topic: agriculture. Although the structure of the Canadian economy has undergone considerable changes over the past several years, we still depend substantially on the agricultural sector. In 1996, our exports of wheat alone earned us $2.4 billion in terms of 1986 dollars; other agricultural products earned us a further $16 billion. First, we will pay some attention to the role of agriculture in the Canadian economy. Then we will study some of the special problems that farmers must face. Microeconomic concepts and tools will help us to explain these problems. Next, we will consider some policies to deal with the problems of agriculture, and finally, we will examine some government programs for assisting farmers.

AGRICULTURE IN THE CANADIAN ECONOMY

Learning Objective 1:
agriculture in the Canadian economy

As an economy develops, the share of agriculture in total output tends to diminish.

Most countries single out the agricultural sector for special treatment. Canada is no exception. After all, this is the sector that produces food for the population. As the population grows, more food is needed. A country that relies very heavily on imported food is obviously in a very vulnerable position. It makes good economic sense, therefore, to allocate resources to the agricultural sector to ensure that food is available for Canadians. It can be stated as a general rule that, as an economy develops, the share of agriculture in the total output of the economy declines. This general principle applies to the Canadian economy. The share of agriculture in the total output of the Canadian economy fell from over 16% in 1931 to 0.2% in 1997. Figure 17.1 shows farm income as a percent of total income for selected years from 1965 to 1997.

FIGURE 17.1

Farm income as a percentage of total income

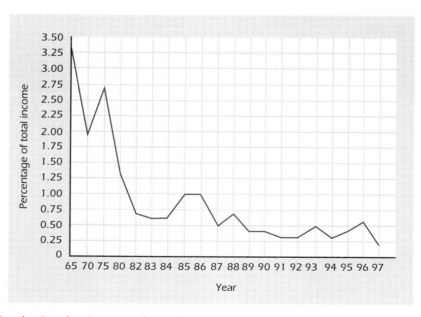

Source: Statistics Canada, *Canadian Economic Observer* (Cat. 11-210-XBP), 1997–98: 2

It has been observed also that as economic growth proceeds, the proportion of the labour force engaged in agriculture also declines. The Canadian economy exemplifies this fact. In 1950, the proportion of the labour force employed in agriculture was over 18%. By 1960, this figure had fallen to 10.7% and in 1997, it had reached 2.8%. Figure 17.2 shows the proportion of the labour force in agriculture from 1978 to 1997.

These facts notwithstanding, agriculture is still an important economic activity in the Canadian economy. It provides employment directly for about 450 000 people, and indirectly to several hundred thousand more who work in related fields such as transportation, marketing, and the processing of agricultural products. There are over 275 000 farms in Canada. Many of these farms are relatively small, with annual sales of less than $5000. On the other hand, some large farms average over $75 000 in annual sales. An important pattern can be observed in Canadian agriculture: the number of large farms has increased over the years while the number of small farms has decreased. Canadian farms, on average, are 22% larger today than they were 20 years ago. The average size of a farm in 1976 was 499 acres, while in 1996, the average size was 608 acres (1 acre = 0.4 hectares). In Canada, farm size varies from province to province. The average size of a farm in Newfoundland in 1996 was 146 acres, while in Saskatchewan it was 1152 acres. The tendency towards larger and fewer farms in Canada means that fewer farmers are producing more food than ever before, but it may also suggest that farming is becoming less competitive as an industry. These farms are of various types including dairy, cattle, wheat, field crops, and fruit and vegetable farms. The most common types of farms are cattle, wheat, small grains other than wheat, and dairy farms. Ontario, Saskatchewan, and Alberta are the provinces with the most farms in the country.

Canadian farmers produce a wide variety of agricultural products including milk and cream, maple sugar and maple syrup, eggs, and a variety of field crops. Table 17.1 contains data on some of Canada's agricultural products, with the cash receipts from each item.

Over time, the number of small farms has decreased while the number of large farms has increased.

Canadian farmers produce a wide variety of agricultural products.

FIGURE 17.2

Employment in agriculture in Canada, 1978–97.

As an economy develops, the proportion of the labour force engaged in agriculture tends to decline.

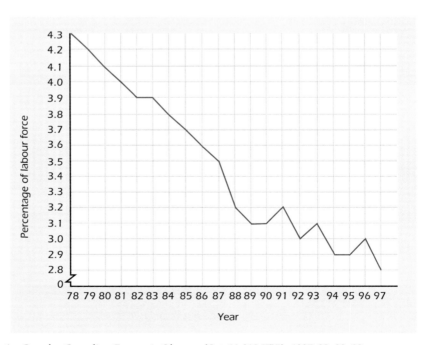

Source: Statistics Canada, *Canadian Economic Observer* (Cat. 11-210-XBP), 1997–98: 32, 33.

	Product	Cash receipts ($million)
TABLE 17.1 Farm cash receipts, selected products, 1997.	Wheat	3 626
	Canola	1 999
	Livestock & products	14 539
	Vegetables	1 001

Source: Statistics Canada, *Canadian Economic Observer* (Cat. 11-010-XPB), July 1998: 41.

Canadian agricultural production can be arranged into five major agricultural sectors. In terms of cash receipts, the most important sector is the grains and oilseeds sector with 34% of total farm cash receipts. The other major sectors are red meats, dairy, horticulture, and poultry and eggs. The five major agricultural production sectors in Canada are shown in Figure 17.3.

FIGURE 17.3

Major agricultural production sectors.

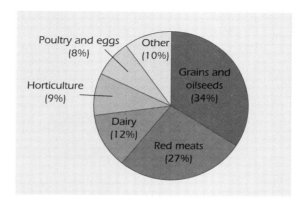

Source: Canadian Federation of Agriculture, *Commodities*, Ottawa, March 1998: 1

THE AGRI-FOOD INDUSTRY IN CANADA

So far, we have been focusing on agriculture specifically. However, in order to really appreciate the important role that agriculture plays in the economic life of the country, we need to pay some attention to the agri-food industry. The agri-food industry includes, in addition to primary agriculture, such activities as food processing, food services, beverage and processed exports and imports related to food. In 1996, the agri-food industry contributed in excess of $70 billion worth of goods and services to the Canadian economy, representing about 8.8% of the total value of all goods and services produced in the country. Of this $70 billion, primary agriculture accounted for over 24%. The rest was accounted for by food and beverage processing, retail, wholesale and food service industries.

The agri-food industry also contributes to the Canadian economy through employment. Approximately two million people were employed in food-related jobs in 1996, representing about 14% of the total number of people employed in Canada. The agri-food industry's greatest employers are hotels, restaurants and institutions. Other high employers are the wholesale and retail sectors and primary agriculture. Primary agriculture has traditionally been dominated by men, but the proportion of women has been increasing slowly, reaching 33% in 1996.

THE ROLE OF COOPERATIVES

Cooperatives are business organizations that are owned, financed, and controlled by their member-patrons, who share the risks and benefits in proportion to their patronage. In 1995, there were over 800 agriculture-based cooperatives in Canada, with membership totalling over 620 000 producers. The cooperatives play an important role, particularly in the marketing of certain products. With a combined volume of business exceeding $11.8 billion, agricultural marketing and processing cooperatives deserve some attention.

AGRICULTURAL TRADE

International trade is a vital part of the Canadian economy, and the Canadian agri-food industry is an important part of that trade. In 1996, we exported about 70% of the value of our total agricultural production and imported about 47% of our agricultural and food products. The dollar value of our agricultural exports, including food, feed, beverages and tobacco, amounted to approximately $19.9 billion and represented about 7.4% of total Canadian exports. At the same time, we imported about $13.2 billion worth of agricultural goods, representing about 5.7% of all goods and services imported into Canada. Thus, these trading activities resulted in a surplus in agricultural trade of $6.7 billion. As Figure 17.4 shows, the major purchasers of our agri-food exports are the United States (51.4%), Japan (10.5%), European Union (7.1%), and China (5.8%).

FIGURE 17.4

Destination of Canada's agricultural exports.

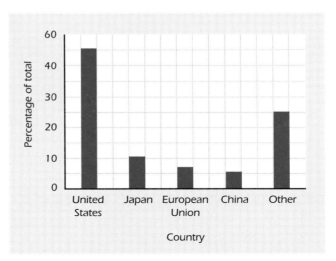

Source: The Canadian Federation of Agriculture, *Agricultural Trade*, Ottawa, March 1998: 2

SOME PROBLEMS OF AGRICULTURE

Learning Objective 2:
some problems of agriculture

The prices of farm products and farm incomes tend to fluctuate significantly because the demand for farm products is inelastic.

FLUCTUATIONS IN PRICES AND INCOME

One of the major problems facing agriculture is the wide fluctuation in the prices of farm products and in the incomes of farmers. Changes in total income and farm income are graphed in Figures 17.5A and 17.5B to demonstrate the difference in the degree of fluctuation between farm income and total income. Figure 17.5A shows total income while Figure 17.5B shows agricultural income.

It is not very difficult to find a reason for the fluctuations in farmers' incomes. A fall in the price of farm products does not cause people to increase their purchases of

FIGURE 17.5A

Farm income compared with total income.

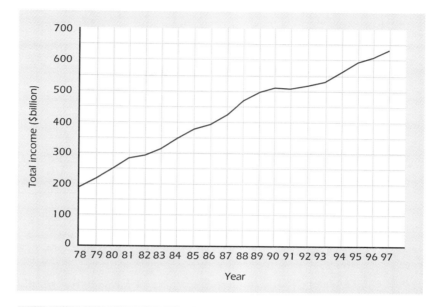

FIGURE 17.5B

Farm income compared with total income.

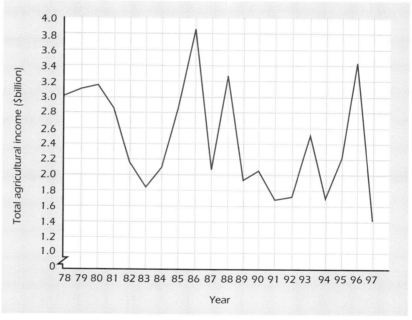

Source: Statistics Canada, Canadian Economic Observer (Cat. 11-210-XPB, 1997-98: 2

these products substantially. Similarly, an increase in the price of farm products does not cause people to reduce their purchases of these products substantially. In other words, the quantity demanded does not respond significantly to price changes: the demand for farm products is inelastic.

Consider Figure 17.6. The demand curve DD is relatively inelastic. If in a particular year farm production increases because of good weather or because of a significant

FIGURE 17.6

Effect of an increase in supply when demand is inelastic.

The inelastic demand causes a substantial price decrease when supply increases.

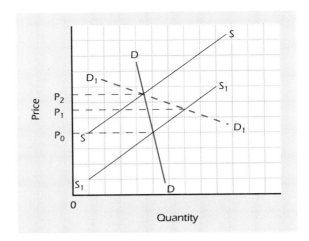

increase in the productivity of farmers, the supply curve shifts from SS to S_1S_1. This increase in supply causes price to fall from P_2 to P_0. Note that if the demand curve were more elastic, such as D_1D_1, the price would have fallen only to P_1. Thus, we see that because the demand for farm products is inelastic, an increase in supply results in substantial reductions in price. And since the lower prices do not stimulate corresponding increases in purchases, the incomes of farmers decline.

On the other hand, consider Figure 17.7. If supply falls from SS to S_0S_0, given demand DD, the price increases from P_0 to P_2. A more elastic demand such as D_1D_1 would have resulted in a smaller increase in price (P_1 instead of P_2). The increase in price from P_0 to P_2 does not lead to a corresponding fall in the quantity purchased. Hence, the income of farmers increases. It is well known that the supply of particular farm products is subject to severe fluctuations from year to year because of weather, diseases, insects, floods, and a host of other factors quite beyond the control of the farmer.

FIGURE 17.7

Effect of a fall in supply when demand is inelastic.

Because the demand is inelastic, a decrease in supply causes a substantial increase in price.

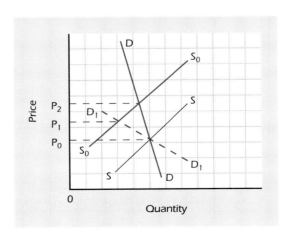

LOW INCOME ELASTICITY

Engel's Law states that as income rises, the percentage spent on food will diminish.

Another problem farmers face is that as total income in the economy increases, the demand for farm products does not increase as fast as the demand for other products. As income increases, a smaller proportion is spent on food — for there is obviously a limit to the amount of food that people can eat! The observation that the percentage of income spent on food declines as income increases has been called **Engel's Law**, named after statistician Ernst Engel. Engel's Law can be stated in terms of income elasticity of demand (introduced in Chapter 5). Because farm products have a low income elasticity of demand, income from farm operations does not increase as fast as total income does. Farm income fell in eight of the 20 years between 1978 and 1997, falling by as much as 59% in 1997. On the other hand, total income rose in every single year during the same period, except in 1991 when the economy experienced a recession. It is ironical that the agricultural sector has recorded the most spectacular increase in productivity, yet farmers have not really benefited from their fabulous performance.

PROBLEM SOLVING 17-1

The price elasticity of demand for farm products has been estimated to be about 0.2. What light does this information throw on the farm problem?

POLICIES TO DEAL WITH THE PROBLEMS OF AGRICULTURE

Learning Objective 3: policies dealing with the problems of agriculture

Many solutions for the problems of agriculture have been suggested and many of these have been implemented by the government. Among policies dealing with the economic problems of agriculture are price support, deficiency payments, direct income subsidies, market quotas, easy credit to farmers, and various fiscal and monetary policies. Let us look at each of these in turn.

PRICE SUPPORTS (OFFERS TO PURCHASE)

Price supports (offers to purchase): a system of markets and prices that determines what to produce, how to produce, and for whom to produce.

A government may establish a **price-support** system to prevent the prices of certain farm products from falling below a certain level. Let us assume that the government wants to support the price of a certain agricultural product. You will recall from Chapter 4 that a price support will be effective only if the price floor is set above the market equilibrium price. Diagram A of Figure 17. 8 will help us to analyze a price-support program. The equilibrium price and quantity are $5 and 55 000 units respectively. Suppose now that the government sets a price of $8. At this price, consumers are willing to buy only 40 000 units of the product, while producers are willing to offer 80 000 units for sale. There will therefore be a surplus of 40 000 units (80 000 – 40 000). At a price of $8, the value of this surplus is $320 000, and is shown by the shaded rectangle in Diagram A.

One obvious result of the price-support program is that it results in a surplus of the product on the market. To maintain the artificially high price of $8, the government offers to purchase the surplus. This surplus tells us that more resources are put into the production of this product than society requires. Resources are misallocated. Furthermore the government-purchased surpluses must be stored, and this could result in high storage costs.

Let us now examine the effects of a price-support program on producers and consumers.

FIGURE 17.8

Price support and
deficiency payment.

DIAGRAM A
Price Support

DIAGRAM B
Deficiency Payment

Producers

Clearly, if a program of price supports is initiated, the farmers gain. In the absence of the price-support program, they would produce 55 000 units at a price of $5, and receive a total revenue of $275 000, that is (55 000 × $5). With the price-support program, they produce 80 000 units at a price of $8, and receive a total revenue of $640 000, that is (80 000 × $8). The price support increases their revenue by $365 000 ($640 000 − $275 000).

Consumers

With the price-support program, consumers pay a price of $8 instead of the market equilibrium price of $5. Also, they consume a smaller quantity of the product (40 000 units instead of 55 000). On this count, they lose. Moreover, the surplus of 40 000 units, which the government must buy, will increase consumers' tax burden by the amount of the surplus ($320 000). And that is not all. Storage costs must be added to this amount.

ELASTICITY AND PRICE SUPPORT

The demand curve DD in Diagram A of Figure 17.8 is inelastic. Let us assume instead that the demand for the product is elastic, as shown by the demand curve dd in Diagram A. A price floor of $8 would result in a quantity of zero being demanded by consumers. In this case, the government would have to purchase the entire output of 80 000 and give it away to consumers. The following conclusion can be drawn:

> **A price-support program in which a price floor is set should not be used if the demand for the product is elastic with respect to the price.**

DEFICIENCY PAYMENTS

Deficiency payments: a subsidy to farmers given at a certain amount per unit.

Diagram B of Figure 17.8 will help us to analyze how **deficiency payments** work. The demand and supply curves are DD and SS respectively, and the equilibrium price and quantity are $5 and 55 000 units. Let us assume that the government, instead of setting a price of $8, allows the price to be determined by the market, but guarantees a price of $8 to farmers. At this price, farmers respond by moving up the supply curve and producing an output of 80 000 units. According to the demand curve, however, this quantity will be purchased only at a price of $3.50. The government therefore gives a deficiency payment (a subsidy) of $4.50 per unit — a total of $360 000, which is shown by the shaded area in Diagram B. How are producers and consumers affected by deficiency payments? Let us investigate.

Producers

Without the deficiency payment, farmers would have produced 55 000 units at a price of $5. Their total revenue would have been $275 000. The guaranteed price of $8 causes farmers to produce 80 000 units. Their total revenue is therefore $640 000. As in the case of a price support, farmers' gross receipts increase by $365 000.

Consumers

Without the deficiency payment, consumers would have purchased 55 000 units at a price of $5 per unit. With the deficiency payment, they purchase 80 000 units at a price of $3.50 per unit. In this sense, consumers gain. They get $1.50 out of the $4.50 deficiency payment. But let us dig a little deeper. The deficiency payment of $360 000 must be paid for out of taxes, so consumers must bear this tax burden. The total payment by consumers is therefore $640 000 ($280 000 + $360 000) — the same as in a price-support scheme.

ELASTICITY AND DEFICIENCY PAYMENTS

The demand curve DD in Diagram B is elastic. Suppose instead that the demand curve was inelastic as in dd. With a guaranteed price of $8, farmers produce 80 000 units, but consumers will not be willing to pay any positive price for this output. The government would therefore have to purchase the entire output of 80 000. Obviously, this does not make sense. We can therefore draw the following conclusion:

> **A deficiency-payment system should not be used if the demand for the product is inelastic with respect to price.**

EVALUATION OF PRICE SUPPORTS AND DEFICIENCY PAYMENTS

Our analysis shows that the benefits that farmers derive from price supports and deficiency payments are identical. In each example, they obtained a total revenue of $640 000. We have also seen that although consumers obtain a greater quantity of the product at a lower price under a deficiency-payment system than under a price-support system, when the tax burden is considered, they pay the same total amount under both schemes.

A price-support program results in a surplus, whereas a deficiency-payment program does not. In both cases, however, a greater amount of society's resources are channelled into the production of the product than society requires. Farmers produce more of the product than consumers want at the equilibrium market price. In this sense, both schemes result in a misallocation of resources.

Price supports and deficiency payments have another disadvantage in common. They benefit the larger commercial farmers. To see why this is so, let us take the case of a price support of $2 per unit. A farmer who sells 100 units receives $200 in support, while a farmer who sells 1000 units receives $2000 in support. If the larger commercial farmers have lower unit costs than the smaller farmers do (which is usually the case), then the system of price supports will benefit least those farmers who need it most. The same argument applies in the case of a deficiency payment. To conclude, both systems prevent the price system from doing its job efficiently. By artificially maintaining high prices for farmers, both systems prevent resources from moving out of agriculture and into other industries where they would be more efficient.

DIRECT INCOME SUBSIDIES

Another policy that may be used to improve the low incomes of farmers is the payment of direct income subsidies. Under this scheme, the determination of prices for agricultural products would be left entirely to the market. Referring to Figure 17.8, we see that under this system, the price would be $5 and the quantity would be 55 000 units. No surplus would exist.

Two major criticisms have been levelled at this program of assistance. First, determining the criteria on which to base the income subsidy is likely to be difficult, and the program would likely be costly to administer. Second, if farmers are subsidized, why not some other groups as well? Thus, we could end up with a situation in which the government is subsidizing an unreasonably large number of industries, thus creating a huge tax burden for taxpayers.

MARKET QUOTAS

Another solution to the agricultural problem is the use of **market quotas**. Under this system, producers would receive marketing quotas for each commodity. Each producer would receive a prescribed number of marketing certificates for each product. Thus, a producer who had fifty certificates for peas could sell only fifty units of peas. In this way, the supply of any particular farm product is controlled. Price fluctuations can therefore be greatly reduced. Two major problems are encountered with the use of this policy, however. First, the direct restriction of output in order to raise the price of the product may be socially undesirable. You may recall that this was precisely one of the problems we mentioned in our discussion of monopolistic firms. Second, farmers have shown a strong tendency to resist this type of control.

EASY CREDIT TO FARMERS

Another policy to deal with the problems of agriculture is the granting of loans to farmers on easy terms. This policy provides more funds to farmers and reduces their costs by reducing their interest payments.

FISCAL AND MONETARY POLICIES

A poor economic performance and an unstable economy may cause changes in demand for all products, including agricultural products. If total income in the economy falls, then the demand for agricultural products will also fall, and this fall in demand will result in a fall in agricultural prices, other things being equal. Lower agricultural prices will, in turn, result in lower incomes for farmers. It follows that government economic policies designed to promote a healthy economy will help to stabilize agricultural prices, and hence the incomes of farmers.

PROBLEM SOLVING 17-2

Which of these policies — price supports, income subsidies to farmers, or market quotas — is best from the consumers' point of view, assuming that the tax burden is equal in all cases?

Policies to assist agriculture include offers to purchase, deficiency payments, income subsidies, market quotas, easy credit, and general economic policies.

Producers in a market-quota system are permitted to sell only the amount of their quota.

THE ROLE OF GOVERNMENT IN AGRICULTURE

Learning Objective 4:
the role of government in
agriculture

Through Agriculture and Agri-Food Canada (the federal department of agriculture and agri-food), and through its support of various programs and initiatives pertaining to agriculture, the federal government engages in research into various aspects of agriculture and agri-food, and offers various types of assistance to farmers. The following are just a few of the federal agencies that offer services to the agricultural and agri-food sector.

THE CANADIAN GRAIN COMMISSION

A number of federal agencies have been established to offer a variety of services to the agricultural sector.

The Board of Grain Commissioners, established in 1912, became the Canadian Grain Commission in April 1971. Its responsibilities include the weighing, inspection, and storage of grain, the establishment of grading standards, and the licensing of grain elevator operators. In addition, the Canadian Grain Commission conducts research relating to grains. Through its Grain Research Laboratory and Corporate Services, the Commission conducts economic studies and collects and publishes relevant statistics. The Commission employs about 700 people.

THE CANADIAN WHEAT BOARD (CWB)

Established in 1935, the Canadian Wheat Board (CWB) is the marketing agency for Western Canadian wheat and barley growers. Its role is to market Canadian wheat and barley at the best possible prices. The net proceeds from the marketing of wheat and barley are passed on to the farmers. With annual revenue of more than $6 billion, the CWB is one of the world's largest grain marketing organizations. The CWB has what is called a *single-desk policy,* which means essentially that the Board has a monopoly in the export of Western Canadian wheat and barley. The federal government guarantees the loans of the CWB, allowing it to finance its operations at lower rates of interest than would otherwise be the case. Thus, Canadian farmers realize significant savings.

THE CANADIAN DAIRY COMMISSION

The Canadian Dairy Commission (CDC) was established through the Canadian Dairy Commission Act of 1996. Funded partly by the federal government, the CDC promotes the interests of dairy producers, processors, exporters, the public, and governments. It administers the federal government's subsidy of about $145 million to dairy producers, and employs about 62 people. The stated objectives of the CDC are to provide an opportunity for efficient producers of milk and cream to obtain a fair return, and to ensure that consumers obtain an adequate supply of high quality dairy products. Among other activities, the CDC establishes support prices for butter and skim milk powder, and recommends the target level of national milk production for industrial milk.

THE CANADIAN FOOD INSPECTION AGENCY (CFIA)

Canada exports a good amount of food and food products. It is important for our customers around the world to be able to rely on the safety and high quality of our food exports. It is also important that the food and food products imported into Canada meet Canadian safety and quality standards. The Canadian Food Inspection Agency (CFIA) provides these assurances. The CFIA is a federal government agency with the objective of helping to build a thriving and competitive agri-food and seafood industry. Any farmer knows how devastating animal and plant diseases can be to agriculture. The Canadian Food Inspection Agency tries to prevent foreign diseases and pests from entering Canada, and to control or eradicate them if they do happen to enter. With over 4500 employees, the Agency works to help growers succeed and to ensure food safety for all consumers.

THE FARM CREDIT CORPORATION (FCC)

The Farm Credit Corporation (FCC), a federal Crown Corporation, was established in 1959, and is now Canada's largest agricultural lender. The Corporation employs about 900 people and provides services from over 100 offices in farming communities across Canada. The main focus of the FCC's lending operations is the family farm. The FCC makes loans for any agricultural or farm-related purpose, such as the purchase of land, equipment and livestock, the construction of farm buildings including houses, and improvement of land and buildings. In short, the FCC grants loans for any purpose that will help farm businesses to grow and prosper. Terms of payment can be arranged to suit the particular circumstances of the borrower, and may be made for as long as 29 years.

Note: The foregoing list of federal programs is representative rather than exhaustive. In addition, the provincial governments have introduced a number of programs to aid farmers and the agricultural sector.

CHAPTER SUMMARY

1. The Canadian economy exemplifies the general principle that, as an economy develops, the share of agriculture in total output declines. The proportion of the labour force engaged in agriculture in Canada has in fact declined.

2. Agriculture is an important sector of the economy, providing employment for nearly half a million people, adding over $18 billion to the country's output of goods and services, and providing food for the country's population.

3. Among the agricultural products produced in Canada are: livestock, wheat, corn, milk, cream, maple sugar and syrup, eggs, and a variety of field crops.

4. Wide fluctuations in the prices of farm products and in the incomes of farmers have created difficulties for farmers. This is due to the fact that the demand for farm products is inelastic, agricultural output is subject to a substantial degree of variation, and farm products have a low income elasticity of demand.

5. Solutions to the agricultural problem include price supports or offers to purchase, deficiency payments, direct income subsidies to farmers, market quotas, easy credit to farmers, and economic policies to enhance economic performance.

6. The federal and provincial governments have designed a variety of programs to assist the agricultural sector of the economy.

TERMS FOR REVIEW

Engel's Law (293)   deficiency payments (294)
price supports (offers to purchase) (293)   market quotas (296)

QUESTIONS FOR REVIEW AND DISCUSSION

1. Why has the share of agriculture in the total output of the Canadian economy declined over the years? (L.O.1)
2. Briefly discuss the importance of agriculture to the Canadian economy. (L.O.1)
3. What is the composition of Canada's agricultural output? (L.O.1)
4. What are the major problems faced by farmers? (L.O.2)
5. Explain why farm prices and incomes are subject to wide fluctuations. (L.O.2)

6. What arguments can you offer in support of government assistance to agriculture? (L.O.3)

7. Discuss some measures that deal with the problems of agriculture. (L.O.3)

8. What are the disadvantages of each of the following? (L.O.3,4)

   (a) price supports (offers to purchase)

   (b) deficiency payments

   (c) market quotas

9. Briefly discuss the role of the federal government in providing assistance to the agricultural sector. (L.O.4)

PROBLEMS AND EXERCISES

1. Technological advances have substantially increased the productivity of farmers. Use a graph to show the effect of this increase in productivity on the farm problem. (L.O.2)

2. The farm population has declined considerably over the years, both in absolute and relative terms. Would farmers have been better off if this decline had not occurred? (L.O.2)

3. Do you agree with the statement that everyone except farmers has benefited from the success of agriculture? Discuss. (L.O.2)

4. Figure 17.9 shows the market for a particular farm product. The government wants the price of the product to be $6. The government may use either offers to purchase or a deficiency-payment scheme. Assume that there is no storage cost. (L.O.3)

FIGURE 17.9

Demand and supply for a farm product.

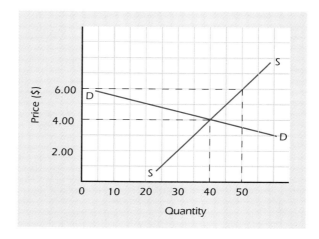

(a) What method should the government use to ensure a price of $6?

(b) How much would consumers spend in purchasing this product?

(c) Would a surplus exist in this case? If so, what would be its value?

(d) How much total revenue would producers receive?

(e) How much would this program cost the government?

5. Figure 17.10 shows the demand and supply for a particular farm product. The government wants the price of the product to be $6. There is no storage cost, and the government has the option of using either offers to purchase or deficiency payments. (L.O.3)

FIGURE 17.10

Demand and supply of a farm product.

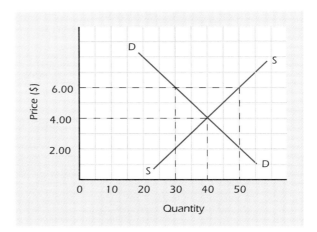

(a) What method should the government use to ensure a price of $6?

(b) How much would consumers spend in purchasing this product?

(c) Would a surplus exist in this case? If so, what would be its value?

(d) What would be the total revenue of farmers?

(e) How much would this program cost the government?

6. (a) "The agricultural and agri-food industry is the most important industry in Canada."

(b) "The agricultural and agri-food sector is not that important. If it were, agricultural product prices would be higher, more people would enter that industry, and there would be no need for government assistance to farmers."

Write down as many points as you can to support or defend each of the statements above.

Internet Site

http://www.agr.ca

This is the main site for Agriculture and Agri-Food Canada. It will expose you to a great deal of information about Canadian agriculture.

http://www.cfa-fca.ca

This site is filled with information about various aspects of agriculture in Canada. It is the home page for the Canadian Federation of Agriculture (CFA).

INTERNET EXERCISE

1. Go to the Canadian Federation of Agriculture (CFA) Web site indicated above, and write a brief description of the CFA, including its mission, its aims and objectives, and its membership.

2. Follow the link *Members of CFA* to *Chicken Farmers of Canada*, and write a paragraph or two about chicken farmers.

18

C H A P T E R

PUBLIC FINANCE

Learning Objectives

After studying this chapter, you should be able to:

1 explain the growth in government expenditure

2 discuss the role of government in society

3 discuss the expenditures of various levels of government

4 discuss sources of government revenue

5 distinguish between different taxation systems

6 explain the Laffer curve

7 analyze the effects of taxes

Those who pay no taxes, disposing by their votes of other people's money, have every motive to be lavish and none to economise. As far as money matters are concerned, any power of voting possessed by them is a violation of the fundamental principle of free government....It amounts to allowing them to put their hands into other people's pockets for any purpose which they think fit to call a public one.

John Stuart Mill, *Considerations on Representative Government*

INTRODUCTION

Public finance is the study of the microeconomic aspects of government spending and taxation.

The study of government behaviour in the areas of spending and taxation is known as **public finance**. The first part of this chapter deals with government spending. Government spending has significant impact on the economic life of the country. You should, therefore, have at least a general idea of the spending activities of the government in order to understand certain aspects of the operation of the economy. One of the objectives of this chapter is to provide you with that general idea. The second part of the chapter deals with government revenues. Since taxes constitute the largest source of revenue for the government, we shall spend a great deal of time studying taxes. We shall look at various principles of taxation, and at different types of taxes. We shall also consider the effects of taxes. Finally, we shall study the revenues of the various levels of government.

Let us begin by looking at the magnitude of government expenditure. Major reasons for the growth of government spending will then be given, followed by a discussion of government responsibilities. All levels of government are considered collectively and individually.

THE GROWTH IN GOVERNMENT EXPENDITURE

Government expenditure has grown tremendously over the years.

Learning Objective 1: explain the growth in government expenditure

Government expenditure increased from $14 million in 1870 to $385 275 million (i.e., $385.28 billion) in 1997. In 1926, total government expenditure accounted for about 13% of the Gross Domestic Product (GDP)— the market value of all goods and services produced in the country. By 1974, government spending climbed to about 33%. By 1997, it was 45% of Gross Domestic Product. Today, the government buys about 20% of everything that the economy produces. Figure 18.1 shows government expenditure as a percentage of Gross Domestic Product from 1978 to 1997.

The principal expenditure items are social services, interest on the public debt, health, and education. Expenditures on these four items alone in 1995 constituted over 69% of total consolidated government expenditure. Figure 18.2 gives a breakdown of total consolidated government expenditure by function for 1995.

FIGURE 18.1

Government expenditure as a percentage of Gross Domestic Product, 1978–97.

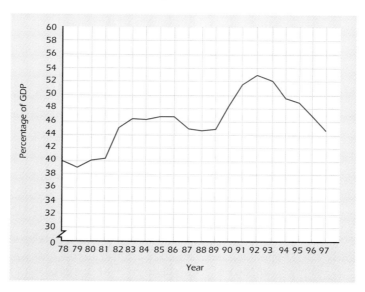

Source: Statistics Canada, *Canadian Economic Observer* (Cat. 11-210-XPB), 1997/98: 2, 15.

FIGURE 18.2

Consolidated government expenditure by major function, 1995.

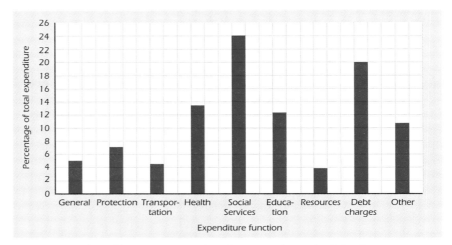

Source: Statistics Canada, *Public Sector Finance* (Cat. 68–212-XPB), March 1996: 168.

GOVERNMENT PURCHASES OF GOODS AND SERVICES VERSUS TRANSFER PAYMENTS

A transfer payment is a payment representing a transfer of purchasing power from one individual or group to another.

Government purchases of goods and services, though they account for over 20% of total purchases, do not really tell the whole story of the magnitude of government expenditures. In addition to purchasing goods and services, government also spends a great deal of money in the form of **transfer payments**, which represent transfers of purchasing power from one group in the society to another. Examples of transfer payments are old age security payments, family allowances, and employment insurance benefits. These payments represent income to their recipients, but they do not represent payments for goods and services. The government also spends a large amount of money in interest payments on its debt. In 1997, interest on the public debt amounted to $74.9 billion, or 19.4% of total government expenditure. Government transfer payments and interest on the public debt together now account for about 50% of total government expenditure.

Figure 18.3 shows the share of government purchases of goods and services and government transfer payments to persons in total government expenditure for selected years from 1961 to 1997.

WAGNER'S LAW

Wagner's Law states that government spending will rise faster than total spending.

The German economist Adolf Wagner postulated over one hundred years ago that the rate of increase in government spending would eventually outrun the rate of growth of total spending on goods and services. This means that the government's share of the total output of the economy would increase. According to **Wagner's Law**, economic development would increase the complexity of government activity, thus making government more expensive.

To what extent does Wagner's Law apply to Canada? Total expenditure on goods and services from 1926 to 1997 increased by more than 13 000% while government expenditure during the same period increased by over 47 000%. On this basis alone, one could conclude that Wagner's Law does apply to Canada. But in order to see more clearly the relation between the growth rate of total spending and the growth rate of government spending, we can compare the annual percentage change in government expenditure with that of total spending. The necessary information is contained in Figure 18.4. In general, the growth rate of government spending has outstripped that of total spending.

FIGURE 18.3

Relation between government purchases of goods and services and transfer payments, 1961–97.

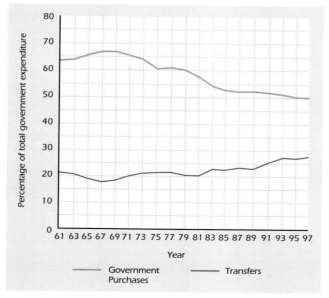

Source: Statistics Canada, *Canadian Economic Observer* (Cat. 11–210-XPB), 1997–98: 15.

FIGURE 18.4

Growth rates of government spending and total spending, 1978–97.

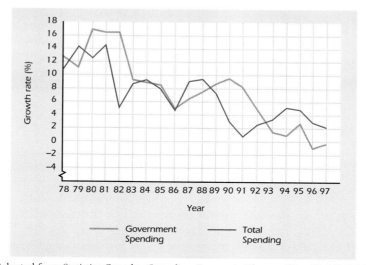

Source: Adapted from Statistics Canada, *Canadian Economic Observer* (Cat. 11–210-XPB), 1997–98: 5, 15.

REASONS FOR THE GROWTH IN GOVERNMENT SPENDING

Several factors are responsible for the growth of public sector expenditure over the years. Among them are increasing government responsibilities for certain services, inflation, and population growth. Let us discuss each of these in turn.

Greater responsibility

The government has assumed increasing responsibility for providing certain services such as health care, education, and social programs. Total expenditure on these three functions amounted to $7.8 billion in 1966. By 1995, the figure had reached $176.8 billion. The government's tax revenues have not been enough to cover its expenditures. The government until recently has been running its budget at a deficit. It has been borrowing money. And just like any other economic unit, when the government borrows money, it pays interest on its debt. In 1966, debt charges for all levels of government were only $1.7 billion. By 1995, these charges amounted to $71.3 billion. They have certainly added to the growth in government spending.

Inflation

Relatively rapid rates of price increases (inflation) over the years mean that the government has had to pay higher prices for the goods and services that it purchases. Between 1948 and 1995, prices rose above 8% annually in 1948, 1951, 1973–76, and 1979–82. The rate of inflation was particularly high in 1974, when a rate of over 14% was recorded. Also, wages and salaries have risen substantially over the years, and this means that the government must pay more to civil servants for their services.

Population growth

An important factor in the growth of government spending is the increase in population. Obviously, we can expect the government's budget to increase as population increases, because there will be a larger number of people for whom services must be provided. The population of Canada increased from 10 376 786 in 1931 to 27 000 400 in 1991 — an increase of approximately 160%. For the 1971–91 period alone, the increase was over 25%. The population now stands at about 30 million. Moreover, the Canadian population has been aging (that is, the proportion of elderly people in the population is increasing). This means that there are increasingly more people who depend on government for financial assistance, and this implies an increase in government spending.

THE ROLE OF GOVERNMENT

In Chapter 3, we discussed the role of government in a market economy. It would be a good idea for you to review that section now. It is generally agreed that it is the responsibility of the government to provide the services that would not be profitable for private individuals to provide but that are socially desirable. It is generally agreed also that the government should engage in those activities where government is more efficient than private individuals. Thus, the provision of law and order and the protection of persons and property are considered the province of government.

It is now an accepted view that education benefits the society and not just the individual who receives that education. Hence, most people would probably agree that the government should provide at least elementary and secondary education out of the public purse. The government pays for elementary and secondary education, and it subsidizes college and university education quite heavily. Whether education beyond the secondary level should be provided by the government without a direct charge is still much debated.

It is also considered desirable for the government to provide sanitation and health services. Another function generally considered essential for the government to undertake is the provision of social welfare services. Such services, it is felt, should not be left in the hands of private enterprise. It is also believed that it should be the responsibility of the government to build and maintain water supply systems, roads, and sewage systems.

Finally, it is believed that the government should play a role in the efficient operation of the economy. For example, most people would agree that the government should regulate certain industries. But just how active the government should be in these areas is still an unsettled issue. The generation of electrical energy in Quebec, for example, is undertaken by the government-owned Hydro-Quebec. Would the community benefit more if Hydro-Quebec were privately owned? Would Canadians get more efficient mail service if Canada Post Corporation were privately owned? There is no certain answer.

In the Canadian confederation, the federal government has the responsibility for certain functions, while the provincial and local governments have jurisdiction over certain other functions. In a political arrangement such as ours, a certain amount of duplication is inevitable. We can gain some insight into the distribution of responsibilities between the three levels of government by examining the expenditure pattern of each. Let us begin with the federal government.

FEDERAL GOVERNMENT EXPENDITURE

The largest share of government spending goes to social services.

As can be seen in Table 18.1, total federal government expenditure in 1995–96 was $177 billion. The three leading expenditure items of the federal government were social services (32.2%), debt charges (26.9%), and protection of persons and property (8.2%). Thus, these three functions alone accounted for 67% of the total expenditure of the federal government.

TABLE 18.1

Federal government expenditure by function, 1995–96.

Learning Objective 3: discuss the expenditures of various levels of government

Function	Amount ($million)	% of Total
General services	7 633	4.3
Protection of persons and property	14 642	8.2
Transportation and communications	3 258	1.8
Health	8 288	4.7
Social services	57 276	32.2
Education	5 129	2.9
Resource conservation and industrial development	8 128	4.6
Environment	915	0.5
Recreation and culture	780	0.4
Labour, employment, and immigration	1 632	0.9
Housing	2 026	1.1
Foreign affairs and international assistance	3 371	1.9
Regional planning and development	447	0.3
Research	1 284	0.7
General purpose transfers to other levels of government	10 606	6.0
Transfers to own enterprises	1 981	1.1
Debt charges	47 800	26.9
Other expenditures	2 509	1.4
TOTAL	177 705	100.0

Source: Statistics Canada, *Public Sector Finance* (Cat. 68-212-XPB), 1995-96: 114.

The largest expenditure item in the social services group was social security, which accounted for over 40% of the social service budget. Other important items in this group are unemployment insurance, social welfare, and family allowances. Interest on the public debt accounts for about 95% of total debt charges. The magnitude of the public debt has given rise to considerable controversy, which we shall examine in a later chapter.

PROBLEM SOLVING 18-1

It has been reported that the Canadian population is getting older. What effect can we expect this aging of the population to have on government expenditure?

PROVINCIAL GOVERNMENT EXPENDITURE

Health, education, and social services are important expenditure items for the provinces.

Turning now to the expenditures of the provincial governments, we see a somewhat different expenditure pattern. This pattern reveals the difference in the responsibilities of the federal government and those of the provincial governments. As Table 18.2 indicates, the largest expenditure items here are health (26.4%), education (17.9%), and social services (18.7%). Thus, these three items account for over 63% of the total expenditure of the provincial governments.

TABLE 18.2

Gross general expenditures of the provincial and territorial governments, 1995.

Learning Objective 3: discuss the expenditures of various levels of government

Function	Amount ($ million)	% of total
General services	7 258.7	4.1
Protection of persons and property	5 004.0	2.9
Transportation and communications	7 343.7	4.2
Health	45 179.7	25.8
Social services	34 560.0	19.7
Education	32 017.4	18.3
Resource conservation and industrial development	7 417.8	4.2
Environment	1 973.2	1.1
Recreation and culture	1 632.0	0.9
Labour, employment, and immigration	825.5	0.5
Housing	1 281.4	0.7
Regional planning and development	692.8	0.4
Research establishments	513.3	0.3
General purpose transfers to other levels of government	2 034.0	1.2
Transfers to own enterprises	1 485.3	0.8
Debt charges	26 209.7	14.9
Other expenditures	6.0	0.0
TOTAL	175 434.5	100.0

Source: Statistics Canada, *Public Sector Finance* (Cat. 68-212-XPB), March 1996: 140.

Other provincial government expenditure items of significance are debt charges, which account for nearly 15% of the total provincial expenditure; transportation and communications, which use up 4.2% of the budget; and general services, which account for 4.1% of the total provincial government expenditure.

LOCAL GOVERNMENT EXPENDITURE

Expenditure on elementary and secondary education accounts for nearly 40% of the total expenditure of the local governments.

The expenditures of the local governments (municipalities) are shown in Table 18.3. Education (elementary and secondary) is the largest single expenditure item, accounting for about 39% of total general expenditures of local governments. Other heavy expenditure items for the local governments include transportation and communications, the environment, protection of persons and property, recreation and culture, and debt charges. And whereas expenditures on health and social services account for significant percentages of the total budget of the provinces, expenditures on these items represent only 5.0% and 7.7% respectively of local governments' budget.

	Function	Amount ($million)	% of total
TABLE 18.3	General services	3 701.3	5.1
Gross general	Protection of persons and property	5 750.4	8.0
expenditures of local	Transportation and communications	6 609.2	9.2
governments, 1994.	Health	3 577.7	5.0
	Social services	5 570.7	7.7
	Education	28 341.0	39.4
	Resource conservation and industrial development	684.5	1.0
Learning Objective 3:	Environment	6 181.4	8.6
discuss the expenditure of	Recreation and culture	4 485.2	6.2
various levels of	Housing	655.5	0.9
government	Regional planning and development	647.4	0.9
	Transfers to own enterprises	1 425.1	2.0
	Debt charges	4 222.6	5.9
	Other expenditures	134.8	0.2
	TOTAL	71 986.7	100.0

Source: Statistics Canada, *Public Sector Finance* (Cat. 68-212-XPB), 1995-96: 166.

TAXATION

Learning Objective 4: discuss sources of government revenue

Taxes are compulsory payments levied by governments.

The government must have funds in order to carry out the various functions that it has assumed. The main source of such funds is taxation. A **tax** is a compulsory payment levied by a government to pay for goods and services provided for the benefit of the community. Taxes obviously impose some degree of hardship on the taxpayer, yet they are necessary and will most likely continue to be the most important source of government revenue. Evidently, a great deal of truth lies in the time-honoured saying that if there are only two things that are certain, they are death and taxes!

DESIRABLE CHARACTERISTICS OF A TAX

To the taxpayer, there is probably no such thing as a good tax, but to the government that imposes the tax, it obviously has some merit. The resentment that many people feel about taxes notwithstanding, we can still discuss the essentials of a good tax.

It should yield adequate revenue

Generally, a tax is designed to produce revenue for the government. It follows that a tax should be such that it can be relied upon to supply a fairly adequate revenue. We should remember that some taxes are designed to achieve objectives other than raising revenue. The primary objective of some taxes may be to discourage the consumption of certain goods. For example, the government may impose a surtax on gasoline during a period of gas shortage to discourage consumption. In such cases, the revenue function will be subordinate to the primary function. As a general principle, however, we can say that the greater the revenue from the tax, the better the tax. It is not only the amount of revenue that the tax yields that is important. Significant consideration must also be given to the dependability of the revenue. The personal income tax is a steady revenue yielder. Tax on capital gains is a much less steady revenue yielder. Any tax that yields a fairly steady stream of revenue from year to year will be preferred to one that yields a widely fluctuating stream, other things being equal.

It should be fair

This principle is much easier to state than to achieve. While most people may agree that a tax should be equitable, they may disagree over what constitutes equity. One criterion by which equity may be judged is the **benefit principle**, which states that the tax paid should be proportional to the benefits received. This implies that if Conrad Small, say, benefits more than Marina Mendez from the provision of a certain service, then Conrad should be taxed more for that service. There are some problems associated with this criterion. How does one measure the amount of benefit received by each person from a certain service? Furthermore, it is often quite difficult to identify which groups benefit. For example, a playground or a park obviously benefits those who use the facilities, but it also benefits other residents who do not like the noise of children playing in the streets, or who have no patience for the accidents — like broken windows — caused by children playing in inappropriate places.

Another criterion for assessing equity is based on the principle that people in similar circumstances should be affected similarly by the tax. This criterion, known as the **ability to pay principle**, implies also that high-income earners should pay more than low-income earners. That is, taxpayers should be taxed according to their abilities to pay. Using this criterion, an income tax is equitable if people with similar incomes and exemptions are taxed similarly. This criterion does not work when it is impossible to determine whether or not people are in similar economic circumstances. For example, is it accurate to say that people with similar incomes and exemptions are in similar circumstances? Moreover, some forms of incomes are not easily identified. What may appear to be equal incomes, therefore, may turn out to be quite unequal. A further difficulty arises in deciding how much more should be paid in taxes as income rises. That is, how rapid should the graduation of the tax rate be?

A tax should not impede the operation of the market system

A tax should not, in general, impede the operation of the market system, and it should not discourage work effort. If additional income is taxed extremely heavily, individuals will have no incentive to earn extra income. Similarly, if profit taxes are exorbitant, businesspeople may lose their drive and initiative. Investment, then, will fall off. If a tax is generally considered to be unreasonable, attempts to evade it may become widespread.

A tax should be as convenient as possible

This means that taxpayers should not have to put themselves through too much trouble to pay their taxes. A sales tax is very convenient in this sense: the tax is simply included in the price of the product. A tax should also be easy to administer, and collection should not entail much difficulty.

A tax should be simple

A tax should not be so complicated as to make it impossible for all but a few experts to understand it. Although the actual computation of taxable income is apparently becoming more and more difficult, most taxpayers understand the basic idea that the amount of tax to be paid depends on the amount of income that they earn and the amount of tax deductions to which they are entitled.

Needless to say, it is difficult to find taxes that possess all of the desirable characteristics that we have mentioned. A tax that is considered good because it yields an adequate revenue may be bad because it is not equitable. And a tax that is considered good because it is equitable may be bad because it is undependable.

PROGRESSIVE, PROPORTIONAL, AND REGRESSIVE TAXES

A tax may be progressive, proportional, or regressive. In this section, we discuss each of these types of taxes.

Progressive tax

A **progressive tax** is one for which the percentage of income paid in taxes increases as income rises. Thus, a progressive tax claims a higher percentage from high-income earners.

Proportional tax

A **proportional tax** is one for which the percentage of income paid in taxes remains constant as income increases. An example of proportional tax is a property tax. If the property tax is 1.5% of the value of the property, then regardless of the value of the property, the tax rate will be the same. The tax on a property valued at $40 000 will be $600 while the tax on a property valued at $150 000 will be $2250. Taxable income in Canada, over a wide range of income up to $29 590, is taxed at a constant rate of 17% and is therefore a proportional tax. Beyond that level of taxable income, however, the tax becomes progressive.

Regressive tax

A tax is said to be **regressive** if the percentage of income paid in taxes decreases as income increases. A tax of $10 imposed on each passenger who boards an aircraft is regressive. For passengers with incomes of $100 per week, the tax represents 10% of their income. For passengers with incomes of $200 per week, the tax paid is only 5% of their income.

Examples of progressive, proportional, and regressive taxes are presented in Table 18.4 and illustrated graphically in Figure 18.5. We have defined progressive, proportional, and regressive taxes with respect to income. This kind of definition is common practice. But these terms can also be defined in terms of property value or some other magnitude.

Income ($)	Progressive tax ($)	Progressive rate (%)	Proportional tax ($)	Proportional rate (%)	Regressive tax ($)	Regressive rate (%)
100	10	10	10	10	10	10.0
200	24	12	20	10	18	9.0
300	42	14	30	10	24	8.0
400	64	16	40	10	28	7.0
500	90	18	50	10	30	6.0
600	120	20	60	10	33	5.3
700	154	22	70	10	35	5.0

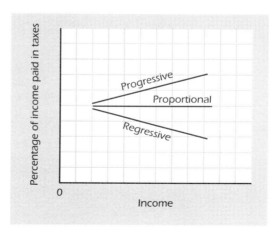

TAX RATES AND TAX REVENUE (THE LAFFER CURVE)

Learning Objective 6:
explain the Laffer curve

The Laffer curve shows that if tax rates are too high, total revenue may be reduced as a consequence.

Named after economist Arthur Laffer, the Laffer curve is a useful analytical device for illustrating the relation between tax rates and tax revenues. The **Laffer curve** is based on the view that as the tax rate increases, tax revenue will increase, but economic activity will decrease, thus lowering incomes and ultimately tax revenue. The Laffer curve depicted in Figure 18.6 shows that as the tax rate increases from 0 to *t*, tax revenue rises from 0 to R. But, as the tax rate rises beyond *t*, tax revenue declines. Note that a tax rate of 100% results in no tax revenue. Presumably, people will not work if the entire amount of their income is going to be taxed away.

FIGURE 18.6

The Laffer curve.

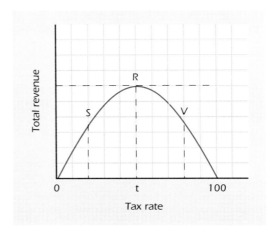

The optimum tax rate for a revenue tax is the rate that maximizes tax revenue.

The tax rate (*t* in our illustration) that maximizes tax revenue may be called the **optimum tax rate**, assuming that the tax is a revenue tax. The optimum tax rate for a revenue tax is the rate that maximizes tax revenue.

If the economy is at point S on the curve, then an increase in the tax rate will yield greater tax revenue. If, however, the economy is at point V, then an increase in tax revenues requires a reduction — not an increase — in the tax rate.

PROBLEM SOLVING 18-2

"A government can always raise additional tax revenues by simply raising the tax rate." Comment on this statement.

TYPES OF TAXES

There are many different types of taxes. There are personal income taxes, corporate income taxes, consumption taxes, and property taxes. We shall study each type in turn, beginning with the personal income tax.

THE PERSONAL INCOME TAX

Personal income tax: taxes, based on income, paid by individuals to federal and provincial governments.

The **personal income tax** has become the most important single source of revenue for the federal and provincial governments. Canadians pay personal income taxes to the federal government in addition to the personal income tax paid to the provinces. The federal government collects personal income taxes for all the provinces except Quebec, which collects its own personal income tax. Taxpayers are allowed to deduct certain

Taxable income is the gross income minus allowed deductions.

amounts from their total income. The amount left after these deductions have been made is known as **taxable income**, and it is on this amount that income taxes are levied.

The personal income tax has certain obviously desirable characteristics. It produces a fairly adequate and dependable revenue. It is relatively fair (at least in principle) in the sense that people with equal incomes and deductions pay the same amount of tax. Tax deductions at source (that is, by the employer) make the personal income tax convenient. It is relatively easy to collect. And in most cases, even though the actual calculations may present some difficulty (extreme difficulty in some cases), it is sufficiently simple for most taxpayers to understand the basic principle.

Major types of taxes are personal income taxes, corporation income taxes, and consumption taxes.

Despite these desirable features, the personal income tax has certain defects. Various loopholes make tax evasion possible, and many people feel that high-income earners are most able to take advantage of tax evasion and tax avoidance. For example, contributions to a registered retirement savings plan (RRSP) are tax deductible. To take advantage of such a plan, however, you must be able to afford the contributions. A second criticism of the personal income tax is that it may be so progressive that it discourages individuals from earning extra income and so restricts economic activity. Actually, this criticism applies to the structure of the tax, rather than to the fact that personal income is taxed.

THE CORPORATE INCOME TAX

In addition to levying personal income taxes, the government also imposes a tax on the profits of corporations. The revenue from this tax represents approximately 5% of total public sector revenue. One of the criticisms made against the **corporate income tax** is that it discourages new investment by firms, and may thus slow down economic activity. Some people argue also that the corporate income tax represents a double taxation of income since the profit of the corporation is taxed and the income of the shareholders is taxed again when it is distributed to them as dividends. A third criticism that has been made against the corporate income tax is that it is passed on to consumers in the form of higher prices for goods and services. In other words, the **incidence** (burden) of the tax falls not on corporations but on consumers. The extent to which this criticism is justified is still being debated by economists.

Corporate income tax: a tax on the profits of corporations.

The incidence of a tax is its burden.

THE CONSUMPTION TAX

Another source of tax revenue for the government is taxes on consumption. **Consumption taxes** include excise taxes and sales taxes. An **excise tax** is a tax levied on a specific commodity, while a **sales tax** is a tax levied on broad groups of goods and services. Excise taxes are levied, for example, on motive fuel (any fuel used to produce motion) and tobacco products. Sales taxes are levied on a large variety of goods and services. Since these taxes are added to the prices of the goods and services bought by the consumer, they are, in effect, taxes on consumption. As can be seen from Figure 18.7, consumption taxes account for approximately 20.3% of consolidated government revenue.

An excise tax is a tax on the sale of a particular good. A sales tax is a tax on the sale of a broad group of goods and services. Both of these are consumption taxes.

Sales taxes and excise taxes produce a dependable revenue. They are convenient and easy to collect (the consumer pays them at the time of purchase since they are added to the price of the product). And the only way for the taxpayer to evade these taxes is to refrain from purchasing the goods and services on which the tax is levied. The major disadvantage of these taxes is that they tend to be regressive. For example, although the sales tax is expressed as a given percentage of total purchases, high income earners will pay a smaller share of their income in sales taxes than low income earners will. An example of a consumption tax is the very controversial **Goods and Services Tax (GST)**. On

The Goods and Services Tax is an example of a consumption tax.

FIGURE 18.7

Consolidated govern-
ment revenue by
major sources, 1995.

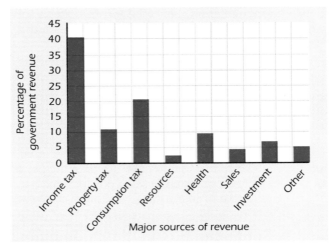

Source: Statistics Canada, *Public Sector Finance* (Cat. 68-212-XPB), March 1996: 167.

January 1, 1991, the GST replaced the manufacturers' sales tax (a tax on manufactured goods). The GST is a tax levied on almost all transactions and is applied to services as well as goods.

PROPERTY TAX

Property tax is levied mainly on real estate.

As the name implies, a **property tax** is a tax levied on property — mainly real estate (land and buildings). The revenue from property and related taxes accounts for over 11% of total consolidated government revenue. It will be seen that property taxes account for a substantial portion of the total revenues of the local governments.

EFFECTS OF TAXES

Learning Objective 7:
analyze the effects of taxes

It is evident that the economic effects of a tax depend on the type of tax. Sales taxes and excise taxes tend to take a larger percentage of the incomes of low-income earners and hence tend to increase income inequality. Also, because these taxes are consumption taxes, they tend to reduce consumption (and hence production) of goods on which the taxes are levied. Resources will tend to shift away from industries producing the taxed goods and into other industries. Hence, these taxes affect resource allocation.

Sales and excise taxes definitely result in higher prices for the consumer. But there is little agreement on the extent to which firms are able to shift the incidence of corporate income taxes onto consumers in the form of higher prices. The effect of corporate income taxes on prices, however, is not expected to be significant. But high corporate income taxes do restrict business expansion, and impede economic growth.

If personal income tax is progressive, it will tend to reduce income inequality. This is so because, other things being equal, high-income groups are taxed more heavily than low-income groups. If the personal income tax rate is too steeply graduated, it will tend to reduce incentive. Individuals will be reluctant to expend effort to earn extra income if most of that extra income will be taxed away.

PROBLEM SOLVING 18-3
How can a consumption tax reduce production?

REVENUES OF VARIOUS LEVELS OF GOVERNMENT

Learning Objective 4:
discuss sources of government revenue

Figure 18.7 shows revenue sources for all levels of government (consolidated government revenue). The various revenue sources are not equally important to all levels of government. An important revenue source for one level of government may not be important at all for another level of government. For example, income tax is the major source of revenue for the federal and provincial governments, but it is not an important source of local government revenue. Let us now examine the revenues of each level of government.

FEDERAL GOVERNMENT REVENUE

Personal income tax is the main source of revenue for the federal government.

The major source of revenue for the federal government is personal income taxes. The revenue from this source accounts for over 45% of the total revenues of the federal government from all sources. Corporation taxes also provide a substantial portion of the revenues of the federal government. In fact, income taxes alone provide 56% of the federal government's total revenue. Other important tax revenue sources are general sales taxes, customs duties, unemployment insurance contributions, and universal pension plan levies. Approximately 90% of the total revenue of the federal government is derived from various types of taxes.

Other revenue sources besides taxes are sales of goods and services and return on investment. These two sources together provide just about 6% of the total revenue. Table 18.5 gives details on the revenues of the federal government.

TABLE 18.5

Federal government revenue, 1995–96.

Source	Amount ($million)	% of total
Income taxes:		
Personal	65 602	45.1
Corporation	14 350	9.9
On payments to non-residents	1 523	1.0
TOTAL INCOME TAXES	81 475	56.0
Consumption taxes:		
General sales	22 130	15.2
Motive fuel	4 180	0.3
Alcoholic beverages and tobacco	2 892	2.0
Custom duties	3 270	2.2
Other consumption taxes	794	0.5
TOTAL CONSUMPTION TAXES	33 266	22.9
Health and social insurance levies	19 520	13.4
Miscellaneous taxes	504	0.3
Natural resource revenues	45	0.0
Privileges, licences, and permits	559	0.4
Sales of goods and services	3 523	2.4
Return on investments	4 952	3.4
Other revenue from own sources	1 530	1.1
Transfers from other levels of government	38	0.0
Transfers from government enterprises	41	0.0
TOTAL REVENUE	145 453	100.0

Source: Statistics Canada, *Public Sector Finance* (Cat. 68-212-XPB), 1995-96: 113.

PROVINCIAL GOVERNMENT REVENUE

Personal income tax and sales tax are the major sources of revenue for the provinces.

As in the case of the federal government, the main source of revenue for the provincial governments is personal income taxes, which account for 25.4% of total provincial revenue. The second most important tax source of revenue for the provincial governments is general sales taxes, which provide over 13% of the total revenue of the provinces. An examination of Table 18.6 reveals that corporation taxes, motive fuel taxes, and health insurance premiums and taxes are other important tax sources of revenue for the provinces.

TABLE 18.6	Source	Amount ($million)	% of total
Provincial and territorial government revenue, 1995.	Personal income taxes	40 479.7	25.4
	Corporate income taxes	6 575.9	4.1
	Property and related taxes	6 736.9	4.2
	General sales taxes	21 145.1	13.2
	Motive fuel taxes	6 197.8	3.9
	Alcoholic beverages and tobacco taxes	1 835.1	1.2
	Other consumption taxes	291.1	0.2
	Health and social insurance levies	10 434.4	6.5
	Miscellaneous taxes	4 676.4	3.0
	Natural resource revenues	7 562.4	4.7
	Privileges, licences, and permits	3 969.9	2.5
	Sales of goods and services	3 392.4	2.1
	Return on investments	14 578.3	9.1
	Other revenue from own sources	1 130.8	0.7
	Transfers from other levels of government	30 407.2	19.0
	Transfers from government enterprises	220.3	0.1
	TOTAL REVENUE	159 633.7	100.0

Source: Statistics Canada, *Public Sector Finance* (Cat. 68-212-XPB), March 1996: 127.

Important non-tax sources of revenue for the provincial governments include natural resource revenue, and general and specific purpose transfers from the federal government. Provincial government revenue may be divided into two categories: revenue from own sources, and transfers. Approximately 80% of the total revenue of the provincial governments is derived from their own sources. The remaining 20% takes the form of transfers from other levels of government. The most sizable transfers from the federal government to the provinces include equalization payments (transfers to the provinces to reduce income inequality among the provinces), social services, and other special purpose transfers.

LOCAL GOVERNMENT REVENUE

Property tax is the main revenue source for the local governments.

Table 18.7 shows that the largest single revenue item of the local governments (municipalities) is real property taxes, which account for over 37% of their total revenues and over 69% of revenues from their own sources. Local government revenues can be divided into revenues from own sources and transfers. Local governments raise about 54% of their total revenue from their own sources while the remaining 46% comes from transfers mainly from the provincial governments. Other important sources of revenue for local governments are sales of goods and services, business taxes, and return on investments.

TABLE 18.7	Source	Amount ($million)	% of total
Local government revenue, 1994.	Property and related taxes	26 731.7	37.9
	General sales taxes	44.3	0.1
	Other consumption taxes	3.1	0.0
	Miscellaneous taxes	124.7	0.2
	Privileges, licences, and permits	403.1	0.6
	Sales of goods and services	8 147.6	11.6
	Return on investments	1 664.5	2.4
	Other revenue from own sources	1 467.2	2.1
	Transfers from other levels of government	31 066.9	44.1
	Transfers from government enterprises	804.9	1.1
	TOTAL REVENUE	70 458.0	100.0

Source: Statistics Canada, *Public Sector Finance* (Cat. 68-212-XPB), 1995-96: 153.

GLOBAL PERSPECTIVE

International Comparisons of Total Government Expenditures

One important indicator of government involvement in an economy is the ratio of government expenditure to the value of goods and services produced in that economy. In this chapter, we have studied the expenditures of all levels of government. In this capsule, we now compare Canada with some other countries.

The accompanying graph shows that in 1998, Canada's expenditure as a percentage of the value of goods and services produced was fourth behind those of France, Italy, and Germany. The U.S. was the lowest, followed by Japan.

Almost everyone complains about high taxes in Canada. Does our government take a larger proportion of the value of total production of goods and services in taxes than do governments in other industrialized countries? The graph also shows that among the so-called G-7 countries, Canada took about 42.4% of the value of total production in taxes. Only France, Italy, and Germany took a larger share of the value of their countries' total production of goods and services.

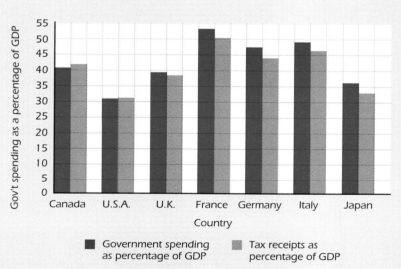

Source: OECD, *Economic Outlook*, December 1995: A31.

CHAPTER SUMMARY

1. Public finance deals with government taxation and spending behaviour.

2. Wagner's Law states that government spending will grow at a faster rate than total spending.

3. Government expenditure has increased substantially over the years mainly because of increasing government responsibilities, inflation, and population growth.

4. Because of different responsibilities, the patterns of expenditure for the various levels of government are different.

5. Social services, resource conservation and industrial development, debt charges, and protection of persons and property are chief items of federal government expenditure.

6. Health, education, and social services are among the chief expenditure items of the provincial governments, while elementary and secondary education, transportation and communications, the environment, and protection of persons and property are among the chief expenditure items of the municipalities.

7. It is generally agreed that government activity in certain areas is desirable. It is also generally agreed that the government should intervene to prevent widespread unemployment and rapid inflation.

8. A tax is a compulsory payment levied by a government to pay for goods and services provided for the benefit of the community.

9. A revenue tax should produce an adequate and dependable revenue. In general, a tax should be fair, it should not impede the operation of the market, it should not discourage work incentive, and it should be convenient, simple to collect, and easy to understand.

10. A progressive tax is one for which the percentage of income paid in taxes increases as income rises. A proportional tax is one for which the percentage of income paid in taxes remains constant as income rises, and a regressive tax is one for which the percentage of income paid in taxes falls as income rises.

11. The Laffer curve shows the relation between tax rates and tax revenues. Tax revenue increases as the tax rate rises. But after a point, further increases in the tax rate result in lower tax revenue.

12. Taxes levied by the federal and provincial governments include personal income taxes, corporate income taxes, and consumption taxes. The property tax is the major tax levied by the municipal governments.

13. The economic effects of taxes include changes in income distribution, consumption, production, and resource allocation. Some taxes also result in higher prices for consumers, and may dampen individual and business incentive to earn extra income.

14. Other sources of revenue include licences and permits, the sale of goods and services, and investment. Transfers from the federal government to the provincial governments, and from the provincial governments to the municipalities are important revenue sources.

TERMS FOR REVIEW

public finance (303)
transfer payments (304)
Wagner's Law (304)
tax (309)
benefit principle (310)
ability to pay principle (310)
progressive tax (311)
proportional tax (311)
regressive tax (311)
Laffer curve (312)

optimum tax rate (312)
personal income tax (312)
taxable income (313)
corporate income tax (313)
incidence of tax (313)
consumption tax (313)
excise tax (313)
sales tax (313)
Goods and Services Tax (GST) (313)
property tax (314)

QUESTIONS FOR REVIEW AND DISCUSSION

1. What are some of the major functions performed by our governments in Canada? (L.O.2)

2. What are the major factors responsible for the growth in government expenditure? (L.O.2)

3. What is Wagner's Law? Does it apply to Canada? (L.O.2)

4. It is sometimes said that government expenditure could be reduced if the government left certain functions to private enterprise. What functions do you think could effectively be carried out by private enterprise? (L.O.2)

5. Explain the difference in the expenditure patterns of the different levels of government. (L.O.3)

6. Identify the level of government that has jurisdiction over the following: (L.O.3)

   (a) primary and secondary education

   (b) national defence

   (c) hospitals

7. Do you believe that the public sector in Canada is too large? (L.O.2)

8. In what way(s) is a school tax of $300 a year different from a tuition fee of $300 a year? (L.O.4)

9. What are the essentials of a good tax? Do you consider the personal income tax to be a good tax? (L.O.4)

10. On what criteria can the fairness of a tax be judged? (General)

11. Give one example each of: (L.O.5)

    (a) a progressive tax

    (b) a proportional tax

    (c) a regressive tax

12. "A sales tax is progressive because it is expressed as a given percentage of total purchases, which means that the more you buy, the more you pay." Do you agree with this statement? Defend your position. (L.O.5)

13. List the major sources of revenue for: (L.O.4)

    (a) the federal government

    (b) the provincial governments

    (c) the local governments

14. Discuss the effects of taxes on prices, income, income distribution, and resource allocation. (L.O.7)

PROBLEMS AND EXERCISES

1. Complete Table 18.8 from data contained in the chapter. (L.O.3)

TABLE 18.8

Government expenditures.

Level of government	Total expenditure	% of total
Federal		
Provincial		
Local		
TOTAL (all levels)		100

2. Study the federal government expenditure by function. Then explain why it is difficult for the federal government to reduce its spending. (L.O.2)

3. How does an income tax based on the benefit principle affect low-income earners? (General)

4. Give an example of each of the following: (General)
   (a) a tax yielding dependable revenue
   (b) a tax which may discourage consumption
   (c) a tax based on the ability to pay principle
   (d) a tax based on the benefit principle

5. Construct arithmetic examples of: (L.O.5)
   (a) a progressive tax
   (b) a proportional tax
   (c) a regressive tax

6. Describe a situation in which a regressive income tax system may benefit an economy. (L.O.5)

7. Construct an arithmetic example showing that sales taxes are regressive. (L.O.5)

8. Table 18.9 shows tax rates and the tax revenue associated with each rate. (L.O.6)
   (a) Plot the information on a graph.
   (b) On your graph, indicate the optimum tax rate.
   (c) Indicate the maximum revenue.
   (d) What is the name of the curve that you have plotted?

9. Taxes in Canada are based on income, wealth, and expenditure. Give an example of a tax that is based on: (General)
   (a) income
   (b) wealth
   (c) expenditure

TABLE 18.9	Tax rate (%)	Tax revenue ($million)
Tax rate and tax revenue.	8	150
	9	200
	10	260
	11	310
	12	350
	13	380
	14	400
	15	410
	16	400
	17	370
	18	320
	19	260
	20	180

10. Health care has become a major issue in Canada. Governments have reduced expenditures on health care and many people have to wait for a very long time (sometimes months) to obtain certain medical services. The federal government has announced that it will make health care a priority. Do you agree that user fees (some kind of direct payment by those who use medical services) should be introduced into the health care system? Why or why not?

Internet Site

http://www.rc.gc.ca

This is the Web site of Revenue Canada. It contains useful information about tax collection and it has links to other useful sites. It also has a *search* option.

INTERNET EXERCISE

1. Go to the Revenue Canada Web site.
2. Click on the *About Revenue Canada* button.
3. Click on the *README: About Revenue Canada* button.
4. Jot down some points about Revenue Canada.
5. Click on the *back* button.
6. Click on the *Revenue Canada's Collection Policies* button.
7. Click on the *T4060 Revenue Canada's Collection Policies* button.
8. Click on the *Your Obligations as a Tax Debtor* button.
9. Write down in point form:
   a) your obligations as a taxpayer
   b) your rights as a taxpayer.

CHAPTER 19

INTERNATIONAL TRADE

Learning Objectives

After studying this chapter, you should know about:

1 the basis for international trade

2 the gains from trade

3 the principle of comparative advantage

4 Canada's exports

5 Canada's imports

Each individual is better off if he receives more of every commodity while rendering less of every productive device.

Paul A. Samuelson, *The Gains from International Trade*

INTRODUCTION

International trade is the exchange of goods and services between nations.

Each year, Canadians consume a huge amount of goods and services not produced in Canada. Coffee, tea, and cane sugar are common items of consumption for many of us. Oranges, bananas, and other tropical fruits are other common items of consumption. We consume these items, but we do not produce them. On the other hand, consumers in other countries enjoy a host of goods and services produced in Canada. All this is made possible through **international trade**.

The Canadian economy depends greatly on international trade. Our exports play a major role in our country's economic growth and development. Among other things, international trade deals with the import and export of goods and services, and with the effects of these flows on the economy. The theory of international trade is quite involved. In this chapter, you will study the reasons for trade between nations, and the sources of gains from international trade. You will also have an opportunity to look at Canada's trade statistics, which teach us something about Canada's international economic activity.

THE BASIS FOR INTERNATIONAL TRADE

The basis for international trade is that different countries are differently endowed with resources. This is called regional specialization.

Learning Objective 1: the basis for international trade

In Chapter 7, we noted that certain advantages resulted from the specialization of labour. These advantages are not limited to labour specialization, however. They extend equally to **regional specialization**, which is the basis for international trade. The main reason for regional specialization is that different regions are differently endowed with resources and technical know-how. Some regions, for instance, are heavily endowed with natural resources. Others are less favourably endowed. Some regions (or nations) are rich in capital. Others suffer from a lack of capital relative to other resources. And human resources vary among regions. Some countries have more highly skilled labour forces than others. Some regions have larger populations than others. Moreover, technological capabilities are not evenly distributed across nations. Country A may have a technological edge over country B in the production of telecommunication equipment while country B may have a technological advantage over country A in the production of books.

A country well endowed with labour can be expected to have lower wage rates than a country with scarce labour resources. Consequently, we can expect the cost of manufacturing a product requiring a large amount of labour to be lower in a labour-abundant country than in a labour-scarce country. Similarly, we would expect the cost of growing tropical fruits such as oranges and bananas in a tropical climate to be much lower than it would be in a temperate climate. Consider the amount of resources that would have to be used to grow citrus fruits in northern Canada!

THE GAINS FROM TRADE

Learning Objective 2: the gains from trade

There are some obvious gains from trade. For example, Canadians can enjoy tropical fruits at relatively low prices, and people in tropical countries can enjoy McIntosh apples grown in Canada at relatively low costs. But some gains from trade are not quite so obvious. Let us now look at two fundamental principles that explain why countries benefit from international trade.

THE PRINCIPLE OF ABSOLUTE ADVANTAGE

A country has an absolute advantage if it can produce a commodity at lower cost, in terms of resources, than another country.

A country is said to have an **absolute advantage** over another country in the production of a commodity if it can produce the commodity more efficiently, that is, with fewer resources, than the other country can. In other words, if country A is more efficient than country B in the production of a certain commodity, country A has an absolute advantage in the production of that commodity. The following numerical example will help to illustrate the concept of absolute advantage.

Suppose that a Canadian worker can produce five cars per year while a worker in Labouria (a fictitious country) can produce only two cars per year. Suppose also that a Labourian worker can produce ten tonnes of grain per year, while a Canadian worker can produce only eight tonnes of grain per year. Table 19.1 contains the relevant data. A Canadian worker is 2.5 times as efficient as a Labourian worker in car production, but a Labourian worker is 1.25 times as efficient as a Canadian worker in grain production. In this case, Canada has an absolute advantage in the production of cars, while Labouria has an absolute advantage in the production of grain.

TABLE 19.1		Cars (units)	Grain (tonnes)
Hypothetical output per worker in Canada and Labouria.	Canada	5	8
	Labouria	2	10

The following example illustrates that the combined output of cars and grain in both countries will increase if Canada specializes in the production of cars and Labouria specializes in the production of grain. Suppose a Canadian worker is transferred from grain production into car production. The output of cars in Canada would increase by five while the output of grain would fall by eight tonnes. If, at the same time, a Labourian worker is transferred from car production into grain production, the output of cars in Labouria would fall by two, but the output of grain would increase by 10 tonnes. The net effect then would be that car production would increase by three while grain production would increase by two tonnes.

The existence of absolute advantage makes trade beneficial to both trading partners.

If each country has an absolute advantage in the production of a commodity, both countries can benefit if each specializes in the production of the commodity in which it has an absolute advantage, and trades with the other.

Learning Objective 3: the principle of comparative advantage

If one country is more efficient than another in the production of two goods, and its efficiency is greater in the production of one commodity, it has a comparative advantage in that commodity.

THE PRINCIPLE OF COMPARATIVE ADVANTAGE

The previous section showed that two countries can gain by trading if each specializes in the production of the commodity in which it has an absolute advantage. But what if one country has an absolute advantage in the production of both commodities? Will trade still benefit both countries? The **principle of comparative advantage** provides the answer.

Let us assume that a Canadian worker can produce either 10 cars or five tonnes of grain per year, while a Labourian worker can produce either three cars or three tonnes of grain per year (see Table 19.2). A Canadian worker is therefore more efficient than a Labourian worker in the production of both commodities. Canada has an absolute advantage in the production of cars and in the production of grain.

TABLE 19.2		Cars (units)	Grain (tonnes)
Hypothetical output per worker in Canada and Labouria.	Canada	10	5
	Labouria	3	3

Instead of producing 10 cars, a Canadian worker could have produced five tonnes of grain. Hence, the opportunity cost of a car in Canada is 0.5 tonnes of grain. That is, in order to produce one car, Canada must sacrifice 0.5 tonnes of grain. On the other hand, instead of producing three cars, a Labourian worker could have produced three tonnes of grain. Hence, the opportunity cost of a car in Labouria is one tonne of grain. Since the opportunity cost of a car in Canada is less than the opportunity cost of a car in Labouria, Canada is said to have a comparative advantage in the production of cars.

The opportunity cost of a tonne of grain in Canada is two cars, while the opportunity cost of a tonne of grain in Labouria is one car. Since the opportunity cost of grain in Labouria is less than the opportunity cost of grain in Canada, Labouria has a comparative advantage in the production of grain.

A country has a comparative advantage in the production of a commodity if it can produce that commodity at a lower opportunity cost than another country.

We are now in a position to demonstrate the mutual gain from trade with comparative advantage. In the absence of trade, Canada must give up 0.5 tonnes of grain for one car while Labouria must give up one tonne of grain for a car. Let us assume that Canada and Labouria can exchange cars for grain at a rate somewhere between the ratio 1:0.5 and 1:1; let us say one car for 0.75 tonnes of grain (1:0.75). The actual rate at which cars will exchange for grain (called the **terms of trade**) is determined by cost and by demand for these two commodities in both countries.

For every worker transferred from grain production into car production in Canada, the output of grain falls by five tonnes, but the output of cars rises by 10. Each of those cars can now be exported to Labouria for 0.75 tonnes of grain, resulting in a net gain of $(0.75 - 0.5) = 0.25$ tonnes of grain per car for Canada. Does Labouria also gain from this transaction? Let us investigate. To produce one car, Labouria would have to give up one tonne of grain. By trading with Canada, Labouria obtains the car for only 0.75 tonnes of grain — a clear gain of 0.25 tonnes of grain.

If each country has a comparative advantage in the production of a commodity, both countries will benefit if each specializes in the production of the commodity in which it has a comparative advantage, and trades with the other.

Note that trade between the two countries is mutually beneficial only because of a difference in opportunity cost between the two countries. If the opportunity cost were identical in both countries, there would be no comparative advantage and therefore no gain from trade.

GRAPHICAL ILLUSTRATION OF COMPARATIVE ADVANTAGE

The principle of comparative advantage and the gains from trade can also be illustrated graphically. For simplicity, let us assume that Canada and Labouria each has only one worker, and that production in both nations takes place under conditions of constant opportunity cost, so that the production possibility curves are linear, as shown in Figure 19.1.

Canada's production possibility curve shows that if Canada uses all of its resources to produce grain, it can produce five tonnes of grain. Alternatively, if it uses all its resources to produce only cars, it can produce 10 cars. On the other hand, with full utilization of all its resources, Labouria can produce six cars or six tonnes of grain. Note that as before, Canada has a comparative advantage in the production of cars while Labouria has a comparative advantage in the production of grain.

Terms of trade are the rates at which a country's exports are exchanged for its imports.

Output will increase if each country specializes in the production of the commodity in which it has a comparative advantage.

FIGURE 19.1

Comparative
advantage.

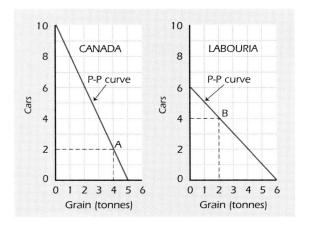

Let us assume that both countries want both grain and cars. In the absence of inter-national trade, each country would have to produce some quantities of both goods. Suppose that Canada decides to produce two cars and four tonnes of grain, thus operating at point A on its production possibility curve. Suppose also that Labouria decides to produce four cars and two tonnes of grain, thus operating at point B on its production possibility curve. The total output of both countries is six cars and six tonnes of grain. Note that each country is operating efficiently because each is operating on its production possibility curve.

Now, let us introduce specialization and trade. Suppose that Canada specializes in the production of cars (in which it has a comparative advantage), and Labouria specializes in the production of grain (in which it has a comparative advantage). With Canada producing only cars, and Labouria producing only grain, the combined output of both countries would be 10 cars and six tonnes of grain. Because of specialization, the output of cars increases from six to 10 while the output of grain remains unchanged at six tonnes. But Canada has only cars, and Labouria has only grain. Here, trade can be beneficial to both countries.

Recall that in the absence of trade, Canada would operate at point A on its production possibility curve (Figure 19.1), producing two cars and four tonnes of grain. Labouria on the other hand, would operate at point B on its production possibility curve, producing four cars and two tonnes of grain. Note that Canada must sacrifice one tonne of grain in order to produce two cars. For Canada, one tonne of grain costs two cars. However, Canada would like to obtain one tonne of grain for less than two cars.

Recall that for Labouria, one car costs one tonne of grain. Therefore two cars cost two tonnes of grain. Suppose Canada offers to pay Labouria one car for 0.75 tonnes of grain (that is, two cars for 1.5 tonnes of grain) and Labouria accepts the offer. The terms of trade (one car for 0.75 tonnes of grain) would mean that Canada would obtain a tonne of grain more cheaply (for 1.33 cars instead of two cars), and Labouria would obtain a car more cheaply (for 0.75 tonnes instead of one tonne of grain). Figure 19.2 shows the gain from specialization and trade.

The production possibility curves for Canada and Labouria are the same as in Figure 19.1. With trade and specialization, Canada can specialize in car production, but now it can trade 10 cars, at the terms of trade, for 7.5 tonnes of grain. Canada's **trading curve** is illustrated in Figure 19.2. Labouria can specialize in grain production, but now it can trade six tonnes of grain, at the terms of trade, for eight cars. Labouria's trading curve is

The trading curve shows all combinations of goods and services available through specialization and trade.

FIGURE 19.2

The gains from specialization and trade.

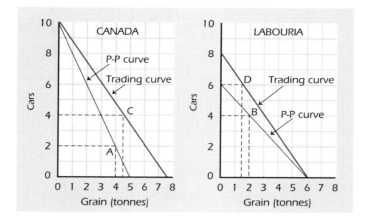

also shown in Figure 19.2. Note that because the trading curve is above the production possibility curve, any point on the trading curve is preferable to any point on the production possibility curve.

It would be inefficient for Canada and Labouria to remain on their production possibility curves when trade is possible. Canada can produce 10 cars and then trade (export) six cars to Labouria for 4.5 tonnes of grain, thus moving to point C on its trading curve. Canada is unambiguously better off at C than at A. But what about Labouria? If Labouria specializes in the production of grain, it can sell 4.5 tonnes of grain to Canada for six cars, thus moving to point D on its trading curve. Labouria is better off at point D than at point B.

PROBLEM SOLVING 19-1
What items of trade would you expect between Canada and Japan?

DETERMINANTS OF COMPARATIVE ADVANTAGE

NATURAL ENDOWMENT

The Caribbean islands have numerous white sandy beaches and a warm (sometimes hot) climate all year round, naturally. They therefore are a natural attraction for tourists who want to get away for a week or two between December and March, when it is cold and snowing in Canada. The comparative advantage enjoyed by the Caribbean islands in this field is a matter of natural endowment. In this case, the comparative advantage is geographically determined — hence the concept of **geographical determinism**, the theory that comparative advantage is determined by natural endowment. This theory has been around for a long time, but, despite its age, it still has relevance in explaining comparative advantage in some instances.

The theory of geographical determinism suggests that comparative advantage is determined by natural endowments.

ACQUIRED ADVANTAGE

In the same way that some individuals work hard to develop and improve whatever abilities may have been bestowed on them, so too can nations, by their own efforts, acquire comparative advantage in certain lines of production. Japan is often cited as the classic example of a nation that has compensated for its lack of natural endowments by saving and by making huge investment in capital, both physical and human.

SPECIAL KNOWLEDGE

Whether by accident or design, some countries have special knowledge that gives them a comparative advantage in the production of certain products. A country that comes to mind in this regard is Switzerland, with its reputation for watch-making. There is little doubt that Switzerland's expertise in watch-making is partly a result of many years of concentration on that activity.

FURTHER GAINS FROM TRADE

Learning Objective 2:
the gains from trade

In addition to the gains described above, gains can come from two other sources: greater efficiency and economies of scale. Let us examine each of these in turn.

Further gains from trade may result from increased efficiency.

Increased efficiency

We can reasonably assume that, as Canada specializes in the production of cars and Labouria specializes in the production of grain, Canadian workers will acquire greater skills and expertise in the production of cars. Labourians will likewise acquire greater skills and expertise in the production of grain. Thus, each country, by specializing, will experience an increase in worker productivity.

Economies of scale

Further gains may result from economies of scale made possible through trade.

Production costs may fall as the volume of output increases. If this is the case, then the average cost of producing cars in Canada will fall, because specialization in car manufacturing will have increased the volume of output. Similarly, the average cost of producing grain will fall in Labouria, because specialization in grain manufacturing will have increased the volume of output.

Canada has comparative advantage in a number of economic activities. Among these are the production of electricity, certain agricultural items, forestry items, certain minerals, and certain kinds of high technology such as communication. Canada's large supply of electric power attracts industries that require large amounts of electricity. Table 19.3 cites some products whose manufacture requires high and average levels of electricity.

TABLE 19.3	High	Medium
Products requiring high and medium levels of electricity.	Newsprint	Other pulp and paper
	Aluminum	Titanium
	Magnesium	Steel works
	Zinc and cadmium	Carbon steel mill
	Silicon carbide	Copper
	Chlorine & sodium hydroxide	Glass
	Phosphorus	Melted alumina — 95%

PROBLEM SOLVING 19-2

Why would you expect Quebec to be an exporter of newsprint?

CANADA'S EXPORTS

Learning Objective 4:
Canada's exports

Trade is very important to the Canadian economy. In 1997, exports of goods and services from Canada amounted to $343.5 billion, accounting for approximately 40% of the total amount of goods and services produced in Canada. Major export items include motor vehicles and parts, wheat, petroleum, natural gas, lumber, minerals, wood pulp, newsprint, chemicals, various metals, and transportation and communications equipment. Note that

Canada exports a wide variety of products.

a significant part of Canada's exports consists of raw materials and that only a few items — such as paper, automobiles, and communications equipment — undergo extensive processing before being exported. However, the largest single export item (motor vehicles and parts) undergoes complete processing in Canada. Table 19.4 shows the value and percentage of Canadian export items in 1996. The values are in 1986 dollars.

TABLE 19.4

Value and percentage of export items, 1996.

Item	Value ($ million)	%
Food:		
Wheat	2 421	1.0
Other farm and fish products	15 962	6.5
Energy materials:		
Crude petroleum	7 264	3.0
Natural gas	9 433	3.8
Other energy products	7 351	3.0
Other (natural resource) materials:		
Lumber and sawmill products	9 390	3.8
Pulp and paper	14 695	6.0
Other metals and minerals	24 359	9.9
Chemicals and fertilizers	13 419	5.4
Motor vehicles and parts	57 867	23.6
Other manufactured goods	83 406	34.0
TOTAL	245 567	100.0

Source: *Bank of Canada Review*, Summer 1998: s105.

Canada's largest export market is the United States. In 1995, over 80% of Canada's merchandise exports went to that country. Other important export markets are Japan, Great Britain, Germany, the Netherlands, the People's Republic of China, and France. Figure 19.3 shows Canada's leading export markets along with the percentage of total exports destined for each.

In 1997, Canadian merchandise exports to the European Union amounted to $16.7 billion or over 5% of our total merchandise exports. There is also a lively trade between Canada and Japan. Our exports of goods to Japan in 1997 totaled $12.1 billion, accounting for 4% of our total merchandise exports. We sold $4.4 billion worth of goods to the United Kingdom and $7.9 billion to other countries of the Organization for Economic Cooperation and Development (OECD).

FIGURE 19.3

Canada's major export markets, 1997.

The United States is the main buyer of Canada's exports.

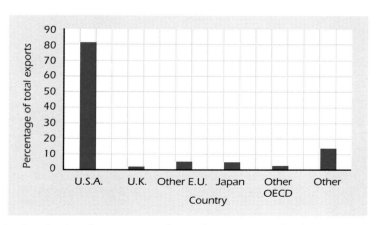

Source: Statistics Canada, *Canadian Economic Observer* (Cat. 11–010–XPB), July 1998: 31.

Canada's merchandise exports are grouped into several broad categories. Data on the value of merchandise exports in each category are shown in Table 19.5.

TABLE 19.5

Classification of Canada's merchandise exports, 1997.

Category	Value ($million)	% of total
Agricultural and fish products	24 705	8.5
Energy products	26 820	9.2
Forest products	34 896	12.0
Industrial goods	55 602	19.1
Machines and equipment	67 983	23.4
Automobile products	70 057	24.1
Consumer goods	10 650	3.7
TOTAL	290 703	100.0

Source: Statistics Canada, *Canadian Economic Observer* (Cat. 11-010-XPB), July 1998: 31.

CANADA'S IMPORTS

Learning Objective 5:
Canada's imports

The United States is the main supplier of Canada's imports.

To get a general overall picture of our international trade, we should really have some idea of Canada's imports. In 1997, Canada imported a total of $329.2 billion worth of goods and services, and its merchandise imports alone amounted to $276.8 billion. Table 19.6 provides information on Canada's imports. The values are in 1986 dollars.

Most of Canada's imports come from the United States. In 1997, imports from that country accounted for over 76% of our total merchandise imports. Figure 19.4 shows the major countries that supply Canada's imports.

In 1997, Canada purchased $6.1 billion worth of goods from the United Kingdom. Our imports from Japan were valued at over $8 billion — about 3% of our merchandise imports. Imports from other countries in the European Union amounted to $18 billion, or over 6.5% of imports from all countries. Other OECD countries supplied us with over $11 billion worth of goods.

TABLE 19.6

Value and percentage of import items, 1996.

Item	Value ($million)	%
Food	12 692	5.4
Energy materials:		
Crude petroleum	5 267	2.3
Other energy products	2 505	1.1
Other (natural resource) materials:		
Construction materials	2 683	1.1
Industrial materials	37 582	16.1
Motor vehicles and parts	54 657	23.4
Other manufactured goods	98 490	42.2
Other consumer goods	19 735	8.4
TOTAL	233 611	100.0

Source: *Bank of Canada Review*, Summer 1998: s106.

Just as we have categorized Canada's exports, so too can we categorize our imports. The value of imports in each category is shown in Table 19.7.

FIGURE 19.4

Major suppliers of
Canada's imports,
1997.

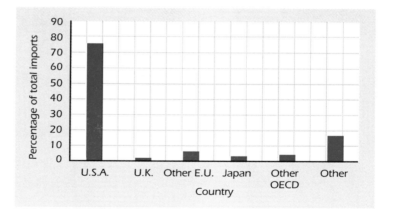

Source: Statistics Canada, *Canadian Economic Observer* (Cat. 11–010–XPB), July 1998: 32.

TABLE 19.7

Classification of
Canada's merchandise
imports, 1997.

Category	Value ($million)	% of total
Agricultural and fish products	15 579	5.9
Energy products	10 603	4.0
Forest products	2 373	0.9
Industrial goods	54 370	20.6
Machines and equipment	91 203	34.5
Automobile products	60 630	22.9
Consumer goods	29 588	11.2
TOTAL	264 345	100.0

Source: Statistics Canada, *Canadian Economic Observer* (Cat. 11-010-XPB), Summer 1998: 32.

CHAPTER SUMMARY

1. International trade concerns the import and export of goods and services and their effects on the economy.

2. The advantages derived from labour specialization apply also to regional specialization. Trade can mutually benefit two or more trading partners if each specializes in the production of the commodity in which it has an absolute advantage.

3. Trade will also mutually benefit trading partners if each specializes in the production of the commodity in which it has a comparative advantage. Thus, trade can benefit partners even in cases where one trading partner has an absolute advantage in the production of all goods.

4. Comparative advantage may result from natural endowment, acquired advantage, or from special knowledge.

5. Canada's major export items include motor vehicles and parts, newsprint paper, wood pulp, communications and electronic equipment, lumber, and wheat.

6. Canada's largest export market is the United States, which buys over 80% of Canada's merchandise exports.

7. Canada imports a wide variety of products, including motor vehicles and parts,

GLOBAL PERSPECTIVE

Export Growth in Seven Countries

The growth of a country's exports measures its sales of goods and services to other countries over time. The economic fortunes of many countries are directly linked to the growth of their export sectors. In this capsule, we compare the growth of Canada's export sector with that of some other industrial countries.

The accompanying graph shows the average rate of growth of exports from 1990 to 1999. As can be seen from the graph, the U.S.A. led the pack with an annual average growth rate of 6.7% in exports. C anada was second with its exports growing at an annual average of 6.3%. Japan was third, with an annual average of 5.6%, followed in order by Germany (5.4%), Italy (4.6%), and France (4.5%). Over the same period, the United Kingdom managed to increase its exports by an annual average of just 4.1%.

Caveat: Students are warned that conclusions about comparative overall economic performance cannot be drawn on the basis of the performance of any one sector of the economy.

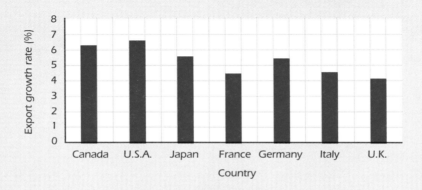

Source: International Monetary Fund, *World Economic Outlook*, May 1998: 176.

industrial machinery, chemicals and plastics, communications and electronic equipment, and crude petroleum.

8. The United States is our largest supplier of imports. Japan, Great Britain, and Germany are also important suppliers of our imports.

TERMS FOR REVIEW
international trade (323)
regional specialization (323)
absolute advantage (323)
principle of comparative advantage (324)

terms of trade (325)
trading curve (326)
geographical determinism (327)

QUESTIONS FOR REVIEW AND DISCUSSION
1. What is the importance of international trade to the Canadian economy? (General)

2. How would you respond to the question, "Why do nations trade?" (L.O.1,2)

3. Assume that Canada is the most efficient country in the world in the production of agricultural goods. Could Canada still benefit by importing food? Explain. (L.O.3)

4. Use an arithmetic example to explain the principle of comparative advantage. (L.O.3)

5. Explain why wheat and newsprint paper are among the leading products exported from Canada. (L.O.3)

6. Discuss the major determinants of comparative advantage. (L.O.3)

7. Name the major countries to which Canada exports goods. Which of these is the main buyer of Canadian exports? (L.O.4)

8. Name the major countries from which Canada imports goods. Which of these is the main supplier of Canadian imports? (L.O.5)

PROBLEMS AND EXERCISES

1. The country of Keylandia (a fictitious country) can produce a typewriter or 20 pairs of shoes. The country of Cloggon (another fictitious country) can produce a similar typewriter or 80 pairs of shoes. (L.O.1,2,3)

   (a) Which of these two countries has an advantage in the production of typewriters?

   (b) Is this advantage absolute or comparative?

   (c) Which country has an advantage in the production of shoes?

   (d) Is this advantage absolute or comparative?

   (e) Would trade benefit these two countries?

2. Suppose Keylandia can produce 75 000 typewriters and 100 000 pairs of shoes per year, while Cloggon can produce 1500 typewriters and 500 000 pairs of shoes per year. (L.O.2)

   (a) On the basis of this information, complete Table 19.8.

TABLE 19.8	Country	Typewriters	Pairs of shoes
Production of type-writers and shoes in Keylandia and Cloggon.	Keylandia Cloggon TOTAL		

   (b) Now, suppose that Keylandia specializes in the production of typewriters while Cloggon specializes in the production of shoes. Use the figures in Exercise 1 to complete post-specialization Table 19.9.

TABLE 19.9	Country	Typewriters	Pairs of shoes
Production of type-writers and shoes in Keylandia and Cloggon.	Keylandia Cloggon TOTAL	0	0

3. Economia and Simpletonia are neighbouring countries. A worker in Economia can produce either six units of clothing or three units of food. A worker in Simpletonia can produce either four units of clothing or one unit of food. (L.O.2,3)

   (a) Does either country have an absolute advantage in the production of both products? If so, which country?

   (b) Fill in the blanks.

_____ has a comparative advantage in the production of clothing while _____ has a comparative advantage in the production of food.

(c) The production of clothing and food in Economia and Simpletonia is shown in Table 19.10.

TABLE 19.10

Production of clothing and food in Economia and Simpletonia.

Country	Clothing	Food
Economia	5000 units	15 000 units
Simpletonia	50 units	10 000 units
TOTAL	5050 units	25 000 units

If Economia specializes in the production of clothing while Simpletonia specializes in the production of food, use the opportunity cost figures given above to complete post-specialization Table 19.11.

TABLE 19.11

Production of clothing and food in Economia and Simpletonia.

Country	Clothing	Food
Economia		0
Simpletonia	0	
TOTAL		

4. "Canada is much too dependent on foreign trade. We depend on foreigners to buy 40% of our goods and services and we buy 38% of our goods and services from foreigners. Canada should be more self-sufficient." Discuss.

Internet Site

http://www.dfait-maeci.gc.ca
This site is for the Department of Foreign Affairs and International Trade. It is a great source of information about Canada's foreign affairs and international trade.

INTERNET EXERCISE

1. Go to **http://www.infoexport.gc.ca/menu-e.asp**.
2. Click on *Canada's Trade Development Agenda*.
3. Click on *Team Canada Trade Mission*.
4. Click on *What is Team Canada?*
   Answer the following questions:
   a) What is Team Canada?
   b) What is the main function of Team Canada?
   c) Write down some trade facts from the 1998 Trade Mission to Latin America.

CHAPTER 20

TARIFFS AND TRADE POLICY ISSUES

Learning Objectives

After studying this chapter, you should understand:

1 the reasons for tariffs

2 classification of tariffs

3 tariff structure

4 arguments in favour of tariffs

5 arguments against tariffs

6 the optimum tariff

7 other restrictive and control devices

8 economic integration

9 an analysis of Separatism

10 the great free-trade debate

11 views on the North American Free Trade Agreement

The degree of protection should be roughly equal to the advantage of foreign producers in this market as a result of their lower labour standards, modified by relative productivity.

The National Labor-Management Council on Foreign Trade Policy.

INTRODUCTION

In the Canadian confederation, certain powers are given to the federal government and certain powers to the provinces. One of the areas over which the federal government has jurisdiction is the imposition of tariffs. As is to be expected, the tariff policies of the federal government affect economic activity all over the country.

We have seen that, through trade and specialization, countries can increase their well-being both individually and collectively. Despite the obvious advantages of free trade, we live not in a world of free trade but in a world with numerous restrictions on trade. The tariff is the most widely used of these restrictions. In this chapter, you will study some of the issues surrounding tariffs.

This chapter will also introduce you to various forms of economic integration. Economic integration is practised among many countries of the world. In 1987, Canada and the United States signed a free-trade agreement. In the summer of 1992, Canada, the United States, and Mexico reached a preliminary agreement on free trade between the three countries which is now in effect. Indeed, tariffs and trade policies are very topical issues.

WHY TARIFFS?

A tariff makes the imported good more expensive.

Learning Objective 1: the reasons for tariffs

A tariff is a tax imposed on imported goods.

When we import goods from Japan or another country, we pay a tax or **duty** on those goods. Similarly, when Canadian exporters sell their goods to foreign countries, those countries impose a tax or duty on our goods. This duty, or **tariff** as it is called, raises the price of the product to the buyer.

A question well worth asking is "Why do nations impose tariffs?" There are many reasons. Nations may impose tariffs:

1. as a device for redistributing income from one group to another;

2. as a means of raising revenue for the government;

3. as a means of improving the country's balance-of-payments position;

4. as a means of dealing with the unemployment problem in the country;

5. as a means of restricting the consumption of certain goods that may be considered socially or economically undesirable;

6. as a means of improving the country's terms of trade, and thus increasing its share of the gains from trade;

7. as a means of protecting certain industries from the full force of international competition;

8. as a means of encouraging certain industries considered to be vital from an economic, military, or political point of view.

From the above list, it is clear that there is no shortage of reasons for imposing tariffs. A tariff can usually be defended (rightly or wrongly) on one or more of the grounds listed above.

CLASSIFICATION OF TARIFFS

Learning Objective 2: classification of tariffs

Tariffs can be classified according to their main objectives. If the main objective of the tariff is to raise revenue for the government, than the tariff is called a **revenue tariff**. If the objective is to protect domestic producers, then the tariff is called a **protective tariff**. Protective tariffs are much more common in Canada than revenue tariffs. In

Revenue tariffs raise revenue for the government.

Protective tariffs protect domestic producers. Canadian tariffs are mainly protective.

A specific tariff is an amount per unit of the imported item.

An ad valorem tariff is a fixed percentage of the value of the imported item.

A compound tariff is a combination of specific and ad valorem tariffs.

Learning Objective 3: tariff structure

Canada, customs duties account for less than 5% of the total revenue of the federal government.

Tariffs can also be classified as specific, ad valorem, or compound. A **specific tariff** is expressed as so much per unit of the imported item. Thus, a tariff of $0.40 imposed on each 100-g bottle of hot sauce imported would be a specific tariff. An **ad valorem tariff** is expressed as a fixed percentage of the value of the imported item. Thus, a tariff of 35% of the value of textiles imported into Canada would be an ad valorem tariff. A **compound tariff** is a combination of specific and ad valorem tariffs. A tariff expressed as $0.25 per kilogram for the first 50 kg and 10% of the value of any amount over 50 kg is an example of a compound tariff. We shall examine arguments for and against tariffs in subsequent sections of this chapter.

TARIFF STRUCTURE

Four main categories of tariff rates apply to goods imported into Canada. These are: British preferential, most-favoured-nation, general, and general preferential.

British preferential

This rate applies to goods imported from British commonwealth countries, which enjoy the benefits of the British Commonwealth preferential tariff.

Most-favoured-nation

This rate is usually higher than the British preferential rate but lower than the general tariff rate, and applies to goods imported from countries with which Canada has trade agreements, such as the General Agreement of Tariffs and Trade (GATT).

General

This rate applies to goods imported from those countries with which Canada has no trade agreements.

General preferential

On July 1, 1974, Canada agreed to a generalized system of preferences designed to allow lower rates on goods imported from developing countries. This rate generally consists of the British preferential rate or the most-favoured-nation rate minus one third, whichever is less.

ARGUMENTS IN FAVOUR OF TARIFFS

Learning Objective 4: arguments in favour of tariffs

Several arguments have been advanced in favour of tariffs. These include both economic and non-economic arguments. In this section, we shall discuss some popular economic arguments in support of tariffs.

THE INFANT INDUSTRY ARGUMENT

Tariffs protect infant industries.

One argument put forward by supporters of tariffs is the **infant industry argument**. The argument is as follows. New domestic industries cannot compete with older and better established industries in foreign countries; hence, new domestic industries need to be protected by tariffs. New domestic industries, moreover, may have the potential to develop a comparative advantage. This potential may never be realized unless such industries are allowed to grow to maturity with the assistance of tariffs. In order for this argument to carry much weight, the tariff would have to be temporary — in place only until the industry matured. In practice, however, an industry is often protected for such a long time that we begin to wonder whether or not the infant will ever grow up! Moreover, protection is valid only if the gains from such protection cannot be claimed exclusively by the firms' owners in the form of eventual profits. In other words, the infant industry argument is significantly strengthened when external economies, in the form of benefits to the society, are present.

THE EMPLOYMENT ARGUMENT

Another argument often used to support the use of tariffs is that they help to create jobs. The imposition of tariffs, it is argued, keeps out foreign goods and thus increases domestic production. The increase in employment in domestic industries competing with the imported goods will spread to other industries. For example, increased employment in the communications industry will increase total income in that industry. This increase in income will increase demand for goods produced by other industries and thus increase employment in those industries. Additional investment may also be undertaken to produce domestic substitutes. When considering this argument, it is important to realize that the reduction of our imports due to tariffs means a reduction of exports from our trading partners, which may result in unemployment, falling incomes, and reduced imports abroad. Our exports will then also be reduced, and we, too, may suffer unemployment and falling incomes.

Tariffs create and protect jobs.

THE TERMS OF TRADE ARGUMENT

A third argument in favour of tariffs is that a country can improve its terms of trade by imposing tariffs on goods imported from other countries. Recall that the phrase **terms of trade** refers to the rate at which a country's exports can be exchanged for its imports. The imposition of a tariff means that a larger quantity of imports will be required for any given quantity of exports. Improvement in a country's terms of trade can make the country better off, but this is not a necessary consequence of higher tariffs. If the tariff is so high that it reduces imports to zero, then the country may be worse off than if the tariff had not been imposed. There is therefore some level of tariff that is optimal in terms of increasing the benefits derived from the terms of trade. The concept of an optimum tariff will be discussed below.

Tariffs can improve the terms of trade.

DIVERSIFICATION AND INDUSTRIALIZATION

It is often argued that protection of domestic industries by tariffs is necessary in order to promote diversification and industrialization. This argument seems to rest on the assumption that industrialization and diversification are desirable because they result in an increase in real income. If industrialization and diversification are desirable for their own sake, then protection by tariffs is one way (though not necessarily the most efficient way) of achieving these ends. We must understand, however, that diversification and industrialization do not necessarily lead to an increase in real income or purchasing power. Indeed, the pursuit of industrialization and diversification may lead to severe misallocation of resources and, consequently, to a reduction in real income. Of course, non-economic arguments exist in support of tariffs, but, as indicated earlier, we are concerned here only with the economic arguments.

Tariffs promote industrialization and diversification.

ARGUMENTS AGAINST TARIFFS

COMPARATIVE ADVANTAGE

The main economic argument against tariffs is that they interfere with the principle of comparative advantage. Thus, they reduce or negate the gains from specialization and trade.

Tariffs interfere with the principle of comparative advantage.

Learning Objective 5:
arguments against tariffs

We have seen that international trade benefits each trading partner and increases total production. The imposition of tariffs, on the other hand, can result in each trading partner being worse off.

EFFICIENCY

Tariffs are inefficient.

Another argument against tariffs is that the objectives that they are designed to achieve can, in most cases, be achieved by other, more efficient means. For example, the objective of industrialization can be achieved more efficiently by subsidization than by the imposition of tariffs. Also, in cases where a temporary tariff may achieve a specific objective, it becomes extremely difficult to remove the tariff once the objective has been achieved; tariffs tend to become permanent once they are imposed.

 PROBLEM SOLVING 20-1
Could Canadian consumers benefit from a gradual elimination of the tariff on shoes?

THE OPTIMUM TARIFF

If a country's terms of trade improve, it will secure a larger share of the gains from trade and specialization. The imposition of a tariff is one way of improving a country's terms of trade. As a country raises its tariffs (assuming that other countries do not retaliate), its terms of trade increase, but its volume of trade decreases. The benefits from the improvement in the terms of trade, however, are likely to more than compensate for the loss resulting from the reduction in trade volume. Hence, the country obtains a net gain.

Learning Objective 6:
the optimum tariff

The optimum tariff is the tariff that maximizes the country's welfare.

After a point, however, the loss resulting from the reduction in the volume of trade will begin to outweigh the benefits from the improvement in the terms of trade. It follows that a tariff exists that maximizes the benefits to the country. Such a tariff is called an **optimum tariff**. Figure 20.1 shows that as the tariff increases from 0 to *t*, community welfare increases. Beyond *t*, however, the tariff chokes off trade so much that community welfare declines. The optimum tariff *t* maximizes community welfare.

FIGURE 20.1

The optimum tariff.

APPLICATION

The Effects of Tariffs

Let us use simple demand and supply graphs to help us to analyze the effects of a tariff. To avoid unnecessary complications, we assume that there are only two countries in the world: Canada and Rest of the World (ROW). For simplicity also, we assume that Canada and ROW use a common currency called the dollar ($). Diagram A shows the demand and supply curves for wheat in Canada while Diagram B shows the demand and supply curves for wheat in ROW. The world price of wheat is P. At that price, Canadian wheat producers supply X units to the Canadian market, but the quantity demanded at that price is X_2. At the world price, there is a shortage of X_2 - X units of wheat in Canada.

What about ROW? Let's take a look. The quantity demanded at the world price is Y, while the quantity supplied by ROW producers is Y_2 units. There is therefore a surplus of Y_2 - Y in ROW. This surplus is exactly equal to the shortage in Canada. Is this a coincidence? Not really. The total quantity of wheat demanded in both countries must be equal to the total quantity supplied at

the world price. If Canada and ROW are allowed to trade freely, Canada will import X_2 - X units of wheat from ROW, and ROW will export Y_2_Y units to Canada.

Let's assume now that Canada imposes a tariff of 50% on wheat imported from ROW. The Canadian price of wheat is now P_t. Canadian wheat growers increase the quantity supplied from X to X_1 units, and consumers reduce the quantity demanded from X_2 to X_1. ROW has lost its export market. This loss of the Canadian market forces the ROW price down from P to P_0 in Diagram B. ROW wheat growers reduce the quantity supplied from Y_2 to Y_1 while ROW consumers increase their purchases of ROW wheat from Y to Y_1.

What has the tariff done? Canadian consumers are paying a higher price and getting a smaller quantity of wheat. But Canadian wheat farmers are happy. They are getting a great deal more money — P_t . X_1 instead of P.X in Diagram A. And what has happened in ROW? Wheat farmers there must be a sorrowful group. They are hurting. They are selling less wheat at a lower price.

Canada

DIAGRAM A

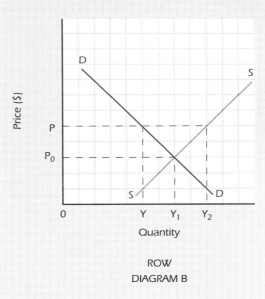

ROW

DIAGRAM B

OTHER RESTRICTIVE AND CONTROL DEVICES

The tariff is not the only device that restricts and controls the volume of trade between countries. Other such devices include import quotas, export subsidies, and voluntary restrictions.

Import quotas

An **import quota** is the maximum amount of a commodity that may be permitted to enter the country during a given period of time. To ensure that the quota is not exceeded, the government requires each importer to obtain an import licence for the amount to be imported.

Export subsidies

A government may offer assistance to its exporters by paying them a subsidy. Such **export subsidies** reduce the exporters' costs, thus enabling them to reduce their prices and so compete more effectively with foreign producers. Some countries use export subsidies rather liberally to promote their industries.

Voluntary restrictions

Imports from a certain country may adversely affect a domestic industry. In this case, a government may ask the exporting country to cooperate by voluntarily restricting its exports. An example of voluntary restrictions has occurred between Canada and Japan. Canada has asked Japan to restrict its exports of radios and cars to Canada, and this has prevented a flood of low-priced goods on the market, enabling Canadian manufacturers to compete.

TARIFFS VERSUS QUOTAS

Both tariffs and quotas raise the domestic price of the product and reduce the volume of trade. There are, however, differences in the effects of tariffs and quotas.

First, import quotas are likely to be more effective than tariffs in limiting the quantity of imports entering a country. If the preference for an imported good is very strong, some amount of that good is likely to be imported in spite of a high tariff. Some consumers may be willing and able to pay the price. But in the case of an import quota, the quota establishes the limit and it cannot be exceeded. The government may even ban the importation of certain goods.

Second, a tariff, as we have seen, raises the price of the imported product and thus reduces the quantity demanded of that product. The proceeds from the tariff accrue to the government as added tax revenues. The tax burden is borne by Canadian consumers of the imported product in the form of increased prices, and also by the foreign exporters in the form of reduced quantities demanded. Domestic producers of the product are thus at an advantage, because the tariff does not apply to their product. A quota, on the other hand, reduces the supply of the product on the domestic market, and hence pushes its price up. The higher prices are paid to foreign exporters of the product and also to domestic producers. They do not accrue to the government as tax revenues as in the case of a tariff.

Finally, a tariff is non-discriminatory in the sense that it applies equally to all foreign exporters. Thus, all domestic importers of the product pay the same tariff. On the other hand, import licences may be awarded on the basis of criteria that have nothing to do with efficiency. For example, import licences may be granted to some importers for political reasons, while more efficient importers may be denied import licences. In such cases, the consumers will be the main losers.

ECONOMIC INTEGRATION

The economic analysis of economic associations among sovereign states belongs to the theory of economic integration. We shall discuss, at a very elementary level, the major forms of economic integration. The objective is to provide you with an inkling of the concepts so that you will not be entirely lost in discussions of the issues relating to economic association.

Economic integration is an arrangement between two or more countries to *abolish* certain discriminatory practices between them. But let us not confuse economic integration with economic cooperation. **Economic cooperation** is an arrangement between two or more countries to *reduce* certain forms of discrimination among them. An example of economic integration is an agreement between Canada and the United States to abolish trade barriers between the two countries. An example of economic cooperation is an agreement to reduce tariffs.

FORMS OF ECONOMIC INTEGRATION

Integration arrangements can take various forms. These forms depend on the degree of integration involved. It is now customary to distinguish five major forms of economic integration. These are:

1. free-trade area

2. customs union

3. common market

4. economic union

5. complete economic integration

Each of these forms of economic integration will be discussed in turn.

Free-trade area

A **free-trade area** agreement entails the lowest degree of economic integration. It involves an agreement whereby goods and services flow freely (without tariffs) between the member countries. Each participating country, however, retains its own tariffs against the rest of the world.

Two main problems surround this form of economic integration: tariff evasion and industrial distribution. **Tariff evasion** is an attempt to avoid a tariff by rerouting imports. This may occur in the following manner. Let us suppose that two countries, A and B, agree to form a free-trade area. Let us assume also that countries A and B impose tariffs of 20% and 30% respectively on the value of goods imported from a third country, C. An importer in country B who wishes to import a product from country C can arrange for the imported product to enter the free-trade area at A, where the tariff is lower than at B. The importer can then transport the product to B and thus avoid B's higher tariff. Such an arrangement will benefit the importer only if transportation costs from A to B are sufficiently low to make the arrangement worthwhile. In any case, the possibility of such tariff evasions in a free-trade area presents a threat to the objectives of B's tariff, and imposes severe strains on the free-trade area agreement.

The problem of *industrial distribution* is actually a byproduct of tariff evasion. To understand this, let us return to our three-country example. If producers want to establish industries within the free-trade area, they must consider the sources of their inputs and the cost of obtaining those inputs. Let us assume that most of their inputs will be imported from country C, which is outside the free-trade area. Given the different tariff rates in A and B, these producers are likely to set up the industries in country A, where the tariff is lower, other things being equal.

We noted earlier that tariffs are used as a device to protect domestic industries. This being the case, a number of industries will tend to be established in the member country whose tariff policies offer greatest protection. Thus, we can see that as long as each member country is allowed to pursue its own tariff policies with the rest of the world, there will be unfavourable consequences. This partly explains why free-trade areas tend to be relatively short-lived and serve mainly as stepping grounds for higher levels of economic integration.

Customs union

A customs union is a form of economic integration in which member countries remove all tariffs among themselves, but erect a common tariff against the rest of the world.

A customs union is a higher form of integration than a free-trade area.

The problems inherent in the free-trade area arrangement have led countries to favour a higher level of economic integration. The problems mentioned above in connection with a free-trade area stem from the fact that member countries do not have a common tariff on trade with the rest of the world. A level of economic integration higher than the free-trade area is a **customs union**, in which a common tariff is levied on goods imported from outside the customs union. In a customs union, an agreement must be reached on how to distribute customs revenues among the members of the customs union.

Although this form of economic integration avoids the problems associated with a free-trade area, it has problems of its own. One such problem is the levying of a common tariff against the rest of the world. Let us assume that each country's tariff structure is consistent with its own interests. Negotiations for a common tariff, then, are likely to be quite difficult. Each participating country will try to secure a tariff that protects its own industries.

A second problem with this form of economic integration is that agreeing on how to distribute joint customs revenues among the participating countries can be very difficult. At first glance, an obvious solution appears to be to divide the proceeds proportionately according to each member country's volume of imports. But the formation of the customs union is likely to affect the volume of imports of each member of the union. We must take this fact into account.

A third problem with customs unions is the difficulty of ensuring that the rules of the common tariff structure are interpreted and applied in the same manner in each member country. If countries interpret and administer the customs laws differently, then the problem of tariff evasion discussed in connection with a free-trade area will certainly resurface in a customs union arrangement.

Common market

A common market is a form of economic integration in which goods flow freely between member countries, a common tariff exists with non-member countries, and there are no restrictions on the movement of labour and capital between the members.

A common market is a higher form of integration than a customs union.

In a **common market**, not only is there free movement of goods between the member countries, but there is no restriction on the free movement of the factors of production. Thus, in a common market, capital and labour move freely between the member countries.

This greater degree of integration requires a greater coordination of policies among the independent member countries. Their economies are united. They must therefore act in concert on a number of important issues. For example, widespread unemployment in one of the member countries will result in an exodus of people from that country to another member country where there are better job prospects. This labour mobility may be economically desirable, but undesirable politically. Since economic and political considerations are fused in a common market, a central body must coordinate the policies of the member states.

Economic union

An **economic union** is an even more highly integrated form of association than the common market. It permits not only free movement of goods and factors of production, but a greater degree of harmonization of national economic policies than a common market does.

Complete economic integration

The most highly integrated form of economic association is complete economic integration. At this level of integration, a supra-national authority is responsible for the monetary, fiscal, and social policies of the integrated group. Decisions taken by this authority are binding on the participating members.

SOME EFFECTS OF ECONOMIC INTEGRATION

Economic integration is extremely popular in many parts of the world today. Although the idea is not new, it has certainly picked up momentum in recent years in both developed and underdeveloped countries. We can reasonably assume that countries agree to enter into the various forms of economic integration because they expect to obtain some benefits. Conventional analysis of the benefits of economic integration concerns trade creation and trade diversion.

Trade creation results from a shift from high-cost domestic production to low-cost production due to economic integration in a member country. Thus, if country A is a high-cost producer of a certain product and country B is a low-cost producer of the same product, country A may produce the product under tariff protection. If these two countries now decide to eliminate tariffs between them, country A will find it more economical to import supplies of the product from country B. This is trade creation.

Trade diversion, on the other hand, results from a shift from the lowest-cost external producer to a higher-cost member producer due to economic integration. Trade creation is felt to be beneficial since it involves shifting resources into more efficient uses. Trade diversion, on the other hand, is felt to be harmful if it shifts resources into less efficient uses.

Economic integration appears to be advantageous because of its effect on the terms of trade. A group of countries bargaining as a unit can win trade concessions from the rest of the world — concessions that probably could not be won if each country bargained individually. These concessions contribute to improved terms of trade.

Another argument in favour of economic integration is that it increases competition. Sometimes, industries are established by erecting high tariff walls. Because of the high degree of protection for these industries, they do not have to compete with similar industries in other countries. This can result in high-cost, inefficient production. Competition forces industries either to seek more efficient methods of production or to leave the market. Lack of competition allows industries to produce inefficiently and at high cost. Now, suppose some countries agree to integrate. This will jeopardize the high-cost inefficient firms because imports can now come from member countries without a tariff. The increase in competition among member countries will result in a more efficient use of resources. Costs and prices will then tend to decrease.

Another advantage of economic integration is that it promotes technological change. Limited domestic markets, on the other hand, impede technological change. In response to the larger market, existing firms will tend to expand. Resources may then flow into research and development. Possibly, latent comparative advantage may also be realized, and the area could become an exporter to non-member countries. All in all, technological change is a positive force, because it promotes economic growth.

Economic integration also dispels fears that markets may disappear due to changes in tariffs, quotas, and other forms of trade restrictions. The market stability ensured by economic integration reduces risk and uncertainty, and promotes a more favourable climate for domestic investment. Foreign investment may also increase as a result of economic integration.

Economic integration may lead to the realization of economies of scale.

Finally, economic integration provides an opportunity to take advantage of economies of scale. Economic integration promotes the development of a larger domestic market. This larger domestic market encourages firms to set up plants and equipment that facilitate economies of scale, since these firms will be supplying a larger regional market.

 PROBLEM SOLVING 20-2

Claude Depapier operates a paper mill in Quebec. Is Claude likely to favour free trade between Canada and the United States?

SEPARATISM: AN ECONOMIC VIEW

A SOVEREIGN QUEBEC

On October 30, 1995, Quebecers went to the polls to vote on the question of separation from Canada. The majority of Quebecers voted in favour of remaining in Canada, but the threat of separation in Quebec is a real and powerful force. Premier Lucien Bouchard has made no secret of the fact that his intention is sovereignty for Quebec. He has promised that another referendum on separation will not be held until after the next provincial election.

Learning Objective 9: an analysis of Separatism

The question of the unilateral declaration of independence by Quebec was brought before the Supreme Court of Canada, and the Court's ruling was handed down on August 20, 1998. The gist of the judgment is that if a "clear majority" of Quebecers, on a "clear" question vote to secede from Canada, then Canada would be obliged to *negotiate* the terms of separation with Quebec. Clearly, the issue is far from settled.

The seriousness of the threat of Quebec separating from Canada has sparked serious discussions about the divisibility of Quebec. As the saying goes, "If Canada is divisible, then so is Quebec." The partition of Quebec, in whatever form it may take, has far reaching economic consequences for both Quebec and Canada. The issues are quite complicated and need not detain us here. Instead, let us turn our attention to an analysis of the consequences of Quebec's secession from Canada.

Let us suppose that Quebec did indeed become a sovereign state. Presumably, it would proceed to negotiate some type of agreement with the rest of Canada — probably an economic union. It could be, however, that so much hostility might result from Quebec's secession, that any meaningful negotiations would be impossible. Quebec would therefore find itself as an independent sovereign state with no economic association with Canada. Canada would then impose tariffs on goods imported from Quebec, and Quebec too would impose tariffs on goods imported from Canada. Depending on the height of the tariff walls, both Quebec and Canada could end up getting supplies from a third country. In other words, Quebec could end up losing its Canadian market and Canada could end up losing its Quebec market. Needless to say, this loss of markets could result in unemployment in both Quebec and Canada. To deal with this problem, still higher tariffs might be imposed to protect domestic producers in Canada and Quebec. These tariffs would result in higher domestic prices, a reduction in the volume of trade, and a misallocation of resources. The standard of living would then fall in both Canada and Quebec.

Let us now suppose that Canada would be willing to negotiate an association with a sovereign Quebec. Let us assume further that the type of association to be negotiated would be a customs union. The decision to negotiate implies an acknowledgement of potential benefits from the association. One major problem would be to agree on how to distribute the benefits from the union among the member states. Conceivably, a union could also result in gains for one state and losses for the other, even though a net gain might be realized by the union as a whole. The country that gained would then have to compensate the country that lost. Agreement on compensatory transfers is one of the major problems of economic integration.

A matter often discussed is how secession might affect manufacturing establishments in Canada and in Quebec. Let us examine this issue briefly. Again, we shall consider two cases: Quebec as a sovereign state with no association with Canada, and a sovereign Quebec in a customs union with Canada. In a sovereign-state Quebec, Quebec industries catering to the large Quebec-Canada market would tend to move out of Quebec and re-establish elsewhere in Canada, assuming that the move was economically feasible. Quebec industries that catered mainly to the Quebec market would tend to remain in Quebec. Quebec industries supplying the American market (these account for about 60% of Quebec's total exports) would also tend to remain in Quebec. In a sovereign-associate Quebec, no logical economic reason would exist to expect an exodus of firms from Quebec or Canada. What is likely to affect investment in Canada and in Quebec is the great uncertainty caused by the threat of secession. This is so because investment does not thrive well in a climate of uncertainty.

THE GREAT FREE-TRADE DEBATE

HISTORICAL BACKGROUND

Several attempts have been made to establish free trade between Canada and the United States.

Learning Objective 10:
the great free-trade debate

Notions of free trade between Canada and the United States are not new. On the basis of the gains from trade discussed earlier, proposals for free trade between the two countries can be traced as far back as pre-Confederation Canada. In 1854, a free-trade agreement was signed between Britain and the United States, ensuring the removal of artificial barriers to trade between Canada and the United States. This agreement lasted until 1866. Successive attempts were made in the three decades following 1866 to return to the 1854 protocol, but each attempt failed.

An agreement of sorts was reached in 1911, but lack of enthusiasm for the agreement both in Canada and in the United States, coupled with the defeat of the government of Sir Wilfrid Laurier in the same year, sounded the death knell of the 1911 accord. It was not until 1935 that another trade agreement was negotiated by the two countries. The 1935 agreement marked the beginning of trade liberalization between Canada and the United States.

In October 1947, the General Agreement on Tariffs and Trade (GATT) was signed at Geneva. The objective of the GATT was to increase trade flows between the countries of the world by tariff reduction. Under the GATT, Canada and the United States negotiated further tariff reductions. In 1953, President Eisenhower showed interest in a more comprehensive trade agreement, but the Canadian government was content with the GATT. But two accords merit our attention. In 1941, an agreement between Canada and the United States made free trade in defence equipment a virtual reality; and in 1965, the Auto Pact brought free trade between the two countries into the auto industry.

In 1985, then-President Ronald Reagan and then-Prime Minister Brian Mulroney met in Quebec City on March 17 (St. Patrick's Day). This so-called "Shamrock Summit" involv-

The most comprehensive trade agreement between Canada and the U.S. was signed in 1987.

ing the two leaders paved the way for a comprehensive trade agreement between Canada and the United States, which was signed in 1987. This Canada–U.S. trade agreement is by far the most important trade agreement that Canada has ever negotiated. Table 20.1 is a summary of the history of free trade between Canada and the United States.

TABLE 20.1

Summary of historical background of Canada-U.S. free trade, 1854–1987.

1854	Free-trade agreement signed between the United States and Britain.
1870–1890	Several abortive attempts made at free trade.
1911	Short-lived trade agreement reached between Canada and the U.S.
1935	Trade agreement reached. This was the beginning of significant tariff reductions on trade between the two countries.
1941	Free trade in defence equipment.
1947	The establishment of the GATT. Further tariff reductions negotiated.
1953	U.S. expressed interest in more comprehensive trade agreement; Canada preferred to stay with the GATT.
1965	The Auto Pact: free trade in the auto industry.
1985	Commitment to free trade at the Shamrock Summit.
1987	Comprehensive trade agreement signed.

THE GREAT 1988 DEBATE

The trade agreement between Canada and the United States, signed on October 4, 1987, produced one of the biggest debates in recent Canadian history. It was the main issue in the 1988 federal election. The liberals, led by John Turner, and the New Democratic Party, led by Ed Broadbent, opposed the trade deal. The Conservatives, on the other hand, led by Brian Mulroney, argued in favour of the deal. By returning the Conservatives to power, Canadian voters knew that they were accepting a free-trade arrangement with the United States.

The trade agreement between Canada and the United States is a rather complex document. We can, however, point out some of the possible consequences of such an arrangement.

POSSIBLE BENEFITS FOR CANADA

Increased income

The trade agreement could lead to increased income for Canada.

The removal of tariffs on goods flowing between Canada and the United States means that the tariff previously paid to the U.S. government by Canadian exporters now reverts to the Canadian producers and ultimately to Canadian factor owners. Thus domestic income is likely to increase.

Economies of scale

It could lead to economies of scale.

The trade agreement with the United States will likely benefit Canadian manufacturers who are able to take advantage of economies of scale. To help you to understand this point, let us assume that tariffs are imposed on goods flowing between the two countries. Consider a small Canadian firm producing a relatively small quantity of some product for a small domestic market. Because of the small size of the market, the Canadian producer operates at a relatively high average cost. On the other hand, an American firm producing a similar product for a much larger U.S. market operates at a much lower average cost. The Canadian producer will find it extremely difficult, if not impossible, to compete with the American producer in the U.S. market. The U.S. firm, however, may be able to compete in the Canadian market because its lower unit cost may more than offset the Canadian tariff. The elimination of tariffs between the two countries will give the Canadian firm easier access to the huge U.S. market, enabling it to take advantage of economies of scale, and compete effectively with the U.S. producer.

Lower-priced imports

The free-trade agreement will benefit Canadian consumers by reducing prices.

The removal of tariffs on imports into Canada from the United States will cause the prices of such imported goods to fall, resulting in an increase in the quantity of imported goods demanded. Canadian consumers will benefit as they replace high-cost (inefficient) domestic production with low-cost imports.

POSSIBLE COSTS TO CANADA

Unemployment

The free-trade agreement may cause unemployment in Canada.

One possible effect of the trade agreement between Canada and the United States is that American firms with subsidiaries established in Canada (to cater to the Canadian market without having to face high tariffs) will close the Canadian subsidiaries and concentrate production in the United States. This, of course, will result in the loss of many jobs in Canada. It may also be argued that the removal of tariffs on U.S. imports will make it impossible for Canadian firms to compete with low-cost imports from the United States. Canadian firms will be forced to close, thus causing unemployment. Another argument related to the unemployment issue is that with the trade agreement, Canadian industries will be forced to reorganize into larger firms to be able to compete with U.S. firms. This so-called "rationalization" of Canadian industries will be the cause of many lost jobs.

Loss of independence

The free-trade agreement could lead to a loss of independence.

Another possible effect of the Canada–U.S. trade agreement is greater reliance on the U.S. market. Once Canadian industries have adjusted to the new trade arrangements, many of our industries will be supplying the U.S. market, thus our industries will be heavily dependent on that market. Knowing that Canadian industries are so heavily dependent on the U.S. market, the United States could conceivably use this heavy reliance as a tool to influence decisions in Canada, even though such decisions may not be in the best interest of Canada. For example, the United States could threaten to dissolve the trade agreement in order to gain certain political concessions. Although there are good reasons for believing that the United States would not resort to this type of tactic, this possible loss of political independence is a cost that should not be ignored.

NORTH AMERICAN FREE TRADE AGREEMENT

Learning Objective 11: views on the North American Free Trade Agreement

While the merits and drawbacks of the free-trade arrangement between Canada and the United States are still being debated, an even wider free-trade area including Mexico has been negotiated. A preliminary North American Free Trade Agreement (NAFTA) between Canada, the United States, and Mexico, reached in the summer of 1992, is now in effect. Supporters of NAFTA argue that such an agreement will open up new opportunities for Canadian firms to penetrate the huge Mexican market. Opponents of NAFTA, on the other hand, claim that free trade between Canada, the United States, and Mexico will be disastrous for Canada.

Two main arguments are presented in support of this pessimistic view. First, opponents claim that firms will relocate to Mexico, where the wage rate is substantially below the Canadian average and pollution standards are almost non-existent. This movement of firms out of Canada will result in a tremendous loss of jobs. Second, opponents of NAFTA argue that because of the huge wage discrepancy between Canada and Mexico, it will be virtually impossible for Canadian products to compete with products made with Mexican cheap labour. In reply to this last argument, supporters of free trade point out that Canada has a comparative advantage over Mexico in the production of many goods, and will therefore benefit from trade. As is usually the case in these matters, the truth probably lies somewhere between these two positions.

NAFTA has been in effect since January 1, 1994. The trade agreement between Canada, the United States, and Mexico calls for tariff reductions between the three countries. By the year 2009, 15 years after NAFTA came into effect, all tariffs between Canada, the United States, and Mexico will be eliminated. Is Canada benefiting from NAFTA? Will Canada benefit from NAFTA? Are some members of NAFTA benefiting at Canada's expense? There is still much debate on these issues. Some are extolling the virtues of NAFTA while others are condemning it.

In April 1998, the NAFTA Commission, in Paris at its fifth meeting, stressed the importance of NAFTA in promoting trade, investment, economic growth and jobs in the three member countries. The commission pointed out that since NAFTA came into effect, trade within North America has grown by nearly 65%. In 1993, trade between Canada, the United States, and Mexico was under U.S. $300 billion. By 1997, trade between the three countries had reached almost U.S. $500 billion. The commission hailed these figures as constituting a clear indication of NAFTA's success in its first four years of implementation. Could this be a case of the *post hoc, ergo propter hoc* fallacy? In addition, Sergio Marchi, the International Trade Minister, said in 1998 that NAFTA has been a tremendous benefit to Canadians of all walks of life. These are powerful claims.

These pronouncements notwithstanding, the Economic Policy Institute (EPI), a Washington-based think tank, has argued that NAFTA has been a failure and should be repealed or drastically revised. The EPI and other organizations including the Institute for Policy Studies, the International Labour Rights Fund, Public Citizen's Global Trade Watch, the Sierra Club, and the U.S. Business Industrial Council Educational Foundation, claimed that NAFTA has, among other things, displaced more than 400 000 jobs in the United States, eliminated more than 2 million jobs and caused the failure of more than 28 000 small businesses. And what damage has NAFTA done to Canada? Well, according to the CPI, NAFTA has increased unemployment in Canada and forced Canada to begin to dismantle its long-standing social safety net, resulting in falling standards of living for the average Canadian. If this is food for thought, perhaps it should be taken with a grain of salt.

CHAPTER SUMMARY

1. A tariff or import duty is a tax imposed on goods from foreign countries. A revenue tariff is designed mainly to raise revenue for the government, while a protective tariff is designed to protect domestic industries from foreign competition.

2. A specific tariff is stated as a given amount per unit of the imported item. An ad valorem tariff is a percentage of the value of the imported item. A compound tariff is a combination of a specific and an ad valorem tariff.

The European Union and the World Trade Organization

NAFTA is not an isolated case of a free trade agreement. Free-trade areas have been formed all over the world. For example, free-trade areas have been formed between groups of developing countries, and a free-trade area has been established between Australia and New Zealand. These agreements among nations to reduce or eliminate trade barriers between themselves are not limited to countries in close proximity. For example, a free-trade area has been established between the United States and Israel. Our concern here, however, is with two organizations — one regional (the European Union), the other global (the World Trade Organization) — whose objectives include the promotion of free trade and international cooperation.

The European Union (EU) is a group of 15 countries — Austria, Belgium, Denmark, Finland, France, Germany, Greece, Ireland, Italy, Luxembourg, The Netherlands, Portugal, Spain, Sweden, and the United Kingdom — that have agreed to form a trading bloc, and to create by this union a stable and predictable environment with the certainty that the rules of the game will not be changed by capricious government behaviour.

One of the main objectives of the EU is to promote free trade. With a population of 370 million, the EU is indeed a force to be reckoned with. It accounts for one-fifth of the total global trade in goods. The EU is much more tightly integrated than NAFTA. It has its own flag, its own anthem, its own 626-member parliament, its own budget, and a single currency. Thus, the EU is more than a free-trade area. It is a political entity.

A look at some statistics might help to place the EU in some perspective. The 15 member countries cover a total area of 1 249 000 square miles. The GDP of the EU is U.S. $8093.4 billion, and it has an unemployment rate of 10.7%. It exports 9.1% of its GDP (the value of all goods and services produced), and its imports account for 9.4% of its GDP. It is interesting to note that the EU and the United States, though economic competitors, have agreed on a plan to promote cooperation, partnership and joint action in areas ranging from trade liberalization to security. They have agreed to contribute to the expansion of world trade and closer economic relations.

The World Trade Organization (WTO), with its headquarters in Geneva, Switzerland, was established on January 1, 1995, following the Uruguay Round of negotiations (1986-94). The WTO was preceded by the General Agreement on Tariffs and Trade (GATT), which is now part of the WTO agreements. Whereas the GATT was established as a *provisional* body, the WTO is a permanent organization with the same legal foundation and legitimate status as the International Monetary Fund (IMF). The GATT dealt only with trade in goods, but the WTO deals with trade in goods and services, and with issues such as copyright, trademarks, and patents — the so-called intellectual property.

The WTO consists of 132 countries and its secretariat employs a staff of 500. The functions of the WTO include administering WTO trade agreements, providing a forum for trade negotiations, handling trade disputes among member countries, monitoring national trade policies to ensure that they do not violate the terms of the WTO agreements, providing technical assistance and training for developing countries, and cooperation with other international organizations. The work of the WTO is conducted by its committees and councils.

3. Economic arguments in favour of tariffs include the infant industry argument, the employment argument, the terms of trade argument, and the diversification and industrialization argument. The main anti-tariff argument is that tariffs interfere with the operation of the principle of comparative advantage.

4. Other devices (besides tariffs) used to control trade flows include import quotas, export subsidies, and voluntary restrictions. Import quotas are often more restrictive than tariffs.

5. Economic integration is an agreement between two or more countries to abolish certain discriminatory practices among them.

6. Economic integration may take the form of a free-trade area, a customs union, a common market, an economic union, or complete economic integration.

7. An economic integration that causes a participating country to shift from high-cost domestic production to lower-cost production results in trade creation.

8. An economic integration that causes a shift from the lowest-cost external producer to a higher-cost member producer results in trade diversion.

9. Economic integration is beneficial because it improves the terms of trade of the integrated group. Other advantages of economic integration include increased competition, technological change, and investment.

10. A sovereign Quebec with no economic association with the rest of Canada would result in tariffs between the two countries. These tariffs could result in a lower standard of living in both countries.

11. An economic union between Canada and a sovereign Quebec would face the problem of agreeing how to distribute benefits and costs resulting from the union.

12. Possible benefits to Canada from the Canada–U.S. trade agreement include increased income, gains from economies of scale, and lower-priced imports. Possible costs include unemployment and loss of independence.

13. The North American Free Trade Agreement brings certain benefits to Canada, but there are some costs as well.

TERMS FOR REVIEW

tariff or import duty (336)
revenue tariff (336)
protective tariff (336)
specific tariff (337)
ad valorem tariff (337)
compound tariff (337)
infant industry argument (337)
terms of trade (338)
optimum tariff (339)
import quota (341)

export subsidies (341)
economic integration (342)
economic cooperation (342)
free-trade area (342)
tariff evasion (342)
customs union (343)
common market (343)
economic union (344)
trade creation (344)
trade diversion (344)

QUESTIONS FOR REVIEW AND DISCUSSION

1. What is the difference between a revenue tariff and a protective tariff? What kind of tariffs does Canada usually impose? (L.O.2)

2. Name some techniques used by Canada to restrict its imports. Do these restrictions benefit Canadian industries? If so, how? (L.O.1,7)

3. List the main features of the infant industry argument in favour of tariffs. Is there a problem with this argument? If so, what is it? (L.O.4)

4. State the employment argument in favour of tariffs. Is it a valid argument? Discuss. (L.O.4)

5. What is meant by terms of trade? Does an improvement in a country's terms of trade necessarily result in an improvement in the country's economic well-being? (L.O.6)

6. List the arguments against restricting trade through tariffs. (L.O.5)

7. Compare tariffs and quotas as restrictive devices. (L.O.7)

8. What is the difference between economic integration and economic cooperation? (L.O.8)

9. List the major forms of economic integration. (L.O.8)

10. Briefly explain how tariff evasion may occur by the formation of a free-trade area. (L.O.8)

11. What problems are likely to result from a customs union arrangement? (L.O.8)

12. Name some advantages of economic integration. (L.O.8)

13. What is the difference between trade creation and trade diversion? (L.O.8)

14. We often hear that if Quebec secedes from Canada, a large-scale exodus of firms from Quebec will result. Do you agree? Why or why not? (L.O.9)

15. "The secession of Quebec from Canada, with no economic association with Canada, is likely to result in lower living standards in both Canada and Quebec." Discuss. (L.O.9)

16. Provide a historical background to the Canada–U.S. free-trade agreement. (L.O.10)

17. What are the possible benefits to Canada from the trade agreement with the United States? (L.O.10)

18. What are the possible costs to Canada from the Canada–U.S. trade agreement? (L.O.10)

19. Discuss the benefits and costs to Canada of NAFTA. (L.O.11)

PROBLEMS AND EXERCISES

1. Do you support a gradual elimination of the tariff on shoes imported into Canada? Why or why not? (L.O.1,4,5)

2. Let us suppose that Canada and the United States agree to trade freely in all goods. Let us suppose also that Quebec decides to opt out of the free-trade agreement. Explain how a Quebec importer can import goods from the United States and thus avoid the tariff. (L.O.8)

3. You are a low-cost producer of forestry products in British Columbia. Do you favour free trade with the United States? (L.O.10)

4. Why would many Canadian producers favour import quotas over tariffs? (L.O.7)

5. Table 20.2 contains data on the various quantities of picture frames demanded (Q_d) in Canada at various prices. The various quantities supplied by Canadian producers (Q_sc) and by foreign producers (Q_sf) are also shown. (General)

TABLE 20.2	Price ($)	Q_d	Q_sc	Q_sf	Q_s	$Q_{st}f$	Q_{st}
Demand and supply for picture frames.	10.00	800	1150	650			
	9.60	900	1100	600			
	9.20	1000	1050	550			
	8.80	1100	1000	500			
	8.40	1200	950	450			
	8.00	1300	900	400			
	7.60	1400	850	350			
	7.20	1500	800	300			
	6.80	1600	750	250			
	6.40	1700	700	200			
	6.00	1800	650	150			

(a) Fill in the total quantity supplied (Q_s) column.

(b) At what price would the market be in equilibrium?

(c) What quantity would be exchanged at that price?

(d) Given a tariff imposed by Canada of $1.20 per frame, compute the new quantities that would be supplied by foreign producers after the tariff ($Q_{st}f$). Then fill in the ($Q_{st}f$) column.

(e) Fill in the column showing the total quantity supplied after the tariff (Q_{st}).

(f) Estimate the new equilibrium price and the new equilibrium quantity.

 6. "When we buy from others, we send money out of the country. When we buy from ourselves, the money stays in the country. By extension, when province A buys from another province, money leaves province A. Therefore, by eliminating interprovincial trade in Canada, each province will keep its money and the entire country will be better off." Discuss.

Internet Site

http://europa.eu.int

This is a good starting place for general information on the European Union. The site explains the mission and operation of the European Union.

http://www.wto.org

This is the Web site for the World Trade Organization. Information on the WTO can be obtained here.

INTERNET EXERCISE

1. Go to **http://www.eurunion.org.**

2. Click on *Information Resources* .

3. Click on *General information about the EU.*

4. Click on *Facts and Figures on the EU and the U.S.*

5. Compare the EU with the U.S. in terms of:

   a) Area (sq. miles);

   b) Population;

   c) Unemployment;

   d) GDP;

   e) Trade (imports and exports) as a percentage of GDP.

VIDEO CASE

Environmental Threat to Salmon

How far must suffering and misery go before we see that even in the day of vast cities and powerful machines, the good earth is our mother and that if we destroy her, we destroy ourselves.

(Paul Bingelow Sears)

Introduction

The market mechanism does many things well, but it does not do all things well; the forces of demand and supply don't take care of everything. A serious problem that our price system does not take care of is pollution. After many years of trying to cope with this mammoth environmental problem, we are still faced with many and varied forms of pollution. Four years ago, it was reported that some of our rivers and lakes were polluted to the extent that they could no longer sustain life. Environment Canada reported that many lakes and rivers in Ontario and Nova Scotia could no longer support salmon fry or trout. Pollution was threatening the salmon industry.

International conflict

Canada and the United States have generally enjoyed a relatively peaceful coexistence, however some issues have caused conflict between the two normally friendly neighbours. The Canadian-American Pacific Salmon Conflict is one such issue.

At the heart of the conflict is each country's contention that the other is intercepting too many of its fish, with disastrous economic and environmental consequences — reduced revenue and overfishing that will seriously deplete fish stocks. The annual catch of Pacific salmon is valued at $300 million. In 1985, the Pacific Salmon Treaty was signed by Canada and the United States, with the intent of equity in sharing the catch, while conserving dwindling stocks. Each country would limit its catch on the basis of estimates of how many salmon originate in its rivers. Negotiations have failed to establish agreeable limits however, and since 1993,

each country has attempted to establish its own limits.

In 1997, Canadians accused Americans of catching five to six million more salmon annually than they were entitled to. On the other hand, Americans have accused Canadians of overfishing salmon headed for rivers in Washington and Oregon states. The conflict is clearly not one that can be easily resolved.

An equally serious problem

A problem as serious as the Canada-United States Pacific salmon conflict is the shortage of salmon from British Columbia. The problem of overfishing mentioned earlier is compounded by the destruction of salmon habitat due to pollution, particularly from an old copper mine that has poisoned a British Columbian salmon lake. If that type of pollution continues, the conflict over who is catching whose fish will be a moot point, because there will be no salmon to catch. The situation is critical, and the governments on both sides must take decisive action to end the pollution of our waters and the destruction of salmon and other habitat.

QUESTIONS

1. Itemize the main points in this case.

2. In what sense would you consider the issue raised in this case a matter of market failure?

3. Canada and the United States agreed to limit their catch of salmon by negotiating quotas based on estimates of how many salmon originate in each country's rivers. What problem or problems do you see arising out of this agreement?

4. Paint a word picture of the seriousness of the Pacific salmon issue discussed in this case.

Video Resource: "Salmon Pak," *National Magazine* (June 1998).

CHAPTER 21

AN OVERVIEW OF MACROECONOMICS

Learning Objectives

After studying this chapter, you should be able to:

1 differentiate microeconomics from macroeconomics

2 discuss the origin of macroeconomics

3 identify the great macroeconomic questions

4 discuss the importance of macroeconomics

5 explain how macroeconomists study the economy

6 understand the interaction between macroeconomic markets

7 construct a simple circular flow model of the economy

8 give an account of the behaviour of the Canadian economy over the past few decades

Inflation and depression are economic phenomena; social strife, revolutions, and wars, while not uniquely economic in their causation, usually have some economic basis. If fear of these monsters is to be exorcised by scientists, the task must fall largely to economists.

Benjamin Higgins, *What Do Economists Know?*

INTRODUCTION

In Chapter 1, we made a distinction between the two main branches of economics: **microeconomics** and **macroeconomics**. In microeconomics, the major focus of attention is on decision-making and behaviour in individual economic units such as households and firms. For example, in microeconomics, we study how individual households make decisions in order to maximize their satisfaction, and how individual firms make decisions in order to maximize their profits. In macroeconomics, on the other hand, we concentrate more on the behaviour of all households together and on the behaviour of all firms together. Our focus is on the **aggregate** (total) rather than on the individual. Thus in macroeconomics, we are interested in the total output of all goods and services in the economy, total employment, and the movements of the total price level.

One would expect macroeconomics and microeconomics to be related, and in fact, they are. After all, to a large extent, macroeconomic behaviour reflects the sum total of decisions made by individual decision-making units. For example, if a household's expenditure on consumer goods and services depends on its income, then we should expect total expenditure on goods and services in the economy to depend on total (aggregate) income. Similarly, we should expect total employment to be equal to the sum of the total number of workers hired by each individual economic unit.

Yet the field of microeconomics is much more settled than that of macroeconomics. There is hardly any disagreement among microeconomists about how consumers maximize satisfaction or about how pricing and output decisions of firms are made in particular market situations. In macroeconomics, however, there are different models about the behaviour of the macroeconomy. Although there is more agreement now in macroeconomics than there was 15 or 20 years ago, this branch of economics is still in a state of flux.

In our approach to the study of macroeconomics, we shall rely on some of the principles of microeconomics. In other words, we shall consider the microeconomic foundations of macroeconomics. This approach is in keeping with the modern trend in macroeconomics, and it provides a rationale for the behaviour of many of the aggregate economic variables that we shall study.

THE ORIGIN OF MACROECONOMICS

In a sense, macroeconomics is as old as economics itself. Adam Smith, in *The Wealth of Nations*, was concerned with the factors that would contribute to a country's wealth. But his approach was not a macroeconomic approach as we know it today. Much of his work dealt with the market mechanism or, as he called it, the "**invisible hand**." Prior to the 1930s, economics was essentially microeconomics.

The **Great Depression** of the 1930s led to a revival of thinking about economics and the economy. This was a period of great economic woe. In 1929, only 116 000 Canadians were unemployed. By 1933, the number had jumped to 826 000. Whereas the unemployment rate was only 2.9% in 1929, it exceeded 19% in 1933. In 1933, the total output of goods and services in the Canadian economy fell by 7.2%. There were widespread bankruptcies and economic hardship everywhere.

CLASSICAL ECONOMICS

There were no macroeconomic models to explain the phenomenon of the Great Depression. The only models available were microeconomic models, which were nevertheless applied to the macroeconomy. These **classical economic models**, as they are called, were incapable of explaining prolonged involuntary unemployment. The popular economic view at the time was as follows. If unemployment developed (perhaps because of a fall in output and consequently a fall in the quantity demanded), there would be a surplus of workers on the labour market. This would cause the wage rate to fall. As wages fell, employers would be willing to hire more workers at the lower wage rate. Workers would be hired until the excess labour was taken off the market.

Something was obviously wrong with this model because it did not explain the economic reality of the time. It was in this economic environment that macroeconomics originated.

KEYNESIAN MACROECONOMICS

Learning Objective 2:
discuss the origin of macroeconomics

Keynes introduced the idea that government spending and taxes could be used to control economic activity.

The failure of classical economic models to explain the Great Depression led an economist named John Maynard Keynes to formulate a new economic model that could explain the economic situation during the 1930s. In his classic work, *The General Theory of Employment, Interest and Money*, published in 1936, Keynes developed a framework that was to become the foundation of macroeconomics. Instead of focusing on wages and prices, Keynes shifted emphasis to total spending as the major determinant of the level of employment in an economy.

Fiscal policy involves changes in government spending and taxation designed to promote economic stability.

Keynes' ideas became quite popular as both economists and politicians adopted his views on the macroeconomy. Largely as a result of Keynes' work, the idea that government spending and taxation could be used to regulate economic activity gained widespread acceptance. In the 1960s, **fiscal policy** (changing government spending and taxes to regulate unemployment and inflation) was in its heyday. Many economists believed that the government could use this macroeconomic tool to achieve high employment and relatively stable prices.

DEVELOPMENTS SINCE THE 1970S

Keynesian economics: economics based on the premise that total output is determined by total spending. The demand side of the economy is emphasized.

The popularity of **Keynesian economics** waned during the 1970s. One of the reasons was that the economy did not seem to respond to Keynesian prescriptions. There were significant fluctuations in output and employment, and the economy experienced inflation. For example, the rate of growth of output fell from 7.7% in 1973 to only 2.6% in 1975. Worse yet, output actually fell by 3.2% in 1982 when the economy experienced a serious recession. The rate of inflation remained high during much of the 1970s and into the early 1980s.

Stagflation: high inflation and high unemployment rates.

Simple Keynesian economics prescribed increased spending to combat recession and reduced spending to combat inflation. This prescription was appropriate prior to the 1970s, when inflation was observed only during periods of rapid economic growth when the rate of unemployment was low. But in the 1970s, economists observed high rates of inflation and high rates of unemployment. This combination of inflation and recession, called **stagflation**, was a new phenomenon. This was a situation beyond the scope of the simple Keynesian model.

The supply side is the production side of the economy.

New classical economists emphasize rapid macro-economic adjustment.

Since the mid-1970s, macroeconomists have been considering new macroeconomic theories which they hope will help them to understand better how the macroeconomy behaves. Keynesian theory emphasized manipulation of total spending or demand. One of the "new" approaches is to place emphasis on the production or **supply side**. This approach became quite popular during the administration of President Reagan in the United States.

Today, there are two leading schools of thought in macroeconomics: the new classical and the new Keynesian schools. **New classical economists** place emphasis on wage and price flexibility and rapid macroeconomic adjustment. They are called new classical

New Keynesians emphasize why the labour market does not clear.

economists because their views are somewhat similar to those of the classical (pre-Keynesian) economists. **New Keynesian economists** attempt to explain why wages and prices fail to adjust to clear the labour market. Because their explanation closely resembles Keynesian ideas, they are called new Keynesians. There is an important similarity between the two schools of thought. They both agree that macroeconomics should be based on microeconomic principles.

GREAT MACROECONOMIC QUESTIONS

Learning Objective 3: understand the great macroeconomic questions

The great macroeconomic questions are: unemployment, inflation, the business cycle, the international economy, and economic growth.

What are the major problems and issues with which macroeconomics is concerned? The list of macroeconomic problems and issues is arbitrary, but we can identify five areas fundamental to macroeconomics. First, macroeconomics is concerned with unemployment. Why is it that the economy cannot always provide jobs for people who want to work? How does unemployment affect the economy? Second, macroeconomics is concerned with movements in the aggregate price level or inflation. What causes inflation? What are its effects? What can be done about it? A third concern of macroeconomics is the aggregate output of goods and services. Why does output sometimes fall below the economy's productive capacity? Can anything be done to keep the economy working at or close to its capability? Fourth, macroeconomics is concerned with the international economy. What is the relationship between the domestic economy and the rest of the world? Such international concerns are of tremendous importance to Canada since a large part of our economy deals with exports and imports of goods and services. Finally, macroeconomics is concerned with economic growth. It is important for an economy to be able to increase its output of goods and services on a long-term basis. How can this be achieved? What are the factors involved? Let us examine each of these concerns in a little more detail.

UNEMPLOYMENT

Not only macroeconomists, but government and households are keenly interested in the rate of unemployment. Although a zero rate of unemployment is hardly expected, economists are interested in knowing why there is so much more unemployment than what can be expected from normal business failures and from new workers entering the labour market.

Unemployment is a situation in which people are unable to find jobs.

Unemployment can be viewed as an excess amount of labour on the labour market. According to microeconomic theory, when there is a surplus on the market, the price of the item falls. This fall in price tends to increase the quantity demanded and to reduce the quantity supplied. Thus, when there is unemployment, one would expect the wage rate to fall. As this happens, ideally, firms hire more workers (quantity demanded increases) and fewer workers look for work (quantity supplied falls) until equilibrium (market clearing) occurs. So why does this adjustment to equilibrium not seem to happen in the case of unemployment? Is there something about the labour market that we do not understand? The problem of unemployment will receive due attention in later chapters.

INFLATION

Inflation is a sustained increase in the average level of prices over time.

Most people dread **inflation**, or rapidly rising prices. Most of us have heard the horror stories of inflation in Germany in the 1920s, and you are probably aware of the efforts of the government and the Bank of Canada to keep inflation under control. Most people dislike inflation because they realize that they have to spend more money to acquire a given amount of goods and services.

Some countries have lived with rates of inflation of 200% and higher. Fortunately, we in Canada have not had to cope with inflationary situations of such magnitude. Yet, economists are aware of the dangers of high rates of inflation, and are constantly seeking a better understanding of the inflationary process.

AGGREGATE OUTPUT

An economy's total output of goods and services is important for obvious reasons. Our standard of living depends to a great extent on what we are able to produce. If a society can keep the total output of goods and services close to the economy's potential, its citizens will be better off. Although the total output of goods and services has increased over time, there have been fluctuations. These ups and downs in the **aggregate output** of goods and services have been given the term **business cycle**. Macroeconomists are very much interested in understanding and explaining why there is so much economic fluctuation.

In the 1960s, many economists believed that it was possible, through macroeconomic policy, to prevent economic fluctuations. Some even talked about **fine tuning** the economy, suggesting that policymakers had the ability to dictate the pulse of the economy. Events since the 1970s suggest that controlling the business cycle is not such an easy matter.

THE INTERNATIONAL ECONOMY

Over the past several years, the economies of the world have become more interdependent than ever. Trading blocs are being formed, and countries are looking for markets outside their own borders. An understanding of how the macroeconomy functions requires an understanding of how the domestic economy is affected by economic events in the rest of the world. As a specific example of how economic events abroad can affect the domestic economy, during the 1970s the price of oil from OPEC (Organization of Petroleum Exporting Countries) rose dramatically, resulting in a striking impact on the Canadian economy.

ECONOMIC GROWTH

The Canadian economy has experienced **economic growth** over the past several decades. We are now producing more goods and services than we did in the 1950s or in the 1960s; consequently, our standard of living has increased. Economic growth requires not only that we use our resources efficiently, but also that we increase our productive capacity.

These concepts may be clarified by invoking the concept of the **production possibility curve,** introduced in Chapter 3 and illustrated in Figure 21.1. The production possibility curve in Diagram A shows the maximum amounts of capital goods and consumer goods that the economy can produce, given its resources and its technology. If the economy is operating at point A, it is not using all its resources, or it is inefficient. By using its idle human and nonhuman resources or by using them more efficiently, the economy could expand its production of consumer goods and capital goods to a point such as B on the production possibility curve.

But macroeconomics is concerned also with an increase in the economy's productive potential. Consider Diagram B of Figure 21.1. If the economy could move from point B on the original production possibility curve to a point such as C, then it would be able to produce more consumer goods and more capital goods. This can be achieved by augmenting the economy's resources through investment and by an increase in technology. We will return to the issue of economic growth in a later chapter.

The aggregate output is a measure of the total production of goods and services.

Business cycles are alternative periods of ups and downs in economic activity.

Economists hoped to fine tune the economy, or control some of the ups and downs.

Economic growth is an increase in per capita output.

A production possibility curve shows the combinations of goods and services that can be produced if resources are fully utilized.

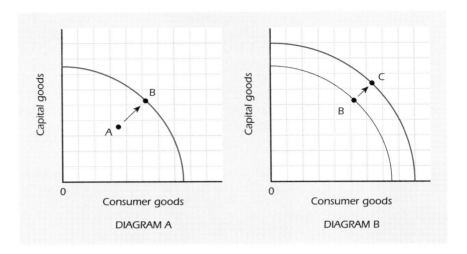

DIAGRAM A   DIAGRAM B

THE IMPORTANCE OF MACROECONOMICS

Learning Objective 4:
discuss the importance of
macroeconomics

Macroeconomic policy:
deliberate government
action taken to achieve
certain economic objec-
tives.

Both government and
businesses use macro-
economics in their
decision-making.

The central bank imple-
ments monetary policy in
order to achieve stability.

Governments implement
incomes policies to attempt
to curb inflation.

Prior to the appearance of macroeconomics, governments in free enterprise economic systems were not considered to be responsible for how the economy functioned. In fact,
there was no such thing as **macroeconomic policy** in which deliberate action is taken
by the government to achieve certain economic objectives. Governments adopted a
laissez-faire attitude toward the economy. Today, major responsibility for regulating
macroeconomic activity and keeping the economy on an even keel rests with governments.
    Macroeconomic theory provides a basis for government macroeconomic policy.
Keynes suggested that government spending and taxes could be used to regulate the
economy. Fiscal policy (government spending and taxing decisions) is now an important
tool of the government to try to stabilize the economy. In addition to fiscal policy, the
government also has some control over the quantity of money and credit in the economy.
Manipulation of the quantity of money and credit by the central bank is referred to as
monetary policy, which is used to bring about certain desired macroeconomic conditions. The government also uses macroeconomics when it imposes direct controls on
wages and prices — an instrument known as **incomes policies**. Because incomes policies prevent the price system from functioning, they are not generally well regarded by
most economists.
    Macroeconomics is also useful for business decision-making. Business decisions are
made not only within a microeconomic framework, but also with due consideration for
the macroeconomic environment. A firm's profitability depends not only on its pricing
and output decisions and on the actions and reactions of other firms in the industry,
but also on the performance of the whole economy. For example, during a period of rapid
economic growth, the demand for the firm's product might be expected to increase.
The firm's decisions should reflect this possibility.

MACROECONOMIC METHODOLOGY

Learning Objective 5:
explain how macroecon-
omists study the economy

Macroeconomists use models to study the behaviour of economic aggregates. Because
macroeconomics is still in an evolutionary stage, there are different models to explain different macroeconomic phenomena. Economists are not in agreement on which is the
"best" model, but most modern macroeconomists try to explain macroeconomic behaviour by focusing on three markets: the product market, the labour market, and the finan-

cial market. As will be seen later, the three markets are related. But a study of all three markets simultaneously is too complicated at this point; consequently, we will study these markets one at a time. An understanding of the interaction of demand and supply in each of these markets will provide considerable information about the major macroeconomic problems and issues.

MACROECONOMIC MARKET INTERACTION

Learning Objective 6:
understand the interaction between macroeconomic markets

Goods and services are traded in the product market.

Labour is traded in the labour market.

Funds are lent and borrowed in the financial market.

Households, firms, and government interact economically through markets: the **product market**, where goods and services are traded; the **labour market**, where labour services are exchanged for wages; and the **financial market**, where funds are lent and borrowed. The relationships between the three markets are shown in Figure 21.2.

Households, firms, and the government purchase goods and services from firms in the product market. Note that some firms purchase goods from other firms. A publishing company, for example, buys paper from other firms to produce books. In the diagram, there is an arrow representing the flow of goods and services from firms to the product market. There are also three arrows representing the purchase of goods and services by households, firms, and the government from the product market.

FIGURE 21.2

Interaction of the three markets.

The three markets are interrelated.

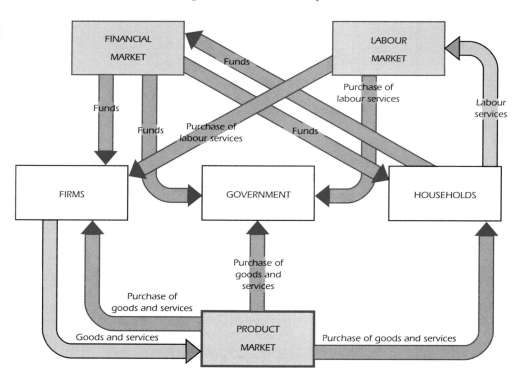

The players in the labour market are households, firms, and the government. Firms and the government purchase labour services from households in the labour market. In Figure 21.2, there is an arrow representing the flow of labour services from households to the labour market, and two arrows representing the purchase of labour services by firms and the government from the labour market. The total amount of labour services offered for sale is a result of the decisions made by households about whether or not to enter the labour market and the extent of their involvement in the labour force (i.e., the number of hours that they decide to work). The demand for labour services is the result of decisions made by firms and the government about how many workers they will hire.

A deficit occurs when spending exceeds income.

Households, firms, and the government borrow funds in the financial market. Households borrow to finance their purchases of consumer goods and services. Firms borrow to finance investment projects, and the government borrows (issues bonds) in order to spend more than it collects in taxes (i.e., to finance its **deficit**). Households purchase stocks and bonds in the financial market from firms. They also purchase bonds from the government. Firms also purchase bonds in the financial market.

Corporations issue bonds and stocks in order to raise funds.

A brief word about stocks and bonds might be in order here. A company that wants to raise funds can sell shares (**stocks**) or **bonds**. The purchasers of the stocks actually own a part of the capital stock of the business and are entitled to a share of the firm's profits in the form of dividends. The purchasers of bonds do not own any part of the firm's assets, but the firm contracts to pay them a certain amount annually, representing the principal (the amount of bonds bought) plus interest payment. Hence, when a company issues bonds, it is actually borrowing money from the purchasers of its bonds.

The government borrows money by selling bonds and Treasury bills.

The government also borrows money by issuing bonds or securities. The most popular of these bonds, Canada Savings Bonds (CSBs), are put on sale each year. The Canadian government also gives **Treasury bills** (T-bills) in exchange for money. A Treasury bill is an evidence of short-term debt issued by the federal government.

In Figure 21.2, there are three arrows from the financial market representing the borrowing of funds from the financial market by households, firms, and the government. There is also an arrow representing the lending of funds by households in the financial market. Financial institutions such as banks and trust companies are important actors in the financial market.

THE CIRCULAR FLOW

The discussion in the previous section provides one way of looking at relationships in the macroeconomy, emphasizing relationships between the basic macroeconomic markets. In this section, we look at the interaction among households, firms, and the government. The interaction between these three sectors can be illustrated by the **circular flow** diagram shown in Figure 21.3.

Learning Objective 7: construct a simple circular flow model of the economy

Households sell labour services to firms and receive wages and salaries in exchange. They also invest in firms by buying shares (stocks), and lend to firms by buying corporate bonds. For this they receive **dividend** and **interest** income. Some households work for the government and receive wages and salaries. Some may also purchase government bonds for which they receive interest, and others may receive other payments such as welfare payments and family allowances from the government. Such payments are called **transfer payments**. Figure 21.3 therefore shows resources flowing from the households to the firms and the government. It also shows wages, interest, and dividends flowing from firms to households; wages, interest, and transfer payments flowing from the government to households.

Investors receive dividends and/or interest when they lend money in the financial market.

Transfer payments do not represent a reward for productive services.

With their income, households purchase goods and services from firms, and pay taxes to the government. Firms supply goods and services to the government, and also pay taxes. They receive payment from the government. Figure 21.3 shows a flow of goods and services from firms to households, and a flow of payment for goods and services from households to firms. The diagram also shows a flow of taxes from households to the government, a flow of goods and services and taxes from firms to the government, and a flow of payment from the government to the firms.

It is important to note that the expenditure of any sector becomes the receipt of some other sector. This should not be surprising. If I purchase a car from General Motors, then the payment for the car becomes income to General Motors. Every economic transaction has two sides: a buyer and a seller. Any payment made must be received by someone. This is one of the main points illustrated by the circular flow model.

FIGURE 21.3

The circular flow diagram.

The circular flow shows that the spending of one sector becomes a receipt by some other sector.

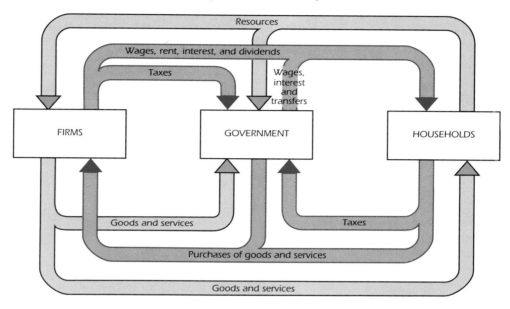

THE BEHAVIOUR OF THE CANADIAN ECONOMY

What has been the Canadian economic experience over the past four decades? We shall attempt to answer this question by looking at three macroeconomic variables: output, unemployment, and inflation.

GROWTH OF OUTPUT

The gross domestic product (GDP) is the value of all the goods and services produced in a country during a period of time.

The total value of goods and services produced in the Canadian economy, or what is referred to as the **gross domestic product (GDP)**, grew from $13.9 billion in 1947 to $855.1 billion in 1997. Throughout this period, the average rate of growth of output was 6.0%. But throughout this period also, there were short-term fluctuations. In some years, the growth rate of GDP was over 19%. In other years it was considerably less than 4%. Figure 21.4 gives us a clear picture of the growth rate of output in the Canadian economy from 1962 to 1997.

THE UNEMPLOYMENT RATE

The Canadian economy has experienced inflationary and recessionary periods, but it has performed reasonably well.

The unemployment rate is the number of people unemployed expressed as a percentage of the labour force.

The **unemployment rate** measures the percentage of the labour force that is unemployed. If the unemployment rate is high, then the economy is not operating at its potential. If the unemployed workers could be gainfully put to work, than the economy's output would expand. A high rate of unemployment is a signal that the economy is not very healthy. The unemployment rate in Canada has shown considerable fluctuation. In some years, it has fallen well below 3%, whereas in other years it has risen above 11%. The unemployment rate was relatively low between 1947 and 1953, and relatively high between 1982 and 1986, and again in 1991 and 1992. Figure 21.5 shows the unemployment rate from 1976 to 1997.

FIGURE 21.4 Growth rate of GDP since 1962.

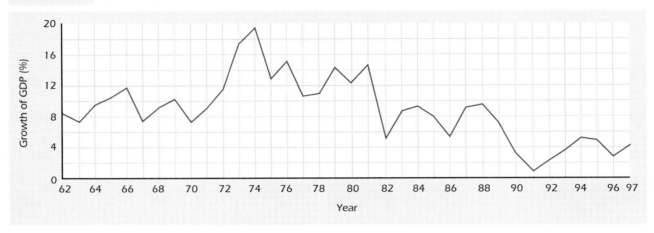

Source: Statistics Canada, *Canadian Economic Observer* (Cat. 11–210-XPB), 1997–98: 5.

FIGURE 21.5

Unemployment rate from 1976 to 1997.

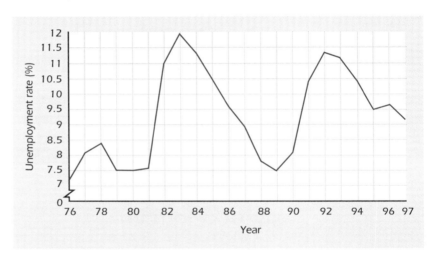

Source: Statistics Canada, *Canadian Economic Observer* (Cat. 11–210-XPB), 1997–98: 34.

THE BEHAVIOUR OF THE PRICE LEVEL

Price indexes show changes in prices over a period of time.

As we noted earlier, the rate of inflation is an important area of concern for macroeconomics. Economists use **price indexes** to measure changes in the average level of prices. One such index is the GDP deflator, an index of prices of all goods and services produced in Canada. (Price indexes will be discussed in the next chapter.) The rate of inflation was particularly high in 1948 and again in 1974, reaching over 13%. The Canadian economy experienced relative price stability during the 1953-63 decade, and as Figure 21.6 shows, prices have been fairly stable since 1990.

A large part of macroeconomics concerns changes in GDP, the unemployment rate, and the rate of inflation. As you study the remaining chapters, you will learn more about the relationships among these important macroeconomic variables. This knowledge will help you to understand how the macroeconomy works. You will be able to make sense of many of the policies that are implemented in an attempt to improve the functioning of the economy.

FIGURE 21.6

The rate of inflation from 1970 to 1997.

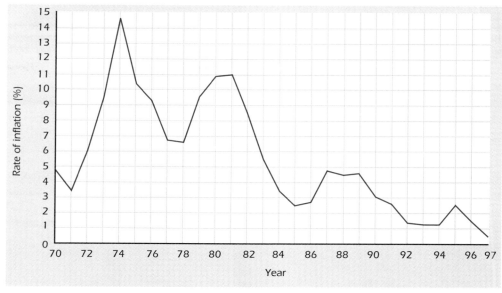

Source: Statistics Canada, *Canadian Economic Observer* (Cat. 11–210-XPB), 1997–98: 46.

CHAPTER SUMMARY

1. Macroeconomics is concerned with the behaviour of broad economic aggregates that reflect the sum total of decisions of households, firms, and the government.

2. The modern approach to studying macroeconomics is to consider the microeconomic principles on which economic decisions are based.

3. Modern macroeconomics owes its origin to the work of John Maynard Keynes, whose ideas provided an explanation for the Great Depression of the 1930s.

4. New classical economics emphasizes rapid macroeconomic adjustment, whereas new Keynesian economics emphasizes the failure of wages and prices to adjust and the consequences of such failure.

5. Among the great macroeconomic problems and issues of our time are the failure of the economy to provide employment for those who want to work, rapidly rising prices, fluctuations in aggregate output, and the international economy.

6. The government uses macroeconomics when it conducts fiscal policy and monetary policy, and businesses use information about macroeconomics when they make decisions.

7. Macroeconomists study the macroeconomy by concentrating on the market for goods and services, the labour market, the financial market, and the interrelationships among these three markets.

8. Firms acquire funds by selling stocks and bonds in the financial market. The government raises money by issuing bonds. Households supply funds to the financial market by purchasing stocks and bonds from firms, and by purchasing bonds from the government.

9. A circular flow diagram can be used to show the interaction between households, firms, and the government. The diagram illustrates that any payment becomes a receipt.

GLOBAL PERSPECTIVE

How Does Canada Compare?

The Canadian economy functions within an international context. One consequence of this fact is the need to pay increased attention to Canada's comparative economic performance. In this capsule, we compare Canada's economic performance with that of other industrialized countries over the past decade, using unemployment, inflation, and economic growth as the frame of reference.

The figures show the rate of unemployment, the rate of inflation, and the growth rate of real per capita output for the G-7 countries. As can be seen from the graph, only Italy and France had higher unemployment rates than Canada over the 1990–99 period. The unemployment rate in Japan was only 2.9% over the 10-year period. Germany had the highest growth rate with an average annual rate of 2.5%. Canada had the third highest growth rate with an average of 1.9% over the period. When we look at the rate of inflation, we see that Italy had the highest rate, with an average of 4.4%. Japan had the lowest inflation rate with 0.7% over the period. Canada's average inflation rate was 1.7%, which was second lowest among the G-7 countries.

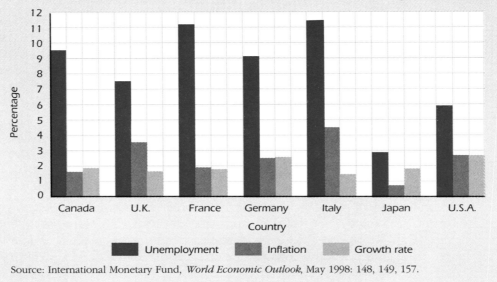

Source: International Monetary Fund, *World Economic Outlook*, May 1998: 148, 149, 157.

TERMS FOR REVIEW

microeconomics and
  macroeconomics (356)
aggregate (356)
invisible hand (356)
Great Depression (356)
classical economic model (356)
fiscal policy (357)
Keynesian economics (357)
stagflation (357)
supply side (357)
new classical economists (357)
new Keynesian economists (358)
unemployment (358)
inflation (358)

aggregate output (359)
business cycle (359)
fine tuning (359)
economic growth (359)
production possibility curve (359)
macroeconomic policy (360)
monetary policy (360)
incomes policies (360)
product market (361)
labour market (361)
financial market (361)
deficit (362)
stocks (shares) (362)
bonds (securities) (362)

Treasury bills (362)
circular flow (362)
interest and dividends (362)
transfer payments (362)

gross domestic product (GDP) (363)
unemployment rate (363)
price indexes (364)

QUESTIONS FOR REVIEW AND DISCUSSION

1. What is the relationship between microeconomics and macroeconomics? What is the difference between them? (L.O.1)

2. What particular economic events gave rise to the birth of modern macroeconomics? (L.O.2)

3. What was the classical economists' view of unemployment? How was this different from the ideas of Keynes? (L.O.2)

4. Why did the popularity of Keynesian economics decline during the 1970s? (L.O.2)

5. In what way are new Keynesian economists different from new classical economists? What do they have in common in their approaches to the study of macroeconomics? (L.O.5)

6. List the four major macroeconomic issues or problems and comment briefly on each one. (L.O.3)

7. What is the business cycle? Why are economists interested in the business cycle? (L.O.3)

8. Give examples of international economic events that are likely to affect the Canadian economy. (General)

9. Explain how the product market, the labour market, and the financial market are related. (L.O.6)

PROBLEMS AND EXERCISES

1. Draw a diagram similar to Figure 21.2 in the text. Use your diagram to explain how the three markets are related. (L.O.6)

2. Do you think that by studying the relations between macroeconomic markets, you would learn something about the behaviour of households, firms, and the government? Explain. (L.O.6,7)

3. Draw a circular flow diagram similar to Figure 21.3. Use your diagram to explain how the three sectors (households, firms, and the government) are related. (L.O.6)

4. Do you think that by studying the relation between the three sectors, you would learn something about how the product, labour, and financial markets are related? Explain. (L.O.6,7)

Internet Site

http://www.bionomics.org
This Web site for the Bionomics Institute provides a totally unconventional look at economics.

INTERNET EXERCISE

1. Go to the Bionomics web site above.
2. Click on *Introduction*.
3. Click on *Bionomics 101*.
4. Briefly explain how Bionomics differs from conventional economics.

C H A P T E R

NATIONAL INCOME AND PRODUCT ACCOUNTS

Learning Objectives

After studying this chapter, you should understand:

1 the meaning of GDP

2 how to measure GDP

3 several national income accounting concepts

4 some issues in national income accounting

5 the relation between GDP and economic well-being

In the statistical measurement of national income the question reduces itself to what commodities and services should be excluded because, by and large, they do not contribute to the goal of economic activity — satisfaction of consumers' wants.

Simon S. Kuznets, *National Income: A Summary of Findings.*

INTRODUCTION

The level of economic activity taking place in an economy is of vital importance because it determines the amount of goods and services that will be produced in the economy. That, in turn, gives an indication (but only an indication) of the economic (material) well-being of the population. Each year, the Canadian economy produces a wide variety of goods and services: medical services, legal services, buildings, farm products, houses, banking services, electricity, textbooks, etc. The more of these goods and services that the economy produces, the more we will have available for consumption, and presumably, the better off we will be.

In this chapter, you will learn how the total output of the Canadian economy is measured, and why it is important to have good estimates of the economy's output of goods and services. You will also become familiar with the uses and limitations of national income accounting data, and be introduced to a variety of national income concepts and how they are related. In studying the behaviour of the macroeconomy, economists make extensive use of economic data, most of which are collected by an agency of the federal government called Statistics Canada. Data such as total output, total income, total investment, total consumption, and total employment are all very important in studying macroeconomics. Many of the concepts you will learn in this chapter will be extremely important for a proper understanding of macroeconomic theory. Let us begin by defining national income accounting.

NATIONAL INCOME ACCOUNTING

National income data give important information about how the economy is functioning.

How does a business firm know how well it is doing? How does it know whether it has made a profit or a loss during the last year? And if it has incurred a loss, how does it know what steps can be taken to improve its earnings? The firm can find answers to all these questions by looking at its accounting figures. In the same way, national income accounting provides us with useful information about how well the economy is performing. We can define **national income accounting** as the whole process of measuring and recording various economic aggregates which give some indication of the economic health of the country over time.

Statistics Canada collects and publishes economic and social statistics.

The agency of the federal government charged with the responsibility of collecting and publishing national income statistics is Statistics Canada (formerly the Dominion Bureau of Statistics, or DBS). National income accounts provide information on the pattern of economic activity. These statistics are of great importance to economists and other researchers in their attempts to explain economic and social phenomena, and also to policymakers in formulating good economic policies both in government and in private industry. It is no wonder then that national income statistics are among the most closely watched figures collected by statisticians.

TOTAL OUTPUT

Learning Objective 1: *understand the meaning of GDP*

A country's economic well-being could conceivably be measured in a variety of ways. One could, for example, survey the members of the economy and come up with some index of economic well-being based on people's responses to certain questions. It is widely believed, however, that the economy's total production of goods and services is a fairly good measure of the country's economic well-being. This measure, which is officially known as the **gross domestic product** or **GDP** for short, is defined as the market value of all final goods and services produced in the economy during a period of time, usually one year. There are several important points to note in our definition of GDP. Let us discuss them.

The GDP is the value of all output in a country during a period of time.

A flow concept

Note that the GDP is a flow concept rather than a stock. GDP refers to the *flow* of output during the year and not to the *stock* of goods and services measured at some point in the year.

GDP is expressed in monetary terms

The Canadian economy produces a large variety of different goods and services annually. How do we add all of these millions of different goods and services together to arrive at a single number which indicates total output? We do it by using money as a common denominator and adding the value in monetary terms of all the items produced during the year. That is the meaning of the term *market value* in our definition. To see how the calculation is done, let us assume that we have a very simple economy which produces only 100 000 kg of potatoes, 10 000 shirts, 8000 bottles of grape juice, and 500 bicycles in a year. Let us assume also that potatoes are sold at $0.50 per kilogram, shirts at $10 each, grape juice at $2 per bottle, and bicycles at $50 each. The total value of the goods produced in this simple economy (its GDP) would be $191 000, consisting of $50 000 worth of potatoes, $100 000 worth of shirts, $16 000 worth of grape juice and $25 000 worth of bicycles.

Avoidance of double-counting

In adding up the value of all goods and services produced in a year, we want to make sure that we count each good or service once and once only. Counting an item more than once is called **double counting**. The following example illustrates how double counting could arise. Suppose that farmers produce $60 million worth of wheat. The farmers then sell the wheat to flour mills. The flour mills produce flour, which they sell to bakeries for $100 million. The bakeries produce bread, which they sell for $150 million to retail grocery outlets. The grocers sell the bread to consumers for $180 million. Table 22.1 illustrates this process.

Double counting over-estimates the value of total output.

If we add the value of production at each stage of production, we arrive at a value of $490 million. This figure, however, over-estimates the value of production because of double counting. The flour, for instance, was made from $60 million worth of wheat that we had already counted. In fact, then, the flour producers added only $40 million to the production process. Similarly, the $150 million worth of bread sold by the bakeries contains $100 million worth of flour which we had already counted in the output of the flour mills, so the bakeries added only $50 million of production. In other words, **value added** by the flour producers is $40 million and by the bakeries is $50 million. The wheat bought by the flour mills and the flour bought by the bakeries are called **intermediate products**, which are outputs of one firm or industry used as inputs by other firms or industries. The bread sold by the retail grocers is a **final product**, which is a good or service bought for final use and not intended for resale or to be subjected to further processing. If we include the values of both intermediate and final goods in our computation of GDP, there will be double counting because the value of final goods includes

Value added is the output value minus the input value.

Intermediate products are the outputs of one industry used as inputs in another.

A final product is bought for final use, not for resale.

TABLE 22.1	Production	Value of product ($million)	Value added ($million)
Value added in production.	Wheat production	60	60
	Flour production	100	40
	Bread production	150	50
	Sales by retail grocers	180	30
	TOTAL	490	180

all intermediate transactions. To avoid double counting, we must calculate only the values added at each stage of production or the total value of the final products.

Treatment of non-productive transactions

Non-productive transactions are excluded because they do not represent current production.

GDP measures the value of current production, not current sales. Thus, purely financial transactions which do not reflect current production are excluded from GDP. Examples of financial transactions that do not represent values of current production are government transfer payments, private transfer payments, and the sale and purchase of securities such as bonds issued by corporations. **Government transfer payments** are payments made by the government to individuals — payments for which no goods or services are produced. Examples of transfer payments are unemployment insurance, family allowances, and welfare payments. **Private transfer payments** are transfers of purchasing power from one individual or group to another. For example, a grant from a private organization to a student would be a private transfer payment. Such transfers are not included in GDP because they do not represent payments for goods and services produced. The buying and selling of stocks and bonds are excluded from GDP because such transactions merely represent the exchange of financial instruments (certificates of debt) between people. They do not represent payments for production.

Government and private transfer payments do not represent payments for production.

Treatment of used or second-hand goods

Second-hand sales do not represent current production.

Recall that the GDP attempts to measure the value of goods and services produced during a certain period. When a car is produced, its value is included in GDP. If the original purchaser of the new car sells it after six months, the amount obtained from that sale should not be included in GDP. To include it would constitute double counting.

? PROBLEM SOLVING 22-1

An economics professor gives an allowance of $50 a week to his daughter who is attending university. Should we include this amount when measuring the gross domestic product?

MEASURING THE TOTAL OUTPUT

Learning Objective 2:
how to measure GDP

We can measure the total value of goods and services produced in an economy over a period of time in two ways. We can measure income, or we can measure expenditure. Both methods should give the same result since both measure the same thing. You will soon see why.

The two approaches can be illustrated by a simple circular flow diagram similar to the one introduced in Chapter 21, and presented here as Figure 22.1.

We can measure the value of the goods and services produced in this simple model by measuring the total income earned by those who contribute to the production of the total output. This approach would be equivalent to measuring the inner flow in the top section of Figure 22.1. By so doing, we would be adding the incomes earned by the owners of the resources used in production. This method is called the **income approach**. If a person earns an annual salary of $20 000, then this person's labour services contribute $20 000 to total output. Thus the total amount earned by the factors of production and accruing to factor owners as income represents the total value of goods and services produced.

The income approach measures the total income of those involved in production.

Alternatively, we can measure the value of the goods and services produced in the economy by measuring the total amount spent in purchasing the total output. This approach would be equivalent to measuring the inner flow in the bottom section of

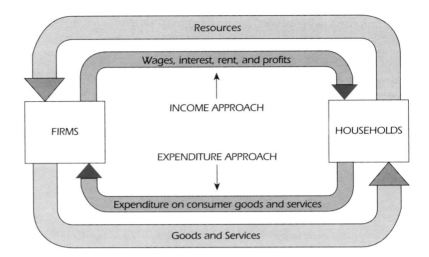

FIGURE 22.1

The circular flow of income and expenditure.

GDP can be measured either by the income method or by the expenditure method.

The expenditure approach measures the total amount spent on the total output.

Figure 22.1. This method is called the **output** or **expenditure approach**. If $500 000 is spent in purchasing the economy's output of goods and services, then the value of those goods and services must be $500 000.

Let us look a little more closely at these two approaches. All expenditures on goods and services are received as income by those who contribute to the production of the goods and services. Thus we arrive at the following identity:

$$\text{Total expenditure on the economy's output} \equiv \text{Total income earned in producing it}$$

THE INCOME APPROACH

Recall that the incomes derived from labour, land, capital, and entrepreneurial services are wages and salaries, rent, interest, and profits respectively. Thus, the income approach to measuring GDP involves adding up these various types of factor incomes. You will see later that an adjustment has to be made to arrive at GDP from summing the factor incomes. Table 22.2 shows GDP for Canada in 1997 using the income approach. Let us examine the various categories in that table.

TABLE 22.2

Gross domestic product, income based, 1997.

Item	Value ($million)
Labour income	445 804
Corporate profits before taxes	78 988
Government enterprise profits	6 707
Interest and investment income	46 187
Accrued net farm income	1 422
Unincorporated business income	52 978
Inventory valuation adjustment	-1 622
Net domestic income at factor cost	630 464
Indirect taxes, less subsidies	114 501
Capital consumption allowances	110 722
Statistical discrepancy	-584
GDP at market prices	855 103

Source: Statistics Canada, *Canadian Economic Observer* (Cat. 11-010-XPB), July 1998: 3

LABOUR INCOME

Labor income includes wages, salaries, and supplementary labour income. Wages and salaries are payments made to the hundreds of thousands of workers employed in the private and public sectors of the economy, including the salaries of military personnel. Business executives, civil servants, nurses, teachers, engineers, computer programmers, salespeople, factory workers, secretaries, garbage collectors, and fire fighters all earn wages and salaries. Supplementary labour income includes other payroll costs such as unemployment insurance contributions and pension funds, which employers pay on behalf of their employees. In 1997, wages, salaries, and supplementary labour income amounted to over $445.8 billion — about 71% of total factor income.

CORPORATION PROFITS BEFORE TAXES

You can best understand this income category by considering the disposition of the total income (profits) earned by corporations. First, the government levies a tax on the incomes of corporations. Second, corporations pay out a part of their profits to their shareholders as dividends. Third, a part of the corporations' profits may be withheld to be reinvested. Thus, this income category consists of three items: corporation income taxes, dividends paid out to shareholders, and retained earnings or undistributed profits. In 1997, corporation profits before taxes amounted to almost $79 billion or just over 12.5% of total factor income.

GOVERNMENT ENTERPRISE PROFITS

The government operates some enterprises that may earn profits. These profits must be included as an income category. You can think of the government as the entrepreneur, and the profits from government enterprises as the income (reward) for the entrepreneurial services provided by the government. In 1997, profits from government enterprises amounted to $6.7 billion, representing just over 1% of total factor income.

INTEREST AND MISCELLANEOUS INVESTMENT INCOME

Included in this income category are interest payments made by private businesses to individuals who provided financial capital. Interest payments made by the government are not included because they are not payments for current goods and services. The interest on the public debt, for example, is considered a transfer payment and is therefore excluded from this income category. Miscellaneous investment income includes returns such as royalties paid to individuals. Interest and miscellaneous investment income in 1997 was $46.2 billion, accounting for about 7.3% of total factor income.

ACCRUED NET INCOME OF FARM OPERATORS FROM FARM PRODUCTION

To arrive at the figure in this income category, the following items are added: (1) total revenue from the sale of farm products; (2) the total value of farm products not sold but consumed on the farm; and (3) the value of the change in inventories of farm output. Since the figure we want to arrive at is net farm income, we subtract all expenses incurred in operating the farms and the depreciation of the real capital stock (farm machinery, equipment, and buildings) of the farms during the year. In 1997, this income category amounted to about $1.4 billion, or just 0.2% of total factor income.

NET INCOME OF NON-FARM UNINCORPORATED BUSINESS, INCLUDING RENT

This category includes incomes of single proprietorships, partnerships, self-employed people, and any other type of income other than corporation income and income derived from farm operations. Rent is included here as the income of landlords. Clearly, this category contains different types of incomes but no attempt is made to sort them into their respective classes as labour income or investment income. Net income of non-farm unincorporated business, including rent, totalled over $52.9 billion, or roughly 8% of total factor income in 1997.

INVENTORY VALUATION ADJUSTMENT

During any period, the value of inventories may change because of changes in prices. Since the objective of national income accounting is to measure current production, an appropriate adjustment is made for windfall profits resulting from valuing inventories at higher prices.

NET DOMESTIC INCOME AT FACTOR COST

Net domestic income at factor cost is the total income earned by the factors of production.

By adding all of the above income categories and making the appropriate adjustment, we obtain a national income accounting figure known as **net domestic income at factor cost**. This aggregate is really the total income earned by the factors of production. Net domestic income at factor cost in 1997 was $630.5 billion. The following two points should be noted. First, this is a net figure, and second, it is evaluated at factor cost. The significance of these points will be shown later.

It will be helpful to summarize the foregoing discussion. Let us use W to denote the income category wages, salaries, and supplementary labour income; P_r to denote corporation profits before taxes and government enterprise prifits; i to denote interest and miscellaneous investment income; R to denote net income of non-farm unincorporated business including rent; and O to denote accrued net income of farm operators. If we ignore the adjustment for inventory evaluation, net domestic income at factor cost (NDI) can then be expressed by the following equation:

$$NDI = W + P_r + i + R + O$$

INDIRECT TAXES LESS SUBSIDIES

Indirect taxes are taxes other than income taxes. They include sales taxes, excise taxes, customs duties, and property taxes. The firms treat these taxes as a part of their production costs and thus take them into consideration when pricing their products. The Canadian government gives certain production and consumption subsidies. For example, some farm production is subsidized and so is Via Rail. Subsidies cause market prices to be lower than they would otherwise be. They must therefore be subtracted from factor costs in order to arrive at market prices. By adding indirect business taxes to factor costs and subtracting subsidies, we obtain market prices. Indirect taxes less subsidies were estimated at over $114.5 billion in 1997. We will use T_{ib} to denote indirect taxes less subsidies.

CAPITAL CONSUMPTION ALLOWANCES

A capital consumption allowance allows for the depreciation of capital during production.

During any given year, the plant and equipment used to produce the national output suffer some loss of value due to wear and tear. This loss of value in the economy's capital stock is called depreciation or **capital consumption allowance** because it measures the value of the capital "consumed" during the year. By including capital consumption allowances, we convert our net figure to a gross figure. Capital consumption allowances amounted to $110.7 billion in 1997. The letter **D** will be used to denote capital consumption allowances.

STATISTICAL DISCREPANCY

Although Statistics Canada tries to obtain accurate and reliable estimates of GDP, it is unlikely that both approaches to measuring GDP will produce exactly the same result. The difference between the results obtained from using the income and the expenditure approaches to GDP is attributed to statistical error. We will return to the treatment of this discrepancy when we discuss the expenditure approach below. If we assume that there is no statistical discrepancy, then income-based GDP may be expressed as:

$$GDP = W + P_r + i + R + O + T_{ib} + D$$

THE EXPENDITURE APPROACH

If an economy produced only wheat, we could find out the value of the wheat produced by finding out the total amount of money spent in buying wheat. Similarly, by finding out the total expenditure on the economy's output of goods and services, we arrive at the market value of total production — GDP. With the help of Table 22.3, we will see how Statistics Canada classifies the various groups that purchase the economy's output in order to arrive at expenditure-based GDP.

TABLE 22.3

Gross domestic product, expenditure-based, 1997.

Item		Value ($million)
Personal expenditure on consumer goods and services		505 896
Government current expenditure on goods and services		168 459
Government investment:		
Fixed capital	18 241	
Inventories	5	
Total		18 246
Business fixed capital:		
Residential construction	45 965	
Non-residential construction	39 230	
Machinery and equipment	55 130	
Total		140 325
Business inventories:		
Non-farm	8 648	
Farm	−1 397	
Total		7 251
Exports of goods and services		343 536
Imports of goods and services		−329 193
Statistical discrepancy		583
Gross domestic product at market prices		855 103

Source: Statistics Canada, *Canadian Economic Observer* (Cat. 11–010–XPB), July 1998: 3.

PERSONAL EXPENDITURE ON CONSUMER GOODS AND SERVICES

By far the largest component of total spending is expenditure on consumer goods and services. In the national accounts, this item is referred to as personal expenditure on consumer goods and services, and only includes spending by households on different types of consumer goods and services. Consumer goods and services include durable consumer goods (such as cars, washing machines, stereo systems, home computers, and refrigerators), semi-durable consumer goods (such as clothing and automobile tires), non-durable consumer goods (such as hamburgers, orange juice, milk, chicken, soap, and cheese), and services such as transportation services, legal services, dental services, plumbing services, etc.

Note that the purchase of a house is not included in the category of personal expenditure on consumer goods and services. Instead, Statistics Canada treats this expenditure as an investment expenditure (to be discussed below). Note also that government purchases of consumer goods and services are likewise excluded from this category. This expenditure category does not therefore represent total expenditures on consumer goods and services, but only households' expenditures on consumer goods and services. In 1997, personal expenditure on consumer goods and services amounted to $505.9 billion or about 60% of total expenditures. We will use the letter **C** to represent this economic aggregate.

GOVERNMENT CURRENT EXPENDITURE ON GOODS AND SERVICES

This expenditure category includes purchases of currently produced goods and services by the various levels of government. Purchases of uniforms, police services, educational services, and health and defence spending are all included in this category. Remember, however, that government transfer payments are not included in this category because they do not represent expenditures for current production. As Table 22.3 shows, government current expenditure on goods and services amounted to $168.5 billion in 1997. We will use **G** to symbolize government current expenditure on goods and services.

GOVERNMENT INVESTMENT

Table 22.3 lists two items under this expenditure category: fixed capital and inventories. An example of fixed capital investment by the government is the construction of a dam. Inventories are stocks of finished and semi-finished goods. These are, of course, unsold, but they are treated as if the government buys them. Government investment was $18.2 billion in 1997 — just over 2% of total spending.

BUSINESS FIXED CAPITAL

There are three items in this expenditure category: residential construction, non-residential construction, and machinery and equipment. Residential construction includes dwellings. Some types of dwellings are acquired and rented out to earn a return, so it is relatively easy to see why these are categorized as investment. But even if the owner occupies the dwelling, it is still considered an investment and not consumption since the owner could rent it out and earn a return. Perhaps it is easier to see the investment aspect of residential construction if viewed from the perspective of a developer. Developers construct new homes strictly as an investment. Non-residential construction includes the construction of such items as warehouses, office buildings, and commercial spaces. Machinery and equipment include tools and the various types of machines that are purchased by businesses. In 1997, the three items in the business fixed capital category totalled $140.3 billion.

BUSINESS INVENTORIES

Business inventories are treated similarly to government inventories — we assume that the firms that own them buy them. It is important to note that it is the value of the physical change in inventories that is recorded in the national accounts. If firms start the year with an inventory of 500 tonnes of flour, and end the year with 575 tonnes, then the difference of 75 tonnes must have been produced during the year, and must therefore be added to the year's production. By similar reasoning, a decrease in inventories means that total expenditures during the year exceeded that year's production. Thus, increases in inventories are added to business investment while decreases are subtracted from it.

Note: Total investment or gross capital formation, as it is sometimes called, consists of government and business investment in fixed capital and inventories. We will see later how firms respond to changes in their inventories, and how such responses affect total production of goods and services. The letter **I** will be used to represent investment.

EXPORTS OF GOODS AND SERVICES

A significant part of our domestic production is bought by foreigners. Expenditures by foreigners on goods and services produced in Canada are referred to as exports of goods and services. Clearly, the value of exports must be included in our GDP. In 1997, we exported a total of $343.5 billion worth of goods and services. To put this in proper perspective, foreigners purchased about 40% of our total output. We shall use **X** to designate this expenditure item.

IMPORTS OF GOODS AND SERVICES

Just as foreign countries purchase a significant portion of our total output, Canada buys a considerable amount of goods and services from foreign countries. Purchases of goods and services from foreign countries constitute imports. GDP is a measure of the value of the goods and services produced in Canada. Since expenditures on imports do not represent expenditures on domestic production, they must be deducted from GDP calculations. To include them would overstate the value of our total output. In 1997, our imports of goods and services amounted to over $329.2 billion. We shall use the letter **M** to denote imports of goods and services.

Net exports equals total exports minus total imports.

Note: National income statisticians usually deduct imports from exports and refer to the result as net exports. **Net exports (X–M)** is the difference between our sales of goods and services to foreigners and our purchases of goods and services from foreigners.

STATISTICAL DISCREPANCY

This is actually a balancing item in the national income and expenditure accounts. Statistics Canada compares the figures obtained from both approaches to GDP. The difference between the two amounts is then divided by two. This amount (half of the difference) is then added to the smaller GDP figure and subtracted from the larger GDP figure, thus ensuring that GDP income-based and GDP expenditure-based are identical. We can summarize the GDP expenditure-based as follows:

$$GDP = C + I + G + (X - M)$$

Let us take a closer look at the investment component in the GDP equation above. **Gross investment** or **gross fixed capital formation** is the value of capital produced during the year. If from this value we deduct the depreciation suffered by the capital stock, we obtain **net capital formation** or **net investment**.

Gross investment is the total expenditure on investment goods.

Net investment is gross investment minus depreciation.

If we let I_g represent gross investment, I_n net investment, and **D** depreciation or capital consumption allowances, then we have the following equation relating gross investment and net investment.

$$I_g - I_n = D$$

COMPARISON OF INCOME AND EXPENDITURE APPROACHES

It would be interesting to be able to compare the shares of the various components of GDP using the income and expenditure approaches. Such a comparison is shown in Figure 22.2.

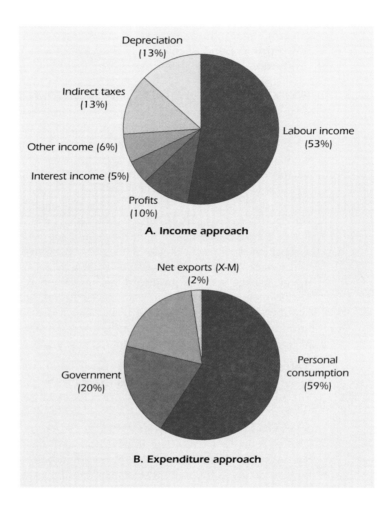

A. Income approach

B. Expenditure approach

In the income approach, the profit component includes corporate profits and government enterprise profits. Other income includes accrued net farm income, unincorporated business income, and inventory valuation adjustment. In the expenditure approach, the investment component includes both business and government investment. In both the income and expenditure approaches, the statistical discrepancy is distributed over all components.

SOME RELATED CONCEPTS

Learning Objective 3:
several national income accounting concepts

The gross national product (GNP) is the value of all output produced by a country's factors, regardless of where the factors are located.

There are other national income accounting concepts with which you should become familiar. Some of these are discussed in this section.

GROSS NATIONAL PRODUCT (GNP)

Many people in Canada are more familiar with the term **gross national product**, or GNP for short, than they are with GDP. A major reason for this familiarity with GNP is the fact that up to 1986, Statistics Canada used GNP as the basic measure of the economy's output. In 1986, Canada joined the majority of western nations in using GDP as the major national income accounting aggregate, leaving the United States, at that time, as the only major exception. In 1991, the United States switched from using GNP as the basic measure of the total output of the economy. Like Canada, it now uses the GDP.

The difference between GDP and GNP is not difficult to grasp. GDP measures the market value of all final goods and services produced within the borders of Canada, regardless of who owns the productive resources. GNP, on the other hand, is the market value of all goods and services produced by Canadian factors, regardless of where those factors are located. Foreigners own some factors of production located in Canada. Payments to those factors do not accrue to Canadians as income. They are included in GDP but not in GNP. Also, Canadians own factors of production located abroad. Payments to those factors accrue to Canadians as income. They are included in GNP but not in GDP. Thus, to obtain GNP from GDP, we must add investment income received from non-residents, and deduct investment income paid to non-residents. That is, we must add net investment income received from non-residents.

$$\text{GDP} + \text{net investment income from non-residents} = \text{GNP}$$

NET NATIONAL INCOME AT FACTOR COST

Net national income at factor cost is the total income earned by a country's factors of production.

Net national income at factor cost or just *national income* (NI) for short is the total income earned by Canadian-owned factors of production. To obtain this figure, we must deduct from GNP those components which do not accrue to factor owners as income. These are indirect taxes less subsidies and capital consumption allowances or depreciation.

Thus:

$$\text{NI} = \text{GNP} - \text{indirect taxes} - \text{D}$$

PERSONAL INCOME

Personal income is income received by the owners of the factors of production.

A discrepancy exists between the total income *earned* by individuals and total income *received* by individuals. **Personal income** is the income received by persons from all sources. Personal income includes wages, salaries, rental income, interest and dividends, and certain transfer payments from government and business.

The discrepancy between income earned and income received results from the fact that factor owners do not receive a part of the earned income. This includes undistributed corporation profits or retained earnings and corporation income tax. Also, some households receive income that is not currently earned by them. This income comprises transfer payments such as welfare payments, old age security, unemployment insurance benefits, Canada and Quebec Pension Plan benefits, etc. We can calculate personal income, therefore, by subtracting undistributed corporation profits and corporation income tax from national income, then adding transfer payments. Personal income in 1995 was $694.9 billion.

PERSONAL DISPOSABLE INCOME

Personal disposable income is personal income minus personal taxes and personal transfers to government.

Personal saving is the part of the disposable income not spent on consumer goods and services.

Individuals have to pay taxes and make other contributions to the government. Personal transfers to the government include Canada and Quebec Pension Plans and employment insurance. Taxes include personal income taxes and personal property taxes. These deductions from personal income result in a figure called **personal disposable income**. Consumers spend a part of their personal disposable income on consumer goods and services. The remainder is **personal saving**.

INFLATING AND DEFLATING THE GROSS DOMESTIC PRODUCT

Since GDP is expressed in monetary terms, price changes can affect our measure of the total output of the economy. The following example illustrates the effect of price changes on GDP. Suppose an economy produces only one product: potatoes. Let us assume that in Year 1, the output of potatoes was 500 000 kg. If potatoes were sold at $0.50 per kilogram, the gross domestic product of our hypothetical economy would be

$$500\ 000 \times \$0.50 = \$250\ 000.$$

In Year 2, if the output was 520 000 kg of potatoes and the price had risen to $0.75 per kilogram, the gross domestic product would be

$$520\ 000 \times \$0.75 = \$390\ 000.$$

The GDP would therefore show an increase of 56%, but the output of potatoes would show an increase of only 4%. This is the effect of valuing the output at market prices. In making comparisons, we must adjust the GDP for price changes.

Let us see how we could adjust the gross domestic product of our hypothetical economy in Year 2 to account for price changes. In this example, we use Year 1 as our reference point or **base year**. We then construct **price indexes** for each year, based on the percentage change in prices. In Year 1, the price was $0.50. In Year 2, the price rose to $0.75 — an increase of 50%. We give the base year an index of 100. We must then give Year 2 an index of 150 to indicate the 50% price increase. To calculate the real increase in output, we deflate the gross domestic product by dividing it by the price index and multiplying it by 100. Thus, we can calculate the *real gross domestic product* for Year 2 as follows:

A base year is a year chosen as a reference point in a comparison.

Price indexes show changes in prices over a period of time.

$$\frac{\$390\ 000 \times 100}{150} = \$260\ 000$$

In general, the formula for converting GDP to real GDP is

$$\text{Real GDP} = \frac{\text{GDP}}{\text{P}} \times 100$$

where P is the price index.

We can calculate the price index for a hypothetical one-product economy quite easily. However, for a modern economy with a vast amount of different goods and services, the calculation of price indexes is difficult. Once we have calculated the price indexes, we can deflate the gross domestic product easily. That is, we can easily express the gross domestic product in real terms.

Table 22.4 shows how we can express the gross domestic product in real terms. All the figures for the years prior to 1971 (the base year) have been inflated, and the figures for the years after 1971 have been deflated. We can now compare the figures in column four, because they are all expressed in the same unit — 1971 dollars. The figures for gross domestic product in column two are expressed in current dollars. We call these figures **nominal income**. The figures for gross domestic product in column 4 are expressed in constant (1971) dollars. We call these figures **real income**. Comparing the figures in columns two and four, in this hypothetical situation, we see that a sum of $185 million in 1950 was equivalent to $308 million in 1971, and that a sum of $1 590 million (or $1.59 billion) in 1975 was worth only $1 144 million (or $1.14 billion) in 1971 dollars. Table 22.5 shows figures for real gross domestic product in Canada in 1997.

Nominal income is income expressed in current dollars.

Real income is income expressed in constant dollars.

TABLE 22.4 Deflating gross domestic product for price level changes (hypothetical data).	Year (1)	Nominal GDP ($million) (2)	Price index (1971 = 100) (3)	Calculation of real GDP (in 1971 dollars) (4)
	1950	185	60	$\frac{185 \times 100}{60} = 308$
	1955	290	71	$\frac{290 \times 100}{71} = 408$
	1960	384	77	$\frac{384 \times 100}{77} = 499$
	1970	860	98	$\frac{860 \times 100}{98} = 878$
	1971	980	100	$\frac{980 \times 100}{100} = 980$
	1974	1 350	125	$\frac{1\ 350 \times 100}{125} = 1\ 080$
	1975	1 590	139	$\frac{1\ 590 \times 100}{139} = 1\ 144$

TABLE 22.5

GDP in constant dollars, Canada 1997.

Item	Value (1992 $million)
Personal expenditure on consumer goods and services	470 177
Government current expenditure on goods and services	162 988
Government investment	17 765
Business fixed capital:	
Residential construction 42 912	
Non-residential construction..36 637	
Machinery and equipment..52 596	
Total	132 135
Business inventories..	6 977
Exports of goods and services	296 534
Imports of goods and services	288 933
Statistical discrepancy...	540
Gross domestic product at market prices	798 183

Source: Statistics Canada, *Canadian Economic Observer* (Cat. 11–010–XPB), July 1998: 4.

PROBLEM SOLVING 22-2

Explain how a country's gross domestic product can increase even if its total production falls.

GROSS DOMESTIC PRODUCT AS A MEASURE OF ECONOMIC WELL-BEING

Learning Objective 4: some issues in national income accounting

Learning Objective 5: the relation between GDP and economic well-being

At the beginning of this chapter, we stated that gross domestic product provided an indication of the material well-being of the population. In this context, the relevant concept is real GDP. However, for a number of reasons which we will discuss below, the real GDP of a country may not adequately indicate how well off the society is. The size of the population, non-marketed goods and services, leisure, and the quality of life are all important factors in determining the well-being of a society. Let us discuss each of these factors.

THE SIZE OF THE POPULATION

The GDP does not tell us anything about the number of people who must share in the total output of goods and services. The real GDP of a country may increase from one year to another, but if the population increases more quickly than the output does, then the people will be worse off. A more meaningful measure of economic well-being is real per capita output.

Real GDP per capita is real GDP divided by the population.

> **Real per capita output, or output per person, tells how much each individual in the country would receive if the total output were divided equally among them.**

Thus, we can obtain a figure for **real GDP per capita** by dividing real GDP by the population.

$$\text{real GDP per capita} = \frac{\text{real GDP}}{\text{population}}$$

Table 22.6 shows a steady increase in real GDP from Year 1 to Year 5. During the same time, however, population increased at the same rate as GDP. Real GDP per capita, therefore, did not change during this period.

TABLE 22.6

Real GDP, population, and real GDP per capita (hypothetical data).

Year	Real GDP ($)	Population	Real GDP per capita ($)
1	10 000	200	50
2	12 000	240	50
3	13 000	260	50
4	15 000	300	50
5	16 000	320	50

THE DISTRIBUTION OF OUTPUT

Although the real GDP per capita is a more meaningful measure of economic well-being than is real GDP, we should remember that per capita output is just an average; it tells us nothing about the distribution of total output among households. For example, compare two societies. In one, an output of $50 000 000 is fairly evenly distributed among households. In the other, the same volume of output is divided so that 10% of the population receives 90% of the total output while the majority barely manages to survive.

NON-MARKETED GOODS AND SERVICES

The GDP measures only the market value of goods and services produced. Many goods and services produced do not get counted in the GDP because they are not sold. These include housework, home garden cultivation, garage chores, and volunteer work. To the extent that we omit these productive services from GDP*, we underestimate the recorded GDP figures. This suggests that the society might be better off than is indicated by the GDP figures.

THE UNDERGROUND ECONOMY

The underground economy is neither recorded by statisticians nor observed for tax purposes.

The **underground economy** refers to economic activities that take place but are not recorded by national income statisticians, and not observed for tax purposes. Such transactions include illegal activities such as prostitution and illicit drug trading, and so-called "under-the-table" transactions such as the payment of cash to a roofer without any receipt.

It is debatable whether illegal activities increase well-being. The individuals who willingly engage in such activities must feel that they do derive some net benefits. From the viewpoint of the society as a whole, however, these activities may be considered as discommodities (i.e. bads rather than goods). The case of under-the-table transactions is different. Each year, a variety of services are provided by babysitters, dentists, carpenters, accountants, etc. Such services do increase the total amount of goods and services produced during the year, and therefore add to our economic well-being. They are, however, not reflected in the national accounts if they are paid for "under the table."

LEISURE

The number of hours spent to produce the GDP has decreased considerably over the years. This means that there has been an increase in leisure time, which obviously is a gain in well-being. This gain in well-being, however, is not reflected in the national income accounts. We could produce a greater GDP by working 50 hours a week instead of 40. If we choose to work only 40 hours a week, it is because we feel that we are better off working 40 hours instead of 50 hours a week.

QUALITY OF LIFE

In discussing how well off we are, we are in fact discussing the quality of life. Other things being equal, the more we produce, the better will be the quality of life for us. But our production and consumption of goods and services cause a certain amount of environmental damage (see Chapter 16). Polluted rivers and lakes, destroyed vegetation and animal life, noise, and foul air are just some of the environmental problems that plague us. These things obviously reduce the quality of life, but they are not reflected in the GDP.

A BETTER MEASURE OF ECONOMIC WELFARE

A better measure of economic well-being can be obtained by making certain adjustments to GDP.

The discussion so far has pointed to a number of flaws in using GDP as a measure of economic and societal welfare or well-being. A **better measure of economic well-being** (BMEW) would require some adjustments to the GDP. By adding certain items to GDP and by subtracting some other items, we can arrive at a better measure of economic well-being. Thus:

$$\textbf{GDP} + \frac{\text{Non-Marketed Goods}}{\text{and Services}} + \frac{\text{Under-the-Table}}{\text{Transactions}} - \frac{\text{Environmental}}{\text{Damage}} = \textbf{BMEW}$$

---

* The recorded GDP figures underestimate the true GDP.

PROBLEM SOLVING 22-3

Would Canada's GDP be affected if Canadian homemakers were paid for their services? Would society have more services as a result?

A P P L I C A T I O N

Business Managers Also Need Them

National income accounting figures provide useful information about the performance of the economy. Managerial decision-making does not occur in a vacuum, but within some general economic environment. Other things being equal, the more information managers have about the economic environment, the bet-ter the decisions that they are likely to make. For example, if national income accounting figures reveal that investment is on an upward trend, business decision-makers can expect an increase in income and may consider appropriate inventory adjustments to meet the expected rise in demand.

CHAPTER SUMMARY

1. National income accounting is the entire exercise involved in measuring and recording various economic aggregates. National income accounting data provide information on how well the economy is performing.

2. We can measure the total output of goods and services produced in the economy (the GDP) by adding up the incomes earned in the process of production (the income approach) or by adding up all expenditures on the economy's output (the expenditure approach).

3. In measuring the GDP, we measure only final goods and services. If we measure intermediate goods as well as final goods, we will be double counting, and thus overestimate the value of total output.

4. In measuring the GDP, we exclude non-productive transactions and second-hand goods because they do not represent current production.

5. Net domestic income at factor cost is the total income earned by the owners of productive factors located in Canada.

6. GDP differs from GNP in that GDP measures the value of output produced within the borders of Canada whereas GNP measures the value of output produced by Canadian factors wherever they may be located.

7. Personal income is the income actually received by persons from all sources. We can calculate personal income by subtracting undistributed corporation profits and corporation income tax from national income, then adding transfer payments.

8. Personal disposable income is what remains of personal income after deducting personal income taxes, personal property taxes, and personal transfers to government.

9. To compare one year's GDP with another, we must express the figure for GDP in constant (real) dollars. To do this, we deflate each year's GDP by the appropriate price index.

10. GDP does not measure well-being adequately because (1) it ignores the size of the population, (2) it ignores the distribution of output, (3) it omits non-marketed goods and services, (4) it does not account for leisure, and (5) it does not measure the quality of life.

11. A better measure of economic well-being can be obtained by adjusting GDP; that is, by adding to it non-marketed goods and under-the-table transactions, and by subtracting environmental damage resulting from economic activity.

TERMS FOR REVIEW

national income accounting (369)
gross domestic product (GDP) (369)
double counting (370)
value added (370)
intermediate products (370)
final product (370)
Government transfer payments (371)
private transfer payments (371)
income approach (371)
expenditure (output) approach (372)
net domestic income at factor cost (374)
capital consumption allowance (374)
net exports (377)
gross investment (gross fixed capital formation) (377)

net capital formation (net investment) (377)
gross national product (GNP) (379)
net national income at factor cost (379)
personal income (379)
personal disposable income (380)
personal saving (380)
base year (380)
price indexes (380)
nominal income (current prices) (381)
real income (constant prices) (381)
real GDP per capita (382)
underground economy (383)
better measure of economic well-being (BMEW) (383)

QUESTIONS FOR REVIEW AND DISCUSSION

1. What is national income accounting, and which government agency has the responsibility for Canada's national income accounting? (General)

2. Why is it important to know national income figures? (General)

3. What is the gross domestic product of a country? (L.O.1)

4. Explain how to measure the value of the output of the Canadian economy. (L.O.2)

5. What is double counting? Give an example. (L.O.2)

6. Explain why GDP is not equal to total sales. (L.O.1,2)

7. Mr. Brown, a public servant in Ottawa, analyzes economic data. During the year, the government hires Mr. Green. Now, Mr. Brown and Mr. Green both do what Mr. Brown alone used to do. There is no increase in output. Has the hiring of Mr. Green affected the GDP? (L.O.1,2)

8. Explain why total expenditure on the economy's output equals the total income earned in producing that output. (General)

9. Distinguish between GDP and GNP. (L.O.3)

10. What is the difference between national income at factor cost and personal income? (L.O.3)

11. Of the various measures of the total output of the economy discussed in this chapter, which do you think gives the most accurate picture of the standard of living of Canadian consumers? (L.O.5)

12. (a) Does GDP adequately measure the well-being of a country? Explain why or why not. (L.O.4,5)

    (b) If GDP does not adequately measure economic well-being, what adjustments can be made to obtain a better measure of economic well-being? (L.O.5)

PROBLEMS AND EXERCISES

1. Table 22.7 gives data for the Canadian economy in 1960.

TABLE 22.7

National income and product data, Canada 1960.

Item	$million
Personal expenditure on consumer goods and services	25 280
Government current expenditure on goods and services	5 181
Indirect taxes less subsidies	4 587
Wages and salaries	20 141
Accrued net income of farm operators	1 026
Exports of goods and services	6 709
Capital consumption allowances	4 769
Gross investment	9 153
Corporation profits before taxes	3 946
Interest and miscellaneous investment income	1 174
Imports of goods and services	7 222
Net income of non-farm unincorporated business, including rent	3 458

Source: Statistics Canada, *Canadian Economic Observer* (Cat. 11-210), July 1993: 4.

Compute each of the following: (L.O.1,2)

(a) net domestic income at factor cost;

(b) GDP, income-based;

(c) GDP, expenditure-based.

2. Using the data in Table 22.7, compute net investment. (L.O.2)

3. In April 1995, you sold your 1988 GM car to one of your college buddies for $1500. A few days later, you bought a new car for $12 000 which you sold a few weeks later to another college friend for $10 500, because you decided to leave the country. Which of these transactions would be included in the GDP for 1995? Why? (L.O.1)

4. Under which heading in the national income accounts would you include each of the following? (L.O.2)

(a) The purchase of a brand-new family car;

(b) Income paid to a gardener for his or her services;

(c) The purchase of a new machine by a manufacturer;

(d) The purchase of micro-computers by a school board in your province from a local producer;

(e) The purchase of new television sets from Japan;

(f) The sale of a shipment of newly made Canadian refrigerators to France;

(g) The payment of interest to Canadians by Canadian banks.

5. You are given the following data:

Consumption   = $5 400 000

Personal saving = $1 200 000

Personal taxes   = $2 000 000

Compute: (L.O.2,3)

(a) Personal income;

(b) Personal disposable income.

6. The following data are available for the economy of Balancia, a fictitious country. The figures are in millions of dollars. (L.O.2)

TABLE 22.8

Data for Balancia.

Item	$million
Rents	$ 120
Personal consumption expenditures	5 400
Indirect taxes less subsidies	815
Net exports	35
Corporate income taxes	325
Undistributed profits	90
Interest and dividends	585
Wages and salaries	5 140
Income from unincorporated business	485
Gross investment	1 200
Capital consumption allowances	900
Government purchases of goods and services	1 825

(a) Compute Balancia's GDP using
   (i) the expenditure method;
   (ii) the income method.

(b) Compute net domestic income at factor cost.

(c) Compute net investment.

7. Table 22.9 gives data for the state of Simpleville. (L.O.2)

(a) Calculate the GDP for 1960, 1970, and 1980.

(b) Using 1970 as the base year, give price indexes for 1960 and 1980.

(c) Using the price indexes calculated in (b), express GDP in Simpleville for 1960, 1970, and 1980 in constant (1970) dollars.

TABLE 22.9

Output and price level.

Year	Average level of prices ($)	Quantity of output
1960	15	650
1970	20	1 000
1980	25	1 500

8. Table 22.10 gives hypothetical data for an economy. Fill in the blanks. (L.O.2)

TABLE 22.10

Hypothetical economic data.

Year	Real GDP (1980 $)	GDP (current $)	Price index (1980=100)
1940	300	_____	25
1960	_____	750	85
1980	1500	_____	_____
1990	_____	3000	200

9. The Ignoreconomists strike again! The Ignoreconomists are a group of economic charlatans. Under the impression that more money necessarily increases economic well-being, the Ignoreconomists persuaded the government of Ignoramia to increase the money supply tenfold, and to distribute this new money to Ignoramians. Will this measure improve the well-being of Ignoramians? Explain your position. (L.O.5)

10. Given the information shown in Table 12.11 about an economy, how much did real GDP grow between 1970 and 1980? How much did it grow between 1980 and 1990? (L.O.2)

TABLE 22.11		**1965**	**1970**	**1975**	**1980**	**1985**	**1990**
Hypothetical GDP data.	Nominal GDP ($million)	800	1 100	1 500	2 500	3 500	5 000
	Price index	100	120	160	250	300	420

11. Explain what would happen to the Canadian GDP if: (L.O.1,2)
    (a) all housekeepers decided to marry their employers;
    (b) prostitution and illicit drug dealing were legalized;
    (c) homemakers were paid for their services.

12. Explain what would happen to the Canadian GNP and GDP if: (L.O.1,3)
    (a) a number of foreign companies established subsidiaries in Canada;
    (b) some Canadian firms relocated in Mexico;
    (c) there was a global increase in the productivity of all workers.

Internet Site

http://www.statcan.ca
Data, data, everywhere. The Statistics Canada site contains a plethora of data on virtually all aspects of the Canadian economy and society.

INTERNET EXERCISE

1. Go to the Statistics Canada site.
2. Click on *About Statistics Canada.*
3. Write a paragraph about Statistics Canada.
4. Go back to the Statistics Canada site
5. Click on *Canadian Statistics.*
6. Click on *The Economy in Detail.*
7. Click on *Economic conditions.*
8. Click on *Gross domestic product, the provinces and territories.*
9. a) Which province has the highest GDP?
   b) Which province has the lowest GDP?
   c) List each province in order according to its GDP.

CHAPTER

UNEMPLOYMENT AND INFLATION

Learning Objectives

After studying this chapter, you should be able to:

1 define unemployment

2 discuss the various types of unemployment

3 understand how unemployment is measured

4 explain the incidence of unemployment

5 discuss the costs of unemployment

6 explain the classical and Keynesian theories of unemployment

7 define inflation

8 understand how inflation is measured

9 discuss the effects of inflation

10 understand the relationship between inflation and unemployment

If we would consider …. the problem of economic disturbances it is clear that these represent the heaviest burden to which our economic and social system is exposed.

Wilhelm Ropke, *Civitas Humana.*

INTRODUCTION

In our discussion of great macroeconomic concerns in Chapter 21, we noted that inflation and unemployment were two of the most important macroeconomic problems. Accordingly, a major part of macroeconomic theory and policy is devoted to these two economic evils. The number of people unemployed in Canada in 1997 was about 1.4 million, or 9% of the labour force, and the average level of prices was rising at an annual rate of about 0.5%. Compared with some previous years, the rate of inflation was relatively low, but the rate of unemployment was relatively high. For example, between 1962 and 1969, the unemployment rate was consistently below 5%, whereas in 1974, the rate of inflation was above 14%. From the point of view of employment, 1990-92 was a bad period.

The unemployment rate and the rate of inflation are among the most important indicators of how well (or poorly) the economy is performing. Politicians, economists, businesspeople, and ordinary citizens are all keenly interested in these indicators, and one of the main objectives of government economic policy is to control unemployment and inflation, keeping both at reasonably low levels.

The inflation rate and the unemployment rate are important indicators of performance.

This chapter is divided into two parts. In the first part, you will study unemployment. The objective here is to help you to understand why unemployment is considered to be such a serious problem. You will also study various theories of unemployment. The second part of the chapter deals with inflation. You will learn how to distinguish inflation from a once-and-for-all increase in the price level, how inflation is measured, and what the effects of inflation are. A brief discussion of the relationship between inflation and unemployment concludes the chapter. Inflation and unemployment will be further analyzed in Chapter 33.

A. UNEMPLOYMENT

Learning Objective 1:
define unemployment

People who are unemployed or have experienced unemployment are well aware of the hardships caused by the economic monster. And even those who have never been unemployed shudder at the thought of being without a job. As you will see later, unemployment can wreak havoc on the unemployed, their families, and on the economy as a whole. Unemployment is indeed a fearful term.

Statistics Canada defines the unemployed as those who are without jobs and who are actively looking and available for work. People can be unemployed for several reasons. Consequently, it is important to be able to distinguish between the different types of unemployment.

TYPES OF UNEMPLOYMENT

Unemployment can be classified as frictional, seasonal, structural, or cyclical.

Unemployed individuals are not much concerned with the type of unemployment that disrupts their lives. However, the type of unemployment is important to economists because different types of unemployment require different remedies. It has become common practice among economists to group unemployment into four broad categories: frictional unemployment, seasonal unemployment, structural unemployment, and cyclical unemployment. We shall discuss each of these in turn.

FRICTIONAL UNEMPLOYMENT

Learning Objective 2:
discuss the various types of unemployment

In an economic system in which people are free to change their jobs and in which employers may dismiss inefficient or redundant employees, frictional unemployment cannot be eliminated, and may even be desirable. Frictional unemployment results from people leaving jobs before they have another one lined up, or people entering the labour force for the first time. After you graduate from school, it may take you a little while to find a job. Until you do, you will be frictionally unemployed. **Frictional unemployment** is unemployment which results from people moving between jobs, and new workers entering the labour force. This type of unemployment can be reduced to some extent by providing better information about job opportunities and available workers, and by human resource planning so that workers will possess the skills required by the economy. However, we cannot hope to completely eliminate frictional unemployment. Since a certain amount of frictional unemployment is inevitable, allowance is made for this fact when we use the term **full employment**. If we consider a frictional unemployment rate of 4% to be inevitable, then we define full employment as the employment of 96% of the labour force.

Frictional unemployment results from people between jobs or entering the labour force.

Full employment involves the entire labour force minus the frictionally unemployed.

SEASONAL UNEMPLOYMENT

It is natural that unemployment varies with the seasons in a country where the seasons are pronounced. **Seasonal unemployment** is unemployment which is caused by economic slowdowns related to seasonal variations. In our part of the world, agricultural activities slow down during winter, and unemployment in this sector therefore increases. Construction activities also decrease significantly during winter; unemployment therefore increases in that sector also. During summer, unemployment increases among people whose jobs are related to winter activities such as ice skating and skiing. Obviously, the scope for policies to reduce seasonal unemployment is severely limited.

Seasonal unemployment is caused by seasonal variations.

STRUCTURAL UNEMPLOYMENT

A growing economy is constantly undergoing structural changes. Demand patterns change. Techniques of production also change. **Structural unemployment** is unemployment that is caused by structural changes in demand patterns. If there is a permanent decline in the demand for textiles, then the industry will demand fewer workers and unemployment will result. The introduction of labour-saving machines in various industries has created a special kind of structural unemployment. We call it **technological unemployment**. Consider the number of people whose jobs have become obsolete because of the introduction of computers into various aspects of business. Do not forget, however, that the introduction of computers has created employment for a number of people: programmers, computer technicians, and computer course instructors, for example.

Structural unemployment is caused by structural changes in demand patterns.

Technological unemployment is a type of structural employment caused by the introduction of labour-saving equipment or methods.

There is a misconception that only uneducated, unskilled, or untrained workers are subject to technological unemployment. In fact, even the skills of highly trained individuals can become obsolete in the wake of rapid technological progress and structural changes in the economy. Structural unemployment can be reduced by providing retraining for those whose skills are no longer in demand. This may prove to be a difficult task, however, especially in the case of older workers.

CYCLICAL UNEMPLOYMENT

A reduction in total spending may cause firms to be unable to sell their output of goods and services. This deficiency of aggregate expenditure results in a decrease in production and an increase in unemployment. A market economy goes through ups and downs known as business fluctuations or business cycles. When the economy is on the upswing, employment rises, and when it is on the downswing, unemployment increases. **Cyclical unemployment** is unemployment that is due to cyclical changes in economic activity. A large part of government macroeconomic policy is aimed at reducing these fluctuations in economic activity. You will study more about business fluctuations in a later chapter.

Cyclical unemployment is due to cyclical changes in the economy.

THE MEASUREMENT OF UNEMPLOYMENT

THE UNEMPLOYMENT RATE

You have repeatedly heard statistics on the rate of unemployment. But what exactly is the rate of unemployment, and how is it measured? Let us first define the unemployment rate, and then we will see how Statistics Canada determines it. The **unemployment rate** expresses the number of people unemployed as a percentage of the labour force. The **labour force** (LF) comprises all unemployed (U) and employed (E) persons. That is,

$$LF = U + E$$

Symbolically, the unemployment rate (UR) can be expressed as

$$UR = \frac{U}{LF} \times 100$$

If there are 100 000 people in the labour force, 10 000 of whom are unemployed, then the unemployment rate is calculated as follows:

$$UR = \frac{U}{LF} \times 100 = \frac{10\ 000}{100\ 000} \times 100 = 10$$

The unemployment rate, in this case, is 10%. It is worth noting that our reference to unemployment relates to only one factor of production: labour. An unemployment rate of 10% does not tell us anything directly about the employment of land or capital. We would, of course, expect that a high unemployment rate would result in a low level of utilization of capital and other factor inputs. Another labour force statistic with which you should be familiar is the **labour force participation rate**, which is defined as the labour force expressed as a percentage of the population 15 years and over.

THE MEASUREMENT OF UNEMPLOYMENT

Each month, Statistics Canada conducts a survey of Canadian households, interviewing about 50 000 of them to determine their employment status. Based on the results of the survey, Statistics Canada makes an inference of the unemployment rate for Canada. Although most people regard the estimate as fairly reliable, there are several problems. In order to understand the conceptual problems involved, you must understand the definitions of certain terms used in the survey.

First, the survey defines as "employed" any person who had a job at the time of the interview, or who was away from work for reasons such as illness, vacation, strikes or lockouts, familial obligations, etc. Second, the survey defines as "unemployed" any person who was actively looking for work and was actually available for work during the past month, or who was laid off for not more than 26 weeks, even if he or she was not looking for another job. Third, the survey defines the adult population as persons 15 years of age and older, excluding people in the armed forces, inmates of institutions, and native people on reserves.

Let us now address some of the issues involved. Just how "actively" must people be looking for work before they are numbered among the unemployed? Consider the following situation. John is a young man from a well-to-do family. He reads the classified ads hoping to find a well-paying job of his liking just to have something to do. John would be classified as unemployed if he told the interviewer that he has been trying to find a job for the past several months by looking for jobs in the newspapers.

The unemployment rate is the number of unemployed expressed as a percentage of the labour force.

All employed and unemployed people make up the labour force.

The labour force participation rate is the labour force as a percentage of the adult population.

Statistics Canada conducts a monthly survey of about 50 000 people to determine the rate of unemployment.

Learning Objective 3: *understand how unemployment is measured*

Some people accept employment on a part-time basis, or are doing a job that is well below the types of jobs that are consistent with their education, training, and skills. Such people are underemployed, but the survey would classify them as being employed. In such cases, the unemployment statistics do not adequately reflect the extent of unemployment.

The official labour force statistics do not accurately measure the extent of unemployment and under-employment.

To be officially unemployed, a person must be in the labour force. Hence, if Lydia has looked for work for several weeks without success, and then gives up looking actively because she is convinced that nothing is available, the survey would list her as not being in the labour force and therefore not among the unemployed, even though she would be only too happy to accept employment if she were offered a job. Such **discouraged workers** who are not actively seeking employment are not counted as unemployed. If they were, the unemployment rate would be higher than the figure reported by the official statistic. To take account of such discouraged workers, Statistics Canada conducts a special survey every six months to determine the number of workers who are not in the labour force.

Discouraged workers are not actively seeking work and are not counted as "unemployed."

The unemployment rate does not tell us anything about how long the average unemployed worker is out of a job. It measures unemployment at a particular time. It certainly makes a difference whether the duration of the unemployment of the average worker is four weeks or four months.

It is important to note also that national unemployment figures do not tell us anything about how the unemployment is distributed among the various regions. When we say that the unemployment rate is 10%, we must realize that it may be 5% in some regions and 15% in others.

The foregoing discussion suggests that care should be taken when looking at official unemployment statistics. Despite the problems mentioned above, however, the consistency with which the monthly labour force statistics are measured makes the unemployment rate a fairly reliable indicator of movements in the labour force.

THE INCIDENCE OF UNEMPLOYMENT

Learning Objective 4:
explain the incidence of unemployment

All groups in society are not equally likely to be unemployed. For example, in general, a skilled worker is less likely to be laid off than an unskilled worker. A skilled worker is also likely to find a job more quickly than an unskilled worker. Also, unemployment among the young is likely to be higher than among older workers. This is due partly to the fact that high-school drop-outs experience considerable difficulty in finding jobs, and partly to the fact that it often takes a while for high-school and college graduates to find jobs after they enter the labour force. Perhaps the unemployment rate among teenagers would be lower if employers were allowed to hire them for less than the minimum wage.

The unemployment rate among women is also usually higher than among men although it may not be reflected in the statistics. The unemployment statistics count only those actively looking for a job, and women are more likely than men to be homemakers in lieu of continuing to look for outside employment. The higher rate among women is due in large part to discrimination against women in the labour market. Efforts to end discrimination against women seem to be reducing somewhat the incidence of unemployment among this group.

Table 23.1 gives unemployment rates according to age and sex.

Notice that unemployment is highest among people between the ages of 15 and 24. The unemployment rate is lowest among people aged 25 years and over.

		Unemployment
TABLE 23.1	**Category**	**rate (%)**
	Total	
Unemployment rates	Both sexes	9.2
according to age and	Men	9.2
sex, 1997.	Women	9.2
	Ages 15-24	16.7
The unemployment rate is	Ages 25 and over	7.8

The unemployment rate is
highest among young
workers between the ages
of 15 and 24.

Source: Statistics Canada, *Canadian Economic Observer* (Cat. 11–010–XPB), July 1998: 16.

THE COSTS OF UNEMPLOYMENT

The costs of unemployment refer to the adverse effects that unemployment has on the economy, on the unemployed and their families, and on the society as a whole. For the purpose of this discussion, we shall divide the costs of unemployment into economic costs and noneconomic costs.

ECONOMIC COSTS

Learning Objective 5: discuss the costs of unemployment

The economic cost of unemployment can be measured as lost income or output.

Unemployment imposes costs on the individual and on the society as a whole. Unemployment hurts individuals economically because it reduces their incomes. Individuals and their families may then be forced to curtail their consumption drastically. The loss of income may also force individuals to liquidate their real assets — often at a loss — in order to meet financial obligations.

Unemployment causes a loss of the output of goods and services that could have been produced by the unemployed. Employment insurance certainly helps to reduce some of the financial hardships that the unemployed have to face. But it does not compensate for the reduction in output. An economy with a high unemployment rate is producing a level of output substantially below its potential. The total output available for distribution is less than it could have been with full employment. Consequently, everybody loses.

Potential GDP: the level of gross domestic product that an economy could produce if full employment existed. Also called full-employment gross domestic product.

Actual output: the level of output actually produced by the economy.

The economic cost of unemployment can be measured as a loss in total output or as a loss in total income. The level of output that the economy would be able to produce with full employment is called **potential GDP** or full-employment output. The output actually produced by the economy and recorded in the national income and product accounts is called **actual output**. If we subtract actual from potential output, we get the **output (income) gap**, which represents the loss of output due to unemployment.

The economic cost of unemployment can be measured as the difference between potential GDP and actual GDP.

Figure 23.1 shows the economic cost of unemployment from 1976 to 1997.

The gap between potential GDP and actual GDP is a measure of the economic cost of unemployment. As a specific example of the economic cost of unemployment, let us consider 1983 — a year in which the unemployment rate climbed to 11.8%. In that year, the gap between potential output and actual output was about $31.4 billion at 1981 prices or $35.8 billion at 1983 prices. This means that the unemployment rate of 11.8% in 1983 caused the Canadian economy to lose $35.8 billion of goods and services. Exactly how large was this loss? To get a clearer perspective of the magnitude of

FIGURE 23.1

The economic cost of unemployment.

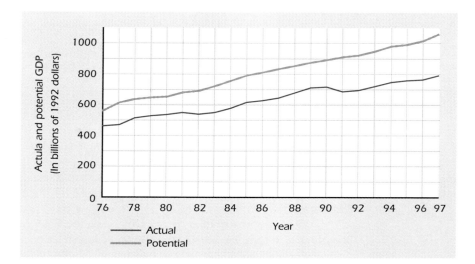

The potential GDP minus the actual output equals the output (income) gap.

The output gap is the economic cost of unemployment.

the loss of output, consider the following. If the $35.8 billion were divided equally among every household in Canada in 1983, each would have received nearly $4000. Or, to look at it another way, the amount was enough to purchase a new car for every person in Manitoba, Saskatchewan, and Alberta.

Okun's Law

Okun's Law states that output falls by 3% for every 1% rise in the unemployment rate above that defined as full employment.

Another way of measuring the economic cost of unemployment is to use **Okun's Law**, named after the late and famous American economist, Arthur Okun. Okun's Law states that for every 1% rise in the unemployment rate above the rate defined as full employment (4% in our case), output falls by 3%. Since Okun discovered the relationship, later economists have adjusted the 1:3 ratio to 1:2.5 or 1:2. It is believed that an **Okun ratio** of 1:2 is applicable to Canada. Let us use this ratio to calculate the loss in output in the Canadian economy in 1983. The output in 1983 was $309.9 billion, and the unemployment rate was 11.8%, that is, 7.8 percentage points above our 4% defined as full employment. Applying Okun's Law, we can conclude that the economy produced 7.8% × 2 = 15.6% less than its potential for that year. The potential output was therefore $358.2 billion (that is, 15.6% more than $309.9 billion). The loss of output was therefore $358.2 − $309.9 = $48.3 billion — even greater than our previous estimate.

NONECONOMIC COSTS

Noneconomic costs of unemployment include emotional and psychological problems faced by the unemployed and their families.

We turn now to the noneconomic costs of unemployment. Unemployed individuals may become discouraged and frustrated because of their inability to secure jobs. These feelings may lead to antisocial activities: violence, theft, the destruction of property, and various other forms of crime. Family happiness may be permanently ruined. The self-esteem of the unemployed person may be destroyed. Moreover, the children of the unemployed may bear a tremendous cost in the form of loss of education and good health, which may affect them adversely for many years in the future. Unemployment statistics cannot adequately measure the misery, suffering, and indignity that the unemployed must endure. But the costs, nevertheless, are real and significant.

THEORIES OF UNEMPLOYMENT

Classical economists thought that flexible wages and prices would lead to full employment.

In this section, we shall discuss two theories of unemployment: the classical theory and the Keynesian theory. The economists of the 19th and early 20th centuries are generally referred to as **classical economists**. Their views on the workings of the economy dominated economic thinking until the 1930s.

THE CLASSICAL THEORY OF UNEMPLOYMENT

Learning Objective 6: explain the classical and Keynesian theories of unemployment

According to the classical economists, the economy would tend to move towards full employment, provided that interest rates, wages, and prices were flexible. The classical economists thought that, if spending by households and firms was insufficient to produce full employment, firms would end up with a surplus of consumer and investment goods. This surplus would exert a downward pressure on prices which, in turn, would stimulate spending on consumer and investment goods.

A decrease in spending by consumers, on the other hand, implies an increase in savings. This, in turn, means that the supply of loanable funds increases. This increase in the supply of loanable funds, according to classical thinking, would exert a downward pressure on the rate of interest. Also, in the classical scheme of things, a decrease in spending by firms would represent a fall in the demand for loanable funds for investment purposes. This decrease in demand would cause the rate of interest to fall. Now, because of this lower interest rate, consumer and investment spending would increase.

The classical economists also felt that, if there was unemployment in the economy, competition among workers for the available jobs would cause wages to fall. Lower wages would act as an incentive for firms to hire more workers and thus restore full employment. Thus, as far as the classical economists were concerned, lapses from full employment would be of short duration only, since forces would be set in motion automatically to eliminate any unemployment which might emerge.

The classical economists, then, would argue that unemployment occurs because the wage rate is set too high, and for some reason, is not allowed to fall. Their position is illustrated by the familiar diagram shown as Figure 23.2.

The equilibrium wage rate is W, where the demand and supply curves for labour intersect. If the wage rate is fixed at W_1, then the quantity of labour supplied, i.e. L_1, will exceed the quantity demanded, L_0. This excess of labour on the market, represented by $L_1 - L_0$, is unemployment. In summary, the classical economists believed that the economy

FIGURE 23.2

Classical unemployment.

The classical economists claimed that the wage rate would fall to restore full employment.

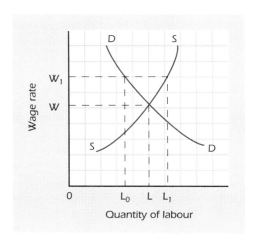

would operate at full employment provided that all output prices and input prices were flexible. Because of their belief in automatic full employment, the classical economists placed a great deal more emphasis on inflation than they did on unemployment.

Say's Law states that supply creates its own demand.

How did the classical economists arrive at their conclusion of automatic full employment? The basis of the classical theory of employment is **Say's Law**, named after the French economist, Jean Baptiste Say (1867-1932). Say's Law is usually summarized by the phrase *supply creates its own demand*. The law can be explained as follows. People engage in economic activity, supplying goods and services, not so much for the sake of work, but in order to be able to buy goods and services to satisfy their wants. This implies that production in itself constitutes the demand for goods and services. That being the case, then a situation in which the total output of goods and services exceeded the total amount that the economy's customers would want to buy is impossible. The mere existence of production represents a corresponding demand for the output which results from that production.

THE KEYNESIAN THEORY OF EMPLOYMENT

Learning Objective 6: explain the classical and Keynesian theories of unemployment

The Great Depression of the late 1920s and early 1930s — a period of severe and prolonged unemployment — caused economists to seriously re-examine the classical conclusion of automatic full employment. A British economist by the name of John Maynard Keynes was foremost among those who attacked the classical framework. In 1936, before the industrialized world had recovered from the Great Depression, Keynes published his book *The General Theory of Employment, Interest, and Money* — one of the most influential books ever written.

Keynes claimed that a deficiency in aggregate expenditure could result in unemployment.

In this book (*The General Theory*, for short), Keynes showed that unemployment could result from a deficiency of aggregate expenditure. Simply stated, Keynes' theory of unemployment says that if total spending was insufficient to enable firms to sell off their total output, they would reduce their production levels, lay off workers, and thus cause the economy to settle down to a less-than-full employment equilibrium. Such a case would necessitate direct intervention in the form of government spending and taxing powers to restore the economy to full employment. The Keynesian theory will occupy our attention in subsequent chapters.

B. INFLATION

Inflation is a sustained rise in the average level of prices.

Learning Objective 7: define inflation

You have probably not heard a great deal of talk about inflation. Why? Because the Canadian economy is now experiencing relative price stability. But this has not always been the case, and hardly anyone would state categorically that inflation will never again surface as a major economic problem in Canada. Let us define **inflation** as a persistent rise in the average level of prices. We should, however, distinguish between an increase in the price of a product resulting from changes in demand and supply and an increase in the average level of prices. If the demand for butter increases, other things being equal, the price of butter will rise. This increase in the price of butter, however, is a change in relative price. It may not indicate the presence of inflationary forces, because other prices may be falling due to changes in demand and supply. For inflation to exist, most prices must be rising.

It is also important to distinguish between a persistent rise in the price level and a once-and-for-all increase in the price level. The difference is illustrated in Figure 23.3. The steadily rising line PS shows a persistent rise in the price level from 100 in Year 0 to 200 in Year 5. We describe this situation as inflationary.

FIGURE 23.3

Inflation vs. a
once-only rise in the
price level.

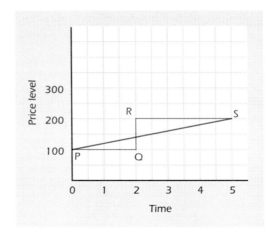

The price level may, however, remain constant at 100 from Year 0 to Year 2 as shown by the horizontal line PQ. Then at Year 2, the price level may suddenly increase from 100 to 200, as shown by the line QR, and then remain constant at 200 for the remaining three years. This situation is described as a once-and-for-all increase in the price level in Year 2. We cannot describe this situation as inflationary. In an inflationary situation, the purchasing power of money falls. Five dollars will buy less today than it did last year, and more today than it will next year.

THE MEASUREMENT OF INFLATION

Inflation is measured by
changes in the price level.

The consumer price index
measures price changes in
consumer goods.

The wholesale price index
measures price changes in
primary goods.

The implicit price deflator
measures changes in the
average price level of all
final goods.

We can measure changes in the price level by using price indexes. Let us recall Chapter 22, in which we determined that price indexes could be used to deflate the GDP. Three popular price indexes are the consumer price index (CPI), the wholesale price index (WPI), and the GDP deflator or the implicit GDP price index. Of these three price indexes, the CPI is used most often. The **consumer price index** measures changes in the prices of consumer goods and services. In constructing the CPI, Statistics Canada collects information on the prices of about 400 different items. The **wholesale price index** measures changes in the prices of goods bought by manufacturers (primary goods). The **implicit price deflator** (also called the gross domestic product deflator) measures changes in the average level of prices for all final goods and services. The implicit price deflator is therefore the most comprehensive among the three price indexes.

PROBLEM SOLVING 23-1
Can inflation occur in a barter economy?

THE RULE OF 70

The rule of 70 allows quick
calculation of the number
of years required for the
price level to double.

When inflation exists, by definition, the price level must rise. The so-called **rule of 70** provides a quick method for calculating the number of years required for the price level to double, given the rate of inflation. According to this rule, the number of years required for a doubling of the price level is determined by dividing 70 by the annual rate of inflation. That is,

$$N = \frac{70}{\text{rate of inflation}}$$

where N is the number of years necessary for the price level to double. If the rate of inflation is 5% per year, then the price level will double in (70 ÷ 5) =14 years. If the rate of inflation of 4.8% in 1987 had been maintained, then the consumer price index would have doubled in (70 ÷ 4.8 = 14.4) years or by 2001.

THE EFFECTS OF INFLATION

Learning Objective 9:
discuss the effects of inflation

In order to examine properly the consequences of inflation, we must make the distinction between anticipated and unanticipated inflation. If everyone expects a rate of inflation of 12% next year and that rate materializes, then we say that the inflation is fully *anticipated*. On the other hand, if everyone expects an inflation rate of 9% next year and the actual rate turns out to be 13%, then we say that the inflation is *unanticipated*. Because different rates of inflation have quite different effects, it is also important to distinguish between different rates of inflation and to be familiar with the terminology used to describe these different rates. Economists have classified inflation into three categories: creeping inflation, galloping inflation, and hyperinflation or runaway inflation. These classifications are arbitrary and there is no specific line of demarcation between them. However, the following will provide a useful way of looking at each category.

CREEPING INFLATION

Creeping inflation creeps at a rate lower than 10%.

Moderate increases in the average level of prices constitute **creeping inflation**. But what is moderate? Most economists would probably agree that inflation rates of less than 10% annually should be classified as creeping inflation. Canadian inflationary experiences would fall within this category. Although moderate increases in the price level do not seem to do great harm to the health of the economy, there is always the danger that a creeping inflation might develop into a more serious inflation. Creeping inflation is like being threatened by the enemy.

GALLOPING INFLATION

Galloping inflation gallops at a rate between about 10% and 1000%.

This type of inflation occurs when the annual rate of increase of the price level climbs to double and triple digits. Inflation rates in the order of 25, 100, and 400% would be classified as **galloping inflation**. Brazil, Italy, and Israel experienced galloping inflation in the 1970s. Although galloping inflation is a real threat to the proper functioning of the economy, some countries seem to be able to cope with it, and even to prosper. Galloping inflation is like having sanctions imposed by the enemy.

HYPERINFLATION

Hyperinflation rates are more than 1000%.

This type of inflation exists when the price level is rising at rates of 1000% and more. The classic example of **hyperinflation** is Germany in the early 1920s, when the annual inflation rate was well over 1 000 000 percent. To add some perspective to these staggering rates of inflation, just imagine what the situation would be like if the amount of money required to purchase a huge mansion in one year was not enough to purchase a box of matches one year later. Some Latin American countries have experienced what many would describe as hyperinflation or runaway inflation. Hyperinflation is like being bombed by the enemy.

WINNERS AND LOSERS

Learning Objective 9:
discuss the effects of inflation

Why is inflation harmful? Probably one of the most popular answers to this question is that, given a fixed sum of money, we have to pay increasingly higher prices for goods and services. Although it is true that inflation reduces some (probably most) people's purchasing power, we must not lose sight of the fact that the high prices which people pay for goods and services are received by someone else. In any inflation, there are winners and losers.

The winners

Inflation results in a redistribution of income and wealth.

Those who benefit during an inflation include debtors, producers (sellers), and owners of real assets. Debtors gain from inflation because they repay their debts with money whose value has fallen. Producers of goods and services benefit from inflation for two main reasons. First, during a period of inflation, the prices of goods and services tend to rise at a faster rate than the rate of increase in the prices of inputs. This implies that profits increase during inflationary periods. Second, the firms buy their factor inputs at current prices but their output is sold at future higher prices, thus profits increase. Owners of real assets benefit from inflation because during an inflation, the value of real assets such as real estate increases.

The losers

Those who lose as a result of inflation include creditors, people on fixed incomes, and owners of financial assets. Creditors lose because, when they are repaid, the money they receive will have lost some purchasing power. People on fixed incomes and salaries lose because, as inflation proceeds, they have to put out a larger sum of money for a given quantity of goods and services while their incomes remain unchanged. To see how inflation harms owners of financial assets, consider an individual with a savings account of $5000. If the price level increases annually by 10%, that individual's $5000 will be able to buy 10% fewer goods and services after one year. In other words, the original $5000 will be worth only $4500 in real terms — a loss of $500.

You should realize that the effects of inflation on various groups apply mainly in the case of unanticipated inflation. For example, creditors who anticipate an inflation rate of 10% may protect themselves from loss by adding this rate to the rate of interest that would have been charged had there been no inflation. People on contractual income may protect their purchasing power by having their income indexed to the inflation rate. This means that if prices rise by 6%, incomes will automatically rise by 6%. Such cost of living adjustment (COLA) clauses are common in many employment contracts.

THE EFFECTS OF INFLATION ON THE ECONOMY

Inflation may cause resources to be misallocated.

Learning Objective 9:
discuss the effects of inflation

The previous section showed that the effect of inflation on individuals is to redistribute income among various groups. The redistributive effect of inflation is only a part of the story. Inflation also affects the entire economy through its effect on resource allocation. In an inflationary period, people will try to protect their savings by taking them out of bank accounts and purchasing real assets, many of which may be non-productive. These savings will not then be available to firms for productive investment. As a consequence, the economy's productive capacity may decrease.

Some economists argue, moreover, that inflation destroys the incentive to work. Since real income declines in a period of inflation, people may consider it pointless to work harder. They may even lose heart and work less. Production may therefore decline. And all of this occurs before we consider the effect of taxes. Inflation tends to push people into higher income brackets. If the tax system is progressive, the proportion of income spent in taxes will increase. To avoid the higher tax bracket occasioned by the higher income bracket, people may reduce their work effort (refuse to work overtime, take time off from work without pay, etc.). While some economists claim that a creeping inflation may stimulate profits and investment, the fear is very real that even a mild inflation may burgeon into a galloping inflation and eventually into a hyperinflation.

Hyperinflation may result in economic collapse.

Because money loses its value so fast during hyperinflation, people try to spend it as fast as they get it. The situation could degenerate to the point where people refuse to accept it as payment for goods and services, and revert to an inefficient barter system where goods and services are exchanged without the use of money. Hyperinflation may require monetary reform or the entire economy could collapse.

APPLICATION

Protection from Inflation

Can people do anything to protect themselves from inflation? By understanding the effects of inflation, we can apply some of the concepts in order to protect ourselves from some of those effects. For example, we have seen that during a period of inflation, the values of real assets rise, whereas the values of financial assets such as savings accounts fall. This suggests that we can protect ourselves from inflation, to some extent, by switching our assets out of savings and into real estate, for example. By using our savings to purchase real assets, we could actually benefit from inflation.

C. THE UNEMPLOYMENT-INFLATION RELATIONSHIP

The relationship between unemployment and inflation is an important one in macroeconomics, and will be examined in considerable depth in later sections of this book. In this section, we merely skim the surface of that important and sometimes controversial relationship. Figure 23.4 will help us with the analysis.

Learning Objective 10: understand the relationship between inflation and unemployment

You will see later that the level of total spending in an economy affects both the rate of inflation and the rate of unemployment. If total spending falls to very low levels, firms will find themselves with a large volume of goods and services which are unsold (inventories). They will lay off workers, and they will certainly not raise their prices. The economy will be operating in Section A of Figure 23.4, where output and employment are well below their full employment levels denoted by F. The unemployment rate will be high.

FIGURE 23.4

Relation between inflation and unemployment.

Some economists believe that there is an inverse relationship between inflation and unemployment.

GLOBAL PERSPECTIVE

An International Look at Unemployment and Inflation

In Chapter 21, we compared unemployment, inflation, and economic growth in Canada and the other G-7 countries, and we saw Canada's performance as measured by those performance indexes. But how does Canada compare with other countries in terms of unemployment and inflation? In this capsule, we select 14 advanced economies other than G-7 countries and compare their unemployment and inflation situation with Canada's over the period 1990-99.

As the chart shows, of the 15 countries on our list, Luxembourg had the lowest unemployment rate with an average of only 2.7% over the 1990-99 period. Spain had the highest average annual rate at 20.2%. Canada tied with Denmark for the countries with the tenth lowest (or fifth highest) unemployment rate among our selected countries. Turning to the rate of inflation for the same period, we observe that a completely different picture emerges. Only Ireland, with an average annual rate of inflation of 1.5% had a lower rate than Canada's 1.7%. Luxembourg also had a relatively low rate at 1.9%. At the other end, Greece had the highest average annual rate of inflation at 11.3%. Portugal had the second highest average annual rate at 6.6%.

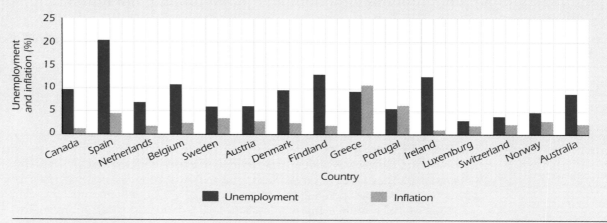

Source: Intrenational Monetary Fund, *World Economic Outlook,* May 1998: 149, 157.

If total spending rises, firms will notice an increase in demand for their goods and services. Their inventories may even fall below desired levels, so they hire more workers in order to increase their production, and the unemployment rate falls. As this continues, resources become relatively more scarce, and resource prices rise. Labour also demands wage increases, and firms are less reluctant to grant such increases. For these reasons, the price level begins to rise. The economy will be operating in Section B of Figure 23.4, which shows the price level rising and output and employment rising (the unemployment rate falling).

If total spending continues to rise, the economy will eventually reach the full employment level (point F on Figure 23.4). Output and employment cannot rise beyond this level, that is, the unemployment rate cannot fall any more. The pressure of spending on the fixed total output results in a high rate of inflation as shown by Section C of Figure 23.4.

The analysis above demonstrates an inverse relationship between inflation and unemployment. On the basis of this relationship, some economists argue that it may be necessary to tolerate a certain amount of inflation in order to reduce the rate of unemployment. Other economists argue that this type of trade-off is only possible in the short run, but in the long run, increases in inflation produce very few gains in terms of a reduction in the unemployment rate. We will return to this controversial issue in a later chapter.

CHAPTER SUMMARY

1. Inflation and unemployment are among the most serious economic problems.

2. The main types of unemployment are frictional unemployment, seasonal unemployment, structural unemployment, and cyclical unemployment.

3. The unemployed are those workers who are without jobs and who are actively looking and available for work. The unemployed plus the employed make up the labour force. The unemployment rate is obtained by expressing the unemployed as a percentage of the labour force.

4. The groups most likely to be unemployed are unskilled workers, those between the ages of 15 and 24, and women.

5. The economic cost of unemployment can be measured in terms of the lost output or income resulting from unemployment. The noneconomic costs include the mental anguish, the frustration, and the loss of dignity and self-worth that the unemployed must suffer.

6. Okun's Law states that for every 1% rise in the unemployment rate above that defined as full employment, output falls by 3% below its potential. The Okun ratio for Canada is about 1:2.

7. According to the classical economists, automatic full employment was assured provided that wages and prices were flexible. The basis of their theory was Say's Law, which states that supply creates its own demand.

8. The Keynesian theory of unemployment states that a deficiency of total spending could cause the economy to achieve a less-than-full employment equilibrium, and that government intervention may be necessary to push the economy towards full employment.

9. Inflation is a sustained increase in the average level of prices and should not be confused with an increase in relative prices due to changes in demand and supply for particular products.

10. Price indexes measure changes in the average level of prices. Three common indexes are the consumer price index, the wholesale price index, and the gross domestic product deflator. Changes in the consumer price index are often used as a measure of the rate of inflation.

11. The rule of 70 allows you to determine easily the number of years required for the price level to double, given the rate of inflation. The number of years is obtained by dividing 70 by the annual rate of inflation.

12. Economists have classified inflation into three categories according to its intensity or severity. A moderate annual increase in the price level is called creeping inflation; double and triple digit inflation is classified as galloping inflation; and extremely high rates of inflation constitute hyperinflation.

13. The effects of inflation depend on the severity of the inflation. A mild inflation does not seem to disrupt the economy very much, but galloping inflation redistributes income and wealth. Hyperinflation may cause economic collapse.

14. Some economists claim that an inverse relationship exists between inflation and unemployment. This view, however, is not supported by all economists.

TERMS FOR REVIEW

frictional unemployment (391)
full employment (391)
seasonal unemployment (391)
structural unemployment (391)
technological unemployment (391)
cyclical unemployment (391)
unemployment rate (392)
labour force (392)
labour force participation rate (392)
discouraged workers (393)
potential GDP (394)
actual output (394

output (income) gap (394)
Okun's Law/ratio (395)
classical economists (396)
Say's law (397)
inflation (397)
consumer price index (398)
wholesale price index (398)
implicit price deflator (398)
rule of 70 (398)
creeping inflation (399)
galloping inflation (399)
hyperinflation (399)

QUESTIONS FOR REVIEW AND DISCUSSION

1. What is meant by the unemployment rate? How does Statistics Canada arrive at the unemployment rate statistic? (L.O.1)

2. What are some of the problems associated with the official unemployment statistic? (L.O.1)

3. What do economists mean by the term full employment? (L.O.1)

4. List the major types of unemployment and discuss any two of them. (L.O.2)

5. What groups of workers are most susceptible to unemployment and why? (L.O.4)

6. "Unemployment is not such a serious problem because we have unemployment insurance." Discuss this statement. (L.O.5)

7. What are the costs of unemployment? (L.O.5)

8. "Unemployment hurts only the unemployed." Is this statement true? Why or why not? (L.O.5)

9. State Okun's Law. What is its significance? (L.O.5)

10. Explain Say's Law. (L.O.6)

11. Summarize the classical theory of unemployment. (L.O.6)

12. According to Keynesian theory, what is the cause of unemployment? (L.O.6)

13. Why do most people consider inflation to be such a serious problem? (L.O.7,9)

14. What is the difference between a sustained rise in the price level and a once-and-for-all increase in the average level of prices? (L.O.7)

15. What is the importance of the rule of 70? (General)

16. How is the rate of inflation measured? (L.O.8)

17. Distinguish between the consumer price index and the implicit price deflator. (L.O.8)

18. Define each of the following: (L.O.9)

    (a) creeping inflation;

    (b) galloping inflation;

    (c) hyperinflation.

19. Do you agree that a mild inflation (less than 5%) is healthy for the economy? Why or why not? (L.O.9)

20. During inflationary periods, many firms declare huge profits. Explain this. (General)

21. Which groups are hurt most by unanticipated inflation? Which groups benefit? (L.O.9)

22. Name some ways by which various groups attempt to protect themselves from anticipated inflation. (L.O.9)

23. How does inflation affect the economy as a whole? (L.O.9)

24. Why do some economists believe that it may be necessary to live with a certain amount of inflation in order to keep the unemployment rate at a low level? (L.O.10)

PROBLEMS AND EXERCISES

1. Table 23.2 gives information for an economy.

TABLE 23.2	Item	Number
Labour force data.	Population (15 & over)	16 000 500
	Labour force	10 100 000
	Employed	9 200 000
	Unemployed	900 000

Calculate: (L.O.1,3)

(a) the participation rate;

(b) the unemployment rate.

2. The data contained in Table 23.3 are for the economy of Grandstand. Complete the table by filling in the blank spaces. (L.O.3)

TABLE 23.3		
Labour force data, 1992.	Labour force	10.5 million
	Unemployment rate (%)	10.5
	Employment rate (%)	—
	Number employed	—
	Number unemployed	—

3. In 1980, the unemployment rate in Megatronia was 15%, and the total output in that year was $200 billion. If an employment rate of 95% is considered to be full employment, use Okun's Law (with a ratio of 1:2) to calculate the loss of output attributable to unemployment. (L.O.5)

4. Classify each of the following as employed, unemployed, or not in the labour force. (L.O.1)

    (a) a spouse who stays at home and takes care of the children;

    (b) a 13-year-old person who does odd jobs for the neighbours for pocket money;

(c) an economics professor who has a job but is actively looking for another job as a consultant;

(d) an adult who has a part-time job, would like to work full-time, but has no time to look for a full-time job;

(e) a painter who has been laid off but expects to be called back to work within three days;

(f) a 19-year-old college graduate looking for a job for the first time;

(g) a radio announcer who has looked for work for several months, would like to work, but has now given up hope of ever finding a job;

(h) the spouse of a wealthy person who stays at home and reads the want ads occasionally to find an interesting job.

5. Classify each of the following into one of the main categories of unemployment: (L.O.2)

(a) high school graduates looking for their first jobs;

(b) coal miners who have been dismissed because of a permanent decline in the demand for coal;

(c) construction workers who have been laid off for the winter;

(d) workers who have been dismissed because of a general decrease in the total demand for goods and services;

(e) workers who have been dismissed because of automation.

6. Table 23.4 contains data for the Canadian economy.

TABLE 23.4	Year	Price index
GDP implicit price indexes.	1950	18.3
	1955	21.7
	1960	24.1
	1965	26.5
	1970	32.8
	1975	49.0
	1980	73.0
	1985	97.6
	1987	104.8
	1989	114.9
	1991	121.9

Plot the data on a graph, and use your graph to comment on inflation in Canada from 1950 to 1991. (L.O.8)

7. Table 23.5 contains data on the CPI for Canada from 1977 to 1991. Calculate the value (purchasing power) of the Canadian dollar in each year from 1977 to 1991, and fill in the last column of the table. (L.O.8)

TABLE 23.5	Year	CPI	Purchasing power of $ at 1986 prices
CPI for Canada, 1977–91.	1977	51.3	
	1978	55.9	
	1979	61.0	
	1980	67.2	
	1981	75.5	
	1982	83.7	
	1983	88.5	
	1984	92.4	
	1985	96.0	
	1986	100.0	$1.00
	1987	104.4	
	1988	108.6	
	1989	114.0	
	1990	119.5	
	1991	126.2	

8. The rate of inflation in an economy has been relatively high for a number of years. A group of economists known as Ignoreconomists have been advising households to purchase financial assets in order to protect themselves from the effects of inflation. What is wrong with their advice? (L.O.9)

9. "Minimum wage legislation only creates unemployment. All provinces should repeal their minimum wage laws and allow market forces to determine the wage rate." Discuss.

Internet Site

http://www.statcan.ca
This, of course, is the Web site for Statistics Canada that you visited in Chapter 22.

INTERNET EXERCISE

1. Go to the Statistics Canada site.
2. Click on *Canadian Statistics*.
3. Click on *The Economy in Detail*.
4. Click on *Economic conditions*.
5. Click on *Consumer price index, ... Canada and provinces*.
6. Select your province and record its inflation rate.

C H A P T E R

AGGREGATE DEMAND AND AGGREGATE SUPPLY

To the extent that increased spending can be brought about, it will either raise prices or expand business activity, or both.

Edward Chamberlin, *The Economics of Recovery Program.*

INTRODUCTION

When we use the terms demand and supply, markets come to mind. You will recall that in our overview of the economy in Chapter 21, we discussed the three basic markets of macroeconomic concern: the product market, the labour market, and the financial market. In this chapter, our business is to understand how demand and supply for all goods and services interact in the product market to determine the volume of output and the price level. One of the objectives of macroeconomic theory is to help us understand the behaviour of total output (GDP), employment, and the price level. If we understand the factors that cause movements in these variables, policymakers, we hope, will be able to implement policies to improve their performance. In Chapter 4, we studied demand and supply for a particular product like school textbooks, and you learned how to use demand and supply curves to analyze the determination of price and output in individual markets. In a similar manner, we can use demand and supply curves for the whole economy to analyze changes in total output and the price level.

First, we will define the concept of aggregate demand and discuss the shape of the aggregate demand curve. Then we will define aggregate supply and study the shape of the aggregate supply curve. We will then be in a position to use these tools to describe the equilibrium level of total real output and the equilibrium price level. Our understanding of inflation and unemployment will improve if we know what causes changes in the price level and in total output.

AGGREGATE DEMAND

Learning Objective 1: understand aggregate demand

Aggregate demand is the total amount of output that will be bought at various price levels.

An aggregate demand curve illustrates aggregate demand.

When we speak of aggregate demand, we refer to the total demand for all goods and services. **Aggregate demand** (AD) refers to the various levels of real output that will be demanded at various price levels. You will notice the analogy between this definition of aggregate demand and the definition of the demand for a single product given in Chapter 4.

THE AGGREGATE DEMAND CURVE

Just as we use a demand curve to portray the demand for an individual good or service, so too, we can use an aggregate demand curve to depict the total demand for all goods and services. The **aggregate demand curve** is a graph showing the various levels of total real output that will be demanded at various price levels. You will probably expect the aggregate demand curve to slope downward since the demand curve for a particular product slopes downward from left to right. That is indeed the case, as is illustrated in Figure 24.1.

As the price level rises, the total amount of real output that will be demanded falls, other things being equal; and as the price level falls, the total amount of real output that will be demanded rises.

Let us review the fundamental reasons for the negative slope of the demand curve for an individual good or service. First, as the price of a good or service falls, consumers tend to purchase a greater quantity of it because it becomes less expensive relative to other goods and services (the substitution effect). Second, as the price of a good or service falls, a given income can purchase a larger quantity of this good or service. In other words, the consumer's real income or purchasing power increases, so it is likely that a greater quantity of this good or service will be bought (the income effect).

It is tempting to think that the aggregate demand curve slopes downward to the right for the same reasons that the demand curve for an individual good or service slopes downward to the right. It is also tempting to think that the aggregate demand curve

The aggregate
demand curve.

As the price level falls, a
greater quantity of real output will be demanded.

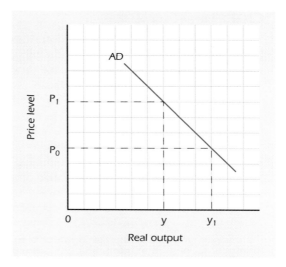

can be obtained by adding up the market demand curves for individual goods and services. These, however, are misconceptions. Although the aggregate demand curve slopes
downward, its shape cannot be explained by the same reasons given for the shape of the
demand curve for an individual good or service. Why not? Let's investigate this in the following section.

REASONS FOR THE SHAPE OF THE AGGREGATE DEMAND CURVE

If the price of a particular commodity rises, consumers will be relatively worse off and
therefore will purchase a smaller quantity of the commodity, given the consumer's
money income. Such is not the case with aggregate demand. If we were to add the
individual demand curves in an attempt to arrive at the aggregate demand curve, we
would be guilty of what is called the **fallacy of composition** — the assumption that what
is true of the parts must also be true of the whole. When the price level rises, factor
prices also rise so that incomes rise too. With larger incomes, more goods and services
can be bought.

The fallacy of composition
is the assumption that what
is true of the part must also
be true of the whole.

The following example will help to illustrate the fallacy of composition. Suppose, for
simplicity, that there are only two products, A and B. If the price of A rises, other things
being equal, consumers are worse off because a given sum of money now buys less
than previously. But if the price of A, the price of B, and income all rise by say 5%,
then consumers on the whole are not worse off.

Why then does the aggregate demand curve slope downward to the right? The price
level, you recall, is an average price of all goods and services. What effect does a rise in
the price level have on the total amount of goods and services that will be demanded?
Let us investigate. Remember that total expenditure or aggregate expenditure (AE) on the
economy's output of goods and services is the sum of consumer spending, investment,
government purchases, and net exports. That is:

$$AE = C + I + G + (X - M)$$

To see the effect of changes in the price level on the total output of goods and services
that will be demanded, we can examine the effect of changes in the price level on the
components of aggregate expenditure.

First, an increase in the price level means that, on average, everything that households and firms have to buy is now more expensive. Hence, households and firms need more money to make these purchases. This increase in the demand for money, other things being equal, causes interest rates to rise. When interest rates rise, it is more costly to borrow money, so firms that borrow funds to invest in capital goods reduce their spending. Thus investment falls. Also, consumers who borrow money to purchase items such as automobiles, furniture, household appliances, and vacations reduce their purchases of these items. (These issues will be further explored in later chapters.) We can conclude that as the price level rises, the C and I components of AE fall. This fall in AE implies that less of the total output will be demanded. The effect of changes in interest rates on C and I is often referred to as the *interest rate effect.*

Second, an increase in the price level in Canada means that, on average, Canadian goods are now more expensive in foreign countries than before the price level increase, and foreign goods are less expensive to Canadians. Other things being equal, Canadians will buy more foreign goods, and foreign countries will buy fewer Canadian goods. Thus, as the price level rises, the (X – M) component of aggregate expenditure falls; this fall implies that less of the total output will be demanded. This is called the *trade effect.*

Third, as the price level rises, holders of financial assets such as savings accounts and bonds lose purchasing power. Their real wealth decreases. This decrease in real wealth results in a fall in expenditures on consumer goods and services. In other words, as the price level rises, the C component of aggregate expenditure falls; and this fall implies that less of the total output will be demanded. This is called the *wealth effect.*

FACTORS THAT SHIFT THE AD CURVE

You should note that changes in the price level will not cause the AD curve to shift; instead, they will cause movements along the curve (recall the discussion on the demand curve in Chapter 4). An increase in aggregate demand means that at any given price level, a greater quantity of total output is demanded. The AD curve will shift if there is a change in aggregate expenditure (AE). Thus, if any of the components of AE changes, then the AD curve will shift. For example, an increase in government spending, a decrease in imports, or an increase in investment will raise AE and cause the AD curve to shift to the right, as shown in Diagram A of Figure 24.2. A decrease in government

FIGURE 24.2

Changes in aggregate demand.

An increase in aggregate demand is shown by a shift in the AD curve to the right.

A decrease in aggregate demand is shown by a shift in the AD curve to the left.

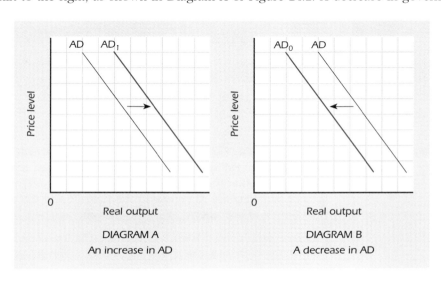

DIAGRAM A
An increase in AD

DIAGRAM B
A decrease in AD

spending, an increase in imports, or a fall in investment will cause the AD curve to shift to the left, as shown in Diagram B of Figure 24.2.

ANALYSIS OF AD SHIFTERS

Let us look again at the components of aggregate expenditure (AE).

$$AE = C + I + G + (X - M)$$

Anything other than changes in the price level that affects any of the components of AE will cause the AD curve to shift. In this section, we shall identify some major AD shifters (or demand-side shocks) and briefly analyze their effects on AD. We begin our analysis with consumption.

Consumption

What are some of the non-price level determinants of consumer spending? Consumer wealth, taxes, expectations and interest rates are good candidates.

Consumer wealth   If the price level remains constant and consumer wealth increases, perhaps because of an increase in property values, then consumers will tend to increase their spending, increasing AE and thus shifting the AD curve to the right. Similarly, a fall in property values reduces consumer wealth, reduces consumption and shifts the AD curve to the left.

Taxes   A fall in personal income taxes increases disposable income (take-home pay). At each price level, consumers are able to purchase more goods and services, so AE increases and the AD curve shifts to the right. Tax hikes will reduce consumer spending, lower AE, and shift the AD curve to the left.

Expectations   If consumers have good reasons to be optimistic about their immediate future economic circumstances, they will increase their current consumption, increasing AE and shifting the AD curve to the right. If they expect their real income to fall, they will reduce their current consumption and thus cause the AD curve to shift to the left.

Interest rates   Certain types of consumer spending are sensitive to changes in interest rates. If the price level remains constant and interest rates fall, consumer loans become more affordable and consumers will tend to borrow more to purchase items such as automobiles, furniture and appliances, and vacation packages. Thus, falling interest rates increase consumer spending and shift the AD curve to the right. Similarly, rising interest rates will lower consumer spending and shift the AD curve to the left.

Investment

Investment refers to the purchase of capital goods and is an important component of AE. If investment changes, other things being equal, then AE will change and the AD curve will shift. Important non-price level determinants of investment spending include interest rates, changes in income, perceived profitability of investment projects, and technological advance.

Interest rates   Falling interest rates, given the price level, reduce the cost of acquiring investment funds and thus increase investment spending. More investment means more AE, which shifts the AD curve to the right. Rising interest rates will reduce investment spending and shift the AD curve to the left.

Changes in income   With a constant price level, an increase in income causes consumers to purchase more goods and services. This increase in demand for goods and services will likely lead to investment by firms, unless they have excess capacity. The AD curve will then shift to the right.

Perceived profitability of investment projects   If business people perceive investment projects to be profitable, they will likely invest in those projects, raising AE and shifting the AD curve to the right. On the other hand, if the prospects for profitable investment opportunities appear to be gloomy, investment spending will fall and the AD curve will shift to the left.

Technological advance   Increases in technology open up new investment opportunities. Just consider the vast investment expenditures that have been made as a direct result of increases in computer technology. Such technological advances increase investment and cause the AD curve to shift to the right.

Government Spending

An increase in government purchases of goods and services at each price level will increase AE and shift the AD curve to the right, other things being equal. For example, if the federal government purchases a new fleet of helicopters to replace an aging fleet, AE will rise and the AD curve will shift to the right. Reductions in government spending in the areas of health and education, for example, will reduce AE and cause the AD curve to shift to the left.

Net Exports

Any non-price level factor that affects exports (X) or imports (M) will affect net exports (X – M) and shift the AD curve. If, for example, income in the U.S. increases, Americans will purchase more Canadian goods, so Canada's exports to the U.S. will increase. Other things being equal, this increase in Canada's exports will increase AE and shift the AD curve to the right. If the value of the Canadian dollar falls in terms of the U.S. dollar, thus making Canadian goods more attractive to Americans, Canadian exports to the U.S. will rise. At the same time, U.S. goods will be relatively more expensive to Canadians, so Canadian imports from the U.S. will fall. This means that (X-M) will rise, AE will increase, and the AD curve will shift to the right.

AGGREGATE SUPPLY

Learning Objective 2:
understand aggregate supply

Aggregate supply is the levels of output supplied at various price levels.

By aggregate supply we mean the total supply of all goods and services. **Aggregate supply** (AS) refers to the various levels of real output that will be supplied at various price levels. Note again that the definition of aggregate supply is analogous to the definition of the supply of an individual good or service. As might be expected, the aggregate supply curve slopes upward from left to right. This signifies that, other things being equal, as the price level rises, the total output of goods and services supplied increases; and as the price level falls, other things being equal, the total output of goods and services supplied decreases.

Can we derive the aggregate supply curve by adding the supply curves of all the individual commodities? No. Just as it would be erroneous to try to derive the aggregate demand curve by adding the demand curves for individual commodities together, so too would it be erroneous to attempt to derive the aggregate supply curve by adding together the supply curves of individual goods and services. In constructing the supply curve of an individual commodity, only the price of the commodity being studied is allowed to vary. But in constructing the aggregate supply curve, the average level of all prices is allowed to vary.

THE AGGREGATE SUPPLY CURVE

An aggregate supply curve illustrates the total supply of goods and services.

The aggregate supply curve can be used to illustrate the total supply of all goods and services in much the same way as a supply curve can be used to depict the supply of an individual good or service. The **aggregate supply curve** is a graph showing the various levels of real output that will be supplied at various price levels. You would probably expect the aggregate supply curve to be upward sloping, simply because the supply curve of an individual good or service is upward sloping. In fact, the aggregate supply curve may be upward sloping. But as we shall see shortly, certain sections of the aggregate supply curve may have different shapes.

REASONS FOR THE SHAPE OF THE AGGREGATE SUPPLY CURVE

The aggregate supply curve may be divided into three sections or ranges as shown in Figure 24.3.

FIGURE 24.3

The aggregate supply curve.

The aggregate supply curve may have a horizontal section, an intermediate section, and a vertical section.

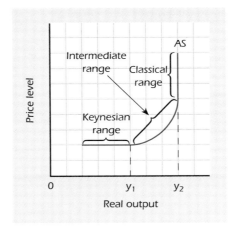

For a level of real output from 0 to y_1, the aggregate supply curve is horizontal (flat). For output levels between y_1 and y_2, it is upward sloping, and when output reaches y_2, the aggregate supply curve becomes vertical. Let us investigate the reasons for the existence of these three ranges of the aggregate supply curve.

The horizontal section

The horizontal section of an AS curve, the Keynesian range, represents high unemployment.

If the economy is operating at low levels of real output and employment, it will be possible to increase real output without any increase in the price level. This horizontal section of the aggregate supply curve is called the **Keynesian range** since it represents substantial unemployment, a topic of great concern to John Maynard Keynes during the Great Depression of the 1930s. Because there are significant amounts of unemployed workers and other resources which can be used to increase real output, average cost will tend to be constant as output increases. And since average cost is constant, firms do not need to receive higher prices for their output in order to induce them to increase production.

The intermediate section

As output continues to increase beyond y_1, factor inputs will become relatively more scarce. Competition among firms for the (now) scarcer inputs will bid up input prices and increase production costs. Firms will have to receive higher prices to induce them to expand production. Also, as output expands, an increasing number of industries will approach their capacities, making it increasingly difficult and costly to continue to increase output. Thus, in this **intermediate range**, there is a direct relationship between real output and the price level. The aggregate supply curve is upward sloping in this section. As output rises, the AS curve becomes steeper.

In the intermediate (upward sloping) range of an AS curve, real output and price level are related.

The vertical section

Once the full employment level of real output is reached (at y_2), it is virtually impossible to increase output beyond that level, regardless of the increase in the price level. Hence, the aggregate supply curve becomes vertical. This vertical section of the aggregate supply curve is called the **classical range** because it relates to the situation with which the classical economists were concerned. You will recall that in Chapter 22, you learned that the classical economists believed that the economy would tend to operate at full employment.

In the classical (vertical) range of an AS curve, output is at a maximum.

> ### COMMENT 24-1
>
> The horizontal (Keynesian) range and the vertical (classical) range are generally regarded as extreme cases, rather than as exact descriptions of how the economy behaves. Nevertheless, there are times when the economy may be operating well below capacity and it may then be possible to increase output without exerting much upward pressure on prices. There are also times when the economy is operating at high levels of output. At such times, further output expansion may be extremely difficult and will exert upward pressure on prices. Of course, it will be possible to squeeze a little more output out of existing resources by running the machines a little harder and by employing labour resources overtime. The Keynesian and classical ranges of the aggregate supply curve are intended as approximations of these situations.

FACTORS THAT SHIFT THE AS CURVE

Recall that a change in the price of a particular commodity will not shift the supply curve. So too, a change in the price level will not shift the aggregate supply curve. The aggregate supply curve is based on the behaviour of all the firms that produce the total output of goods and services. If the costs of production change, then at any given price level, the firms will produce a different volume of output. A reduction in production costs will cause the AS curve to shift to the right as shown in Diagram A of Figure 24.4, while an increase in costs will cause it to shift upward to the left as shown in Diagram B of Figure 24.4. A national disaster such as an earthquake may also cause the AS curve to shift.

ANALYSIS OF AS SHIFTERS

The economy's total output of goods and services is produced by numerous firms operating under different conditions. Non-price level factors that affect the firms' decisions will affect the AS curve. These supply-side shocks include production costs, changes in resources, changes in technology, tax policies, and natural disasters.

Production Costs

As noted earlier, changes in the costs of production will cause the AS curve to shift. For example, if labour costs increase because of a shortage of labour, firms will observe a significant increase in their production costs. Or if the price of an important input

FIGURE 24.4

Changes in aggregate supply.

An increase in aggregate supply is shown by a shift in the AS curve to the right.

A decrease in aggregate supply is shown by an upward shift in the AS curve to the left.

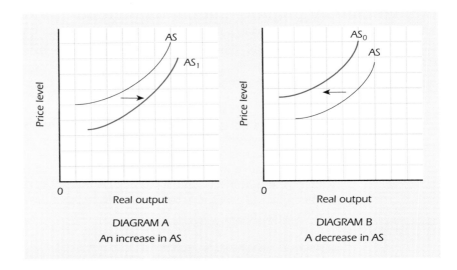

such as oil increases, production cost will rise. Such increases in costs will shift the AS curve to the left. Cost reductions will shift the AS curve to the right.

Changes in Resources

If an economy acquires more resources (land, labour, capital, and entrepreneurial ability), then its AS curve will shift to the right. If resources are destroyed, then its AS curve will shift to the left. For example, other things being equal, Canada's AS curve will shift to the right if it adopts a more liberal immigration stance and allows more immigrants to take up residence in Canada. On the other hand, the destruction of the fish stock through overfishing or pollution will shift the AS curve to the left.

Changes in Technology

Technological advances enhance a country's ability to produce goods and services. If Canada develops technologies that allow firms to use their resources more productively, the economy will be able to obtain a greater volume of output from given resources, and the AS curve will shift to the right.

Tax Policies

Tax policies that are favourable to business will shift the AS curve to the right, while unfavourable or hostile tax policies will shift the AS curve to the left. A reduction in business taxes reduces the cost of doing business and thus shifts the AS curve to the right. On the other hand, some economists believe that the introduction of the goods and services tax (GST) in Canada in 1991 shifted the AS curve to the left.

Natural and Other Disasters

Earthquakes, tornadoes, hurricanes, and other natural disasters can seriously hamper the economy's ability to produce goods and services; so too can forest fires, severe and prolonged droughts, and insects and diseases. These occurrences will shift the AS curve to the left.

SUMMARY OF AD AND AS SHIFTERS

AD Shifters

1. Consumption
   a) consumer wealth
   b) taxes
   c) expectations
   d) interest rates

2. Investment
   a) interest rates
   b) changes in income
   c) perceived profitability of investment projects
   d) technological advance

3. Government Spending

4. Net Exports
   a) increases in income abroad
   b) changes in exchange rates

AS Shifters

1. Production Costs
   a) labour costs
   b) changes in other input prices

2. Changes in Resources
   a) land
   b) labour
   c) capital
   d) entrepreneurial ability

3. Changes in Technology

4. Tax Policies

5. Natural and other Disasters

EQUILIBRIUM REAL OUTPUT AND THE PRICE LEVEL

Learning Objective 3:
explain the determination of equilibrium real output and the price level

We can now bring aggregate demand and aggregate supply together to see how the equilibrium level of real output and the price level are simultaneously determined. This is done in Figure 24.5.

The analysis here parallels that presented in Chapter 4 where we discussed the equilibrium price and output in the market for a single product. Any price level above P (such as P_1) results in the production of an output level which exceeds the total amount that will be demanded at that price level. Consequently, the price level and real output will tend to fall. Any price level below P (such as P_0) will result in a lower level of production than the economy's customers are willing to purchase at that price level. Consequently, the price level and real output will tend to increase. But at a price level

FIGURE 24.5

Equilibrium output and the price level.

The equilibrium level of real output and the price level occur at the intersection of the aggregate demand and the aggregate supply curves.

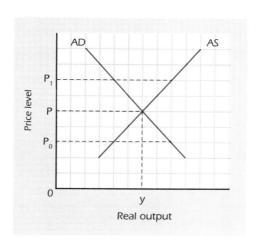

of P, the total amount of all goods and services that will be demanded just equals the total amount of all goods and services that will be supplied. Hence, P is the **equilibrium price level** and y is the **equilibrium level of real output**.

EFFECTS OF CHANGES IN AGGREGATE DEMAND

Learning Objective 4: *discuss the effects of changes in aggregate demand*

What effects do changes in aggregate demand have on real income and the price level? This depends on the shape of the aggregate supply curve where the aggregate demand curve intersects it. If the aggregate supply curve slopes upward when it cuts the aggregate demand curve, as shown in Figure 24.6, then an increase in aggregate demand, other things being equal, will cause the price level and real output to rise. An increase in aggregate demand is shown by an upward shift of the aggregate demand curve from AD to AD_1. This results in a rise in the price level from P to P_1, and an increase in real output from y to y_1.

FIGURE 24.6

The effect of an increase in AD in the intermediate range.

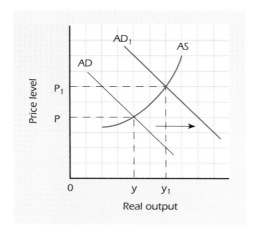

An increase in aggregate demand in the intermediate range results in an increase in the price level and an increase in real output.

But suppose that the AS curve is horizontal (that is, in the Keynesian range) as shown by Figure 24.7. An increase in aggregate demand from AD to AD_1 results in an increase in real output from y_0 to y_1, while the price level remains unchanged at P. This is due to the existence of a considerable amount of unused resources, which allows the production of more output without any increase in prices. Finally, if the AS curve is vertical (that is, in the classical range), as shown in Figure 24.8, an increase in aggregate demand from AD_2 to AD_3 results in an increase in the price level from P_1 to P_2. But note that no increase in real output occurs, because the economy is operating at the full employment level of output, y_f. You can easily work out the effects of a decrease in aggregate demand in each of the three sections of the aggregate supply curve.

DEMAND-SIDE POLICIES

The government can shift the AD curve through its monetary and fiscal policies.

We have seen that changes in aggregate demand can affect real output and the price level, depending on the shape of the aggregate supply curve. The government can affect aggregate expenditure and can therefore shift the aggregate demand curve to the right or to the left. The government has two main policies that it can use to affect the AD curve — fiscal policy and monetary policy. **Fiscal policy** refers to changes in government spending and taxes, designed to change aggregate demand. **Monetary policy** refers

FIGURE 24.7

The effects of an increase in AD in the Keynesian range.

An increase in aggregate demand in the Keynesian range results in an increase in real output, but no change in the price level.

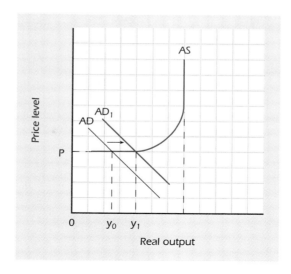

FIGURE 24.8

The effects of an increase in AD in the classical range.

An increase in aggregate demand in the classical range results in an increase in the price level, but no change in real output.

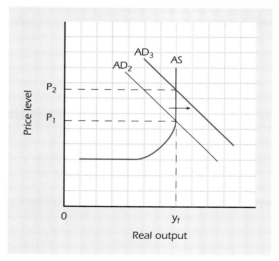

to changes in the money supply and interest rates in an attempt to influence aggregate demand. Because monetary and fiscal policies are so important in macroeconomics, we will spend a great deal of time in later chapters studying these policies.

Since government purchases of goods and services (G) are a component of AE, the government can shift the AD curve by changing its own spending. For example, it can shift the AD curve to the right by increasing its own spending, and/or by using its taxing powers to encourage consumers and firms to increase their spending. Also, the government, through the central bank (the Bank of Canada), can shift the AD curve to the right by lowering interest rates. Lower interest rates will stimulate investment and consumer spending and thus increase AE.

GOVERNMENT POLICIES TO REDUCE UNEMPLOYMENT

Let us suppose that the economy is experiencing substantial unemployment (a 20% unemployment rate, for example), like the situation that existed in the early 1930s during the Great Depression. The economy would thus be operating at a level of real output well below its potential. Such a situation is illustrated in Figure 24.9, where the economy is operating at an output level of y_0 within the horizontal section of the AS curve. The aggregate demand is AD_0. In order to move the economy towards full employment, the government can shift the aggregate demand curve from AD_0 to AD_1 by using its monetary and fiscal policies. Note that because the economy is operating substantially below capacity, the expansionary demand policies of the government will not exert any significant upward pressure on the price level.

FIGURE 24.9

Government policies to reduce unemployment.

Expansionary demand policies can reduce unemployment.

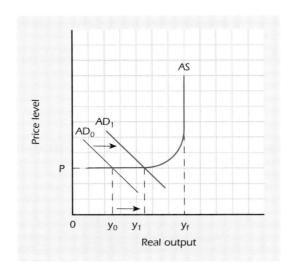

GOVERNMENT POLICIES TO REDUCE INFLATION

In the same way that monetary and fiscal policies can be used to shift the AD curve to the right, so too can they be used to shift the AD curve to the left. Suppose that the economy is going through a severe bout of inflation, such as occurred in Canada in the 1970s. (In 1974, the inflation rate as measured by the consumer price index was almost 11%.) The situation may be illustrated by Figure 24.10, where the economy is operating in the vertical section of the AS curve (the classical range).

The initial price level is P_1 with aggregate demand at AD. In order to lower the price level and relieve the inflationary pressure, the government can shift the aggregate demand curve from AD to AD_0, by using its monetary and fiscal policies. Specifically, through the Bank of Canada, the government can raise interest rates. Higher interest rates will tend to reduce the investment and consumption components of AE. The government can also reduce its own spending and raise taxes to reduce consumer spending. Such contractionary demand policies will reduce AE and thus shift the aggregate demand curve to the left. The result is a fall in the price level from P_1 to P_0 in Figure 24.10.

You probably realize that monetary and fiscal policies to combat unemployment and inflation are more complicated than presented here. Subsequent chapters will present more detailed accounts of monetary and fiscal policies and how they can be used to improve the performance of the economy.

FIGURE 24.10

Government policies to
reduce inflation.

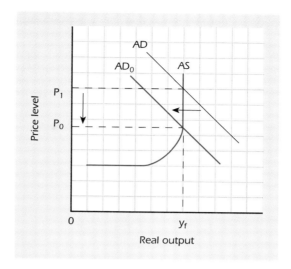

Contractionary demand
policies can reduce
inflation.

EFFECTS OF CHANGES IN AGGREGATE SUPPLY

The price of an individual good or service and the quantity demanded and supplied of
that good or service can change if the supply curve for that good or service shifts. So too,
the price level and real output of all goods and services will change if the aggregate
supply curve shifts. In this section, we shall examine the effects of changes in aggregate
supply on real output and the price level. Aggregate supply changes as a result of a
supply-side shock such as a crop failure and/or a change in production costs. An increase
in aggregate supply causes the aggregate supply curve to shift to the right, while a
decrease in aggregate supply causes the aggregate supply curve to shift to the left. An
improvement in technology or an increase in productivity, for example, will cause the
aggregate supply curve to shift to the right, signifying that a greater quantity of real output will be supplied at each price level than before.

Changes in production
costs, technology, and
productivity can shift the
aggregate supply curve.

Learning Objective 5:
discuss the effects
of changes in aggregate
supply

Let us assume that the economy is in equilibrium in the intermediate range, as
shown in Figure 24.11. The equilibrium level of real output is y and the price level is P.
An increase in aggregate supply from AS to AS_1 causes real output to rise from y to y_1
and the price level to fall from P to P_0.

FIGURE 24.11

The effect of an
increase in aggregate
supply.

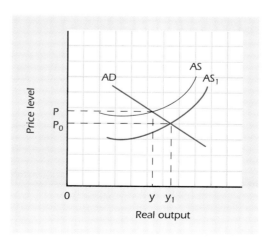

An increase in AS results in
an increase in real output
and a fall in the price level.

Suppose now that the aggregate supply curve shifts to the left because of a global shortage of an important input such as oil which pushes production costs up. The effect of such a shift is illustrated in Figure 24.12. The initial aggregate demand and aggregate supply curves are AD and AS respectively. A shift in the aggregate supply curve from AS to AS_1 results in an increase in the price level from P to P_1, and a fall in real output from y to y_0.

FIGURE 24.12

The effect of a decrease in aggregate supply.

A decrease in AS results in a fall in real output and a rise in the price level.

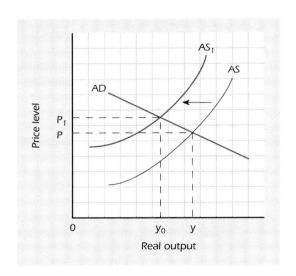

SUPPLY-SIDE POLICIES

Supply-side economics stresses incentives to work, save and invest.

During the Reagan administration, we heard a great deal about supply-side economics. The purpose of this section is to help you to understand the fundamental argument of **supply-side economics**. Keynesian economics emphasizes the management of aggregate demand by controlling the components of aggregate expenditure. Supply-side economics, on the other hand, is concerned mainly with policies to influence the supply side, that is, the AS curve, by affecting incentives to work, save, and invest.

Learning Objective 6: discuss the policy implications of the AD-AS model

Our analysis of changes in aggregate demand in a previous section of this chapter suggests that a reduction in aggregate demand may result in an increase in unemployment. So, instead of shifting aggregate demand to reduce prices, supply-side economists prefer to stimulate aggregate supply. The thinking is that unemployment and inflation can be solved by greater productivity and growth in real output.

The marginal tax rate is the ratio of the change in taxes to the change in income.

The concept of the marginal tax rate is important for an understanding of supply-side policies. The **marginal tax rate** (MTR) is the change in tax receipts resulting from a change in income. That is,

$$MTR = \frac{\Delta T}{\Delta Y}$$

where T represents taxes and Y represents income. A marginal tax rate of 0.3 means that an increase in income of $100 million will result in an increase in taxes of $30 million.

Learning Objective 7: understand the basis of supply-side policies

Supporters of supply-side economics favour changing taxes, reducing government deficit spending, and deregulating industries to stimulate the supply side of the economy. Tax cuts designed to encourage consumer saving provide funds for business investment. Lower marginal tax rates provide an incentive for workers to do extra work since the extra income earned is not as heavily taxed as before the tax cut. Greater investment tax credits and lower business taxes encourage capital investment. Relieving business enterprises from many of the burdens of government regulation and reducing the level of government deficit spending provide greater scope for business activity. All these measures, according to supply-siders, increase productivity and therefore shift the AS curve to the right.

The Laffer curve helps to explain supply-side philosophy.

The **Laffer curve** discussed in Chapter 18 and shown here as Figure 24.13 helps to explain the argument of supply-side economists. A tax rate of t_1 is so high that it discourages work effort. A reduction in the tax rate from t_1 to t will provide incentives for people to work harder and thus increase total output. This increase in total output (income) will result in greater tax revenues. In the view of supply-siders, the current combination of tax rate and tax revenues lies on the declining portion of the Laffer curve.

FIGURE 24.13

The Laffer curve.

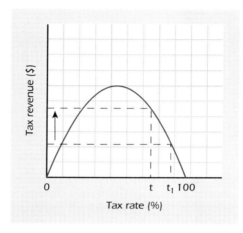

How effective are supply-side policies? Supply-side economists contend that supply-side measures to increase incentives have significant effects on growth and productivity. Critics of supply-side economics claim that the effects of supply-side policies on labour supply, saving, and investment are likely to be quite small. Nobel laureate Paul Samuelson, who has had a long association with the Massachusetts Institute of Technology, is particularly critical of supply-side economics. He claims that the 1982 recession in the United States was attributable to the failure of supply-side policies. The effectiveness of supply-side policies continues to be a controversial issue.

There is considerable controversy over the effectiveness of government supply-side policies.

 A P P L I C A T I O N

Reducing the Deficit

The budget deficit is defined as the amount by which government expenditures exceed tax revenues. Clearly, the deficit will be reduced by reducing government spending, by raising taxes, or by using some combination of both. But the Laffer curve suggests that it may be possible to reduce the deficit by reducing taxes, that is, the tax rate. If a reduction in the tax rate increases work effort, then increases in output and income may result, and this could lead to an increase in tax revenues for the government, and a reduction in the budget deficit.

CHAPTER SUMMARY

1. Aggregate demand refers to the various amounts of real output of all goods and services that will be demanded at various price levels. The aggregate demand curve slopes downward, indicating that a smaller quantity of all goods and services will be demanded as the price level rises.

2. The fallacy of composition arises when we assume that what is true for an individual or a part is true automatically for the whole.

3. The AD curve will shift if any of the components of aggregate expenditure changes. It will not shift as a result of changes in the price level.

4. Aggregate supply refers to the various quantities of real output that will be supplied at various price levels.

5. The aggregate supply curve may have three sections: a horizontal (Keynesian) section, a rising (intermediate) section, and a vertical (classical) section.

6. The aggregate supply curve will shift in response to supply-side shocks such as changes in production costs, technology, crop failure, etc. It will not shift as a result of changes in the price level.

7. The equilibrium level of real output and the price level are simultaneously determined by the intersection of the aggregate demand and aggregate supply curves.

8. The effect of an increase in aggregate demand depends on the shape of the aggregate supply curve. Government can use its monetary and fiscal policies to shift the aggregate demand curve in an attempt to reduce unemployment and inflation.

9. Aggregate supply shocks such as a shortage of an important input can cause the aggregate supply curve to shift to the left. An improvement in technology or an increase in productivity can cause the aggregate supply curve to shift to the right.

10. An increase in aggregate supply can reduce the price level and increase real output. A reduction in aggregate supply can raise the price level and reduce real output.

11. Supply-side economics emphasizes changes in supply as a means of solving inflation and unemployment problems. Tax measures and other means of affecting incentives to work, save, and invest are stressed by supply-siders.

12. There is a lively ongoing debate between supporters and critics of supply-side economics regarding the effects of supply-side policies on real output.

TERMS FOR REVIEW

aggregate demand (409)
aggregate demand curve (409)
fallacy of composition (410)
aggregate supply (413)
aggregate supply curve (414)
Keynesian range (of the AS curve) (414)
classical range (of the AS curve) (415)
intermediate range (of the AS curve) (415)

equilibrium real output and the price level (418)
fiscal policy (418)
monetary policy (418)
supply-side economics (422)
marginal tax rate (MTR) (422)
Laffer curve (423)

QUESTIONS FOR REVIEW AND DISCUSSION

1. What is meant by aggregate demand? (L.O.1)
2. What is the aggregate demand curve? (L.O.1)

3. What is the fallacy of composition? Give an example to illustrate the fallacy. (General)

4. Explain why the aggregate demand curve cannot be derived by adding all the demand curves for individual goods and services. (L.O.1)

5. Explain the shape of the aggregate demand curve (i.e., why does it slope downward to the right?). (L.O.1)

6. What is meant by aggregate supply? (L.O.2)

7. What is the aggregate supply curve? (L.O.2)

8. Explain the three ranges of the aggregate supply curve. (L.O.2)

9. Use aggregate demand-aggregate supply analysis to explain the determination of aggregate real output and the price level. (L.O.3)

10. Explain how the government can use monetary and fiscal policies to combat (L.O.6)
    (a) inflation
    (b) unemployment

11. Discuss the basic argument of supply-side economists. (L.O.7)

PROBLEMS AND EXERCISES

1. Table 24.1 contains data for the economy of Aggregatia (a hypothetical economy). (L.O.1,2)

TABLE 24.1

Data for the economy of Aggregatia.

Price level (index)	Quantity of real output demanded ($million)	Quantity of real output supplied ($million)
92	80	20
96	70	30
100	60	40
104	50	50
108	40	60
112	30	70
116	20	80
120	10	90

(a) Draw the aggregate demand curve.

(b) On the same graph, draw the aggregate supply curve.

(c) Use your graph to determine the equilibrium price level and the equilibrium real output.

2. Referring to the data in Table 24.1, suppose the quantity of real output increases by $20 million at each and every price level, while the aggregate supply remains unchanged. (L.O.3)

(a) Graph the original and the new aggregate demand curves.

(b) On the same diagram, graph the original aggregate supply curve.

(c) From your diagram, determine the equilibrium level of real output and the corresponding price level.

3. Assume that an economy is operating in the intermediate range of the aggregate supply curve. Use diagrams to show the effect of each of the following on the economy's equilibrium real output and price level. (L.O.3)

(a) Firms become optimistic and increase their investment spending.

(b) A tax cut increases personal disposable income.

(c) The discovery of an important productive input reduces production costs.

(d) Active research results in an overall improvement in technology.

(e) Labour becomes more productive, and workers are successfully induced to work harder.

(f) Americans increase their purchases of Canadian goods.

4. Use aggregate demand and aggregate supply curves to show that expansionary monetary and fiscal policies need not be inflationary. Under what circumstances will these expansionary demand policies most likely be inflationary? (L.O.6)

5. Under what circumstances would you advocate the following?

(a) a contractionary demand policy

(b) an expansionary demand policy

6. Supply-side economists support tax cuts as a means of providing incentive to work. Draw a Laffer curve and indicate on the curve the situation assumed by supply-side economists. (L.O.7)

C H A P T E R

EQUILIBRIUM IN THE PRODUCT MARKET

Learning Objectives

After studying this chapter, you should be able to:

1 understand how households and firms interact in the product market to determine the level of income

2 describe the relation between income and consumption

3 distinguish between ex ante and ex post concepts

4 understand the saving-income relation

5 integrate the aggregate expenditure-aggregate output and the injections-withdrawals approaches

Once the fundamental ideas are clear, the rest falls easily into place.
Dudley Dillard, *The Economics of John Maynard Keynes.*

INTRODUCTION

In our overview of the macroeconomy in Chapter 21, we noted that households, firms, and the government interact in three markets. In this chapter, we develop a model of a simple economy that will form the basis for more complicated models. Here we will study how households and firms interact in the product market. In later chapters, we will study the financial market and the determination of the rate of interest.

The AD-AS model developed in Chapter 24 is highly aggregated. The present chapter is our starting point in getting behind the curves in the AD-AS model. Many of the concepts and ideas used in this chapter were developed by Keynes.

A SIMPLE KEYNESIAN MODEL OF INCOME DETERMINATION

SIMPLIFYING ASSUMPTIONS

To explain the determination of the equilibrium level of income in the product market with the Keynesian model, it is helpful to make some simplifying assumptions. We will relax these assumptions as we extend the model in subsequent chapters. For the moment, however, we assume that:

A closed economy does not engage in foreign trade.

1. we are dealing with a **closed economy** (i.e., there are neither exports nor imports);

2. there are no government expenditures and there are no taxes and government transfer payments;

3. households' spending and saving decisions depend only on their incomes;

Autonomous investment is independent of income.

4. firms decide to spend a fixed amount for new investment (net investment) each period, and the amount does not depend on the level of income. In other words, investment is **autonomous** (i.e., independent of income);

5. the economy is operating with unemployed labour and other resources;

6. the price level is constant. Relative prices may change because of changes in demand and supply in individual markets, but the average level of prices remains unchanged.

Because assumptions 5 and 6 resemble the situation in which the economy is operating in the Keynesian (horizontal) range of the aggregate supply curve, we refer to this model as the Keynesian model. In presenting this simple Keynesian model, we will follow two alternative approaches: the aggregate expenditure-aggregate output approach and the injections-withdrawals approach. To facilitate your understanding of the process of equilibrium income determination, we will present the analysis in arithmetical, tabular and graphical forms.

EX ANTE AND EX POST CONCEPTS

Ex ante concepts rather than ex post concepts are relevant in the process of equilibrium income determination.

Learning Objective 3: *distinguish between ex ante and ex post concepts*

In discussing the forces that lead to macroequilibrium, we must understand the distinction between ex ante and ex post concepts. The latin phrases **ex ante** and **ex post** mean *before the fact* and *after the fact* respectively. Ex ante concepts relate to plans or intentions; ex post concepts relate to realized or actual (historical) facts. In an ex post sense, total expenditure on the economy's output of goods and services must be equal to the total value of that output. Thus, we have the following identity:

$$\text{Total expenditure} \equiv \text{Value of total output}$$

This identity holds for any level of income or output. While the above expression is a tautology in an ex post sense, that is not the case in an ex ante sense. Households and firms may plan to spend more or less than the total output of the economy; hence total desired expenditure need not be equal to total output. You will see also that the plans of households and firms may not always be realized. When we discuss equilibrium income (output), it is ex ante concepts that are relevant.

THE AGGREGATE EXPENDITURE-AGGREGATE OUTPUT APPROACH

Learning Objective 1: understand how households and firms interact in the product market to determine the level of income

Aggregate expenditure is the total spending in an economy.

Aggregate output is the total production of goods and services in an economy.

In this simple Keynesian model, national income and personal disposable income are assumed to be the same. We shall use Y to denote income or output. Note that the terms used here are **aggregate expenditure** (AE) and **aggregate output** (AO) rather than *aggregate demand* (AD) and *aggregate supply* (AS). Aggregate expenditure and aggregate output mean simply *total spending* and *total production* respectively, whereas aggregate demand and aggregate supply relate total quantities demanded and total quantities supplied to the price level (see Chapter 24).

Since we are dealing here with a hypothetical economy in which there is no foreign trade and in which government neither spends nor taxes, aggregate expenditure is the sum of consumption spending (C) and investment spending (I). That is,

$$AE = C + I$$

The other components of AE are all zero by assumption.

ARITHMETICAL ANALYSIS

Suppose that, at a current output of $70 million, consumers plan to spend $65 million on consumer goods and services, while firms plan to purchase $10 million worth of investment goods. Desired aggregate expenditure will exceed current output of goods and services. This excess expenditure may result in a reduction of inventories of goods previously produced, or in queues of unsatisfied buyers. In either case, there is a clear signal that a greater quantity of output could have been sold if it were produced. Since we have assumed that all resources are not fully employed, the firms can be expected to respond to this signal by increasing production. This, of course, means an increase in income. Thus:

> **If desired aggregate expenditure exceeds aggregate output, inventories will fall below desired levels. Firms will then tend to increase their production, and the level of income will tend to rise.**

Let us now investigate the situation in which desired aggregate expenditure falls short of aggregate output. Suppose that, at an output of $90 million, consumers plan to spend $75 million on consumer goods and services, while firms plan to invest $10 million. This total desired expenditure of $85 million is not enough to allow the firms to sell their entire output. There will therefore be a buildup of unplanned inventories of unsold goods. The firms will reduce their levels of output, thus causing income to fall. We can conclude that:

> **If desired aggregate expenditure falls short of aggregate output, there will be an unintended increase in inventories; firms will tend to reduce their production, and income will tend to fall.**

Suppose now that total output of goods and services in the economy is $80 million. At this output level, if desired consumption expenditures amount to $70 million and investment expenditures amount to $10 million, then desired aggregate expenditure is

$80 million — exactly equal to aggregate output. No unintentional stockpiling of unsold goods and no unintentional reduction of inventories will occur. Therefore, firms will tend not to alter their volume of output. Income (output) will be at its **equilibrium income** level. Hence, we can draw the following conclusion:

Income is at its equilibrium level when aggregate expenditure equals aggregate output.

> **The economy will be in equilibrium when desired aggregate expenditure equals aggregate output.**

PROBLEM SOLVING 25-1
How do unintended changes in inventories signal producers to vary their outputs?

TABULAR AND GRAPHICAL ANALYSES

Various possible levels of output with associated consumption and investment expenditures are presented in Table 25.1. At any level of output below $80 million, desired aggregate expenditure is greater than aggregate output. Output and income will therefore tend to rise. Consider a level of output of $50 million. At this level of output, desired aggregate expenditure is $65 million. Firms will attempt to increase their output to meet this level of expenditure, thus output and income will tend to rise. At any level of output above $80 million, desired aggregate expenditure is less than aggregate output. Income and output will therefore tend to fall. At an output level of $80 million, desired aggregate expenditure equals aggregate output. Output will therefore be at its equilibrium level.

TABLE 25.1

Consumption, investment, and aggregate expenditure (hypothetical data).

Value of output ($million)	Desired consumption expenditure ($million)	Desired investment expenditure ($million)	Desired aggregate expenditure ($million)	Pressure on income
0	30	10	40	upward
40	50	10	60	upward
50	55	10	65	upward
60	60	10	70	upward
70	65	10	75	upward
80	70	10	80	none
90	75	10	85	downward
100	80	10	90	downward
110	85	10	95	downward
120	90	10	100	downward

THE CONSUMPTION-INCOME RELATION

To continue our analysis, we now need some new analytical tools. The first two columns of Table 25.1 give us a **consumption schedule**. This schedule shows the relation between total income and total consumption. The other analytical tools needed are the average propensity to consume and save, and the marginal propensity to consume and save. We shall define each of these concepts in turn.

A consumption schedule relates total income and total consumption.

The **average propensity to consume** (APC) is defined as the fraction of total income that is allocated to consumption. That is,

The average propensity to consume is the ratio of consumption to income.

$$APC = \frac{C}{Y}$$

where C is consumption and Y is income. If out of an income of $100 million, total

Learning Objective 2:
describe the relation
between income and
consumption

consumption is $80 million, then

$$APC = \frac{80}{100} = 0.8$$

*The average propensity to
save is the ratio of saving to
income.*

The **average propensity to save** (APS) is defined as the fraction of total income that is saved. That is,

$$APC = \frac{S}{Y}$$

where S is saving and Y is income. Out of an income of $100 million, for example, if total saving is $20 million, then

$$APC = \frac{20}{100} = 0.2$$

It should be evident that APC + APS = 1. If I consume three fifths of my disposable income, it follows that I save two fifths. This can be shown by simple algebra. Disposable income is either consumed or saved. Hence,

$$Y = C + S$$

By dividing each term by Y, we obtain

$$\frac{Y}{Y} = \frac{C}{Y} + \frac{S}{Y}$$

That is,

$$1 = APC + APS$$

*The marginal propensity to
consume is the ratio of the
change in consumption to
the change in income.*

The **marginal propensity to consume** (MPC) is defined as the fraction of extra income allocated to consumption. That is,

$$MPC = \frac{\Delta C}{\Delta Y}$$

where ΔC is the change in consumption and ΔY is the change in income. For example, if an increase in income of $10 million causes consumption to increase by $7 million, then

$$MPC = \frac{7}{10} = 0.7$$

*The marginal propensity to
save is the ratio of the
change in saving to the
change in income.*

The **marginal propensity to save** (MPS) is defined as the fraction of extra income that is saved. That is,

$$MPS = \frac{\Delta S}{\Delta Y}$$

where ΔS is a change in saving and ΔY is a change in income. For example, if an increase in income of $10 million results in an increase in total saving of $3 million, then

$$MPS = \frac{3}{10} = 0.3$$

Note also that MPC + MPS = 1. Again, this result can be derived algebraically as follows:

$$Y = C + S$$

$$\Delta Y = \Delta C + \Delta S$$

Dividing by ΔY we obtain

$$\frac{\Delta Y}{\Delta Y} = \frac{\Delta C}{\Delta Y} + \frac{\Delta S}{\Delta Y}$$

That is,

$$1 = MPC + MPS$$

At a break-even level of income, saving is zero.

Table 25.2 shows the average propensity to consume, the average propensity to save, the marginal propensity to consume, and the marginal propensity to save for a hypothetical economy. At an income level of $60 million, households spend exactly $60 million on consumer goods and services. This means, of course, that saving is zero. This level of income is called the **break-even level of income**. Note that at the break-even level of income, the APC equals 1 because consumption and income are equal. Below the break-even level, APC > 1 because consumption is greater than income; above the break-even level of income, APC < 1 because consumption is less than income. Note that even at a current level of income of $0, consumers still spend $40 million purchasing consumer goods and services. How is this possible? This is possible if consumers borrow or if they finance a part of their current consumption out of past savings — a concept referred to as dissaving. **Dissaving** occurs when consumers spend more than their current income on current consumption.

Dissaving occurs when consumers finance consumption by borrowing or from past savings.

The data in the first two columns of Table 25.2 are plotted in Figure 25.1, which shows the relation between income and consumption.

Note that as income increases, consumption also increases. We shall refer to this relationship as the consumption curve. The **consumption curve** shows the direct relationship between current income and current consumption.

A consumption curve illustrates a consumption schedule of current income and consumption.

Let us consider the consumption curve in Figure 25.1. Its slope is

$$\frac{\Delta C}{\Delta Y}$$

TABLE 25.2	Income ($million)	Consumption ($million)	MPC	MPS	APC	APS
Consumption schedule with MPC, MPS, APC and APS.	0	30			—	—
			0.50	0.50		
	40	50			1.25	–0.25
			0.50	0.50		
	50	55			1.10	–0.10
			0.50	0.50		
	60	60			1.00	0.00
			0.50	0.50		
	70	65			0.93	0.07
			0.50	0.50		
	80	70			0.88	0.12
			0.50	0.50		
	90	75			0.83	0.17
			0.50	0.50		
	100	80			0.80	0.20
			0.50	0.50		
	110	85			0.77	0.23
			0.50	0.50		
	120	90			0.75	0.25

FIGURE 25.1

The consumption curve.

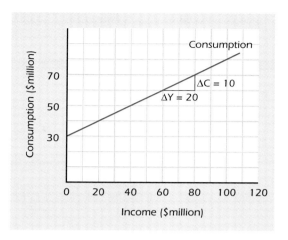

Does that ratio remind you of anything? Well, it is exactly how we earlier defined the marginal propensity to consume . We have just made the following discovery:

The marginal propensity to consume is the slope of the consumption curve.

Special Note: The consumption curve shown in Figure 25.1 is linear. This is only a simplifying assumption, and it should not be interpreted to mean that consumption curves are always linear. In a subsequent chapter, we shall explore more fully the shape of the consumption curve.

Before we can use the AE-AO approach to determine the equilibrium level of income graphically, we need to introduce just one more piece of analytical equipment. That is the 45-degree line. This line will prove to be quite convenient in future analyses. Figure 25.2 shows a 45-degree line.

Note that if aggregate expenditure and income are on the axes, any point on the 45-degree line represents the equality of aggregate expenditure and aggregate output. Thus, at point E, aggregate expenditure ($70 million) equals income ($70 million). Note also that an income of $70 million can be measured vertically upward from 70 to the 45-degree line.

We know that for equilibrium to exist, AE and AO must be equal. But AE and AO are equal only along the 45-degree line. Hence equilibrium must occur along the

FIGURE 25.2

The 45-degree line.

Any point on the 45-degree line represents the equality of total expenditure and total income.

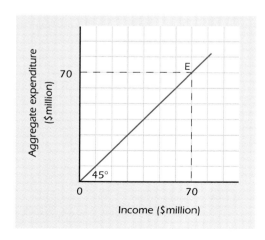

45-degree line. The graph of the equilibrium level of income, illustrated in Figure 25.3, is often referred to as the **Keynesian cross**.

The equilibrium level of income.

Equilibrium in the closed economy without government is shown graphically by the intersection of the C + I line and the 45-degree line.

Keynesian cross: the 45-degree diagram showing aggregate expenditure and aggregate output.

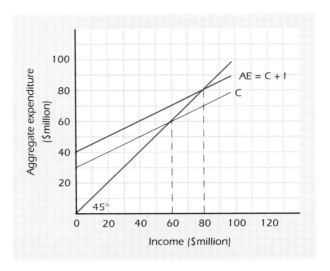

The consumption curve C representing consumption, and the line C + I representing the sum of consumption and investment (AE in this case), are derived from Table 25.1. The C + I line is parallel to the consumption curve because fixed investment has been added to consumption. The equilibrium level of income is $80 million where total intended expenditure (C + I) just equals total output. At any other level of income, there would be an imbalance between desired aggregate expenditure and aggregate output. For reasons already discussed, such a level of income would not be maintained.

THE INJECTIONS-WITHDRAWALS APPROACH

Before you can understand the injections-withdrawals approach to the determination of equilibrium income, you must understand the concepts of injections and withdrawals. Any income that is injected into the flow of income and expenditure is referred to as an **injection**. Injections will tend to increase the level of income in the income-expenditure stream. Injections include investment (I), government purchases (G), and exports (X). On the other hand, any income that is taken out of the income-expenditure stream is referred to as a **withdrawal** or a leakage. Withdrawals will tend to reduce the level of the flow of income and expenditure. Withdrawals include saving (S), taxes (T), and imports (M). Under our simplifying assumptions, the only injection in our hypothetical economy is investment, and the only withdrawal is saving.

An injection tends to increase the flow of income while a withdrawal tends to reduce it.

ARITHMETICAL ANALYSIS

Suppose that the economy produces a total output of $70 million. Suppose also that at that level of output, households decide to save $5 million, while firms plan to invest $10 million. Clearly, if households save $5 million out of a total personal disposable income of $70 million, they must be consuming $65 million. The current level of output is not enough to allow both households and firms to realize their plans. Firms will therefore tend to increase their output, which will cause income to rise. We can therefore draw the following conclusion:

In a closed economy in which the government neither spends nor taxes, if planned investment exceeds planned saving, the level of income will tend to rise.

Let us now suppose that at an output of $100 million, consumers desire to save $20 million while firms plan to invest $10 million. This implies that consumers want to spend $80 million on consumer goods and services. The volume of output produced is thus greater than that required for the plans of households and firms to be realized. Firms will tend to reduce their production levels, and in so doing, income will fall. Hence:

In a closed economy in which there is neither government spending nor taxes, if intended investment is less than intended saving, the level of income will tend to fall.

If, however, the level of output is $80 million, and households plan to save $10 million while firms plan to invest $10 million, both groups will be able to realize their plans and there will be no incentive for a different level of output to be produced. The equilibrium level of income will be $80 million. This leads to the following conclusion:

A closed economy in which there is neither government spending nor taxes will be in equilibrium when intended saving equals intended investment.

TABULAR AND GRAPHICAL ANALYSES

The break-even level of income is that level at which saving is 0.

Table 25.3 shows various possible levels of income and the amounts that consumers desire to save at each level of income. The saving schedule is drawn up on the assumption that as income increases, saving also increases. At an income level of $40 million, consumers will be dissaving. At an income level of $60 million, saving will be zero; hence the break-even level of income is $60 million.

At any level of income below $80 million, the amount that firms want to invest exceeds the amount that households want to save. For example, at an income level of $70 million, the amount that firms want to invest is $10 million. The amount that households want to save, however, is only $5 million. This injection by firms is greater than the withdrawal by households. Income will therefore tend to rise.

On the other hand, if income is at a level of $90 million, the withdrawal by households ($15 million) will exceed the injection by firms ($10 million). Income will therefore tend to fall. Only at an income level of $80 million will the saving decisions of households coincide with the investment decisions of the firms. Hence the equilibrium level of income is $80 million.

TABLE 25.3

Saving and investment schedules (hypothetical data).

Income ($million) (1)	Consumption ($million) (2)	Saving ($million) (3)	Investment ($million) (4)	Pressure on income (5)
0	30	−30	10	upward
40	50	−10	10	upward
50	55	−5	10	upward
60	60	0	10	upward
70	65	5	10	upward
80	70	10	10	none
90	75	15	10	downward
100	80	20	10	downward
110	85	25	10	downward
120	90	30	10	downward

THE SAVING-INCOME RELATION

Learning Objective 4:
understand the saving-income relation

Columns one and three of Table 25.3 give us a saving schedule. If we plot this information on a graph, we obtain the **saving curve** shown in Figure 25.4. Note that the slope of the saving curve is

$$\frac{\Delta S}{\Delta Y}$$

which is the marginal propensity to save. You should note that the linear saving curve results from our simplifying assumption that the MPS is constant. It should not be inferred that the actual relation between saving and disposable income is linear.

FIGURE 25.4

The saving curve.

The slope of the saving curve is the marginal propensity to save.

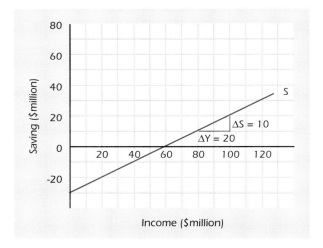

The equilibrium level of income can also be illustrated graphically, as shown in Figure 25.5. Saving and investment are measured along the vertical axis and income is measured along the horizontal axis. Investment is drawn as a horizontal line because of the assumption that investment does not vary with income. The saving curve is derived from the saving schedule in Table 25.3. The equilibrium level of income is determined

FIGURE 25.5

The equilibrium level of income.

In a closed economy without government, equilibrium income occurs at the intersection of the saving curve and the investment line.

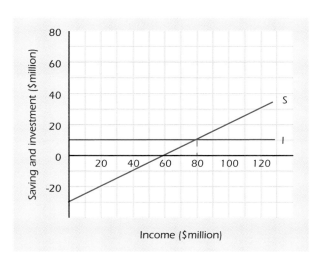

by the intersection of the saving curve and the investment line. This occurs at an output level of $80 million.

 PROBLEM SOLVING 25-2

The economy will be in equilibrium as long as saving equals investment. True or false?

INTEGRATING THE AGGREGATE EXPENDITURE-AGGREGATE OUTPUT AND THE INJECTIONS-WITHDRAWALS APPROACHES

Learning Objective 5: integrate the aggregate expenditures-aggregate output and the injections-withdrawals approaches

We have examined two techniques within the Keynesian model of income determination. We have seen also that these two techniques are just different ways of looking at the same thing. In this section, you will see how the two techniques can be lined up to illustrate their relationship to the determination of equilibrium income.

Figure 25.6A shows the AE-AO approach while Figure 25.6B shows the injections-withdrawals approach. A positive consumption when income is zero implies negative saving when income is zero. The break-even level of income ($60 million) is shown in

FIGURE 25.6

Equilibrium income.

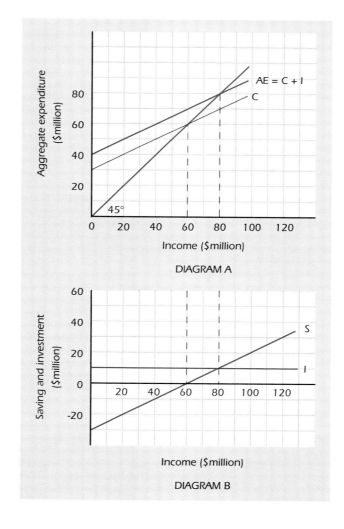

Diagram A, where consumption and income are equal, and in Diagram B, where saving is zero. Finally, note that the aggregate expenditure line intersects the 45-degree line at the same level of income at which the saving and investment lines intersect.

PROBLEM SOLVING 25-3

Demonstrate algebraically that the equilibrium condition Y = C + I is identical to the equilibrium condition S = I.

RECONCILIATION OF AE-AO WITH AD-AS ANALYSIS

Most likely, you believe intuitively that there is a close relationship between the AE-AO analysis of this chapter and the AD-AS analysis presented in Chapter 24. The purpose of this section is to formally reconcile the AE-AO and AD-AS analyses. The Keynesian cross diagram presented in Figure 25.7 (Diagram A) shows the equilibrium level of income occurring at the point where the AE line crosses the 45-degree line. According to this analysis, firms adjust their output levels to suit aggregate expenditure at the existing price level. (Recall our assumption that the price level is constant). If AE exceeds AO, output expands; if AE is less than AO, then output contracts.

FIGURE 25.7

Reconciliation of AE-AO with AD-AS analysis.

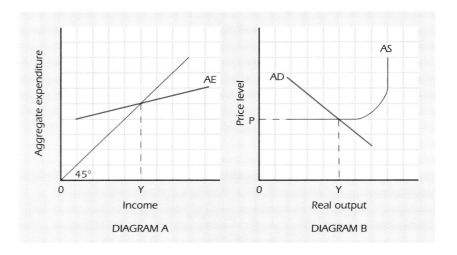

DIAGRAM A   DIAGRAM B

The fact that firms are able to increase their production levels without any increase in the price level assumes that the economy is operating in the Keynesian (horizontal) section of the AS curve. Diagram B of Figure 25.7 shows the AD curve intersecting the AS curve in the horizontal range. The two diagrams are lined up to emphasize the relation between the two approaches. In Diagram A, we assume that the price level is P. The equilibrium level of income is Y, where desired aggregate expenditure equals aggregate output. This is the same level of income shown in Diagram B where aggregate demand equals aggregate supply at a price level of P.

LIMITATIONS OF THE SIMPLE MODEL

The simple model of income determination presented in this chapter has certain limitations. First, it is not a complete model of the macroeconomy. The model does not analyze what is happening in the money market and in the labour market. It deals exclusively with the product market.

Second, the model is a demand-side model in the sense that the level of output (income) is determined exclusively by aggregate expenditure. If aggregate expenditure increases, aggregate output will increase. If aggregate expenditure falls, aggregate output will fall. In this model then, expenditure creates output.

Third, this simple model assumes that the price level is fixed, and that the economy is operating with idle human and non-human resources that can be employed as long as there is enough expenditure to purchase the goods and services produced. In other words, the economy is assumed to be operating along the horizontal portion of the aggregate supply curve, where it is possible to increase production without any increase in prices. But in reality, price levels do change, and a more complete model must address this fact.

GLOBAL PERSPECTIVE

Are Canadians Really Big Savers?

Canadians have a reputation of being big savers. In this capsule, we examine saving in some advanced economies with a view to determining how Canadians stack up against other economically advanced economies in terms of saving. We look at two measures of saving: gross national saving as a percentage of GDP and household saving as a percentage of disposable household income. The chart shows the average of national saving as a percentage of GDP for the period 1986-95, and the average of household saving as a percentage of disposable household income for the 10-year period from 1989 to 1998.

Let us first consider gross national saving as a percentage of GDP. Of the countries considered, Japan had the highest saving rate at over 32% of GDP. Other countries with relatively high saving rates were Austria (23.6%), Germany (22.2%), and Spain (20.8%). At the other end

of the scale were the U.K. with the lowest saving rate of 14.4% of GDP, the United States (15.4%), and Sweden (16.3%). Canada's saving rate was 16.7% for a ninth place ranking among the 12 countries considered.

When we look at household saving as a percentage of disposable household income over the 1989-98 period, we observe that of the 12 countries investigated, Belgium had the highest average rate of disposable housing income at 17.5%. Italy, France, and Japan had relatively high rates at 14.9%, 13.3%, and 12.5% respectively. Sweden's household saving rate of 3.8% of disposable household income was the lowest of the 12 countries observed. Canada occupied nineteenth place with a household saving rate of 7.2% of disposable household income.

Are Canadians big savers? You have seen the evidence, and you be the judge.

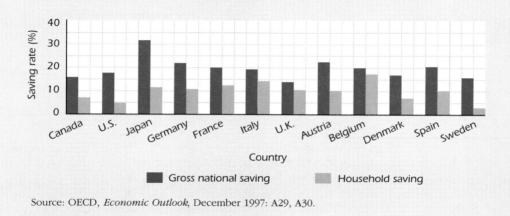

Source: OECD, *Economic Outlook*, December 1997: A29, A30.

CHAPTER SUMMARY

1. Autonomous investment is investment that is independent of income.

2. Ex ante concepts relate to plans; ex post concepts relate to historical facts. Ex ante concepts are relevant when we describe equilibrium conditions.

3. The consumption curve shows the direct relationship between consumption and personal disposable income.

4. The average propensity to consume (save) is the ratio of consumption (saving) to income. The marginal propensity to consume (save) is the ratio of the change in consumption (saving) to the change in income.

5. In a closed economy in which government neither spends nor taxes, equilibrium income occurs when desired aggregate expenditure equals aggregate output.

6. Injections tend to increase the level of income while withdrawals tend to reduce it.

7. The saving curve shows the direct relationship between saving and personal disposable income.

8. In a closed economy in which there is no government spending and no taxes, equilibrium income occurs where the saving curve and the investment line intersect.

9. The limitations of the simple model of income determination presented in this chapter include the fact that the model concentrates only on the product market, it focuses only on the demand-side, and it does not allow for changes in the price level.

TERMS FOR REVIEW

closed economy (428)
autonomous investment (428)
ex ante, ex post (428)
aggregate expenditure (429)
aggregate output (429)
equilibrium income (430)
consumption schedule (430)
average propensity to consume (APC) (430)
average propensity to save (APS) (431)

marginal propensity to consume (MPC) (431)
marginal propensity to save (MPS) (431)
break-even level of income (432)
dissaving (432)
consumption curve (432)
Keynesian cross (434)
injection (434)
withdrawal (434)
saving curve (436)

QUESTIONS FOR REVIEW AND DISCUSSION

1. Explain why planned investment might be different from realized investment. (General)

2. What is the difference between ex ante and ex post concepts such as saving and investment? (L.O.3)

3. How is it possible for current consumption to exceed current income? What is this phenomenon called? (General)

4. Define aggregate expenditure and aggregate output. Are they always equal? Can they ever be equal? (General)

5. What is the difference between the aggregate expenditure curve and the aggregate demand curve? (General)

6. What is the relation between (a) the marginal propensity to consume (MPC) and the marginal propensity to save (MPS), and (b) the average propensity to consume (APC) and the average propensity to save (APS)? (L.O.2)

7. In the aggregate expenditure-aggregate output approach to income determination, equilibrium will always occur along the 45-degree line. Is this true or false? Explain. (L.O.1)

8. What is an injection? What effect do injections have on equilibrium income? (L.O.1)

9. What are withdrawals? What effect do they have on equilibrium income? (L.O.1)

10. Define the break-even level of income. (L.O.4)

11. If injections exceed withdrawals, what will be the effect on equilibrium income? (L.O.1)

12. "In a closed economy without government, the equilibrium level of income occurs where intended saving and investment are equal." Explain why. (L.O.1)

13. What are the limitations of the simple model of income determination presented in this chapter? (General)

14. In what sense can it be said that the simple model of income determination is a demand-side only model? (General)

PROBLEMS AND EXERCISES

1. Table 25.4 shows income and saving data for a simple economy. There is no government spending and there are no taxes. (L.O.2,4)

TABLE 25.4	Disposable income ($million)	Saving ($million)	Consumption ($million)
Income and saving data.	350	–4	
	360	0	
	370	4	
	380	8	
	390	12	
	400	16	
	410	20	

(a) Complete the consumption column.
(b) Graph the saving curve and the consumption curve on the same diagram.
(c) On your graph, indicate the break-even level of income.

2. Table 25.5 gives data on disposable income and consumption. (L.O.2)

TABLE 25.5	Income	Consumption	APC	APS	MPC	MPS
Income and consumption data.	400	320				
	500	400				
	600	480				
	700	560				
	800	640				
	900	720				
	1000	800				

(a) Complete the table.

(b) Draw the consumption curve.

(c) Calculate the slope of the consumption curve and compare your answer with the MPC.

3. The following table contains data on personal disposable income and consumption. Autonomous investment is 15. (L.O.1)

TABLE 25.6

Income and consumption data.

Income	C	I	AE = C + I
60	70		
80	85		
100	100		
120	115		
140	130		
160	145		
180	160		
200	175		

(a) Complete the table.

(b) On a 45-degree diagram, draw in the consumption curve and the AE line, and indicate the equilibrium level of income.

4. The data shown in Table 25.7 are for a closed economy without government. (L.O.1)

TABLE 25.7

Consumption and income data ($million).

Disposable income	Consumption	Saving	AE
400	420		
500	500		
600	580		
700	660		
800	740		
900	820		
1000	900		

(a) Complete the saving column.

(b) If investment is fixed at $40 million for each and every level of income, what is the equilibrium level of income?

(c) With investment constant at $40 million, complete the AE column.

(d) At what level of income does aggregate expenditure equal aggregate output? Compare this with your answer for part (b).

5. Table 25.8 gives data for the hypothetical economy of Tamalai. (General)

TABLE 25.8

Data for Tamalai.

Item	Amount ($million)
Investment	45
Consumption	400
Disposable income	360
Government purchases	15
Imports	10
Taxes	10
Exports	25

(a) What are total injections?

(b) What are total withdrawals?

6. Table 25.9 gives data for Durban, a hypothetical economy without government and without foreign trade. (L.O.1)

TABLE 25.9	Income	Saving	Investment
Saving and investment data for Durban.	60	−10	15
	80	−5	15
	100	0	15
	120	5	15
	140	10	15
	160	15	15
	180	20	15
	200	25	15

(a) On a graph, draw the saving curve and the investment line.

(b) On your graph, indicate the break-even level of income.

(c) On your graph, indicate the equilibrium level of income.

(d) Calculate the slope of the saving curve.

7. "When AE and AO are equal in a closed economy with neither government spending nor taxes, the economy is in equilibrium. AE and AO are always equal, by definition; therefore, the closed economy with no government spending and no taxes is always in equilibrium." Discuss. (L.O.3)

8. Show that the AE-AO and the injections-withdrawals approaches to the determination of equilibrium income are different ways of looking at the same thing. (L.O.5)

9. In the hypothetical economy of Bayan Obo, intended aggregate expenditure is $300 million and the value of total output is $250 million. Carefully describe the process by which equilibrium will be reached. If total output were $250 million and total desired expenditure $210 million, describe the process by which equilibrium would be reached. (L.O.1)

Internet Site

http://mobydicks.com/lecture/Keyneshall/wwwboard.html

Many of the concepts and ideas that you studied in this chapter were introduced into economic literature by John Maynard Keynes. This Web site is about Keynes. You can read others' opinions of Keynes and express your own opinions at this site.

INTERNET EXERCISE

1. Explore the Keynes Lecture Hall at the above address.

2. Write your opinion (one short paragraph) of Keynes.

MATHEMATICAL APPENDIX

Simple mathematical tools can be used to explain the Keynesian model. This appendix should familiarize you with the simple mathematics of income determination. This presentation is not a different theory of income determination. It is the same theory presented earlier in the chapter, but the analytical tools are different. Here also, we assume that we are dealing with a closed economy and that government neither spends nor taxes.

THE CONSUMPTION FUNCTION

If we assume that personal disposable income is the only determinant of consumption, then we can express the consumption function as:

$$C = C(Y_d) \tag{1}$$

where C is consumption, and Y_d is disposable income. Let us assume that the relationship between consumption and disposable income is linear. The consumption-income relation can then be expressed as:

$$C = a + bY_d, \ a > 0, \ b > 0 \tag{2}$$

Here, the value of a represents the amount of consumption that will take place when income is zero. In other words, a is autonomous consumption, and b is the slope of the consumption curve or the marginal propensity to consume. Since we assume a linear relation between C and Y_d, b is constant. The consumption function, for example, could be represented by the equation:

$$C = 30 + 0.5Y_d \tag{3}$$

THE INVESTMENT FUNCTION

We assume that investment is a fixed amount each period and does not vary with the level of income. The investment function can be expressed as:

$$I = I_a \tag{4}$$

where I_a is a fixed amount. For example, investment could be represented as:

$$I = 20 \tag{5}$$

On a graph, equation (5) would be represented as a horizontal straight line.

THE EQUILIBRIUM LEVEL OF INCOME

We know that the equilibrium level of income occurs where desired aggregate expenditure equals aggregate output. This equilibrium condition can be expressed as:

$$Y_d = C + I \tag{6}$$

We can now collect all the equations to show the complete model:

$$C = a + bY_d \tag{7}$$

$$I = I_a \tag{8}$$

$$Y_d = C + I \tag{9}$$

By solving these equations for Y_d, we can obtain the equilibrium value of Y_d. Thus:

$$Y_d = C + I \tag{10}$$

But

$$C = a + bY_d \tag{11}$$

By substituting $a + bY_d$ for C in equation (10), we obtain:

$$Y_d = a + bY_d + I \tag{12}$$

By transposing, we obtain:

$$Y_d - bY_d = a + I \tag{13}$$

By factoring, we obtain:

$$Y_d(1 - b) = a + I \tag{14}$$

$$Y_d = \frac{a + 1}{1 - b} \tag{15}$$

But $a + I$ is autonomous expenditure consisting of autonomous consumption and autonomous investment. If we use A to denote autonomous expenditure, we can rewrite equation (15) as:

$$Y_d = \frac{A}{1 - b} = \frac{1}{1 - b} \cdot A \tag{16}$$

EXAMPLE 25-1

Consider the following set of equations.

$$C = 30 + 0.5Y_d$$
$$I = 20$$

The equilibrium condition is given by

$$Y_d = C + I$$

Here A = 50 (autonomous consumption + autonomous investment) and $b = 0.5$

Therefore,

$$Y_d = \frac{A}{1-b} = \frac{50}{1-0.5} = 100$$

The equilibrium level of income is therefore 100.

EXERCISES

1. You are given the following consumption equation:

$$C = 16 + 0.7Y_d$$

   (a) What is autonomous consumption?

   (b) What is the MPC?

   (c) If autonomous investment is 15, what is autonomous expenditure?

2. If the consumption function is given by the equation $C = 8 + 0.8Y_d$,
   (a) What is the MPS?

   (b) What is autonomous consumption?

3. If the MPC in an economy is 0.9 and autonomous expenditure is 25, what is the equilibrium level of income?

4. If consumption in a certain economy is given by $C = 12 + 0.8Y_d$, what is consumption when disposable income is the following?

   (a) 80

   (b) 100

   (c) 120

5. If consumption is $C = 15 + 0.9Y_d$, what is the break-even level of disposable income?

6. Use each of the following sets of equations to determine the equilibrium level of income:

   (a) $C = 10 + 0.5Y_d$
       $I = 30$

   (b) $C = 8 + 0.8Y_d$
       $I = 10$

   (c) $C = 4 + 0.9Y_d$
       $I = 10$

7. You are given the following consumption equation:
$$C = 20 + 0.8Y_d$$
   If autonomous investment is 8,

   (a) complete the following consumption and AE schedules;

Y_d	C	I	AE = C + I
0			
20			
40			
60			
80			
100			
120			
140			
160			

   (b) use your schedules to determine the equilibrium level of income;

   (c) prove your answer mathematically.

CHANGES IN INCOME AND THE MULTIPLIER

Learning Objectives

After studying this chapter, you should understand:

1 the effects of changes in investment

2 the effects of changes in saving

3 the multiplier effect

4 the inflationary and deflationary gaps

If saving is the pill and consumption is the jam, the extra jam has to be proportional to the size of the additional pill.

J. M. Keynes, *The General Theory*

INTRODUCTION

From our analysis of the determination of the equilibrium level of income presented in the previous chapter, it is clear that changes in investment and changes in consumption (or saving) will cause changes in aggregate expenditure and hence in the equilibrium level of income. The purpose of this chapter is to study the effects of changes in investment and consumption on the equilibrium level of income and employment. We will pay some attention to the multiplier as this adds to our understanding of how changes in aggregate expenditure affect the equilibrium level of income in the product market. The chapter ends with a discussion of the inflationary and recessionary gaps. In this chapter, we maintain the simplifying assumptions that the economy is closed and that government neither spends nor taxes.

THE INCOME EFFECTS OF CHANGES IN INVESTMENT

Learning Objective 1:
the effects of changes in investment

One of the questions that we would like to answer is, "How does the equilibrium level of income respond to a change in planned investment?" One way to visualize the problem is to realize that investment is an injection. We should expect, therefore, that an increase in investment will increase the equilibrium level of income, while a fall in investment will reduce it. But we can view the situation another way.

Consider the saving and investment schedules in Table 26.1. At a level of investment of $10 million, the equilibrium level of income is $80 million. Now, suppose that firms decide to invest $15 million instead of the original $10 million. How will this increase in investment affect the equilibrium level of income?

	Income	Consumption	Saving	Original level of investment	New level of investment
TABLE 26.1					
Saving and investment schedules (hypothetical data in $million).	40	50	−10	10	15
	50	55	−5	10	15
	60	60	0	10	15
	70	65	5	10	15
	80	70	10	10	15
	90	75	15	10	15
	100	80	20	10	15
	110	85	25	10	15
	120	90	30	10	15

When investment increases to $15 million, the level of income at which saving equals investment is $90 million — an increase of $10 million over the initial level. Thus, an increase in investment of $5 million has generated an even greater increase in income — $10 million. The mechanism through which this occurs will be discussed below. Note that if investment had fallen to only $5 million, total income would have fallen from its initial level of $80 million to $70 million. A given reduction in investment generates an even greater reduction in the equilibrium level of income.

A given change in investment will lead to an even greater change in income.

The effects of changes in investment on the equilibrium level of income can be illustrated graphically. In Diagram A of Figure 26.1, S and I are the initial saving and investment lines respectively. The equilibrium level of income occurs at $80 million where the S and I lines intersect. The new level of investment is represented by I_1. The new investment line intersects the saving line at a level of income of $90 million.

FIGURE 26.1

The effect of an
increase in investment.

*An increase in investment
spending increases equilibrium income.*

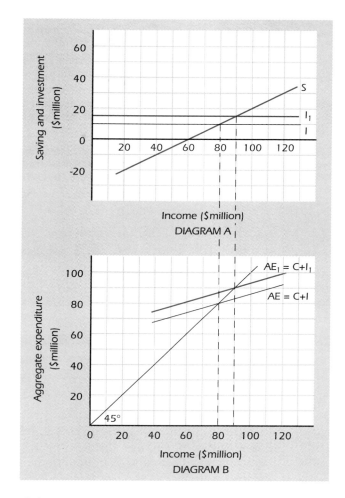

DIAGRAM A

DIAGRAM B

The effects of changes in investment on the equilibrium level of income can also be illustrated by the aggregate expenditure-aggregate output diagram. In Diagram B of Figure 26.1, the initial equilibrium level of income is shown to be $80 million where AE and the 45-degree line intersect. The increase in investment causes the AE curve to shift to AE_1. The new equilibrium level of income is now $90 million. It is left as an exercise for the student to demonstrate the effect on income of a reduction in investment. Note that, throughout the analysis, we assume that saving remains unchanged; thus, the saving line does not shift.

THE INCOME EFFECTS OF CHANGES IN SAVING

Learning Objective 2:
*the effects of changes in
saving*

Let us now consider the effects of changes in saving on the level of income. Here, we are considering changes in saving resulting from changes in non-income determinants. Hence, an increase in saving means that, at any given level of income, a greater amount is saved. A decrease in saving means that a smaller amount is saved out of any given level of income. Thus, a change in saving in this context means that the entire saving schedule changes, or the saving curve shifts.

Table 26.2 reproduces the initial saving and investment schedules of Table 26.1, and shows a new saving schedule, which has resulted from an increase in saving of

$5 million at each level of income. We assume that investment remains fixed throughout the analysis. Recall that the equilibrium level of income generated by the original saving and investment schedules was $80 million. With the increase in saving, the new equilibrium level of income is $70 million, where the new level of saving equals investment. Thus we conclude:

Other things being equal, an increase in saving results in a reduction in total income.

This conclusion can also be illustrated diagramatically. In Figure 26.2, S and I are the original saving and investment lines derived from the saving and investment schedules in Table 26.2. The new higher level of saving is represented by the saving curve S_1, which intersects the investment line at a level of income of $70 million.

TABLE 26.2

Saving and investment schedules (hypothetical data in $million).

Income	Initial saving	New saving	Investment
40	−10	−5	10
50	−5	0	10
60	0	5	10
70	5	10	10
80	10	15	10
90	15	20	10
100	20	25	10
110	25	30	10
120	30	35	10

THE PARADOX OF THRIFT

We have seen that an increase in saving, other things being equal, results in a fall in income. We know also that when income falls, saving falls. This rather interesting result has been termed the paradox of thrift or the paradox of saving. The **paradox of thrift (saving)** states that an increase in intended aggregate saving, other things being equal, will lead to a fall in total income, and hence to a fall in actual aggregate saving.

The paradox may be viewed in a different way. Saving by individuals makes them better off in the future (provided that inflation does not wipe out the value of their sav-

The paradox of thrift (saving) states that an increase in intended aggregate saving results in a decrease in actual saving.

FIGURE 26.2

The effect of an increase in saving.

An increase in saving reduces equilibrium income.

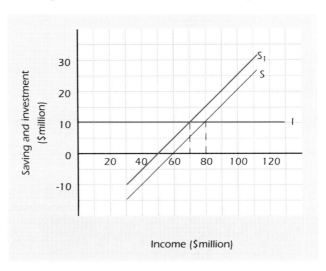

ing) and is therefore usually considered a virtue. But from society's point of view, thrift is a social vice since it makes the society worse off in the future.

The paradox of thrift can be illustrated very clearly by a graph. To do this, we assume that investment is induced by changes in income. Thus, investment increases as income increases. Figure 26.3 shows saving curve S and investment curve I intersecting at an equilibrium level of income of 0Y. The saving curve S_1 represents the higher level of saving. The equilibrium level of income falls to $0Y_0$. Note that the new level of saving, Y_0A is less than the initial level, YE. Now, you can try to demonstrate graphically the effect of a reduction in aggregate saving on the equilibrium level of income.

It is important to note that the paradox of thrift applies to a situation in which aggregate saving increases with no offsetting changes in investment. We have examined only the effects of changes in saving and investment on the equilibrium level of income. But our analysis can be extended to include any injection and any withdrawal. An increase in total injections will tend to increase income. An increase in total withdrawals will tend to reduce total income. Stated somewhat differently, anything that causes the AE curve to shift upward will increase the equilibrium level of income in the product market; anything that causes it to shift downward will reduce the level of income.

FIGURE 26.3

The paradox of thrift.

An upward shift of the saving curve reduces the level of actual saving.

APPLICATION

Pick Up the Clue

Economic theory tells us that if there is an increase in aggregate saving with no offsetting increase in investment (or other injections), we can expect a fall in total income. This is useful information for government policymakers and for business decision-makers. For government policymakers, it means that increases in the saving rates of Canadians may need to be offset by poli-

cies such as lower interest rates, which tend to reduce saving and increase spending. For business decision-makers, it may mean a fall in demand for their products, which may require a reevaluation of their production plans. In their decision-making, business managers will of course take into account any policies adopted by the government.

PROBLEM SOLVING 26-1

An increase in saving by consumers may be good or bad for the economy. Can you explain why?

THE MULTIPLIER

Learning Objective 3:
the multiplier effect

Multiplier effect: the result
that the ultimate change is
greater than the initial
change by some multiple.

In discussing the effect of an increase in investment on the equilibrium level of income, we noted that an increase in investment of $5 million led to an increase in income of $10 million. Let us now examine, in some detail, the curious result known as the **multiplier effect**. Suppose that there is an increase in expenditure of $100 million on investment goods. This may come about because of an anticipated increase in the demand for automobiles. Automobile dealers will purchase more cars from auto manufacturers, causing an unplanned decline in the inventories of auto manufacturers. In response to this unplanned decline in their inventories, these producers increase their output.

Now what is the effect of this increase in planned investment of $100 million? In order to manufacture additional automobiles, the automobile producers must employ more workers or require the existing workers to put in more hours. They must also purchase more steel, more tires, more tin, more leather or fabric, more electrical parts, etc. The auto manufacturers and their suppliers will pay out more in wages and salaries, a part of which will be spent, resulting in an increase in planned aggregate expenditure.

What happens then is that extra production leads to extra income, which leads to extra spending on consumer goods and services. People will buy more furniture and appliances, more television and stereo sets, more shoes, more computers, more clothes, and more suitcases to go on more trips. Sellers of these consumer goods and services will experience an unplanned decline in their inventories, and this will cause them to place new orders. This will result in a further increase in production and further increases in income in the manner explained earlier.

What should be clear from our analysis so far is that an increase in planned investment results in an increase in output and expenditure that is greater than the initial investment. But by how much greater is the increase in income? This depends on the amount of additional spending that occurs out of additional income. In other words, it depends on the marginal propensity to consume.

Now, let us assume that the society's marginal propensity to consume is constant at 0.8. If firms initially spend $100 million, then under this assumption there will be a second round of spending of $80 million (0.8 of $100 million). This additional spending will result in another increase in income, which will again lead to additional expenditure, and so on. The process is illustrated in Table 26.3. Since the initial increase in investment of $100 million leads to an increase in total income of $500 million, we say that the multiplier is 5.

Note: A formula for finding the total income generated will be presented shortly.

TABLE 26.3	Expenditure ($million)	Income generated ($million)
The multiplier process.	Initial increase in spending = 100.00	100.00
	2nd round spending = (0.8 x 100) = 80.00	80.00
	3rd round spending = (0.8 x 80) = 64.00	64.00
	4th round spending = (0.8 x 64) = 51.20	51.20
	5th round spending = (0.8 x 51.20) = 40.96	40.96
	6th round spending = (0.8 x 40.96) = 32.77	32.77
	etc.	
	TOTAL (all rounds) 500.00	

GRAPHICAL ILLUSTRATION OF THE MULTIPLIER EFFECT

The multiplier effect can also be illustrated graphically. In Figure 26.4, S and I are the initial saving and investment lines. The equilibrium level of income associated with these levels of saving and investment is Y. The diagram shows that an increase in investment from I to I_1 causes income to increase from Y to Y_1. Note that the change in income is greater than the change in investment that generated it. The number by which the change in investment is multiplied to get the change in income is called the **multiplier**, and can be calculated from the following formula:

The multiplier tells the amount by which a change in spending will change income.

$$\text{Multiplier} = \frac{\Delta Y}{\Delta I} = \frac{Y_1 - Y}{I_1 - I}$$

FIGURE 26.4

The multiplier effect.

The change in income is greater than the change in investment that caused it.

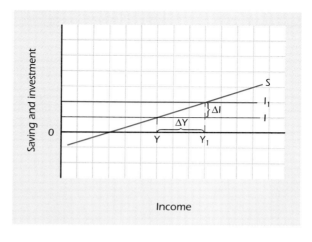

RELATION BETWEEN THE MULTIPLIER, THE MPC, AND THE MPS

It is evident that if the marginal propensity to consume in Table 26.3 were greater than 0.8, the increase in income would be greater than $500 million. In other words, the value of the multiplier would be greater than 5. We have just defined the multiplier as the change in income divided by the change in investment. That is, the multiplier is

$$\frac{\Delta Y}{\Delta I}$$

Refer to Figure 26.4 and you will observe that the slope of the saving line, which is the MPS, is

$$\frac{\Delta I}{\Delta Y}$$

Hence the multiplier is the inverse of the marginal propensity to save.

$$\text{The multiplier} = \frac{1}{\text{MPS}}$$

Since MPC + MPS = 1, it follows that MPS = 1 − MPC.

The multiplier is the reciprocal of the MPS.

Hence the formula for the **multiplier** can be expressed as follows:

$$\text{The multiplier} = \frac{1}{1 - \text{MPC}}$$

For example, given a marginal propensity to consume of $\frac{7}{9}$, the marginal propensity to save would be

$$1 - \frac{7}{9} = \frac{2}{9}$$

and the multiplier would be $\frac{9}{2} = 4.5$.

It is easy to see that the smaller the marginal propensity to save, the larger the multiplier will be. Mathematically, the marginal propensity to save measures the slope (steepness) of the saving curve. The steeper the saving curve (that is, the higher the marginal propensity to save), the less the multiplier effect will be. Figure 26.5 shows two saving curves, S and S_1, with different slopes.

FIGURE 26.5

Relation between the multiplier and the slope of the saving curve.

The flatter the saving curve, the greater the multiplier effect.

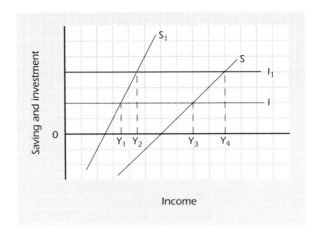

With the less steep saving curve S, an increase in investment from I to I_1 causes an increase in income from Y_3 to Y_4. With the steeper saving curve S_1, a similar increase in investment causes a much lower increase in income — from Y_1 to Y_2.

A MORE REALISTIC MULTIPLIER

The discussion of the multiplier, so far, assumes that saving is the only withdrawal from the income-expenditure stream. But in fact, as we saw in Chapter 25, taxes and imports are also withdrawals from the flow of income and expenditure. When these other withdrawals are recognized, the formula for the multiplier must be modified. The simple multiplier (1/MPS) will no longer be valid. The fraction of extra income allocated to saving, taxes, and imports may be termed the **marginal propensity to withdraw** (MPW), which may be expressed as

The marginal propensity to withdraw is the fraction of extra income allocated to savings, taxes, and imports.

$$MPW = \frac{\Delta W}{\Delta Y}$$

The generalized multiplier is the reciprocal of the marginal propensity to withdraw.

The formula for the more realistic multiplier, sometimes called the **generalized multiplier**, is

$$1/MPW$$

The generalized multiplier is smaller than the simple multiplier because some portion of income is allocated to taxes and imports.

ESTIMATING THE MULTIPLIER FOR CANADA

Between 1996 and 1997, the GDP of Canada increased by $34.8 billion. In the same period, total withdrawals increased by $25.4 billion. Details are presented in Table 26.4.

The marginal propensity to withdraw, as shown in Table 26.4, is 0.73. Since the multiplier is the reciprocal of the marginal propensity to withdraw, then an estimate of the multiplier for Canada (1996–97) is 1.37.

TABLE 26.4	Item	($billion)
Estimating the multiplier for Canada between 1996 and 1997.	Change in GDP Change in withdrawals	34.5 25.4
	$MPW = \dfrac{\Delta W}{\Delta Y} = \dfrac{25.4}{34.8} = 0.7299$	
	$\text{Multiplier} = \dfrac{1}{0.7299} = 1.37$	

THE FULL EMPLOYMENT GAPS

Learning Objective 4:
the inflationary and deflationary gaps

One of the predictions that followed from our analysis of the equilibrium level of income in Chapter 25 was that if desired total spending is greater than total output, the firms will expand production. Total income will then increase. On the other hand, if intended aggregate expenditure falls short of aggregate output, firms will reduce production. Total income will then fall. When equilibrium is reached, it will not necessarily be at the full-employment level of output. These predictions were based on the assumption that the economy's resources were not fully employed and that output could expand without any rise in the price level. In other words, we assumed we were operating in the horizontal section of the AS curve. We will now examine situations in which aggregate expenditure exceeds or falls short of the full-employment level of output. To do so, we relax the restrictions that the economy operates with a constant price level and that output is below the full-employment level.

THE INFLATIONARY GAP

The inflationary gap equals the desired aggregate expenditure minus the full-employment output.

Consider a situation in which the economy's resources are fully employed, and aggregate expenditure exceeds that full-employment level of output. In such a situation, real output tends to be stable since it cannot expand beyond the full-employment level. Prices, however, will tend to move upward. Table 26.5 shows desired aggregate expenditure and aggregate output for a simple closed economy with no government spending or taxation.

TABLE 26.5	Output	Consumption	Investment	Aggregate expenditure
Aggregate expenditure and aggregate output (hypothetical data in $million).	40	50	10	60
	50	55	10	65
	60	60	10	70
	70	65	10	75
	80	70	10	80
	90	75	10	85
	100	80	10	90
	110	85	10	95
	120	90	10	100

The equilibrium level of income is $80 million where intended aggregate expenditure equals aggregate output. Now, let us suppose that $60 million is the full-employment level of output. At that level of output, desired aggregate expenditure is $70 million. Desired consumption and investment spending together exceed the full-employment output. Prices then tend to rise. There is an inflationary gap. The **inflationary gap** is the amount by which desired aggregate expenditure exceeds aggregate output at full employment.

An inflationary gap results when total spending exceeds the full-employment level of output.

Intended aggregate expenditure would have to fall by $10 million (in our example) to reach the full-employment level of output; hence the inflationary gap is $10 million. Note that the inflationary gap of $10 million with a multiplier of 2, in our example, will cause income to increase by $20 million (from $60 million to $80 million). This increase is, of course, not in real terms but in nominal terms. It is due to inflation of prices. The inflationary gap is illustrated in Figure 26.6.

FIGURE 26.6

The inflationary gap.

The distance GH measures the excess of spending over full-employment output.

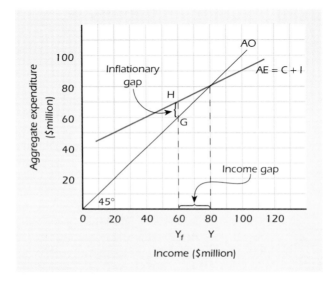

At the full-employment level of output, intended aggregate expenditure exceeds full employment aggregate output by GH; hence GH represents the inflationary gap. The gap between the full-employment level of output and the equilibrium level of output is the income or output gap.

THE DEFLATIONARY GAP

Consider now a situation in which, at full employment, desired aggregate expenditure is less than aggregate output. In such a situation, the economy's resources will not be fully employed, and prices may even fall. A deflationary situation exists. A deflationary situation, strictly speaking, refers to a situation of falling prices. In this situation, we are likely to witness a reduction in production levels and an increase in unemployment much sooner than a fall in prices. For this reason, the term *recessionary* seems to be preferable.

Let us look once more at Table 26.5. Suppose that the full-employment level of output is $100 million. At that level of output, desired aggregate expenditure is $90 million. Because total intended spending falls short of the full-employment output, the

A deflationary (recessionary) gap exists when total spending is less than the full-employment output.

economy cannot attain its full-employment level of output, so some resources are unemployed. There is a deflationary gap or a recessionary gap. The **recessionary gap** or **deflationary gap** is the amount by which desired aggregate expenditure falls short of aggregate output at full employment.

In our example, aggregate expenditure would have to increase by $10 million to reach the full-employment level of output; hence, the size of the recessionary gap is $10 million. Note that a recessionary gap of $10 million with a multiplier of 2 gives a $20 million difference between the full-employment output of $100 million and the equilibrium level of income of $80 million. Figure 26.7 illustrates the deflationary gap. At the full-employment level of output, desired aggregate expenditure falls short of the full-employment output by EF. Thus, EF represents the recessionary gap.

FIGURE 26.7

The recessionary gap.

The distance EF measures the deficiency of total spending below the full employment output.

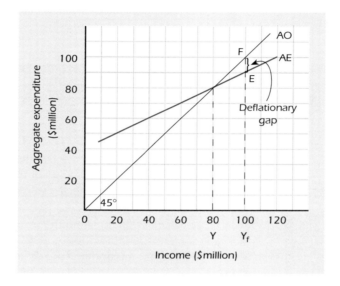

THE NEED FOR POLICY

One of the objectives of macroeconomic policy is to achieve full employment without inflation. When a gap exists between the equilibrium level of income and the full-employment level of income, economic policy may be used to close the gap. In the inflationary gap situation shown in Diagram A of Figure 26.8, there is a need for economic policies that will reduce desired aggregate expenditure from AE to AE_0, and thus eliminate the gap. Desired aggregate expenditure will then exactly equal the full-employment output. Equilibrium will occur at full employment without inflation.

In the deflationary gap situation shown in Diagram B of Figure 26.8, there is a need for macroeconomic policies that will raise the desired aggregate expenditure curve from AE to AE_1. Equilibrium will then be at the full-employment level, and there will be no inflation. Appropriate macroeconomic policies designed to change desired aggregate expenditure will be discussed in subsequent chapters.

FIGURE 26.8

Closing the full-employment gaps.

Policies may be required to shift AE in order to close the gaps.

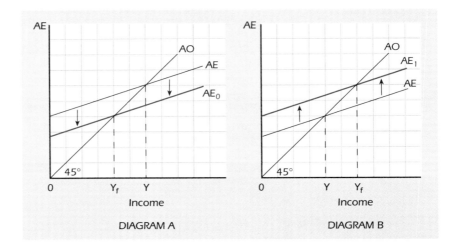

DIAGRAM A   DIAGRAM B

CHAPTER SUMMARY

1. A given change in investment spending will generate an even greater change in the equilibrium level of income.

2. The paradox of thrift refers to the fact that an increase in desired aggregate saving, other things being equal, leads to a fall in total income and hence to a fall in actual aggregate saving.

3. The multiplier effect refers to the fact that an increase in spending generates an even greater increase in equilibrium income. For a simple closed economy with neither government spending nor taxation, the multiplier is the reciprocal of the MPS. More generally, the multiplier is the reciprocal of the marginal propensity to withdraw.

4. The marginal propensity to withdraw in Canada in 1996-97 was approximately 0.73. This gives an estimate of 1.37 for the multiplier for Canada.

5. The inflationary gap is the amount by which aggregate expenditure exceeds aggregate output at full employment. When there is an inflationary gap, prices will tend to rise.

6. The recessionary gap is the amount by which aggregate expenditure falls short of the full-employment output. When there is a recessionary gap, output and employment will tend to fall. Depending on the size of the gap, prices may also fall.

7. Macroeconomic policies can be used to shift the aggregate expenditure curve and thus close inflationary and recessionary gaps.

TERMS FOR REVIEW

paradox of thrift (saving) (450)   generalized multiplier (454)
multiplier effect (452)   inflationary gap (456)
multiplier (453)   deflationary (recessionary) gap (457)
marginal propensity to withdraw (454)

QUESTIONS FOR REVIEW AND DISCUSSION

1. What effect will an increase in investment have on the equilibrium level of income in the product market? (L.O.1)

2. Why might firms decide to increase their investment spending? (General)

3. What would happen to the equilibrium level of income in Canada if Canadian households increased their saving? (L.O.2)

4. Explain the paradox of thrift. (L.O.2)

5. If Ms. Jones decides to save an additional $100, her saving increases by $100. If, however, everyone decides to save an extra $100, total saving does not increase. Explain. (L.O.2)

6. What is the multiplier? Briefly explain how it works. (L.O.3)

7. What is the relationship between the marginal propensity to consume, the marginal propensity to save, and the multiplier in a simple closed economy with neither government spending nor taxation? (L.O.3)

8. Explain how you would estimate the multiplier for Canada. (L.O.3)

9. Explain how full-employment gaps may originate. (L.O.4)

10. What is the difference between the inflationary gap and the recessionary (deflationary) gap? What is the implication of these gaps for economic policy? (L.O.4)

11. What is the relationship between the deflationary gap and the output (income) gap? (L.O.4)

PROBLEMS AND EXERCISES

1. Use a saving-investment diagram similar to Figure 26.1 (Diagram A) to show the effect of a reduction in investment on the equilibrium level of income. Compare the change in investment with the resulting change in income. (L.O.1)

2. Demonstrate graphically the effect of a reduction in saving, given the level of income, on the equilibrium level of income. (L.O.2)

3. An expenditure of $15 million is made to repair a part of the Trans-Canada Highway. If the marginal propensity to withdraw in Canada is 5/9, what effect will such an expenditure have on total income in Canada? (L.O.2,3)

4. In a simple closed economy with no government spending and no taxes, an increase in investment from $60 million to $90 million results in an increase in income from $400 million to $520 million. What is the MPC in this economy? (L.O.3)

5. Table 26.6 gives data for a simple closed economy with no government spending and no taxes. (L.O.4)

TABLE 26.6	Income	Consumption
Income and consumption data in $million.	6000	5000
	6100	5075
	6200	5150
	6300	5225
	6400	5300
	6500	5375
	6600	5450
	6700	5525
	6800	5600
	6900	5675

(a) Calculate the marginal propensity to consume at an income level of $6400 million.

(b) Calculate the marginal propensity to save at an income level of $6400 million.

(c) If the full-employment output is $6700 million and investment is fixed at $1200 million, is there an inflationary gap or a deflationary gap? What is the size of the gap (if any)?

(d) If the full-employment output is $6900 million and investment is fixed at $1200 million, is there an inflationary gap or a recessionary gap? What is the size of the gap (if any)?

6. Table 26.7 gives data for a simple closed economy in which government neither spends nor taxes. (L.O.3,4)

TABLE 26.7

Consumption and investment data.

Income (output)	Consumption	Investment	Aggregate expenditure
30	45	10	55
40	50	10	60
50	55	10	65
60	60	10	70
70	65	10	75
80	70	10	80
90	75	10	85
100	80	10	90
110	85	10	95
120	90	10	100

(a) If the full-employment output is 120, calculate the amount by which this full-employment output exceeds the equilibrium level of income.

(b) Calculate the gap between the full-employment output and aggregate expenditure. Is this an inflationary gap or a recessionary gap?

(c) Calculate the multiplier.

(d) Multiply your answer for part (b) by your answer for part (c). The result now should be the same as your answer for part (a).

7. Table 26.8 contains data on income and consumption for a closed economy with no government spending and no taxes. (L.O.3)

TABLE 26.8

Consumption schedule.

Income	Consumption
100	80
200	160
300	240
400	320
500	400
600	480
700	560

(a) Draw the consumption curve.

(b) On the same graph, draw the saving curve.

(c) Calculate the slope of the saving curve.

(d) Calculate the multiplier.

27

C H A P T E R

CONSUMPTION AND INVESTMENT

Learning Objectives

After studying this chapter, you should know about:

1 the consumption function

2 the factors that influence consumption expenditure

3 the difference between a movement along the consumption function and a shift of the consumption function

4 the life-cycle and permanent-income hypotheses

5 the different categories of investment

6 the determinants of investment spending

7 how interest rates affect investment

8 the difference between a movement along the investment demand curve and a shift of the investment demand curve

---

Clearly, it is very important to understand what determines the amount of investment that actually takes place.

Dudley Dillard, *The Economics of John Maynard Keynes*

INTRODUCTION

Our analysis of the equilibrium level of income in the product market in Chapter 25 and the discussion of changes in aggregate expenditure and income in Chapter 26 suggest that an understanding of aggregate expenditure is vital for an understanding of how the macroeconomy functions. You will recall that aggregate expenditure (AE) is the sum of consumption (C), investment (I), government purchases of goods and services (G), and net exports (X – M). That is,

$$AE = C + I + G + (X - M)$$

To understand aggregate expenditure, we must examine its components. In this chapter, we study the first two components (C and I), and in later chapters, we shall examine the other components — government spending and net exports. We have studied the effects of changes in saving or consumption and changes in investment on the equilibrium level of income. But what are the factors that cause consumption and investment to change? That is the question that will occupy our attention in this chapter.

THE CONSUMPTION FUNCTION

Learning Objective 1:
the consumption function

In Chapter 25, we discussed an important relationship between consumption and personal disposable income. There, personal disposable income was assumed to be the only determinant of current consumption. Consequently, the consumption function was expressed as

$$C = C(Y_d)$$

where C represents consumption and Y_d disposable income. But personal disposable income is not the only determinant of consumption.

What are the factors that determine the amount of consumption expenditure that takes place in an economy? Strictly speaking, the factors are numerous; however, economists have singled out certain ones that are considered to be particularly important. These factors are

- the level of disposable income
- wealth
- availability of credit
- interest rates
- stock of durable consumer goods
- expectations
- income distribution

The consumption function is the relation between consumption spending and its determining factors.

When we express consumption as a function of these determinants, we obtain the consumption function. The **consumption function** is the relationship between current consumption and all of the factors that influence consumer spending.

Using the functional notation, we can express the consumption function as

$$C = C(Y_d, W, CR, r, DG, Ex, Y_{dis})$$

where C = consumer spending, Y_d = personal disposable income, W = wealth, CR = availability of credit, r = interest rates, DG = stock of durable consumer goods, Ex = expectations, and Y_{dis} = income distribution. This expression is just a technical way of saying that consumption is affected by changes in any of these variables. We shall discuss each of the determinants of consumption expenditure in turn.

DETERMINANTS OF CONSUMPTION EXPENDITURE

THE LEVEL OF INCOME

The level of current disposable income is an important determinant of consumer spending.

Learning Objective 2: the factors that influence consumption expenditure

The level of current disposable income is certainly one of the most important factors affecting consumer spending. For many economists, including Keynes, income was the principal determinant of consumer spending. The following quotation from Keynes' revolutionary book, *The General Theory of Employment, Interest and Money*, indicates the importance of income as a determinant of consumption expenditure.

> The fundamental psychological law, upon which we are entitled to depend with great confidence both *a priori* from our knowledge of human nature and from the detailed facts of experience, is that men are disposed, as a rule and on the average, to increase their consumption as their income increases, but not by as much as the increase in their income.*

The above passage says, in effect, that the marginal propensity to consume is greater than 0 but less than 1:

$$0 < MPC < 1$$

Keynes' fundamental psychological law states that people increase consumption as their income increases, but by less than the increase in income.

This **fundamental psychological law** is consistent with a linear income-consumption relation that exhibits a constant marginal propensity to consume, or with an income-consumption relation that exhibits a declining marginal propensity to consume. A declining marginal propensity to consume means that, as income increases, a smaller fraction of the increase in income is allocated to consumption. The consumption schedule shown in Table 27.1. shows a consumption-income relation with a declining marginal propensity to consume. The consumption-income data contained in Table 27.1 are plotted in Figure 27.1.

TABLE 27.1	Disposable income	Consumption	MPC
A consumption-income relation with a declining MPC.	100	80	
	150	120	0.80
	200	155	0.70
	250	185	0.60
	300	210	0.50
	350	230	0.40
	400	245	0.30
	450	255	0.20
	500	260	0.10

*J. M. Keynes, *The General Theory of Employment, Interest and Money* (New York: Harcourt, Brace & Co., 1936), p. 96.

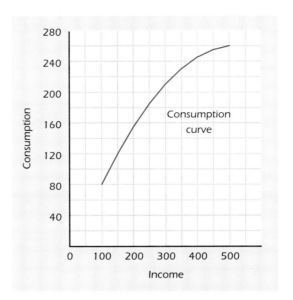

A consumption curve that displays a diminishing marginal propensity to consume implies that high-income earners have relatively low marginal propensities to consume and that low-income earners have relatively high marginal propensities to consume.

PROBLEM SOLVING 27-1

Mr. Adam earns an annual salary of $225 000. Mr. Buntin earns $12 000. If the government takes $5000 in taxes from Mr. Adam and transfers it to Mr. Buntin, what effect will this redistribution of income between Mr. Adam and Mr. Buntin have on total consumption?

WEALTH

Learning Objective 2:
the factors that influence
consumption expenditure

Wealth is the value of one's
assets.

It is important to distinguish between income and wealth. Income is money received during a period of time. **Wealth**, on the other hand, is the dollar value of one's assets at a particular time. Recall the distinction between a stock variable and a flow variable. Income is a flow variable, while wealth is a stock variable. At any given level of current disposable income, wealthier people spend more on consumer goods and services. If people's wealth changes, they are likely to change their consumption somewhat. If, for example, real estate prices rise, owners of real estate will feel better off, and this will tend to cause an increase in their consumption.

PROBLEM SOLVING 27-2

How might a stock market crash affect consumption?

THE AVAILABILITY OF CREDIT

Good credit conditions
favour consumption
spending.

Durable consumer goods such as automobiles, furniture, and appliances are usually purchased on a credit basis. We can expect that, if credit becomes easily available on good terms, expenditure on these items will increase. On the other hand, if it becomes difficult to obtain credit, or if the terms of credit become onerous, then we can expect expenditure on these items to decrease. In a situation where automobiles can be purchased with a low down payment and a long repayment period, consumers are likely to increase their purchases of automobiles. Moreover, easy credit terms on certain items make more funds available to consumers for the purchase of other consumer goods and services. If, for example, I can pay down 10% on a suite of furniture instead of 50%, then I am left with additional funds for other purchases.

THE RATE OF INTEREST

Closely associated with the availability of credit is the rate of interest. In fact, the rate of interest is one of the terms on which credit is available. We can look at the effect of the rate of interest on consumption spending in two ways. First, high interest rates act as a deterrent to consumers who want to borrow in order to purchase certain goods. Low interest rates, on the other hand, reduce the cost of borrowing and thus cause an increase in expenditure on these goods. Second, high interest rates may encourage households to save more. If households save more out of a given level of income, it means that they consume less. High interest rates will therefore cause consumption expenditure to decrease, while low interest rates will cause it to increase.

Low interest rates tend to stimulate consumer spending, while high interest rates discourage consumer spending.

THE EXISTING STOCK OF DURABLE CONSUMER GOODS

If the existing stock of durable consumer goods in an economy happens to fall to unusually low levels, then we can expect an increase in consumer spending. Why? This is so because households will attempt to replenish their holdings of durable consumer goods. The rusted, old 1987 car will need to be replaced, and the old refrigerator, which keeps spoiling expensive cuts of meat, has seen its best days and must be put out for the garbage collectors. A classic example of the effect of the existing stock of durable goods on consumption occurred after World War II. The stock of durable consumer goods had fallen by that time because resources were diverted from the production of consumer durables to the production of military goods. After the war, consumption expenditure on consumer durables rose considerably as households tried to replace old goods.

Consumer spending is affected by the existing stock of durable consumer goods.

EXPECTATIONS

Consumers' expectations about their future circumstances significantly affect the level of consumer spending. If consumers view the future with gloom and uncertainty, they may decide to reduce their consumption until the future appears more optimistic. On the other hand, if consumers have an optimistic outlook about the future (such as a more solid economic position), they may decide to increase their current purchases of goods and services. Expectations regarding changes in prices also tend to influence consumption spending. If consumers expect prices to rise, they tend to increase their current purchases in an attempt to avoid the higher future prices. An expected fall in prices prompts consumers to delay their current purchases in order to take advantage of the lower prices in the future.

Expectations of future changes in prices and incomes affect consumer spending.

INCOME DISTRIBUTION (THE ROBIN HOOD EFFECT)

You have seen, earlier in this chapter, that households with high incomes tend to have a relatively low marginal propensity to consume, while those with low incomes tend to have a relatively high marginal propensity to consume. In other words, the marginal propensity to consume diminishes as income increases. That being the case, a redistribution of income from high-income earners to lower-income earners will result in an increase in aggregate spending on consumer goods and services. The activities of Robin Hood, the medieval English outlaw of Sherwood Forest, must have contributed significantly to total spending on consumer goods and services. We shall refer to the effect of income redistribution on consumption as the **Robin Hood effect**. One of my students

A redistribution of income from high-income earners to low-income earners increases consumer spending. This can be called the Robin Hood effect.

once remarked that the activities of Robin Hood are still being actively carried on in Canada, but under a different name. I asked, "Under what name?" The student replied quite seriously, "The government."

PROBLEM SOLVING 27-3

In a certain country, average income increased over a year. During the same year, the interest rate on consumer loans rose from 10% to 13%. Since consumption is expected to rise as income rises, should furniture dealers be surprised to find their total sales down below the previous year's level?

A SHIFT OF THE CONSUMPTION FUNCTION VERSUS A MOVEMENT ALONG THE CONSUMPTION FUNCTION

Learning Objective 3: the difference between a movement along the consumption function and a shift of the consumption function

Before we proceed, we must understand the difference between a movement along the consumption function and a shift of the consumption function. You will remember that a similar distinction was made between a movement along a demand curve and a shift of the demand curve.

We have postulated that an increase in income, other things being equal, results in an increase in consumption expenditure. Figure 27.2 shows that an increase in income from $200 million to $300 million results in an increase in consumption from $250 million to $300 million. This change in consumption when income changes is represented by a movement from point A to point B along the consumption curve. If consumption spending increases at each and every given level of income, however, a new consumption-income relation will be established.

In Table 27.2, columns one and two show the initial consumption-income relation. Column three shows the new level of consumption spending at each level of income. Note that, in this case, the change in consumption spending is due not to a change in income but to a change in a non-income determinant of consumption such as credit availability, the rate of interest, the existing stock of consumer durables, expectations, or income distribution.

This change in the income-consumption relation is illustrated graphically in Diagram A of Figure 27.3 by a shift of the consumption curve from C_1 to C_2. We have examined an increase in consumption resulting from a change in a non-income determinant, and have demonstrated that this increase results in an upward shift of the consumption

FIGURE 27.2

The effect of an increase in income.

The effect of a change in income is shown as a movement along the consumption curve.

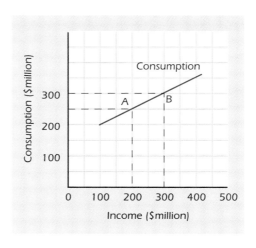

TABLE 27.2

Consumption-income relation (hypothetical data in $million).

A change in a non-income determinant of consumption changes the consumption-income relation.

Income (1)	Initial consumption level (2)	New consumption level (3)
200	250	300
300	300	350
400	350	400
500	400	450
600	450	500
700	500	550
800	550	600
900	600	650
1000	650	700
1100	700	750

FIGURE 27.3

A change in consumption due to a change in a non-income determinant.

The consumption curve shifts when there is a change in a non-income determinant of consumption.

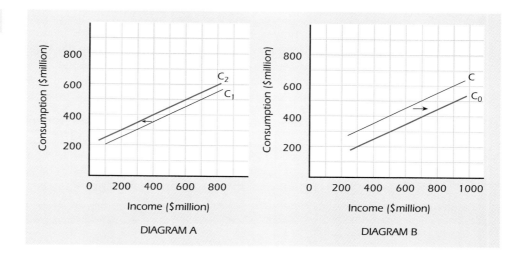

DIAGRAM A

DIAGRAM B

curve. A reduction in consumption spending, given the level of income, would be shown graphically by a downward shift of the consumption function as shown in Diagram B of Figure 27.3. We can summarize the discussion as follows:

> **A change in income causes a movement along the consumption curve; a change in a non-income determinant of consumption causes the consumption curve to shift.**

PROBLEM SOLVING 27-4

The government decides to reduce the tax rate from 20% of taxable income to 15% of taxable income. What is the likely effect of this tax change on private consumption?

THE LIFE-CYCLE AND PERMANENT-INCOME HYPOTHESES

The current-income hypothesis states that a change in a non-income determinant of consumption causes the income-consumption relation to change.

The consumption-income relation discussed in the previous section and in Chapter 25 is a relationship between current consumer spending and current disposable income. We may refer to this relationship as the **current-income hypothesis**, or the *Keynesian consumption function*. It may seem reasonable enough that if current disposable income rises, people will purchase more consumer goods. However, a group of economists including Milton Friedman, Franco Modigliani, and Albert Ando (among others) have argued that current expenditure on consumer goods and services depends not so much on current disposable income, but more so on expected stream of future income over a considerable length of time, and on wealth.

Learning Objective 4:
the life-cycle and perma-
nent-income hypotheses

Consumption may depend
more on permanent
income than on current
income.

The **permanent-income hypothesis** of Milton Friedman and the Modigliani-Ando **life-cycle hypothesis** are different in many ways; yet they are sufficiently similar to justify presenting them together. The central idea is that a transitory increase in income will have little or no effect on households' expenditure on goods and services if it does not significantly affect households' future income expectations.

The following example will illustrate the idea behind the permanent-income and life-cycle hypotheses. It will also serve to demonstrate the difference between these hypotheses and the current-income hypothesis. Suppose a household wins a lottery this year. According to the current-income hypothesis, the household's consumption this year will increase dramatically to reflect the increase in current income, but will return to its normal lower level thereafter. According to the permanent-income and life-cycle hypotheses, however, since the household will not expect to win lotteries in succeeding years, it is more likely to spread the proceeds from the lottery over several years in the future and adjust its consumption pattern to this long-term income.

A graphical illustration will help to highlight the difference between these hypotheses. Diagram A of Figure 27.4 shows a Keynesian consumption function relating cur-

FIGURE 27.4

Illustration of
Keynesian and life-
cycle and permanent-
income hypotheses of
the consumption
function.

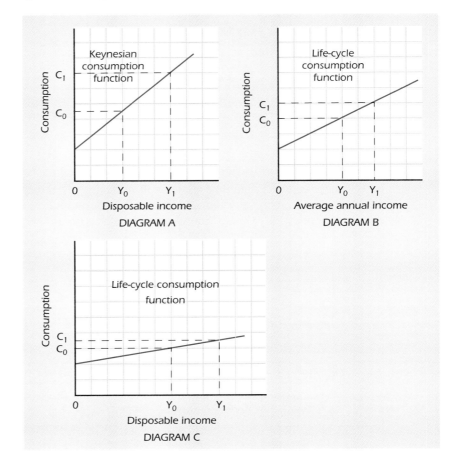

rent consumption to current disposable income. Note that as current disposable income rises, current consumption also rises. Diagram B illustrates the life-cycle/permanent-income consumption function in which current consumption is related to average long-term income. An increase in average long-term income results in an increase in current consumption. Finally, Diagram C illustrates that according to the life-cycle/permanent-income consumption function, current consumption is not affected much by current disposable income. The implications of the life-cycle/permanent-income hypothesis for government fiscal policy will be discussed in a later chapter.

INVESTMENT DEMAND

Investment was an important element in our theory of income determination. Investment refers to expenditure on machinery, equipment, residential and non-residential construction, and inventories, which, as we have already seen, play an important role in the adjustment process of aggregate expenditure and aggregate output. Investment spending accounts for about 15% of aggregate spending.

Learning Objective 5:
the different categories of investment

Residential construction, non-residential construction, and machinery and equipment constitute gross fixed capital formation. Table 27.3 contains data on the main categories of investment in Canada for 1992. Although inventory investment constitutes the smallest percentage of total investment, it is the most volatile of the components of total investment. The instability of inventory investment is believed to be a prime cause of shifts in investment.

TABLE 27.3

Investment categories, 1995.

Investment category	Amount ($million)	% of total
Government investment:		
Fixed capital	17 416	12.1
Inventories	30	0.02
Business fixed capital:		
Residential construction	39 148	27.1
Non residential construction	32 809	22.7
Machinery and equipment	48 198	33.4
Business inventories	6 851	4.7
TOTAL	144 452	100.0

Source: Statistics Canada, *Canadian Economic Observer* (Cat. 11-010XPB), March 1996: 3.

DETERMINANTS OF INVESTMENT SPENDING

Learning Objective 6:
the determinants of investment spending

As in the case of consumer spending, the factors influencing the level of investment spending are numerous. Economists generally agree that the following factors exert significant influence on the level of investment:

- the rate of interest
- retained earnings
- the level of profits
- expectations
- the rate of technological change
- the level of national income
- the rate of change of national income

The investment function is the relation between investment spending and its determining factors.

When we express investment spending as a function of these determinants, we obtain the investment function. The **investment function** is the relation between investment spending and all of the factors that determine it.

Using functional notation, we can express the investment function as

$$I = I(r, RE, \pi, Ex, Tc, Y, \dot{Y})$$

where I = investment, r = rate of interest, RE = retained earnings, π = level of profits, Ex = expectations, Tc = the rate of technological change, Y = income, and $\dot{Y}$ = the rate of change of national income.

If we assume that all of the determinants of investment (except the rate of interest) are fixed, then the investment function is reduced to a relation between two variables — the rate of interest and the level of investment — and appears as

$$I = I(r)$$

We will discuss each of these factors in turn.

THE RATE OF INTEREST

Low interest rates encourage investment, while high interest rates discourage investment.

Learning Objective 7: how interest rates affect investment

We can look at the rate of interest as the cost of borrowing money. If interest rates are high, firms find it more expensive to borrow funds for investment purposes. Hence, a low level of investment is associated with a high rate of interest. On the other hand, if the rate of interest is low, firms find it more profitable to invest. An interest rate of 20% makes an investment loan much more costly than an interest rate of 10% does.

Investment decisions are often made on the basis of a comparison of the rate of interest and the expected rate of return. The expected rate of return from an investment is the expected percentage profit on the money outlay used to acquire capital goods such as new buildings and equipment. Thus, an expected rate of return of 10% means that investors expect to earn an annual profit of 10% on their investment. The effect of the rate of interest on investment decisions can be illustrated by the following example. Suppose a firm is contemplating five investment projects with expected rates of return as shown in Table 27.4. Let us suppose that the firm can borrow money at an interest rate of 8%. At this rate of interest, all five projects are profitable since the expected rate of return on all five exceeds the rate of interest. If the interest rate is 14%, only projects one and two are profitable; and if the interest rate is 20%, none of the projects is profitable. Clearly, high interest rates tend to reduce investment spending, while low interest rates tend to increase investment spending.

TABLE 27.4

Rates of return for investment projects.

Projects	Expected rate of return (%)
1	18
2	16
3	13
4	10
5	9

Marginal efficiency of investment: inverse relation between the rate of interest and the level of investment.

Figure 27.5 shows the relation between the rate of interest and the level of investment. Economists use the term **marginal efficiency of investment** (MEI) to summarize this inverse relation between the rate of interest and the level of investment. The graph shows that, at a rate of interest of 18%, the level of investment is $40 million. When the rate of interest falls to 10%, the level of investment increases to $90 million. This graph is also referred to as the **investment demand curve**.

As the rate of interest falls,
the level of investment
rises.

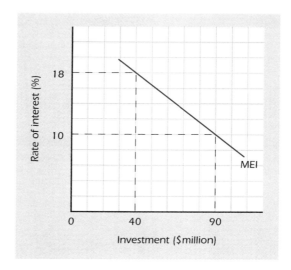

RETAINED EARNINGS

The amount of retained
earnings affects the level of
investment.

Firms do not usually pay out all their after-tax profits to their shareholders. The amount withheld is called **retained earnings** or *undistributed profits*. Obviously, if firms have a large amount of retained earnings, they need not depend so heavily on loans for investment funds. Investment spending can be undertaken with retained earnings. The greater the amount of retained earnings, the greater the level of investment is likely to be.

PROBLEM SOLVING 27-5

Should a firm with sufficient retained earnings to finance its investment projects be concerned with the rate of interest in its investment decisions?

THE LEVEL OF PROFITS

High levels of profits may
encourage investment
spending.

Closely associated with the amount of retained earnings at the firms' disposal is the level of profits. High profit margins enable firms to secure larger undistributed profits which can be allocated to investment. It can also be argued that high profits act as an incentive for firms to expand. And expansion involves purchasing new plant and equipment.

EXPECTATIONS

Business expectations and
confidence influence investment.

The expectations of businesspeople undoubtedly play an important role in determining the amount of investment that takes place in an economy. If firms believe that their sales are going to fall off, they will most likely not undertake new investment. On the other hand, if they have optimistic expectations about the demand for their products, they are likely to purchase new equipment and invest in inventories in order to meet the expected high level of demand.

THE RATE OF TECHNOLOGICAL CHANGE

The rate of technological
change and the rate of
introduction of new prod-
ucts affect investment.

New and more efficient machines are constantly being introduced. The faster the rate at which this occurs, the greater the rate of obsolescence of existing stocks of capital goods — hence, the greater the amount of investment. The development of new products and new production methods may also cause firms to invest in new plants and equipment. For example, the development of synthetic products has resulted in substantial investment.

GLOBAL PERSPECTIVE

A Comparative Look at the Growth of Investment and Consumption

In any economy, the rate of saving is of crucial importance. Saving provides funds for investment purposes. We have seen, however, that if savings are not channelled into investment, then the level of economic activity may decline. This capsule takes a look at the growth rate of fixed investment in the G-7 countries between 1988 and 1997.

The graph illustrates that gross fixed investment grew at an average annual rate of 2.4% in Canada. Thus, Canada ranked fourth among the world's leading industrial countries. Japan took the lead with an average rate of growth in gross fixed investment of 3.9% during the 1988–97 period. Germany was second with

3.1%, while Italy had an average annual rate of less than 1.3%.

Consumption is the largest component of GDP. Personal expenditure on consumer goods and services therefore constitutes an important economic activity. In addition to looking at investment in G-7 countries, this capsule also looks at the growth of consumer spending. As can be seen from the graph, during the 1988-97 period, Japan experienced the highest average annual increase in consumer spending at 3.0%. This was followed by Germany (2.7%), the United States (2.3%), and France (2.0%). Canada and Italy were tied for last place with 1.9% average annual growth in consumer spending.

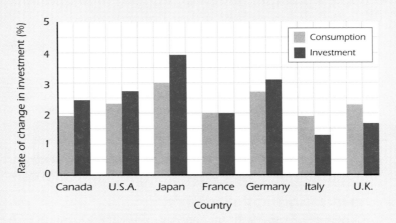

Source: International Monetary Fund, *World Economic Outlook*, October 1996: 169.

THE LEVEL OF INCOME

A direct relation exists between the level of income and the level of investment.

Economists have observed that, when total income is high, investment tends to be high. When total income is low, investment tends to be low. It seems, therefore, that the level of total income has some influence on the level of investment. It could be that a high level of income inspires optimism and confidence, while a low level of income inspires pessimism. As we saw in an earlier section, expectations about future business conditions are likely to affect firms' investment decisions.

THE RATE OF CHANGE OF NATIONAL INCOME

Not only the level of income but also the change in income will affect investment.

An increase in national income leads to an increase in demand for goods and services. In order to produce more goods and services to satisfy this greater demand, firms require a larger capital stock. Investment in plant and equipment must therefore occur. In our preliminary discussion of investment in the previous chapter, we assumed that investment does not depend on changes in income. That is, investment was considered to be

Autonomous investment does not depend on changes in income, whereas induced investment does.

autonomous. We now postulate that investment does depend on changes in income. Investment resulting from changes in income is called **induced investment**.

PROBLEM SOLVING 27-6

The higher the level of income, the greater the amount of investment. Is it surprising that at an income level of $500 million, investment is $15 million, and at an income level of $150 million, investment is $50 million?

Learning Objective 8:
the difference between a movement along the investment demand curve and a shift of the investment demand curve.

Note: You should be careful not to confuse a movement along the investment demand curve with a shift of the curve. A change in the rate of interest will cause a movement along the curve, but any of the other determinants of investment will shift the investment curve.

CHAPTER SUMMARY

1. The consumption function is a relation between consumption and all of the factors that determine consumption. Among the factors that influence the amount of consumer spending are: the level of current income, wealth, credit availability, the rate of interest, existing stocks of consumer durables, expectations, and income distribution.

2. Income is the amount of money received during a period of time. Wealth is the value of one's assets at a particular time. Income is a flow variable, but wealth is a stock variable.

3. The fundamental psychological law states that if income increases, consumption will increase, but not by as much as the increase in income. This sets the value of the marginal propensity to consume between 0 and 1.

4. The marginal propensity to consume declines as income increases; thus, a redistribution of income from high income groups to low income groups will increase total consumption.

5. A change in consumption resulting from a change in income is illustrated by a movement along the consumption curve. A change in consumption resulting from a change in a non-income determinant of consumption is illustrated graphically by a shift of the consumption curve.

6. The permanent-income and life-cycle hypotheses state that consumption depends on permanent income and on wealth.

7. Investment spending accounts for about 20% of total spending.

8. The main categories of investment spending are government investment and business fixed capital, which includes residential construction, non-residential construction, and machinery and equipment.

9. Some of the determinants of investment spending are interest rates, retained earnings, the level of profits, expectations, the rate of technological change, the level of income, and the rate of change in income.

10. The relation between the rate of interest and the level of investment is summarized in the marginal efficiency of investment (MEI) schedule.

TERMS FOR REVIEW

consumption function (462)

fundamental psychological
  law (463)

wealth (464)

Robin Hood effect (465)

movement along vs. shift of the
  consumption curve (467)

current-income hypothesis (467)

permanent-income and life-cycle
  hypotheses (468)

investment function (470)

marginal efficiency of investment
  (MEI) schedule (470)

retained earnings (471)

autonomous investment (473)

induced investment (473)

QUESTIONS FOR REVIEW AND DISCUSSION

1. What are the main factors likely to affect the level of consumer spending in an economy? (L.O.2)

2. What relation would you expect between wealth and consumption? (L.O.2)

3. How does the current-income hypothesis differ from the permanent-income and life-cycle hypotheses? (L.O.1,4)

4. What are some of the non-income factors that influence consumer spending? (L.O.2)

5. Explain how each of the following events affects current consumption: (L.O.2)

    (a) an announcement by economists that the economy will experience a period of rapid economic growth within the very near future

    (b) a significant reduction in personal income taxes

    (c) a law forbidding the extensive use of credit

    (d) a successful advertising campaign by commercial banks to attract savings

    (e) an announcement by the finance minister that all sales taxes will be abolished within three months

    (f) an announcement that there is going to be a general shortage of goods

6. Why might a redistribution of income from wealthy individuals to poorer individuals stimulate total spending on consumer goods and services? (L.O.2)

7. What do economists mean by the term *investment?* What are the major categories of investment? (L.O.5)

8. What are the major determinants of investment? (L.O.6)

9. What is the difference between autonomous investment and induced investment? (General)

10. Explain how each of the following events affects investment: (L.O.6)

    (a) the discovery of a new and more efficient method of producing rubber

    (b) a government announcement of a two-year tax concession for new firms

    (c) a significant increase in the number of marriages

    (d) an announcement by economists that the economy is heading for a long recessionary period

PROBLEMS AND EXERCISES

1. You are given the consumption schedule shown in Table 27.5. (L.O.1)

TABLE 27.5

Income and consumption data.

Income	Consumption	MPC
80	70.00	
90	78.00	
100	85.50	
110	92.50	
120	99.00	
130	105.00	

(a) Compute the marginal propensity to consume and fill in the MPC column.
(b) Graph the consumption curve from the data in Table 27.5.

2. You are given the consumption schedule shown in Table 27.6. (L.O.1,2)

TABLE 27.6

Income and consumption data.

Income	Consumption
60	80
80	90
100	100
120	110
140	120
160	130

(a) Graph the consumption curve.
(b) Construct a new schedule showing the effect of a reduction of the down payment required on most durable consumer goods.
(c) Draw the new consumption curve on the same diagram as (a).

3. Comparing medical students in their final year and Ph.D. economics students in their final year, which group, on average, would you expect to have a higher level of consumption expenditure? Why? (L.O.2,4)

4. After completing your degree in economics, you are hired by a firm of business and economic consultants. One of your clients is asking your advice on whether or not her company should increase production of electrical appliances. Mention three important economic variables that you should study in order to advise your client. (L.O.2)

5. The schedule in Table 27.7 shows the amount of investment that firms are willing to make at different expected rates of return, given that the rate of interest is 10% per year. (L.O.7)

TABLE 27.7

Expected rates of return and investment.

Expected rate of return (%)	Investment ($million)
21	190
19	170
17	140
15	100
13	50
11	40
9	35
7	20
5	10
3	7

(a) Construct a new investment column showing the effect of a rise in interest rates from 10% to 12%. (Make up your own numbers.)

(b) Do you think that the change in the rate of interest affects the expected rate of return? If so, how?

6. Table 27.8 gives interest rates and associated investments. (L.O.7)

TABLE 27.8

Interest rates and investment.

Interest rate (%)	Investment ($million)
20	2
18	12
16	20
14	30
12	42
10	56
8	65

(a) What is this schedule called?

(b) Plot this schedule on a graph with the rate of interest on the vertical axis and investment on the horizontal axis.

(c) What does this relation suggest about a policy to stimulate investment spending?

7. Ask each of six of your friends or acquaintances to compile a short list of four important things that might cause them to spend more on consumer goods and services even if their income did not change. Then compare your lists and see whether or not there are common factors. Check to see whether your lists contain any of the factors listed in this chapter as determinants of consumption.

Internet Site

http://www.economist.com

This is the Web site for the world-famous Economist magazine. As a student of economics, you will find this site to be a useful source of information.

INTERNET EXERCISE

1. Go to the Economist Web site.

2. Click on *current issue*.

3. Write down the name(s) of any article(s) that may be of particular interest to you as a student of economics.

28

C H A P T E R

FISCAL POLICY

Learning Objectives

After studying this chapter, you should be able to:

1 explain how government spending and taxes affect the equilibrium level of net domestic income

2 identify a budget deficit, a budget surplus, and a balanced budget

3 explain the effect of a balanced budget change in spending

4 describe automatic stabilizers and how they work

5 explain how discretionary fiscal policy can be used to close full employment gaps

6 state the significance of the full-employment budget

7 discuss the limitations of fiscal policy

To make fiscal policy work, economists must contaminate themselves with political theory and public administration ... someone must try to bring together the fruits of political, economic, and administrative theory if we are to have a successful fiscal policy.

Arthur Smithies, *Federal Budgeting and Fiscal Policy.*

INTRODUCTION

In Chapters 25 and 26, we studied a simple closed economy in which there was neither government spending nor taxation. Hence the components of aggregate expenditure were assumed to be consumption and investment spending. Thus our aggregate expenditure equation was

$$AE = C + I$$

More realistically, however, government does indeed purchase a significant portion of the economy's output of goods and services. And taxation is a reality — a fact to which anyone who earns income can solemnly attest. In this chapter, our objective is to study the effects of government spending and taxation on income and employment. The introduction of government into our analysis now means that government purchases of goods and services (G) is a component of aggregate expenditure. We continue to assume that the economy is closed, so that

$$AE = C + I + G$$

Throughout the analysis, we assume that changes in planned aggregate expenditure do not affect the rate of interest.

After studying the effects of government spending (G) and taxes (T) on aggregate expenditure and on income and employment, we examine how these variables can be manipulated to promote economic stability.

GOVERNMENT SPENDING AND EQUILIBRIUM NET DOMESTIC INCOME

Learning Objective 1: how government spending and taxes affect the equilibrium level of net domestic income

We assumed that the expenditures of all levels of government (federal, provincial, and local) are independent of the level of income. Thus, changes in income will not affect the level of government spending. Under the assumption that there are neither exports nor imports, aggregate expenditure consists of consumer spending, investment spending, and government spending. If intended AE (C + I + G) exceeds aggregate output, there will either be lines of unsatisfied customers or an unplanned reduction of the inventories of goods previously produced. Either situation will signal firms to increase production, and increased production will result in increased income. On the other hand, if desired (C + I + G) is less than aggregate output, then the inventories of firms will accumulate over their planned levels. This situation will result in a reduction in total production and income. The equilibrium level of income, therefore, will be that level at which desired (C + I + G) equals aggregate output. At this level of income, there will be no change in production levels, because the spending plans of households, firms, and government will coincide with the production plans of firms.

In a closed economy with government spending, equilibrium occurs when Y = C + I + G.

Table 28.1 illustrates the effect of government spending on the equilibrium level of income. Government spending is assumed to be $20 million at each level of income. The consumption and saving schedules are similar to those introduced in Table 25.1. Without government spending, the equilibrium level of net domestic income is $80 million. With government spending of $20 million, desired aggregate expenditure is now $100 million. Since desired AE > AO at an output level of $80 million, firms will increase their production so income rises. Income will reach its equilibrium level at $120 million, where intended aggregate expenditure equals net domestic income. The addition of government spending to intended consumer and investment spending causes the equilibrium level of net domestic income to increase.

	Net domestic income	Desired consumption	Desired investment	Government spending	Desired AE
TABLE 28.1	50	55	10	20	85
	60	60	10	20	90
Government spending	70	65	10	20	95
and equilibrium	80	70	10	20	100
domestic income	90	75	10	20	105
(values in $million).	100	80	10	20	110
	110	85	10	20	115
	120	90	10	20	120
	130	95	10	20	125
	140	100	10	20	130

The equilibrium level of income is illustrated in Figure 28.1. The consumption curve and the C + I line are plotted from the data in Table 28.1. Desired aggregate expenditure is represented by the C + I + G line. At an income level of $80 million, for example, the aggregate expenditure line is above the 45-degree line. This excess of desired aggregate expenditure over aggregate output causes firms to expand their production. At an output level of $140 million, desired aggregate expenditure is below total output. Firms will therefore reduce their production levels. But at a level of income of $120 million, the C + I + G line crosses the 45-degree line. As you now know, the C + I + G line represents desired aggregate spending, and the 45-degree line represents aggregate output. When the two lines intersect, intended aggregate expenditure equals aggregate output — the condition required for equilibrium. The equilibrium level of income is $120 million.

FIGURE 28.1

Equilibrium net domestic income with government spending.

Equilibrium occurs where the C + I + G line intersects the 45-degree line.

EFFECT OF AN INCREASE IN GOVERNMENT SPENDING

Learning Objective 1: how government spending and taxes affect the equilibrium level of net domestic income

It should not be too difficult to figure out the effect caused by a change in government spending on the equilibrium level of net domestic income. Let us consider first the effect of an increase in government spending. Suppose that the economy is in equilibrium at $120 million with government spending at $20 million and consumption and investment as shown in Table 28.1. The situation is illustrated in Figure 28.2. What will be the effect on equilibrium net domestic income of an increase in government spending from $20 million to $30 million? The $10 million increase in government spending will shift the C + I + G line up to C + I + G_1 as shown in Figure 28.2. The effect is an increase in the equilibrium level of net domestic income from $120 million to $140 million.

FIGURE 28.2

Effect of an increase in government spending.

An increase in government spending increases net domestic income.

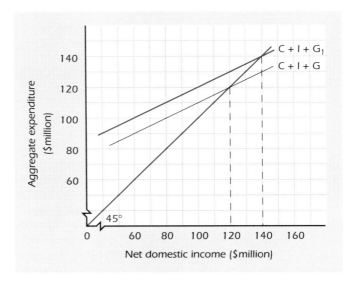

EFFECT OF A DECREASE IN GOVERNMENT SPENDING

Let us now examine the effect of a decrease in government spending. To see how a reduction in government spending affects the equilibrium level of net domestic income we return to our initial equilibrium income of $120 million as shown in Figure 28.3.

Now, suppose that government spending falls from its initial level of $20 million to $10 million. The aggregate expenditure curve will shift downward from C + I + G to C + I + G_0. The $10 million reduction in government spending causes a decrease in the equilibrium net domestic income from $120 million to $100 million.

FIGURE 28.3

Effect of a decrease in government spending.

A reduction in government spending reduces net domestic income.

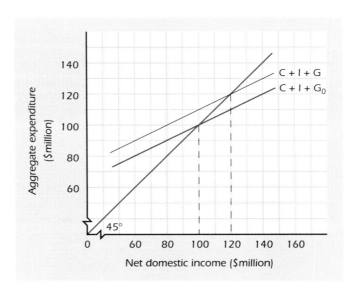

THE GOVERNMENT SPENDING MULTIPLIER

The government spending multiplier, like the investment multiplier, is the reciprocal of the MPS.

You will recall that the simple multiplier for a change in investment spending is the reciprocal of the MPS. You have also seen that a change in government spending produces a change in the equilibrium level of net domestic income that is greater than the change in government spending. For example, a $10 million increase in government spending, given the data in Table 28.1, leads to a $20 million rise in equilibrium net domestic income. The government spending multiplier in this case is 2. A quick look at Table 28.1 will reveal that the MPS is 0.5, and that the investment spending multiplier is 2. The **government spending multiplier** is exactly the same as the investment multiplier. Each is the reciprocal of the marginal propensity to save.

TAXATION AND EQUILIBRIUM NET DOMESTIC INCOME

The imposition of a tax reduces net domestic income.

Learning Objective 1: how government spending and taxes affect the equilibrium level of net domestic income

A lump-sum tax is a fixed tax, independent of income level.

To avoid complicating the analysis, we have assumed, up to this point, that the government does not impose any taxes. Inasmuch as many of us might like that to be true, it is far removed from reality. We must now remove that restriction in order to examine the effect of taxation on the equilibrium level of net domestic income. In order to focus on the effect of taxation, we assume that government spending is zero. To avoid unnecessary complications at this point, we assume also that the government collects a fixed amount of taxes at each and every level of income. Such a tax is referred to as a **lump-sum tax**. Let us suppose now that the amount of the tax is $20 million, and that it is levied on personal income.

The immediate effect of such a tax is to reduce personal disposable income. And since consumer spending depends on disposable income, the imposition of the tax will reduce consumer spending. We are now in a position to examine the effect of taxation on the equilibrium level of net domestic income.

Table 28.2 contains the relevant data. Note that the imposition of the tax makes net domestic income (NDI) different from personal disposable income. Note also that the relation between consumption and disposable income is the same as in Table 28.1. The equilibrium level of net domestic income occurs where intended aggregate expenditure equals aggregate output. This occurs at a net domestic income level of $60 million. In the absence of the tax, the equilibrium level of net domestic income is $80 million. Thus we see that the effect of the tax is to reduce the equilibrium level of net domestic income.

Figure 28.4 shows the equilibrium level of net domestic income with the tax included. Without the tax, the equilibrium level of net domestic income is $80 million, where the C + I line intersects the 45-degree line. With the tax, the relevant desired aggregate

TABLE 28.2	Personal income = NDI	Taxes	Personal disposable income	Desired consumption	Desired investment	Desired AE
Taxation and equilibrium net domestic income (values in $million).	50	20	30	45	10	55
	60	20	40	50	10	60
	70	20	50	55	10	65
	80	20	60	60	10	70
	90	20	70	65	10	75
	100	20	80	70	10	80
	110	20	90	75	10	85
	120	20	100	80	10	90
	130	20	110	85	10	95
	140	20	120	90	10	100

FIGURE 28.4

The equilibrium level of
net domestic income
with taxation.

A tax reduces the aggre-
gate expenditure line.

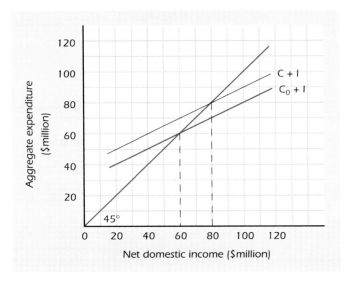

expenditure line is $C_0 + I$. The tax reduces consumption and thus reduces aggregate
expenditure. The equilibrium level of net domestic income is $60 million, where the
$C_0 + I$ line intersects the 45-degree line.

THE EFFECT OF AN INCREASE IN TAXES

Given the data in Table 28.2, the equilibrium level of net domestic income is $60 million.
Now, suppose that taxes increase by $10 million (from $20 million to $30 million). The
$10 million increase in taxes causes personal disposable income to fall by $10 million.
Because the MPC in our example is 0.5, this fall in disposable income causes consumption to fall by $5 million and saving to fall by $5 million. The $5 million fall in
consumption causes the C + I line in Figure 28.5 to shift downward to $C_0 + I$. The equilibrium level of net domestic income falls from $60 million to $50 million.

FIGURE 28.5

Effect of an increase in
taxes.

An increase in taxes
reduces net domestic
income.

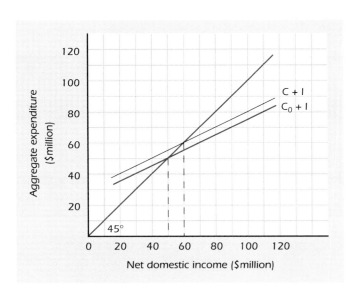

EFFECT OF A DECREASE IN TAXES

Let us now consider something more palatable to most taxpayers — a reduction in taxes. We assume that the initial situation is as shown in Figure 28.6, where the aggregate expenditure line is C + I and the equilibrium level of net domestic income is $60 million. Suppose now that there is a reduction in taxes of $10 million. This will result in an increase of $10 million in personal disposable income. Consumption will consequently increase by $5 million (the MPC is 0.5), causing the C + I line to shift upward to C_1 + I as shown in Figure 28.6. The equilibrium level of income rises from $60 million to $70 million.

FIGURE 28.6

Effect of a decrease in taxes.

A decrease in taxes increases net domestic income.

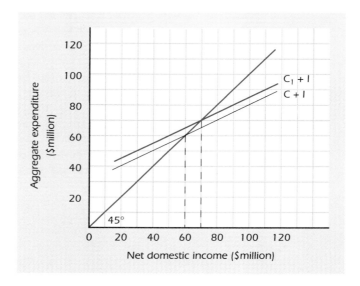

EQUILIBRIUM NET DOMESTIC INCOME WITH GOVERNMENT SPENDING AND TAXES

How will the equilibrium level of net domestic income be affected by government spending and taxation? In this section, we include both government spending and taxes in our model. We assume that the government spends $20 million and collects $20 million in taxes. We continue to assume that the tax is a lump-sum tax, independent of the level of income, and that government spending is autonomous. Consumption and investment remain as before. The relevant data are contained in Table 28.3.

TABLE 28.3

Equilibrium with government spending and taxation (values in $million).

Net domestic income = PI	Taxes	Disposable income	Desired consumption	Desired saving	Desired investment	Government spending	AE
50	20	30	45	−15	10	20	75
60	20	40	50	−10	10	20	80
70	20	50	55	−5	10	20	85
80	20	60	60	0	10	20	90
90	20	70	65	5	10	20	95
100	20	80	70	10	10	20	100
110	20	90	75	15	10	20	105
120	20	100	80	20	10	20	110
130	20	110	85	25	10	20	115
140	20	120	90	30	10	20	120

At a net domestic income of $100 million, desired aggregate expenditure is just equal to aggregate output. At any other level of net domestic income, desired aggregate expenditure will be either greater or less than aggregate output, and firms will tend to increase or reduce their production levels accordingly. Hence, the equilibrium level of net domestic income is $100 million.

THE INJECTIONS-WITHDRAWALS APPROACH

In a closed economy with government spending and taxation, equilibrium net domestic income occurs when I + G = S + T.

In Chapter 25, the injections-withdrawals approach was used, along with the aggregate expenditure-aggregate output approach, to determine the equilibrium level of net domestic income in a closed economy without government. Here too, we can use the injections-withdrawals approach to determine the equilibrium level of net domestic income in a closed economy in which there is government spending and taxation. Recall that equilibrium occurs when the sum of desired injections equals the sum of desired withdrawals.

Government spending injects money into the income-expenditure stream. For example, if the government spends money to extend a highway, the incomes of firms supplying the materials and of people hired to do the work will increase. Taxes levied on the incomes of households reduce the amount that they can spend on the output of firms. Taxes therefore represent a withdrawal or leakage from the income-expenditure stream.

Under our present assumption, the withdrawals are savings and taxes. The injections are investment and government spending. Equilibrium occurs when the sum of desired withdrawals equals the sum of desired injections. That is, when

$$S + T = I + G$$

From Table 28.3, we can see that the only level of net domestic income at which desired $S + T$ = desired $I + G$ is $100 million. At a net domestic income of $120 million, for example, desired $S + T = \$40$ million while desired $I + G = \$30$ million. Because desired withdrawals exceed desired injections, the level of net domestic income will tend to fall. On the other hand, at a net domestic income of $90 million, for example, desired injections $(I + G) = \$30$ million, while desired withdrawals $(S + T) = \$25$ million. Since desired injections exceed desired withdrawals, the level of net domestic income will tend to rise. The equilibrium level of net domestic income is $100 million.

The injections-withdrawals approach can also be illustrated graphically. Figure 28.7 shows the $I + G$ and $S + T$ lines derived from the data in Table 28.3. The injections $(I + G)$ line intersects the withdrawals $(S + T)$ line at a net domestic income of $100 million — the equilibrium level of net domestic income.

FIGURE 28.7

The equilibrium level of net domestic income.

The intersection of the injections line and the withdrawals line determines the equilibrium level of net domestic income.

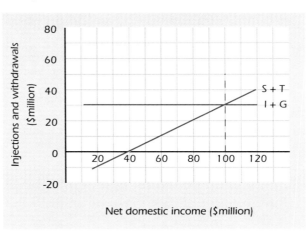

A PROPORTIONAL TAX AND EQUILIBRIUM NET DOMESTIC INCOME

The major advantage of the assumption of a lump-sum tax is its simplicity. The major disadvantage is that it is highly unrealistic. We can move a great deal closer to reality by assuming that taxes are proportional to net domestic income. Let us assume that taxes are set at 20% of net domestic income as shown in Table 28.4. Pre-tax consumption is shown so that the effect of the proportional tax can be easily discerned. Column one shows that before the tax is imposed, net domestic income (NDI), personal income (PI), and personal disposable income (PDI) are all equal. Column two shows desired consumption prior to the imposition of the tax. The consumption-income relation is similar to that assumed in earlier tables. The proportional tax of 20% of NDI is shown in column three. The tax reduces personal disposable income as shown in column four; and since consumption varies with disposable income, the after-tax consumption is less than the pre-tax consumption, as can be seen by comparing columns two and five. In Figure 28.8, the pre-tax consumption is shown by the C line, and the after-tax consumption by the C_1 line. Note that the consumption curve with the proportional tax is flatter than the consumption curve without the tax.

Suppose that the tax were 30% of net domestic income instead of 20%. How would the consumption curve be affected? Let us investigate. As can be seen from Figure 28.8,

	Pre-tax NDI = PI = PDI (1)	Desired pre-tax consumption (2)	Taxes (3)	After-tax PDI (4)	Desired after-tax consumption (5)
TABLE 28.4	50	55	10	40	50
	60	60	12	48	54
The effect of a propor-	70	65	14	56	58
tional tax. Values in	80	70	16	64	62
$million.	90	75	18	72	66
	100	80	20	80	70
	110	85	22	88	74
	120	90	24	96	78
	130	95	26	104	82
	140	100	28	112	86

FIGURE 28.8

The effect of a proportional tax on consumption.

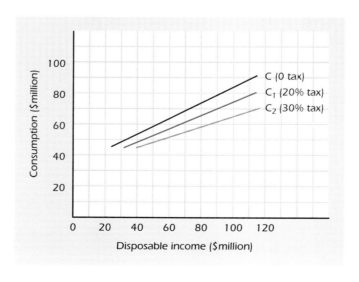

An increase in the tax rate
lowers the marginal
propensity to consume.

an increase in the tax rate from 20% to 30% lowers the consumption curve. Is desired aggregate expenditure also affected? The answer is yes. Since the tax rate affects the consumption curve, it also affects the aggregate expenditure. An increase in the tax rate also reduces the slope of the consumption curve (the MPC) and, therefore, increases the MPS. Thus, it reduces the multiplier. We have reached the following conclusion:

An increase in the tax rate reduces desired consumer spending and hence desired aggregate expenditure. An increase in the tax rate also reduces the slope of the consumption curve and hence reduces the size of the multiplier.

BUDGET POSITIONS

Learning Objective 2: identifying a budget deficit, a budget surplus, and a balanced budget

Discussion of government spending and taxation inevitably leads to the use of certain terms that you must understand. These terms relate to the position of the government's budget and include budget deficit, budget surplus, and balanced budget. We shall now define each of these concepts.

Budget deficit

A budget deficit occurs when the government spends more than it collects in taxes.

A **budget deficit** is said to exist when the government currently spends more than it collects in taxes. The size of the deficit is the difference between government spending (G) and taxes (T).

$$\text{Budget Deficit} = G - T$$

Budget surplus

A budget surplus occurs when the government collects in taxes more than it spends.

A **budget surplus** is said to exist when the government currently spends less than it collects in taxes. The size of the surplus is the difference between taxes and government spending.

$$\text{Budget Surplus} = T - G$$

Balanced budget

A balanced budget occurs when government's expenditures and income from taxes are the same.

A **balanced budget** is said to exist when the government currently spends exactly as much as it collects in taxes. There is no surplus and there is no deficit.

Figure 28.9 will help to clarify these concepts. In the diagram, we assume that government spending is a fixed amount, independent of the level of income, and that taxes

FIGURE 28.9

Budget positions.

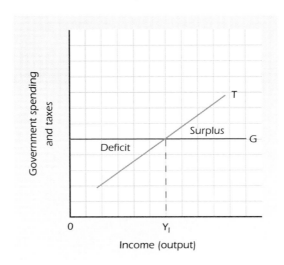

are proportional to income. At a level of income of Y_1, G = T. The budget, therefore, is balanced. At any income level below Y_1, the budget is in deficit. And at any income level above Y_1, the budget is in surplus. The classical economists firmly believed that sound government finance consisted of balancing the budget. We shall see shortly that, following Keynesian economics, **functional finance** (that is, intentional budget deficits and surpluses) can be used as an effective weapon against recessionary and inflationary situations.

Functional finance is intentional budget deficits and surpluses.

THE BALANCED BUDGET MULTIPLIER

Learning Objective 3: the effect of a balanced budget change in spending

A balanced budget increase in spending is expansionary.

Our analysis so far has shown that an increase in government spending tends to increase desired aggregate expenditure and hence net domestic income, whereas an increase in taxes tends to reduce intended aggregate expenditure and hence net domestic income. But what happens if the increase in government spending equals the increase in taxes? In such a case, we say that there is a **balanced budget change in spending**. You may be tempted to conclude that a balanced budget increase in spending would leave income unchanged. But before you come to that conclusion, recall that in an earlier example in this chapter, we showed that an increase in government spending of $10 million resulted in an increase in net domestic income of $20 million, whereas an increase in taxes of $10 million caused net domestic income to fall, not by $20 million, but by $10 million. Thus a given change in government spending seems to have a more powerful effect on net domestic income than does an equivalent change in taxes. Let us see why this is so.

Let us assume that the multiplier is 2 throughout the economy. An increase in government spending of $10 million will generate an increase in net domestic income of $20 million. A government spending multiplier of 2 implies a marginal propensity to consume of 0.5. An increase in taxes of $10 million will therefore cause domestic spending to fall initially not by $10 million but by $5 million (one half of $10 million). With a multiplier of 2, the total decrease in income will be $10 million. When these two effects are combined, there is a net increase in net domestic income of $10 million. Thus we see that a balanced budget change in spending is not neutral. In fact, the result we have derived is called the **balanced budget theorem,** which states that if government spending and taxes increase by the same amount, the resulting increase in net domestic income will equal the increase in government spending.

The balanced budget theorem states that the balanced budget multiplier equals 1.

Looked at another way, we can say that the balanced budget multiplier is 1. An increase in government spending of $50 million followed by an increase in taxes of $50 million will increase net domestic income by $50 million.

AUTOMATIC STABILIZERS

Automatic fiscal policy is built into the economy.

Discretionary fiscal policy is deliberate change in government spending and/or taxes.

Automatic (built-in) stabilizers reduce economic fluctuations.

Learning Objective 4: automatic stabilizers and how they work

Fiscal policy (i.e., changes in government spending and taxes) is one of the main macroeconomic policy tools available to the government. It is analytically useful to distinguish between **automatic fiscal policy** and discretionary fiscal policy. Certain fiscal policy measures have been built into the economic system. These measures operate automatically to increase the budget surplus in inflationary periods and increase the budget deficit in periods of recession. Because they tend to stabilize the economy, they are called **automatic (built-in) stabilizers**. On the other hand, some fiscal policy measures are not built into the system and therefore have to be formulated and implemented deliberately. These measures are called **discretionary fiscal policy**.

Examples of automatic stabilizers are progressive taxes, government assistance to agriculture, and unemployment compensation. Let us examine each of these briefly.

PROGRESSIVE TAXES

In a progressive tax system, the tax rate increases as income increases.

As income increases in a **progressive tax** structure, the proportion paid in taxes increases. Since taxes are withdrawals from the income-expenditure stream, they tend to have a contractionary effect on net domestic income. Progressive taxes prevent the economy from expanding as fast as it would in the absence of progressive taxes. On the other hand, when the economy is in a recession, income tends to fall. And in a progressive tax system, taxes fall even faster. This decrease in taxes prevents the economy from falling as deeply into the recession as would be the case in the absence of progressive taxes.

GOVERNMENT ASSISTANCE TO AGRICULTURE

If the economy is in a recession or a depression, income and aggregate expenditure will both fall. The demand for goods and services (including the demand for agricultural products) will fall. Other things being equal, the price of agricultural products will fall, resulting in a fall in the incomes of farmers. This fall in incomes in the agricultural sector will result in an increase in government spending to support the agricultural sector. The increase in government spending will tend to lessen the severity of the recession. In a period of rapid economic expansion, farmers will require less subsidizing, hence government spending in this area declines. The decline in government spending slows down the rapid expansion in expenditure, which might otherwise be inflationary.

UNEMPLOYMENT COMPENSATION

In a period of economic slowdown and increasing unemployment, the number of people eligible for employment insurance benefits increases. Consequently, there is an increase in government spending, which tends to promote economic activity. On the other hand, if the economy is expanding rapidly and heading for an inflationary period, unemployment will fall, employment insurance benefits will decrease, and consequently, government spending will fall, resulting in a contraction of aggregate expenditure.

THE FISCAL DRAG

We have seen that built-in stabilizers help to prevent the economy from accelerating into an inflation and decelerating into a recession. This type of stability is desirable. But built-in stability is not always desirable. Let us consider a situation in which the economy is recovering from a state of severe unemployment and low level of economic activity. As income increases, in a progressive tax system, taxes increase at a faster rate. The increase in taxes will exert a downward pressure on the economy and will thus hamper economic recovery. This built-in stabilization is called **fiscal drag**, defined as an undesirable built-in stabilizer that prevents the economy from recovering from a state of high unemployment and low economic activity.

The fiscal drag is a hindrance to economic recovery.

Discretionary fiscal policy may be required to counteract the fiscal drag. Although the automatic stabilizers help to reduce instability in the economy, they do not do the job completely. Assistance from direct fiscal policy is often considered to be necessary.

PROBLEM SOLVING 28-1

What tax policy would you suggest to offset the fiscal drag?

DISCRETIONARY FISCAL POLICY: CLOSING THE GAPS

Our analysis of the effect of changes in government spending and taxes on aggregate expenditure and net domestic income suggests that fiscal policy can be used to reduce inflation and unemployment. The objective of fiscal policy is to move the economy toward its full-employment level of net domestic income without inflation. In other words, the objective is to achieve equilibrium at full employment. Let us see how fiscal policy can be used to combat inflation and unemployment.

ANTI-INFLATIONARY FISCAL POLICY

A contractionary fiscal policy reduces inflation.

Learning Objective 5: how discretionary fiscal policy can be used to close full-employment gaps

An inflationary situation is illustrated in Figure 28.10. There is an inflationary gap because at the full employment level of output (Y_f), intended aggregate expenditure exceeds aggregate output. There is a tendency, therefore, for prices to move upward. Desired aggregate expenditure must be reduced to eliminate the inflationary gap. The appropriate fiscal policy in this situation is a reduction in government spending or an increase in taxes, or some combination of both. In other words, a reduction of the deficit or an increase in the surplus is required.

FIGURE 28.10

An inflationary gap.

Fiscal policy can reduce AE and thus close an inflationary gap.

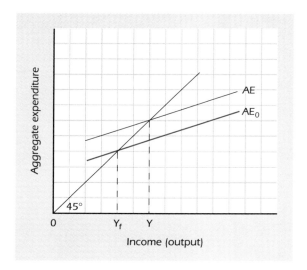

A reduction in government spending reduces desired aggregate expenditure and hence net domestic income. The reduction in income causes a reduction in planned consumption and investment. Figure 28.10 shows decreased intended aggregate expenditure as a shift in the expenditure line from AE to AE_0. The inflationary gap disappears as equilibrium occurs at the full-employment level of income. A similar result can be obtained by increasing taxes. An increase in taxes reduces disposable income, which in turn decreases planned consumption and investment spending. As before, the aggregate expenditure line shifts downward, reducing or eliminating the inflationary gap. Decreases in government spending or increases in taxes are referred to as **contractionary fiscal policies** because they result in a contraction in the economy.

> **If the economy is experiencing inflation without unemployment, the appropriate fiscal policy to eliminate the inflationary pressure is a contractionary or restrictive fiscal policy.**

FISCAL POLICY TO COMBAT UNEMPLOYMENT

An expansionary fiscal policy reduces unemployment.

Learning Objective 5: how discretionary fiscal policy can be used to close full-employment gaps

Let us assume now that the economy is experiencing unemployment and a low level of net domestic income. There is a recessionary gap as shown in Figure 28.11. An increase in government spending or a reduction in taxes or both will stimulate the economy towards full employment. That is, an increase in the deficit or a reduction in the surplus is required. At the full employment level of net domestic income (Y_f), aggregate output exceeds desired aggregate expenditure. In order for the economy to achieve full employment, desired aggregate expenditure must increase. An increase in government spending will result in an increase in desired aggregate expenditure and, hence, an increase in net domestic income. The increase in net domestic income will cause planned consumption and investment to increase. The aggregate expenditure line will shift upward from AE to AE_1 as shown in Figure 28.11. The recessionary gap is thus eliminated. A reduction in taxes will produce a similar result. A fall in taxes increases disposable income, which in turn increases consumption and investment spending. As before, the aggregate expenditure line shifts upward, eliminating the recessionary gap. Increases in government spending and reductions in taxes are called **expansionary fiscal policies** because they result in an expansion of aggregate expenditure, income, and employment.

If the economy is experiencing a recession, with high unemployment and no inflation, the appropriate fiscal policy to move the economy towards full employment is an expansionary fiscal policy.

FIGURE 28.11

A recessionary gap.

Fiscal policy can increase AE and thus close a recessionary gap.

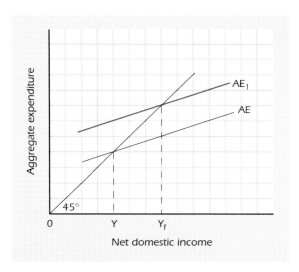

GOVERNMENT SPENDING OR TAXES? THE PROS AND CONS

Government spending or taxes can be used to reduce or eliminate an inflationary or a recessionary gap. Does it matter which of these two fiscal policy tools the government uses to control the economy? Let us examine the arguments for and against each of the tools of fiscal policy.

GOVERNMENT SPENDING

The pros

One of the advantages of using government spending to control macroeconomic activity is that it is a more powerful tool than tax changes. A $20 million increase in government spending will have a greater impact on the economy than a tax cut of the same magnitude. (Recall our discussion of the balanced budget theorem.)

Another advantage of changes in government spending over tax changes is that changes in government spending can be focused on certain regions. For example, if there is widespread unemployment in certain regions but not in others, a tax cut designed to reduce unemployment in those regions may cause inflation in other regions. In such a case, government spending programs can be designed to increase aggregate expenditure in regions suffering from high unemployment.

The cons

A major disadvantage of government spending programs is that they take a long time to get under way. Highway construction and other public works programs require a considerable amount of planning time. Some of the reasons for the delays in government spending will be discussed in a later section of this chapter.

Another disadvantage of government spending as a fiscal policy tool is the difficulty of reversing certain government spending programs. Indeed, it may be political suicide to try to eliminate certain programs. Moreover, certain projects, once in progress, cannot be abandoned without an immense waste of resources. What good is an incomplete highway from a city to an airport!

CHANGES IN TAXES

The pros

A tax cut designed to stimulate the economy is likely to be more favourably received by the public than an increase in government spending. The tax cut will likely benefit more people directly as it increases their disposable income. Furthermore, people who believe that the government is already too big will resist increases in government spending.

Another advantage of using changes in taxes is that it may be easier and less wasteful to change taxes when economic conditions change. For example, if a tax cut is instituted to combat high unemployment, it may be easier to reimpose taxes when the situation improves than to cut certain government programs. This, however, is not to suggest that tax changes are easy.

Yet another advantage of tax changes over changes in government spending is the relative speed with which tax changes can be implemented. In cases where a quick change is desired, tax changes may be preferable to changes in government spending.

The cons

One big disadvantage of using tax changes as a fiscal policy tool is that its effect is national rather than regional. And, as we have seen earlier, regional considerations may be an important element in macroeconomic policy decisions.

Another disadvantage of tax changes is that they are less effective, dollar for dollar, than changes in government spending. Thus, during periods of severe unemployment and undesirably low aggregate expenditure, the choice of fiscal policy tool may favour an increase in government spending over tax cuts.

THE FULL-EMPLOYMENT BUDGET

Learning Objective 6:
the significance of the full-employment budget

We have seen that a government may intentionally put its budget in deficit or in surplus as a means of regulating economic activity. Can we conclude that the existence of a budget deficit reflects an expansionary fiscal policy while a surplus reflects a contractionary fiscal policy? Let us examine this issue. In times of economic prosperity, with rising incomes, government tax receipts increase. Since people find themselves generally in better economic circumstances, government transfer payments tend to fall automatically. The budget may change passively, therefore, from a deficit position to a surplus position. Likewise, in recessionary times, government tax receipts fall. Government spending on items such as unemployment compensation, welfare payments, and subsidies then increases automatically as more and more people find themselves in straitened circumstances. As a result, the budget may change passively from a surplus position to a deficit position.

In order to distinguish between policy-induced (intentional) changes in the budget and automatic (passive) changes, we may use the concept of the **full-employment budget** or **high-employment budget**, defined as the position of the budget if the economy were at full employment, given the level of government spending and taxes.

Figure 28.12 illustrates the concept of the full-employment budget. If the full-employment level of income is Y_2, then the full-employment surplus is Y_2C. If the full-employment level of income is Y_1, then the full-employment deficit is Y_1A.

Full-employment budget: the position of the budget if the economy were at full employment.

FIGURE 28.12

The full-employment budget.

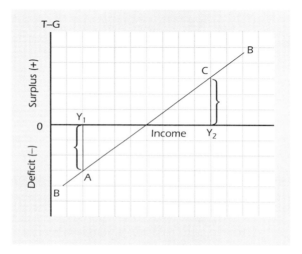

Now consider Figure 28.13. If income increases from Y_1 to Y_f, without any policy-induced changes in government spending and taxes, the actual budget deficit will decrease from Y_1A to Y_fC. The full-employment deficit would remain unchanged,

FIGURE 28.13

Fiscal policy and the full-employment budget.

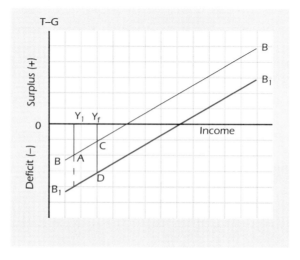

however, at Y_fC. If the government intentionally increased the deficit to move the economy from Y_1 to Y_f, then the budget line would shift from BB to B_1B_1. As a result, the full-employment budget deficit would increase from Y_fC to Y_fD. Thus, we can draw the following conclusion:

Changes in the budget do not necessarily indicate changes in fiscal policy. Changes in the full-employment budget, however, do indicate changes in fiscal policy.

LIMITATIONS OF FISCAL POLICY

Time lags reduce the effectiveness of fiscal policy.

Learning Objective 7: *the limitations of fiscal policy*

A recognition lag is the time required to recognize a problem.

A decision lag is the time required to decide what to do.

An implementation lag is the time required for decisions to be implemented.

An impact lag is the time required for decisions to take effect.

Inflexibility in government spending and tax measures may reduce the impact of fiscal policy.

Poor coordination between various levels of government may reduce the effectiveness of fiscal policy.

Four main problems are associated with fiscal policy. First, let us consider the problem of time lags. First, there is a **recognition lag**. A problem (inflation or unemployment) may begin and be in progress for some time before it is recognized. The economy could well be in a recession before the statistics tell the tale. Second, there is a **decision lag**. Once the problem is recognized, decision-makers need time to decide what action to take. They must decide whether to change government spending or taxes, and the specific forms that these changes will take. Third, there is an **implementation lag**. After the decision is made as to the type of fiscal policy that will be used, there will be some time before the policy is actually implemented. A tax change, for example, may not take effect immediately; and a program of government expenditure may require a considerable length of time before it is actually launched. Plans have to be drawn up, tenders invited and considered, and contracts awarded. The actual construction period can be quite long, depending on the nature of the project. Finally, there is an **impact lag** or an *effect lag* — the lag that elapses between the implementation of the policy and its effects on aggregate expenditure, output, and employment. The implication is that the entire process may take so long that the effects of the policy may be felt only after the need for the policy has passed.

A second limitation of fiscal policy is the difficulty of varying government spending and taxes as the need arises. Many expenditure items cannot be varied to any appreciable extent. For example, the salaries of civil servants cannot be varied as a means of stabilizing the economy. Similarly, the amounts spent on defence and as interest payment on the public debt cannot be varied in response to fluctuations in economic activity. To see just how difficult it can be to vary government spending, try to write down on paper some areas where you think cuts in government spending can be made — and consider the political and social repercussions.

How about tax changes? To the government, tax cuts are attractive because voters like them. Tax increases are a great deal less popular. So while it may be relatively easy to reduce taxes, it may be considerably more difficult to increase them when the economic situation so dictates.

A third problem associated with fiscal policy relates to our governmental structure. During a recession, an expansionary fiscal policy is appropriate; but the revenues of governments decline during a recession. Government spending, then, also tends to decline. Thus, the actions of provincial and municipal governments may reduce the effectiveness of the fiscal policy being pursued by the federal government. Greater cooperation between the various levels of government will make fiscal policy a more effective stabilization tool.

A fourth problem with using fiscal policy is that during periods of heavy national debt when the government is committed to reducing the deficit and to arresting the growth of the national debt, it may be difficult for the government to use expansionary fiscal policy to stimulate the economy. We shall return to this issue in Chapter 37 when we discuss the deficit and the national debt.

CHAPTER SUMMARY

1. In a closed economy with government spending, net domestic income will be at its equilibrium level when desired (C + I + G) equals aggregate output.

2. An increase in government spending, other things being equal, will cause an increase in net domestic income. A decrease in government spending, other things being equal, will cause a reduction in net domestic income.

3. The government spending multiplier is 1/MPS, which is the same as the investment multiplier.

4. An increase in taxes, other things being equal, results in a fall in net domestic income. A reduction in taxes, other things being equal, results in an increase in net domestic income.

5. In a closed economy in which government spends and collects taxes, the equilibrium level of net domestic income occurs where the sum of saving and taxes equals the sum of investment and government spending.

6. A budget deficit exists when government spending exceeds tax receipts. A budget surplus exists when tax receipts exceed government spending. A balanced budget exists when government spending equals tax receipts.

7. The balanced budget theorem states that if government spending and taxes increase by the same amount, then income will increase by an amount equal to the increase in government spending. That is, the balanced budget multiplier is 1.

8. Automatic stabilizers are built-in fiscal policy measures that operate automatically to produce economic stability. They include progressive taxes, assistance to agriculture, and unemployment compensation.

9. In an inflationary situation, the appropriate fiscal policy is to reduce government spending and increase taxes. In a recessionary situation, the appropriate fiscal policy is to increase government spending and reduce taxes.

10. Advantages of government spending as a fiscal policy tool are that government spending is more powerful than taxes and can be directed to certain regions. Disadvantages of government spending include time lags, and the difficulty of reversing government spending programs.

11. Advantages of tax changes as a fiscal policy tool are that they may be more favourably received, less wasteful, and faster to implement than government spending. Major disadvantages are that their effects are national rather than regional, and they are less effective than government spending.

12. The major limitations of fiscal policy are the difficulties imposed by time lags, varying government spending in response to business fluctuations, coordinating expenditures between the various levels of government, and the restriction imposed by a huge deficit and the public debt.

TERMS FOR REVIEW

government spending multiplier (481)
lump-sum tax (481)
budget deficit (486)
budget surplus (486)
balanced budget (486)
functional finance (487)

balanced budget change
 in spending (487)
balanced budget theorem (487)
automatic fiscal policy (487)
automatic (built-in) stabilizers (487)
discretionary fiscal policy (487)

progressive tax (488)
fiscal drag (488)
contractionary fiscal policy (489)
expansionary fiscal policy (490)
full-employment budget (492)

recognition lag (493)
decision lag (493)
implementation lag (493)
impact lag (493)

QUESTIONS FOR REVIEW AND DISCUSSION

1. Briefly explain why an increase in government spending will increase net domestic income. (L.O.1)

2. "A tax cut is expansionary." Explain. (L.O.1)

3. What is fiscal policy? What fiscal policy measures can be taken to reduce or eliminate (a) an inflationary gap, (b) a deflationary gap? (L.O.1,5)

4. What problems are associated with the use of fiscal policy? (L.O.7)

5. What is the difference between automatic fiscal policy and discretionary fiscal policy? (L.O.4,5)

6. Mention two automatic stabilizers, and explain how they work. (L.O.4)

7. What are the limitations of automatic stabilizers? (L.O.4)

8. What is the fiscal drag? (L.O.4)

9. Use an arithmetic example to show that the balanced budget multiplier is 1. (L.O.3)

10. Compare government spending and taxes as fiscal policy tools. (L.O.5)

11. Can the government stimulate the economy without changing the size of its deficit? Explain. (L.O.3)

12. Explain why a government that is seriously committed to slowing down the growth of the public debt may have difficulty using expansionary fiscal policy to combat a recession. (L.O.7)

PROBLEMS AND EXERCISES

1. Use the case of a closed economy with government spending and taxation to show that the injections-withdrawals approach and the aggregate expenditure-aggregate output approach are just different ways of looking at the same thing. (General)

2. Table 28.5 contains data for the economy of Freeland — a hypothetical closed economy in which the government does not collect any taxes. (L.O.1)

TABLE 28.5	NDI = PI = DI	C
Data for Freeland.	400	420
	500	500
	600	580
	700	660
	800	740
	900	820
	1000	900

(a) If planned investment is 40, and government spending is 0, what is the equilibrium level of net domestic income?

(b) Assume now that government spending is 20 at each level of net domestic income. What is the new equilibrium level of net domestic income?

(c) Illustrate graphically the equilibrium level of net domestic income with government spending at 20.

3. Refer to Table 28.5. If government spending increases from 20 to 40, (L.O.1)

(a) what will be the new equilibrium level of net domestic income?

(b) what is the government spending multiplier?

4. Table 28.6 contains data for a hypothetical economy. Intended investment is fixed at 15, government spending at each level of NDI is 10. (L.O.1)

TABLE 28.6	NDI = PI	C	I	G	AE	T
Data for a hypothetical economy.	100	100				
	120	115				
	140	130				
	160	145				
	180	160				
	200	175				
	220	190				
	240	205				

(a) Complete the table (except for the tax column) and determine the equilibrium level of net domestic income.

(b) Suppose now that the government imposes a lump sum tax of 20. Make a new table showing disposable income and consumption.

(c) What will be the new equilibrium level of net domestic income?

5. Refer to Table 28.6. If government spending increases by 20 (from 10 to 30) and at the same time taxes rise by 20 (from 20 to 40), what will be the new equilibrium net domestic income? (L.O.3)

6. In a recession, what changes would you expect in each of the following variables? (General)

(a) consumer spending

(b) investment spending

(c) government spending

7. In a hypothetical economy, the unemployment rate is considered to be dangerously high and the government feels that it must do something about it. At the same time, the budget deficit and the public debt have reached such high levels that the government is greatly concerned about them. How will each of the following affect the deficit and the public debt? (L.O.7)

(a) an increase in government spending

(b) a reduction in taxes

(c) a combination of tax cuts and increases in government spending.

 8. Depending on the state of the economy, it may sometimes be necessary to reduce government spending. This means cuts in certain government programs and services. Assume that your group or class has been asked to prepare a program to reduce government spending. In what areas would you recommend cuts? What would be the likely effects of your recommendations? (In your discussion, consider reactions from interest groups).

Internet Site

http://www.fin.gc.ca

This Department of Finance (federal) site contains useful information about government fiscal actions.

INTERNET EXERCISE

1. Go to the Department of Finance Web site.
2. Click on *Budget Info*.
3. Click on the most recent budget (for example, 19xx Budget).
4. Click on *General Info*.
5. Click on *Budget in Brief*.
6. Click on *Highlights of the 19xx Budget*.
7. List five highlights of the budget that you have chosen.

CHAPTER 29

BUSINESS FLUCTUATIONS

Learning Objectives

After studying this chapter, you should understand:

1 the meaning of business cycles

2 the phases of the cycle

3 economic causes of business fluctuations

4 politics and the business cycle

5 the real business cycle

6 forecasting of business cycles

Business cycles, fluctuations in the general output of the economy, have for many years absorbed the interests of the world's best economists.

Gottfried Haberler, *Prosperity and Depression*

INTRODUCTION

The real output of the Canadian economy has increased significantly over the years. This increase, however, has not been even. There have been times of rapid increase, and there have been times of slow increase. For example, real gross domestic product increased at an annual rate of more than 8% in 1952, 1955, and 1956; at an annual rate of more than 6% in 1950, 1962, 1964, 1965, 1966, 1973, 1976, and 1984; but at an annual rate of less than 3% in 1948, 1954, 1957, 1958, 1960, 1967, 1970, 1975, 1980, and 1982. In 1954, real gross domestic product fell by 1.1%, in 1982, it fell by 3.2%, and in 1990 and 1991, it fell by 0.5% and 1.7% respectively. Clearly, these were bad years, but not as difficult as 1933, when real output fell by more than 6% and the unemployment rate soared to over 19%. More recently, real gross domestic product grew at annual rates of 2.4% in 1989, 2.2% in 1993 and 3.7% in 1997. Figure 29.1 shows the rate of change of real gross domestic product from 1973 to 1997.

FIGURE 29.1

Growth rate of real gross domestic product.

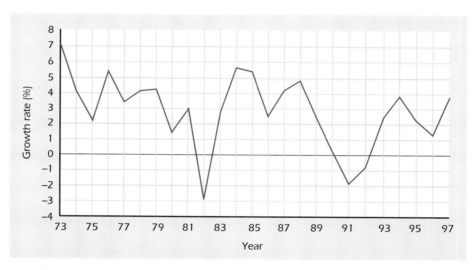

Source: Statistics Canada, *Canadian Economic Observer* (Cat. 11–210-XPB), 1997–98: 7.

Learning Objective 1:
the meaning of business cycles

Business cycles are alternating periods of ups and downs in the economy.

These fluctuating economic fortunes have come to be known as *business fluctuations* or **business cycles**. Some of these cycles last for a long period. Others are of short duration. Some cycles are severe; others are mild. But, despite the fact that each cycle has its own peculiar characteristics, certain features appear to be common to all cycles.

What causes these ups and downs in economic activity? Why do we sometimes have periods of high employment and satisfactory increases in real output, while at other times, we have high unemployment rates and low output growth? We shall try to answer these questions in this chapter. We shall also discuss the theory of the real business cycle and whether business cycles can effectively be controlled.

PHASES OF THE CYCLE

Learning Objective 2:
the phases of the cycle

The use of the term "cycles" to describe economic fluctuations should not be interpreted to mean that they occur at regular intervals. In fact, they are quite irregular. Nevertheless, each one, whether mild or severe, whether short or long, goes through the same four phases. These are: trough, expansion, peak, and recession. These four phases are illustrated in Figure 29.2, which shows that real GDP tends to fluctuate around an upward trend. Let us examine each of these phases.

FIGURE 29.2

Phases of a business
cycle.

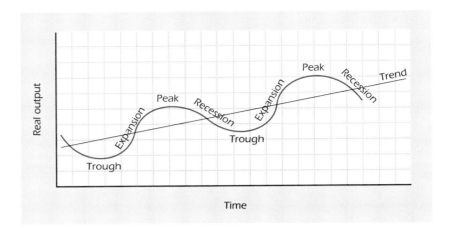

A business cycle shows four
distinct phases: peak,
recession, trough, and
expansion.

TROUGH

A trough is the lowest point
in a business cycle.

The **trough** is the lowest point or bottom of the cycle. Here, actual output might be significantly less than potential output. Unemployment is likely to be high, business-people's expectations about the future will be pessimistic and, as a result, investment will be low. Total demand for consumer goods will also be low. Moreover, banks will experience an increase in the amount of money available for loans because of an inability to find good and willing borrowers. If the fall in real output and the increase in unemployment are severe, the economy will be said to be in a **depression**. You are, by now, quite familiar with the Great Depression of the early 1930s.

A depression is a severe
trough.

EXPANSION

During the expansion
(recovery) phase, output
expands and income
increases.

Expansion is the phase that follows the trough. In this phase of the cycle, output begins to expand, and income increases. Consumption expenditures and employment also increase. Businesspeople become optimistic about the future and increase their investment spending. People are confident and feel quite good about the economy. The prime minister and the government are usually popular. This is a good time to call an election. Since the economy appears to be recovering from a state of low growth or stagnation, we say that it has entered a period of **recovery**.

PEAK

In the peak phase, real
GDP is at its highest level.

But alas, all good things must end, and an expansion is no exception. The end comes when the use of the economy's resources has reached capacity. When this occurs, we say that the economy has entered a phase called the **peak**. During a peak, real gross domestic product has reached its highest level. And, because the economy's resources are fully employed, increases in demand lead not to increases in real output but to increases in prices. In fact, prices will tend to begin to rise even before the economy has peaked.

RECESSION

During the recession
phase, income and con-
sumption decline.

The phase that follows the peak is called a **recession**. In this phase of the cycle, consumption and investment spending decline. Many business ventures that were profitable during the expansion phase now become unprofitable. Business failures occur more frequently and may even become widespread. Real output decreases and unemployment increases. This is no time to call an election, unless the government believes that the situation will get even worse.

LENGTH AND INTENSITY OF PHASES

Business cycles vary in frequency and intensity.

It is important to note that no definitive statement can be made about the length or intensity of any phase of the cycle. A recession, for example, may be quite mild and of short duration, such as the 1970 recession; or it may be long and severe with widespread unemployment, such as the Great Depression. Similarly, the expansion phase may extend over several years, such as the expansion of the 1960s; or it may be so short that the effects of the previous trough may still be evident in many sectors of the economy. The 1976 expansion was short-lived.

 PROBLEM SOLVING 29-1

During the Christmas season, spending usually increases. In January and February, spending usually declines. Is this an example of a business cycle?

 ### APPLICATION

After the Recession, What?

Business cycle theory and concepts have important implications for business decision-making. We know that a recession is followed by a trough. In other words, the recession will "bottom out." After that, there will be a period of recovery or expansion. Good business decision-making requires that careful attention be paid to the business cycle. Managers should plan ahead. Planning takes place in an environment of uncertainty. A knowledge of the phases of the business cycle reduces the uncertainty under which decisions can be made. Predicting the length and severity of the phases of the cycle, however, remains a critical issue.

ECONOMIC CAUSES OF BUSINESS FLUCTUATIONS

Learning Objective 3: economic causes of business fluctuations

Despite the fact that business cycles have been with us for quite a long time, economists do not generally agree on their causes. Several theories have been advanced as explanations of the causes of business cycles. Let us examine some of these theories.

THE UNDER-CONSUMPTION THEORY

Variations in consumer spending cause economic fluctuations.

By looking at national income accounting figures, we can see that expenditure on consumer goods and services is the largest component of aggregate expenditure. If consumption changes (other things being equal) then aggregate expenditure also changes. Output then changes as well. The under-consumption theory of the business cycle states that, as income increases, a smaller proportion is spent on consumption, and a larger proportion is saved. This situation may cause planned saving to exceed planned investment, resulting in a fall in income. When income falls, a larger proportion is spent on consumer goods and services, and a smaller proportion is saved. At this level of income, intended investment may exceed intended saving, resulting in an increase in output and income. To summarize then, the under-consumption theory states that fluctuations in consumer spending result in an imbalance between intended saving and investment which, in turn, causes ups and downs in income and employment.

THE VOLATILE INVESTMENT THEORY

Of all of the components of aggregate expenditure, investment is the most volatile. Because investment fluctuates substantially from one period to the next, many economists consider it to be the prime cause of fluctuations in economic activity. Inventory investment is relatively small but highly unstable. Its instability is the major cause of fluctuations in total investment. This fact has led to the use of the term **inventory cycles** when referring to the volatile investment theory of the business cycle. During a period of low economic activity, according to this theory, businesspeople run down their inventories. They reduce their production levels in response to reductions in their orders, and unemployment results. When the economy recovers, they restore their inventory levels. This investment in inventories increases employment and income.

Inventory cycles: changes in inventory investment cause fluctuations in economic activity.

GOVERNMENT SPENDING

According to the government spending theory of the business cycle, variations in government spending contribute to economic instability. During wars, national disasters, or other emergency situations, government spending will rise sharply. Such rapid increases in government spending cause increases in income and employment, which may exert upward pressure on the price level. But when the emergency passes, government spending is reduced, and this reduction in government spending, according to supporters of this theory, may result in a significant reduction in output and employment. In this way, government spending can be a destabilizing force.

Changes in government spending may be destabilizing.

THE EXPECTATIONS THEORY

This theory states that expectations of businesspeople play a key role in business fluctuations. In a recession, according to this theory, businesspeople become pessimistic about the future. This pessimism results in postponement of investment spending and possibly leads to cutbacks in certain ventures. Certain investment projects remain on the drawing boards and others are shelved. Output and employment decrease as a result. If economic activity revives, businesspeople will become optimistic about the future. Projects that were shelved are now reactivated and investment spending increases. Consequently, employment, income, and output also increase.

Changes in expectations cause business cycles.

THE INNOVATIONS THEORY

The innovations theory of the business cycle owes its origin to the work of Joseph Schumpeter, an Austrian-born economist who worked at Harvard University. According to the proponents of this theory, innovations are the main cause of business cycles. Those who subscribe to this view argue that innovations are introduced when economic activity is on the upswing. The introduction of these innovations is accompanied by a flood of economic activity that sooner or later subsides. After a period of low economic activity, another set of innovations is introduced, and this leads to another round of increased business activity.

Innovations are a prime cause of business cycles.

THE MONETARY THEORY

You will not fully understand the effect of money on economic activity until we have studied monetary theory and policy. That should not, however, prevent you from getting an idea of the role of money in economic fluctuations. Those who support the monetary theory of the business cycle argue that, when the economy is in the expansion phase, business ventures are profitable. Banks are therefore willing to extend loans. Eventually, the amount of money available for loans diminishes. The demand for loans then causes banks to increase their interest rates. It also becomes increasingly difficult for businesspeople to secure loans. This tight credit situation results in a reduction in economic activity. When banks acquire more lending money, credit becomes easier, and the economy then re-enters an expansion phase.

Changes in the availability of money and interest rates cause business fluctuations.

THE MULTIPLIER-ACCELERATOR THEORY

To understand the multiplier-accelerator theory of business cycles, you must first understand the acceleration principle. The acceleration principle, or simply the accelerator, is closely associated with the concept of induced investment, which you have already learned. The **acceleration principle** states that an increase in income leads to an accelerated increase in investment. Table 29.1 illustrates the operation of this principle. We assume that there is no depreciation of capital. There is therefore no difference between gross and net investment. We assume also that it takes $4 worth of capital to produce $1 of output per year. In other words, the **capital-output ratio** (that is, the ratio of the value of capital to total output) is assumed to be 4:1. You may question the wisdom of spending $4 on capital to produce only $1 of output. Note, however, that the $4 expenditure on capital will yield a stream of output of $1 in successive years. The investment can therefore be profitable.

The acceleration principle suggests that the level of investment is proportional to the rate of change of output.

The capital-output ratio is the ratio of the value of capital to total output.

TABLE 29.1

The acceleration principle.

Year	Total output ($thousand)	Required capital stock ($thousand)	Investment ($thousand)
1	50	200	0
2	52	208	8
3	52	208	0
4	54	216	8
5	56	224	8
6	58	232	8
7	59	236	4
8	62	248	12
9	66	264	16
10	70	280	16

Table 29.1 shows that an annual output of $50 000 requires a capital stock of $200 000. An increase in output of $2000 in Year 2 requires an increase in capital stock from $200 000 to $208 000 — that is, an investment of $8000. The table shows that if total output increases at a constant rate (as in Years 4 to 6), investment will remain at a constant level. If the rate of increase in output falls off (as from Year 6 to Year 7), investment will fall. Investment will increase when total output increases at an increasing rate as in Years 7 to 9. It is important to note also that investment is proportional to the change in total output. Given the change in total output, the amount of investment required can be calculated by multiplying the change in output by the capital-output ratio — or the accelerator, as it is often called.

A change in income leads to an accelerated change in investment.

The formula for the required investment can be developed by using simple algebra.

$$K = \text{required capital stock}$$
$$Y = \text{total output}$$
$$\text{Let } K/Y = v, \text{ where } v \text{ is constant}$$
$$\text{then } K = vY$$
$$\Delta K = v\Delta Y$$

that is, $I = v\Delta Y$ where I is the required investment.

The following example illustrates how the formula may be used.

EXAMPLE 29-1

Given a capital-output ratio of 4, how much investment is required to increase output from $56 000 to $58 000?

Solution: $K/Y = v = 4;$ $\qquad Y = 2000$

$$I = v\Delta Y$$

$$I = 4 \times 2000 = 8000$$

The required investment is $8000.

The simple accelerator principle assumes that an increase in demand for consumer goods and services translates into demand for the capital goods that produce these consumer goods and services. This implies that there is no excess capacity in the industries producing consumer goods. You should keep in mind, however, that firms sometimes do have excess capacity. In cases where they do, it is unlikely that they will purchase new equipment as soon as there is an increase in demand. Firms are more likely to use up any excess capacity before undertaking new investment. The simple acceleration principle assumes also that excess capacity exists in the industries producing capital goods. However, it must be noted that in certain circumstances, the capital goods industries may not be able to respond immediately to increases in demand for capital goods. Investment may thus be delayed.

PROBLEM SOLVING 29-2

Does it make good economic sense for the business sector to undertake (new) investment as soon as there is an increase in demand for goods and services?

Multiplier-accelerator interaction intensifies the business cycle.

Now that you have studied the principle of acceleration, we can proceed to an examination of the role of the accelerator in business cycles. Professor Paul Samuelson has demonstrated that the interaction of the multiplier and the accelerator can produce wide fluctuations in economic activity. If the economy is expanding, the increase in income accelerates investment. The increased investment generates an even greater increase in income. But as the economy's resources become fully employed, the acceleration of output slows down. And, as we have seen in Chapter 26, a deceleration in output hinders investment. The decreased investment causes an even greater reduction in output via the multiplier. Hence, the interaction of the multiplier and the accelerator acts to intensify fluctuations in economic activity.

PROBLEM SOLVING 29-3

What effect can the maturation of industries be expected to have on economic fluctuations?

IS THERE A DOMINANT CAUSE?

A question well worth asking is which of these variables contributes most to business fluctuations? Is it consumption, investment, government spending, or some other factor? Figure 29.3 shows the behaviour of consumption, investment, and government spending in Canada from 1973 to 1997. The inventory component of investment is shown separately in the second diagram in order to emphasize its volatility. Clearly, investment spending and government spending have fluctuated much more from year to year than has consumer spending.

FIGURE 29.3

Variations in consumption, investment, and government spending.

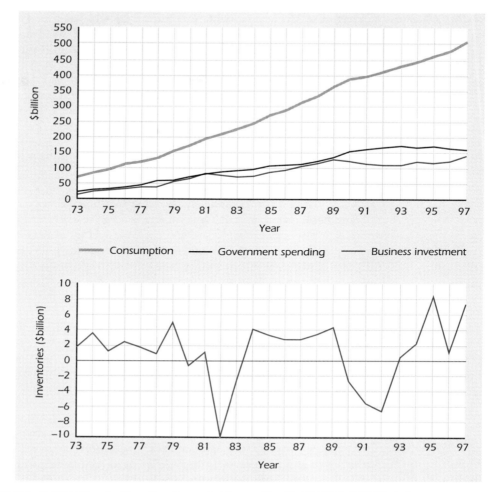

Source: Statistics Canada, *Canadian Economic Observer* (Cat. 11-210-XPB), 1997–98: 4, 5.

It is likely that combinations of these and other factors, rather than any single dominant factor, provide the reasons for fluctuations in economic activity.

POLITICS AND THE BUSINESS CYCLE

Learning Objective 4:
politics and the business cycle

The political business cycle is caused by the government's use of its spending and taxing powers to secure its political future.

Several economists have argued that many business cycles can be attributed to political factors. According to proponents of this view, elected government officials may use (or abuse) certain tools of economic policy, not to achieve economic stability, but to advance their own political objectives.

Fluctuations in economic activity caused by the use of economic policy tools to further political ends are referred to as **political business cycles**. To understand how subscribers to the idea of political business cycles explain their position, consider the following set of circumstances. The main objective of elected government officials is to be re-elected. Prior to an election, the government in office pursues expansionary economic policies — introducing a variety of spending programs and tax cuts — whether or not the economic situation warrants such policies. These expansionary policies increase income and employment (at least in the short run). Voters are pleased with the present state of the economy, so they return the government to power. To express the situation in more graphic terms, the government buys the election.

Once the election has been won, however, the longer-term impact of the expansionary economic policies begins to be felt. If the economic stimulus occurred when the economy was operating close to full employment, the increase in aggregate expenditure is likely to result in inflation some time after the election. The electorate begins to complain, and the opposition parties begin to scream for anti-inflationary action. The government then reduces its spending and may also raise taxes to eliminate the inflationary pressures and appease those crying for policies to combat inflation. These contractionary policies plunge the economy into a recession. The recession succeeds in eliminating the inflationary pressures. By the time this process is completed, it is again close to another election, and the government is again ready to engage in another round of pre-election spending that will simply start the whole process again.

Actual events seem to lend some credence to the political business cycle. During election periods, the economy tends to expand more frequently than it contracts. This correlation, however, may be due to the fact that governments are much more likely to call elections during periods of prosperity than during periods of high unemployment and low economic growth.

THE REAL BUSINESS CYCLE

Learning Objective 5:
the real business cycle

The real business cycle theory suggests that the main causes of business cycles are shifts in aggregate supply.

According to the **real business cycle** theory, economic fluctuations are caused mainly by shifts in the aggregate supply (AS) curve. Real business cycle theorists claim that nominal shocks do not affect real output and employment, because the economy will quickly adjust to its natural levels of output and employment.

Supporters of the real business cycle theory believe that a business cycle can be initiated by any severe supply-side shock such as a prolonged drought that adversely affects agricultural production. Other supply-side changes such as changes in technology or changes in the supply of labour that occur constantly or simultaneously in several industries can also generate business cycles.

The real business cycle theory can be explained with the help of the AD-AS model developed earlier in this text. In Figure 29.4, we assume that the AS curve is vertical. The economy is initially in equilibrium at a real output of y and a price level of P.

FIGURE 29.4

Illustration of the real business cycle.

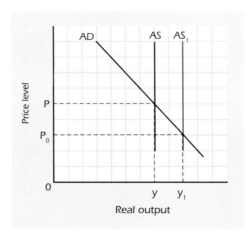

Let us assume that a supply shock shifts the AS curve to the right from AS to AS$_1$. Consequently, real output increases from y to y$_1$, while the price level falls from P to P$_0$. An unfavourable aggregate supply shock such as a massive increase in energy prices would shift the AS curve to the left, resulting in a fall in real output. Such changes in aggregate supply result in fluctuations in real output and employment.

HAVE WE CONQUERED THE BUSINESS CYCLE?

Through the correct use of stabilization policies, we have managed to avoid severe depressions.

One of the main reasons for developing theories about economic phenomena is to be able to understand them and, hopefully, to control them. Following the publication of *The General Theory* and the understanding of the general message of Keynesian economics, many economists and policymakers believed that with the judicious use of macroeconomic policies, business cycles could be avoided.

Whether or not this view is too optimistic has been the subject of considerable debate. There is considerable agreement, however, that our increased ability to predict business fluctuations and the proper use of macroeconomic policy tools have enabled us to reduce both the frequency and intensity of business cycles. We have been successful in avoiding major depressions of the magnitude of the Great Depression of the 1930s.

Although our knowledge of the operation of the economy has improved greatly since the 1930s, to the point where another Great Depression is unlikely, our knowledge is still imperfect. We can expect mild ups and downs in economic activity, resulting from any of the causes that we have discussed in this chapter. There will be fluctuations in private sector investment (including inventories) and government spending, and changes in taxes — all of which are potentially destabilizing. We do not yet possess the knowledge of how to "fine tune" the system to the state where we can iron out all of the wrinkles and ripples. This is a continuing challenge.

FORECASTING BUSINESS CYCLES

Learning Objective 6: *forecasting of business cycles*

The ability to forecast business cycles would greatly improve our ability to control them. Economists have made some advances in forecasting economic fluctuations. You must remember, however, that economics is not an exact science, and our forecasts, though useful, are not exact. A very simple method of forecasting business cycles is to use *leading indicators.*

Leading indicators turn downward before the cycle peaks and upward before the trough.

Coincidental indicators coincide exactly with the business cycle.

Lagging indicators turn downward after the cycle peaks and upward after the trough.

Economists use leading indicators to help them to forecast business cycles.

Indicators of economic activity fall into three main categories: leading indicators, coincidental indicators, and lagging indicators. **Leading indicators** are economic variables that typically turn downward before the cycle has reached its peak, and turn upward before the trough. Examples of leading indicators are stock prices, orders for durable goods, and the rate of change of the money supply. **Coincidental indicators** are variables that coincide exactly with the business cycle. Their peaks and troughs coincide with the peaks and troughs of the business cycle. Examples of coincidental indicators are gross domestic product, employment, and business profits. **Lagging indicators** are variables that turn downward after the peak and upward after the trough. Examples of lagging indicators are inventories and personal income.

Economists rely on leading indicators to forecast peaks and troughs in the business cycle. For example, if the leading indicators turn upward, economists suspect that a trough is imminent. If they turn downward, economists suspect that the economy is about to peak. Unfortunately, economic forecasting is a more difficult exercise than just looking at leading indicators. Moreover, these leading indicators sometimes send false messages. For these reasons, economists combine the use of leading indicators with other forecasting techniques, and a great deal of effort is expended in improving the existing tools and in developing new and more reliable methods.

CHAPTER SUMMARY

1. The economy has been subject to periods of economic fluctuations or business cycles. Each cycle has its own peculiarities, but we can identify four phases common to all cycles. These phases are the trough, expansion, peak, and recession.

2. Among the theories advanced to explain business cycles are the under-consumption theory, the volatile investment theory, the government spending theory, the expectations theory, the innovations theory, the monetary theory, and the multiplier-accelerator theory.

3. The acceleration principle states that investment depends on the rate of change of income. As income increases, the demand for consumer goods increases. If this occurs, then a larger capital stock is required to produce a larger volume of consumer goods. Investment will then also increase.

4. The capital-output ratio refers to the amount of capital required to produce $1 of output per year. It is the ratio of the value of capital to the annual value of output.

5. The political business cycle is the result of changes in government spending and taxes by elected government officials in an attempt to secure their political position rather than to stabilize the economy.

6. The business cycle is likely to be the result of a combination of factors — some economic, some political.

7. The real business cycle theory states that business fluctuations are due mainly to aggregate supply shocks.

8. Because of our increased understanding of the operation of the economy, we are able to avoid serious depressions. However, dips and bumps are likely to remain in economic activity.

9. Leading indicators tend to turn downward before the peak and upward before the trough. Economists use leading indicators to help them forecast business cycles.

TERMS FOR REVIEW

business cycles (499)
trough (500)
depression (500)
expansion (recovery) (500)
peak (500)
recession (500)
inventory cycles (502)

acceleration principle (503)
capital-output ratio (503)
political business cycle (505)
the real business cycle (506)
leading indicators (507)
coincidental indicators (507)
lagging indicators (507)

QUESTIONS FOR REVIEW AND DISCUSSION

1. What are business cycles? (L.O.1)

2. What are the phases of a business cycle? Mention the characteristics of each phase. (L.O.2)

3. Briefly explain each of the following theories of the business cycle: (L.O.3)
   (a) under-consumption theory
   (b) volatile investment theory
   (c) government spending theory
4. Explain how each of the following may be destabilizing: (L.O.3)
   (a) innovations
   (b) monetary factors
   (c) multiplier-accelerator interaction
5. Briefly explain the acceleration theory. (L.O.3)
6. What relation, if any, exists between the accelerator and the capital-output ratio? (General)
7. Explain the so-called political business cycle. (L.O.4)
8. Briefly explain the real business cycle theory (L.O.5).
9. Can we effectively control economic fluctuations? (General)
10. What are leading indicators? How can they be used to forecast business cycles? (L.O.6)

PROBLEMS AND EXERCISES

1. Table 29.2 gives data for the economy of Cyclicalona. (L.O.2)

TABLE 29.2

GDP of Cyclicalona.

Period	Real GDP ($billion)
1	40.7
2	43.6
3	47.8
4	53.6
5	50.2
6	46.0
7	42.9
8	44.3
9	48.7
10	55.6
11	61.2
12	56.0

Plot the information on a graph and indicate each of the following:
(a) peak
(b) trough
(c) recession
(d) recovery

2. "The innovations theory of business cycles loses credibility because innovations do not occur in unison." Discuss. (L.O.3)
3. The total demand for goods and services in an economy increases from $205 billion to $215 billion. Given a capital-output ratio of 3, compute the amount of investment required to meet this increase in total demand. (General)

4. Assume that you are one of the economic advisers of the finance minister of Canada. All the leading indicators have just turned downward. What advice would you give to the minister in terms of fiscal policy measures? (L.O.5)

Internet Site

http://www.businessweek.com
This is the Web site for the Business Week publication. The Business Week is read world wide. The site is full of information on business and economics.

INTERNET EXERCISE

1. Go to the Business Week site above.
2. Click on *Current Issue*.
3. Scroll down to *Economic Trends*.
4. Click on a topic from the list. (You may have to register, but it's free.)
5. Jot down the main points of the topic that you selected.

VIDEO CASE

The Hibernia Investment Project

Introduction

Discovered in 1979, the Hibernia oil field is a massive source of energy consisting of two oil and gas reservoirs located 315 km east-southeast of St. John's, Newfoundland, on the continental shelf of the Grand Banks. The Hibernia oil field is estimated to contain more than 615 million barrels of recoverable oil, making it the fifth largest oil field ever discovered in Canada. In addition to this huge amount of oil, the Hibernia field is estimated to contain nearly 29 billion cubic metres of natural gas, and almost 18 million cubic metres (111 million barrels) of natural gas liquids. In January 1990, Hibernia was declared to be commercially viable, and, a 25-year production licence was issued three months later. November 17, 1997 was a momentous day when oil began flowing on the platform of the Hibernia oil field, 18 years after the reservoir was discovered.

Management and Ownership

Hibernia is currently managed and operated by Hibernia Management and Development Company Ltd. (HMDC). This company is responsible for designing, engineering, and constructing the drilling and production platform, and for all drilling and reservoir management activities. Hibernia is owned by a group of companies comprising Mobil Oil Canada Ltd., Chevron Canada Resources Ltd., Petro-Canada, Canada Hibernia Holding Co. Ltd., Murphy Atlantic Offshore Oil Company Ltd., Chevron Hibernia Holding Company Ltd., Mobil Canada Hibernia Holding Company Ltd., and Norsk Hydro Canada. The share of each owner is indicated below:

Owner	Percentage of Ownership
Mobil Oil Canada Ltd.	28.125
Chevron Canada Resources Ltd.	21.875
Petro-Canada	20.00
Canada Hibernia Holding Co. Ltd.	8.50
Murphy Atlantic Offshore Oil Company Ltd.	6.50
Chevron Hibernia Holding Company Ltd.	5.00
Mobil Canada Hibernia Holding Company Ltd.	5.00
Norsk Hydro Canada	5.00
Total	100.0

Economic Impact

Between the years 2000 and 2006, production is expected to average 125 000 barrels per day. Production is expected to end in 2016 after 19 years of production activity. For the first nine months of 1995, approximately 7500 people found employment on the Hibernia project. Since construction began in 1990, spending on the project has exceeded $6 billion. During production, about 800 workers will be required to operate the Hibernia platform.

According to economic theory, investment increases income by more than the amount of the investment (the multiplier theory). An investment expenditure of the magnitude of the Hibernia project is therefore expected to affect income and employment positively. The economy of Newfoundland and the entire Canadian economy should benefit from the Hibernia investment.

QUESTIONS

1. Summarize, in point form, the main points of this case.

2. What are some of the economic benefits that can be expected from Hibernia?

3. Given that the multiplier for Canada is about 1.4, what effect will the Hibernia project have on the level of income in Canada?

4. How will the governments of Canada and Newfoundland benefit from Hibernia? How will ordinary Canadians benefit?

Video Resource: "Hybernia," *National Magazine* (May 1998).

CHAPTER 30

MONEY: ITS NATURE AND FUNCTIONS

Learning Objectives

After studying this chapter, you should be able to:

1 define money

2 discuss the functions of money

3 distinguish between money and money substitutes

4 understand how the money supply is measured in Canada

5 describe the Canadian payments system

6 understand the meaning of the value of money

7 discuss the relationship between the money supply and inflation, and between the money supply and unemployment

When we want to induce a man to do something for us we generally offer him money.

Alfred Marshall, *Principles of Economics*

INTRODUCTION

Up to this point in our study, we have not really said much about money and what effect it might have on the economy. Intuitively, you know that money is important. You probably also suspect that your knowledge of economics would be incomplete without some knowledge of what money is and what it does. You are correct on both counts.

Money is extremely important for the efficient functioning of a modern economy. We receive our wages and salaries in the form of money. We pay our rent and our mortgages with money, and we buy our groceries with money. Firms use money to purchase the inputs that they need to produce goods and services. Money is the oil that lubricates the wheels of economic activity. Too much money in the system can lead to inflation. Too little can result in unemployment.

In the previous chapter, you saw that changes in the money supply could contribute to business cycles. But what exactly is meant by the money supply? And how do we measure the quantity of money in an economy? In this chapter, we attempt to answer those questions. You will study the functions of money; you will know what things perform the functions of money in our society; and you will have a good idea of how money affects economic activity. Let us begin by answering the important question, what is money?

WHAT IS MONEY?

Money is anything accepted to pay for goods and services or to settle a debt.

Money is best defined in terms of its functions.

Learning Objective 1:
define money

It may seem strange to ask, "What is money?" After all, doesn't everybody know what money is? You will soon see, however, that there are differing views as to what constitutes money. Most Canadians recognize the items we use as money: quarters, dimes, two-dollar coins, ten-dollar bills, etc. But because these items are money in Canada now does not mean that these same items have been money all through the ages and in different societies. What is money at one time may not be money at some other time, and what is money in one society may not be money in some other society. For this reason, economists prefer to define money in terms of its functions rather than in terms of some concrete items. We define **money** as anything that is generally accepted by the members of a community as payment for goods and services or as settlement of a debt.

This abstract definition of money avoids identifying money with any particular object which may, at one time or another, be used as money. All sorts of things have served as money throughout the ages: beads, salt, stones, gold, silver, paper, cattle. When the word money is mentioned, the things that first spring to the minds of most people are the notes (bills) and coins that they carry around in their pockets, wallets, and purses. Some will think also of their chequing and savings accounts at banks and other financial institutions. In other words, people tend to think of money as the items used as money. What functions are performed by items when used as money? We answer this question in the next section.

FUNCTIONS OF MONEY

Learning Objective 2:
discuss the functions of money

Money functions as a medium of exchange when it is used to purchase things.

Money performs three basic functions: a medium of exchange, a unit of account, and a store of value. Let us now briefly discuss each of these functions.

Medium of exchange

The main function of money is to serve as a **medium of exchange**. Without money, exchange would take place by means of barter. **Barter** is the direct exchange of one good or service for another good or service. In a very simple economy with very limited specialization, barter exchange might be tolerable. As the economy develops, however, exchange by barter becomes quite inefficient.

Obviously, barter is quite cumbersome — far less efficient than exchange with the use of money. Under a barter system of exchange, a double coincidence of wants is a precondition for exchange to occur. By **double coincidence of wants** we mean that traders must find other traders who want what they have and who have what they want. A person who has wheat and wants to exchange it for shoes must find someone who has shoes and wants wheat in exchange.

This need to have a double coincidence of wants makes exchange by barter quite costly. A great deal of time must be spent searching for a trading partner (someone who has what you want and who wants what you have) — time that could be spent in actual production. With the use of money, a double coincidence of wants is not necessary for exchange to take place. The person who has wheat can sell it to anybody who wants wheat. With the money obtained from the sale of wheat, the person can buy shoes from any seller. Money serves as a medium of exchange when we use it for such purposes as buying movie tickets, buying groceries, paying utility bills, paying taxes, buying lunch in the school cafeteria — and paying for this economics textbook!

Unit of account

A second important function of money is to serve as a **unit of account**. Money is used to express the values of goods and services in a society. The annual output of goods and services of the Canadian economy consists of a wide variety of products. Yet we can express the economy's annual output as a single value. When we say that the Gross Domestic Product of Canada is over $500 billion, we are using money as a unit of account or as a **measure of value**, as it is also called. Distance is measured in kilometres, and weight is measured in kilograms. So too, value is measured in terms of money. When we see a pair of shoes with a price tag of $89.99 in a store window, we are witnessing an example of money serving as a measure of value. It is convenient for the item that serves as a medium of exchange to serve also as the unit of account. Thus, we use dollars to purchase textbooks whose prices are expressed in dollars. But this is not a necessity. The unit of account could be the dollar, while the medium of exchange could be beads or trinkets. All prices would be expressed in dollars, but we would pay our rent and receive our wages in beads or cigarettes.

Store of value

A third important function of money is to serve as a **store of value**. We do not always spend all of our current income on consumer goods and services. We put some of it away for future use. The money we deposit in a savings account serves as a store of value: it represents stored-up purchasing power. Money is not the only thing that is used to perform the store-of-value function. Real estate, paintings, and other non-monetary assets also serve as stores of value.

It may be desirable to convert the store of value quickly into the medium of exchange. The ease with which an asset can be converted into the medium of exchange without much loss is called **liquidity**. Money is, of course, the most liquid of all assets. If the value of an item deteriorates substantially with the passage of time, then it will not qualify as a good store of value.

(margin notes)

Exchange by barter requires a double coincidence of wants.

As a unit of account (measure of value), money is used to express values.

As a store of value, money is used as a liquid asset.

Liquidity refers to the ease of converting a store of value into the medium of exchange.

PROBLEM SOLVING 30-1

When is money not a good store of value?

KINDS OF MONEY

Notes and coins constitute currency.

We commonly use three kinds of money in Canada to carry on transactions: coins, notes, and chequing accounts. Coins and notes are often called **currency**. You are quite familiar with the nickels, dimes, dollar coins, etc., that make up our supply of metallic currency. You are likewise familiar with the various bills ($5, $10, $20, etc.) that make up our supply of paper currency. A point worth noting, however, is that our coins and paper currency are worth much less as commodity than as money. A $20 bill purchases $20 worth of goods and services. But consider the value of the paper used to make it! A $20 bill would sell for very little as paper in the market.

Canadian currency is fiat money, not backed by gold or any other precious metal.

An interesting question which may be asked is: "Why do people give up goods and services in exchange for metallic and paper money with little or no intrinsic value?" Many would answer this question by saying that our paper money is backed by gold. But this is just one of the many misconceptions people hold regarding our currency. In fact, the Canadian dollar is **fiat money**. Fiat money is money that circulates as money by government decree. It is not backed by gold or any other precious metal, and cannot be converted into gold as a matter of right. Prior to 1940, Canadian paper currency was backed by gold. This means that the holder of a $20 bill could present it for payment of $20 in gold. The gold backing was abandoned in 1940. Ironically, Canadian paper currency continued to carry the statement "will pay to the bearer on demand" for 14 years after the gold backing was removed. If a $20 bill were presented for payment, the holder would simply be given $20 in paper currency. Of course, paper currency can be used to buy gold, just as it can be used to buy anything else.

Legal tender money must be accepted in settlement of debts.

People are willing to accept paper money in exchange for valuable goods and services because other people are willing to accept it from them in exchange for goods and services. The declaration in law that our currency is **legal tender** has helped to increase its general acceptability. This is so because declaring money to be legal tender means that if it is offered in payment of a debt, it must be accepted; otherwise, the debt is considered to be legally discharged. Fiat money is legal tender.

The face value of good money is equal to the value of the metal that it contains.

The face value of bad money is greater than the metal's value.

Gresham's Law states that bad money drives out good money.

There was a time when the face value of metallic money equaled the value of the commodity from which it was made. That type of money was referred to as **good money**. If the face value were greater than the value of the commodity from which it was made, it was called **bad money**. If good money and bad money were in circulation at the same time, people tended to hold on to the good money and spend the bad money instead. Ultimately, only the bad money would remain in circulation. This tendency to hoard the good money and spend the bad money has come to be known as **Gresham's Law**, named after Sir Thomas Gresham, a financial adviser of Queen Elizabeth I. Gresham's Law is often stated as, "Bad money will drive good money out of circulation."

Chequing accounts are bank deposits that are transferable by cheques.

We have discussed coins and paper currency. We must now discuss chequing accounts. Chequing accounts are deposits in banks on which the depositor may write cheques. Because the depositor can withdraw money from this type of account without giving the bank any notice, economists call these accounts **demand deposits**. We should note that it is the chequing accounts (that is, the deposits) and not the cheques themselves that are considered money. The cheque is just an order to the bank to transfer funds from the account on which the cheque is drawn to another account, or to convert funds from a chequing account into cash.

NEAR MONEY AND MONEY SUBSTITUTES

Learning Objective 3: distinguish between money and money substitutes

Money, as a medium of exchange in the form of currency and chequing accounts, is not the only instrument that can be used to obtain goods and services. And there is considerable debate as to whether the medium of exchange concept of money should be extended to include other highly liquid assets. This leads us into a discussion of near money and money substitutes.

NEAR MONEY

Notice deposits are interest-earning deposits subject to notice before withdrawal.

There are some assets, other than currency and demand deposits, that can be readily converted into currency and demand deposits. Examples of such assets are **notice deposits** (savings accounts, for example) in commercial banks, deposits in other financial institutions such as credit unions and caisses populaires, trust companies, and Canada Savings Bonds (CSBs). You will observe that these assets serve as temporary stores of value, but they do not directly perform the medium of exchange function. They can, however, be readily converted into cash or demand deposits. Because these assets are so closely related to money, economists call them **near money**.

Near money is any highly liquid asset that can easily be converted into currency or demand deposits without much loss of value.

When you hold your assets in the form of currency and chequing accounts, you earn little or no interest. When you hold assets in the form of near money (such as CSBs), you do earn interest. Why then, you may ask, do people not hold their liquid assets entirely in the form of near money? If people did not hold some currency and demand deposits, they would have to make frequent trips to the bank — every time they wanted to purchase something. The convenience of being able to make payments by writing cheques clearly outweighs the interest earning that could have been made if the money were deposited in a non-chequable interest-earning account.

MONEY SUBSTITUTES

Credit cards are not money; they are money substitutes.

The common use of major credit cards such as Visa, MasterCard, and American Express and their fairly wide acceptance as a means of obtaining goods and services in recent times have caused some people to confuse them with money. In fact, credit cards have been called plastic money. But are they really money? Let us answer this question by looking at two cases: one in which a transaction is carried out with the use of currency or demand deposits, the other in which a transaction is carried out with the use of a credit card. Henry and Irma were in a flower shop purchasing flowers. Irma purchased her carnations by using currency or by writing a cheque drawn on her account at the Town Bank. Henry used his credit card to obtain his roses. Several days after, Henry received a bill from the credit card company demanding that payment be made. Irma received no such bill from anyone. Why? Irma's debt was discharged when she paid for her carnations. She used money. Henry's debt was not discharged. He did not use money. Henry must now pay his bill with currency or demand deposit. He cannot discharge his debt by using a credit card. It is quite clear that credit cards are not money. They are temporary substitutes for money, because they enable us to obtain goods and services without immediately using money. We may summarize the difference between money and credit cards as follows:

> **The use of money in transactions discharges debts, but the use of credit cards establishes debts that must ultimately be discharged by using money.**

THE MONEY SUPPLY IN CANADA

The narrow definition of money (M1) emphasizes the medium of exchange function.

Learning Objective 4: understand how the money supply is measured in Canada

We can define the money supply in various ways. Narrowly defined, the money supply includes currency outside banks and demand deposits, less private sector float (mainly cheques issued by the Bank of Canada to the public, but which have not yet been deposited in their accounts). This narrow definition of the money supply focuses on the medium of exchange function and is usually referred to as **M1**. Many economists believe that this concept of the money supply is too narrow. They contend that daily interest chequable and non-personal notice deposits should be included in the definition of money. This concept of money, which includes currency, demand deposits, daily interest chequable and non-personal notice deposits, is referred to as **M1A**.

M1 = currency outside banks + demand deposits in chartered banks − private sector float.

M1A = M1 + daily interest chequable and non-personal notice deposits.

Broader definitions of money (such as M1A) include notice deposits and other highly liquid assets.

One very important aspect of studying money is to determine its effect on aggregate expenditure. Notice and personal term deposits certainly affect spending. (Term deposits are amounts deposited for specific periods of time.) In certain circumstances, it may be desirable to include them in the definition of the money supply. The measure of the money supply thus derived is known as **M2**, which is even broader than M1A. We have been concentrating on deposits in chartered banks. But many Canadians have deposits in financial institutions other than chartered banks. How are these accounted for? Well, there is a monetary aggregate called **M2+**, which consists of M2 and deposits in trust and mortgage loan companies, and deposits and shares at caisses populaires and credit unions.

M2 = M1A + other notice deposits + personal term deposits.

M2+ = M2 + deposits at trust and mortgage loan companies + deposits and shares at caisses populaires and credit unions.

Businesses usually deposit large sums, typically over $100 000, in the form of Certificates of Deposits (CDs) for a fixed term. Some Canadians hold foreign currency deposits (mainly in U.S. funds) in Canadian banks. It can be argued that these items should also be included in the money supply. The money supply, defined to include these items, is called **M3**.

M3 = M2 + other non-personal fixed-term deposits + foreign currency deposits of residents of Canada.

Table 30.1 shows various measures of the money supply in Canada. You will notice that these monetary aggregates omit liquid assets such as Canada Savings Bonds and short-term marketable securities. Although we do not include them in our definition of the money supply, such near monies cannot be neglected when studying the determinants of aggregate expenditure.

Our coins are issued by the Royal Canadian Mint. Although coins represent only a small proportion of our money supply, they are, nevertheless, quite important. They enable us to make purchases of low-priced items. Coins also provide us with change when the amount offered as payment exceeds the value of the transaction. Coins make our money more divisible.

Notes are now issued only by the Bank of Canada. Table 30.2 shows the various denominations for notes. Quantitatively, notes are about ten times more significant than coins. Notes and coins together constitute about 43% of the money supply defined narrowly as M1, and about 7% of the money supply defined broadly as M2. Some notes pre-

	Item	Amount ($million)
TABLE 30.1	Currency outside banks	$ 29 340
	Demand deposits	53 063
Monetary aggregates, December 1997.	M1	81 572
	M2	407 318
	M2+	632 110
	M3	554 198

Source: Bank of Canada Review, *Monetary Aggregates,* December 1997, Summer 1995: S50–S51.

	Denomination ($)	Amount ($thousand)
TABLE 30.2	1	161 112
	2	238 268
Bank of Canada note liabilities as of December 31, 1997.	5	778 697
	10	995 189
	20	8 881 353
	25	46
	50	3 916 443
	100	12 450 299
	500	23
	1000	3 107 656
	TOTAL	30 529 056

Source: *Bank of Canada Review*, Summer 1998: S103.

viously issued are now being retired. These include chartered banks' notes, Dominion of Canada notes, notes issued by the provinces, and defunct banks' notes.

Demand deposits are now the most important type of money (narrowly defined) in Canada. Quantitatively, they are substantially more important than notes and coins together. Demand deposits constitute about 55% of narrow money. Payment by cheque represents a very high proportion (probably as high as 90%) of the total dollar volume of all transactions.

> *Demand deposits are the most important type of money in Canada.*

 PROBLEM SOLVING 30-2

Can the money supply increase even if the Bank of Canada does not print more money?

THE CANADIAN PAYMENTS SYSTEM

Learning Objective 5: describe the Canadian payments system

The Canadian payments system has evolved from a very simple system using commodity money to a highly sophisticated system using electronic devices.

In any exchange economy, there must be some arrangements for exchanging purchasing power among individuals. The **payments system** includes the whole set of arrangements whereby the exchange of goods and services is effected. Through what mechanism do people acquire the goods and services they require to satisfy their wants? The answer depends on the payments system.

The Canadian payments system is one of evolution — from the *wampum* of the Native peoples to animal skins and *card money* (ordinary playing cards) in New France in the mid-1680s, to gold and silver coins and paper money in British North America, to fiat and deposit money today.

THE PRESENT PAYMENTS SYSTEM

Today, coins and Bank of Canada notes are used extensively to effect payment. But, in terms of the dollar value of transactions, chequing accounts are the most important medium of exchange. Generally, the smaller purchases are made with currency. Purchasing a small pocket calculator, a $35.00 watch, a newspaper, or a pen would typically be done with currency. But purchasing a car, a new set of furniture, an expensive stereo set, or a Caribbean cruise would normally be done with chequing accounts. Of course, credit cards are used in many transactions. We have shown, however, that in such circumstances, final settlement must be made with currency or deposit money.

The Canadian Payments Association facilitates transfers between financial institutions.

A relatively recent development in the Canadian payments system was the establishment of the **Canadian Payments Association** (CPA) in 1980. The CPA is responsible for clearing and settling accounts between depository institutions, that is, financial institutions that accept deposits. All chartered banks in Canada must be members of the CPA. Trust and mortgage loan companies, caisses populaires, and credit unions have the option to be or not to be members. The banks hold deposit accounts with the Bank of Canada. Let us consider the following situation. Mr. Andrews, who has an account at Bank A, writes a cheque for $500.00 to Mr. Barnes, who has an account at Bank B. At the same time, Ms. Browne, who has an account at Bank B, writes a cheque for $800.00 to Mr. Arrow, who has his account at Bank A. The outcome of these transactions is that Bank A owes Bank B $500.00 while Bank B owes Bank A $800.00. The net indebtedness between Bank A and Bank B, then, is that Bank B owes Bank A $300.00. The debt is settled by increasing Bank A's account at the Bank of Canada by $300.00 and reducing Bank B's account by $300.00. Since 1984 the clearing system has been automated through the use of computers.

We are deep in the electronic age. It is not at all surprising, therefore, that electronic technology is used in the payments system. Corporations are now sending payment instructions to financial institutions by using electronically encoded tapes. The institutions then make the appropriate entries in their accounts.

Another recent development worthy of note is the introduction of **automatic teller machines (ATMs)**. Financial institutions install these machines at convenient locations, so that their clients can have easy access to them at any time. These machines allow clients to perform a wide variety of banking activities, including withdrawing and depositing, transferring funds from one account to another, paying bills, and checking account balances.

THE PAYMENTS SYSTEM OF THE FUTURE

The payments system of the future depends to a great extent on technological developments and on our ability to use the technology to transfer purchasing power from individual to individual. It is therefore very difficult, if not impossible, to predict with any degree of accuracy what kind of payments system will emerge in the distant future. We can, however, say something about the payments system of the immediate future. The writing is on the wall.

The electronic funds transfer system transfers funds instantly between accounts.

The use of debit cards permits the instantaneous transfer of purchasing power.

A comprehensive system of transferring funds electronically — the **electronic funds transfer system (EFTS)** — allows for the instantaneous transfer of funds by electronic computers. This system is now being used nationwide. This is how the system works. People are given **payment cards** also known as **debit cards**, and merchants are equipped with computer terminals at the point of sale. When customers make purchases, their debit cards are inserted into the computer terminals. Within a matter of seconds, the funds are transferred from the customers' accounts to the merchants' accounts. Note that the use of debit cards, unlike the use of credit cards, requires the necessary funds to be currently in the customers' accounts. Some people have predicted that moving in this direction will lead to a cashless society. Only time will tell.

THE VALUE OF MONEY

In a previous section, you saw that money in Canada consists of coins, Bank of Canada notes, and deposits in banks. You know also that our currency is fiat money with no gold backing and with little or no intrinsic value. A bank account is merely a figure in the bank's books. Yet you know that money is valuable. You want money because you can buy things with it. If you were trying to sell your stereo set in order to purchase a new one, you would not accept pieces of paper with numbers on them for your set unless you were confident that the seller of the new set will also accept those pieces of paper. We can conclude then, that money is valuable because people will accept it as payment for goods and services.

It is important to note that when we talk about the value of money, we are not talking about the value of the Canadian dollar in terms of the U.S. dollar or the British pound. That is a different matter — the exchange rate — which will be studied later in this book. When we talk about the value of money, we are talking about what money will buy. If a dollar can buy more goods and services today than it could have bought a year ago, then prices have fallen and the value of the dollar has risen. On the other hand, if a dollar can buy fewer goods and services than it could have bought a year ago, then prices have risen and the value of the dollar has fallen. Thus, the value of the dollar depends on the price level.

During periods of high inflation, a given amount of money buys less this year than it did last year, and more this year than it will next year. The value of money is inversely related to the price level. What can we say about the stability of the value of the Canadian dollar in recent decades? Although we have not had runaway inflation in this country, we have had years of fairly rapid increases in the price level. To give you some idea of how the value of the dollar has fallen over the years, in 1960, $24.10 could purchase the same amount of goods and services that $121.90 could buy in 1991. To put it another way, $1 in 1991 was worth only about $.60 in terms of what you could buy with it in 1980. In the last 25 years, the price level has more than quadrupled — money has lost more than three quarters of its purchasing power.

THE MONEY SUPPLY AND INFLATION

In Chapter 21, you studied the record of inflation in Canada, and you have seen that although we have not had hyperinflation here, we have had some periods of price increases, which caused some anxiety. What causes inflation? There are several theories of inflation, and these will be taken up in a subsequent chapter. In this section, though, we will sketch the role of the money supply in inflation.

Severe inflations have resulted from excessive increases in the money supply. When the quantity of money (the money supply) increases, people get more money. Desired aggregate expenditure will therefore increase. As the economy reaches full employment, further increases in the money supply result in further increases in desired aggregate expenditure and inflation. Further increases in the money supply at this point simply add fuel to the inflation.

With money losing its value so fast, people will try to spend it quickly. They may even refuse to accept it as payment for goods and services, and may resort to barter exchange instead. In this situation, money will cease to perform its most important economic function, that is, to serve as a medium of exchange.

Continuous increases in the money supply at a tremendously rapid rate will result in severe inflation.

THE MONEY SUPPLY AND UNEMPLOYMENT

Inadequate growth in the money supply can cause unemployment.

Learning Objective 7:
discuss the relationship between the money supply and unemployment

No doubt you have suspected already that if rapid increases in the money supply result in inflation, then drastic reductions in the money supply may cause unemployment. Well, this section will confirm your suspicion. In our study of business cycles in Chapter 29, we noted that recessions could be caused by inadequate growth of the money supply.

Consider the following scenario. The Bank of Canada reduces the rate of growth of the money supply. Consequently, there is a slowdown in desired aggregate expenditure. This reduction in desired aggregate expenditure leads to a reduction in net domestic income and an increase in unemployment.

Reductions or inadequate increases in the money supply may result in economic slowdowns and increases in unemployment.

GLOBAL PERSPECTIVE

Money Here, Money There: How Fast Does It Grow?

In the latter part of this chapter, we studied the possible impact of the growth of the money supply on the economy, focusing on how the growth of the money supply affects inflation and unemployment. How fast does the money supply grow in Canada, and how does this growth rate compare with the growth rate of the money supply in other countries? That is the question we will try to address in this capsule.

The monetary aggregate that we shall consider is M1 — the narrow concept of the money supply and we shall consider the average annual percent growth for the period 1990-97 in the G-7 countries. The accompanying graph helps to tell the story.

Of the seven countries considered, Germany had the highest average annual percent growth in money supply (almost 10%). Canada had the second highest money supply growth with an annual average of 7.9%. Japan was third with an annual average of 7.6%. The country with the lowest average annual growth rate of the money supply over the 1990-97 period was France with a 2.3% average. The United States had the second lowest with a rate of 4%. The United Kingdom and Italy had almost identical money supply growth with 5.0% and 5.2% respectively.

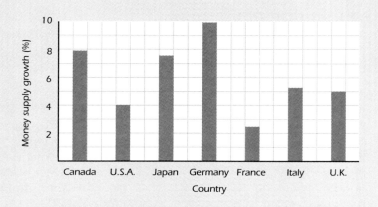

Source: International Monetary Fund, *World Economic Outlook.*, May 1998: 168

CHAPTER SUMMARY

1. Money is anything that is generally accepted by the members of a society as payment for goods and services or as settlement of a debt.

2. A barter system is a system by which goods and services are exchanged for other goods and services. Exchange by barter requires a double coincidence of wants, and is inefficient.

3. The most important function of money is to serve as a medium of exchange. Other important functions of money are the unit of account and the store of value functions.

4. The three kinds of money in common use in Canada are coins, Bank of Canada notes, and chequing accounts. Our coins and notes have a greater face value than the value of the commodity from which they are made.

5. Our currency is fiat money, which means that it is money by government decree. It is not backed by gold or by any other precious metal. Nevertheless, we accept it in exchange for valuable goods and services because other people will accept it from us.

6. The declaration that our currency is legal tender means that it must be accepted if it is offered in payment of a debt. Otherwise, the debt is considered to be legally discharged.

7. Gresham's Law states that bad money will drive good money out of circulation.

8. Near monies are assets such as notice deposits and Canada savings bonds, which can readily be converted into cash or demand deposits without much loss.

9. The money supply, narrowly defined as M1, consists of currency outside banks, and demand deposits. The M2 definition of money consists of currency outside banks, demand deposits, and notice and personal term deposits. Demand deposits are the most important type of money in Canada.

10. The Canadian payments system has evolved from a simple system of exchange using useful commodities as money, to a very advanced system whereby funds are transferred electronically. A cashless society may not be too far away.

11. The value of money is inversely related to the price level. The Canadian dollar has lost value gradually over the years as the price level has risen.

12. Rapid increases in the money supply are likely to cause inflation. Inadequate increases or reductions in the money supply may lead to unemployment.

TERMS FOR REVIEW

money (513)
medium of exchange (513)
barter (513)
double coincidence of wants (514)
unit of account (measure of value) (514)
store of value (514)
liquidity (514)
currency (515)
fiat money (515)
legal tender (515)
good money (515)
bad money (515)
Gresham's law (515)
demand deposits (515)

notice deposits (516)
near money (516)
M1 (517)
M1A (517)
M2 (517)
M2+ (517)
M3 (517)
payments system (518)
Canadian Payments Association (CPA) (519)
automatic teller machines (ATMs) (519)
electronic funds transfer
  system (EFTS) (519)
debit (payment) cards (519)

QUESTIONS FOR REVIEW AND DISCUSSION

1. Discuss briefly the main functions of money. (L.O.2)
2. What are the main types of money in common use in Canada? (L.O.1)
3. State Gresham's Law and briefly explain why it might be expected to hold. (General)
4. How is the money supply defined? Do you think that Canada Savings Bonds should be included in the money supply? Why or why not? (L.O.4)
5. What is the electronic funds transfer system (EFTS)? (L.O.5)
6. What are debit cards? How do they differ from credit cards? (L.O.5)
7. Why is a $20 bill worth more than the paper on which it is printed? (L.O.6)
8. How does inflation affect the value of money? (L.O.6)
9. Is there any relationship between the money supply and inflation? (L.O.7)
10. Explain how a reduction in the money supply might cause unemployment. (L.O.7)

PROBLEMS AND EXERCISES

1. You are given the information shown in Table 30.3.

TABLE 30.3

Money items.

Item	Amount ($million)
Notes	1 169
Demand deposits	11 258
Coins	219
Notice and personal term deposits	25 268

Calculate: (L.O.4)
(a) the amount of currency
(b) M1
(c) M2

2. Which function of money is evident in each of the following? (L.O.2)
   (a) You purchase a set of books from the bookstore and pay $126.00.
   (b) You put $1500.00 in a savings account.
   (c) You are told that the price of a compact disk player is $750.00.
   (d) You use $45.00 to purchase a gift.
   (e) I write a cheque to you for $150.00.
   (f) Your friend says to you, "That company is worth millions of dollars."

3. Which of the following items are money in Canada? (L.O.1,4)
   (a) shares in Air Canada
   (b) Bank of Canada notes
   (c) Canadian Tire coupons
   (d) Bell Canada stocks
   (e) a chequing account at a chartered bank
   (f) gold bars
   (g) Canada Savings Bonds
   (h) American Express credit cards
   (i) an Eaton's store credit card
   (j) coins issued by the Royal Canadian Mint that have no intrinsic value.

4. Canadian Tire stores issue coupons (popularly called Canadian Tire money) to their customers when they purchase items in Canadian Tire stores. These coupons can be used for purchases at Canadian Tire stores across the country. Assume that there are no laws forbidding the use of any item as money. Could Canadian Tire coupons become real money? If so, explain the process by which this could occur.

Internet Site

http://www.rcmint.ca/index.html
This is the Web site for the Royal Canadian Mint. It contains useful information on our coins and other interesting material.

http://www.bank-banque-canada.ca
This site for the Bank of Canada contains information on our central bank and our paper money.

INTERNET EXERCISES

1. Go to the Royal Canadian Mint site above
   a) Click on *CIRCULATION*.
   b) What are circulation coins?
   c) Click on any coin (for example, *One Cent*, *Fifty Cent*, etc.) and write a short paragraph about the coin you have chosen.
2. Go to the Bank of Canada site indicated above.
   a) Click on *About the Bank*.
   b) Click on *General information about the Bank*.
   c) Click on *bank notes*.
   d) Scroll down and learn how to spot a counterfeit bank note.

THE BANKING SYSTEM AND THE MONEY SUPPLY

Learning Objectives

After studying this chapter, you should be able to:

1 describe the Canadian banking system

2 state the objectives and functions of the Bank of Canada

3 identify the major items on the balance sheet of the Bank of Canada

4 discuss the origins of modern banking

5 discuss the services provided by chartered banks

6 describe the main items on the balance sheet of chartered banks

7 explain the expansion of the money supply by the chartered banks

8 discuss the role of near banks in the financial system

If when loans are repaid to a bank, the bank merely keeps the cash instead of lending it out or investing it, then total purchasing power is reduced.

Arthur D. Gayer and W.W. Rostow, *How Money Works*

INTRODUCTION

The banking system is an important aspect of our economy. We studied the nature and functions of money in Chapter 30, and we know, at least intuitively, that a close relationship exists between money and banks. In this chapter, you will learn about Canada's central bank — the Bank of Canada and about the origin of modern banking, the sources and uses of bank funds, and the creation of deposit money by chartered banks. Near banks (caisses populaires and credit unions, and trust and mortgage loan companies) play an important role in the Canadian financial system. We shall briefly study their activities by examining their main sources and uses of funds as revealed by their balance sheets.

THE CANADIAN BANKING SYSTEM

Learning Objective 1:
the Canadian banking system

The Canadian banking system consists of a central bank and a number of chartered banks.

Near banks include credit unions, trust companies, and mortgage loan companies.

The Canadian **banking system** is a subset of a larger system — the financial system — which consists of the following financial institutions:

1. the Bank of Canada;

2. chartered banks;

3. near banks;

4. other financial institutions.

The *Bank of Canada* is Canada's *central bank*. As you will see later, it occupies a most important position in the Canadian financial system. Chartered banks are financial institutions such as the Royal Bank of Canada, the Bank of Montreal, the Canadian Imperial Bank of Commerce, etc., where most of us do our banking. **Near banks** are financial institutions other than chartered banks that accept deposits from the public. They include caisses populaires and credit unions, trust companies, and mortgage loan companies. The last group of financial institutions — those we referred to as "other financial institutions" — does not accept deposits from the public. This group includes financial institutions such as mutual funds, sales finance companies, consumer loan companies, and insurance companies. The banking system, which is our main concern in this chapter and the following one, consists of the central bank (the Bank of Canada) and the chartered banks. Because the near banks provide services that are so similar to the services provided by the chartered banks, we shall pay some attention to their activities. The activities and influence of non-depository financial institutions, though important in the financial system, lie outside the scope of our present study.

CANADA'S CENTRAL BANK

ESTABLISHMENT OF THE BANK OF CANADA

The Bank of Canada was established in response to calls for better monetary management.

Central banks are a characteristic feature of modern economies. Canada's central bank is the Bank of Canada. Prior to the establishment of the Bank of Canada, the Department of Finance conducted central banking operations for the country. Suggestions were made as early as 1914 to establish a central bank, but no action to that effect was taken. During the Great Depression, it was felt that the economy would perform better if there was better management of the country's monetary system. Consequently, in 1933, the Royal Commission on Banking and Finance, chaired by Lord Macmillan, was appointed. The mandate of the Macmillan Commission was to inquire into the desirability of establishing a central bank in Canada.

In the fall of 1933, the Macmillan Commission submitted its report in favour of establishing a central bank. It is interesting to note that the chartered banks were not in favour of the commission's recommendation. However, the **Bank of Canada Act** establishing the central bank was passed in 1934, and the Bank of Canada thus became a reality. The Bank of Canada began to operate in 1935 as a privately owned bank, but the federal government acquired complete ownership in 1938.

ORGANIZATION AND MANAGEMENT OF THE BANK OF CANADA

The Bank of Canada is managed by a board of directors.

The Bank of Canada is under the management of a board of directors. This board comprises the governor of the Bank, the deputy governor, and twelve directors. The governor and deputy governor are appointed by the directors (with the approval of the Cabinet) for terms of seven years. The directors are appointed by the Minister of Finance for terms of three years each. Directors must be under 75 years of age, and must be Canadian citizens. Moreover, they must not be full-time employees of the federal or any provincial government, and must not be directors, partners, or employees of an institution that deals directly with the Bank of Canada. The executive committee, which acts on behalf of the board of directors, consists of the governor, the deputy governor, and from two to four directors. The executive committee meets at least once a week. The Deputy Minister of Finance is a member of the Board, but has no voting rights.

THE OBJECTIVES AND FUNCTIONS OF THE BANK OF CANADA

OBJECTIVES

Learning Objective 2: *state the objectives and functions of the Bank of Canada*

The main objectives of the Bank of Canada are set out in the preamble to the Bank of Canada Act as follows:

> to regulate credit and currency in the best interest of the economic life of the nation, to control and protect the external value of the national monetary unit and to mitigate by influence fluctuations in the general level of production, trade, prices and employment so far as may be possible within the scope of monetary action, and generally to promote the economic and financial welfare of the Dominion.

Restated, the Bank of Canada is charged with the responsibility of conducting monetary policy to achieve economic stability, economic growth, and a viable balance of payments. The achievement of these objectives is no easy matter! And, since measures taken to achieve one objective often push us further away from achieving other objectives, the task can become very difficult indeed.

FUNCTIONS

The Bank of Canada, like other central banks, performs five basic functions. Let us look at each of these functions in turn.

Controller of the money supply

The Bank of Canada is responsible for providing an adequate supply of currency.

We have already seen that the quantity of money has an important effect on the levels of output and prices in the economy. If the money supply increases too rapidly, inflation may result. On the other hand, an inadequate money supply may result in unemployment. Controlling the money supply is thus an important function of any central bank. In Canada, the only institution empowered to issue bank notes is the Bank of Canada.

Banker to the commercial banks

The Bank acts as a lender of last resort.

Another important function of the Bank of Canada is to serve as banker to the commercial banks. We have already seen that Canadian chartered banks keep a fraction of their deposits as desired cash reserves. Cash reserves of chartered banks are deposited with and are liabilities of the Bank of Canada.

If a commercial bank or any other member of the Canadian Payments Association finds itself with insufficient cash to meet its depositors' demands, it could borrow, as a last resort, from the Bank of Canada. This function of extending loans to members of the Canadian Payments Association has become known as the **lender of last resort** function. Although Canadian chartered banks do not often take advantage of this privilege, the Bank of Canada stands ready to aid them should the need arise.

Fiscal agent and financial advisor to the government

The Bank serves as the government's bank.

The Bank of Canada also serves as fiscal agent and financial advisor to the government. The Canadian government keeps a chequing account with the Bank of Canada. The government of Canada also borrows money from the Bank of Canada. The Bank of Canada grants these loans by buying securities from the government and paying for them by crediting the government's account with a deposit for the amount of the securities. For example, if the government wants to borrow $10 million from the Bank of Canada, it prints $10 million worth of bonds and sells them to the Bank of Canada. The Bank of Canada then credits the government's account with a deposit of $10 million. Thus, the Bank of Canada acts as the government's bank. Also, the Bank of Canada is staffed with experts in various areas of finance and monetary affairs, and is therefore well equipped to act as financial advisor to the federal government.

Manager of the country's monetary policy

Conduct of the country's monetary policy is entrusted to the Bank of Canada.

The Bank of Canada, in consultation with the federal government, conducts the country's monetary policy. While the Bank of Canada enjoys a certain degree of independence in establishing and implementing monetary policy, the federal government reserves the right — and the responsibility — to instruct the Bank on the country's monetary policy. Mr. Louis Rasminsky, when he assumed the governorship of the Bank in 1961, formalized this principle as follows:

> …in the ordinary course of events, the Bank has the responsibility for monetary policy, and if the government disapproves of the monetary policy being carried out by the Bank, it has the right and responsibility to direct the Bank as to the policy which the Bank is to carry out.

These sentiments have now been clearly expressed in the Bank of Canada Act since its amendment in 1967. The Bank of Canada Act now specifies that: (1) there must be ongoing consultation between the federal government and the Bank of Canada; (2) if the government and the Bank disagree over monetary policy, the Minister of Finance may, with the approval of the Cabinet, and after consulting the governor of the Bank, give a written directive to the governor stating the monetary policy that should be followed; and (3) if such a directive is given, it must be for a specified period of time and the Bank of Canada must comply.

Supporter of the financial system

The Bank tries to maintain confidence in the monetary system.

The Canadian monetary system is based on confidence. We accept paper currency from other people in exchange for valuable goods and services mainly because we are confident that others will, in turn, accept it from us. Likewise, we accept entries in banks' books (deposit accounts) as money because others accept them as money. If we lose confidence in the system, and rush to the banks to cash in all our deposit accounts, there will be chaos. The Bank of Canada supports the financial system and prevents the loss of confidence that might cause panic and ensuing bank failures.

THE BALANCE SHEET OF THE BANK OF CANADA

A balance sheet is a statement of assets, liabilities, and owner's equity.

Learning Objective 3:
list the major items on the balance sheet of the Bank of Canada

Familiarity with the concept of a balance sheet will enhance our comprehension of much of the material presented in later sections of this chapter. A **balance sheet** is a statement of the assets and liabilities of an economic unit. An **asset** is anything that is owned by the unit. A **liability** is anything owed by the unit. The difference between the total assets and the total liabilities is called **capital** or **owner's equity**.

The composition of the balance sheet of the Bank of Canada helps to reveal its functions and responsibilities. In the same way that we learned something about the activities of other financial institutions from their balance sheets, so too can we learn something about the Bank of Canada from its balance sheet. Table 31.1 shows the balance sheet of the Bank of Canada.

ASSETS OF THE BANK OF CANADA

Government of Canada Securities

The main asset of the Bank of Canada is Government of Canada securities.

As can be seen from Table 31.1, the most important asset item is Government of Canada securities. In June 1998, Government of Canada bonds accounted for over 90% of the total assets of the Bank of Canada. This tells us explicitly that the Bank of Canada makes substantial loans to the government of Canada. This is one sense in which the Bank of Canada is the government's bank.

TABLE 31.1		**Amount ($million)**
Balance sheet of the Bank of Canada, June 30, 1998.	ASSETS	
	Government of Canada securities	29 099
	Advances to members of the Canadian Payments Association	224
	Other investments	1 954
	Foreign currency deposits	326
	Accrued interest on investments	288
	All other assets	220
	TOTAL ASSETS	32 111
	LIABILITIES	
	Notes in circulation:	30 364
	Canadian dollar deposits:	
	Government of Canada	8
	Chartered banks	797
	Other members of the Canadian Payments Association	68
	Foreign central banks and official institutions	158
	Other	135
	Foreign currency liabilities	169
	Bank of Canada cheques outstanding	6
	All other liabilities	406
	TOTAL LIABILITIES	32 111

Source: *Bank of Canada Review,* Summer 1998: s8–S9.

Advances to members of the Canadian Payments Association

The function of the Bank of Canada as lender of last resort is reflected in this item in the Bank's asset portfolio. Total advances to members of the Canadian Payments Association at the end of June 1998 were $224 million.

Other investments and accrued interest on investments

The Bank of Canada engages in investment activities. These items amounted to about $1.9 billion at the end of June 1997.

Foreign currency deposits

This item represents deposits which the Bank of Canada keeps with other central banks. These deposits are a part of our country's foreign exchange reserves. In June 1997, foreign currency deposits amounted to $326 million.

LIABILITIES OF THE BANK OF CANADA

Bank of Canada notes

The main liability of the Bank of Canada is Bank of Canada notes in circulation.

As you already know, the Bank of Canada has a monopoly on note issue. All of our paper currency is issued by the Bank of Canada. Notes in circulation at the end of June 1997 amounted to $30 billion, accounting for over 94% of the total liabilities of the central bank.

Canadian dollar deposits

The items under this heading reveal that the government of Canada, the chartered banks and other members of the Canadian Payments Association, and foreign central banks all have deposits at the Bank of Canada. Recall that the chartered banks hold desired cash reserves on deposit at the Bank of Canada. Deposits of chartered banks and other members of the Canadian Payments Association totalled $0.86 billion at the end of June 1997, representing about 3% of the total liabilities of the Bank of Canada.

Foreign currency liabilities

These are foreign currency deposits held at the Bank of Canada by the federal government and by foreign central banks. Foreign currency liabilities amounted to $169 million in June 1997.

THE ORIGINS OF MODERN BANKING

Modern banking can be traced to the seventeenth century, when goldsmiths accepted gold deposits and issued paper receipts.

Learning Objective 4:
the origins of modern banking

We can trace the origin of modern banking to seventeenth-century England, where goldsmiths accepted gold deposits for safekeeping in their secure safes. Depositors of gold received receipts from the goldsmiths certifying that the deposits were made. Upon presentation of the receipts to the goldsmiths, they were obliged to deliver the stipulated amount of gold to the owner of the receipt. Since the gold was redeemable on demand, the goldsmiths had to ensure that the gold was always available whenever a receipt was presented.

If a depositor (let's call her Cathy) wanted to purchase an item from Ben, she could go to her goldsmith, withdraw some of her gold and use it to pay Ben for the item. Ben could then take the gold to the goldsmith for safekeeping. As time progressed, people realized that they could save the time of going back and forth to their goldsmiths if a purchaser simply handed the goldsmith's receipt to a seller. Provided that the goldsmith who issued the receipt was reputable, the seller would normally be willing to accept the receipt since it could be presented to the goldsmith at any time for gold.

Goldsmiths' receipts became money once they were generally accepted.

For convenience, depositors began to ask for receipts to be given in smaller denominations. For example, instead of having one receipt for ten pounds of gold, depositors were choosing to have ten receipts, each for one pound of gold. The goldsmiths became an issuer of paper money. This function was later performed by the commercial banks, but now is performed exclusively by the Bank of Canada.

Once these receipts began to circulate and to be widely accepted, the goldsmiths observed that they had gold in their possession for long periods of time. They began to make loans. But, instead of lending gold, they lent notes (receipts). Thus, the total value of all receipts exceeded the value of gold deposited with the goldsmith. You will see shortly that this situation bears a striking resemblance to our present fractional reserve banking system.

THE COMMERCIAL (CHARTERED) BANKS

A commercial (chartered) bank is a financial institution chartered by the government.

Learning Objective 5: commercial (chartered) banks

When banks were first established, their main function was to cater to the needs of commerce by extending commercial loans; hence the term **commercial banks**. Commercial loans were typically short-term loans (not exceeding one year) granted to merchants and traders for such purposes as acquiring inventories and paying for raw materials. Such loans were considered to be appropriate because the goods would be sold within a short period of time and the loan could be repaid from the proceeds of the sale. Although bank lending is not presently limited to commercial loans, the term "commercial bank" still persists. In Canada, commercial banks are also called **chartered banks** because prior to 1980, a bank could be established in Canada only by a special charter granted by the federal Parliament.

STRUCTURE OF CANADIAN BANKING

The Canadian banking system is a branch banking system.

The Bank Act governs the operation of commercial banks in Canada.

A unit banking system has many independent banks.

Schedule A banks are Canadian-owned; Schedule B banks are foreign.

The banking structure of Canada has changed from one of over fifty banks in the years following Confederation — a period of rapid bank expansion — to a structure with only a few Canadian-owned banks. The major Canadian banks have many branches all over the country. The Canadian banking structure is, therefore, **a branch banking system**. This is in sharp contrast to the **unit banking system** typical of the United States where there are several thousand independent banks without branches.

The act that governs the operations of chartered banks in Canada is a federal legislation known as the Bank Act. This act is subject to review every ten years. The revision of the Bank Act in 1980 allowed foreign banks to operate in Canada. Foreign banks established under the 1980 provisions are called **Schedule B banks**. Canadian banks operating at the time of the revision were classified as **Schedule A banks**.

THE BUSINESS OF COMMERCIAL BANKING

Commercial banks must strike a balance between profitability and liquidity.

Commercial banks are privately owned, and therefore they seek to earn a return for their shareholders. At the same time, commercial banks must keep sufficient funds to meet the needs of their depositors. The problem that confronts the banker is the fact that assets that yield high earnings tend to be non-liquid. On the other hand, liquid assets tend to yield little or no earnings. For example, if a bank keeps all of its assets in cash, it will be 100% liquid, but it will earn nothing for its shareholders. If it keeps all of its assets in loans and long-term securities, which have high interest earnings, it will have a major liquidity problem. It will not survive.

Banks therefore face conflicting needs for profitability on the one hand and liquidity on the other. Good banking consists of being able to use bank funds profitably while at the same time having due regard for liquidity needs.

Canadian chartered banks perform a variety of services including the granting of loans, the establishment of convenient chequing accounts, the establishment of savings accounts, the safekeeping of valuables, foreign exchange services, automatic teller machine services, funds transfer between accounts, mail banking, and bill payment services.

Commercial banks earn income by making profitable loans and investments.

Chartered banks obtain some of their earnings by charging a fee for some of the services they provide. Their largest earnings, however, are derived from the various loans that they make to borrowers. Like other businesses, banks too have expenses. For example, they pay interest on some deposits, they pay rent for their facilities, and they pay salaries to their employees. Table 31.2 shows revenues and expenses of all chartered banks in Canada in 1997.

TABLE 31.2	
Chartered banks' consolidated statement of revenue and expense, 1997.	

Items	Amount ($million)
Interest Income:	
Loans	49 436.6
Securities	10 730.4
Deposits with banks	4 514.0
TOTAL including dividends	64 681.1
Interest Expense:	
Deposits	32 132.5
Bank debentures	1 685.0
Liabilities other than deposits	7 777.2
TOTAL	41 594.9
Net interest income	23 086.1
Provision for loan losses	(2 079.9)
Other income	15 787.7
Net interest and other income	40 043.4
Non-Interest Expense:	
Salaries and benefits	14 767.1
Premises and equipment	5 050.2
Other	7 333.5
TOTAL	27 150.7
Net income before provision for income taxes	12 892.7
Provision for income taxes	(4 784.3)
Net income before minority interest in subsidiaries and extraordinary items	8 108.4
Minority interest in subsidiaries	(178.7)
Extraordinary items	25.5
Net Income	7955.2

Source: *Bank of Canada Review*, Summer 1998: s107.

BALANCE SHEETS OF CHARTERED BANKS

Learning Objective 6:
the balance sheet of chartered banks

The assets of chartered banks include notes and deposits with the Bank of Canada, deposits in banks in currencies other than Canadian, cheques and other items in transit, government of Canada treasury bills, loans, and mortgages. Table 31.3 shows the assets of chartered banks.

An asset is owned, a liability is owed, and capital (owner's equity) is the difference between total assets and total liabilities.

Liabilities represent claims on the assets of the individual or institution. Among the liabilities of commercial banks are deposits by various groups, advances from the Bank of Canada, acceptances, guarantees, and letters of credit. Table 31.4 shows liabilities of chartered banks.

TABLE 31.3

Assets of chartered banks, April 30, 1998.

Items	Amount ($million)
Canadian dollar liquid assets:	
Bank of Canada deposits, notes and coin	3 842
Treasury bills	20 829
Government of Canada bonds	45 213
Call and short loans	1 014
TOTAL	70 898
Less liquid Canadian dollar assets:	
Loans in Canadian dollars:	
Federal, provincial and municipal governments	1 906
General loans	300 053
Residential mortgages	229 648
Non-residential mortgages	13 907
Leasing receivables	2 593
TOTAL	548 108
Canadian securities:	
Provincial and municipal	11 918
Corporate	46 167
TOTAL	58 085
Total liquid and less liquid assets	677 090
Canadian dollar deposits with other regulated financial institutions	16 090
Canadian dollar items in transit	−4 336
Customers' liability under acceptances	42 868
Other Canadian dollar assets	39 853
Total Canadian dollar assets	771 565
Total foreign currency assets	535 097
TOTAL ASSETS	1 306 662

Source: *Bank of Canada Review*, Summer 1998: s18-s19.

TABLE 31.4

Liabilities of chartered banks, April 30, 1998.

Items	Amount ($million)
Canadian dollar deposits:	
Personal savings deposits	288 157
Non-personal and term deposits	135 722
Gross demand deposits	52 691
Government of Canada	1 627
TOTAL	478 198
Advances from Bank of Canada	367
Bankers' acceptances	42 870
Liabilities of subsidiaries other than deposits	2 590
Other liabilities	142 321
Non-controlling interest in subsidiaries	902
Subordinated debt	15 301
Shareholders' equity	57 369
Total Canadian dollar liabilities	739 917
Total foreign currency liabilities	566 745
TOTAL LIABILITIES	1 306 662

Source: *Bank of Canada Review*, Summer 1998: s20-s21.

An examination of the balance sheet of chartered banks tells us a great deal about their activities. Specifically, the balance sheet provides useful information about the banks' sources and uses of funds.

MAIN SOURCES OF FUNDS

Customers' deposits provide the main source of funds for commercial banks.

From what sources do commercial banks obtain their funds? This question can be answered easily by looking at the liabilities of the banks. As can be seen from Table 31.4, the most important source of funds for chartered banks is the deposits of their customers. At the end of April 1998, total Canadian dollar deposits amounted to $478.2 billion. In addition, Canadian chartered banks obtained a substantial amount of deposits in foreign currencies.

Personal savings deposits

Most of these deposits are personal savings deposits of Canadians. At the end of April 1998, total personal savings deposits amounted to $288.2 billion or 60% of total Canadian dollar deposits.

Non-personal term and notice deposits

These deposits also provide funds for commercial banks. These deposits amounted to $135.7 billion or about 28% of total Canadian dollar deposits at the end of April 1998.

Government of Canada

Another source of funds for chartered banks is the federal government. The government of Canada holds deposits at the chartered banks. As we shall see later, these deposits are used partly to control the money supply. At the end of April 1998, government of Canada deposits at chartered banks amounted to $1.6 billion.

Capital and debentures (Subordinated debt)

Debentures are bonds secured by the credit-worthiness of the borrower.

The banks' capital and debentures also provide funds for the banks' operations. **Debentures** are bonds that are secured by the credit-worthiness of the issuer rather than by specific tangible assets. In addition to providing funds for their operations, banks' capital funds also provide a margin of safety for the banks' depositors. At the end of April 1998, bank debentures amounted to almost $15.3 billion while retained earnings, a part of shareholders' equity, amounted to just over $31.9 billion.

MAIN USES OF FUNDS

The major use of bank funds is loans extended to customers.

Everyone knows that banks are in the business of lending money. By looking at the asset side of the banks' balance sheet, we can get a pretty good picture of the uses to which banks allocate their funds and the types of lending in which they are involved.

CASH RESERVES AND HIGHLY LIQUID ASSETS

The Bank Act is a federal legislation that governs the chartered banks.

The **Bank Act** (1980 version) stipulated that chartered banks must keep a minimum cash reserve of 10% of demand deposits, 2% of the first $500 million of notice deposits and 3% on the balance, and 3% of foreign currency deposits. Legal cash reserves were held on deposit with the Bank of Canada. The ratio of the legal reserve to total deposits is called the *minimum legal reserve ratio*. Because the chartered banks were obliged to keep in cash only a fraction of the total amount deposited with them, the system has been called a **fractional reserve banking system**. Legal **reserve requirements** have now been phased out.

The reserve ratio is the ratio of reserves to deposits.

Cash reserve requirements were originally instituted in order to protect the deposits of customers. Today, each person's deposit at a Canadian chartered bank is insured

Canada Deposit Insurance Corporation (CDIC): government agency that insures deposits in chartered banks, trust companies, and loan companies up to a maximum of $60 000 per depositor.

Primary reserves: cash reserves held by banks.

Secondary reserves: excess cash reserves, treasury bills, and day-to-day loans hold by banks.

against loss by the **Canada Deposit Insurance Corporation (CDIC)** up to a maximum of $60 000. You will see later that the legal reserve requirement was a means whereby the money supply could be controlled.

You will recall that a large proportion of the banks' deposit liabilities is payable on demand or on short notice. Therefore, chartered banks keep a certain amount of their assets in the form of cash (**primary reserves**) and other liquid assets called **secondary reserves**. Secondary reserves consist of currency, day-to-day loans, treasury bills, and call and short loans. At the end of April 1998, primary and secondary reserves amounted to $25.7 billion.

Government of Canada bonds

Government of Canada bonds are liquid assets that earn interest income for their holders. The chartered banks use some of their funds to acquire these bonds. At the end of April 1998, the chartered banks held a total of $45.2 billion worth of Government of Canada bonds.

Loans in Canadian dollars

Most of the funds collected by chartered banks are used to grant general loans to businesses and individuals. At the end of April 1998, general loans by chartered banks amounted to $300 billion — about 55% of total loans in Canadian dollars and 39% of total Canadian-dollar assests. In addition, chartered banks extend loans to the provinces and the municipalities. Since 1967, when banks were first allowed to engage in conventional mortgage lending, they have increased their activities in this area of lending substantially. At the end of April 1998, mortgage lending by chartered banks totalled $244 billion, of which 94% was allocated to residential mortgages.

Canadian securities

Chartered banks also use some of their funds to purchase Canadian securities issued by provincial and municipal governments and by corporations. The total value of these securities was estimated at $58.1 billion at the end of April 1998, 80% of which was corporate securities.

Foreign operations

Canadian chartered banks are quite active on the international banking scene.

Canadian chartered banks are active on the international banking scene. Canadian banks have over 300 branches and offices in more than 55 countries around the world. They extend loans for a variety of purposes, including the financing of dams, airports, office buildings, and public utilities. At the end of April 1998, total foreign currency assets of the chartered banks amounted to $535.1 billion. This is a considerable amount since it represents nearly 70% of total Canadian dollar assets.

THE EXPANSION OF THE MONEY SUPPLY BY THE COMMERCIAL BANKS

Learning Objective 7: the expansion of the money supply by the chartered banks

Commercial banks are in business to earn a profit for their shareholders. It will be seen that by going about their business of trying to earn a profit, commercial banks actually affect the money supply. To see how changes in the money supply result from the operation of the banking system, let us make the following simplifying assumptions:

1. Commercial banks desire to keep a cash reserve of 10%.

2. All deposits are demand deposits.

3. The banks invest their funds in loans only.

4. They are successful in extending as much in loans as they possibly can.

Let us assume that a customer, Mr. Berber, deposits $1000 cash into his chequing account at the Muskoka Bank. T-accounts show changes in the balance sheet resulting from transactions. The $1000 deposit will cause changes in the balance sheet of the Muskoka Bank. These changes are shown in Table 31.5. The Muskoka Bank desires to keep as cash reserves only 10% of the $1000 deposited. The bank therefore has excess reserves of $900. Since the bank is a profit-seeking institution, it will likely not allow $900 to lie idly in its vault.

TABLE 31.5

Balance sheet changes at the Muskoka Bank.

Muskoka Bank				
Assets			**Liabilities**	
Desired reserves	+$ 100		Demand deposits:	
Excess reserves	+ 900		Mr. Berber	+$1000
TOTAL	+$1000		TOTAL	+$1000

Let us suppose that another customer, Mr. Strada, goes to the bank to borrow $900 to purchase a refrigerator. The bank grants the loan by adding $900 to Mr. Strada's chequing account. Note that the bank does not give the customer its excess reserves of $900. Instead, it has created a new deposit by granting the loan to the customer. The new deposit, however, is an amount equal to the bank's excess reserves. Table 31.6 shows how the loan transaction will affect the bank's balance sheet.

TABLE 31.6

Balance sheet changes at the Muskoka Bank.

Muskoka Bank				
Assets			**Liabilities**	
Cash:			Demand deposits:	
Desired reserves	+$ 190		Mr. Berber	+$1000
Excess reserves	+ 810		Mr. Strada	+ 900
Loans	+ 900			
TOTAL	+$1900		TOTAL	+$1900

Let us take a brief look at what has happened to the money supply up to this point. Mr. Berber's deposit of $1000 did not affect the money supply. It was just a matter of converting one type of money (cash) into another type (demand deposits). The loan granted to Mr. Strada, however, has resulted in an increase in the money supply of $900. By creating a new deposit, the bank has increased the money supply. Mr. Strada now has $900 that did not previously exist.

Banks increase the money supply by creating deposits.

Mr. Strada has taken out the loan to buy a refrigerator. He then learns that Bracebridge Appliances has a sale. Naturally, he rushes to this store and buys a refrigerator, paying for it by writing a cheque for $900. Bracebridge Appliances deposits the cheque in its account at the Georgian Bank. The Georgian Bank now has a cheque written on Mr. Strada's account at the Muskoka Bank. How does the Georgian Bank collect from the Muskoka Bank? Let us investigate. It is quite likely that the Muskoka Bank will have cheques written on accounts at the Georgian Bank also. Through the clearing system discussed in Chapter 30, the net indebtedness of each bank is determined. If the Muskoka Bank has to make a net payment to the Georgian Bank, the Muskoka Bank's account at the central bank will be reduced by the amount of the payment, and the Georgian Bank's account will then be increased by an equivalent amount. Note that the settlement is accomplished by bookkeeping entries at the central bank rather than by physical transfers of funds. The role of the Canadian Payments Association in the clearing mechanism was examined in Chapter 30.

Let us resume our discussion of the process of money creation. The transaction between Mr. Strada and Bracebridge Appliances will change the Muskoka Bank's balance sheet. Table 31.7 shows this change. It is important also to note the changes in the balance sheet of the Georgian Bank. Table 31.8 shows the effect of the transaction on the Georgian Bank's position. Note that the purchase of the refrigerator has not resulted in any change in the money supply. The Muskoka Bank has lost $900 in reserves. But the Georgian Bank has gained $900 in new demand deposits.

TABLE 31.7

Balance sheet changes at the Muskoka Bank.

Muskoka Bank

Assets		Liabilities	
Desired reserves	+$ 100	Demand deposits:	
Loan	+ 900	Mr. Berber	+$1000
TOTAL	+$1000	TOTAL	+$1000

TABLE 31.8

Balance sheet changes at the Georgian Bank.

Georgian Bank

Assets		Liabilities	
Desired reserves	+$ 90	Demand deposits:	
Excess reserves	+ 810	Bracebridge Appliances	+$900
TOTAL	+$900	TOTAL	+$900

Now let us suppose that another customer, Ms. Kiyat, goes into the Georgian Bank and borrows $810. The Georgian Bank grants the loan by adding $810 to Ms. Kiyat's chequing account. Table 31.9 shows how this loan transaction will affect the Georgian Bank's balance sheet. The granting of the loan of $810 by the Georgian Bank has led to an additional increase of $810 in the money supply. The initial deposit of $1000 on the Muskoka Bank has resulted so far in an increase in the money supply of $1710 in the form of deposit liabilities of commercial banks.

TABLE 31.9

Balance sheet changes at the Georgian Bank.

Georgian Bank

Assets		Liabilities	
Desired reserves	+$ 171	Demand deposits:	
Excess reserves	+ 729	Bracebridge Appliances	+$ 900
Loans	+ 810	Ms. Kiyat	+ 810
TOTAL	+$1710	TOTAL	+$1710

Suppose Ms. Kiyat writes a cheque for $810 to pay for an airline ticket purchased from Rapid Airlines. Rapid Airlines deposits the cheque into its account at the Huron Bank. After the cheque is cleared, the Georgian Bank's position will be as shown in Table 31.10, and the Huron Bank's position, will be as shown in Table 31.11.

Now, the Huron Bank has excess reserves — and the process of money (deposit) creation could go on and on. Money creation would come to an end when the entire initial deposit of $1000 becomes desired reserves. Since the ratio of desired reserves to deposits is assumed to be 10%, then total reserves of $1000 could support total deposits of $10 000.

TABLE 31.10

Balance sheet changes
at the Georgian Bank.

	Georgian Bank			
Assets		**Liabilities**		
Desired reserves	+$ 90	Demand deposits:		
Loans	+ 810	Bracebridge Appliances	+$900	
TOTAL	+$900	TOTAL	+$900	

TABLE 31.11

Balance sheet changes
at the Huron Bank.

	Huron Bank			
Assets		**Liabilities**		
Desired reserves	+$ 81	Demand deposits:		
Excess reserves	+ 729	Rapid Airlines	+$810	
TOTAL	+$810	TOTAL	+$810	

Money (deposit) expansion
multiplier (bank multiplier):
the reciprocal of the reserve
ratio.

Observe that the amount of deposits can be obtained by multiplying the initial deposit by the reciprocal of the reserve ratio. The reciprocal of the reserve ratio is called the **money (deposit) expansion multiplier** or the **bank multiplier**.

$$MM = 1/rr$$

where MM is the money multiplier and rr is the reserve ratio. Thus, if the reserve ratio is 10%, the money expansion multiplier is $1/10\% = 10$. If the reserve ratio is 20%, then the money expansion multiplier is $1/20\% = 5$. In our example above, the money supply increased by $9000. Table 31.12 summarizes the step-by-step approach that we have taken.

Commercial banks increase the money supply by creating deposits when they extend loans.

We have concentrated on how banks create money. You should be aware, however, that the process works in reverse also. A reduction in the reserves of the commercial banking system causes demand deposits to fall by several times the reduction in reserves. We used a multi-bank system in our illustration of the process of money creation (deposit expansion). The result would have been the same if we had assumed a monopoly bank situation.

TABLE 31.12

The deposit expansion
process.

Steps	Deposits ($)	Desired reserves ($)	Loans = excess reserves ($)
1	1000.00	100.00	900.00
2	900.00	90.00	810.00
3	810.00	81.00	729.00
4	729.00	72.90	656.10
5	656.10	65.61	590.49
6	590.49	59.05	531.44
.	.	.	.
.	.	.	.
.	.	.	.
Sum (all steps)	10 000.00	1 000.00	9 000.00

PROBLEM SOLVING 31-1

It has been said that banks create money by lending out their excess reserves. Is this true?

A MORE REALISTIC EXPANSION MULTIPLIER

The money expansion multiplier that we have derived is a maximum expansion multiplier because it shows the maximum amount of money the banks can create. This has resulted from the simplifying assumptions we made. In practice, however, it is unlikely that our assumptions will hold. The non-fulfillment of these conditions will therefore alter the value of the money expansion multiplier. Indeed, a more realistic multiplier will be considerably smaller than the one derived above.

Let us now discuss the main reasons for this assertion. First, we assumed that people deposited all the extra funds they obtained into their chequing accounts. In the real world, it is likely that people will keep some funds in the form of currency. Thus, the entire amount of a cheque written on an account at one bank may not be deposited into another bank. This being the case, the money expansion multiplier will be somewhat smaller than we have indicated.

Second, we assumed that households and firms will always want to borrow as much as the banks want to lend. This is why the banks in our illustration had no trouble finding willing borrowers. Inability on the part of the banks to lend out the maximum amount possible will obviously result in an expansion multiplier that is smaller than the maximum.

Third, we assumed that the banks do not keep any excess reserves. That is, the banks want to be "fully loaned up." Banks however, do keep excess reserves, so the money expansion multiplier will be somewhat smaller than the reciprocal of the desired reserve ratio. A smaller money expansion multiplier in turn reduces the banks' ability to increase the money supply. Our analysis illustrates that banks make loans by creating new deposits. These deposits, moreover, increase the money supply. But we should remember that banks make investments other than loans. If, for example, the banks buy bonds and pay for them by writing cheques, the cheques will be deposited into accounts at the banks; and the money expansion process will then be exactly as illustrated above.

THE NEAR BANKS

Learning Objective 8:
near banks

In this section, we shall study financial institutions whose main liabilities are very close substitutes for the deposit liabilities of commercial banks. These are, of course, the near banks. In the past, banks and near banks were quite distinct. Today, however, the distinction between them is not nearly as sharp.

CAISSES POPULAIRES AND CREDIT UNIONS

Caisses populaires and credit unions are important to the financial sector of the Canadian economy. The credit union movement is of particular interest to Quebec because it is one of those institutions originating in Quebec and organized by Quebecers. In 1900, the caisses populaires were founded in Levis, Quebec, by Alphonse Desjardins. It should not be surprising then that the credit union movement is more popular in Quebec than in any other province of Canada.

Unlike chartered banks, caisses populaires and credit unions operate under provincial legislation. The local credit unions and caisses populaires in each province belong to a central credit union operating in the province.

Sources and uses of funds

The sources and uses of funds for caisses populaires and credit unions are revealed in their balance sheet (see Table 31.13). By looking at their liabilities, we see that their major sources of funds are deposits and members' equity. You will notice the similarity between the deposit liabilities of credit unions and caisses populaires and those of the chartered banks. At the end of 1997, deposit liabilities of caisses populaires and credit unions amounted to $90.9 billion. Members' equity provided $7.1 billion of additional funds.

The main purpose for which the funds of caisses populaires and credit unions are used is mortgage lending. Personal cash loans and other cash loans are also important uses for the funds of caisses populaires and credit unions. Mortgage loans amounted to just under $60 billion at the end of 1997, while personal and other loans amounted to $27.2 billion.

Credit unions and caisses populaires obtain most of their funds from customers' deposits.

Credit unions' and caisses populaires' funds are used mainly for mortgage lending and cash loans.

TABLE 31.13

Assets and liabilities of caisses populaires and credit unions, end of 1997.

Items	Amount ($million)
ASSETS	
Cash and demand and notice deposits	6 978
Term deposits	7 688
Government of Canada securities	199
Provincial and municipal securities	303
Shares in central credit unions	545
Personal and other loans	27 184
Mortgages	59 345
Other assets	4 758
TOTAL ASSETS	107 000
LIABILITIES	
Loans payable	6 558
Deposits	90 892
Other liabilities	2 454
Members' equity	7 096
Total liabilities	107 000

Source: *Bank of Canada Review*, Summer 1998, s42, s43.

TRUST AND MORTGAGE LOAN COMPANIES

Trust and mortgage loan companies are similar in many ways in terms of their operations. In fact, trust companies and mortgage loan companies sometimes operate their businesses as one unit. As would be expected, mortgage loan companies have a greater proportion of their assets as mortgage loans than trust companies do.

Main sources and uses of funds

As can be seen from the liabilities section in Table 31.14, trust and mortgage loan companies obtain a great deal of their funds from term deposits. They also obtain funds from chequable and non-chequable deposits. At the end of 1997, term deposits, guaranteed investment certificates, and debentures amounted to $37.1 billion, accounting for about 76% of total deposits. Chequable savings deposits were estimated at $7.9 billion and non-chequable savings deposits were estimated at $3.7 billion.

As for the uses of funds, the asset section of Table 31.14 provides the answer. Since trust and mortgage loan companies offer chequing accounts, we can expect them to keep a certain portion of their assets in very liquid form. Consequently, in 1997, they held $456 million in cash and demand and notice deposits. In addition, trust and mortgage loan

Term deposits constitute the main source of funds for trust and mortgage loan companies.

TABLE 33.14	**Items**	**Amount ($million)**
Assets and liabilities of trust and mortgage loan companies, end of 1997.	**ASSETS**	
	Cash and demand and notice deposits	456
	Items in transit	281
	Term deposits	168
	Government of Canada treasury bills	2 156
	Short-term paper and bankers' acceptances	3 396
	Government of Canada bonds	2 294
	Provincial and municipal bonds	529
	Corporate bonds	976
	Residential and non-residential mortgages	25 065
	Personal loans	13 625
	Other loans	786
	Leasing contracts	360
	Canadian preferred and common shares	1 351
	Other assets	3 659
	TOTAL ASSETS	55 102
	LIABILITIES	
	Savings deposits	11 558
	Term deposits, guaranteed investment certificates, and debentures	37 061
	Loans and overdrafts	317
	Promissory notes and debentures	1 625
	Other liabilities	2 033
	Shareholders' equity	2 508
	TOTAL LIABILITIES	55 102

Source: *Bank of Canada Review*, Summer 1998, s40–S41.

companies extended personal loans amounting to over $13.6 billion at the end of 1997. Most of their funds, however, are used to grant mortgage loans. At the end of 1997, mortgage loans amounted to over $25 billion or 45% of the total assets of trust and mortgage loan companies.

CHAPTER SUMMARY

1. The Bank of Canada and a number of chartered banks make up the Canadian banking system.

2. The Bank of Canada was established in 1934 as Canada's central bank, following the recommendation of the Royal Commission on Banking and Finance headed by Lord Macmillan.

3. A board of directors comprising the governor of the Bank of Canada, the deputy governor, and twelve directors is responsible for the management of the Bank of Canada.

4. The main functions of the Bank of Canada are to issue currency in adequate quantities, to act as banker to the chartered banks, to act as fiscal agent and financial advisor to the government, to conduct the country's monetary policy, and to support the financial system.

5. Near banks are financial institutions other than commercial banks that accept deposits from the public. They include caisses populaires and credit unions, trust companies, and mortgage loan companies.

GLOBAL PERSPECTIVE

Canadian Banks Merge to Face Global Competition

On January 23, 1998, two of Canada's largest banks—the Royal Bank of Canada and the Bank of Montreal — announced that they had worked out a merger agreement between them to form a megabank that will be able to compete on a global scale. Three months later, on April 17, 1998, two other Canadian banks — the Canadian Imperial Bank of Commerce (CIBC) and the Toronto-Dominion Bank (TD Bank) — announced that they too would merge to form a megabank in order to compete, not only with domestic competitors but also "with powerful competitors from all over the world."

Much can be argued about the advantages and disadvantages of such bank mergers. For example, the banks that want to merge claim that being bigger will make them more secure and stable, enable them to pay more dividends to bank shareholders, generate jobs, investments and taxes that will benefit Canadians. They claim also that their customers will be able to get "the most complete range of services at the best price" and that their employees will benefit from more investment in employee training.

On the other hand, opponents of bank mergers argue that size and stability do not necessarily correlate, observing that size did not prevent megabanks in Japan from experiencing serious financial instability. They claim that far from creating jobs, bank mergers will result in job losses for between 9000 and 20 000 people. In addition, they claim that bank mergers will lead to branch clo-

sures, reduced competition in the banking industry, and higher fees for banking services.

The main question before us, however, is this: Do Canadian banks need to be bigger to compete internationally or to face competition at home from foreign banks? The banks that want to merge say yes. On the other hand, opponents point to two crucial issues. First, they claim that megabanks may not necessarily be stronger internationally, and in any event, the proposed mergers will produce a bank which is still relatively small when compared with such giants as NationsBank-Bank of America in the United States and the Japanese megabanks. They also point out that even a relatively small bank like the Bank of Nova Scotia (Scotiabank) is a very active player on the international financial stage in 53 countries. The second plank in their opposition platform is that Canadian banks do not now face much competition from foreign banks in Canada.

To give you some perspective on the sizes of the merged banks in terms of big banks, the Bank of Tokyo-Mitsubishi has assets of about U.S. $720 billion, and the new Bank of America has assets of about U.S. $574 billion. On the other hand, the combined assets of the Royal Bank and the Bank of Montreal amount to about U.S. $308 billion. The accompanying graph places the Canadian banks in the midst of a selected number of banks for comparison.

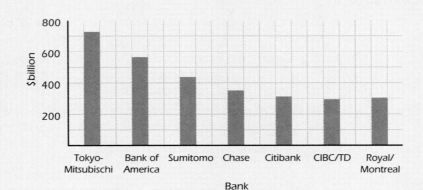

Most of the funds of trust and mortgage loan companies are used for mortgage lending.

6. The origin of modern banking can be traced to the seventeenth century, when goldsmiths in England accepted gold deposits and issued certificates of deposit.

7. Commercial banks operating in Canada are classified as Schedule A banks or Schedule B banks. Their operations are governed by the provisions of the Bank Act.

8. Banks must try to strike a balance between profitability on the one hand and liquidity on the other.

9. Banks make a profit by charging a higher rate of interest on money they lend out than the rate they pay their depositors.

10. Customers' deposits are the most important source of funds for chartered banks. The main use of chartered banks' funds is to grant loans to customers.

11. The reserve ratio is the ratio of the amount of cash reserves the banks keep to their total deposit liabilities.

12. Chartered banks increase the money supply by extending loans to borrowers and by crediting the amount of the loan to their deposit accounts. Borrowers are not given cash. The reciprocal of the desired reserve ratio gives the maximum money expansion multiplier.

13. The caisses populaires were founded in Quebec in 1900 by Alphonse Desjardins. The main functions of credit unions and caisses populaires are to encourage saving and to make loans available to their members at reasonable rates of interest.

14. The main sources of funds for credit unions and caisses populaires are deposits and members' equity. Funds are allocated mainly to mortgage lending and cash loans to members.

15. Term deposits constitute the major source of funds for trust companies and mortgage loan companies. The main use of their funds is mortgage lending.

TERMS FOR REVIEW

banking system (526)
near bank (526)
Bank of Canada Act (527)
lender of last resort (528)
balance sheet (529)
asset (529)
liability (529)
capital (owner's equity) (529)
commercial (chartered) bank (531)
branch banking system (531)
unit banking system (531)

Schedule A banks (531)
Schedule B banks (531)
Bank Act (534)
fractional reserve banking system (534)
reserve requirement (534)
Canada Deposit Insurance Corporation (535)
primary reserves (535)
secondary reserves (535)
money (deposit) expansion multiplier (bank multiplier) (538)

QUESTIONS FOR REVIEW AND DISCUSSION

1. What constitutes the Canadian banking system? (L.O.1)

2. How does the banking system differ from the financial system? (L.O.1)

3. What circumstances led to the establishment of the Bank of Canada? (L.O.2)

4. What are the main objectives and functions of the Bank of Canada? (L.O.2)

5. Give a brief account of the organization and management of the Bank of Canada. (General)

6. Distinguish between the Bank Act and the Bank of Canada Act. (General)

7. What is a chartered (commercial) bank? What services do chartered banks provide? (L.O.5)

8. Trace the origin of modern banking. (L.O.4)

9. How did paper receipts become money? (L.O.4)

10. "The banker must walk a tightrope between profitability and safety." Discuss. (L.O.5)

11. Why is the Canadian banking system called a fractional reserve banking system? (L.O.5)

12. What is the most important asset of a chartered bank? What is its most important liability? (L.O.6)

13. What are the main sources of funds for chartered banks? What are the main uses of funds? (L.O.6)

14. "Only the central bank can create money. Chartered banks merely lend out funds deposited with them and earn a return by charging interest on their loans." Discuss. (L.O.7)

15. Briefly explain the process of money (deposit) expansion by commercial banks. (L.O.7)

16. What are the factors that limit the amount of deposits that commercial banks can create? (L.O.7)

17. Why is the credit union movement of particular significance to Quebec? (L.O.8)

18. What are the main sources and uses of funds for caisses populaires and credit unions? (L.O.8)

19. What are the main sources and uses of funds for trust and mortgage loan companies? (L.O.8)

PROBLEMS AND EXERCISES

1. Draw up a hypothetical balance sheet for a central bank, listing major assets and liabilities. (L.O.3)

2. State whether each of the following statements is true or false, and briefly explain your reason.

   (a) The Bank of Canada is owned and operated by the major Canadian chartered banks. (General)

   (b) The Bank of Canada is completely independent of the government and is therefore free to pursue any monetary policy it pleases. (General)

   (c) The paper currency we use is recorded on the asset side of the Bank's balance sheet. (L.O.3)

3. Draw a hypothetical balance sheet for a chartered bank showing only the major assets and liabilities. (L.O.6)

4. Draw a table showing the main sources and uses of funds for a chartered bank. (L.O.6)

5. Draw a table showing the main sources and uses of funds for a credit union or caisse populaire. (L.O.8)

6. Draw a table showing the main sources and uses of funds for a trust or mortgage loan company. (L.O.8)

7. Use T-accounts to illustrate the effects of each of the following transactions on a bank's balance sheet: (L.O.6)

   (a) Customer Harrison Kennedy deposits $500 in his chequing account.

   (b) Customer Sheng Song withdraws $100 from her savings account.

   (c) Customer Camile Turner makes a cash payment of $250 on her loan account.

   (d) Natalya Zola writes a cheque for $75 and the cheque is cashed.

8. Assume that:

   (i)   all banks decide to keep 10% of their deposit liabilities as cash reserves;

   (ii) they keep no excess reserves;

   (iii) they can lend as much money as they wish.

   How much money will the banking system be able to create from a deposit of $5000?

9. Referring to Question 8, if banks keep 5% of their deposit liabilities as cash reserves instead of 10%, how much money will they be able to create from a deposit of $5000?

 10. Compose a list of as many advantages and disadvantages of bank mergers as you can think of, and then try to determine whether Canadians will be better or worse off as a result of bank mergers.

Internet Sites

http://www.cdic.ca
This is the Web site for the Canada Deposit Insurance Corporation. The site contains useful information on the functions of the CDIC, as well as information on Canadian and other financial institutions.

http://www.cba.ca
Above is the Web site for the Canadian Bankers' Association. You can learn a great deal about our chartered banks and commercial banking in Canada from this site. Just click on *banking facts*.

INTERNET EXERCISE

1. Visit the CDIC site above.

2. Write up a list of 20 financial institutions that are members of the CDIC.

CHAPTER 32

MONETARY THEORY AND POLICY

Learning Objectives

After studying this chapter, you should understand:

1 the quantity theory of money

2 the Keynesian theory of money

3 the liquidity preference theory of interest

4 the relationship between the money supply and net domestic income

5 the instruments of monetary policy

6 how monetary policy works

7 the effectiveness and limitations of monetary policy

8 Canadian monetary policy since 1968

If, however, we are tempted to assert that money is the drink which stimulates the system to activity, we must remind ourselves that there may be several slips between the cup and the lip.

J. M. Keynes, *The General Theory*

INTRODUCTION

Monetary theory deals with the effects of the demand and supply of money on income, output, and the price level.

One of the messages that this book has tried to convey is that good economic policies should be based on sound economic theory. Hence, in order to understand how the money supply can be used as an instrument of economic policy, you must first understand how changes in the money supply affect economic activity. In this chapter, you will study different theories of the economic impact of money, and in the process, you will be introduced to an economic viewpoint called monetarism.

The subject of this chapter is monetary theory and policy. We can define monetary theory as the study of the demand for money, the supply of money, and the effect of these variables on the economy. Although there is general agreement that money affects the economy, there is considerable controversy over just how money exerts influence on the economy. We shall study the Bank of Canada in its role as Canada's monetary policy maker.

THE QUANTITY THEORY OF MONEY

Learning Objective 1: the quantity theory of money

The quantity theory of money states that price level changes are due to changes in the quantity of money.

An important segment of classical economics was the quantity theory of money, which commanded a great deal of respect and attention prior to 1930. In its crudest form, the **quantity theory of money** states that changes in the average level of prices are due mainly to changes in the quantity of money. In the nineteenth and early twentieth centuries, this theory was in its heyday. The quantity theory and much of classical economics fell from prominence in the 1930s and was supplanted, though not usurped, by Keynesian theory which apparently did a better job of explaining the Great Depression. Largely as a result of the work of Professor Milton Friedman, and the apparent failure of Keynesian economics to explain the co-existence of inflation and unemployment, the quantity theory has had a resurgence under the name of monetarism. Let us now look at the crude quantity theory of money.

THE CRUDE QUANTITY THEORY OF MONEY

The crude quantity theory states that the money supply is directly proportional to the price level.

The classical economists established a relationship between the quantity of money and the price level. Specifically, the simple version of this theory (called the crude quantity theory), states that the price level is proportional to the money supply. A doubling of the money supply would result in a doubling of the price level.

To see how the classical economists arrived at this conclusion, we need to introduce two new concepts: the velocity of circulation of money and the equation of exchange.

The velocity of circulation of money

The velocity of circulation is GDP divided by the money supply.

This is the number of times, on average, that a unit of money (such as a dollar) is spent per year in purchasing final goods and services. For example, if the gross domestic product is $500 billion, and the money supply is $50 billion, then it means that, on average, each dollar buys $10 worth of the economy's output of goods and services; that is, each dollar is spent 10 times a year, on average — the velocity of circulation is 10. The **velocity of circulation** may be expressed symbolically as

$$V = GDP/M$$

where V is the velocity of circulation, GDP is gross domestic product, and M is the money supply.

When the concept of the velocity of circulation of money was first developed, there was no measure for gross domestic product. How then could the velocity of circulation be expressed? You will recall from Chapter 22 that real gross domestic product is nominal gross domestic product divided by the price level. That is,

$$\text{Real GDP} = \text{GDP}/P$$

$$\text{or GDP} = P \times \text{real GDP}$$

where P is the price level. If Q denotes real gross domestic product, we have

$$\text{GDP} = P \times Q$$

We can now express the velocity of circulation as

$$V = \text{GDP}/M = (P \times Q)/M$$

The velocity of circulation of money can be computed by multiplying real gross domestic product by the price level, and dividing the result by the money supply.

The equation of exchange

The equation of exchange is an important element of the quantity theory of money.

The next step en route to the quantity theory of money is the equation of exchange developed by Irving Fisher in the 1900s. The **equation of exchange** may be expressed as the following identity:

$$MV = PQ$$

where M, V, P, and Q have exactly the same meanings as in the velocity equation in the previous section. As a matter of fact, we can obtain the equation of exchange simply by multiplying the velocity equation by M.

Let us examine the equation of exchange a little more closely. The left-hand side of the equation (MV) is simply the amount spent in purchasing goods and services. If the money supply is $50 billion and each dollar is spent 10 times a year on average, then total spending must be $500 billion. As we have seen earlier, the right-hand side of the equation (PQ) is gross domestic product in nominal terms. Since the total amount spent on the economy's output of goods and services must equal the value of that output, the equation of exchange is a truism or tautology (meaning that it is true by definition). MV and PQ are just different ways of looking at the same thing.

The Theory

As it stands, the equation of exchange is not a theory at all, since it tells us nothing about how anything is determined. The classical economists, however, made certain assumptions about the variables in the equation of exchange which enabled them to arrive at a theory of money and the price level. These assumptions are as follows:

1. The money supply is exogenously determined by the monetary authorities. Hence M is given.

2. V, the velocity of circulation, is determined by institutional factors such as the payment habits of individuals and the frequency of receipt of income, and is therefore independent of M, P, and Q. Therefore, V is a constant.

3. Real gross domestic product, Q, would remain fixed at the full-employment level, at least in the short run.

Thus, P, the average level of prices, is the only passive variable in the equation. This means that the price level does not affect the other variables, but it may be affected by them. The effect of these assumptions can be seen readily if we divide the equation of exchange by V to obtain

$$M = Q/V \times P$$

Clearly, with Q/V being constant, M is directly proportional to P. The conclusion of the quantity theorists is as follows:

The price level is determined by the money supply. Changes in the money supply cause proportional changes in the price level.

The logic behind the quantity theory of money is that any increase in the money supply will cause households and firms to end up with more money than they wish to hold for transactions. According to the classical economists, money was held for transaction purposes only. Households and firms tend to keep some portion of their wealth in the form of cash and demand deposits so that they can pay for the goods and services they want. The classical economists saw no reason for holding more money than was required for this purpose. They based their argument on the fact that assets held in the form of cash and demand deposits earn little or no interest. Because of the assumption of full employment, output cannot increase in response to the increase in total spending. Prices are therefore forced up.

Limitations of the Crude Quantity Theory

The version of the quantity theory discussed above has been called the *crude* or *naive* quantity theory. The assumption that output remains constant at the full-employment level is one of the weaknesses of the theory. The economy is quite often operating at less than full employment as we have seen from previous chapters. Consequently, the output of goods and services is subject to a considerable degree of variation. With Q variable, the possibility arises that an increase in M may lead to an increase in Q rather than to an increase in P. Or an increase in M may affect both P and Q. But the increase in P may not be proportional to the increase in M.

A second limitation of the crude quantity theory is that it assumes the velocity of circulation to be constant. The velocity of circulation may be fairly constant under certain circumstances. However, in times of rapid inflation, households and firms will be unwilling to hold money since the value of money will decrease. Thus, the velocity of circulation tends to increase sharply during periods of rapid inflation. Figure 32.1 shows the velocity of circulation in Canada over a 25-year period from 1973 to 1997. The velocity of circulation has followed a fluctuating but upward trend from just over 9 in 1973 to a high of 16.5 in 1990. It was just over 11 in 1997.

The assumptions of a constant velocity of circulation and constant output are the main weaknesses of the crude quantity theory.

FIGURE 32.1

The velocity of circulation.

The velocity of circulation in Canada has moved steadily upward over the years.

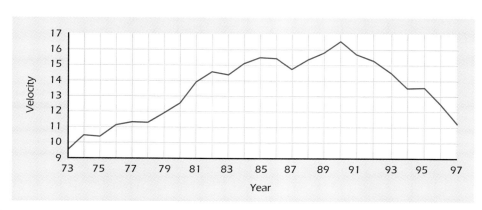

Source: Statistics Canada, *Canadian Economic Observer* (Cat. 11-210-XPB), 1997–98: 3, 96.

THE NEW QUANTITY THEORY (MONETARISM)

The limitations of the crude quantity theory — the assumptions that (1) output remains constant at the full-employment level, and (2) the velocity of circulation of money is constant — have led to the development of a new and more sophisticated version of the quantity theory of money. In this new version, output is allowed to vary since the economy may be operating at less than full employment. The velocity of circulation is assumed to vary only slightly over time and such variations are considered to be predictable. Where the crude quantity theory stressed the relation between the money supply and the price level, the modified version emphasizes the relation between the money supply and nominal (money) income. This relation is expressed in the following form:

$$M = (1/V)P \times Q$$

The new quantity theory links the money supply to nominal income.

If V were assumed to be constant, 1/V (which we may denote by k) would also be a constant. The product of P and Q is simply total income, which we may denote by Y. We can rewrite the above equation as:

$$M = kY$$

It is clear that, if k is a constant, the money supply will be proportional to total income. But, because V is assumed to vary slightly over time, k is not a constant. The new quantity theory predicts, therefore, that increases in the money supply will increase net domestic income, while reductions in the money supply will decrease net domestic income.

The revival of interest in the quantity theory is due largely to the work of Milton Friedman, a very prominent economist who proposed a restatement of the quantity theory. According to Friedman, the quantity theory is a theory about the demand for money. Specifically, it is assumed that the demand for money is a stable function of income and the rate of interest. Without going through the details of Friedman's restatement of the quantity theory, we can state the main conclusions:

Monetarism: the school of thought that claims that changes in the money supply are the major cause of economic fluctuations, and that macroeconomic stability can be achieved by a steady increase in the money supply.

1. The demand for money varies directly with the price level.

2. Real income is an important determinant of the demand for money.

3. There is a consistent direct relation between the money supply and the growth rate of nominal income.

Because of its emphasis on money the new quantity theory is often referred to as the monetarist model or **monetarism**.

THE KEYNESIAN THEORY OF MONEY

Learning Objective 2:
the Keynesian theory of money

We have completed our study of the classical quantity theory of money. We now present an alternative theory — the Keynesian theory of money. We shall begin by looking at the demand for money. The demand for money in this context is the demand for money to hold. The question is, why do people hold money? Following Keynes, we may note three reasons for holding money: for transaction purposes, for precautionary purposes, and for speculative purposes. Let us discuss each of these motives for holding money.

THE TRANSACTIONS DEMAND FOR MONEY

The transactions demand for money depends on the level of income.

In our study of the classical theory of money, we saw that households and firms will hold a part of their wealth in the form of cash and demand deposits so that they can carry out certain transactions. The amount of money that will be demanded for transaction purposes will depend on the number of anticipated transactions, which, in turn, depends on the level of income. If the annual income of a family increases from $20 000 to $30 000, we can expect that family to keep more money for transaction purposes. In the same way then, if total income in the economy increases, we expect the demand for money for transaction purposes to increase. The **transactions demand for money** varies directly with the level of income.

Transactions demand for money: the desire to hold money for transactions purposes.

THE PRECAUTIONARY DEMAND FOR MONEY

In addition to holding money for regular transactions such as paying rent, buying food, purchasing gasoline, etc., people will tend to hold some money to meet unexpected contingencies such as a broken furnace, a blown muffler, or a really big sale at a major department store. This motive for holding money is called the **precautionary demand for money**. Clearly, the precautionary demand for money is closely related to the transactions demand. In times of uncertainty, a greater amount of money is held for precautionary purposes. We can expect the level of income to influence the precautionary demand for money. Like the transactions demand for money, the precautionary demand for money varies directly with the level of income.

Precautionary demand for money: the desire to hold money for unexpected contingencies.

The precautionary demand depends on the level of income.

THE SPECULATIVE DEMAND FOR MONEY

Finally, people hold money for speculative purposes. When the purchasing power of money is rising (prices are falling), people will tend to hold more money. By so doing, they hope to gain by purchasing goods at lower prices in the future. When money is losing its value (prices are rising), people will tend to convert their money into goods to avoid incurring a loss. The desire to hold money in the hope of gaining financially from price changes is called the **speculative demand for money**.

In order to illustrate the concept of the speculative demand for money, let us assume that the public can hold its wealth in two forms only: (1) money that earns no interest, and (2) bonds that do earn interest. The price of a bond, like the price of any other commodity the price of which is not controlled, varies with changes in demand and supply. If a $100 bond is issued at a 10% rate of interest, the purchaser of the bond will receive $10 annually. If the owner of the bond sells it for $200, the new owner will still receive $10 annually. As far as the new owner is concerned, 5% will be earned annually on the bond purchase. Thus, to say that bond prices rise is equivalent to saying that interest rates fall.

Speculative demand for money: the desire to hold money in anticipation of the movement of the prices of financial assets.

The speculative demand depends on the rate of interest.

If interest rates are high (bond prices are low) and people expect them to fall (bond prices will rise), they will buy bonds now, hoping to sell them for future profit. This implies that the higher the rate of interest, the smaller the amount of money that will be held. If interest rates are expected to rise (bond prices are expected to fall), people will convert their bonds into cash before prices fall. The lower the rate of interest, the greater the amount of money that people will wish to hold. The quantity of money demanded for speculative purposes is inversely related to the rate of interest.

PROBLEM SOLVING 32-1

Do you think that credit cards have had any effect on the precautionary motive for holding money?

THE TOTAL DEMAND FOR MONEY

The various demands for money discussed above can be combined to give the total demand for money. The desire to hold wealth in the form of money rather than in the form of interest-earning assets is called **liquidity preference**. There is a cost for holding money since, instead of holding money, people have the option of buying interest-earning assets. The rate of interest can therefore be viewed as the opportunity cost of holding money. Given the level of income, when interest rates are high, interest-earning assets are more attractive than money; less money is then held. When interest rates are low, more money will be held since the cost of holding money (in terms of lost interest earnings) will be low.

This inverse relation between the rate of interest and the quantity of money that people are willing to hold is shown graphically in Figure 32.2. The demand curve for money shown in the diagram is often called the **liquidity preference curve**.

FIGURE 32.2

The liquidity preference or demand for money curve.

The liquidity preference curve shows that as the rate of interest falls, the amount of money that people will hold increases.

EFFECT OF CHANGES IN INCOME ON THE DEMAND FOR MONEY

How will a change in income affect the demand curve for money? Let us investigate. Consider the demand for money curve, LP (liquidity preference), shown in Diagram A of Figure 32.3. The demand curve is drawn on the assumption that income is held constant. If the level of income increases, households and firms will want to hold more

FIGURE 32.3

Effect of a change in income on the demand for money.

An increase in income causes the demand curve for money to shift to the right; a decrease causes the curve to shift to the left.

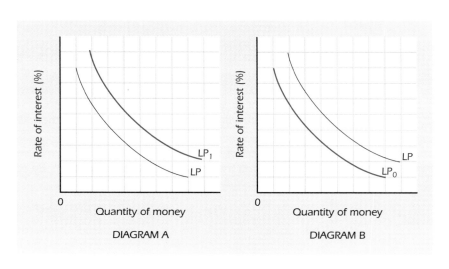

money at each and every rate of interest. The demand curve will shift to the right from LP to LP_1 as shown in Diagram A. If the level of income falls, the demand curve for money will shift to the left from LP to LP_0 as shown in Diagram B.

INTEREST RATE DETERMINATION (LIQUIDITY PREFERENCE THEORY)

Learning Objective 3:
the liquidity preference theory of interest

In Chapter 14, we presented the loanable funds theory of interest rate determination, in which the rate of interest is determined by the demand for and supply of loans. In this section, we present an alternative theory — the Keynesian liquidity preference theory of interest. We have seen in the previous section that the demand curve for money (the liquidity preference curve) is downward sloping when plotted against the rate of interest as shown in Figure 32.4.

FIGURE 32.4

Demand for money curve.

At higher interest rates, a smaller quantity of money will be held by the public. We need to determine the rate of interest at which the amount of money that the public wants to hold equals the quantity supplied by the monetary authorities.

To simplify our analysis, we assume that the money supply is fixed by the monetary authorities. In other words, the money supply is exogenously determined. Since, by assumption, changes in the rate of interest will not affect the money supply, we draw the money supply curve as the vertical line SS shown in Figure 32.5.

FIGURE 32.5

Money supply curve.

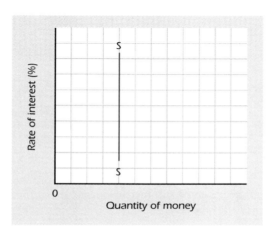

By bringing the demand for money and the supply of money together, we can illustrate the equilibrium rate of interest. This is done in Figure 32.6. At an interest rate of 15%, the quantity of money the public wishes to hold is $30 billion, but the quantity of money supplied is $40 billion. Clearly, the interest rate is too high for the quantity demanded to equal the quantity supplied. The rate of interest will therefore fall. At a rate of interest of 5%, the quantity of money the public wishes to hold is $50 billion, but the quantity supplied is only $40 billion. The excess quantity demanded (shortage) will exert an upward pressure on the rate of interest. Now, consider a rate of interest of 10%. At this rate of interest, the amount of money that the public wants to hold is $40 billion, which exactly equals the quantity supplied by the monetary authorities. The equilibrium rate of interest is therefore 10%.

FIGURE 32.6

The equilibrium rate of interest.

The equilibrium rate of interest occurs at the intersection of the demand and supply curves for money.

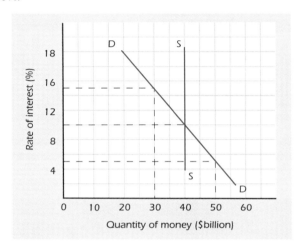

CHANGES IN THE MONEY SUPPLY AND NET DOMESTIC INCOME

Learning Objective 4: the relationship between the money supply and net domestic income

One of the conclusions of the quantity theory of money is that increases in the money supply will increase net domestic income, whereas decreases in the money supply will reduce net domestic income. Does the Keynesian model also lead to these conclusions? Let's investigate.

EFFECTS OF AN INCREASE IN THE MONEY SUPPLY

Suppose that the demand for money curve is as shown in Diagram A of Figure 32.7. The money supply is $40 billion, and the equilibrium rate of interest is 10%. Suppose also that under these conditions, the equilibrium level of net domestic income is $500 billion as shown in Diagram B of Figure 32.7. Now, let's see what happens when the monetary authorities increase the money supply from $40 billion to $60 billion. The money supply curve shifts to the right from SS to S_1S_1 as shown in Diagram A, and the rate of interest falls to 8%. You will recall that a fall in the rate of interest leads to an increase in investment. The increase in investment causes the aggregate expenditure curve in Diagram B to shift upward from AE to AE_1, resulting in an increase in net domestic income from $500 billion to $700 billion.

> **An increase in the money supply causes the rate of interest to fall. The fall in the rate of interest increases investment, which, in turn, increases net domestic income.**

FIGURE 32.7

Effect of an increase in
the money supply on
net domestic income.

An increase in the money
supply increases net
domestic income.

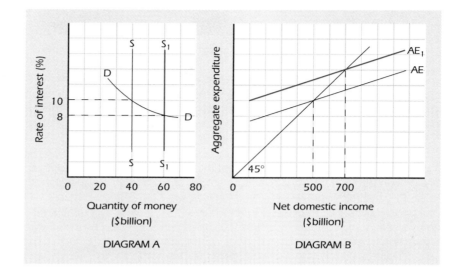

DIAGRAM A   DIAGRAM B

EFFECTS OF A DECREASE IN THE MONEY SUPPLY

Let us now examine the effects of a decrease in the money supply. Suppose that the demand for money, the supply of money, and the equilibrium rate of interest are as shown in Diagram A of Figure 32.8. Suppose further that the equilibrium level of net domestic income is $500 billion as shown in Diagram B. If the money supply falls from $40 billion to $20 billion, the supply curve shifts to the left from SS to S_0S_0. This fall in the money supply results in an excess in quantity demanded (shortage) which forces the rate of interest up from 10% to 12%. As the rate of interest rises, the level of intended investment falls, resulting in a shift in the aggregate expenditure curve from AE to AE_0. The fall in desired aggregate expenditure leads to a reduction in net domestic income from $500 billion to $300 billion.

A decrease in the money supply causes the rate of interest to rise. The increase in the rate of interest reduces investment which, in turn, reduces net domestic income.

FIGURE 32.8

Effect of a decrease in
the money supply on
net domestic income.

A decrease in the money
supply reduces net
domestic income.

DIAGRAM A   DIAGRAM B

GLOBAL PERSPECTIVE

International Interest Rates

There can be little doubt that the rate of interest is an extremely important macroeconomic variable. Interest rates affect the economy largely through their effects on aggregate expenditure. For example, lower interest rates encourage consumption and investment, while higher interest rates encourage saving and discourage investment. Also, interest rates affect the amount of interest payment on the public debt. As a specific example of the effects of interest rates on the level of economic activity, many people claim that the recession that plagued the Canadian economy in the early 1990s was directly related to a high interest rate policy in Canada aimed at fighting inflation. Once inflation was considered to be under control, however, interest rates were brought down in an effort to kickstart the economy.

The graph shows the annual averages of both short-term and long-term interest rates in seven industrial countries over the period from 1990 to 1998. The annual average short-term rate in Japan over this period was only about 2.8%. This compares with 4.9% for the United States and 6.4% for Canada. Short-term interest rates were highest in Italy and the United Kingdom with annual averages of 10% and 8.3% respectively. Long-term interest rates were highest in Italy (10.5%), followed in order by the United Kingdom (8.4%), Canada (7.9%), France (7.4%), Germany (6.9%), the United States (6.8%), and Japan (4.1%). The annual averages of long-term rates were higher than short-term rates.

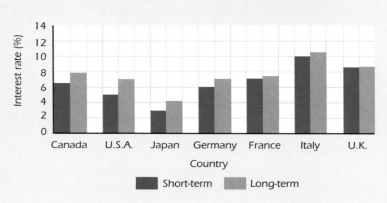

Source: International Monetary Fund, *World Economic Outlook*, May 1998: 169.

THE INSTRUMENTS OF MONETARY POLICY

Learning Objective 5:
explain the instruments of monetary policy

Monetary policy, implemented by the Bank of Canada, is designed to affect general economic activity.

Monetary policy is one of two major economic policies available to the government to influence economic activity. The other is fiscal policy, which we have already studied in Chapter 28. **Monetary policy** refers to the activities of the Bank of Canada designed to bring about changes in the money supply, the availability of credit, and the level of interest rates in order to affect general economic activity.

The main instruments or tools available to the Bank of Canada for controlling the money supply and interest rates are (1) open-market operations, (2) changes in the bank rate, (3) switches of government deposits, and (4) moral suasion. Let us deal with each in turn.

OPEN-MARKET OPERATIONS

Open-market operation is the purchase or sale of government securities by the Bank of Canada on the open market.

The term **open-market operations** refers to the buying and selling of government securities by the Bank of Canada on the open market. *Open* signifies public involvement in the transactions. The purchase or sale of government securities on the open market is the most important technique available to the Bank of Canada for controlling the money supply. If the Bank of Canada wants to increase the money supply, it can purchase securities on the open market. If these securities are bought from chartered banks, the Bank of Canada pays for them by increasing the deposits of the chartered banks at the central bank. This transaction results in an increase in the reserves of the chartered banks. The process of deposit expansion outlined in the previous chapter is then activated.

If the securities are purchased from the general public, the Bank of Canada pays for them by issuing to the sellers cheques drawn on the Bank of Canada. These cheques are deposited in chartered banks. In effect, the public has exchanged one type of asset, securities (which are not money), for another type of asset, deposits on chartered banks (which are money). Hence, the money supply increases. But this is not the whole story. When the chartered banks present these cheques to the Bank of Canada for payment, the Bank of Canada settles the account by increasing the deposits of the chartered banks at the Bank of Canada. Thus, a purchase of securities from the public by the Bank of Canada results in an increase in the reserves of the chartered banks, and hence in an increase in the money supply by the multiplier process.

If the Bank of Canada wishes to reduce the money supply, it can sell government securities on the open market. The purchasers of these securities pay for them by cheques drawn on chartered banks. The central bank presents these cheques to the chartered banks for payment and the account is settled by reducing the deposits of the chartered banks at the Bank of Canada. The reserves of the chartered banks are reduced and this results in a contraction in the money supply.

Open-market purchases of securities by the Bank of Canada increase the money supply. Open-market sales reduce the money supply.

CHANGES IN THE BANK RATE

The bank rate is the interest rate charged by the Bank of Canada to financial institutions.

By changing the bank rate, the Bank of Canada influences interest rates and credit.

The **bank rate** is the interest rate that the Bank of Canada charges for loans or advances that it makes to chartered banks and other members of the Canadian Payments Association. The use of the bank rate as a technique for controlling the money supply is based on the principle that, if the bank rate increases, it is more expensive for the chartered banks to borrow from the Bank of Canada. Chartered banks are thus likely to keep large cash reserves to minimize the need to borrow from the Bank of Canada. And, if chartered banks keep large cash reserves, then their ability to extend loans and thus expand deposits will be small. A reduction in the bank rate, on the other hand, would cause the chartered banks to keep small cash reserves. Small cash reserves would in turn increase their ability to extend loans and increase deposits.

Canadian chartered banks, however, do not often exercise their privilege of borrowing from the Bank of Canada. Nevertheless, the bank rate still serves as an important instrument of monetary policy in Canada. It provides a signal to the chartered banks of the monetary policy the Bank of Canada wishes to pursue. An increase in the bank rate, for example, will likely result in chartered banks raising interest rates and restricting loans. A reduction in the bank rate, on the other hand, will likely result in chartered banks lowering interest rates and making loans easily available. From 1962 to March 1980, the bank rate was fixed and was changed only at the discretion of the central bank. Since mid-March 1980, the Bank of Canada has adopted the policy of floating the bank rate. The bank rate is now set at a quarter of a percentage point above the rate set for 91-day treasury bills at the weekly auction.

> **Reductions in the bank rate lower interest rates and increase the money supply. Increases in the bank rate raise interest rates and reduce the money supply.**

DEPOSIT SWITCHING

The Bank of Canada may switch its deposits as a control device.

Another technique commonly used by the Bank of Canada to change the reserves of the chartered banks and hence the money supply is **deposit switching**: switching federal government deposits from the Bank of Canada to the chartered banks and vice versa. If the Bank of Canada wants to increase the money supply, it can transfer funds from the government's account at the Bank of Canada to the government's account at the chartered banks — a process known as a **redeposit**. This transaction results in an increase in the chartered banks' cash reserves and hence an expansion of bank deposits. If the Bank of Canada wishes to reduce the money supply, it can switch funds from the government's account at the chartered banks to the government's account at the Bank of Canada — a process known as **drawdown**. The chartered banks' cash reserves will then diminish, resulting in a contraction in the money supply.

> **Switching funds from the government's account at the Bank of Canada to the chartered banks results in an increase in the money supply; switching funds from the government's account at the chartered banks to the central bank results in a reduction in the money supply.**

MORAL SUASION

The Bank of Canada uses moral suasion to control the money supply and to regulate credit.

Moral suasion refers to influence exerted by the central bank on the chartered banks in an effort to enlist their support in achieving specific objectives of monetary policy, but without legal obligation. Let us suppose that the Bank of Canada wants to increase the money supply and make credit more easily available. It can announce its intention to the chartered banks and enlist their support. Because there are so few chartered banks in Canada, it is relatively easy to establish and maintain channels of communication between the Bank of Canada and the chartered banks. This situation makes it relatively easy to use moral suasion as an instrument of monetary policy.

CLOSING THE GAPS WITH MONETARY POLICY

Learning Objective 6: *understand how monetary policy works*

We have already seen that changes in the money supply can affect output, employment, and the price level. We have also studied the various instruments available to the Bank of Canada for controlling the money supply and interest rates. Let us now consider the circumstances under which the Bank of Canada might use expansionary or contractionary monetary policy.

MONETARY POLICY AGAINST UNEMPLOYMENT

Let us assume that the economy is experiencing unemployment and that the Bank of Canada wants to use monetary policy to move the economy towards full employment. Figure 32.9 will help us to analyze the situation. Diagram A shows that the economy is in equilibrium at Y, which is below the full-employment level of net domestic income, Y_f. In Diagram B, the equilibrium level of real output is Y, where the aggregate demand and aggregate supply curves intersect. For simplicity, we have omitted the intermediate section of the aggregate supply curve.

FIGURE 32.9

Monetary policy against unemployment.

The Bank may use an expansionary monetary policy to reduce or eliminate a recessionary gap.

DIAGRAM A

DIAGRAM B

To deal with the situation, the Bank of Canada may increase the money supply and lower interest rates, using one or more of the instruments of monetary policy. The effect of this expansionary monetary policy is shown in Diagram A of Figure 32.9 by the upward shift of the aggregate expenditure line from AE to AE_1, and in Diagram B by the outward shift of the aggregate demand curve from AD to AD_1. The economy moves to full employment.

MONETARY POLICY AGAINST INFLATION

Let us now suppose that the economy is going through an inflationary period as shown in Figure 32.10. In Diagram A, the inflationary situation is illustrated by the fact that aggregate expenditure exceeds full-employment net domestic income. In Diagram B, it is reflected in the fact that aggregate demand, AD, is higher than what is required for full employment without inflation. In either case, the result is an increase in the price level. The Bank of Canada can move to relieve the inflationary pressure by implementing a restrictive or contractionary monetary policy. Such a policy will reduce aggregate expen-

FIGURE 32.10

Monetary policy against inflation.

The Bank may use a restrictive monetary policy to eliminate or reduce an inflationary gap.

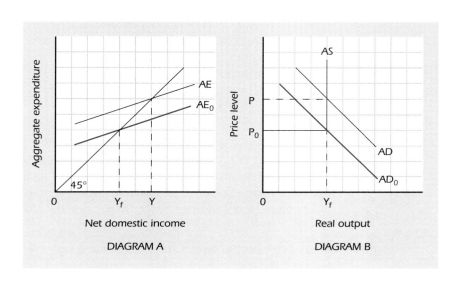

DIAGRAM A

DIAGRAM B

diture as shown in Diagram A by the downward shift of the aggregate expenditure curve from AE to AE_0, or in Diagram B by the leftward shift in the aggregate demand curve from AD to AD_0. Equilibrium occurs at full employment, and the price level falls from P to P_0.

APPLICATION

Decision on the Mortgage

A mortgage may be defined as a long-term loan secured by real estate. Most people who purchase homes do so by taking out mortgages. The interest payment on a mortgage is substantial, so the future direction of the rate of interest is a key factor in determining whether a borrower takes out a mortgage for a longer term or for a shorter term.

If the economy is experiencing a severe recession, one can assume that the Bank of Canada will make an effort to keep interest rates low in order to help to stimulate the economy. This is likely, especially if there is little threat from inflation. Once the economy recovers, interest rates may begin to edge upward. With this kind of knowledge, people who are renewing their mortgages may do well to lock into a long-term deal if interest rates are relatively low and are expected to rise.

THE EFFECTIVENESS AND LIMITATIONS OF MONETARY POLICY

THE EFFECTIVENESS OF MONETARY POLICY

Learning Objective 7: discuss the effectiveness and limitations of monetary policy

A large part of the debate between monetarists and Keynesians concerns the effectiveness of monetary policy. A great deal of attention will be given to this debate in the next chapter; but in this section, we shall discuss two cases where, theoretically at least, monetary policy will be ineffective.

The liquidity trap

Some people have argued that a situation is possible in which increases in the money supply have no effect in reducing the rate of interest. In such a situation, the liquidity preference curve is flat where it intersects the supply curve for money. The situation is illustrated in Figure 32.11. An increase in the money supply from S to S_1 has no effect on the rate of interest. This situation is called a liquidity trap. A **liquidity trap** occurs when the rate of interest is so low that households and firms prefer to hold exceptionally large amounts of money over other forms of assets.

If the economy is in a liquidity trap, according to some economists, monetary policy will be ineffective as a means of stimulating economic activity. Since the liquidity trap occurs at very low rates of interest, and since interest rates have been high for such a long time, most people consider the liquidity trap concept to be of theoretical interest only.

Interest insensitive investment

You will recall how money is purported to affect net domestic income in the Keynesian model: an increase in the money supply leads to a fall in the rate of interest, which in turn leads to an increase in investment, which, via the multiplier, increases net domestic income. Using flow arrows, we can express the series of events as follows:

$$\Delta M \uparrow \rightarrow r \downarrow \rightarrow I \uparrow \rightarrow Y \uparrow$$

where M = money supply, r = rate of interest, I = level of investment, and Y = net domestic income.

FIGURE 32.11

Liquidity trap.

Monetary policy will be ineffective if the economy is in a liquidity trap.

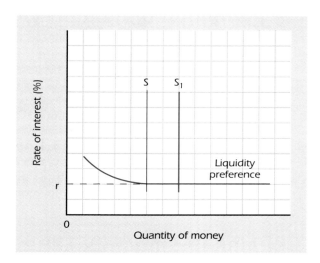

The effect of monetary policy then, depends on the extent to which changes in interest rates affect investment. If the marginal efficiency of investment schedule is flat, a change in the rate of interest will have a greater effect on the level of investment than if the marginal efficiency of investment schedule is steep. Figure 32.12 shows two marginal efficiency of investment schedules: one steep, the other flat. In Diagram A, a fall in the rate of interest from 16% to 10% results in an increase in investment from $4 million to $6 million. In Diagram B, an equivalent fall in the rate of interest has led to a much larger increase in investment — from $4 million to $16 million. In other words, investment is much more sensitive to interest rate changes in Diagram B than in Diagram A.

From the foregoing analysis, it appears that monetary policy is most effective when the liquidity preference curve is steep and the marginal efficiency of investment curve is flat. This combination of curves ensures that increases in the money supply will lower interest rates and that reductions in the rate of interest will stimulate investment and aggregate expenditure.

FIGURE 32.12

Interest rates and investment.

The flatter the marginal efficiency of investment curve, the more effective monetary policy will be.

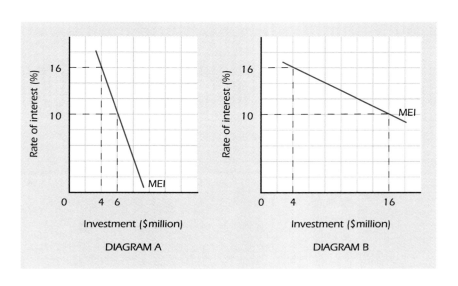

LIMITATIONS OF MONETARY POLICY

Circumstances other than those mentioned in the previous section also may cause monetary policy to be ineffective. During a recession, an expansionary monetary policy may prove to be ineffective. This is so because, although loans may be easily available, households and firms may not wish to borrow if they are pessimistic about the future.

Second, the problem of time lags mentioned in connection with fiscal policy also applies to monetary policy. Keep in mind, however, that monetary authorities are able to act more swiftly than can the makers of fiscal policy. But it is quite possible for the effects of monetary policy to be felt only after the need for such a policy has passed.

Third, a significant amount of investment may be financed out of retained earnings rather than through borrowing from banks and other lending institutions. The interest rate policies of the Bank of Canada may therefore have little or no effect on the investment decisions of firms.

MONETARY POLICY IN CANADA, 1968-PRESENT

Learning Objective 8: comment on monetary policy in Canada since 1968.

The Bank of Canada uses monetary policy on a regular basis.

Figure 32.13 will be helpful to our discussion of Canada's monetary policy since 1968. It shows changes in the money supply and the bank rate.

By 1968, the rate of inflation had risen to 4% from its 1961 level of 1.2%. At the same time, the Bank felt that it was necessary to raise interest rates in order to attract foreign investment into Canada and thus strengthen the Canadian dollar. Accordingly, the bank rate rose from 4.98% in 1967 to 6.79% in 1968. The Bank also implemented a policy of monetary restraint which lasted for the rest of the 1960s.

Unemployment had become a matter of some concern by 1971, as the unemployment rate rose from 3.6% in 1966 to 6.4% in 1971. The Bank instituted an expansionary monetary policy, increasing M1 by 11.3% in 1971 and by 14.3% in 1972. M2 increased by 12.6% in 1971 and by 10.8% in 1972. The bank rate was reduced from 7.1% in 1970 to 5.1% in 1971 to 4.7% in 1972, as can be seen from Figure 34.5.

The rate of inflation rose from 2.8% in 1971 to 7.6% in 1973. Something had to be done to curb this price increase; the bank rate was raised from 4.7% (its 1972 rate) to 6.1%

FIGURE 32.13

Changes in the money supply and the bank rate.

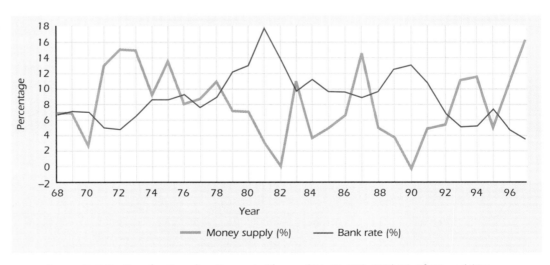

Source: Statistics Canada, *Canadian Economic Observer* (Cat. 11–210), 1994–95: 86, 88; and (Cat. 11–010–XPB), March 1996: 52, 54.

in 1973. But inflation continued and was recorded at 10.9% in 1974, and the rate of monetary expansion slowed to just about 9% between 1973 and 1974.

By 1975, it was clear that inflation was a very serious problem in the Canadian economy. The bank rate remained high, and the Bank of Canada adopted a more restrictive monetary policy between 1975 and 1976. Also, in 1975, the Bank of Canada openly announced a monetarist stance in its monetary policy. That is, it established specific targets for the growth rate of the money supply. The target announced in 1975 was a 10 to 15% annual growth in M1. This target rate was gradually reduced until by 1981, it was set between 4 and 8%.

The policy established in 1975 by the Bank of Canada under then-governor Gerald Bouey — using monetary policy to achieve a long-run low rate of inflation — seems to have continued under governor John Crow. In an attempt to keep inflation under strict control, the Bank of Canada had set a course of high interest rates. In August 1988, the bank rate was above 10%. In January 1989, it was 11.5%, and by May 1989, it had reached 13.5%. Notwithstanding calls for a reduction in interest rates, the Bank of Canada seemed adamant in sticking to its high interest rate policy.

The high interest rate policy pursued by the Bank of Canada succeeded in reducing the rate of inflation to about 2% in 1991. The downside, however, is that the rate of unemployment, which stood at 7.5% in 1989, jumped to 11.5% in 1992. Also, in 1991, the economy experienced a recession, with real output falling by 1.7%. In response, the Bank of Canada reduced the bank rate gradually from over 13% in 1990 to 9% in 1991 to 6% in 1992. Some experts believe that the Bank of Canada was too slow in responding to the slowdown in economic activity, and that when it did move, its measures were not sufficiently drastic. In other words, they think that it was a case of "too little, too late."

There was a significant increase in the bank rate between 1994 and 1995 when the rate moved from 5.77% to 7.31%. This was probably due partly to an upward trend in the consumer price index from December 1994, reaching 2.9% in May 1995; and partly to the growth of the real GDP at a rate of 4.6% in 1994. It seems that the Bank of Canada tried to prevent the economy from being overheated by using a contractionary monetary policy.

Between 1995 and 1997, the rate of inflation in Canada fell from 2.6% to 1.4% to 0.5%. With inflation clearly under control, the Bank probably felt that an easing of interest rates could help to stimulate the economy, the real growth rate of which dipped to 1.2% in 1996, with an unemployment rate of 9.7%. Moreover, interest rates in the United States were pointing downward. The bank rate fell from 7.31% in 1995 to 3.52% in 1997.

CHAPTER SUMMARY

1. The crude quantity theory of money states that changes in the price level are due primarily to changes in the quantity of money.

2. The velocity of circulation and the equation of exchange are key elements in the quantity theory of money.

3. The assumptions that velocity is constant and that output remains constant at the full-employment level are the main weaknesses of the crude quantity theory of money.

4. The new quantity theory (monetarism) states that there is a direct relation between the growth rate of the money supply and the growth rate of nominal income.

5. The Keynesian theory of money identifies three reasons for holding money: (1) transaction purposes, (2) precautionary purposes, and (3) speculative purposes.

6. The desire to hold wealth in the form of money rather than in the form of interest-earning assets is called liquidity preference.

GLOBAL PERSPECTIVE

Bank Rates: An International View

In recent years, the bank rate in Canada has changed rather frequently. In this capsule, we examine two aspects of the bank rate — its level and the extent to which it changes. These two aspects of the bank rate in Canada are compared with their counterparts in other industrial countries. The table shows average annual bank rates in G-7 countries from 1994 to 1997.

Country	1994	1995	1996	1997
Canada	5.77	7.31	4.55	3.52
U.S.A.	3.66	5.25	5.00	5.00
U.K.	5.45	6.69	3.95	6.58
Germany	4.37	3.83	2.63	2.50
Italy	7.42	8.63	8.44	6.40
Japan	1.75	0.98	0.50	0.50

Between 1994 and 1995, the bank rate in Canada rose from 5.77% to 7.31%. It then fell to 4.55% in 1996 and to 3.52% in 1997. In the United States, the bank rate rose from 3.66% in 1994 to 5.25% in 1995. It then fell

to 5% in 1996 and remained at that level in 1997. In 1994, the bank rate in the United Kingdom was 5.45%. It climbed to 6.69% in 1995, fell to 3.95% in 1996, and then rose to 6.58% in 1997. In France and Germany, the bank rate fell over the entire period under consideration. In Italy, the bank rate was 7.42% in 1994 — the highest of all G-7 countries. It rose to 8.63% in 1995 before falling to 8.44% in 1996 and 6.40 % in 1997. Japan's bank rate was the lowest among the G-7 countries, falling from 1.75 % in 1994 to 0.50% in 1997. In 1994, Canada's bank rate was the second highest of the G-7 countries. By 1997, it was the fourth highest behind the United Kingdom, Italy, and the United States.

The following graph compares changes in the bank rate in Canada, the United States, the United Kingdom, Germany, and Italy from April 1997 to March 1998. During that period, the bank rate in the U.S.A. and Germany did not change. Italy's bank rate changed twice, while Canada's and the U.K.'s bank rates changed five and six times respectively.

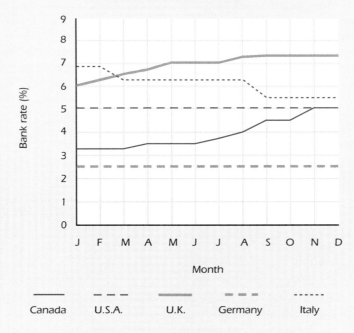

Source for table and figure: Statistics Canada, *Canadian Economic Observer* (Cat. 11-010-XPB), July 1998: 68.

7. The higher the rate of interest, the smaller the quantity of money the public will wish to hold. This inverse relation between the rate of interest and the amount of money the public wishes to hold, if shown on a graph, is usually called the liquidity preference curve or the total demand for money curve.

8. The equilibrium rate of interest is determined by the intersection of the demand and supply curves for money.

9. An increase in the money supply results in a fall in the rate of interest, an increase in investment, and an increase in net domestic income. A decrease in the money supply results in an increase in the rate of interest, a fall in investment, and a reduction in net domestic income.

10. Monetarists and Keynesians are currently engaged in a very interesting and important debate over which model is better. Despite the controversy, both groups agree on the effect of the money supply on net domestic income.

11. The main techniques used by the Bank of Canada to control the money supply and credit are open-market operations, changes in the bank rate, switches in government deposits, and moral suasion.

12. An expansionary monetary policy can be used to eliminate or reduce a recessionary gap. A contractionary monetary policy can be used to eliminate or reduce an inflationary gap.

13. A liquidity trap or an interest insensitive investment schedule may cause monetary policy to be ineffective. The problem of time lags also limits the effectiveness of monetary policy.

14. The Bank of Canada has used monetary policy on many occasions in an effort to achieve certain economic objectives. Until recently, the Bank of Canada pursued a policy of high interest rates in an attempt to keep inflation under control. Now that inflation has fallen, the Bank has lowered interest rates.

TERMS FOR REVIEW

quantity theory of money (547)
velocity of circulation of money (547)
equation of exchange (548)
monetarism (550)
transactions demand for money (551)
precautionary demand for money (551)
speculative demand for money (551)
liquidity preference (552)

liquidity preference curve (552)
monetary policy (556)
open-market operations (557)
bank rate (557)
deposit switching (drawdowns and redeposits) (558)
moral suasion (558)
liquidity trap (560)

QUESTIONS FOR REVIEW AND DISCUSSION

1. According to the crude quantity theory of money, what relation exists between the quantity of money and the price level? (L.O.1)

2. What is the velocity of circulation of money? (L.O.1)

3. What is the equation of exchange? Is this equation a theory of money? (L.O.1)

4. What are the assumptions of the crude quantity theory of money? (L.O.1)

5. Does the Canadian experience in recent years support the assumption of a constant velocity of circulation of money? (L.O.1)

6. How does the new quantity theory differ from the crude quantity theory? (L.O.1)

7. What are the main conclusions of the new quantity theory of money? (L.O.1)

8. According to the classical economists, people hold money for transaction purposes only. What additional reasons (motives) do people have for holding money? (L.O.2)

9. Briefly explain the liquidity preference theory of the rate of interest. (L.O.3)

10. According to the Keynesian model, how does an increase in the money supply affect net domestic income? (L.O.4)

11. "The monetarists and Keynesians disagree fundamentally on the qualitative effect of a change in the money supply on income and output." Discuss. (L.O.5)

12. What techniques are available to the Bank of Canada to control the money supply? (L.O.5)

13. Briefly explain how open-market operations may be used by the Bank of Canada to increase the reserves of the chartered banks. (L.O.5)

14. Briefly explain how monetary policy may be used to (L.O.6)

    (a) curb inflation;

    (b) reduce unemployment.

15. Mention some of the limitations of monetary policy. (L.O.7)

16. Under what circumstances will monetary policy be least effective in stimulating economic activity? (L.O.7)

17. What is the liquidity trap? Why are economists today not terribly concerned about the liquidity trap? (L.O.7)

18. Give a brief account of the use of monetary policy in Canada in recent times. (L.O.8)

PROBLEMS AND EXERCISES

1. Table 32.1 gives data on the money supply and gross domestic product. (L.O.1)

TABLE 32.1

Money supply and GDP.

Year	GDP ($million)	Money supply ($million)	Velocity
1	66 409	7 975	
2	72 586	8 323	
3	79 815	8 919	
4	87 215	9 396	
5	96 470	10 210	
6	102 324	11 129	

   (a) Compute the velocity of circulation and fill in the velocity column.

   (b) In Year 4, $1 bought as much goods and services as $____ would have bought if spent only once.

2. According to the quantity theory, if V = 12, Q = $120 billion, and M = $20 billion, find P. If M increases from $20 billion to $30 billion, find the new price level. (L.O.1)

3. Show graphically the effect of a reduction in the money supply on the rate of interest. (L.O.3)

4. State whether each of the following events will increase or decrease the amount of money that people wish to hold. (L.O.2)

    (a) an increase in the level of income

    (b) a fall in intended expenditures

    (c) the introduction of credit cards

    (d) a rise in the rate of interest

5. Illustrate graphically, using the Keynesian model, that an increase in the money supply will result in an increase in net domestic income. (L.O.4)

6. "Open-market purchases and sales affect the reserves of the commercial banks." Discuss. (L.O.5)

7. Suppose that the Bank of Canada buys $2 billion worth of government bonds from bond holders. What effect will this action have on (L.O.5)

    (a) the rate of interest

    (b) expenditures on durable consumer goods

    (c) real investment spending

8. Explain why an open-market purchase of government securities of $10 million will likely increase the money supply by more than $10 million. (L.O.5)

9. State whether each of the following is true or false, and briefly explain your reason.

    (a) Monetary policy is most effective when the liquidity preference curve is flat. (L.O.7)

    (b) The Bank of Canada uses monetary policy to fight unemployment, not inflation. (L.O.6)

    (c) A reduction in the bank rate will tend to expand economic activity. (L.O.5)

    (d) The Bank of Canada tries to combat inflation with restrictive monetary policy. (L.O.6)

10. It has been suggested that monetary policy in Canada could be made more effective by making the Bank Act applicable to near banks as well as banks. Discuss. (General)

C H A P T E R

INFLATION AND
ANTI-INFLATION POLICIES

Learning Objectives

After studying this chapter, you should be able to:

1 discuss the causes of inflation

2 understand the Phillips curve

3 discuss the accelerationists' position

4 understand policies designed to deal with stagflation

5 explain the rational expectations hypothesis

6 distinguish between the new classical and new Keynesian macroeconomics

My conclusion therefore is that fiscal control must depend on prompt abandonment of antidepression measures and the anti-inflationary safeguards that are built into the long-run program.

Arthur Smithies, *Federal Budgeting and Fiscal Policy*

INTRODUCTION

It would be advisable for you to review Chapter 23 before you begin to study this chapter. By now, you should be familiar with the traditional tools of macroeconomic stabilization policy. In this chapter, you will study various theories of inflation, and you will obtain a better understanding of the relationship between inflation and unemployment. You will also get an idea of how the economy may experience inflation and unemployment at the same time. We introduce the accelerationist view of inflation, and discuss policies to deal with stagflation. We also discuss the rational expectations hypothesis. We end the chapter with a discussion of new classical and new Keynesian macroeconomics.

CAUSES OF INFLATION

Learning Objective 1:
discuss the causes of inflation

Inflation may be classified as demand-pull, cost-push, or both. Several explanations of inflation have been advanced. In this section, we shall discuss some of the main theories of inflation, and indicate the category into which each fits.

DEMAND-PULL INFLATION

Demand-pull inflation results from too much aggregate expenditure.

Demand-pull theories of inflation emphasize demand forces such as excess spending caused by monetary expansion or government deficit spending. In terms of the models that we have studied, demand-pull inflation occurs when aggregate expenditure $(C + I + G + (X - M))$ is too high or when MV is so high that it exerts an upward pressure on the price level. In popular terminology, there is too much money chasing too few goods.

Figure 33.1 illustrates demand-pull inflation. Suppose that the economy is in equilibrium at the full-employment level of real output, y_f, with the price level at P. An increase in aggregate expenditure will cause the aggregate demand curve AD to shift to the right to AD_1 as shown in Figure 33.1. The price level rises from P to P_1. The process of demand-pull inflation has been set in motion. Demand-pull theories of inflation are also called **excess demand inflation** because they emphasize excess aggregate demand.

Webster's Dictionary defines inflation as "a general rise in prices brought about by an increase in the ratio of currency and credit to the goods available." This notion of infla-

FIGURE 33.1

Demand-pull inflation.

Aggregate demand shifts to the right, resulting in an increase in the price level.

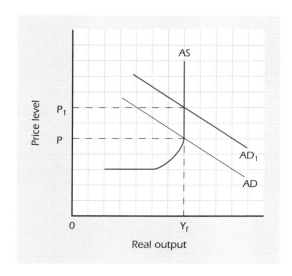

tion is demand-pull inflation. Now, let us study two theories of demand-pull inflation: the monetary theory and the budget deficit theory.

The monetary theory of inflation

We discussed the relation between the quantity of money and the price level when we examined the quantity theory of money. According to the **monetary theory**, inflation is caused by increases in the money supply that occur at a faster rate than the increase of real output in the economy. The theory argues that people wish to hold a certain amount of cash balances. An increase in the money supply will cause people to have larger cash balances than they wish to hold. They will therefore spend the excess money balances on goods and services. If the real output of the economy increases more quickly than the money supply does, then inflation will not result. It is when the money supply increases more quickly than the real output does that the average level of prices rises.

The monetary theory of inflation states that inflation may be caused by rapid monetary expansion.

The budget deficit theory of inflation

The **budget deficit theory** states that government spending in excess of tax revenues is responsible for increases in the average level of prices. The supporters of this theory argue that government deficits increase aggregate expenditure, which in turn results in inflation. To a certain extent, the budget deficit theory of inflation is a variant of the monetary theory of inflation. The proponents of the budget deficit theory claim that government deficits, however financed, are inflationary. Proponents of the monetary theory, on the other hand, claim that government deficits are inflationary only if financed by printing money. They argue that if the deficit is financed by borrowing from households and firms, then the increase in government spending will be offset by an equivalent reduction in spending in the private sector. In other words, there will be a crowding out effect, and there will be no increase in aggregate expenditure, and hence no inflationary pressures.

The budget deficit theory of inflation states that inflation may be caused by government deficit spending.

COST-PUSH INFLATION

Whereas demand-pull theories of inflation emphasize demand forces as the main cause of inflation, **cost-push** theories of inflation, or **sellers' inflation** as it is often called, emphasize supply or cost factors as the dominant cause. According to the cost-push theories, inflation is caused by powerful unions or by powerful firms. The process is explained as follows. Unions demand higher wages for their members. Because unions are so powerful, employers accede to their demands even if there are no increases in productivity. But higher wages mean higher costs for the firms. So in order to protect their profits, the firms raise their prices. These higher prices lead the unions to demand even higher wages. The firms then raise their prices even higher. This **wage-price spiral**, as it is called, continues, and the process becomes a vicious cycle.

Cost-push (sellers') inflation results from supply factors such as increases in costs of production.

Firms, too, can initiate the process. Monopolies, for instance, may raise their prices in order to increase their profits. As a result, unions ask for higher wages to compensate for the higher prices workers have to pay for goods and services. This causes the firms to raise their prices in response. Again, a vicious cycle results.

In a wage-price spiral, increased wages are followed by higher prices, which are followed by higher wages, and so on.

Another relative of the cost-push family of inflation is the so-called **imported inflation**. According to this theory, inflation may be caused by an increase in the prices of imported inputs, or by increases in the prices of imported goods. If the prices of imported inputs rise, importers will raise the prices of their products. Also, if there is inflation abroad, the prices of imported goods will rise, resulting ultimately in domestic inflation. Small open economies such as the Canadian economy are believed to be susceptible to imported inflation.

Imported inflation results from increases in the prices of imported items.

Figure 33.2 illustrates cost-push inflation. Suppose that the economy is operating at a level of real output of y with the price level at P. An increase in the firms' costs will cause the aggregate supply curve to shift from AS to AS_0. Cost-push inflation is initiated with the increase in the price level from P to P_1. Note that cost-push inflation occurs even if the economy is operating below full employment.

FIGURE 33.2

Cost-push inflation.

An upward shift in the aggregate supply curve initiates cost-push inflation.

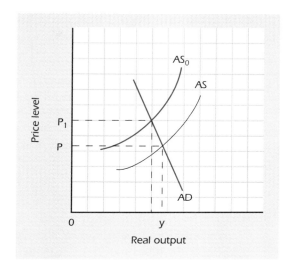

Economists generally agree that an increase in cost will be inflationary only if it is accompanied by an increase in the money supply. Consider the inflation of the 1970s. Many economists cite this case as a classic example of cost-push inflation. OPEC raised the price of oil significantly in 1974. Consequently, the prices of petroleum-related products increased. If these price increases had been offset by price reductions in other sectors of the economy, there would have been no increase in the average level of prices. Why were there no offsetting price reductions elsewhere in the economy? After all, given a certain amount of money, if we spend more on oil and products made from petroleum, then we have a smaller amount to spend on other things. Only if the monetary authorities "validate" the cost-push inflation, i.e., increase the money supply, will there be overall increases in the price level, which is what happened in 1974. It is in this sense that many economists claim that inflation is a purely monetary phenomenon.

PROBLEM SOLVING 33-1

After the rapid increase in the price of OPEC oil in the 1970s, the rate of inflation in Canada rose dramatically. We can therefore conclude that the inflation of the 1970s was due to the increase in the price of oil. Discuss.

EXPECTATIONAL INFLATION

Inflationary expectations may sustain inflation.

Expectational inflation contains elements of both demand-pull and cost-push inflation. The expectational theory of inflation, also called **inertial inflation**, states that inflation is caused by inflationary expectations. If people expect inflation, they will tend to increase their current spending in order to avoid paying higher prices in the future. This is the demand element of expectational inflation. There is also a supply (cost) element. If unions expect inflation, they will ask for wage increases that incorporate the expected rate of inflation. This increase in wage cost will cause firms to respond by raising the prices of their products, thus setting the wage-price spiral in motion.

DEMAND-PULL OR COST-PUSH?

There is no general agreement over the dominant cause of inflation.

Economists disagree over what is the dominant cause of inflation. Many economists believe that all inflations owe their origin to demand pressures. Some economists believe that inflation can originate from wage-push or price-push. Monetarists see monetary expansion as the prime cause of demand-pull inflation. Neo-Keynesians, on the other hand, view aggregate expenditure components such as government spending and investment as the main culprits. Most economists agree that, once inflation has started, it tends to generate inflationary expectations which fuel inflation and keep it going.

In practice, it is quite difficult to determine whether a particular inflation is demand-pull or cost-push. They really do not identify themselves by wearing labels. Consider the following scenario. An increase in government spending raises aggregate expenditure, which, in turn, increases the demand for labour. This increase in the demand for labour results in higher wages, which cause firms to raise prices. The wage-price spiral discussed earlier is now in effect. We have inflation. Is this inflation demand-pull or cost-push? It is demand-pull because it originated as a result of an increase in aggregate expenditure. But it is also cost-push because the immediate cause of the price increase is the rise in wages.

THE PHILLIPS CURVE

Learning Objective 2: understand the Phillips curve

The coexistence of persistent inflation and widespread unemployment is a relatively new phenomenon. Prior to 1950, many economists believed that unemployment and inflation could not exist simultaneously. They argued that inflation resulted from too much spending while unemployment resulted from too little spending. Of course, too much spending and too little spending are mutually exclusive. Nevertheless, unemployment and inflation do, in fact, coexist. In fact, the coexistence of rampant inflation and unemployment in many countries since the 1950s has caused economists to take a closer look at the situation.

The Phillips curve expresses an inverse relation between the rate of increase in wages and the unemployment rate.

To help us better understand the important relation between inflation and unemployment, we should first look at another important economic relationship — the Phillips curve. A British economist by the name of A.W. Phillips was among the first to call attention to the relation between the rate of change in wages and the level of unemployment. He explained it as follows: During a period of severe unemployment, competition among unemployed workers for jobs slows down wage increases. Workers are less likely to demand wage increases when there is a large army of unemployed people. When unemployment is low, competition among employers for scarce labour services bids wages up. Unions are also in a strong position to demand wage increases for their members.

The higher the unemployment rate, the lower will be the rate of increase in wages; and the lower the unemployment rate, the higher the rate of increase in wages.

This inverse relationship between the rate of change in wages and the unemployment rate is called the **Phillips curve**, and is illustrated in Figure 33.3. The curve shows the various combinations of unemployment and changes in wage rate that the economy can attain. It shows, for example, that when the unemployment rate is 10%, wages rise by 3%, and when the unemployment rate is 4%, wages rise by 9%.

FIGURE 33.3

The Phillips curve.

A low rate of unemployment is associated with high increases in the wage rate.

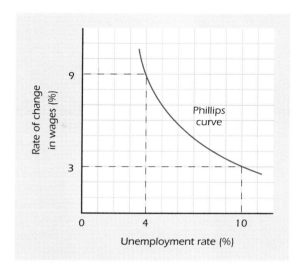

THE RELATION BETWEEN INFLATION AND UNEMPLOYMENT

The Phillips curve expresses a relationship between the rate of change in the wage rate and the rate of unemployment. Can we proceed from the Phillips curve relation to a relationship between inflation and unemployment? Let's investigate. You will recall that the cost-push theory of inflation establishes a relation between changes in wages and inflation. Specifically, it suggests that the percentage change in wages is directly related to the rate of inflation. Thus, by substituting the rate of change in the wage rate in the Phillips curve relation with the rate of inflation, we obtain a relation between inflation and unemployment.

> **The higher the rate of unemployment, the lower will be the rate of inflation; and the lower the rate of unemployment, the higher will be the rate of inflation.**

This inverse relationship between inflation and unemployment is illustrated in Figure 33.4.

The Phillips curve, strictly speaking, is a relation between the rate of change in the wage rate and the rate of unemployment. Today, however, when people talk of the Phillips curve, it is the relation between inflation and unemployment to which they usually refer. In the remainder of this chapter, we shall follow this practice.

THE NATURAL RATE OF UNEMPLOYMENT

This is an opportune time to introduce the concept of the natural rate of unemployment. The natural level of output can be defined as that level of real output that the economy will produce when all adjustments have been made, i.e., when the economy is in long-run macroeconomic equilibrium. With any given level of output is associated some level of employment which will be less than 100% of the labour force. In the long run, wages and prices adjust to clear the labour market. But remember, there will still be some frictional unemployment. Apart from this, in long-run equilibrium, all those who want to find employment at the market-determined wage rate will be able to do so. Thus, any unemployment over and above frictional unemployment will be voluntary.

The level of unemployment that prevails when the economy is in long-run equilibrium is referred to as the natural level of unemployment. It is natural in the sense that the economy will tend toward this level of output and employment in the long run. When the economy is in long-run equilibrium, there is no pressure for inflation to accelerate or decelerate. The rate of inflation will tend to be constant. The rate of unemployment that is consistent with the non-accelerating inflation rate (NAIR) is called the **natural rate of unemployment**. Therefore, we can define the natural rate of unemployment as that unemployment rate that is consistent with a constant rate of inflation. This explains why the natural rate of unemployment is often referred to as the **NAIRU** (non-accelerating rate of unemployment).

The NAIRU is affected by a number of factors, some of which will be discussed briefly here. During any period of time, some people will find jobs while others will lose their jobs. The rate of unemployment per period is determined by the rate at which people find jobs, and the rate at which they lose jobs. The higher the rate of job loss, the higher the rate of unemployment; and the higher the job-finding rate, the lower the rate of unemployment. Anything that reduces the rate of job loss and increases the job-finding rate on a long-term basis lowers the natural rate of unemployment. By the same token, anything that increases the rate of job loss and reduces the job-finding rate raises the natural rate of unemployment. Let us now examine some factors that affect the natural rate of unemployment.

Job search

People have priorities as to the type of work they want to do, and they will expend a certain amount of effort searching for jobs that satisfy those priorities. If a marketing specialist loses her job, she will most likely try to find a job in the field of marketing. If her search is unsuccessful, she will then begin to search for a job in a related field. If her efforts are still unsuccessful, she will consider accepting a job offer in some other field. Clearly, the longer the job search, the longer she will remain unemployed. The natural rate of unemployment is affected by the tendency for unemployed workers to continue to search rather than to accept the first job offer.

Labour market information, training and manpower planning

Information about job vacancies and available workers increases the job-finding rate, and thus reduces the natural rate of unemployment. Training also increases the job-finding rate since people with relevant skills are more likely to find jobs. Through careful human resource planning, current training and skill development can be geared to the future needs of industry. Human resource planning increases the job-finding rate and thus reduces the natural rate of unemployment.

Labour-force growth

If there is an increasing number of would-be workers entering the labour force, then other things being equal, it will be more difficult for the economy to be able to absorb these additional labour force entrants. Labour-force growth reduces the job-finding rate and thus increases the natural rate of unemployment.

Employment insurance

There can be no denying that the existence of employment insurance has prevented many unemployed workers from facing severe hardships and possibly personal bankruptcy. But at the same time, it has had the unfortunate effect of reducing the job-finding rate. Because of employment insurance, there is less pressure for unemployed workers to search for jobs. They may also be more likely to refuse job offers that they consider to be unattractive. These tendencies reduce the job-finding rate. Moreover, knowing that they can receive employment insurance benefits if they lose their jobs, workers may not be so hard pressed to hold on to their jobs. This tendency increases the rate of job loss. For all of these reasons, we can conclude that employment insurance increases the natural rate of unemployment.

POLICY IMPLICATION

The discomfort (misery) index equals inflation plus unemployment.

What is the implication of this trade-off between inflation and unemployment for government macroeconomic stabilization policy? Let us assume for the moment that the curve in Figure 33.4 is fixed. If the government wants to reduce the rate of inflation from 7% to 4.5%, it may do so by implementing restrictive monetary and fiscal policies. The rate of unemployment, however, will rise from 3% to 4%. Lower inflation can be achieved only at the expense of higher unemployment. This, of course, is a real dilemma for policymakers. Since inflation and unemployment are both economic evils, the term **discomfort index** or **misery index** has been used to define the rate of inflation plus the rate of unemployment. Reducing the discomfort index is a tremendous task facing policymakers. The discomfort index = the rate of inflation + the rate of unemployment.

IS THERE A TRADE-OFF?

Over 30 years ago when the Phillips curve was popularized, economists believed that there was a relatively fixed trade-off between inflation and unemployment. They believed that the Phillips curve was stable. In the 1970s, however, it was observed that the Phillips curve had shifted to the right. Referring to Figure 33.4, this means that when the inflation rate was 7%, the unemployment rate was 4% instead of 3%.

Many economists believe that the outward shift of the Phillips curve in the 1970s was due to supply-side shocks such as the rapid increase in the price of oil, which shifted the aggregate supply curve to the left.

AGGREGATE SUPPLY AND STAGFLATION

Stagflation describes the coexistence of inflation and unemployment.

The term **stagflation** has been used to describe the coexistence of inflation and unemployment. The word is made up from stagnation and inflation as follows:

*Stag**nation** + In**flation** = Stagflation*

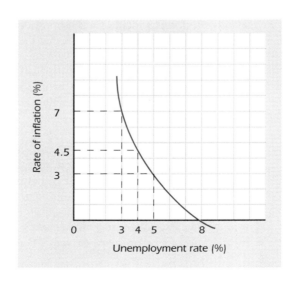

We can use the aggregate demand-aggregate supply analysis that we developed earlier to explain simultaneous increases in the price level and decreases in real output. In Figure 33.5, AD and AS are the initial aggregate demand and aggregate supply curves. The initial equilibrium level of real output is y, and the price level is P. If the aggregate supply curve shifts from AS to AS_0, the level of real output falls from y to y_0. This results in an increase in the price level from P to P_1.

FIGURE 33.5

Aggregate supply and stagflation.

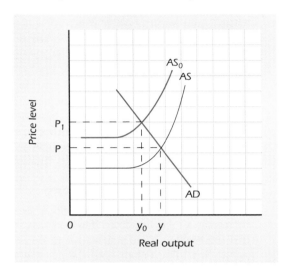

An upward shift in the aggregate supply curve causes output and employment to decrease and the price level to increase.

The aggregate demand-aggregate supply analysis points clearly to supply shifts as a cause of rising prices accompanied by falling output and employment — the phenomenon we have already referred to as stagflation. But, before we look at policies to deal with stagflation, we must realize that not all economists accept the theory of the trade-off between inflation and unemployment. In the next section, we examine opposition to the stable trade-off proposition.

THE ACCELERATIONISTS AND THE LONG-RUN PHILLIPS CURVE

Learning Objective 3: discuss the accelerationists' position

Accelerationists claim that monetary and fiscal policies used to reduce unemployment will result in accelerated inflation.

The proposition of a stable trade-off between inflation and unemployment, according to several economists including Milton Friedman and Edmund Phelps, is valid only in the short run. These economists claim that there is no trade-off in the long run. They believe that the long-run Phillips curve is vertical as shown in Figure 33.6. They contend that expansionary monetary and fiscal policies designed to reduce unemployment will result in accelerated inflation and only a temporary reduction in unemployment. For this reason, proponents of this view are called **accelerationists**. Let us study the argument of these economists.

Suppose that in Figure 33.6 the natural rate of unemployment is 7%, but policymakers attempt to reduce it to 4%, believing that 4% constitutes full employment. They will use expansionary monetary and fiscal policies to increase aggregate expenditure in the manner described in earlier chapters. Because the economy is at its natural rate of unemployment, the increase in aggregate expenditure will cause the price level to rise. If nominal wages remain constant, then the increase in prices raises the profit margins of firms. Higher profits cause businesses to expand, hiring more workers and thus reducing the rate of unemployment from 7% to 4%. The economy thus moves from A to B

FIGURE 33.6

The long-run Phillips curve.

There is a temporary trade-off along the short-run Phillips curve but not along the long-run Phillips curve, which is assumed to be vertical.

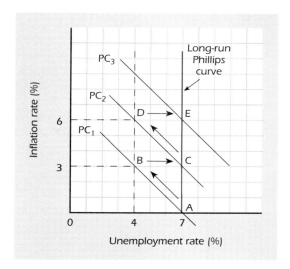

along the short-run Phillips curve PC_1. The rate of inflation has risen from zero at A to 3% at B. The economy has chosen to live with a 3% inflation rate in order to achieve a 4% unemployment rate.

The accelerationists claim, however, that the economy will not long remain at B. This is only a transitory position. Now that the rate of inflation has risen to 3%, workers will adjust their wage demands to compensate for the loss in real wages caused by the increase in the price level. Workers then receive higher money wages, which reduce the firms' profits and cause them to reduce output and employment. The rate of unemployment therefore returns to its natural rate of 7%, but the inflation rate is 3%. The economy is now at C. The short-run Phillips curve has shifted from PC_1 to PC_2.

With the unemployment rate again at 7%, the government tries again to reduce it to 4% by using expansionary monetary and fiscal policies. The unemployment rate falls temporarily to 4%, but the increase in aggregate expenditure causes the rate of inflation to rise from 3% to 6%. The economy moves along the short-run Phillips curve PC_2 from C to D as shown in Figure 33.6.

According to the accelerationists, the economy does not remain at D. As before, workers revise their inflationary expectations, and as before, firms react by reducing output and employment. The unemployment rate returns to its natural rate of 7%, while the inflation rate remains at 6% as shown by point E in Figure 33.6. The short-run Phillips curve shifts from PC_2 to PC_3. The government's attempts to force unemployment below its natural rate have resulted only in raising the rate of inflation from zero to 6%. Further attempts, according to the accelerationists, will meet with a similar fate. Accelerationists therefore conclude that there is no long-run trade-off between inflation and unemployment. The long-run Phillips curve is vertical.

> **The accelerationists claim that attempts to use expansionary monetary and fiscal policies to push unemployment below its natural rate will result only in accelerated inflation.**

POLICIES TO DEAL WITH STAGFLATION

Learning Objective 4:
understand policies designed to deal with stagflation

If we could shift the Phillips curve to the left, we would have either a lower unemployment rate without increasing the rate of inflation or a lower rate of inflation without an increase in the unemployment rate. In other words, we would reduce the discomfort index. Figure 33.7 shows that, by shifting the Phillips curve from position A to position B, the unemployment rate will fall from 12% to 5% while the inflation rate remains at 4%. To deal with the problem of stagflation, the government must adopt policies that will shift the Phillips curve toward the origin. Among the factors that will cause a downward shift in the Phillips curve are greater mobility of labour, the development of relevant skills through education and training, better information about available jobs and available workers, and a reduction in inflationary expectations. All these factors will tend to increase employment without putting undue upward pressure on prices. Hence, the Phillips curve will shift toward the origin.

FIGURE 33.7

The Phillips curve.

A downward shift of the Phillips curve reduces unemployment without raising inflation.

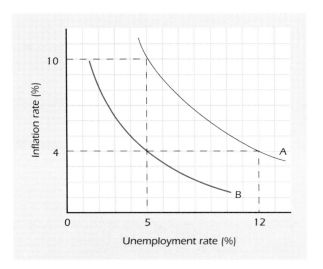

WAGE AND PRICE CONTROLS

The government imposes wage and price controls (incomes policies) to limit increases in both.

Another method of shifting the Phillips curve to the left is the imposition of wage and price controls. **Wage and price controls** are the direct intervention by government to limit increases in wages and prices. Such controls, sometimes referred to as **incomes policies**, occurred in Britain as early as 1948. In August 1971, President Richard Nixon introduced wage and price controls in the United States; and in October 1975, they were introduced in Canada by Prime Minister Pierre Trudeau. Experience with wage and price controls has not been pleasant, since prices continued to rise even in the face of controls. Those who favour wage and price controls claim that the rate of inflation would have been higher had it not been for wage and price controls.

Economists in general do not give overwhelming support for wage and price controls. The main reason for the lack of enthusiasm is that such controls interfere with the efficient working of the price system, resulting in widespread misallocation of resources. Economists claim also that the costs involved in administering the wage and price controls program often outweigh the benefits. These negative views notwithstanding, some economists contend that controls are necessary in certain circumstances.

TAX-BASED INCOMES POLICIES (TIPS)

Tax-based incomes policies may be used to combat stagflation.

Since the 1970s, some economists have suggested the use of **tax-based incomes policies** (TIPS) to increase the effectiveness of incomes policies. There are two different but related forms of the proposal for tax-based incomes policies. In one form, the tax system is seen as a stick to punish nonconformists. The operation of this system may be illustrated as follows. Let us assume that the normal corporate income tax rate is 38% and that the government establishes guidelines specifying a 5% increase in wages and prices as the upper limit. Under this proposal, firms that grant wage increases in excess of the 5% guidelines are penalized by increases in their corporate income tax rate.

Table 33.1 shows that a company that grants wage increases of 5% will be taxed at the normal rate of 38%. If the company grants an increase of only 3%, then the tax rate will be only 34%. On the other hand, if it grants a wage increase of 7%, the tax rate will jump to 42%.

TABLE 33.1

Tax-based incomes policy.

Wage increase granted (%)	Corporate income tax rate (%)
2	32
3	34
4	36
5	38
6	40
7	42
8	44

In the other form of the proposal for tax-based incomes policies, the tax system is seen as a carrot to provide incentive for employees and employers to limit wage and price increases. Let us assume again that the government establishes guidelines specifying a maximum increase of 5% in wages and prices. Under a carrot approach, employers and employees are given tax rebates if they operate within the guidelines. Thus, if a firm manages to keep its prices and wages down to a 3% increase, the firm and its workers will receive tax rebates.

Tax-based incomes policies provide incentives for firms to comply with established wage and price guidelines. However, they do have certain disadvantages. For one thing, the implementation of tax-based incomes policies, some claim, imposes considerable administrative difficulties. Firms may experience hardship in complying with them. Furthermore, union leaders view tax-based incomes policies as an intrusion by the government into the collective bargaining process. Tax-based incomes policies have never been introduced in Canada. But they have attracted considerable attention. The possibility exists that they could be used if policymakers consider them warranted.

RATIONAL EXPECTATIONS HYPOTHESIS (REH)

Learning Objective 5:
understand the rational expectations hypothesis

As we saw in Chapter 24, there is disagreement over supply-side economic policies, and as we shall see in this section, the controversy does not end there. One of the most controversial issues in macroeconomics today is the rational expectations hypothesis (REH).

ADAPTIVE EXPECTATIONS

In order to properly understand the theory of rational expectations, you should grasp the notion of **adaptive expectations**. Quite succinctly stated, the adaptive expectations

The adaptive expectations hypothesis suggests that people's expectations are based on their experiences.

theory assumes that people's inflationary expectations are based solely on past experiences with inflation. For example, if the rate of inflation were 10% last year, people would base their economic decisions on the expectation that the rate of inflation would be 10% this year. If the actual rate of inflation turns out to be different from the anticipated rate, then people will revise their expectations. Unions will revise their wage demands; and firms will revise their pricing decisions. According to the theory of adaptive expectations, people's expectations about the rate of inflation will be wrong most of the time. They will, in fact, be right only if the rate of inflation does not change. The theory of adaptive expectations therefore suggests that most people can be fooled most of the time.

The adaptive expectations theory has been criticized on two counts. First, critics claim that it is unreasonable to assume people's expectations about the rate of inflation to be formed only on the basis of past inflation rates. Other factors such as anti-inflation policies, they argue, will affect people's inflationary expectations. Second, critics of the adaptive expectations theory claim that it is unreasonable to assume that most people can be fooled most of the time.

RATIONAL EXPECTATIONS

The theory of rational expectations assumes that, on average, people's inflationary expectations and thus their wage and price decisions will be correct.

The **rational expectations hypothesis** — a spinoff from monetarism — was developed mainly in response to the criticisms of adaptive expectations. This theory assumes that people understand the factors involved in inflation, and that they use the relevant information in forming their inflationary expectations. The rational expectations theory therefore predicts that, on average, people's inflationary expectations and their consequent wage and price decisions will be correct.

Prominent rational expectations theorists include economists Robert Lucas, Thomas Sargent, and Neil Wallace. According to these economists, people's expectations, and hence their decisions, are based on government policies, the effects of which are known in advance. Rational expectations theorists contend that markets are efficient and that firms use all the available information to make decisions that will accomplish their objective of profit maximization. Unemployment above the natural rate, i.e., the rate consistent with price stability, according to rational expectations theorists, is voluntary because workers know that they can find employment by accepting lower wages.

Critics of the rational expectations hypothesis claim that the theory is not consistent with empirical evidence.

Is the theory of rational expectations rational? Not according to its critics. Critics of this theory claim that the inflationary process is extremely complex and that it is unreasonable to assume that people understand the factors that determine inflation. It is also unreasonable, according to critics, to expect people to know precisely the effects of government policies. Franco Modigliani, whom we have already met in connection with the life-cycle hypothesis, is particularly critical of the rational expectations hypothesis. He claims that the rational expectations hypothesis is not consistent with the evidence. The rational expectations hypothesis leads to the conclusion that unemployment should deviate only slightly from the natural rate, but, according to Modigliani, actual events refute this conclusion.

RATIONAL EXPECTATIONS AND ECONOMIC STABILIZATION

What is the implication of the rational expectations hypothesis for economic stabilization policies? Let us assume that the economy experiences an unemployment rate of 12% and an inflation rate of 5%. Suppose that policymakers move to combat unemployment with expansionary monetary and fiscal policies. According to the theory of rational expectations, people will know the effect of these policies on the rate of inflation. They will expect the rate of inflation to increase. They will also expect interest rates to rise. Accordingly, workers will demand wage increases in order to protect their real wage. With expectations of higher interest rates and higher wages, firms would not find it profitable to undertake new investment projects. Expansionary monetary and fiscal policies will thus be frustrated. Monetary and fiscal policies, then, will be successful only if they come as complete surprises to people.

NEW CLASSICAL AND NEW KEYNESIAN MACROECONOMICS

THE NEW CLASSICAL MACROECONOMIC MODEL

Learning Objective 6:
distinguish between the
new classical and
new Keynesian macro-
economics

In the **new classical macroeconomic model**, wages and prices adjust quickly so that the economy moves quickly to the natural levels of output and employment. If the price level is expected to rise, according to the new classical economists, rational expectations will cause workers to immediately demand higher wages and the demand for goods and services will rise. At the same time, expected higher production costs will cause aggregate supply to fall. Therefore, in the new classical model, wages and prices will rise quickly.

The quick adjustment to long-run equilibrium in the new classical macroeconomic model can be illustrated with the help of the AD-AS model. In Figure 33.8, AD and SRAS are the aggregate demand and short-run aggregate supply curves respectively. The economy is in equilibrium at the natural level of output indicated by y, and at a price level of P. The long-run aggregate supply curve is LRAS. The long-run aggregate supply curve is vertical because as long as wages are flexible (and classical economists assume them to be flexible in the long run), the economy will move to the natural employment level of output.

Let us assume that with the economy in this position, the Bank of Canada implements an expansionary monetary policy. People, having rational expectations, will expect the price level to rise. With this expectation, they increase their purchases of goods and services, so the AD curve shifts to the right from AD to AD_1 as shown in Figure 33.8, and the economy moves to y_1.

The economy does not, however, stay at y_1. The expectation of higher prices causes workers and suppliers of other inputs to demand higher wages and prices. This action

FIGURE 33.8

Adjustment in the new
classical model.

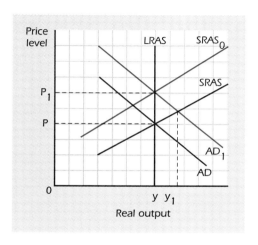

raises the costs of production and shifts the short-run aggregate supply curve to the left from SRAS to $SRAS_0$. Immediately, the price level rises to P_1 and real output instantaneously returns to y. All these rapid adjustments take place automatically, according to new classical economists, so activist macroeconomic stabilization policies are unnecessary.

THE NEW KEYNESIAN MACROECONOMIC MODEL

In the **new Keynesian model of the macroeconomy**, it is assumed that wages are fixed in the very short run. There are several reasons why wages and prices may not adjust in the very short run. First, negotiated wage contracts may fix wages for two to three years, and firms may enter into contracts with their suppliers to supply inputs for some pre-arranged prices. Second, firms may find it more cost efficient not to change certain prices than to change them. New price lists, new catalogues, and new menus may have to be printed following price changes. Such *menu costs*, as they are called, may deter firms from making short-run changes in prices. Third, the practice of using mark-up pricing, whereby firms add a percentage mark-up to arrive at their prices, may prevent firms from changing their prices in response to short-run changes in demand and supply. New Keynesians accept the view that in the long run, wages and prices will be somewhat flexible as time removes the rigidities imposed by contracts, menu costs, and mark-up pricing.

The new Keynesian macroeconomic model can be illustrated with the help of Figure 33.9.

The very short-run aggregate supply curve (VSRAS) is horizontal at a price level of P. Output can vary without affecting the price level. The economy is in full-employment equilibrium at a real output of y and a price level of P. Let us now assume that aggregate demand falls from AD to AD_0. In the short run, the price level is not affected but real output falls from y to y_0. The fall in aggregate demand causes firms to have an undesirable accumulation of inventories. They respond to this situation by cutting back production and laying off workers. Because wages and prices do not adjust, output remains unsold, and workers remain unemployed.

In the long run however, wages and prices adjust downward. This results in lower costs of production, and consequently, the very short-run aggregate supply curve shifts down from VSRAS to $VSRAS_1$ as shown in Figure 33.9. The price level falls from P to P_0, and output and employment increase until full employment is restored at y. Note that the new Keynesian model predicts that in the long run, the economy will return to full-employment equilibrium. New Keynesian economists claim that when wages and prices

FIGURE 33.9

The new Keynesian model.

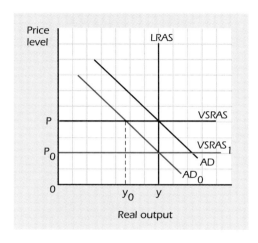

GLOBAL PERSPECTIVE

The Money Supply and Inflation

According to the monetary theory of inflation, increases in the money supply at rates faster than the rate of increase in the economy's real output of goods and services will likely result in inflation. How does this theory stand up empirically? What is the relationship between inflation and money growth in Canada and internationally? In this discussion, we use M1 as the measure of the money supply and changes in the GDP deflator as the measure of inflation.

Diagram A shows the relationship between the rate of growth in the money supply and inflation in Canada from 1990 to 1997. On the basis of this relation alone, there does not seem to be any direct, unambiguous relationship between the growth rate of the money supply in Canada and inflation. For example, between 1990 and 1993, the money supply rose significantly from a growth rate of –1% to 14.7%, but the rate of inflation fell from 3.1% to 1.2 %. And between 1995 and 1996, the growth rate of the money supply increased from 5.9% to 17.3%, while the rate of inflation fell from 2.6% to 1.4%.

Let us look at the situation internationally. During the 1990-97 period, France recorded the lowest increase in the money supply, but Japan recorded the lowest rate of inflation among the G-7 countries. Germany was at the other extreme with the highest growth rate in the money supply, but it had the fourth lowest rate of inflation. One cannot conclude, on the basis of the data under consideration, that increases in the money supply cause inflation. Even if there was greater correlation between the money supply and inflation, one would still need to exercise caution. Recall the caveat in Chapter 1 about correlation and causation.

As Diagram B shows, the United Kingdom had the second highest inflation rate among the seven industrialized countries considered, but the rate of increase in the money supply was the third lowest. Canada, on the other hand, had a much lower rate of inflation than both Italy and the United Kingdom, even though it had a much higher rate of increase in its money supply.

DIAGRAM A

DIAGRAM B

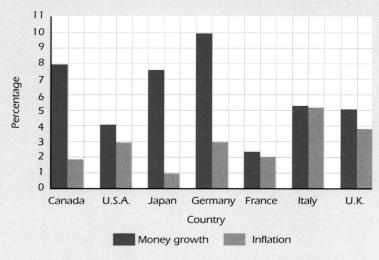

Source: International Monetary Fund, *World Economic Outlook*, May, 1998: 157, 168

adjust too slowly, activist policies should be used to move the economy more quickly to full employment equilibrium.

CHAPTER SUMMARY

1. Demand-pull inflation is due to increases in aggregate expenditure, which exert upward pressure on prices.

2. The monetary theory of inflation states that inflation is caused by increases in the money supply at a faster rate than the increase of real output in the economy. This theory is related to the quantity theory of money and belongs to the family of demand-pull inflation.

3. The budget deficit theory of inflation states that inflation is caused by government deficits, which cause excessive aggregate demand.

4. The cost-push theory of inflation states that inflation is caused by powerful unions demanding high wages and by powerful firms continually raising the prices of their products. These actions produce an inflationary wage-price spiral.

5. Expectational inflation states that inflation is due to inflationary expectations. This type of inflation is both demand-pull and cost-push.

6. The Phillips curve expresses the relationship between the rate of change of wages and the unemployment rate. It is often used in discussions of the trade-off between inflation and unemployment.

7. The natural rate of unemployment is the rate of unemployment necessary for the economy to attain price stability.

8. The coexistence of inflation and unemployment is called stagflation. Stagflation is explained by an upward shift in the aggregate supply curve.

9. The accelerationists believe that the inverse relation between inflation and unemployment exists only in the short run. They believe that the long-run Phillips curve is vertical, and that attempts to push unemployment below its natural rate will result only in accelerated inflation.

10. Policies to solve the problem of stagflation include promoting greater labour mobility, providing better labour market information, reducing inflationary expectations, and establishing incomes policies.

11. The rational expectations hypothesis suggests that government stabilization policies will be unsuccessful because households and firms will respond in a manner that will frustrate economic stabilization policies.

12. The new classical macroeconomic model claims that wages and prices adjust quickly to move the economy to the natural levels of output and employment. Rational expectations ensure the rapid adjustment of wages and prices.

13. The new Keynesian macroeconomic model specifies that wages and prices are fixed in the very short run so that the adjustment to the full-employment level of output may be slow. In the long run however, the rigidities will be removed and the economy will move to full employment.

TERMS FOR REVIEW

demand-pull inflation (569)

excess demand inflation (569)

monetary theory of inflation (570)

budget deficit theory of inflation (570)

cost-push (sellers') inflation (570)

wage-price spiral (570)

imported inflation (570)

expectational (inertial) inflation (571)

Phillips curve (572)

natural rate of unemployment (574)

discomfort (misery) index (575)

stagflation (575)

accelerationists (576)

wage and price controls (578)

incomes policies (578)

tax-based incomes policies (TIPS) (579)

adaptive expectations (5790)

rational expectations hypothesis (580)

new classical economics (581)

new Keynesian economics (582)

QUESTIONS FOR REVIEW AND DISCUSSION

1. What is the difference between demand-pull and cost-push inflation? (L.O.1)

2. What is the main difference between the monetary theory of inflation and the budget deficit theory of inflation? (L.O.1)

3. What role do expectations play in the inflationary process? (L.O.1)

4. Explain the concept of imported inflation. (L.O.1)

5. Why is the Canadian economy considered to be vulnerable to imported inflation? (L.O.1)

6. Explain how inflation and unemployment may occur simultaneously. (L.O.2)

7. Carefully explain the theory of the Phillips curve. (L.O.2)

8. What is the accelerationists' view of the Phillips curve? (L.O.3)

9. Why might expansionary monetary and fiscal policies fail to reduce unemployment? (L.O.3)

10. What policies have been suggested to deal with stagflation? (L.O.4)

11. Why do economists in general have so little enthusiasm for wage and price controls? (L.O.4)

12. What are tax-based incomes policies? How can they be used to combat stagflation? (L.O.4)

13. Briefly explain the rational explanations hypothesis. What is its implication for economic stabilization policy?. (L.O.5).

14. Outline the main arguments of the new classical macroeconomics. (L.O.6).

15. Outline the main arguments of the new Keynesian macroeconomics. (L.O.6).

16. What explanations do new Keynesians offer for sticky wages and prices? (L.O.6).

PROBLEMS AND EXERCISES

1. Table 33.2 gives data for the Canadian economy. Study the data and then answer the following questions.

   (a) Do the data seem to support the monetary theory of inflation? (L.O.1)

   (b) Between 1971 and 1973, the rate of monetary expansion was relatively high yet the rate of inflation was relatively low. Is this a refutation of the monetary theory of inflation? (L.O.1)

TABLE 33.2	Year	% change in M1	% change in real output	% change in CPI	Deficit (–) or surplus ($million)
Economic data for Canada.	1970	2.5	2.5	3.4	266
	1971	12.9	6.9	2.8	–145
	1972	14.3	6.1	4.8	–566
	1973	14.6	7.6	7.6	387
	1974	9.3	3.6	10.9	1 109
	1975	13.8	1.2	10.8	–3 805
	1976	8.1	5.9	7.5	–3 391
	1977	8.4	2.0	8.0	–7 303
	1978	10.1	3.6	8.9	–10 626
	1979	7.1	3.2	9.2	–9 131
	1980	6.3	1.1	10.2	–10 393
	1981	3.9	3.3	12.5	–7 366
	1982	0.6	–4.4	10.8	–18 904

Source: *Bank of Canada Review*, various issues.

(c) In 1982, real output fell by more than 4%. What monetary policy measure would you have prescribed? (General)

(d) Do the data seem to support the budget deficit theory of inflation? (L.O.1)

2. Suppose that in order to combat inflation, the Canadian government introduces legislation forbidding wage settlements in excess of 4% annually. What type of inflation would be assumed by the government? (L.O.1,4)

3. Suppose that the government decides to fight inflation by raising interest rates and increasing taxes on disposable income. What type of inflation would be assumed by the government? (L.O.1,4)

4. "Expectations do not cause inflation, they only sustain an already existing inflation." Do you agree? Why or why not? (L.O.1)

5. Draw a diagram to show that stagflation in the 1970s may have been due, at least partly, to increases in the price of oil. (General,2)

6. The United States is our largest trading partner. Explain how inflation in the United States might be imported into Canada. (L.O.1)

7. Table 33.3 gives information for the Canadian economy from 1970 to 1980. (L.O.2)

TABLE 33.3	Year	Unemployment rate	Inflation rate (%)
Inflation and unemployment data.	1970	5.7	4.6
	1971	6.2	3.2
	1972	6.2	5.6
	1973	5.5	8.8
	1974	5.3	14.4
	1975	6.9	9.9
	1976	7.1	8.7
	1977	8.1	6.2
	1978	8.3	6.0
	1979	7.4	10.0
	1980	7.5	10.8

Source: Dept. of Finance, *Quarterly Economic Review*, Table 43.1; Statistics Canada, *Canadian Economic Observer* (Cat. 11-210), 1991–92: 36.

(a) Plot the Phillips curve.

(b) Is the shape of the curve consistent with the theoretical description?

8. "Canada should allow the market to determine the wage rate and get rid of minimum wage legislation and employment insurance because they cause unemployment." Discuss.

Internet Site

http://www.conferenceboard.ca
The Conference Board of Canada is a "think tank." The site contains information about the Conference Board and its activities.

INTERNET EXERCISE

1. Go to the Conference Board Web page above.
2. Click on *ECONOMICS* under *Knowledge Areas.*
3. Click on *News Releases.*
4. Select an item of interest to you under *News Releases*, click on it, and write up a brief summary of the article.

VIDEO CASE

Canadian Banks Seek Merger Agreement: The Case of the Bank of Montreal and the Royal Bank of Canada

It is our belief that by combining our talents and energies and financial resources, we will deliver to you and to this country a higher standard of banking.

Matthew W. Barrett, CEO, Bank of Montreal
John E. Cleghorn, CEO, Royal Bank of Canada

Background

The Canadian banking scene and the way banking is done have undergone significant changes over the past few years, mainly because of advances in banking technology. But anticipated changes in the structure of the Canadian banking industry threaten to transform the banking landscape even further. Big bank mergers have occurred in Japan and in the United States, and the movement is expected to hit Canada with proposed mergers between the Bank of Montreal and the Royal Bank of Canada, and between the Toronto-Dominion (TD) Bank and the Canadian Imperial Bank of Commerce

(CIBC). There is no guarantee that these proposed mergers will actually occur, because government approval must first be obtained.

The Bank of Montreal and the Royal Bank of Canada have announced their intention to merge to form a bigger and better bank for Canadians. The proposed merger is a controversial issue. Canada's banks have had a long history of contribution to the economic life of the country. In the early days, they helped with the financing of railways, hydroelectric development, and the mining industry. Opponents of the merger fear that bigger will not be better, but worse, as far as banking services to Canadians are concerned.

The Banks' Claim

From the banks' point of view, Canada's banks are finding it increasingly difficult to face global competition from giant financial institutions. The merger is necessary if Canadian banks are to be able to compete head to head with financial institutions delivering financial services in Canada from their European and American bases. Without this merger (so claim the banks), Canadian banks will be unable to provide Canadians with superior products and services at competitive prices, and that's bad.

The Beneficiaries

The banks claim that the following groups will benefit from the proposed bank merger:

1. Shareholders in the banks — some seven million of them — who will realize greater returns on their investment;
2. Individual customers who will be able to receive the highest quality of service and products, and who will be able to exercise greater choice over when, where, and how they do their banking;
3. Small- and medium-sized business customers who will, like individual customers, realize savings in the form of lower service charges;
4. Canadians as a whole as stronger domestic banks will help to ensure that decisions about Canada's economic fate will be made by Canadians for Canadians.

The Bank of Montreal and the Royal Bank of Canada have pledged, through the proposed merger, to reduce personal banking plan fees by not less than 10%. They have pledged also to reduce or eliminate some service charges. They have promised to increase the total number of staffed outlets (branches) from 2500 to 3000. They have promised to allocate $40 billion in loans to small- and medium-sized businesses, thus doubling their current lending to this group. They plan to employ more customer service people to provide more face-to-face banking. And what about rural and remote areas? The banks have pledged that no rural or remote area will lose branch service as a result of the proposed

merger. The banks have tried to educate Canadians as to the benefits of the merger in a booklet, entitled *"Two Banks, One Pledge: A Better Bank for Canadians,"* destined for wide distribution across Canada.

A Quick View From the Other Side

The proposed merger between the Bank of Montreal and the Royal Bank of Canada, if approved, will result in one less bank in Canada. If the proposed merger between the TD Bank and the CIBC happens, then the number of Canadian banks will be reduced further. This may mean even less competition in an industry that is already considered to be non-competitive. Opponents of the merger maintain that bigger is not necessarily better. They fear that the merger will result in higher, not lower, bank charges, and a reduction in the quality of services. They claim also that the merger, instead of creating employment as the banks claim, will result in job losses for many bank employees. Citing evidence and experience from bank mergers in the United States, opponents claim that there is no clear evidence that bank mergers result in greater efficiency.

QUESTIONS

1. Outline the main issues in this case.
2. What advantages do you foresee resulting from a merger between the Bank of Montreal and the Royal Bank of Canada? What disadvantages do you foresee?
3. One of the major issues in the bank merger debate is competition. In your view, what can be done to make the Canadian banking industry more competitive?
4. Do you personally support the bank merger? Why or why not?

Video Resource: "Banks and Panel," *National Magazine* (January 1998).

CHAPTER

DEFICITS, SURPLUSES, AND THE NATIONAL DEBT

Learning Objectives

After studying this chapter, you should be able to:

1 understand the nature of the public debt

2 differentiate between public and private debts

3 explain various budget philosophies

4 discuss the management of deficits and surpluses

5 discuss the problems associated with a public debt

6 determine the benefits of the public debt

7 identify misconceptions about the public debt

Unlike fiscal policy certainly and monetary policy possibly, our thinking about debt policy is in a most primitive stage relative to its probable importance for the economy in the decade ahead.

Paul W. McCracken, *The Debt Problem and Economic Growth*

INTRODUCTION

Since 1995, when Canada was said to be close to hitting the debt wall, the federal and provincial governments have made concerted efforts to reduce their deficits and thus slow the growth of the public debt. Policy makers talk about balancing the budget, and ordinary citizens seem to respond approvingly. Many people seem to want the government to move from a deficit position to a balanced budget, but with no reduction in government services, and definitely no increases in taxes. Do you see any contradiction here?

There seems to be general agreement that efforts must be made to reduce the national debt. The federal government announced a budget surplus in 1997-98, and promised a balanced budget through to 1999-2000. One relevant issue is what should be done with the surplus. Should Canadians get some tax relief now that there is no deficit? Should any surpluses generated over the next few years be used to reduce the debt?

This chapter attempts to address some of the major issues relating to deficits, surpluses, and the public debt. The relationship between deficits and the public debt is sketched briefly at the beginning of the chapter. The important distinction between private and public debts is noted, and various budget philosophies are discussed. This is followed by a treatment of the management of deficits and surpluses, and a discussion of problems and benefits of a public debt. The chapter ends with an examination of two popular misconceptions about the public debt.

DEFINITION OF THE PUBLIC DEBT

Learning Objective 1:
understand the nature of the public debt

The public debt is the money owed by the government to its creditors.

We have heard a great deal about the public debt. There have been warnings of dire consequences from Canada's debt and deficits. Politicians, economists, and the general public seem to worry about the public debt, though perhaps for very different reasons. The **public debt** (also called the national debt) is the amount of money the government owes its creditors. It is the accumulated sum of past deficits. In this chapter, we shall look at why concern exists over the public debt, and whether or not these concerns are justified.

The public debt is very large in absolute terms. In 1940, the net federal debt was $3271.3 million (the net debt is the difference between the gross debt [liabilities] and total assets). By 1964, it had grown to $16 598 million; by 1991, it had reached the enormous sum of $388 429 million; and in 1996, the national debt was estimated at $573 378 million. Figure 34.1 contains information on the growth of the federal debt since 1977.

PUBLIC DEBT VERSUS PRIVATE DEBT

Learning Objective 2:
differentiate between public and private debts

One reason for the great concern over the public debt is the tendency of individuals to equate the public debt with private debts. But in analyzing the public debt, it is crucial to distinguish between the public debt and a private debt. If households borrow money, they can increase their current consumption of goods and services with the proceeds of the loan. But during repayment of the loan, they must sacrifice some goods and services. Repayment of the loan, therefore, imposes a burden on borrowers. By analogy, some people have concluded that a government deficit increases the purchasing power of the nation, but that the citizens must sacrifice some consumption during repayment of the debt. This analogy, however, may be faulty.

We owe an internal debt to ourselves, but we owe an external debt to foreigners.

If the public debt is owed to foreigners, then the analogy is substantially correct. If Canada borrows from the United States or from Germany, then the purchasing power of Canadians will be increased as a result of the loan. But when the principal and interest are repaid, Canadians will suffer a reduction in purchasing power. Such a debt is said to be an **external debt** and may be defined as a debt that is owed to a foreign country.

FIGURE 34.1

Growth of the public debt, 1977–1996.

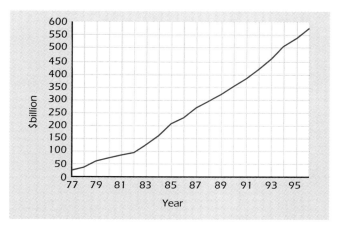

Source: Statistics Canada, *Public Sector Finance, 1995–96* (Cat. 68–212–XPB): 1.

If, however, the debt is owed to Canadians, the analogy ceases to be appropriate. When Canadians lend money to the Canadian government by buying government bonds, total purchasing power is not affected to any significant degree. By buying government bonds, we simply transfer purchasing power to the government. In such a case, the debt is said to be an **internal debt**. This is so because we owe it to ourselves. Between 1967 and 1983, the percentage of the federal government debt owed to foreigners averaged only about 5%. Since 1984, however, the percentage of the debt owed to foreigners increased considerably, averaging over 17% between 1984 and 1991. In 1997, the share of the federal government debt held by foreigners was 24%. Table 34.1 shows the federal (public) debt by type of holder from 1986 to 1997.

Internal debt: a debt that a nation owes to its citizens.

TABLE 34.1

Federal (public) debt by type of holder, 1986-1997, in $million.

Year	Held by Bank of Canada	Held by chartered banks	Held by general public	Held by residents of Canada	Held by non-residents	Total	Percentage held by non-residents
1986	18 422	17 501	199 482	164 349	35 133	220 372	15.9
1987	20 412	14 913	221 160	182 036	39 124	245 199	15.9
1988	20 653	17 669	248 571	195 793	52 778	273 856	19.3
1989	21 176	18 539	268 731	206 999	61 732	294 721	20.9
1990	20 364	19 456	291 608	219 669	71 930	317 087	22.7
1991	22 404	29 512	319 583	239 537	80 046	347 820	23.0
1992	22 639	39 655	345 402	259 458	85 944	373 885	23.0
1993	23 650	65 218	379 142	268 430	110 712	408 246	27.1
1994	25 361	74 396	405 074	295 422	109 652	435 385	25.2
1995	23 609	79 834	431 155	311 518	119 637	460 480	26.0
1996	25 519	74 593	439 993	319 427	120 566	471 513	25.6
1997	27 004	67 034	432 191	320 083	112 108	465 057	24.1

Source: Bank of Canada Review, Summer 1998: s84, s85.

The absolute size of the public debt is misleading. To get a better picture of the public debt, we need to relate it to some other variable. The ratio of the public debt to gross domestic product declined generally from 30.4% in 1961 to 13.9% in 1974. Since 1974, however, the ratio has increased significantly, reaching 57.8% in 1991. By 1996, the figure had risen to about 72%. The ratio was particularly low between 1974 and 1976, when the average dipped to as low as 14%. Figure 34.2 show the federal government debt as a percentage of GDP from 1977 to 1996.

FIGURE 34.2

Federal government debt as a percentage of GDP, 1977–96.

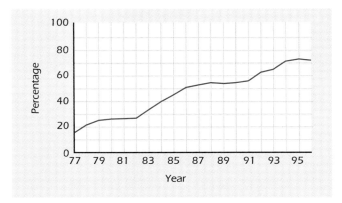

Source: Statistics Canada, *Public Sector Finance* (Cat. 68–212-XPB), March 1996: 4.

People often feel uneasy about the size of the interest payment on the public debt. But in analyzing the interest on the public debt, we must consider two things. First, it is not so much the absolute size of the interest payment that is important, but rather its size in relation to total income. Figure 34.3 shows interest on the debt as a percentage of GDP. In 1967, debt charges claimed only 1.8% of GDP. By 1997, they claimed over 5% of GDP. Second, we must find out whether the interest payment is made to Canadians or to foreigners. If the interest payment is made to residents of Canada, then the situation is less alarming than if it is made to foreigners. Payment of interest to residents in Canada will, of course, result in income redistribution as tax dollars are transferred from taxpayers to bond holders. Now, you have seen that the percentage of the public debt owed to foreigners has increased significantly in recent years. This means that an increasing share of our tax dollars must be used as interest payment to non-residents of Canada.

FIGURE 34.3

Interest on the public debt as a percentage of the GDP.

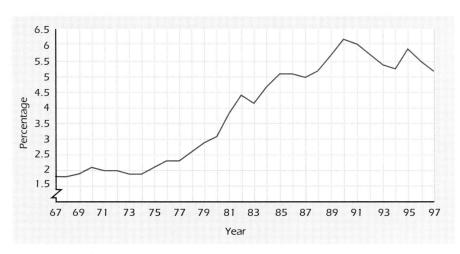

Source: Statistics Canada, *Canadian Economic Observer* (Cat. 11–210-XPB), 1997–98: 3, 17.

BUDGET PHILOSOPHIES

The term **budget philosophy** as used here refers to a general view regarding prudent budgetary policy. We shall discuss three main budget philosophies: balance the budget every year, balance the budget over the business cycle, and use the budget as a tool of fiscal policy.

BALANCE THE BUDGET EVERY YEAR

Prior to the publication of Keynes' seminal work, *The General Theory*, the general philosophy regarding the government budget was that the government should maintain a balanced budget annually. Just as it is considered prudent for a household to live within its means, so too, according to this philosophy, is it prudent and desirable for a government not to be in debt. However, the government has powers that a household does not have, so what is true for a household is not always true for the government.

What are the consequences of accepting this balanced budget philosophy? Balancing the budget every year would mean that the government could no longer conduct fiscal policy as a means of stabilizing the economy. And this inability to use fiscal policy could conceivably result in inflation rates and unemployment rates that are considerably higher than they would be if fiscal policy is used.

BALANCE THE BUDGET OVER THE BUSINESS CYCLE

Business cycles refer to cyclical fluctuations in economic activity. The rate of growth of total output tends to fluctuate over time. You know now that output and employment tend to move together. When output expands, employment increases and the unemployment rate falls. When the rate of output falls, employment falls and the unemployment rate increases. One budget philosophy states that the government should balance the budget over the course of the business cycle. According to this philosophy, an annually balanced budget is not necessary. However, during periods of high employment and rapid economic growth, the government should accumulate a surplus sufficiently large to offset any deficit it will build up during periods of severe unemployment.

This budgetary policy allows the government to pursue policies to combat inflation and unemployment. However, it fails to deal with the problem that would arise when the deficit required to eliminate a recessionary gap is not equal to the surplus required to eliminate an inflationary gap. For example, suppose that there is a prolonged period of severe unemployment, followed by a brief spell of full employment, followed by another prolonged period of severe unemployment. In this case, a balanced budget over the course of the business cycle would be inconsistent with economic stability.

USE THE BUDGET AS A TOOL OF FISCAL POLICY

This budget philosophy states that balancing the budget should be secondary to using it as a tool to combat inflation and unemployment. According to this philosophy, the government should adjust its budget to achieve economic stability, even if this means an unbalanced budget over a long period of time. This is the position we referred to earlier as functional finance. Supporters of functional finance claim that the benefits from reducing inflation and unemployment by running surpluses and deficits outweigh the costs of moderate increases in the public debt that may result from functional finance.

MANAGING DEFICITS AND SURPLUSES

You have seen that the use of discretionary fiscal policy requires the government to run a deficit in times of recession and high unemployment and a surplus in times of inflation. In this section, we discuss certain aspects of managing deficits and surpluses.

DEFICIT FINANCING

What is the usual fiscal position of the government of Canada? A look at Figure 34.4 reveals that prior to 1997–99 Canada had not had a budget surplus since 1974. Canada has had a budget deficit in 24 of the 31 years between 1967 and 1997.

Deficit financing is the policies used to manage a budget deficit.

A question well worth asking is, how do governments go about **deficit financing**? The answer is, they borrow. There are three main sources from which the government of Canada borrows to finance its deficit — the public (including foreigners), the chartered banks, and the Bank of Canada. Let us look briefly at each of these creditors of the government.

FIGURE 34.4

Federal government total revenue and total expenditure.

Source: Statistics Canada, *Canadian Economic Observer* (Cat. 11–210-XPB), 1997–98: 16, 17.

Borrowing from the public

Borrowing from the private sector may crowd out the effect of an expansionary fiscal policy.

Crowding-out effect: the concept that increases in government spending lead to a reduction in private sector spending.

The government may borrow from households and non-bank firms by selling government bonds. If it chooses this option, consumers and firms may divert money from consumption and investment to the purchase of government bonds. Thus, spending by the private sector may fall. This reduction in private sector spending resulting from government borrowing is called the **crowding-out effect**. The crowding-out effect reduces the expansionary effect of the increase in government spending.

Borrowing from the chartered banks

Another source from which the government may borrow is the chartered banks. When the chartered banks purchase government bonds, the government's account at the Bank of Canada increases by the amount of the bond purchase, and at the same time, the chartered banks' accounts at the Bank of Canada decrease by an equivalent amount. The government can then write cheques on its account at the Bank of Canada. If the funds used to purchase government bonds would have been spent by the banks, then total spending would not increase.

Borrowing from the Bank of Canada

Borrowing from the Bank of Canada increases aggregate expenditure.

If the government borrows from the Bank of Canada (our central bank) by selling bonds to the Bank of Canada, it receives new money from the Bank of Canada in exchange for the bonds. When this new money is spent, aggregate expenditure increases. Since, in this case, funds are not diverted from the private sector, there is no crowding out. Thus, the expansionary effect is greater than when the deficit is financed by borrowing from the public.

PROBLEM SOLVING 34-1

Show that an increase in the budget deficit need not mean an increase in overall spending.

HANDLING A SURPLUS

It may have seemed to be of little importance to discuss surpluses in the Canadian context when, for more than a quarter of a century, we had not had a surplus. But economic conditions do change, and students of economics must understand economic problems even though they may not be serious threats at some particular time. On October 14, 1998, Finance Minister Paul Martin announced that, for the first time in 28 years, the Government of Canada had recorded a budget surplus — a surplus of $3.5 billion for the fiscal year 1997-98. The Minister also claimed that the federal government will balance the budget or record surpluses in each of fiscal years 1998-99 and 1999-2000. Thus the budget would be balanced or better for three consecutive years. Let us assume that there will be surpluses. How can they be managed?

If we eliminate simplistic and nonsensical solutions such as throwing the surplus away, there are three ways in which a government can deal with a surplus. First, the government can use the surplus to reduce the government's debt. Second, it can keep the surplus idle in its bank accounts, and third, it can give the surplus back to the taxpayers. Let us examine the effect of each alternative.

Reducing the government's debt

Recall that a budget surplus may result from a government's attempts to balance its budget in order to arrest the growth in the public debt, or it may be intended as a contractionary measure to reduce inflationary pressures. If the surplus is used to reduce the government's debt, then bond holders (households and firms) will receive extra money, some of which will be spent. This increase in total consumption and investment spending will increase aggregate expenditure and thus reduce the anti-inflationary impact of the surplus. The Government of Canada decided to apply the $3.5 billion surplus of 1997-98 directly to the debt. It was the first time the Government of Canada paid down the debt in more than a generation. By reducing the debt, the ratio of debt to GDP will decline.

A part of the public debt is held by the Bank of Canada. The government can pay down some of this debt with the surplus. If the Bank of Canada surrenders some of the government bonds it holds, then the government's accounts at chartered banks will be reduced as cheques are drawn on these accounts to pay the Bank of Canada for the bonds it surrenders. The Bank of Canada then cashes these cheques by reducing the chartered banks' reserves at the Bank of Canada. Thus, the money supply is reduced, and this reduction in the money supply will likely result in a reduction in aggregate expenditure which will amplify the deflationary effect of the surplus.

Keeping the surplus idle

If the funds are held idle in the government's accounts, they become "sterile" as they do not provide extra spending money to the private sector, so no increase in aggregate expenditure results. The anti-inflationary impact of the surplus is not therefore diminished. Furthermore, a surplus, by definition, is the excess of tax receipts over government spending. Therefore, idle surpluses represent tax dollars that could have been spent by taxpayers or held in their bank accounts. To the extent that surpluses represent deposits transferred from private accounts to the government's accounts, the money supply is reduced, and this will likely exert a contractionary effect on the economy.

Giving the surplus back to the taxpayers

Though certainly not impossible, it is unlikely that the government will simply send cheques out to taxpayers totalling the amount of the surplus. However, if it did, aggregate expenditure would increase. It is more likely that the surplus would be given back to taxpayers in the form of expenditures by government on certain services provided for Canadians — services such as health care, education, and social services. In any case, giving the surplus back to taxpayers will increase aggregate expenditure and reduce the anti-inflationary impact of the surplus.

PROBLEMS ASSOCIATED WITH A PUBLIC DEBT

Learning Objective 5:
discuss the problems associated with a public debt

There are certain economic consequences of a large public debt. In this section, we discuss some of the problems caused by a large public debt. These problems include income redistribution, inflation, economic disincentive, high interest rates, and reduced investment.

Income redistribution

The public debt redistributes income.

One problem caused by a large public debt, even if we owe it to ourselves (i.e., it is internally held), is that it leads to a redistribution of income. This redistribution may increase inequality of incomes. The government borrows funds from its citizens by issuing bonds. The government repays the loan plus interest out of taxes. Generally, bonds are owned by people in the higher income groups. Taxes, however, are collected from bond holders and lower income people. Thus, the paying of interest transfers funds from taxpayers to bond holders. This transfer burdens the lower income groups.

Inflation

A public debt may cause inflation.

A second problem sometimes caused by a large public debt is inflation. A public debt can be financed by printing more money, which is potentially inflationary. Also, if the debt is financed through the sale by government of securities to banks, deposits in banks will increase. This increase in bank deposits causes the money supply to increase. And an increase in the money supply may be inflationary.

Economic disincentive

A public debt may reduce incentives.

Because of the higher taxes associated with it, a large public debt may adversely affect economic incentives. It may thus prevent output from being as high as it could be. Also, the public generally interprets a large public debt to mean that the economy is in an unhealthy state. This being the case, a large public debt will discourage investment, which in turn will reduce output and employment.

High interest rates

A public debt may cause higher interest rates.

Continuous borrowing and a growing public debt tend to put upward pressure on interest rates. Lenders fear that the huge debt will lead to inflation or low economic growth or both, so they require higher interest rates as a risk premium.

Reduced investment

A public debt may reduce private investment.

Because of the high interest rates caused by the public debt, private investment declines (recall the inverse relation between investment and interest rates). Also, high interest rates tend to discourage consumer borrowing and hence consumer spending. A reduction in consumer spending tends to reduce investment spending.

Hindrance to fiscal policy

To the extent that a government is committed to a reduction in the public debt or the deficit, it will find it difficult to use expansionary fiscal policy as a means of stimulating the economy should the need arise. Recall that an expansionary fiscal policy increases the deficit and thus adds to the size of the public debt.

APPLICATION

The Public Debt and Private Business

You have probably noticed that the business sector tends to support government attempts at reducing the deficit and the public debt, and you have probably wondered why. When the government reduces its borrowing, it exerts a downward pressure on interest rates. Most businesses regard this as good news. Lower interest rates make it easier for firms to finance their investment projects and to expand their operations. Higher interest rates have the opposite effect. By applying the theory of the relationship between government borrowing and interest rates, we can easily explain the tendency for businesses to support reductions in the deficit and the public debt.

BENEFITS OF THE PUBLIC DEBT

Learning Objective 6:
determine the benefits of the public debt

The public debt makes fiscal policy possible.

The public debt provides a means into which savings can be channelled.

Does the public debt have any benefits associated with it? The answer is yes. We can point to at least two benefits. First, the public debt results from government borrowing to finance its deficits. If there were never any deficits, there would be no public debt. You have seen earlier in this chapter that fiscal policy requires the government to run deficits sometimes in order to stabilize the economy. Thus, the public debt enables the government to conduct economic stabilization policies.

Second, some lucky individuals may consume less than their current income and thus end up with some savings. A part of these savings may be used to purchase government bonds. Thus, the public debt provides a relatively safe form in which individuals may hold their assets. The popularity of government bonds among Canadians is a clear demonstration of the value of this vehicle of saving. Its removal would certainly reduce the level of satisfaction of many Canadians.

TWO POPULAR MISCONCEPTIONS ABOUT THE PUBLIC DEBT

Learning Objective 7:
identify misconceptions about the public debt

The public debt is a matter of great concern. Opinions abound as to the dangers of the public debt. Some of the opinions are based on sound economic theory, but others are simply misconceptions. Two of these misconceptions merit consideration.

Misconception 1:
The public debt will lead the country into bankruptcy

An internal public debt will not result in bankruptcy.

The public continues to express the fear that a large public debt will lead the country into bankruptcy. Let us examine this misconception. Suppose the government owes its citizens x billion. It can always meet its debt obligation by raising x billion in taxes and then use the proceeds to pay off the debt. The government, therefore, cannot go bankrupt like a business or a private individual can if it owes debt to its citizens.

Misconception 2:
The burden of the public debt is passed on to future generations

Many people feel that the burden of the public debt will be passed on to future gener-

An internal debt does not transfer a burden to future generations.

ations. Indeed, an external debt does transfer a burden from the present to the future. If a country increases its present command over goods and services by borrowing externally, the citizens of the future will have to sacrifice some goods and services when payment is made on the loan. Thus, the burden is passed on to them.

An internal debt, however, does not necessarily transfer a burden from the present to the future. It is true that future generations will pay higher taxes because of the loan. But it is equally true that the repayment of the loan is received by future generations. The real burden of an internal debt is not necessarily passed on to future generations. It is borne by those individuals who have given up current consumption of goods and services in order to buy government bonds.

It is worth noting, however, that the reduction in investment that might result from the deficit and the public debt could cause the level of future capital stock to be reduced. If this occurs, then the public debt will place a burden on future generations in the form of reduced capital.

PROBLEM SOLVING 34-2

Most Canadians are confident that the government will honour its debt obligations. Are their expectations rational?

IS GOVERNMENT BORROWING JUSTIFIABLE?

We have seen that some problems exist with a large public debt. Would it not therefore be better if the government did not borrow, but financed its projects out of taxation instead? Government borrowing can be defended on strictly economic grounds in two situations. These situations are (1) during recessionary periods when economic activity is at a very low level, and (2) during times when it is needed to finance public investment.

BORROWING DURING RECESSIONARY PERIODS

It is the responsibility of the government to use its spending and taxing powers to promote economic stability. This means that, in a period of full employment (or very low unemployment) and inflation, the government should spend less than it collects in taxes. In other words, the government should have a budget surplus. A budget surplus will reduce total spending and relieve the inflationary pressure. In a period of full employment and price stability, the government should spend the same amount as it collects in taxes. A balanced budget will have little effect on total spending. In a period of high unemployment and low production levels with stable or falling prices, the government should borrow. A budget deficit tends to increase total spending and thus stimulates economic activity. Government borrowing in periods of recession is therefore justified.

BORROWING FOR PUBLIC INVESTMENT

The government provides certain goods and services for the society. In order to provide these goods and services, the government makes huge outlays on capital goods such as roads, water supply projects, bridges, hospitals, and schools. If such projects are financed completely out of taxation in any given year, the tax burden will be substantial. Borrowing permits the government to lessen the tax burden by spreading it over a period of several years. We must understand, however, that not all borrowing for **public investment** projects can be defended on economic grounds. Government borrowing for public investment can be justified only if the benefits from such investments outweigh the costs.

Public investment: the purchase of new capital or the production of capital goods by the government.

GLOBAL PERSPECTIVE

The Public Debt: How Bad Is Canada's?

We now have a good understanding of the problems associated with a huge public debt. Do other industrial countries also have public debts, or is Canada unique in this regard? If the existence of a public debt is not peculiar to Canada, how does Canada compare? These issues are addressed here. The ratios of the public debt to GDP for selected OECD countries are shown in the following diagram.

In 1998, Canada's net debt was estimated at 62.5% of GDP. Canada's net debt to GDP was the second highest among G-7 countries and third highest among the selected OECD countries. It may be of interest to note that in 1981, Canada's net debt was only 11.7% of GDP. At that time, only France had a lower debt-to-GDP ratio. Italy had the highest debt-to-GDP ratio of all G-7 countries, and the second highest of the selected OECD countries. Belgium had the highest with 115.9%. At 20.7%, Japan had the lowest debt-to-GDP ratio of all the countries considered. Sweden had the second lowest with a ratio of 14.7%.

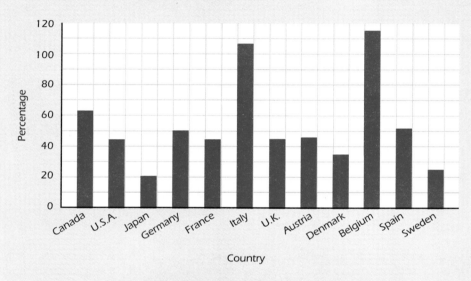

Source: OECD, *Economic Outlook*, December, 1997: A38.

CHAPTER SUMMARY

1. The public debt refers to the amount of money the government owes its creditors. It is the sum of past deficits.

2. The distinction between an external debt and an internal debt is an important one. An external debt is owed to foreigners while an internal debt is owed to one's self. An external debt increases purchasing power when the loan is received, and reduces purchasing power when the principal and interest are repaid. An internal debt, on the other hand, does not significantly affect purchasing power, at least in the short run.

3. The federal public debt is mainly an internal debt, although the percentage of the debt held by foreigners has increased considerably over the past several years.

4. Budget philosophies range from annual balanced budgets to balanced budgets over the business cycle to using the budget as a fiscal policy tool.

5. In order to finance its deficit, the government can borrow from the public, the chartered banks, or the Bank of Canada.

6. Some problems associated with a large public debt are: (1) it may lead to an undesirable redistribution of income, (2) it may be inflationary, (3) it may reduce work effort and initiative and thus adversely affect the total output of the economy, (4) it may raise interest rates, (5) it may reduce the level of investment, and (6) it may make it difficult to use fiscal policy.

7. The public debt enables the government to establish policies to improve the economy, and it provides a secure form in which people may hold their assets.

8. Two popular misconceptions about the public debt are: (1) it may lead the country into bankruptcy and (2) the burden of the debt is necessarily passed on to future generations.

9. Government borrowing can be justified on economic grounds if the debt is used as a weapon against recessions, or if it is used to finance profitable investment projects.

TERMS FOR REVIEW
public debt (590)

external debt (590)

internal debt (591)

budget philosophy (593)

deficit financing (594)

crowding-out effect (594)

public investment (598)

QUESTIONS FOR REVIEW AND DISCUSSION

1. What is meant by the public (national) debt? (L.O.1)

2. What is the relationship between the deficit and the public debt? (L.O.1)

3. What is the difference between a public debt and a private debt? Give an example to illustrate the difference. (L.O.2)

4. What is the difference between an internal debt and an external debt? Give examples to illustrate the difference. (L.O.1)

5. Should the federal government balance its budget every year? Why or why not? (L.O.3)

6. "A government deficit financed by borrowing from the public is less expansionary than a deficit financed by borrowing from the Bank of Canada." Explain why this statement is true. (L.O.4)

7. What problems does a large public debt cause? (L.O.5)

8. What are the benefits of the public debt? (L.O.6)

9. Is the public's concern over the size of the public debt justified? (L.O.7)

10. Comment on each of the following statements:

    (a) "Sooner or later, we must pay off the public debt to avoid bankruptcy." (L.O.7)

    (b) "Interest payment on the public debt will burden future generations." (L.O.7)

PROBLEMS AND EXERCISES

1. *Let's pay off the public debt.* Let us assume that the federal government has a debt of $80 billion on which it pays interest of $7 billion annually. The full amount of the debt is owed to resident Canadians. A powerful interest group (those "ignoreconomists") has succeeded in getting the government to decide to pay off the debt.

(a) How can the government reduce the public debt to zero?

(b) Which group will bear the burden (where will the money come from)?

(c) Which group will benefit (where will the money go)?

(d) How will the Canadian society as a whole be affected? (L.O.1,7)

2. Now suppose 75 percent of the debt referred to in Question 1 were owed to foreigners.

(a) Which group will bear the burden?

(b) Which group will benefit?

(c) How will the Canadian society as a whole be affected? (L.O.1,7)

3. *Let's try to burden our grandchildren and great grandchildren with the national debt.* Assume that the national debt is $320 billion. Let us try to ignore it by getting the government to pass legislation that no payment will be made on the debt until the year 2065, at which time the entire debt will be paid off. The debt is owed entirely to Canadian residents. It is now 2065 and the total debt (including interest charges) has amounted to $900 billion. The government collects $900 billion in taxes and uses the proceeds to pay off the debt.

(a) From whom does the government collect the money?

(b) To whom does the government give the money collected?

(c) Have we succeeded in paying off the debt?

(d) Have we succeeded in passing the burden on to our descendants in 2065?

(d) What lesson have you learned from this exercise? (L.O.1,7)

4. Present an argument to support the view that reducing the deficit would contribute to economic growth. (General)

Internet Site

http://www.fin.ga.ca

This is the Web site for the Department of Finance (federal government). Here you can find useful information about government financial management.

INTERNET EXERCISE

1. Go to the Web site for the Department of Finance.
2. Click on *Budget info.*
3. Click on the most recent budget year.
4. Click on *Budget in Brief.*
5. Select an item under the Table of Contents.
6. Write up a brief summary.

CHAPTER 35

BALANCE OF PAYMENTS AND EXCHANGE RATES

Learning Objectives

After studying this chapter, you should be able to:

1 explain Canada's balance of payments

2 understand exchange rates and how they are determined

3 understand the relationship between inflation and exchange rates

4 discuss fixed and flexible exchange rates

5 understand the relation between foreign exchange transactions and the money supply

6 discuss the international repercussions of monetary and fiscal policies

An attempt to analyse the foreign market with the tools and in the terminology of general price theory helps in avoiding pitfalls into which one is easily led by the often confusing terminology in which foreign exchange theory is usually treated.

Fritz Machlup, *The Theory of Foreign Exchanges*

INTRODUCTION

We have seen that Canada trades with other countries. In fact, the Canadian economy has a relatively large foreign sector. External economic events, particularly events in the United States, do have a significant impact on the Canadian economy. Countries trading internationally keep a record of all economic transactions with the rest of the world. This record is called the **balance of payments**. A country's balance of payments reveals considerable information about the country's dealings with the rest of the world and much about the country's own economy.

This chapter will cover Canada's balance of payments and exchange rates. In earlier chapters, we discussed monetary and fiscal policies without really considering the international repercussions of such policies. In this chapter, we examine the international feedbacks caused by monetary and fiscal policies under different exchange rate regimes.

BALANCE OF PAYMENTS

Learning Objective 1:
Explain Canada's balance of payments

The balance of payments is a record of international economic transactions.

The current account records sales and purchases to and from the rest of the world.

Non-merchandise items are services, investments, and transfers, as noted on the current account.

A country's balance of payments is a summary of all economic transactions between the country and the rest of the world for a period of time. The balance of payments is divided into two main parts: the current account, and the capital account. Let us examine these two parts of the balance of payments by looking at Canada's balance of payments shown in Table 35.1.

CURRENT ACCOUNT

The **current account** contains all sales and purchases of currently produced goods and services to or from the rest of the world. Specifically, it contains exports and imports of goods (merchandise) and services such as tourist services, freight and shipping services, and other services such as insurance and management. The current account also contains an item called *transfers*.

Services, investment income, and transfers are referred to as **non-merchandise transactions** or **invisibles**. Exports are entered as credit items (with plus signs). Imports are entered as debit items (with minus signs). This is so because exports result in payments to Canada from foreign countries, while imports result in payments from Canada to foreign countries.

The difference between total exports of goods and total imports of goods is called the **balance of merchandise trade** or the **balance of visible trade**. The difference between exports of goods and services and imports of goods and services is called the **balance of trade**. Some authors, however, use the term balance of trade to refer to the balance of merchandise trade. When net transfers are added to the balance of trade, we obtain the **current account balance**. We will discuss net transfers in a later section.

The balance of trade is the difference between exports and imports.

Balance of merchandise trade is total goods exported minus total goods imported.

The current account balance is total current receipts from foreigners minus total current payments to foreigners.

A negative balance of trade, also called a **balance of trade deficit**, is a debt owed by a country to the rest of the world. A positive balance of trade, also called a **balance of trade surplus**, is a debt owed by the rest of the world to a country. Table 35.1 indicates that Canada exported $301 101 million worth of goods and $41 572 million worth of services in 1997, for a total of $342 673 million. At the same time, Canada imported $276 846 million worth of goods and $50 316 million worth of services for a total of $327 162 million. Canada therefore had a balance of trade surplus of $15 511 million in 1997. That is, the rest of the world had to pay that amount to Canada on the trade in goods and services account.

Investment income includes interest and dividend income. In 1997, Canada received $29 722 million from foreigners in interest and dividend payments while it paid out $58 649 million in interest and dividends to foreigners. The relatively large net balance

	Current receipts exports (+) ($million)	Current payments imports (–) ($million)	Balance ($million)
TABLE 35.1			
Canada's balance of payments, 1997.			
CURRENT ACCOUNT			
Merchandise exports	301 101		
Merchandise imports		276 846	24 255
Services (exports)	41 572		
Services (imports)		50 316	–8 744
Investment income	29 722	58 649	–28 927
Transfers	4 828	4 227	601
TOTAL CURRENT ACCOUNT	377 223	390 038	–12 815
CAPITAL ACCOUNT			
Capital account			7 609
Financial account:			
Canadian assets net flow			-51 706
Canadian liabilities to non-residents, net flows			63 966
Total capital and financial accounts			19 870
Statistical discrepancy			–7 054

Source: Bank of Canada Review, Summer 1998: s100-s102.

of investment income of $–28 927 is an indication of the large amount of foreign investment in Canada relative to Canadian investment abroad.

Transfers include inheritances and immigrants' funds, personal and institutional remittances, withholding taxes, and official contributions. The funds that immigrants bring into Canada are recorded as a credit item under transfers. The funds they send to their home country are recorded as a debit item. Official contributions include loans and grants made from Canada to foreign countries. A withholding tax is a tax deducted from income payments to non-residents. Total transfers received by Canada in 1997 from the rest of the world amounted to $4828 million. Transfers paid by Canada to the rest of the world amounted to $4227 million. The net balance of transfers, therefore, was $601 million. In 1997, Canada had a current account deficit of $12 815 million.

CAPITAL ACCOUNT

The capital account records capital flows.

The **capital account** is divided into two sections: the capital account and the financial account. The capital account records real capital flows while the financial account records flows of financial assets and financial liabilities. Thus, all transactions with the rest of the world that are not entered in the current account are contained in the capital account. These include long-term capital flows, short-term capital flows, and changes in official reserves (net official monetary movements). *Long-term capital flows* include mainly direct foreign investment and portfolio investment. **Direct foreign investment** is the ownership or control of a business enterprise in a foreign country. The establishment by a Canadian firm of a branch in the Caribbean and the establishment by an American company of a branch in Canada are two examples of direct foreign investment. These investments are recorded in the capital account as long-term capital flows. **Portfolio foreign investment** is the purchase by foreigners of shares and bonds whose term to maturity is more than one year. Portfolio foreign investment does not imply ownership or control. The purchase of Canadian bonds by Americans, therefore, is recorded as portfolio investment in the capital account and entered as long-term capital flows.

Short-term capital flows include financial assets whose term to maturity is less than one year. The holding by Canadians of short-term funds abroad or by foreigners of

Direct foreign investment is control of an enterprise by a foreigner.

Portfolio foreign investment is ownership of shares or bonds by a foreigner.

International payments are made in official reserves, funds such as gold, U.S. dollars, and other foreign currencies.

Canadian funds and short-term paper is recorded in the capital account as short-term capital flows.

The final item in the balance of payments account to be discussed is official reserves. **Official reserves** are funds with which international payments can be made. They consist mainly of gold, American dollars, other foreign currencies, and special drawing rights (SDRs). Special drawing rights are deposits with the International Monetary Fund (IMF). They can be used as international money to settle indebtedness among nations.

The items in the capital account are arranged under three headings in Table 35.1: capital account, Canadian assets (net flows) representing Canadian claims on non-residents, and Canadian liabilities to non-residents (net flows). In 1997, Canadian claims on non-residents (Canadian assets, net flows) amounted to $51 706 million, and Canadian liabilities to non-residents totalled $63 966. Note that the balance of payments always balances, since any imbalance in the current account is made good in the capital account. In other words, the sum of the current account balance and the capital account balance must be zero.

EXCHANGE RATES

Learning Objective 2:
understand exchange rates and how they are determined

The exchange rate is the price of foreign currency.

Trade between nations requires a mechanism through which the currency of one country can be converted into the currency of another country. The rate at which one country's currency exchanges for the currency of another country is called the **exchange rate**. If Canadians have to pay $2.15 for a British pound, then the exchange rate is $2.15 to 1 pound. In other words, the exchange rate is the price of foreign currency. Table 35.2 shows exchange rates for some of Canada's trading partners.

TABLE 35.2

The prices (exchange rates) of various currencies in Canadian dollars (average June 1998).

Foreign currency	Value in Cdn $
United States dollar	1.4653
British pound	2.4184
French franc	0.2438
German mark	0.8174
Swiss franc	0.9804
Japanese yen	0.0145

Source: *Bank of Canada Review*, Summer 1998: s98.

FLEXIBLE AND FIXED EXCHANGE RATES

Flexible exchange rates

A flexible exchange rate is determined by market forces.

A country may decide to leave its exchange rate to be determined by the market forces of demand and supply. Such an exchange rate is said to be a **flexible** or **freely fluctuating** or **floating exchange rate**. Figure 35.1 illustrates how a flexible exchange rate is determined between Canadian dollars and British pounds.

The demand curve DD shown in Figure 35.1 represents the demand for Canadian dollars by the British. There are three reasons why the British might want Canadian dollars (and thus supply British pounds on the foreign exchange market). First, they might want to buy Canadian goods. Since Canadian exporters will want to be paid in Canadian dollars, British importers will need to buy Canadian dollars. Second, the British might want to invest in Canada. For example, if the British want to buy shares in Canadian companies, they will need to convert their pounds into Canadian dollars for such investments. Finally, the British might want to hold Canadian dollars for speculative purposes. If they

FIGURE 35.1

Determination of flexible exchange rates.

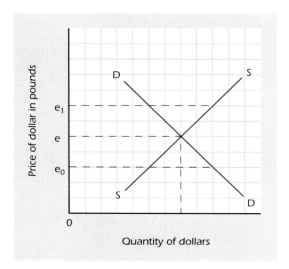

The exchange rate is determined by the demand for and the supply of a country's currency.

expect the value of the Canadian dollar to rise, they might increase their holdings of Canadian dollars in order to enjoy a capital gain if the increase does indeed materialize. The greater the number of pounds that have to be given up for Canadian dollars, the fewer the quantity of dollars demanded by the British. The demand curve, therefore, slopes downward as shown in Figure 35.1.

The supply curve SS shows the supply of dollars by Canadians. Canadians might supply Canadian dollars to the foreign exchange market for the same reasons that the British demand Canadian dollars. Canadians might want to buy British exports (i.e., import British goods), or make investments in Britain, or increase their holdings of British pounds for speculative purposes. If the price of dollars (in terms of pounds) rises, Canadians will offer more dollars (buy more pounds). Thus, the supply curve slopes upward as shown in Figure 35.1.

At an exchange rate of e_1, Canadians are willing to supply more Canadian dollars to the foreign exchange market than the amount that the British want to buy. Thus there will be a surplus of Canadian dollars on the foreign exchange market, which will force the exchange rate down. At an exchange rate of e_0, the British want to buy more Canadian dollars than the amount that Canadians are willing to supply to the foreign exchange market. Therefore, there will be a shortage of Canadian dollars on the foreign exchange market, which will bid the exchange rate up. The only exchange rate at which the amount of Canadian dollars demanded and supplied are equal is e. Hence, the equilibrium exchange rate is e, where the demand and supply curves intersect.

What effect will an increase in the demand for Canadian goods have on the exchange rate? Let us investigate. If the British demand more Canadian goods, they will require more Canadian dollars to pay for those goods. The demand for Canadian dollars will increase from D to D_1 as shown in Figure 35.2. This increase in the demand for Canadian dollars at the exchange rate e results in a shortage of Canadian dollars. This shortage of Canadian dollars will bid up the exchange rate from e to e_1, assuming that other things remain equal. The increase in the value of the Canadian dollar (in terms of pounds) is called an **appreciation** of the Canadian currency. You should work out the effect of a fall in demand for Canadian dollars by foreigners. A fall in the value of the currency is called a **depreciation** of the currency.

Flexible currency appreciates when it gains in value, and depreciates when it declines in value.

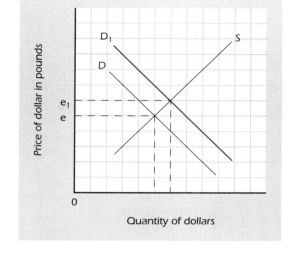

FIGURE 35.2

The effect of an increase in demand for Canadian dollars.

An increase in demand for Canadian dollars increases the value of the Canadian currency.

Fixed exchange rates

A country may decide to fix the value of its currency in relation to some other country's currency. This is called a **fixed exchange rate**, or a *pegged exchange rate*. In order to maintain the exchange rate at its fixed or pegged value, the government enters the market and buys or sells foreign exchange. A country may decide to raise the value at which its currency was pegged. Such an action is referred to as a **revaluation** of its currency. Similarly, a country may reduce the rate at which its currency was fixed. This is called **devaluation**.

> **The terms appreciation and depreciation apply to a regime of flexible exchange rates, whereas the terms revaluation and devaluation apply to a regime of fixed exchange rates.**

As an alternative to a fixed or a flexible exchange rate, a government may adopt a **managed flexible exchange rate**. Under this **dirty float**, as it is called, the exchange rate is neither completely fixed nor allowed to fluctuate freely in response to the market forces of demand and supply. Instead, the government intervenes and manipulates the exchange rate so that it attains a level different from its market equilibrium level. For example, if the market established a value of U.S. $0.65 for Cdn $1, the Bank of Canada might intervene and prop up the Canadian dollar so that it did not reach its U.S. $0.65 level.

POLICY IMPLICATIONS

If a country has a large deficit in its balance of trade, it can improve its situation by devaluing its currency. By so doing, its goods will become less expensive to foreigners. At the same time, foreign goods will become relatively more expensive. Thus, by devaluing its currency, a country can stimulate its exports and discourage imports. This will lead to an improvement in its balance of trade and may generate income and employment within the domestic economy. Recall that in an economy with a foreign sector, aggregate expenditure is C + I + G + (X − M). A devaluation of the currency will increase the (X − M) component of aggregate expenditure and thus stimulate output and employment.

Currency with a fixed exchange rate is pegged to another currency.

Fixed currency revalues when it gains in value, and devalues when it declines in value.

A managed flexible exchange rate is neither fixed nor flexible.

A country may change its exchange rate in an attempt to regulate its economy.

PROBLEM SOLVING 35-1

If Canada succeeds in increasing its exports to the United States, other things being equal, what effect will it have on the value of the Canadian dollar in terms of American funds?

INFLATION AND EXCHANGE RATES

Learning Objective 3:
understand the relationship between inflation and exchange rates

Now that we have studied exchange rates, we can see how domestic inflation affects the exchange value of the Canadian dollar. Let us assume that the Canadian economy is experiencing inflation while prices in the rest of the world are stable. Let us assume also that Canada is operating under a flexible exchange rate regime. Since Canadian prices are rising relative to foreign prices, the quantity of exports from Canada will fall. As a result, the demand for Canadian dollars by foreigners will fall. In other words, the demand for Canadian dollars will shift to the left. Figure 35.3 shows this as a shift in the demand curve from DD to D_0D_0.

FIGURE 35.3

Effect of domestic inflation on the exchange rate.

Inflation in a country may cause a depreciation of its currency.

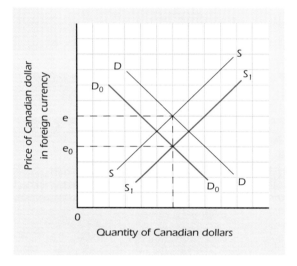

At the same time, imports into Canada will increase, resulting in an increase in the supply of Canadian dollars on the foreign exchange market. Figure 35.3 shows this increase in the supply of Canadian dollars as a shift in the supply curve from SS to S_1S_1. As a result, the exchange rate falls from its initial level of e to e_0.

If there is inflation in the Canadian economy, other things being equal, the value of the Canadian dollar on the foreign exchange market will depreciate.

RELATIONSHIP BETWEEN THE FOREIGN EXCHANGE MARKET AND THE BALANCE OF PAYMENTS

You may have suspected that there is a relationship between exchange rates and the balance of payments. In this section, we will examine the effects of changes in the balance of payments on the exchange rate, and the adjustments that will be made to restore balance of payments equilibrium under flexible and fixed exchange rates.

FLEXIBLE EXCHANGE RATES AND THE BALANCE OF PAYMENTS

To facilitate this discussion, let us assume that there are only two countries in the world — Canada and the Rest of the World (ROW). We assume also that initially, the foreign exchange market is in equilibrium at an exchange rate of e as shown by point **a** in Figure 35.4. The balance of payments is also in equilibrium.

FIGURE 35.4

The foreign exchange market.

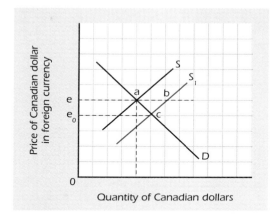

Now, suppose that average income in Canada rises so that Canadians import more goods and services from ROW. Canada will demand more ROW currency to pay for the increased imports, thus providing Canadian dollars in exchange for ROW currency. The supply of Canadian dollars will then increase as shown in the shift in the supply curve from S to S_1 in Figure 35.4. Total payments to ROW will now exceed total receipts from ROW. Canada will have a deficit in its balance of payments account. The foreign exchange market moves from point **a** to point **b**.

Under a flexible exchange rate system, the excess quantity of Canadian dollars supplied (**b** – **a**) will lower the exchange rate. As the exchange rate falls, Canadian goods become more attractive to ROW, and goods from ROW become less attractive to Canadians. As Canadians decrease their imports of goods from ROW, the quantity of Canadian dollars supplied to the foreign exchange market decreases. There is a movement from point **b** to point **c** along the supply curve S_1. At this point, the market is again in equilibrium with the exchange rate at e_0, and the balance of payments deficit is eliminated.

FIXED EXCHANGE RATES AND THE BALANCE OF PAYMENTS

Let us now turn to the case of fixed exchange rates. Let us suppose that Canada fixes its exchange rate, with respect to the ROW currency, at e_1 which is above the equilibrium exchange rate as shown in Diagram A of Figure 35.5.

At an exchange rate of e_1, the quantity of Canadian dollars demanded by ROW to make payments to Canada is Q_0. At the same time, the quantity of Canadian dollars supplied in exchange for ROW currency is Q_1. Thus, payments by Canada to ROW exceed payments by ROW to Canada. Canada has a balance of payments deficit illustrated by $Q_1 – Q_0$ in Diagram A of Figure 35.5.

In a regime of flexible exchange rates, the surplus of Canadian dollars on the foreign exchange market would cause the exchange rate to fall until the surplus is eliminated.

FIGURE 35.5

Fixed exchange rates and the balance of payments.

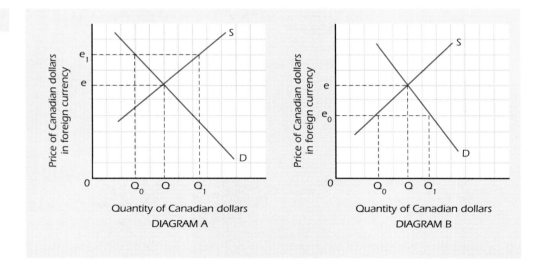

In a fixed exchange rate regime, however, the Bank of Canada must enter the foreign exchange market and use its ROW currency out of its official reserves to buy up the surplus Canadian dollars. If the Bank's reserves are exhausted, a devaluation of the Canadian dollar will occur.

We will now examine the case where Canada fixes its exchange rate at e_0 which is below the market equilibrium exchange rate of e (see Diagram B). At this exchange rate, the quantity of Canadian dollars demanded by ROW to make payments to Canada is Q_1. At the same time, the quantity of Canadian dollars supplied in exchange for ROW currency to make payments to ROW is Q_0. Thus, payments to Canada by ROW exceed payments to ROW by Canada. There is a surplus in Canada's balance of payments illustrated by $Q_1 - Q_0$ in Diagram B of Figure 35.5. In order to prevent the exchange rate from being bid up to the equilibrium level of e, the Bank of Canada would have to supply Canadian dollars in the amount of $Q_1 - Q_0$ to the foreign exchange market in exchange for ROW currency. Canada's holdings of ROW currency would thus increase.

FIXED VERSUS FLEXIBLE EXCHANGE RATES

Learning Objective 4:
discuss fixed and flexible exchange rates

Is the economy of a country better off under fixed exchange rates or under flexible exchange rates? That is the question that we discuss in this section. We shall examine the advantages and disadvantages of flexible and fixed exchange rates.

ADVANTAGES AND DISADVANTAGES OF FLEXIBLE EXCHANGE RATES

One of the advantages of a freely fluctuating exchange rate is that no direct intervention is necessary to achieve equilibrium in the foreign exchange market. The exchange rate will adjust automatically to changes in demand and supply and thus maintain equilibrium. There is therefore no need to maintain foreign reserves in order to "peg" the exchange rate. A flexible exchange rate frees monetary policy so that it may be used in conjunction with fiscal policy to ensure high employment and price stability. Under a fixed exchange rate system, the Bank of Canada has to intervene in the foreign exchange market to maintain the fixed exchange rate. No such intervention is necessary under a flexible exchange rate regime.

A second advantage of a flexible exchange rate is that it helps to insulate a country from foreign inflationary pressures. Suppose that there is inflation in the United States but not in Canada. Canadian exports to the United States will rise as Americans switch to relatively cheaper Canadian goods. Also, imports from the United States will fall as Canadians reduce the quantity of the relatively expensive U.S. goods demanded. The resulting increase in the demand for Canadian goods will tend to increase prices in Canada. Under a fixed exchange rate regime, the money supply will be increased to maintain the "pegged" exchange rate, and consequently, the American inflation will tend to spill over into Canada. Under a system of flexible exchange rates, however, the exchange rate will rise and thus prevent Canadian prices from rising.

A freely fluctuating exchange rate has certain disadvantages also. First, the uncertainty associated with flexible rates discourages international trade. It is important for international traders to know what they will pay for their imports and what they will receive for their exports. Trade cannot be expected to flourish in an environment of uncertainty and insecurity.

A flexible exchange rate may affect the economy in another way. An appreciation of the Canadian dollar means that foreign goods become less expensive to Canadians. Lower-priced imports will then compete with Canadian-made goods, and consumers may buy foreign products instead of made-in-Canada products. This, in turn, may lead to reductions in income and increases in unemployment.

ADVANTAGES AND DISADVANTAGES OF FIXED EXCHANGE RATES

Fixed exchange rates have the great advantage of certainty and security. International traders can arrange their transactions with confidence, knowing that prices and costs will not change in the interim. A serious disadvantage of a fixed exchange rate is that a country may be forced to adopt a monetary policy with undesirable domestic effects just to be able to maintain the exchange rate at its fixed level. For example, a restrictive monetary policy with high interest rates may be necessary to maintain the official level of the exchange rate. Such a policy, however, may result in high unemployment and low economic growth.

WHAT IS THE VERDICT?

No decisive verdict has been reached about which system of exchange rate is better. Although most economists seem to favour a flexible exchange rate, the debate continues. It is worth noting, however, that there are more countries on a fixed exchange rate regime than there are on a flexible exchange rate system.

FOREIGN EXCHANGE TRANSACTIONS AND THE MONEY SUPPLY

Foreign currency transactions affect the money supply only if the central bank is involved in the transaction.

How do foreign exchange transactions affect the domestic money supply? The answer to this question depends on whether Canada is on a flexible or fixed exchange rate regime; that is, whether or not the Bank of Canada intervenes in the foreign exchange market to maintain a fixed exchange rate.

FLEXIBLE EXCHANGE RATES

Let us assume that the country is on a freely fluctuating exchange rate regime. To simplify the calculations and avoid complications, let us assume further that the Canadian dol-

Learning Objective 5:
understand the relation
between foreign
exchange transactions
and the money supply

lar is on par with the U.S. dollar; that is, Cdn $1 = U.S. $1, and that there are no bank charges or commissions. If a customer, Miss Thompson, sells U.S. $1000 to a Canadian chartered bank and deposits the proceeds in her chequing account, her deposits (in Canadian dollars) at the bank increase by $1000. The bank then sells the U.S. $1000 on the foreign exchange market to a buyer, Mr. Mason, who pays for the U.S. dollars with Canadian dollars drawn on his account. Mr. Mason's deposit account falls by Cdn $1000. The combined effect of the foreign exchange transaction on the money supply is zero.

> **Under a flexible exchange rate regime, foreign exchange transactions do not affect the domestic money supply because the central bank does not intervene.**

FIXED EXCHANGE RATES

Does the above conclusion hold under a fixed exchange rate system? Let us investigate. If the central bank does not intervene in the foreign exchange market, our result will not be affected. Under a fixed exchange rate regime, however, the central bank must often intervene to maintain a fixed exchange rate. Suppose that the Bank of Canada sells U.S. $1 000 000 to the chartered banks. We assume here also that the Canadian dollar is set at par with the U.S. dollar.

The chartered banks pay for the U.S. dollars by having their accounts at the Bank of Canada lowered by Cdn $1 000 000. Hence the cash reserves of the chartered banks fall. They reduce their lending activities and the money supply consequently falls. You should work through the effect on the domestic money supply of a purchase of U.S. dollars by the Bank of Canada. Note how closely the purchase and sale of foreign currency on the open market resemble the central bank's open market operations.

> **A sale of foreign currency on the open market by the Bank of Canada reduces the domestic money supply. A purchase of foreign currency on the open market by the Bank of Canada increases the domestic money supply.**

MONETARY POLICY AND EXCHANGE RATES

In previous chapters, when we discussed monetary policy, we ignored the foreign sector. We must now examine the international repercussions of monetary policy.

FLEXIBLE EXCHANGE RATES

Learning Objective 6:
discuss the international
repercussions of mone-
tary and fiscal policies

Let us assume that the Canadian economy is experiencing a recession. To stimulate economic activity, the Bank of Canada implements an expansionary monetary policy, increasing the money supply from S to S_1 as shown in Figure 35.6. As the money supply increases, the rate of interest falls from r_1 to r_0 as shown in Figure 35.6. The fall in the rate of interest will stimulate aggregate expenditure and income, which will cause the demand for money to increase as shown in Figure 35.6 by the shift in the demand for money curve from D to D_1. As a result, the rate of interest rises from r_0 to r, which is lower than the initial level.

Since Canadian interest rates are now lower than they were before the expansionary monetary policy, foreigners will find Canadian securities less attractive than they were previously. Funds will flow out of Canada in search of higher yields elsewhere. The demand for Canadian dollars by foreigners will thus decrease and the supply of Canadian currency will increase. The value of the Canadian currency will fall. As a result, Canadian goods will be relatively less expensive to foreigners, and foreign goods more expen-

FIGURE 35.6

Monetary policy under flexible exchange rates.

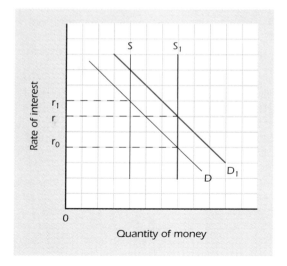

sive to Canadians. Our exports will rise and our imports will fall. The (X – M) component of aggregate expenditure will rise, hence aggregate expenditure will rise.

If a country is on a flexible exchange rate regime, the effects of monetary policy will be amplified by international repercussions.

FIXED EXCHANGE RATES

Consider now what happens when the money supply is increased under a fixed exchange rate system. As in the case of a flexible exchange rate regime, an increase in the money supply causes interest rates to fall. This fall in interest rates, however, will not result in a fall in the value of the Canadian dollar. The Bank of Canada will enter the foreign exchange market and sell foreign currency. As noted above, this sale of foreign currency by the Bank of Canada reduces the money supply. Thus, the net increase in the money supply will be less than the initial increase. Furthermore, the expansionary monetary policy may push the domestic price level upward, resulting in a fall in our exports and an increase in our imports. Moreover, an expansionary monetary policy will likely increase domestic output and income and thus increase imports. Hence, the (X – M) component of aggregate expenditure falls, resulting in a fall in aggregate expenditure.

If a country is on a fixed exchange rate regime, the effects of monetary policy will be dampened by international repercussions.

FISCAL POLICY AND EXCHANGE RATES

Learning Objective 6:
discuss the international repercussions of monetary and fiscal policies

FLEXIBLE EXCHANGE RATES

Assume again that the government adopts an expansionary fiscal policy, increasing government spending, in an attempt to move the economy towards full employment. The increase in aggregate expenditure and net domestic income will cause the demand for money to increase, pushing interest rates up. As interest rates rise, there will be some crowding out so that the expansionary impact of the fiscal policy will be lessened. But what about the international repercussions? Let us investigate.

GLOBAL   PERSPECTIVE

The Current Account Balance: Is Canada Unique?

While Canada has a positive balance in its merchandise trade with the rest of the world, it has a negative balance in its current account. The positive merchandise trade balance is more than offset by the negative balance in its non-merchandise international transactions. In fact, Canada usually has a negative balance on its current account.

As can be seen from the following table, Japan, France, and Italy all had positive current account balances over the five-year period from 1993 to 1997. On the other hand, the U.S.A., Germany, and the U.K. all had negative balances on their current accounts. During this period, Canada had negative balances in all but one year, 1996, when it had a positive balance of $100 million.

To get a perspective of the relative magnitudes of the current account balances, we express that balance as a percentage of GDP for each country, and take the average from 1988 to 1997. The information is presented in the accompanying graph. In these terms, Japan had the largest surplus, representing 2.2% of its GDP over the period. Germany was next with a surplus of 0.6% of GDP. At the other extreme, Canada had a current account deficit representing an average of 2.3% of its GDP from 1988 to 1997. The deficit of the U.S. averaged 1.7% of its GDP, and was the third largest of the seven countries.

Current account balance in seven industrial countries, 1993-97 (U.S. $ billion)

Year	Canada	U.S.A.	Japan	Germany	France	Italy	U.K.
1993	−22.3	−99.9	132.0	−13.5	9.2	11.3	−16.7
1994	−16.2	−148.4	130.6	−19.7	8.0	15.1	−2.9
1995	−8.2	−148.2	111.4	−21.0	18.2	27.3	−8.9
1996	0.1	−149.5	66.7	−18.8	22.5	28.8	−3.5
1997	−1.0	−149.8	70.7	−17.4	24.8	24.1	−3.5

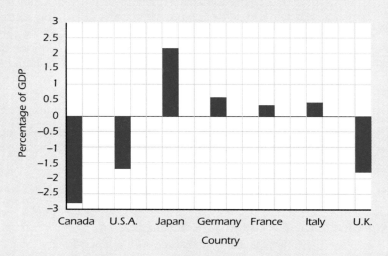

Source of table and figure: International Monetary Fund, *World Economic Outlook*, May 1998: 204.

The increase in domestic interest rates will cause capital funds to flow into the country to profit from higher yields. There will be an increase in demand for Canadian dollars and an increase in the supply of foreign currency. This will cause an increase in the value of the Canadian dollar. Canadian exports will fall as Canadian goods will now be relatively more expensive to foreigners. Our imports will also tend to rise as foreign goods will now be relatively less expensive. The (X – M) component of aggregate expenditure will fall; hence the impact of the fiscal policy will be lessened.

If a country is on a flexible exchange rate regime, the effects of fiscal policy will be dampened by international repercussions.

FIXED EXCHANGE RATES

Assume that the country is on a fixed exchange rate system and that the government increases its spending to reduce unemployment. Higher interest rates will result, and the demand for Canadian dollars by foreigners will rise. This increase in demand will put upward pressure on the value of the Canadian dollar. However, to maintain the fixed value, the Bank of Canada will enter the foreign exchange market and purchase foreign currency. This purchase of foreign currency will result in an increase in the domestic money supply, as discussed earlier. This increase in the money supply actually prevents interest rates from rising as high as they otherwise would, and thus reinforce the effect of the expansionary fiscal policy.

If a country is on a fixed exchange rate regime, the effects of fiscal policy will be amplified by international repercussions.

CHAPTER SUMMARY

1. The balance of payments is a record of all economic transactions made with the rest of the world.

2. The current account contains all sales and purchases of currently produced goods and services to or from the rest of the world.

3. The capital account contains long-term and short-term capital movements and changes in official reserves.

4. Long-term capital flows include direct investment and portfolio investment. Short-term capital flows include financial assets whose term to maturity is less than one year.

5. Official reserves consist of gold, American dollars, other foreign currencies, and special drawing rights.

6. The exchange rate is the rate at which one country's currency exchanges for that of another country. A country's exchange rate may be flexible or fixed. A country may also operate a "dirty float."

7. By changing its exchange rate, a country can help to regulate economic activity.

8. Inflation in an economy operating under a flexible exchange rate system will cause a depreciation of the country's currency.

9. Under a flexible exchange rate system, monetary policy is released to be used as a stabilization device. A flexible exchange rate system also helps to insulate a country against foreign inflation.

10. A flexible exchange rate may adversely affect international trade because of the uncertainty associated with it. A flexible exchange rate may also lead to reduced net domestic income and employment.

11. A fixed exchange rate encourages international trade because it is certain. However, it may force a country to adopt a monetary policy that reduces employment and slows economic growth.

12. Foreign exchange transactions not involving the central bank have no effect on the domestic money supply. Under a fixed exchange rate regime, however, in which the central bank is involved, foreign exchange transactions affect the money supply in a similar manner to open market operations.

13. Under a flexible exchange rate system, international repercussions magnify the effects of monetary policy. Under a fixed exchange rate system, international repercussions dampen the effects of monetary policy.

14. Under a flexible exchange rate system, international repercussions dampen the effects of fiscal policy. Under a fixed exchange rate system, international repercussions amplify the effects of fiscal policy.

TERMS FOR REVIEW

balance of payments (603)
current account (603)
non-merchandise transactions
   (invisibles) (603)
balance of merchandise (visible)
   trade (603)
balance of trade (603)
current account balance (603)
balance of trade deficit (603)
balance of trade surplus (603)
capital account (604)
direct foreign investment (604)

portfolio foreign investment (604)
official reserves (605)
exchange rate (605)
flexible exchange rate (605)
appreciation (606)
depreciation (606)
fixed exchange rate (607)
revaluation (607)
devaluation (607)
managed flexible exchange rate
   (dirty float) (607)

QUESTIONS FOR REVIEW AND DISCUSSION

1. What is the difference between balance of payments and balance of trade? (General)

2. Into which two main categories is the balance of payments divided? What does each section contain? (L.O.1)

3. What is the difference between a balance of trade deficit and a current account deficit? (L.O.1)

4. Explain how a country may use its exchange rate to improve its balance of trade. (L.O.2)

5. What are the advantages and disadvantages of a flexible exchange rate regime? (L.O.2)

6. What are the advantages and disadvantages of fixed exchange rates? (L.O.2)

7. How do foreign exchange transactions affect the money supply under a fixed exchange rate system? Would your answer be different for a regime of flexible exchange rates? (L.O.5)

8. How do international repercussions affect monetary policy under a flexible exchange rate system? (L.O.6)

9. How do international repercussions affect fiscal policy under a fixed exchange rate system? (L.O.6)

PROBLEMS AND EXERCISES

1. How would each of the following transactions be recorded in Canada's balance of payments? (L.O.1)

   (a) a shipment of wheat from Canada to Russia

   (b) an expenditure of $2000 by a Canadian couple vacationing on a West Indian island

   (c) the establishment of a manufacturing company in Canada by a group of American investors

   (d) the transfer of a certain sum of money from a landed immigrant in Canada to a relative in a foreign country

2. Table 35.3 shows the quantities of Canadian dollars demanded and supplied at various prices of Canadian dollars. (L.O.2)

TABLE 35.3

Demand and supply for Canadian dollars.

Price of Cnd S in U.S. $	Quantity of Cnd S demanded	Quantity of Cnd S supplied
1.10	100	180
1.05	110	170
1.00	120	160
.95	130	150
.90	140	140
.85	150	130
.80	160	120
.75	170	110
.70	180	100

   (a) Plot the demand and supply curves on a graph.

   (b) What is the equilibrium exchange rate?

   (c) Show the effect of an increase in income in Canada that results in an increase in imports of goods and services from the United States.

   (d) An increase in income in Canada results in an increase in imports of goods and services from the United States. On your graph, show the effect of this increase in imports on the equilibrium exchange rate.

3. Describe the flow of money between countries when a Canadian exporter sells communication equipment to a U.S. firm for Cdn $50 000. (Assume that Cdn $1 = U.S. $1).
   (General)

Internet Sites

http://www.statcan.ca

You have probably visited the Statistics Canada site previously. Here is where you find numerous economic and social data on Canadian economy and society.

http://www.bank-banque-canada.ca

You have probably visited this site also. It is the Bank of Canada site which contains useful information about the Bank's functions and our money supply.

INTERNET EXERCISES

1   a) Go to the Statistics Canada site.

b) Click on *Canadian statistics.*

c) Click on *The Economy in Detail.*

d) Click on *Economic conditions.*

e) Click on *Balance of international payments.*

What is the current account balance for the latest available year?

2   a) Go to the Bank of Canada Site.

b) Click on *Exchange Rate.*

c) Click on *convert on-line.*

d) Use the on-line converter to do the following:

i)   convert Cdn $500 to U.S. $

ii) convert 500 pounds (sterling) to Cdn $.

CHAPTER

ECONOMIC POLICY IN AN OPEN ECONOMY

Learning Objectives

After studying this chapter, you should be able to:

1 define the trade deficit and the trade surplus

2 discuss the determinants of net exports

3 explain how changes in net exports affect aggregate expenditure and equilibrium income

4 understand the policy implications of the relationship between net exports and aggregate expenditure

5 understand internal and external balance

6 explain how fiscal policy and exchange rate policy can be used for overall balance

7 explain how fiscal policy and monetary policy can be used for overall balance

8 discuss Canada's position in the international arena

Experience has shown, however, that purely unilateral action in regard to exchange rates is not merely undesirable but that it cannot be made effective.

Ragnar Nurkse, *Essays in International Finance*

INTRODUCTION

Our study of the macroeconomy has been focused mainly on internal balance. The Canadian economy is an open economy, and your understanding of how it functions will be greatly enhanced if you know more about the foreign sector, and how it interacts with the rest of the economy. In the previous chapter, you studied balance of payments and exchange rates, and the effects of international repercussions on monetary and fiscal policies.

In this chapter, we shall pay some attention to the final component of aggregate expenditure, that is, (X-M) or net exports. We shall look at the determinants of net exports, consider the relationship between net exports and aggregate expenditure, and policy implications. We shall then study the intricate interrelationship between internal and external equilibrium, and you will understand why a combination of policies will often be necessary to achieve overall balance.

RELATIONSHIP BETWEEN EXPORTS AND IMPORTS

Learning Objective 1:
define the trade deficit and the trade surplus

If a trade surplus exists, X – M is positive. With a trade deficit, X – M is negative.

The advantages of international trade are discussed in detail in Chapter 19 of the microeconomic section of this book. International trade can be mutually beneficial to all trading countries. It is not necessarily a zero-sum game. All countries can gain from international trade, but there may be problems if there is a large and persistent divergence between exports and imports. A **trade surplus** exists when exports exceed imports. A **trade deficit** exists when exports fall short of imports.

Most people regard a trade surplus as good for a country and a trade deficit as bad. But a large and persistent trade surplus may have harmful effects. For example, if our exports consistently exceed our imports, the excessive demand for Canadian goods by foreigners may result in an increase in the average level of prices in Canada.

Canada has generally had a surplus in its trade of goods and services with the rest of the world, but it has had a deficit from time to time. A severe recession in 1982 resulted in a sharp decline in imports, and opened up the trade surplus. The deficit that started about 1989 grew in 1990 and in 1991. The Free Trade Agreement signed by Canada and the United States in 1987, and a wider trade agreement — the North American Free Trade Agreement (NAFTA), that came into effect in January 1994 — have increased the volume of trade between Canada and the other North American economies. Some who worry about the trade deficit argue that Canada should maintain a policy of protectionism to restrict the flow of imports. Such a policy is referred to as a **beggar-thy-neighbour policy**, since the purpose is to improve one's economy at the expense of others. This view, however, is not supported by most economists.

Beggar-thy-neighbour is a policy of trade protectionism that restricts the flow of imports.

THE DETERMINANTS OF NET EXPORTS

Learning Objective 2:
discuss the determinants of net exports

Variations in net exports cannot be understood without a knowledge of the factors that influence exports and imports. The amount of goods and services that Canada is able to sell abroad depends on (1) the prices of our goods relative to prices in other countries, (2) foreigners' incomes, and (3) foreigners' tastes and preferences for Canadian goods and services. The amount of goods that Canadians buy from abroad depends on (1) the prices of those goods relative to Canadian prices, (2) income in Canada, and (3) Canadian tastes and preferences for foreign goods. We shall discuss each of these determinants below.

RELATIVE PRICES

Changes in relative prices affect net exports.

A fall in the prices of foreign goods relative to the prices of Canadian goods will cause Canadians to buy more foreign goods, other things being equal. Also, because Canadian goods will be more expensive relative to foreign goods, Canadian exports will tend to decline. Since exports will fall and imports will rise, $(X - M)$ will fall.

The exchange rate is the value of one country's currency in terms of another's.

Changes in exchange rates affect net exports.

The **exchange rate** measures the value of a country's currency in terms of another country's currency. Thus, the exchange rate between the Canadian dollar and the U.S. dollar may be Cdn $1.00 = U.S. $0.73. When the exchange rate changes, the prices of foreign goods also change. For example, if the value of the Canadian dollar were to fall from U.S. $0.73 to U.S. $0.70, then American goods would become more expensive to Canadians. Of course, this means also that Canadian goods would become less expensive to Americans. Hence, changes in exchange rates affect relative prices and thus net exports.

The relative rate of inflation affects net exports.

If the rate of inflation in Canada is higher than that in the United States, then Canadian goods will become relatively more expensive than U.S. goods, and Canadians will tend to purchase more U.S. goods. At the same time, Americans will tend to purchase fewer Canadian goods. Higher inflation in the United States relative to that in Canada will have the opposite effect. Hence, the rate of inflation affects relative prices, and thus net exports.

PROBLEM SOLVING 36-1

Why might a fall in the value of the Canadian dollar in terms of U.S. funds reduce cross-border shopping by Canadians?

RELATIVE INCOME

Changes in relative income affect net exports.

A rise in income in Canada will tend to increase imports, while a fall in income will tend to reduce imports. Similarly, a rise in incomes in foreign countries will increase the demand for Canadian goods by foreigners, while lower incomes abroad will reduce the demand for Canadian goods. Note that if incomes rise at home and abroad to the same extent, then our exports and our imports will tend to rise together, as foreigners buy more from us, and we buy more from them.

Let us see how an increase in incomes abroad will affect net exports. The increase in foreign incomes will increase Canadian exports as foreigners will buy more Canadian goods. The effect of a fall in foreign incomes is left as an exercise for the student.

TASTES AND PREFERENCES

A change in tastes affects net exports.

If Canadians can succeed in increasing foreign tastes for Canadian goods, then Canadian exports will increase, and this will increase net exports. Suppose Canadian manufacturers are able to convince foreign consumers of the superior quality of Canadian-made goods; then preference for Canadian goods will increase. If a change in tastes and preferences for Canadian goods by foreign consumers results in an increase in Canadian exports, then net exports will increase. If Canadian tastes change in favour of foreign-made goods, then the level of imports into Canada will rise at each level of income, and net exports will fall.

NET EXPORTS AND AGGREGATE EXPENDITURE

In the previous section, we examined the factors that will affect net exports. In this section, we shall study how changes in net exports affect aggregate expenditure and equilibrium income in the product market.

Learning Objective 3: explain how changes in net exports affect aggregate expenditure and equilibrium income

THE EFFECT OF NET EXPORTS

In a **closed economy**, there is no foreign trade; hence, both exports (X) and imports (M) are zero. In an open economy however, we must consider the effects of foreign trade — we must consider net exports. Figure 36.1 illustrates the effect of adding the foreign sector.

Without foreign trade, the product market is in equilibrium at a level of income denoted by Y, where planned aggregate expenditure, AE (C + I + G), equals aggregate output, AO. With foreign trade, aggregate expenditure becomes

$$C + I + G + (X - M)$$

Figure 36.1 assumes that $(X - M) > 0$, hence AE rises. The equilibrium level of income rises from Y to Y_1. If we assume that $(X - M) < 0$, then AE would fall, and the aggregate expenditure line would shift down as depicted in Figure 36.2. The equilibrium level of income would fall from Y to Y_0.

FIGURE 36.1

The effect of net exports.

There is no foreign trade in a closed economy.

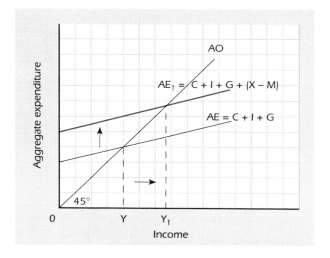

FIGURE 36.2

Effect of net exports.

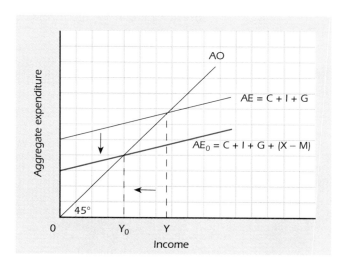

EFFECTS OF CHANGES IN NET EXPORTS

Net exports may change as a result of changes in exports or changes in imports. Let us assume that net exports increase as a result of an increase in exports resulting from an increase in incomes abroad relative to income at home. Figure 36.3 illustrates the situation.

FIGURE 36.3

Effect of an increase in exports.

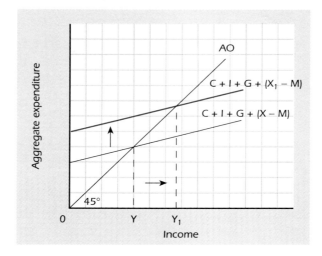

An increase in net exports increases AE and equilibrium income.

The initial AE line is $C + I + G + (X - M)$. Because of the increase in exports, $(X - M)$ increases, and the AE line shifts up to $C + I + G + (X_1 - M)$. As a result, the level of income rises from Y to Y_1. It can easily be seen that a fall in exports would result in a reduction in the equilibrium level of income.

If net exports change because of a change in imports, how will AE and equilibrium income be affected? Let us assume that an increase in the preference for foreign goods results in an increase in imports into Canada, from M to M_1. Net exports would fall, and the AE line would shift downward as shown in Figure 36.4. The equilibrium level of income would fall from Y to Y_0.

FIGURE 36.4

Effect of an increase in exports.

An increase in imports reduces AE and the equilibrium level of income.

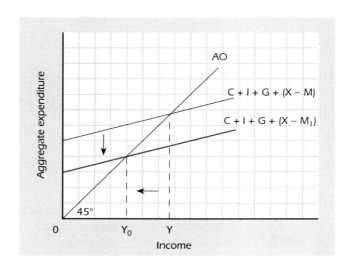

POLICY IMPLICATIONS

Learning Objective 4: understand the policy implications of the relationship between net exports and aggregate expenditure

The analysis that we have done so far suggests that macroeconomic policy may be used to influence net exports and hence aggregate expenditure. Suppose the government wants to stimulate economic activity by increasing AE. We have seen that it may do so by expansionary fiscal policy, but it may also stimulate economic activity by lowering the external value of the Canadian dollar. The effect of such a policy is illustrated in Figure 36.5.

FIGURE 36.5

The effect of a fall in the external value of the dollar.

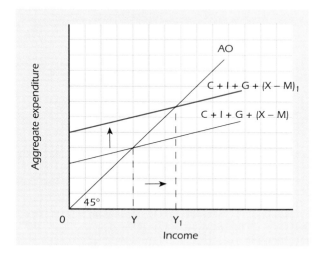

Canadians would find foreign goods relatively more expensive and would therefore reduce their purchases of foreign goods. Foreigners would find Canadian goods relatively less expensive and would therefore increase their purchases of Canadian goods. Thus, exports would increase while imports would decrease, resulting in an increase in net exports. This increase in net exports will shift the AE curve upward and increase the equilibrium level of income from Y to Y_1.

INTERNAL AND EXTERNAL BALANCE

Learning Objective 5: understand internal and external balance

INTERNAL BALANCE

You will recall that we defined macroeconomic equilibrium as the equality of desired aggregate expenditure and aggregate output, or alternatively, as the intersection of the aggregate demand and aggregate supply curves. You will recall also that this equilibrium can occur at any level of employment. If equilibrium occurs at less than full employment, economic policy may be used to move the economy to full employment. If equilibrium occurs at over-full employment (i.e., with inflation), economic policy may be used to eliminate the inflationary pressures. When the economy achieves equilibrium at full employment without inflation, we say that it has achieved **internal balance**, defined as full-employment equilibrium without inflation.

Internal balance occurs when AE equals AO at full employment.

EXTERNAL AND OVERALL BALANCE

External balance is equilibrium in the foreign exchange market.

A combination of policies may be required to achieve overall balance.

External balance is achieved when the foreign exchange market is in equilibrium; that is, when the quantity of foreign exchange demanded is equal to the quantity supplied. Overall balance is attained with the simultaneous achievement of internal and external balance.

GLOBAL PERSPECTIVE

The Export Sector: An International View

The globalization of economic activity is a reality. The degree of economic interaction between national economies has grown at a rapid pace, and nations now recognize their economic interdependence. In this chapter, we concentrated on the foreign sector of the Canadian economy. Canada exports about one quarter of the total value of the goods and services that it produces. How does Canada compare with other industrial countries in this regard?

When Canada is compared with the United States, for example, we find that Canada exports a much larger proportion of its GDP. As the accompanying figure shows, Canada exports a larger percentage of its GDP than does any other G-7 country: over 34% of its GDP. Germany also exports a sizable proportion (27%) of its GDP. On the other hand, the U.S. exports only 10% and Japan only 11.5% of their GDPs. The relevant figures for the G-7 countries are shown on the graph.

When we include five European countries, Belgium, Netherlands, Austria, Norway, and Sweden, we see that they export a larger percentage of their GDP than does Canada. Belgium's exports-to-GDP ratio was highest at 90.9%. The U.S.A. was lowest at 10.1%. Canada's position among the 12 countries selected can easily be determined from the graph. The data are for the year 1997.

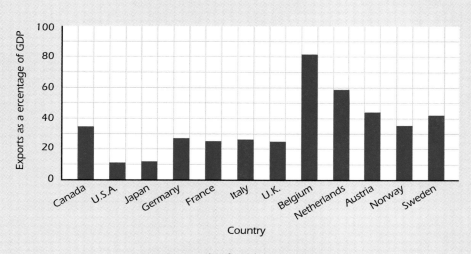

Source: Base on data from the OECD Web page.

Quite often, internal balance and external balance are considered independently. However, an economic policy designed to achieve internal balance will affect external balance. For example, the use of fiscal policy will affect both internal and external balance. Indeed, a combination of policies may be necessary to achieve internal and external balance simultaneously.

FISCAL POLICY AND EXCHANGE RATE POLICY FOR OVERALL BALANCE

Learning Objective 6:
fiscal policy and ex-
change rate policy for
overall balance

In order to facilitate our understanding of how fiscal policy and exchange rate policy may be used simultaneously to achieve overall balance, we shall develop the IB-EB model.

THE IB CURVE

Assume that the economy is in equilibrium at full employment without inflation. From this position, an increase in government spending will be inflationary and the internal balance will be disturbed. However, if the government lowers the price of foreign currency, that is, if it revalues the domestic currency, then our exports would fall and our imports would increase, resulting in a fall in the $(X - M)$ component of aggregate expenditure. The effect of the increase in government spending can thus be offset by a revaluation of our currency. Thus, various combinations of increases in government spending and reductions in the price of foreign currency can maintain internal balance. This is illustrated in Figure 36.6.

FIGURE 36.6

The IB curve.

Any point on the IB curve shows internal balance.

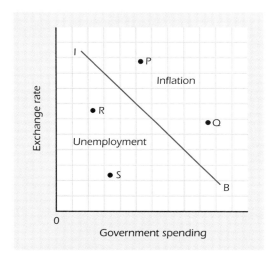

Points above the IB curve, such as P and Q, signify that government spending is too high for desired aggregate expenditure and aggregate output at full employment to be equal. Such points therefore represent inflation. On the other hand, points below the curve, such as R and S, represent unemployment.

The IB curve in Figure 36.6 is negatively sloped, depicting combinations of government spending and exchange rates that will maintain internal balance. We may refer to this curve as the internal balance (IB) curve. The **IB curve** or the **internal balance curve**, with government spending and exchange rate on the axes, shows combinations of government spending and exchange rates that maintain internal balance.

THE EB CURVE

Just as we have shown combinations of government spending and exchange rates that maintain internal balance, so too we can show combinations of these same two variables that maintain external balance. Assume that the foreign exchange market is in equilibrium. An increase in government spending will increase income. As income increases, imports will rise as some portion of the increase in income will be spent on foreign goods. The foreign exchange market will thus be in disequilibrium. To retain external balance, it will be necessary to stimulate exports. This may be achieved by increasing the price of foreign currency, that is, by devaluing our currency. Hence, various combinations of increases in government spending and exchange rates can maintain external balance. Figure 36.7 illustrates these combinations. The EB curve in Figure 36.7 is positively sloped, depicting combinations of government spending and exchange rates that will maintain external balance. Points above the EB curve, such as C and D, signify that the exchange rate will be too high, so that exports will exceed imports and an external surplus will emerge. Points below the EB curve, such as K and L, represent an external deficit. We may refer to this curve as the external balance (EB) curve. The **EB curve** or the **external balance curve**, with government spending and exchange rate on the axes, shows various combinations of government spending and exchange rates that maintain external balance.

FIGURE 36.7

The EB curve.

Any point on the EB curve shows external balance.

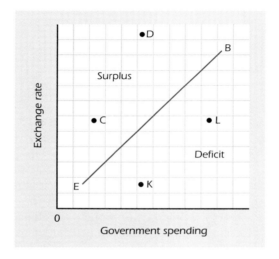

OVERALL BALANCE

We can now bring the IB curve and the EB curve together to illustrate graphically how a combination of policies — fiscal policy and exchange rate policy — may be used to achieve overall balance. In Figure 36.8, the IB curve and the EB curve intersect at E to give overall balance. **Overall balance** is achieved when government spending is G, and when the exchange rate is e. Figure 36.8 shows the following four sections:

>   Section I: Inflation and external deficit
>   Section II: Unemployment and external deficit
>   Section III: Unemployment and external surplus
>   Section IV: Inflation and external surplus

We can therefore use points in Figure 36.8 to represent the situation of the economy in terms of internal or external balance or imbalance. For example, an economy suffering from inflation and an external deficit would be at a point such as F in Section I. A point such as D represents unemployment and external surplus.

Let us assume now that the economy is experiencing inflation but that it has achieved external balance, as shown by point H in Figure 36.8. The objective of macroeconomic policy is to achieve overall balance as illustrated by point E. A reduction in government

FIGURE 36.8

Internal and external balance.

The intersection of the IB curve and the EB curve shows overall balance.

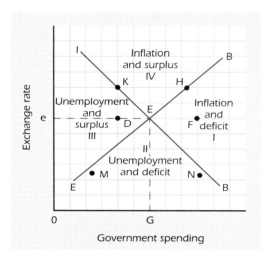

spending will achieve internal balance by moving the economy horizontally from H to K. The reduction in government spending reduces income and expenditure, including expenditure on imports, and thus produces an external surplus. A smaller reduction in government spending together with a fall in the price of foreign currency (that is, a revaluation of the domestic currency) could move the economy to the desired position at E.

Let us examine a case where the economy is experiencing internal and external imbalance. Specifically, let us assume that the economy is at N in Figure 36.8, with unemployment and an external deficit. A reduction in government spending coupled with an increase in the price of foreign currency (that is, a devaluation of the domestic currency), would be appropriate to achieve overall balance. At point M, however, the unemployment and external deficit require a different combination of policies. In this case, the appropriate policy combination would be an increase in government spending together with devaluation.

Rarely will a single policy achieve overall balance.

Will a combination of policies *always* be required to move the economy to overall balance? Not always. Consider point D in Section III, which illustrates unemployment and an external surplus. Clearly, an increase in government spending is all that is required to achieve overall balance.

FISCAL POLICY AND MONETARY POLICY FOR OVERALL BALANCE

Learning Objective 7:
fiscal policy and monetary policy for overall balance

In the previous section, we showed how internal and external balance may be achieved by using fiscal policy and exchange rate policy. In this section, we shall find out whether a combination of monetary policy and fiscal policy can be used to achieve the same objective. Figure 36.9 will help us with the analysis.

Like Figure 36.8, the level of government spending is measured along the horizontal axis. Unlike Figure 36.8, however, the vertical axis measures a monetary policy variable — the rate of interest. Recall that changes in the money supply result in changes in interest rates, and that the Bank of Canada uses the rate of interest as part of its monetary policy.

FIGURE 36.9

Monetary and fiscal
policy for overall
balance.

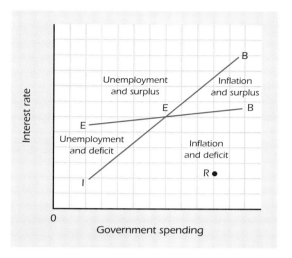

Assume that the economy is at full employment without inflation. A reduction in government spending will result in unemployment. This unemployment, however, can be offset by lower interest rates brought about by increases in the money supply. Combinations of lower government spending and lower interest rates can maintain internal balance. With interest rate and government spending on the axes, the IB curve is positively sloped as shown in Figure 36.9.

Let us now consider the external balance (EB) curve. Assume that the economy is in external balance. An increase in government spending will increase income, resulting in an increase in imports, and an external deficit. This increase in imports may be offset by higher interest rates brought about by reductions in the money supply. Higher interest rates reduce income, which in turn reduces spending, including expenditure on imports. The external balance curve is therefore positively sloped.

To avoid any unnecessary complications, we assume that the EB curve is flatter than the IB curve. The two curves intersect at E, where internal and external balance occur. Suppose the economy is operating at point R with inflation and an external deficit. To achieve internal and external balance, a combination of fiscal policy and monetary policy will be appropriate. By reducing government spending and by raising interest rates through reductions in the money supply, we can achieve our objective of internal and external balance.

External balance can be achieved without using exchange rate policy.

Different economic situations will require different combinations of monetary and fiscal policy to achieve internal and external balance. We can conclude that external balance can be achieved without using exchange rate policy. A combination of policies, however, will normally be required.

CANADA'S POSITION IN THE INTERNATIONAL ARENA

Learning Objective 8:
Canada's position in the international arena

Canada's proximity to the United States and the political relations between the two countries place Canada in a unique situation. Because most of Canada's international economic transactions are dealings with the United States, we shall discuss Canada's position in the international context by focusing on economic transactions between Canada and the United States.

U.S. investment in Canada is substantial. In 1997, Canada paid $58 649 million as investment income to foreigners, mainly Americans, in the form of interest and dividends. These huge payments to U.S. investors are largely responsible for Canada's current account deficit with the United States. In order to pay U.S. investors, Canadian firms must purchase U.S. dollars on the foreign exchange market. This purchase of U.S. currency pushes up the value of the U.S. dollar in terms of Canadian dollars. In other words, our continuous current account deficits with the United States exert downward pressure on the value of our dollar in terms of U.S. funds.

High interest rates are used to deal with Canada's current account deficit with the United States.

How does Canada respond to this problem? To prevent the value of the Canadian dollar from falling below a certain level, the Canadian government, through the Bank of Canada, has maintained domestic interest rates at higher levels than those prevailing in the United States. Higher Canadian interest rates will attract U.S. investment, since investors will favour Canadian securities with higher yields than U.S. securities. The increase in demand for Canadian dollars to purchase Canadian securities prevents the value of the Canadian dollar from falling below a certain level. In addition to maintaining relatively high interest rates to attract foreign investment, the Bank of Canada has also kept interest rates high in order to control inflation.

The Bank of Canada's high interest rate policy has been criticized from many quarters. Critics of the policy claim that lower interest rates would stimulate real investment in Canada and increase employment and net domestic income. They claim further that lower interest rates would result in a lower value of the Canadian dollar, which would stimulate exports and discourage imports. This, the critics contend, would help to relieve the almost chronic deficit in our current account with the United States.

PROBLEM SOLVING 36-2

In what sense could one argue that the levels of Canadian interest rates are determined externally, that is, in the United States?

CHAPTER SUMMARY

1. A trade surplus exists when exports exceed imports, and a trade deficit exists when exports fall short of imports.

2. Canada has generally had a surplus in its trade of goods and services, but it has had occasional deficits.

3. The determinants of net exports include relative prices, relative income, and tastes and preferences. The exchange rate and the relative rate of inflation affect relative prices.

4. An increase in net exports increases AE and raises the equilibrium level of income. A fall in net exports reduces AE and lowers the equilibrium level of income.

5. A government may attempt to influence economic activity by changing AE through manipulating (X – M).

6. Internal balance occurs when the economy is at full employment without inflation.

7. When there is neither an external deficit nor an external surplus, external balance is achieved.

8. The economy is in overall balance when internal balance and external balance are achieved.

9. All points along the IB curve represent positions of full employment without inflation.

10. All points along the EB curve represent positions of equilibrium in the foreign exchange market.

11. The IB-EB model is useful for illustrating economic situations and for showing the appropriate policy mix to achieve overall balance.

12. Combinations of fiscal policy and exchange rate policy may be used to achieve overall balance. Overall balance can also be achieved by using monetary and fiscal policies simultaneously.

13. Canada's perennial current account deficit with the United States is due largely to the magnitude of U.S. investment in Canada. The Bank of Canada has tried to deal with this problem by setting Canadian interest rates somewhat higher than U.S. interest rates.

TERMS FOR REVIEW

trade surplus (620)
trade deficit (620)
beggar-thy-neighbour policy (620)
exchange rate (621)
closed economy (622)

internal balance (624)
external balance (624)
IB curve (626)
EB curve (627)
overall balance (627)

QUESTIONS FOR REVIEW AND DISCUSSION

1. What is the net export function? What are the determinants of net exports? (L.O.2)

2. Explain how a change in exports will affect net exports. (L.O.2)

3. How will an increase in imports affect net exports? (L.O.2)

4. Explain why a fall in the exchange value of the Canadian dollar might stimulate economic activity in Canada. (L.O.3)

5. How does internal balance differ from equilibrium net domestic income? (L.O.5)

6. What does the internal balance (IB) curve show? (L.O.5)

7. Explain why the IB curve slopes downward when government spending and exchange rate are on the horizontal and vertical axes respectively. (L.O.5)

8. What does the external balance (EB) curve show? (L.O.5)

9. Explain why the external balance curve is upward sloping when government spending and exchange rate are on the horizontal and vertical axes respectively. (L.O.5)

10. Explain why the IB curve is positively sloped when government spending and interest rate are measured along the horizontal and vertical axes respectively. (L.O.5)

11. Why are interest rates in Canada usually higher than interest rates in the United States? (General)

12. What change would you expect in international capital flows if the Bank of Canada were to allow interest rates in Canada to fall below those prevailing in the United States? (L.O.8, General)

PROBLEMS AND EXERCISES

1. Suppose that Canadian producers manage to convince foreign consumers that Canadian goods are of superior quality. (L.O.2)

    (a) How would this affect Canada's net exports?

    (b) Draw a graph to show how AE and equilibrium income would be affected.

2. Show how each of the following events would affect Canada's net export function. (L.O.2)

   (a) Canadians develop a preference for foreign goods.

   (b) Foreign income increases relative to Canadian income.

   (c) The rate of inflation in Canada increases relative to inflation in other countries.

   (d) The exchange value of the Canadian dollar falls.

3. Draw diagrams to show how each of the events described in (a) to (d) of Question 2 will affect Canada's AE and the equilibrium level of income. (L.O.3)

4. Which of the following would prefer that the value of the Canadian dollar fall relative to the U.S. dollar. (General)

   (a) a family who has to pay tuition fees for a daughter studying at an American university

   (b) a Canadian manufacturer whose main market is the United States

   (c) importers of goods from the United States

   (d) a Canadian tourist planning to travel in the United States

   (e) an American tourist planning a vacation in Canada

   (f) a student who must purchase some books from an American supplier

5. Explain why an expansionary fiscal policy might lead to a trade deficit if exchange rates remain unchanged. (General)

6. Describe the economic situation illustrated by each of the points P, Q, R, S, and T in Figure 36.10. (L.O.5)

FIGURE 36.10

IB and EB Curves

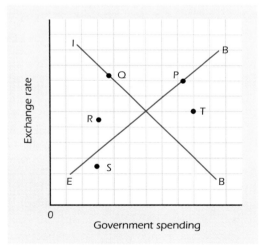

7. Referring to Figure 36.10, what policy or policies would be appropriate to achieve overall balance if the economy were at T? (L.O.6)

8. Referring to Figure 36.10, what policy or policies would be appropriate to achieve overall balance if the economy were at Q? (L.O.6)

9. With the help of a diagram like Figure 36.9, show how monetary policy and fiscal policy can be used to achieve internal and external balance when the economy is in external deficit with unemployment. (L.O.7)

Internet Site

http://www.statcan.ca
This is the Statistics Canada Web site that we have visited before.

INTERNET EXERCISE

1. Go the Statistics Canada Web site.
2. Click on *Canadian Statistics*.
3. Click on *Economy in Detail*.
4. Click on *International Trade*.
5. Compare Canada's exports and imports for 1997 in the Agricultural sector.
6. In what sector of the economy did Canada export the most in 1997?
7. In what sector of the economy did Canada import the most in 1997?

CHAPTER

ECONOMIC GROWTH AND DEVELOPMENT

Learning Objectives

After studying this chapter, you should be able to:

1 explain the meaning of economic growth

2 discuss the desirability of economic growth

3 give a brief account of economic growth in Canada

4 identify the determinants of economic growth

5 discuss measures to promote economic growth

6 discuss growth and regional disparities in Canada

7 understand the problem of economic development in less-developed countries

8 explain Canada's role in international development

If, however, a society improves its techniques too slowly, the old habits will persist and the rise in population will keep pace with the improvement in techniques, thus preventing any improvement in the standards of life.

Kenneth E. Boulding, *The Economics of Peace*

INTRODUCTION

Chapter 1 of this book mentioned economic growth as one of the major objectives of societies. This chapter will examine long-term economic growth. First, we shall briefly review the controversy over the desirability of rapid economic growth in Canada. Then we shall look at Canada's growth record. Also, we shall consider some measures to promote economic growth and those efforts already made by Canada in this regard. In addition to looking at national growth, we shall pay some attention to regional growth. Finally, we shall conclude the chapter with a brief discussion of problems surrounding growth and development in less-developed countries.

THE MEANING OF ECONOMIC GROWTH

Learning Objective 1:
explain the meaning of economic growth

There is a general feeling that economic growth is a good thing. News of the prospects of rapid economic growth in an economy inspires a feeling that good times are coming. News of no growth or of very little growth is received with much less enthusiasm and is viewed as an omen of difficult times. But what exactly do we mean by economic growth? One notion of economic growth is an increase in a country's real gross domestic product. If the real gross domestic product of a country was $100 million in 1985, and it increased steadily to $140 million in 1990, we may say that the country experienced economic growth between 1985 and 1990.

If a country experiences economic growth, we expect its citizens to be better off on the average. Economic growth increases the amount of goods and services that are available. However, if the population grows just as fast as the real gross domestic product, then the citizens will be no better off than before the growth period, despite the increase in real gross domestic product. Because of this fact, it is often necessary to modify the above definition of economic growth to take changes in population into account.

Economic growth is a steady increase in real GDP per capita over time.

Economic growth therefore focuses on changes in real output per capita. **Economic growth** refers to a sustained increase in a country's real gross domestic product per capita over time.

Growth rate is the rate of economic growth.

The term *economic growth* can also describe an increase in a country's productive capacity. This concept of economic growth is usually illustrated by an outward shift of the production possibility curve. Figure 37.1 shows this shift. The outward shift of the curve illustrates an increasing capacity to produce goods and services. The term **growth rate** — frequently used in discussions relating to a country's economic progress — refers to the rate of growth of a country's real gross domestic product.

FIGURE 37.1

Economic growth.

An outward shift of the production possibility curve illustrates economic growth.

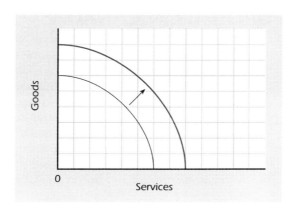

THE DESIRABILITY OF ECONOMIC GROWTH

Learning Objective 2: discuss the desirability of economic growth

Is economic growth desirable? In 1941, the population of Canada was 11 506 655. By 1981 it was over 24 000 000. This means that the population of Canada more than doubled in 40 years. Between 1985 and 1995, Canada's population increased by about 13%. If the rate of growth of real gross domestic product had fallen behind the rate of growth of the population over this period, the standard of living of Canadians would have fallen. But because the economy experienced a rate of growth that exceeded the rate of growth of the population, the standard of living has improved substantially over these years. Thus, in order to maintain our current living standards, our productive capacity must increase over time. And in order to improve our standard of living, our productive capacity must grow at a faster rate than the rate of increase in the population.

Economic growth increases our material well-being.

When an economy is growing, industries are expanding and new industries are being established. These new and expanding industries create new jobs. Hence, economic growth reduces unemployment. We can argue also that economic growth makes it easier for the government to redistribute income in order to reduce economic inequality among persons. Economic growth causes an increase in government revenues. With increased revenues, the government can provide more social services and more opportunities for the less fortunate.

> **Economic growth enables us to maintain and improve our living standards. It also creates employment, and it can help to reduce economic inequality among the population.**

The benefits of economic growth are truly impressive. This fact explains why the objective of economic growth is so ardently pursued by so many countries. The advantages of economic growth, however, should not obscure the reality that economic growth has costs as well as benefits. In fact, recognition of these costs has led to several attacks on the objective of rapid economic growth. Those who oppose further economic growth argue that it causes social problems such as traffic congestion, the destruction of the countryside, and overcrowding in our cities. The present serious pollution problem, according to these critics, results directly from rapid economic growth. As long as we pursue the goal of more economic growth, they conclude, we will continue to damage the environment.

Economic growth involves a cost in terms of sacrificing present consumption.

Other economists argue that a greater output of goods and services will, in fact, not help us to achieve the good life. On the contrary, a greater real gross domestic product, they feel, can be achieved only by lowering current consumption — and by sacrificing leisure.

ECONOMIC GROWTH IN CANADA

Learning Objective 3: give a brief account of economic growth in Canada

In the 1840s, the economy of Canada was based primarily on agriculture and small crafts. Actually, the development of the Canadian economy followed a pattern of development characteristic of other colonies. The colonies exported raw materials and imported manufactured goods. Canada exported furs and lumber to England and imported manufactured goods mainly from England.

Three major shocks helped to transform the Canadian economy. The first was the Industrial Revolution in England. The Industrial Revolution produced changes that significantly reduced England's demand for Canadian products. The second shock was a worldwide economic recession, which started around 1870 and continued for the next twenty years or so. This forced Canada to look inward toward the home market rather than outward toward foreign markets. The third shock was Canada's national policy, which, with regard to land settlement, tariff protection, and transportation, was particularly favourable to the development of the domestic economy.

From the close of the nineteenth century to about 1920, Canada experienced rapid economic growth. The first decade of the twentieth century saw an increase of almost 80% in Canadian manufactured goods. During this period, Canada's manufacturing industries produced wood products, clothing, railway equipment, textiles, tobacco products, footwear, dairy products, and milled flour.

This period of expansion based on light manufacturing gave way to another period of expansion based on the exploitation of Canada's natural resources for the export market. After the Great Depression of the 1930s, Canada's most important industries were those that most directly exploited its natural resources. These were pulp and paper, asbestos, iron ore, copper, and aluminum. We should acknowledge also that these industries rely fairly heavily on electricity, with which Canada is very well endowed.

The Canadian economy has experienced long-term economic growth.

We saw earlier that the Canadian economy has experienced substantial economic growth since 1941, and that the standard of living of Canadians has improved considerably as a result. In 1970, the real gross domestic product (GDP) was $351 434 million when translated into 1992 prices. By 1997, this value had reached $798 183 million. Thus, in about 27 years, Canada increased its real output of goods and services by over 127%. The average annual rate of growth of real GDP from 1988 to 1997 was approximately 2.0%. Figure 37.2 shows the rate of growth of real output between 1990 and 1999.

The real output per capita is the GDP divided by the population.

In order to get a better idea of the economic progress which has occurred in Canada in recent times, let us take a look at the **real output per capita**. Along with the growth rate of real output, Figure 37.2 shows also the growth rate of real output per capita.

There have been times when the rate of growth of real per capita output exceeded 5%, and there have been times when it dropped below 0%. The average rate of growth of real per capita output from 1990 to 1999 was estimated at 0.7%. In Figure 37.2 you will notice that the growth rate of real output per capita is somewhat less than the growth rate of real output, reflecting the effect of population growth.

FIGURE 37.2

Growth rates of real GDP and real GDP per capita.

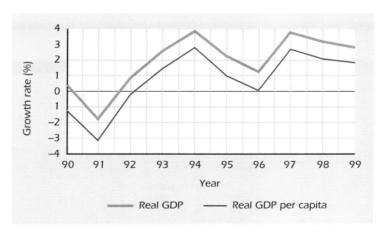

Source:International Monetray Fund, *World Economic Outlook,* May 1998: 146, 149.

DETERMINANTS OF ECONOMIC GROWTH

Learning Objective 4:
identify the determinants of economic growth

Economists still search actively for the factors that explain most fully how economies grow. Although no general agreement exists on the relative importance of these growth factors, the following are usually cited as contributors to a country's long-term economic growth:

1. the size of the labour force;
2. the quality of the labour force;
3. natural resources;
4. capital formation;
5. technological change.

We shall look at each of these factors in turn.

THE SIZE OF THE LABOUR FORCE

The size of a country's labour force determines to a large extent its rate of economic growth. Other things being equal, the larger the labour force, the greater the economy's real output of goods and services. Canada's labour force increased from 4 151 000 in 1931 to 15 354 000 in 1997. The rate of growth of the labour force is shown in Figure 37.3. The average annual rate of increase for the period from 1977 to 1997 was about 1.8%.

Labour must be combined with other productive factors to produce the economy's output. If the labour force increases while the other factors of production and technology remain constant, after a while, diminishing returns will set in. Thus, a given labour force may be too large or too small. The label we give to it depends on its effect on real output per worker. The size of the labour force that leads to the maximum real output per worker is the **optimal labour force**, given the other factors of production.

FIGURE 37.3

Growth rate of the labour force.

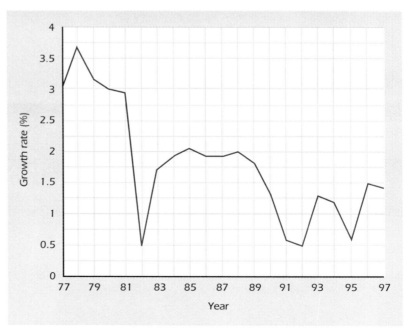

Source: Statistics Canada, *Canadian Economic Observer* (Cat. 11-210-XPNB, 1997-98: 32.

In Figure 37.4, a labour force less than 0L is too small to maximize real output per worker. A labour force greater than 0L is too large to maximize real output per worker. 0L is the optimal labour force since it maximizes output per worker. We should remember, though, that the optimal labour force is not constant. It changes continuously as the other factors of production and technology change.

FIGURE 37.4

The optimal labour force.

The optimal labour force is that which is consistent with maximum real output per worker.

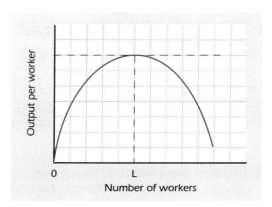

THE QUALITY OF THE LABOUR FORCE

To a large extent, the quality of the labour force determines economic growth. A highly skilled and well-trained labour force will doubtlessly contribute greatly to the amount of goods and services that an economy will be able to produce. The same is true of a healthy, energetic, and imaginative labour force. The educational level of the population 15 years and older is a good approximation of the quality of the Canadian labour force. Table 37.1 gives this information. Over 80% of the Canadian population 15 years and over has attained an education at or above the high school level.

TABLE 37.1

Educational attainment of the Canadian population 15 years and over, 1997.

Level	Population 15 years & over (000)
0-8 years	2 801
High school	4 430
Some post-secondary	2 159
Post-secondary certificate or diploma	6 450
University degree	3 332

Source: Statistics Canada, *Labour Force Update*, (Cat. 71-005-XPB), Spring 1999, p. 34.

Human capital includes the education, skills, and health of the labour force.

The other aspect of the duo that constitutes **human capital** is the state of health of the population. We can get some idea of the state of health of Canadians by looking at the medical facilities and health professionals available to the population. In each province, there are many hospitals with several thousand beds. The Canadian population is well served by highly qualified physicians and surgeons, and by other well-trained health practitioners.

NATURAL RESOURCES

The role of natural resources in economic growth is a controversial issue. The case of Japan is often used to support the argument that a country can achieve rapid economic growth without possessing an abundance of natural resources. But most experts would probably agree that a bountiful supply of natural resources helps enormously to achieve a high growth rate. Mineral and energy resources as well as fertile land contribute to economic growth. Canada is relatively well endowed with a variety of natural resources; and the natural resource sector has played and will continue to play a vital role in the country's economic growth.

CAPITAL ACCUMULATION

Most theories of economic growth have given a central role to capital formation. The greater the economy's stock of plants, equipment, and machinery, the greater its capacity to produce goods and services. Since investment increases an economy's stock of capital, we can expect the rate of investment to influence the rate of economic growth. But we must be careful not to conclude that increases in investment alone ensure rapid economic growth. Other factors must also be taken into consideration.

TECHNOLOGICAL CHANGE

The way in which the economy's resources combine to produce the output of goods and services obviously determines to a large extent the economy's productive capacity. A method of production (technology) that requires few inputs will lead to a larger output than will a technology that requires many inputs, other things being equal.

MEASURES TO PROMOTE ECONOMIC GROWTH

Learning Objective 5: discuss measures to promote economic growth

Our discussion of the forces likely to generate economic growth suggests some measures that may be taken to promote long-term economic growth. First, the government can encourage investment in human capital by providing scholarships, educational grants, and loans to students on easy terms. Financial support to colleges and universities will also help to improve the quality of human capital and thus promote economic growth. Canada, in fact, already has a program of financial assistance to students in the form of loans and grants. A number of government scholarships are also available, and the colleges and universities are heavily subsidized.

Second, the government can promote technological change by encouraging research and development. A number of private firms already undertake research and development. The government can provide incentives to these and other firms to increase their research and development activities. It can also finance some research and development projects of its own. In fact, the federal government already operates a number of programs to promote research in the physical, natural, and social sciences, the arts, and the humanities. These programs are channelled mainly through the Natural Sciences and Engineering Research Council, the Medical Research Council, and the Social Sciences and Humanities Research Council.

Third, the government can foster economic growth by encouraging investment. This can be achieved partly through interest rate policies (low interest rates tend to stimulate real investment), and partly through tax incentives for investment in plant and equipment.

GROWTH AND REGIONAL DISPARITIES

There is considerable income disparity among the various regions in Canada.

Canada's land area is vast. As one moves from one region to another, it is hardly surprising to find significant differences in living standards and economic fortunes. Economic growth and its benefits are not evenly distributed among the various regions. Table 37.2 gives some idea of the extent of regional disparity in Canada. For instance, aver-

TABLE 37.2	Region	Average family income
Average family income, 1996.	Atlantic Provinces	$45 235
	Quebec	50 935
	Ontario	62 614
	Prairie Provinces	55 039
	British Columbia	59 440
	Canada	56 629

Source: Statistics Canada, *Income Distribution by Size in Canada* (Cat. 13-207-XPB), December 1997: 64, 65.

Learning Objective 6:
discuss growth and regional disparities in Canada

age annual family income in Ontario is much higher than it is in Newfoundland, the difference being more than $19 000. Average family income figures, however, cloak the true extent of regional disparity, because they include federal-provincial fiscal transfer payments. These payments are designed to reduce regional income inequality. Without these transfers, regional differences would be even more pronounced.

CAUSES OF REGIONAL ECONOMIC DISPARITY

No single factor can explain income differentials in the various regions of Canada. A multiplicity of contributing factors exists, some of which we will discuss in the following paragraphs. Regional economic disparity is largely a matter of differences in productivity among the various regions. Among the factors that explain regional disparities are: labour quality, capital stock per worker, technology, and management. Let us briefly examine each of these.

Labour quality

Other things being equal, a region with good workers will be more productive than one with bad workers. One measure of the quality of the labour force is the level of educational attainment. Those regions with the highest levels of educational attainment are also those with the highest personal income per capita. It is true, however, that labour quality may be a cause as well as a result of regional economic disparity.

Capital stock per worker

The quantity of capital available to each worker in a region is likely to affect productivity, particularly if the capital is used efficiently. It is generally agreed that the difference in productivity among developed and underdeveloped countries results partly from the availability and efficient use of capital in the developed countries. The same seems to be true of regional differences in income and productivity.

Technology

Technology refers to the method of combining resources into the process of production. An improvement in technology allows either a greater output from given inputs, or the same output from fewer inputs. Other things being equal, those regions that are able to embrace new technology will tend to be more productive — and hence richer — than those that do not employ new technology or do so only on a limited scale.

Management

The availability of a certain technology is one thing. But its adoption may be quite another thing. If managers make poor decisions regarding the adoption of new technology, productivity may indeed suffer. Managerial prowess, though difficult to measure, seems to be concentrated in regions where income (and productivity) are relatively high.

MEASURES TO REDUCE REGIONAL ECONOMIC DISPARITY

The government has taken measures to reduce regional economic disparity, such as Industry Canada, equalization payments, and labour mobility programs.

Measures to reduce regional economic disparity in Canada have taken various forms. Among these are the establishment of Industry Canada, federal-provincial fiscal arrangements, and the labour mobility program.

Industry Canada

This department of the federal government, in collaboration with other federal departments, has established a wide variety of programs to assist in regional development. Programs such as The Atlantic Groundfish Strategy (TAGS) Program, designed to support displaced Atlantic fishers and fish-plant workers, and the Agricultural Employment Service (AES), designed to promote more effective human resource planning in the Quebec agricultural industry, fall into this category.

Equalization payments

By a negotiated agreement between the federal government and the provincial governments, the federal government makes **equalization payments** to some provinces. The purpose of these payments is to reduce the gap between "have" and "have-not" provinces. Such federal-provincial fiscal arrangements are instrumental in reducing regional economic disparity.

Labour mobility program

In 1965, the federal government introduced a **labour mobility program** designed to encourage unemployed workers to move to areas where jobs may be found. The program is administered by the federal Department of Employment and Immigration and involves travel grants for training, relocation grants, living allowances, and temporary employment grants. Although the program applies to all regions of Canada, it tends to benefit the regions with highest unemployment since workers tend to migrate from depressed to more affluent regions.

GROWTH AND DEVELOPMENT IN LESS-DEVELOPED COUNTRIES

Learning Objective 7: understand the problem of economic development in less-developed countries

The electronic media and the press have helped to make Canadians (and others) more aware of living conditions in less developed countries (LDCs). Whether the reports are on famine in Ethiopia, poverty in Haiti, or political and social problems in Somalia, the television camera has made us conscious of the misery being experienced by people in other parts of the world. The recent events in Eastern Europe, the struggle to cope with democracy in Russia, and the tragedy in what was formerly Yugoslavia, revealed not only the political but also the economic situation in those countries. In 1998, well over 50% of the world's population lived in circumstances of extreme suffering and fear.

In this section, we shall examine the main characteristics of underdeveloped countries, explain some reasons for their underdevelopment, and discuss measures to increase their rate of growth and development. Finally, we shall look at Canada's role in promoting development in underdeveloped countries.

DEFINITION OF A LESS-DEVELOPED COUNTRY

A less-developed country is one with a relatively low income per capita.

A **less-developed country** is a country that is poor in an absolute sense. But how poor must a country be to be considered less developed? The answer, of course, is subjective and arbitrary. For present purposes, we shall define a less-developed country as having an income per capita of below $5000. In Chapter 22, we noted the limitations of using income per capita as a measure of well-being. However, even after making allowances for statistical difficulties and for the large size of the subsistence sector (non-marketed goods and services) in the LDCs, a per capita income of less than $5000 would definitely indicate that the country is poor. Table 37.3 contains a partial list of countries and their incomes per capita, according to continent and region. Both developed and underdeveloped countries are included in the list so that you can see the vast difference in income between rich and poor countries.

It staggers the imagination that in 1996, the per capita income in Canada was 52 times that in India and 70 times that in Bangladesh! Even more alarming is the fact that the gap between advanced and less-developed countries is not narrowing. It is widening. Rapid developments in communication have allowed residents in the

TABLE 37.3

A list of selected countries with their per capita incomes, 1996, in U.S. dollars.

Country	Per capita income ($)	Country	Per capita income ($)
		AFRICA	
Algeria	1 534	Mauritius	3 800
Botswana	2 966	Nigeria	856
Cape Verde	985	Rwanda	241
Chad	171	Senegal	592
Ethiopia	101	Togo	329
Kenya	330	Tunisia	2 144
Malawi	222	Zambia	3 204
		NORTH AMERICA	
Canada	19 515	United States	27 420
	CARIBBEAN, LATIN AMERICA, and SOUTH AMERICA		
Antigua	8 484	Haiti	382
Argentina	8 446	Jamaica	2 196
Bolivia	939	Mexico	3 554
Brazil	4 648	Nicaragua	482
Colombia	2 325	Panama	3 029
El Salvador	1 791	Paraguay	1 947
Grenada	2 738	Trinidad	4 178
		Venezuela	3 017
		ASIA	
Bangladesh	279	Jordan	1 301
Hong Kong	24 902	Korea	10 698
India	375	Pakistan	504
Indonesia	1 018	Philippines	1 206
Israel	16 091	Singapore	27 693
Japan	36 658	Sri Lanka	771
		EUROPE	
Austria	28 218	Norway	36 293
Belgium	26 403	Portugal	10 923
France	26 374	Spain	14 641
Ireland	19 902	Sweden	28 546
Italy	21 219	Switzerland	40 746
Netherlands	25 426	United Kingdom	19 847
		Germany	28 728
		OCEANIA	
Australia	22 235	New Zealand	15 291
Fiji	2 639	Papua New Guinea	1 181
Kiribati	573	Tonga	1 819

Source: United Nations Web page, **www.un.org**, Statistics Division.

less-developed countries to become increasingly aware of living conditions in the developed countries. Expectations have risen as a result in less-developed countries. It is well known that the greater the expectations and the lower the standard of living, the greater are the chances of discontent and social unrest. The potential for social uprisings all over the world is tremendous.

CHARACTERISTICS OF LESS-DEVELOPED COUNTRIES

No two less-developed countries are exactly alike, yet they hold certain characteristics in common, as described in the following sections.

Low productivity

Needless to say, incomes are low in less-developed countries because productivity is low. We shall discuss the reasons for low productivity in a later section.

Predominance of agriculture

Agriculture employs a very large proportion of the labour force in less-developed countries. Agriculture also accounts for a significant share of the total output of goods and services.

Extremely uneven income distribution

In many less-developed countries, income is extremely unevenly distributed. It is not uncommon to find a few extremely rich people, while the vast majority lives in abject poverty.

Dualistic economy

In several less-developed countries, two types of economies exist side by side. On the one hand is a modern advanced market economy with fairly well-developed manufacturing and service industries catering to the few rich people or to the export market. On the other hand is a backward subsistence economy using outmoded methods of production, and experiencing very low productivity. Often, the picture presented is of two different worlds.

REASONS FOR UNDERDEVELOPMENT

It is important to understand that underdevelopment is a multidimensional problem. This discussion is merely an introduction to the problems of underdevelopment. Many factors are responsible for the low standards of living in less-developed countries. Among them are low capital formation, backward technology, lack of natural resources, and overpopulation. Let us look at each of these in turn.

LOW CAPITAL FORMATION

Lack of capital, limited natural resources, overpopulation, and outmoded technology impede economic growth.

Lack of capital is very noticeable in most less-developed countries. The vast amounts of plants, equipment, machinery, and tools that are taken for granted in an advanced country like Canada are woefully lacking in most less-developed countries. Why is there such a scarcity of capital there? One of the main reasons is that capital accumulates as a result of saving. Since incomes are so low in these countries, saving is difficult — or impossible.

BACKWARD TECHNOLOGY

The development and utilization of new technology have been crucial in the development and growth of the advanced countries. For a variety of reasons — some cultural, some political, and some economic — many less-developed countries have not been able to adopt new technology. Often, production methods are outmoded. Also, modern technology requires a skilled labour force. Without these skills, it is impossible to introduce new technology. And less-developed countries lack these skills. Even if less-developed countries had the necessary skills, however, the technologies that more-developed countries have adopted may not be appropriate to less-developed countries. This is so because capital in less-developed countries is scarce. New technologies are necessary — new technologies geared to the particular resources of each country wishing to raise its standard of living from poverty to economic prosperity.

LACK OF NATURAL RESOURCES

While a few less-developed countries are richly endowed with natural resources, many have hardly any natural resources at all. Some countries with oil have used oil revenues to achieve growth and development. On the other hand, some countries with very few natural resources — Japan, Switzerland, and Denmark, for example — have managed to secure respectable and enviable standards of living. Much seems to depend on how well available resources are used.

OVERPOPULATION

Recall that output per capita is total output divided by population. If total output increases more quickly than population does, then output per capita will increase. Many less-developed countries have increased their total output substantially, but have not reduced the rate of growth of their population. Consequently, output per capita has not increased. If, for example, total output increases by 4% while population increases by 4%, output per capita will not increase at all.

Why has population grown so fast in less-developed countries? One very important reason is that, over the past several years, modern medical care has been introduced into these countries. As a result, many diseases that formerly claimed many lives have been eradicated. The infant mortality rate has also seen a dramatic decline. Hence, a tremendous increase in population has occurred — a **population explosion**! Moreover, in many less-developed countries, children are viewed both as a source of labour and as a major source of support for their parents in old age. Consequently, large families are still common in many less-developed countries.

MEASURES TO PROMOTE GROWTH AND DEVELOPMENT

The transfer of labour from less-productive use in agriculture to more-productive industrial use promotes growth.

One step taken by less-developed countries to promote growth and development has been to remove surplus labour from the agricultural sector to more-productive use in other sectors. Another method has been to impose heavier taxes and apply the proceeds to development projects. However, these methods, though helpful, have often resulted in inadequate funds for development. Less-developed countries have depended quite heavily, therefore, on foreign aid from more-developed countries. One argument often used against foreign aid is that it has resulted in manipulation of the recipient country by the donor country.

Attempts have also been made to introduce modern technology into less-developed countries. This has been difficult. One area where modern technology has proved successful, however, is agriculture. The development of new types of seeds and fertilizers has resulted in spectacular yields in agriculture. The **green revolution** refers to dramatic increases in agricultural production resulting from the introduction of new types of seeds and improved farming methods in underdeveloped countries.

The green revolution refers to the tremendous increases in agricultural yields.

Curbing rapid population growth assists in raising output per capita.

Recognizing the negative effect of rapid population growth on economic growth and development, less-developed countries have been concentrating on birth control and family planning. Their efforts have been greatly aided by the World Health Organization (WHO). Steps to increase the quality of their labour resources through education and training have also been taken. These measures have helped to promote growth and development in less-developed countries. Without these measures, the plight of these countries would have been worse.

CANADA'S ROLE IN INTERNATIONAL DEVELOPMENT

Through CIDA, Canada takes an active role in world economic development.

Learning Objective 8: explain Canada's role in international development

The more-developed countries have rallied to the aid of less-developed countries. Help continues in the form of food, training, medical supplies, and other necessary items. Canada's official aid is channelled through a special agency called the **Canadian International Development Agency (CIDA)**. In 1992–93, Canada's **official development assistance** (ODA) under a variety of programs amounted to $3250.12 million, less than 0.5% of Canada's gross domestic product.

Although Canada's international assistance budget fell to $2220 million for 1995-96, Canada still stands tall among G-7 countries as far as international assistance is concerned. In terms of the percentage of GNP devoted to international assistance, Canada was second among G-7 countries in 1996, and third in terms of per capita GNP devoted to international assistance. Canada's aid is in the form of grants, and it has forgiven the official development assistance debt owed by the least developed countries.

We have seen that among G-7 countries, Canada is a leading donor of aid to developing countries. Among other donor countries, however, Canada occupied ninth place in 1996 in terms of official development assistance expressed as a percentage of GNP. Norway, Denmark, Sweden and the Netherlands are the world leaders in terms of the percentage of GNP devoted to official development assistance. Figure 37.5 gives us a clear picture of Canada's involvement in assistance to less developed countries, and allows us to compare Canada's contribution with those of other donor countries.

FIGURE 37.5

Assistance to less-developed countries

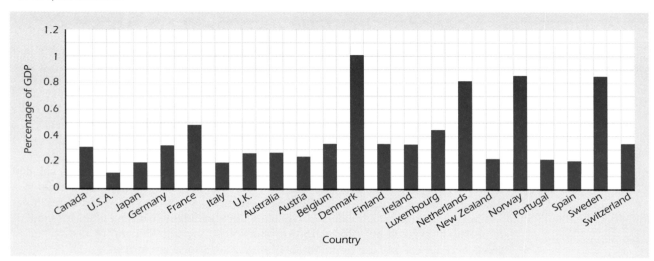

When we consider disaster assistance and humanitarian relief, Canada ranks first among G-7 countries in terms of the proportion of GNP dedicated to such assistance. In addition to official development assistance, donor countries also provide assistance to developing countries through non-governmental organizations (NGO). Among G-7 countries, Canada ranks first in providing assistance through non-governmental organizations.

In conclusion, Canada has been playing quite an active role in international development. Canada's efforts have helped to relieve world hunger and have contributed to the promotion of growth and development in less-developed countries. Most Canadians support these efforts in a substantive way. And it is well that we do. After all, we must not forget that "Tears Are Not Enough" and still, "We Are The World."

CHAPTER SUMMARY

1. Economic growth refers to an increase in real output per capita. The rate of growth measures the rate of increase of real output.

2. Economic growth increases the standard of living, creates employment for a growing population, and reduces inequality among individuals.

3. Among the costs of economic growth are increased pollution, traffic congestion, destruction of the beauty of the countryside, and a reduction in present consumption.

4. Canada has experienced substantial economic growth over the years. Output growth has exceeded population growth, thus output per capita has increased.

5. Among the factors contributing to economic growth are the growth of the labour force, the quality of the labour force, natural resources, capital formation, and technological change.

6. The optimal labour force is that size of labour force which maximizes real output per worker.

7. Measures to promote economic growth include encouraging investment in human capital, the promotion of technological change (through research and development), and investment in plants and equipment.

8. Significant differences in standards of living and economic fortunes exist among the various regions in Canada.

9. Differences in labour quality, capital stock per worker, technology, and management account for regional economic disparity.

10. The government has taken a number of measures to reduce regional economic disparity. These include the establishment of Industry Canada, certain federal-provincial fiscal arrangements, and a labour mobility program.

11. In general, less-developed countries are characterized by low productivity, predominance of agriculture, substantial income inequality, and dual economies.

12. Among the reasons for underdevelopment are low capital formation, backward and inappropriate technology, lack of natural resources, and overpopulation.

13. The less-developed countries have taken some steps towards improving their living standards. The more-developed countries are contributing to growth and development in the less-developed countries. Canada is taking an active role in that process.

TERMS FOR REVIEW

economic growth (635)
growth rate (635)
real output per capita (637)
optimal labour force (638)
human capital (639)
Industry Canada (642)
equalization payments (642)
labour mobility program (642)

less-developed country (LDC) (642)
dualistic economy (644)
population explosion (645)
green revolution (645)
Canadian International Development
  Agency (CIDA) (646)
Official Development Assistance
  (ODA) (646)

QUESTIONS FOR REVIEW AND DISCUSSION

1. Define economic growth. (L.O.1)

2. Many countries pursue economic growth as an important objective. Why? (L.O.2)

3. What are some objections to economic growth? (L.O.2)

4. What are some of the costs of economic growth? (L.O.2)

5. Describe economic growth in Canada over the past 20 years. (L.O.3)

6. What are the main factors that contribute to economic growth? (L.O.4)

7. What measures can a government take to promote long-term economic growth? (L.O.5)

8. What is the extent of economic disparity in Canada? (L.O.6)

9. Give reasons for economic disparity among the various regions in Canada. (L.O.6)

10. What measures are being taken to reduce regional economic disparity in Canada? (L.O.6)

11. What is a less-developed country? Name some characteristics of less-developed countries. (L.O.7)

12. What can be done to help relieve the problem of shortage of capital in less-developed countries? (L.O.7)

13. What is the "population explosion"? What has caused it? (L.O.7)

14. Briefly explain Canada's role in international development. (L.O.8)

15. What is the green revolution? What has caused it? (L.O.7)

PROBLEMS AND EXERCISES

1. A country decides to increase its savings in order to increase its stock of capital goods. With capital goods and consumer goods on the axes, illustrate the effect of this decision with the use of a production possibility graph. What lesson can be learned from this exercise about the growth process? (L.O.1,4)

2. Show that rapid population growth can contribute to as well as hinder economic growth. (L.O.4)

3. Capital accumulation is necessary for economic growth, but it involves a cost to society. What is this cost? (L.O.4)

4. Economic growth requires investment in physical capital as well as investment in human capital. Why? (L.O.4)

5. Why is an increase in real output through capital accumulation preferable to a similar increase in real output through population growth? (L.O.4)

6. Explain the economic pressure that might urge a family in an LDC to have more children than a family in an advanced economy. (General)

7. In a foreign policy statement, the Government of Canada stated that the "purpose of Canada's development assistance is to support sustainable development in order to reduce poverty and contribute to a more secure, equitable and prosperous world." Some people believe that Canada should concentrate its efforts and mobilize resources toward solving its own poverty problem at home, and get out of official development assistance. What are your views?

Internet Sites

http://www.un.org
The United Nations Web page provides information on world development and other issues of interest to economics students.

http://www.oecd.org
The Organization for Economic Cooperation and Development (OECD) is a useful source of economic statistics and other pertinent information.

http://www.acdi-cida.gc.ca
This is the Web page for the Canadian International Development Agency (CIDA) that handles Canada's official development assistance. The site contains useful information on Canada's role in international development assistance.

INTERNET EXERCISE

1. Go to the CIDA Web page
2. Type *ODA* in the search area.
3. Click on *How CIDA Spends ODA Program Funds*.
4. How much does CIDA spend on each of the following:
   a) Basic human needs
   b) Women in development
   c) Infrastructure
   d) Human rights
   e) Environment

VIDEO CASE

Managing the Surplus

The situation

Canadian federal finance ministers have had a great deal of experience in managing deficits and none in managing surpluses over the past 27 years; fiscal 1997-98 was the first time since 1969-70 that the federal budget was not in a deficit position. In 1995, Canada's huge, ever increasing public federal debt even attracted international attention. The federal government got to work to set its financial house in order. The growth of the debt had to be arrested, and this had to be done by raising taxes, reducing government spending, or a combination of both. The government opted to curtail its spending significantly, and this meant drastic cuts in services and in transfers to the provinces.

Now, after a few years of actually working towards eliminating the deficit, the federal government reported a surplus in 1997-98, and expects to have financial surpluses again in 1998-99 and in 1999-2000. This will be the first time in almost 50 years that the federal government will have three consecutive years of budget surpluses. The government has acknowledged that the next fiscal challenge is a reduction in the public debt. It plans to pay down the debt by about $9 billion by 2000-01.

Dealing with the surplus

Now that the deficit years are behind us, at least for now, what options are available to the government in terms of dealing with the surplus? What is to be done with the difference between the government's revenues and its expenditures? Some analysts have suggested too much government spending was cut and that funding to various programs should be restored, particularly to health care, education, and social services.

Another suggestion is to reduce taxes. The deficit was eliminated partly because government spending was reduced, while tax revenues did not fall in line with reductions in government expenditure. It is argued, therefore, that taxpayers should be allowed some tax relief now that the deficit no longer exists. But the absence of a deficit does not imply the absence of debt. Recognizing that a huge public debt still exists, many have argued that the difference between the government's revenues and its expenditure should be allocated in large part towards paying down the debt.

What Canadians think

In a survey to determine what Canadians felt about the use of the surplus, about 40% of respondents felt that the debt should be paid down, while about 37% felt that funding should be supplied to new programs or to those programs from which funding was cut. Canadians often complain of high taxes, so it was perhaps surprising that only about 21% of the respondents favoured tax cuts. The government plans to split the difference between debt reduction, tax relief for Canadians, and new spending initiatives in health, education, and social services.

QUESTIONS

1. Outline the main points in this case.

2. In 1993-94, the budget deficit was estimated at $42 billion. By 1997-98, the government reported a surplus. How did the government manage to accomplish this dramatic turnaround?

3. In your opinion, how should the government split the difference between its revenues and its expenditures? Give reasons for your choice.

Video Resource: "Splitting the Difference," *National Magazine* (February 1998).

APPENDIX I: STATISTICAL TABLES

TABLE S1

CANADA'S GDP BY EXPENDITURE — Current (nominal) $million

Year	Consumption	Investment	Government purchases	Exports	Imports	Statistical discrepancy	GDP	Percentage Change
1952	15 282	5 823	3 620	5 373	4 862	−66	25 170	13.0
1953	16 296	6 583	3 824	5 174	5 311	−171	26 395	4.9
1954	17 078	5 773	3 825	4 944	5 023	−66	26 531	0.5
1955	18 543	7 047	4 036	5 536	5 804	−108	29 250	10.2
1956	20 273	9 379	4 426	6 141	7 007	−310	32 902	12.5
1957	21 699	9 228	4 573	6 158	6 996	−195	34 467	4.8
1958	23 064	8 584	4 854	6 072	6 558	−327	35 689	3.5
1959	24 643	9 421	4 976	6 403	7 168	−398	37 877	6.1
1960	25 780	9 253	5 281	6 728	7 222	−372	39 448	4.1
1961	26 240	8 870	6 166	7 296	7 450	−236	40 886	3.6
1962	27 985	9 928	6 567	7 939	7 977	−34	44 408	8.6
1963	29 846	10 673	6 923	8 748	8 398	−114	47 678	7.4
1964	32 042	12 260	7 526	10 067	9 565	−139	52 191	9.5
1965	34 714	14 960	8 269	10 719	10 832	−307	57 523	10.2
1966	37 952	17 200	9 643	12 564	12 584	−387	64 388	11.9
1967	41 068	16 453	11 092	14 161	13 461	−249	69 064	7.3
1968	44 842	17 229	12 685	16 166	15 186	−318	75 418	9.2
1969	49 093	19 621	14 186	17 844	17 705	−13	83 026	10.1
1970	51 853	19 250	16 448	20 078	17 830	−683	89 116	7.3
1971	56 271	21 941	18 228	21 173	19 531	−792	97 290	9.2
1972	63 021	24 660	20 136	23 737	22 779	−146	108 629	11.7
1973	72 069	30 722	22 851	29 767	28 024	−13	127 372	17.3
1974	84 231	39 372	27 480	37 805	37 366	590	152 111	19.4
1975	97 566	43 213	33 266	38 954	41 362	−97	171 540	12.8
1976	111 500	49 037	38 274	44 252	45 279	140	197 924	15.4
1977	123 555	52 090	43 411	51 183	51 252	−1 108	217 879	10.1
1978	137 427	55 632	47 386	61 152	60 052	59	241 604	10.9
1979	153 390	68 428	52 288	75 073	73 279	198	276 096	14.3
1980	172 416	72 624	59 250	87 579	81 933	−45	309 891	12.2
1981	196 191	87 305	68 792	96 880	93 001	−173	355 994	14.9
1982	210 509	71 574	78 655	96 651	82 598	−349	374 442	5.2
1983	231 452	78 329	84 571	103 444	89 832	−2 247	405 717	8.4
1984	251 645	89 460	89 089	126 035	110 632	−862	444 735	9.6
1985	274 503	96 479	95 519	134 919	123 388	−44	477 988	7.5
1986	297 478	104 117	100 129	138 119	133 369	−808	505 666	5.8
1987	322 769	119 788	105 836	145 416	140 502	−1 710	551 597	9.1
1988	349 937	136 585	114 472	159 309	156 384	1 987	605 906	9.8
1989	378 933	149 682	124 108	163 903	166 079	201	650 748	7.4
1990	399 319	138 541	135 157	168 917	171 223	−1 244	669 467	2.9
1991	411 960	128 766	144 885	164 849	172 805	−1 178	676 477	1.0
1992	422 515	125 164	150 390	181 189	187 254	−1 882	690 122	2.0
1993	436 542	129 987	152 158	209 370	212 534	−2 668	712 855	3.3
1994	452 859	142 014	150 758	249 371	243 756	−1 193	750 053	5.2
1995	466 313	144 452	150 158	288 543	269 223	−216	780 027	4.0
1996	477 927	142 223	168 965	320 739	289 319	−210	820 323	2.7
1997	505 896	165 822	168 459	343 536	329 193	583	855 103	4.2

TABLE S2

CANADA'S GDP BY EXPENDITURE — Constant (real) 1986 $million to 1960, and (real) 1992 $million since 1961

Year	Consump-tion	Invest-ment	Government purchases	Exports	Imports	Statistical discrepancy	GDP	Percentage Change
1952	66 842	21 274	30 676	20 140	17 650	–317	118 627	8.3
1953	71 420	24 295	31 610	19 873	19 247	–860	124 526	5.0
1954	73 994	21 823	30 378	19 166	18 140	–311	123 163	–1.1
1955	80 277	25 815	31 045	20 607	20 652	–519	134 889	9.5
1956	86 413	31 886	31 774	22 259	24 115	–1 471	146 523	8.6
1957	89 538	31 486	31 261	22 445	23 396	–915	150 179	2.5
1958	92 779	29 924	32 205	22 248	21 578	–1 518	153 439	2.2
1959	97 943	31 771	31 931	23 086	23 795	–1 811	159 484	3.9
1960	101 455	31 276	32 703	24 114	23 738	–1 673	164 126	2.9
1961	134 009	31 628	36 968	27 532	23 931	– 485	220 816	3.1
1962	140 860	34 601	53 923	28 775	24 460	264	235 900	6.8
1963	146 731	36 031	55 760	31 347	24 874	–232	247 944	5.1
1964	154 507	39 707	58 702	35 648	28 038	–496	264 174	6.5
1965	163 548	46 215	61 356	37 253	31 820	–604	281 249	6.5
1966	171 654	50 722	66 789	42 333	36 099	–1 154	299 689	6.6
1967	178 057	47 540	72 649	46 762	38 070	–550	308 639	3.0
1968	185 983	49 407	77 397	52 736	42 014	–383	325 147	5.3
1969	195 023	54 079	80 760	56 984	47 446	906	342 468	5.3
1970	198 364	50 644	87 850	62 317	46 595	–1 845	351 434	2.6
1971	210 322	54 953	91 485	65 349	49 957	–2 325	370 859	5.5
1972	224 819	58 097	94 346	70 971	57 145	49	390 702	5.4
1973	240 443	65 584	98 782	78 534	65 509	1 073	418 797	7.2
1974	252 874	73 293	105 059	76 487	72 716	3 009	436 151	4.1
1975	263 377	71 541	112 092	71 547	71 168	1 758	445 813	2.2
1976	277 572	76 452	114 247	79 193	76 830	2 340	470 291	5.5
1977	285 897	76 552	119 590	85 363	77 599	–902	486 562	3.5
1978	295 598	78 027	121 700	94 616	82 016	426	506 413	4.1
1979	303 855	90 386	122 979	98 092	88 772	540	527 703	4.2
1980	309 935	90 197	127 172	99 897	93 296	1 442	535 007	1.4
1981	314 720	103 137	129 157	103 568	103 147	2 481	551 305	3.0
1982	306 931	78 790	131 901	102 305	86 865	1 108	535 113	–2.9
1983	315 693	87 266	134 119	108 822	96 247	–1 154	549 843	2.8
1984	329 926	96 598	135 654	129 078	113 709	–997	581 038	5.7
1985	346 955	106 433	141 501	136 229	123 759	123	612 416	5.4
1986	360 738	110 329	144 166	143 359	134 335	–709	628 575	2.6
1987	375 678	122 040	146 180	148 093	141 920	–1 546	654 360	4.1
1988	392 093	133 110	152 897	162 162	161 382	2 036	686 176	4.9
1989	406 034	142 813	157 195	164 103	171 580	479	703 577	2.5
1990	411 343	131 466	162 937	171 977	175 482	52	705 464	0.3
1991	405 783	122 876	167 541	175 926	181 120	11	692 247	–1.9
1992	412 940	120 483	169 262	189 784	192 393	–1 532	698 544	0.9
1993	420 595	123 857	168 864	212 603	208 046	–1 750	716 123	2.5
1994	433 812	135 045	165 888	237 684	227 054	–1 155	744 220	3.9
1995	441 263	135 860	165 244	259 695	242 306	553	760 309	2.2
1996	451 682	135 534	163 164	274 456	254 908	–198	769 730	1.2
1997	470 177	156 877	162 988	296 534	288 933	540	798 183	3.7

TABLE S3

LABOUR FORCE STATISTICS

Year	Labour Force (000)	Employed (000)	Unemployed (000)	Unemployment rate (%)	Participation rate (%)
1978	11 265	10 320	945	8.4	63.1
1979	11 630	10 761	870	7.5	64.0
1980	11 983	11 082	900	7.5	64.6
1981	12 332	11 398	934	7.6	65.3
1982	12 398	11 035	1 363	11.0	64.7
1983	12 610	11 106	1 504	11.9	64.9
1984	12 853	11 402	1 450	11.3	65.3
1985	13 123	11 742	1 381	10.5	65.8
1986	13 378	12 095	1 283	9.6	66.3
1987	13 631	12 422	1 208	8.9	66.7
1988	13 900	12 819	1 082	7.8	67.2
1989	14 151	13 086	1 065	7.5	67.5
1990	14 329	13 165	1 164	8.1	67.3
1991	14 408	12 916	1 492	10.4	66.7
1992	14 482	12 842	1 640	11.3	65.9
1993	14 663	13 015	1 649	11.2	65.5
1994	14 832	13 292	1 541	10.4	65.3
1995	14 928	13 506	1 422	9.5	64.8
1996	15 145	13 676	1 469	9.7	64.9
1997	15 354	13 941	1 414	9.2	64.8

TABLE S4

MONEY SUPPLY — (Monetary Aggregates)

Year	M1 ($000 000)	M2 ($000 000)	M3 ($000 000)
1973	13 525	41 678	52 069
1974	14 788	50 386	65 377
1975	16 808	57 777	75 155
1976	18 157	65 574	89 154
1977	19 710	75 266	104 059
1978	21 848	84 469	119 534
1979	23 439	98 016	143 069
1980	25 092	116 535	166 908
1981	25 886	134 170	189 344
1982	25 848	146 317	197 844
1983	28 678	155 627	201 023
1984	29 772	164 244	207 295
1985	31 198	180 612	220 921
1986	33 187	198 450	238 040
1987	37 918	223 694	264 222
1988	39 941	242 779	287 154
1989	41 497	275 815	321 340
1990	41 188	306 450	354 668
1991	43 074	327 341	377 662
1992	45 444	339 379	396 935
1993	50 352	372 043	438 752
1994	56 181	379 977	457 258
1995	58 992	394 966	479 477
1996	65 511	407 149	506 554
1997	76 039	406 229	533 469

TABLE S5

INTEREST RATES, EXCHANGE RATES, AND PRICE INDEXES

Year	Interest rates		Exchange rates $Cdn per $US	Price indexes (1992 = 100)		
	Bank rate	Prime rate		GDP deflator	% Change	CPI
1961	3.06	5.60	1.013	24.2	0.8	23.9
1963	3.88	5.75	1.079	19.4	2.2	19.2
1964	4.04	5.75	1.079	19.9	2.8	19.6
1965	4.29	5.77	1.078	20.6	3.6	20.0
1966	5.17	6.00	1.077	21.7	5.0	20.8
1967	4.98	5.92	1.079	22.6	4.4	21.5
1968	6.79	6.92	1.077	23.5	3.7	22.4
1969	7.46	7.96	1.077	24.5	4.6	23.4
1970	7.13	8.17	1.044	25.7	4.8	24.2
1971	5.19	6.48	1.010	26.6	3.4	24.9
1972	4.75	6.00	0.991	28.2	6.0	26.1
1973	6.13	7.65	1.000	30.8	9.4	28.1
1974	8.50	10.75	0.978	35.4	14.7	31.1
1975	8.50	9.42	1.017	39.0	10.3	34.5
1976	9.29	10.04	0.986	42.6	9.2	37.1
1977	7.71	8.50	1.063	45.5	6.8	40.0
1978	8.98	9.69	1.141	48.5	6.6	43.6
1979	12.10	12.90	1.171	53.1	9.6	47.6
1980	12.89	14.25	1.169	58.9	10.9	52.4
1981	17.93	19.29	1.199	65.4	11.0	58.9
1982	13.96	15.81	1.234	71.0	8.5	65.3
1983	9.55	11.17	1.232	74.8	5.4	69.1
1984	11.31	12.06	1.295	77.3	3.4	72.1
1985	9.65	10.58	1.366	79.2	2.5	75.0
1986	9.21	10.52	1.389	81.4	2.8	78.1
1987	8.40	9.52	1.326	85.3	4.8	81.5
1988	9.69	10.83	1.231	89.2	4.5	84.8
1989	12.29	13.33	1.184	93.3	4.6	89.0
1990	13.05	14.06	1.167	96.1	3.1	93.3
1991	9.03	9.94	1.146	98.7	2.7	98.5
1992	6.78	7.48	1.209	100.0	1.3	100.0
1993	5.09	5.94	1.290	101.2	1.2	101.8
1994	5.77	6.88	1.366	102.4	1.2	102.0
1995	7.31	8.65	1.372	105.1	2.6	104.2
1996	4.53	6.06	1.364	106.6	1.4	105.9
1997	3.52	4.96	1.385	107.1	0.5	107.6

ⓘ APPENDIX II:
SOLUTIONS TO PROBLEM SOLVING EXERCISES

1-1 Solution: There are probably a few people in the world who can have anything they want. It is tempting to think that scarcity (lack of resources) is not a problem for such people. But as soon as we consider time as a resource, then it becomes quite obvious that they have to decide whether to spend an afternoon shopping in Paris, or entertaining friends. Every individual is subject to the problem of scarcity.

1-2 Solution: Although economics is not fundamentally a vocational subject, it help us to solve a great number of problems that affect us personally. Moreover, economics help us to develop the skill of logical thinking which is useful in many real-life situations. Many people are concerned with basic economic issues such as, Will I be able to find a job after graduation from school? Will I be able to repay my student loan? Will I be able to finance my car if interest rates rise? What is the opportunity cost of going to college or university? Economics, therefore, is of great practical value.

1-3 Solution: There is a fair amount of disagreement among economists, but there is also considerable agreement among them. In fact, there is much more agreement than disagreement on the positive aspects of economics. But economists, like ordinary human beings, do have different values and opinions on many issues. It is natural, therefore, that they would disagree on normative issues.

Note: Disagreement within any field of inquiry is not a measure of the extent to which it is "scientific." After all, physicists and chemists do sometimes disagree among themselves. For example, there has been disagreement recently about the future of nuclear fusion.

1-4 Solution: In this model, the endogenous variables are consumption, income, and the rate of interest. These variables will be determined within the model. The exogenous variables, i.e., the "givens" of the model, are wealth and income distribution. The values of these variables are predetermined.

1-5 Solution: Economists are well aware that other things are not equal, but without that assumption, it would be extremely difficult to isolate the effect of one variable on another. The assumption greatly simplifies the thinking process.

2-1 Solution:
1. $g = g(h)$
2. $H = H(a)$
3. $M = M(Y)$
4. $S = S(r,Y)$

2-2 Solution:

FIGURE 2.A

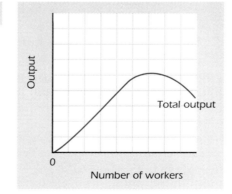

2-3 Solution: We can put interest rates on the vertical axis and the amount of loans on the horizontal axis. Since these two variables move in opposite directions, the resulting curve will be downward sloping as shown in Figure 2.B

FIGURE 2.B

Relation between the rate of interest and the amount of money borrowed.

As the rate of interest falls from r to r_0, the amount of money borrowed rises from L to L_1.

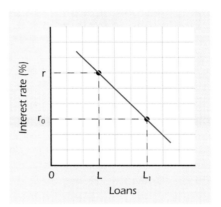

3-1 Solution: Whether or not a car is a capital good depends on the purpose for which the car is used. If the car is for personal use, it is not a capital good but a consumer good. If, however, it is used as a taxi, or as a delivery vehicle for a firm, then it is a capital good.

3-2 Solution: There is no income the source of which is not a resource. On the surface, it may appear that government welfare payments do not originate from resources. However, upon careful reflection, we find that tax dollars pay for welfare programs, and that those tax dollars are derived from some kind of income whose source is either land, labour, capital, or entrepreneurial services.

3-3 Solution: 1. The opportunity cost of watching the hockey game is probably a better score on the test. The opportunity cost of studying for the economics test is the thrill of seeing Gretzky and company do battle against the Canadiens. You have to evaluate each of these opportunity costs subjectively. If the opportunity cost of watching the game outweighs the opportunity cost of studying economics, then you should study for the test. If, on the other hand, the opportunity cost of studying for the test outweighs the opportunity cost of watching the game, then you should watch the hockey game.

3-3 Solution: 2. The production of anti-pollution equipment would cause resources to be diverted from other uses. The opportunity cost would be the goods and services that the economy could not produce because it decided to use some resources to produce anti-pollution equipment.

3-4 Solution: Since the carpenters were unemployed, output would not fall in any sector of the economy by hiring them. Regardless of what they are paid by Antigonish Construction, society does not make any sacrifice in terms of lost output or anything else. Thus the opportunity cost of employing the carpenters for a week is zero.

Note: If the carpenters were employed in pulp and paper at the time they were hired by Antigonish Construction, the opportunity cost would be the fall in output in pulp and paper resulting from transferring them from that industry.

3-5 Solution: A shift in the p-p curve implies a change in the economy's productive capacity. This will happen only if there is a change in technology or in resources. Since the computer programmers already existed, their employment does not affect the economy's productive capacity. Thus, the p-p curve would not shift.

Note: The presence of unemployed computer programmers represents unemployment of resources. This would be illustrated by a production possibility point below the p-p curve. The employment of the programmers would move the economy closer to the p-p curve but the curve would not shift.

3-6 Solution: If we accept the view that the main objective of business firms is to maximize profits, then businesses in Canada are likely to favour capitalism or free enterprise over other economic systems. Businesses would generally prefer government to leave them alone to pursue their own interests. They would tend to favour the system with the least amount of government involvement in the economy. This system is the free enterprise system.

3-7 Solution: We rely on the market mechanism. Authors know that students are willing to buy books, so they write books in the hope of finding publishers who are willing to publish them and pay royalties to the authors. The publishers, on the other hand, publish the books in the hope of making a profit in the process. Although there is no direct command to the authors or the publishers to produce books, they respond to market signals, which indicate to them that writing and publishing textbooks can be a profitable undertaking.

3-8 Solution: Education provides benefits not only to the recipient directly, but also to society. A better-educated population implies a better-educated labour force and a more productive economy. Hence, the entire society benefits and should help to defray the costs. This is done out of tax dollars.

4-1 Solution: It is obvious that a price of $5 is too high for Roisin to be able to sell her entire stock by the end of the day. By lowering her price, Roisin will be able to increase the quantity sold. She may even be able to sell her entire stock if she lowers the price sufficiently. Businesses use the same strategy to increase their sales. Think of designated "sales days" at department stores.

4-2 Solution: 1. Crayons and colouring books are complementary goods. The bookstore can charge a relatively low price for its crayons, because it can obtain them at a relatively low cost. Other things being equal, this will result in an increase in the quantity of crayons that will be bought. As people buy more crayons, however, they will also buy more colouring books since one is used in conjunction with the other.

4-2 Solution: 2. The fact that people buy more gold when the price rises does not refute the law of demand. The law states that less will be bought at higher prices than at lower prices, <u>other things being equal.</u> People may buy more gold when gold prices rise because they expect the price to rise even higher. If their expectations are correct, they make a capital gain. Their behaviour can be explained by changing expectations; other things are not equal.

4-3 Solution: An increase in the quantity of typewriters bought might be a response to falling prices of typewriters and not to an increase in the demand for typewriters. If that is the case, then Vinud would be making a mistake to think that the demand for typewriters was increasing. An increase in quantity demanded may not signify any increase in demand.

Note: Vinud found this out after he took his first course in economics.

4-4 Solution: An increase in wages in the shoe industry will increase the cost of producing shoes, and will therefore reduce the supply of shoes.

4-5 Solution: The following is a plausible explanation. As the price of gold rises, people buy less gold. They substitute silver for gold in their investment portfolios. This increase in demand for silver (an upward shift in the demand curve) results in an increase in the price of silver.

5-1 Solution: A price elasticity of demand of 2.8 means that a certain percentage increase in price causes quantity demanded to fall by 2.8 times the percentage increase in price. Since the increase in price is 15%, the quantity demanded falls by $2.8 \times 15 = 42\%$.

5-2 Solution: 1. When people are ill, medical attention becomes a necessity. Therefore, the demand for the services of medical doctors is likely to be inelastic.

2. The demand for toilet paper is likely to be inelastic for two main reasons. First, this product has no close substitutes. Second, the fraction of the budget spent on it is relatively small.

3. There are many substitutes for diamond necklaces. Moreover, many people would consider them to be luxuries. Therefore, the demand for diamond necklaces is likely to be elastic.

4. Telephone services are essential. A small change in price is unlikely to cause any significant change in the quantity demanded. In other words, the demand is inelastic.

5-3 Solution: 1.   Since the income elasticity of demand for beef is 2.2, then an increase in income of 10% causes the demand for beef to increase by 22% (10 × 2.2). Beef farmers should therefore increase their production of beef by 22%.

5-3 Solution: 2.   Because tea and coffee are substitutes, we know that an increase in the price of tea leads to an increase in the demand for coffee, other things being equal. Since the cross elasticity of demand between coffee and tea is 2.5, then a 6% increase in the price of tea causes the demand for coffee to rise by 6 × 2.5 = 15%.

5-4 Solution: Andrei has incurred a cost of $10 on each unit produced. His minimum acceptable profit is 10%. His reservation price is therefore $11. He will withdraw his glasses from the market unless the price is at least $11. For (a), (b), and (c), the market price is above his reservation price, so he will sell. But a market price of $10 is below his reservation price, so he will withdraw his product from the market.

6-1 Solution: Provided that the marginal utility is positive, additional Cherry Coke consumption will increase your total satisfaction. This is so whether the marginal utility is increasing or decreasing. Since the marginal utility is positive after the third bottle is consumed, you should continue to drink Cherry Coke.

6-2 Solution: With $14, Yuki will now buy $6 worth of A and $8 worth of B in order to maximize her satisfaction. The marginal utility of the last dollar spent on each will be equal at 30.

7-1 Solution: In a partnership, each partner is fully liable, not only for debts resulting from his own actions, but also for those resulting from the actions of the other partners. If one lawyer in the firm bungles a case, it exposes the other lawyers as well to any unfavourable consequences. This is a sort of safety net that ensures that each lawyer in the firm will do his or her best to see that the best decisions are made. It provides an incentive for consultation among the lawyers, which is definitely a great advantage to the firm's clients.

7-2 Solution: 1.   The most effective form of business organization, from the capital-raising perspective, is the corporation. The corporation provides limited liability to its shareholders. Potential investors who are unwilling to invest in an enterprise that does not have limited liabilty can safely do so in a corporation. Should the business go bankrupt, the personal assets of the investors are protected. Therefore, Hitchcock, James, and Chill Filmmakers might be able to raise sufficient capital to expand their operation if they were to form a corporation.

7-2 Solution: 2.   The profits of a corporation are taxed twice: first as corporation income and again as dividend income paid out to shareholders. Thus, governments generally favour the formation of corporations. But a government may lose this tax revenue advantage since the maximum tax rate on corporate profits is lower than that on income from other forms of business organizations. The one source of taxation must be weighed.

7-3 Solution: Under the circumstances, it appears that a single proprietorship is the most appropriate form of organization for this business. The organization of a sole proprietorship entails no legal red tape and is relatively inexpensive. Once the experimental state is over and the idea proves to be good, then some other form of business organization should be considered.

7-4 Solution: Labour costs are an important factor in the decision regarding the location or the establishment of firms. Other things being equal, firms will tend to locate in areas where labour costs are lowest. Industries that use a large quantity of workers who are paid minimum wages will tend to shy away from the province with the highest minimum wage, provided that other factors do not outweigh the labour cost factor.

8-1 Solution: A firm seeking to maximize its profits will be cost conscious. It will tend to hire workers on the basis of their ability to contribute to the output of the firm, and not on the basis of sex or race. In fact, to the extent that workers of a certain sex or race (for example, women and blacks) are skilled and relatively inexpensive, the profit motive dictates that they will be hired in preference to more expensive groups. Discrimination in hiring will not be in the best interest of the firm seeking to maximize its profits.

8-2 Solution: The choice between methods 1 and 2 will be made on the basis of their relative economic efficiency. Using method 1, the value of the inputs is $(10 \times \$5) + (6 \times \$6) = \$86$. The value of the output is $(24 \times \$10) = \$240$. Therefore, the economic efficiency ratio is $240/86 = 2.79$. Using method 2, the value of the inputs is $(15 \times \$5) + (2 \times \$6) = \$87$. The value of the output is $(25 \times \$10) = \$250$. Therefore, the economic efficiency ratio is $250/87 = 2.87$. Method 2 should be chosen, since it is more efficient.

9-1 Solution: Your total revenue is $2000. From this, you must deduct $50 for the advertisement, $550 for paint, brushes, etc. This leaves you with $1400. Is this all profit? Remember, you used your own car to get from one job to the next, so you must deduct something for gas, oil, and wear and tear — let's say $200. This still leaves you with $1200. To determine whether or not you have made a profit, you must estimate the opportunity cost of your time. If you could have earned more than $1200 elsewhere, you have actually incurred a loss. If you could have earned only $800 elsewhere, then you have made a profit of $400.

Note: This problem illustrates the importance of not neglecting implicit costs — in this case, depreciation, your time, and the income you could have made by leasing your car for the summer.

10-1 Solution: No. By definition, a purely competitive firm can sell as much as it can produce at the existing price. Advertising involves a cost. For the purely competitive firm, this cost does not result in any direct benefit to the firm incurring the cost. That being the case, a firm in a purely competitive industry will not advertise its product.

Note: While advertising by a purely competitive <u>firm</u> will not be beneficial to that firm, the <u>industry</u> as a whole may attempt to increase the demand for the product by advertising.

10-2 Solution: Provided that a firm is maximizing its profits, it must be equating its marginal revenue with its marginal cost. This is so whether the firm's manager knows it or not. The economic analyst can examine a firm's operations and advise the firm's managers on adjustments that it may make in order to increase its profits, but if the firm happens to attain the maximum profit position, then its marginal revenue will equal its marginal cost.

10-3 Solution: In certain circumstances, the firm may do better to operate at a loss, in the short run, than to cease operating. This is the case if the firm is in a position where the price of its product is below its average total cost but above its average variable cost. If the firm suspends its operation temporarily, it still has fixed costs but earns nothing to help to defray these costs. If it continues to operate, any earnings above its variable costs can be used to help to pay its fixed costs. If it seems that the firm will continue to incur losses in the long run, it should close its plant.

11-1 Solution: This is one of the popular misconceptions about the monopolistic firm. While the firm in a monopoly situation can manipulate market supply by virtue of being the only firm in the industry, remember that demand plays an important role in price determination. If the monopolistic firm decides to put a certain quantity on the market, the market demand will establish the price. If the monopolistic firm decides to charge a certain price, the quantity that it can sell at that price will be determined by the demand for its product. Except for the exceptional case where the demand for the product is perfectly inelastic, the monopolistic firm cannot charge <u>any</u> price and at the same time sell any quantity at that price. The statement is therefore false.

11-2 Solution: The notion that a monopolistic firm can always increase its profits by raising its price is utterly false. If the firm is charging a price that is less than that at which marginal revenue equals marginal cost, then an increase in price will raise its profits. If it is charging a price higher than that at which marginal revenue equals marginal cost, then an increase in price will reduce its profits. If the firm is charging a price consistent with the MR = MC condition for profit maximization, then any change in its price will result in lower — not higher — profits.

11-3 Solution: The monopolistic firm maximizes its profits when it produces at the point where marginal revenue equals marginal cost. If marginal cost equals zero, then the profit-maximizing monopolist will produce where marginal revenue equals zero. But when marginal revenue is zero, demand is unitary elastic. Hence, it is shown that if marginal cost equals zero, the monopolist will maximize profits by producing where the price elasticity of demand is one.

11-4 Solution: The general conclusion that pure competition results in a lower price and larger quantity than monopoly does is valid, provided that the monopolistic firm faces cost conditions similar to those confronting the purely competitive firm. However, if substantial economies of scale are present, then the general conclusion may no longer hold. A single firm in a purely competitive market may be quite incapable of taking advantage of economies of scale, while a firm in a monopolistic situation may have such a large output that its unit cost may be relatively low. In such a case, the price of the product may be lower in a monopolized market and output may be greater than in a purely competitive market.

12-1 Solution: A pharmacy is a good example of a firm that operates in a monopolistically competitive market structure. Prices could successfully be set slightly above those in other pharmacies if, by product differentiation, you were able to increase demand for your products. However, it would be unwise to charge significantly higher prices. After all, your products may be different, but not that different. And a significantly higher price will result in a significant reduction in your share of the market.

12-2 Solution: The installation of the air-conditioner by the competitor is an example of a type of non-price competition known as quality competition. Other things being equal, patrons will prefer to have coffee in an air-conditioned café. In order to avoid losing customers to your competitor, and perhaps to attract some of his customers to your café, you might try installing an air-conditioner in your café, cutting your price, or advertising.

12-3 Solution: On the surface, price cutting may appear to be a good strategy. But let us not be too hasty; let us analyze the situation. If you cut your prices, your competitors are likely to retaliate with price cuts of their own. They may even undercut your prices. Before you know it, you may be involved in a vicious price war. And what are the likely results? They are lower profits, lower prices, and hardly any change in market shares.

13-1 Solution: The institution of minimum wage laws is actually a type of price control, the price being the price of labour. To see how this type of price control may affect employment, let us study Figure 13.8. DD and SS are the demand and supply curves of labour respectively. The equilibrium wage rate is $0W$, and at that wage rate, the number of workers employed is $0L$. Now, suppose the government legislates a minimum wage of $0W_1$. Firms can no longer legally pay workers a wage rate of $0W$. The quantity of labour demanded at $0W_1$ has fallen to $0L_0$, while the quantity supplied has risen to $0L_1$. A surplus of labour ($0L_1 - 0L_0 = L_0L_1$) has resulted. Thus, the effect of the minimum wage law is to increase unemployment.

FIGURE 13.A

Effect of minimum wage on employment.

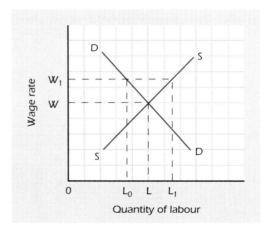

13-2 Solution: A closed shop, though obviously benefiting the union, may also benefit the employer. The closed shop serves as a central employment agency for the employer, from which a pool of workers can be drawn when required. Thus, a closed shop arrangement may reduce the cost to the employer of searching for an employee with the requisite skills. The employer may also benefit from greater industrial peace and harmony resulting from the fact that all of the employees are union members — a fact that will eliminate any conflict between union and non-union members.

13-3 Solution: Many strikes do result in a loss in total output as plants close, but not all strikes do. A strike in a certain factory at a certain time may mean simply that the factory has to work harder and longer at the end of the strike to compensate for the loss of production during the strike. In this case, the strike results in a shifting of the timing of production rather than in the volume of output.

13-4 Solution: If Canadian economists were subjected to a licensing procedure, we could expect some of them to fail the licensing requirements. The total supply of practising economists would therefore decline. Then, assuming no change in the demand for the services of economists, we could expect the average salaries of economists to increase.

Note: This would be a case of an association limiting the number of entrants into a profession and thus shifting the supply curve to the left.

14-1 Solution: The demand for land in the business section of the city is high relative to the demand for land in outlying areas. Consequently, the rental value of land in the downtown area is high relative to the rental value of land in outlying areas. To overcome problems of scarce space and hence high rent, we erect high-rise buildings. In the absence of high-rise buildings, we would have to use a considerable amount of land to obtain the space that is now provided by high-rise buildings. The cost would be astronomical. The abundance of high-rise buildings in many business districts results largely from the high rental value of land in those areas.

14-2 Solution: If Canadians were not such big savers, a smaller amount of loanable funds would be available at any given rate of interest. Figure 14.4 will help to explain how this would affect the rate of interest. D is the original demand curve and S is the original supply curve for loanable funds.

FIGURE 14.A

Demand for and supply of loanable funds

A fall in saving increases the rate of interest.

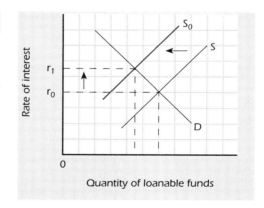

The corresponding equilibrium rate of interest is r_0. A smaller amount of saving by Canadians would cause the supply of loanable funds to fall, other things being equal. (The supply curve will shift from S to S_0.) This results in an increase in the rate of interest from r_0 to r_1.

14-3 Solution: On the surface, the answer to this question seems quite obvious. After all, if you borrow $100 for a year at a 4% interest rate, your interest cost is $4, while at an interest rate of 17%, your interest cost is $17. But let us not be too hasty to jump to any conclusions. Suppose the rate of inflation is only 1% when the rate of interest is 4%. The real interest cost is $3; and if the rate of inflation is 15% when the interest rate is 17%, then the real interest cost is only $2. Clearly, in some circumstances, it is more costly to borrow at 4% than at 17%.

14-4 Solution: A tax levied on the excess profits of a firm may cause the firm to forgo certain economic activities that could earn extra profits. The tax may also weaken the incentive to keep cost down. The firm may then engage in certain programs and projects that could not be justified were it not for the excess-profits tax. For example, excess-profits taxes have resulted in the increased padding of expense accounts.

15-1 Solution: If everyone in Canada were to receive the same income, regardless of contribution to the total output of goods and services in the economy, certain consequences could be expected. Many people have exerted themselves and have taken risks in the pursuit of an income above the average. If income were distributed equally, then the prospect of earning above-average incomes would disappear. Consequently, the incentive to take risks and to work hard would be greatly reduced. Total output would then fall. Additional reward in the form of income for extra effort is an important motivator for economic activity.

15-2 Solution: The prospects of young people finding worthwhile jobs in rural areas are quite limited. Also, for young people, city life is often more exciting than country life. Entertaining hopes of a more appropriate job and greater excitement, unattached individuals may migrate from the rural areas to the urban areas where they may end up being numbered among those living in poverty.

15-3 Solution: Most Canadians do not see poverty to the same extent as the statistics reveal because poverty in Canada is, to a significant degree, invisible; it is hidden. In many cases, the poor live in city slums, which we do not see from the highways and the subways. They also live in rural areas, which many of us hardly ever see. Moreover, many of the poor are old and infirm and remain indoors for much of the time. For all these reasons, the statistics on poverty seem more horrible than our everyday experiences would lead us to believe.

16-1 Solution: Pollution, in its various forms, imposes a cost on society. In the case of a pharmaceutical company that pollutes a river, the society is being robbed of a better environment, of the use of the river for recreational purposes, and of the fish population. All these are costs that we, as members of society, will be forced to bear whether we live upstream or not. Moreover, any tax dollars that may be used to clean up the river represent additional costs. These costs are sufficient reasons for us to concern ourselves about the pollution of the river by the company.

16-2 Solution: It is quite unlikely that an individual producer would voluntarily internalize all its costs. The objective of the producer is to maximize profits. If one producer internalizes all costs, then that producer voluntarily incurs a cost disadvantage vis-à-vis other producers. Thus, the producer's profitability relative to that of competitors would decline.

17-1 Solution: We have stated that the demand for farm products is price inelastic. Now, we know that the elasticity coefficient is 0.2. This means that a 10% fall in the prices of farm products results in only a 2% increase in the quantity of farm products demanded. In order to induce a 10% increase in consumer purchases of farm products, the prices of farm products would have to fall by 50%. Clearly, this is a colossal problem for farmers.

17-2 Solution: Let us examine the effect of each of these policies on consumers. Price supports result in higher prices for consumers. Market quotas result in both fewer farm products and higher unit prices. Subsidies, on the other hand, allow consumers to have more agricultural products at lower unit prices. Therefore, from the consumers' point of view, subsidies to farmers are better than either of the other two policies.

18-1 Solution: A significant portion of government spending is allocated to social service programs, including old age security payments. As the population ages, one expects expenditure for this function to increase. The Canada Pension Plan and the Quebec Pension Plan also provide benefits to persons who have reached the age of 65 years. In addition, expenditure on health services is likely to rise with an aging population.

18-2 Solution: The effect of increasing the tax rate depends on the effect of the higher tax rate on economic activity and hence on income. If the increase in the tax rate does not result in a corresponding decrease in economic activity and income, then tax revenues will increase. If, however, the increase in the tax rate acts as a disincentive to work, then total income may fall to the extent that the higher rate yields a lower — rather than a higher — tax revenue.

18-3 Solution: A tax imposed on a commodity will tend to reduce the quantity of that commodity that will be bought. If producers continue to produce the same quantity as they did before the imposition of the tax, they will notice that their stocks (inventories) will begin to pile up as consumers reduce their purchases of the commodity. In response to this situation, producers will reduce their level of production.

19-1 Solution: Canada is well endowed with fertile agricultural land. Japan, on the other hand, is well endowed with the kind of labour and technology that allows it to produce electronic items cheaply. Hence, we can reasonably expect Canada to export agricultural products to Japan and to import electronic items from Japan.

Note: This is not to suggest that Canada is mainly an agricultural country. Although we have a very strong agricultural sector, we are also well endowed with many high technology industries.

19-2 Solution: Newsprint is an output of the forest industry and Quebec is well endowed with forest resources. Also, the newsprint industry uses a lot of electricity, and Quebec is well endowed with electricity. Consequently, Quebec enjoys a cost advantage in the production of newsprint. We can therefore reasonably expect Quebec to export newsprint.

20-1 Solution: A gradual reduction and ultimate elimination of the tariff on shoes will lead to the importation of relatively inexpensive shoes. Canadian producers, in order to compete with foreign producers, will have to be more efficient and reduce their prices. This means that Canadian consumers will benefit from a reduction in the price of shoes. If Canadian producers cannot compete with foreign manufacturers in the shoe industry, then they will gradually shift resources out of the shoe industry into some other industry where they will be more efficient. This more efficient allocation of resources will also benefit Canadian consumers.

20-2 Solution: Quebec is well endowed with water, electricity, and forest resources. These resources are important inputs in paper production. Claude Depapier is likely to enjoy a comparative cost advantage in the production of paper. Free trade with the United States will extend Claude's market. He may also benefit from economies of scale. It seems to be in Claude's interest to support free trade between Canada and the United States.

22-1 Solution: No, we should not include the allowance of $50 a week when measuring the gross domestic product. Although the money represents income to the student, it does not represent the value of goods produced or of services rendered. It simply represents a transfer of income from father to daughter. Presumably, we already counted the $50 allowance as a part of the payment to the professor for his services. To count it again would be double counting.

22-2 Solution: Gross domestic product is a price times quantity measure. This product can increase if prices, quantities, or both increase. But it can also increase if total production (quantity) falls, provided that the fall in production is more than compensated for by an increase in prices. The following arithmetic example will help to clarify the problem. Let total output (Q) be 200, and let the average price (P) be $5. Thus, the value of total output (P × Q) = 200 × $5 = $1000. Now, assume that total output falls to 180, while the average price rises to $6. The value of the total output (GDP) will now be 180 × $6 = $1080. Here total production falls, but GDP rises. In economic terminology, a nominal increase in GDP can be consistent with a decrease in real GDP.

22-3 Solution: The services of homemakers are now treated as a non-marketed item in national income accounting. As such, they are omitted in GDP calculations. If, however, homemakers were paid for their services, then their output would be valued in the market and would cause the GDP to increase. This increase in output would not imply an increase in the services of homemakers, unless the fact that they are being paid causes them to exert greater effort.

23-1 Solution: Inflation is a sustained increase in the general level of prices. In a barter economy, the price of one good or service is expressed in terms of another good or service. Thus, if the price of one good, say A, doubles in terms of good B, then it means that the price of good B is halved in terms of good A. Hence, in a barter economy, there cannot be an increase in the general level of prices — inflation cannot occur. In that sense then, inflation is a purely monetary phenomenon.

25-1 Solution: Firms keep a certain amount of inventory to meet unanticipated changes in demand. If inventories rise above their intended or planned levels, then the firms' production levels are too high for the current level of demand. An unplanned accumulation of inventories is therefore a signal to producers to reduce their volume of output. On the other hand, if inventories fall below their intended levels, then the firms' production levels are too low for the current level of expenditures. This situation would be a signal to the firms to increase their volume of output. Unintended changes in inventories thus serve as a barometer that the firms may use to adjust their output to the appropriate level.

25-2 Solution: The statement is correct only under certain simplifying assumptions, and only if it refers to ex ante saving and investment. In an ex post sense, saving and investment must always be equal. Saving, by definition, is that part of income that is not spent on current consumption. Investment is the unconsumed part of current output. In this sense, saving and investment are one and the same thing. Their equality does not define equilibrium income. If we are dealing with an economy where government neither spends nor taxes, and which does not engage in foreign trade, then the statement is true, ex ante. If, however, we are dealing with an open economy with government spending and taxing, then the statement is incorrect. In such an economy, total injections and total withdrawals may not be equal even if saving and investment are equal. The economy may not be in equilibrium.

25-3 Solution: Assuming a closed economy with neither government spending nor taxes, and using the injections-withdrawals approach, equilibrium is S = I. Using the AE-AO approach, equilibrium is Y = C + I. Since each approach expresses equilibrium under the same circumstances, both approaches are equivalent. That is,

$$Y = C + I$$

By transposing C, we obtain

$$Y - C = I$$

But Y – C = S by definition; therefore S = I

Thus we see that Y = C + I is identical to S = I.

26-1 Solution: Given the level of income, an increase in saving by consumers means that they are reducing their spending on consumer goods and services. Firms may then notice a reduction in sales, and consequently reduce production, spending less on the factors of production. Thus, income will fall. If, however, consumers increase their saving and at the same time firms, through borrowing, channel those savings into investment, then the economy's capital stock will increase, and the economy's productive capacity will thus increase.

27-1 Solution: Since Mr. Adam has a much larger income than Mr. Buntin does, it follows that Mr. Adam's marginal propensity to consume is lower than Mr. Buntin's. Taking $5000 from Mr. Adam and giving it to Mr. Buntin is actually taking money from where it is not likely to reduce consumption much and putting it where it is likely to increase consumption significantly. The effect is an increase in total consumption.

27-2 Solution: A stock market crash lowers the value of the assets of stock owners. Such individuals will feel a reduction in their wealth, and will tend to reduce their consumption. Some economists believe that the stock market crash of 1929 contributed to the Great Depression by causing a significant decline in consumption.

27-3 Solution: Although income and consumption are directly related, it is quite possible for some non-income determinant of consumption to offset any effect of income changes. In this case, the increase in the rate of interest may have had a greater effect in reducing expenditure on furniture than the positive effect of the increase in income. It is also possible that other determinants of consumption may have been operating.

27-4 Solution: A reduction in the tax rate from 20% to 15% implies an increase in personal disposable income. For example, with a tax rate of 20%, an individual with a taxable income of $20 000 would pay $4000 in taxes, keeping a disposable income of $16 000. With a tax rate of 15%, the same individual would pay $3000 in taxes, keeping a disposable income of $17 000. The fundamental psychological law suggests that a part of this extra $1000 will be allocated to extra consumption.

27-5 Solution: Even if a firm does not need to borrow to finance its investment projects, it should consider the opportunity cost of using its own funds. This cost is measured by the interest earnings that could have been made on these funds. So the rate of interest should feature in this firm's investment decisions.

27-6 Solution: The fact that investment is higher at a lower level of income does not refute the hypothesis that the higher the level of income is, the greater the amount of investment will be. If, at a level of income of $500 million, income increases at only 1% per year while, at a level of $150 million, it is growing at 5% per year, investment could well be higher at the lower income level.

28-1 Solution: The solution to the fiscal drag is to increase spending without at the same time increasing taxes. Thus, the granting of tax rebates will help to offset the fiscal drag. This has been done with some degree of success.

29-1 Solution: Seasonal variations in spending should not be confused with cyclical fluctuations. Seasonal fluctuations occur at specific times, are of relatively short duration, and are quite predictable. Business cycles, on the other hand, exhibit four distinct phases (peak, recession, trough, and recovery). The times of their occurrence and their duration are not easily predictable.

29-2 Solution: An increase in demand for goods and services will induce the business sector to increase production. This can be done by new investment or by working existing plants harder (e.g., utilizing any excess capacity, operating beyond normal capacity, and working overtime). When an increase in production is warranted by an increase in demand for goods and services, it makes good economic sense for firms to run their plants harder until it is ascertained whether the increase in demand is permanent or just transitory. Once it is determined that the increase in demand is permanent, then investment can be justified, because it is costly to run plants beyond their normal capacity for a long period of time.

29-3 Solution: A major explanation of economic fluctuations is changes in investment. Mature industries are industries that have reached their full growth. They will not engage in any net (new) investment. Gross investment is likely to consist mainly of replacement investment. Fluctuations, therefore, are likely to be less than in the case of expanding (or contracting) industries.

30-1 Solution: People choose to hold a part of their wealth in liquid form. Money is ideal for this purpose because of its liquidity. Used in this manner, money serves as a store of value. To perform this function well, money must maintain its purchasing power over time. During inflationary times (that is, in times of rising prices), money loses purchasing power and does not therefore serve as a good store of value.

30-2 Solution: The money supply does not consist only of Bank of Canada notes. In fact, the money supply consists mainly of deposits (accounts) at chartered banks. These accounts can increase even if the Bank of Canada does not print more notes. They can increase, for example, when a chartered bank makes a loan to a customer.

Note: We will pursue this further in the following chapter.

31-1 Solution: The statement is false. This is a common misconception about the deposit expansion process. Although it is possible for a bank to lend out its excess reserves, it is not in its best interest to do so. Instead, the bank grants a loan by creating a deposit for the borrower and keeping the excess reserves to meet its reserve requirement. By so doing, the bank can extend a great deal more loans on which it can earn interest income. The bank does not lend out its excess reserves but it does lend out an amount equivalent to its excess reserves.

32-1 Solution: People hold money for unforeseen emergencies. The existence of credit cards is likely to reduce the amount of money that people will hold for this purpose. In an emergency, it will often be possible to use a credit card instead of money. Of course, money will have to be used to discharge the debt eventually.

33-1 Solution: This is a classic example of what is called the **post hoc, ergo propter hoc** fallacy. **Post hoc, ergo propter hoc** is a Latin expression meaning "after this, therefore because of this." The fallacy lies in the argument that because one event follows another event, it is caused by that other event — an argument that is not necessarily valid. In this problem, the inflation of the 1970s has been attributed to the increase in the price of OPEC oil because it followed the increase in the price of OPEC oil. It is quite possible, however, that the inflation could have been caused by other factors.

34-1 Solution: An increase in the budget deficit means that the government has increased its spending more than it has increased tax receipts. Does this mean an increase in total spending? Not necessarily. If the budget deficit is financed by borrowing funds from the private sector — funds which the private sector would otherwise have spent — then the increased budget deficit represents a shift of purchasing power from the private to the public sector. The increased budget deficit, therefore, does not in this case result in any increase in total spending.

34-2 Solution: The government of Canada depends heavily on the Canadian people as a source of borrowed funds. The Canadian public holds about 69% of the federal government debt. To be able to continue to borrow from the public, the federal government must continue to hold the confidence of the public. How many of us would continue to buy government of Canada bonds if we thought there was a good chance that the government would not honour its debt obligations to us? Moreover, the government of Canada has built up a reputation for repaying its debts. Have you ever heard of a case where a holder of a Canada savings bond (CSB) was unable to collect the principal and interest? We have sufficient reasons to justify our confidence in our debtor, the federal government. Our expectations that the government will honour its obligations to us as lenders are therefore quite rational.

35-1 Solution: An increase in exports to the United States means that Americans will demand more Canadian dollars to pay for their imports from Canada (our exports). This increase in demand for Canadian dollars will tend to increase the value of the Canadian dollar in terms of U.S. funds.

36-1 Solution: Several thousand Canadians who live near the United States cross the border in search of lower prices. If the value of the Canadian dollar falls in terms of U.S. funds, then U.S. prices will rise relative to Canadian prices. This increase in U.S. prices will deter Canadians from shopping in the United States. Consider how expensive American goods would become to Canadians if the value of the Canadian dollar were to fall to about U.S. $0.70.

36-2 Solution: Because of a perennial current account deficit with the United States, the value of the Canadian dollar has been under constant downward pressure. To cope with this problem, the Bank of Canada has kept interest rates in Canada above those in the United States. This policy is intended to increase foreign investment in Canadian securities, increase the demand for Canadian dollars, and thus prevent the value of the Canadian dollar from falling. Because of this tendency to keep Canadian interest rates above U.S. interest rates, it may be argued that Canadian interest rates are externally determined. Once U.S. interest rates are established, the Canadian rates will simply be set at somewhat higher levels.

GLOSSARY

A

Ability-to-pay principle: The idea that people should be taxed according to their ability to pay. The rich should pay more in taxes than the poor.

Absolute advantage: One country is said to have an absolute advantage over another country in the production of a commodity if it can produce the commodity with fewer resources than the other country can.

Absolute price: The monetary price of a good or service. The amount of money that must be spent to obtain one unit of a good or service.

Acceleration principle: The hypothesis that the level of investment is proportional to the rate of change of output (income).

Accelerationists: Economists who claim that attempts to keep unemployment below its natural level will simply accelerate inflation.

Actual output: The level of output actually produced by the economy.

Actual rate of inflation: The percentage rate at which the price level moves upward annually.

Ad valorem tariff: A tariff expressed as a fixed percentage of the value of the imported item.

Adaptive expectations: The hypothesis that people form their expectations solely on the basis of the experience of the recent past. For example, the expected rate of inflation for 1998 is based on the actual rate of inflation in 1997.

Administered price: A price that is controlled rather than determined exclusively by demand and supply.

Aggregate: Total.

Aggregate demand: The total amounts of all goods and services that will be bought at various price levels.

Aggregate demand curve: The curve showing the relation between the total amount of all goods and services that will be purchased and the price level.

Aggregate expenditure: Total spending in an economy, consisting of consumption spending, investment spending, government spending, and net exports.

Aggregate expenditure curve: The curve showing the relation between total spending and total income.

Aggregate output: A measure of the total production of all goods and services.

Aggregate supply: The levels of output supplied at various price levels.

Aggregate supply curve: The curve showing the relation between the total output of all goods and services that will be produced and the average level of prices.

Aggregation problem: The problem encountered in adding up individual units in order to arrive at a single total.

Air pollution: smog mainly due to burning fuels.

Allocative efficiency: A situation in which it is impossible to make someone better off without making someone else worse off by a change in production or consumption.

Appreciation (of exchange rate): A market determined increase in the value of a country's currency in terms of another country's currency.

Arbitrage dealing: Buying in a lower price market in order to resell in a higher price market.

Arbitration: A mechanism for settling disputes in the collective bargaining process whereby a decision is made by an independent person or persons.

Arc elasticity (of demand): A measure of elasticity for a segment of the demand curve.

Asset: Anything that is owned by an economic unit.

Assumptions: Statements about the conditions under which a model operates.

Automatic fiscal policy: Fiscal policy tools built into the system. They automatically help to stabilize the economy. Also called automatic (built-in) stabilizers.

Automatic stabilizers: Built-in measures that increase the budget surplus during inflationary periods and increase the budget deficit during periods of recession.

Automatic teller machines (ATMs): Machines that allow clients to make certain banking transactions without the aid of a bank teller/clerk.

Autonomous investment: Investment that is independent of any other variable.

Average cost (AC): Total cost divided by the number of units produced. Also known as average total cost (ATC) or unit cost.

Average cost pricing: A pricing strategy in which price and average cost are equated. Often used by regulatory agencies in regulating monopolies.

Average fixed cost (AFC): Total fixed cost divided by the number of units produced.

Average product (AP): Total product divided by the quantity of the variable factor employed.

Average propensity to consume (APC): The proportion of total income that goes into consumption. (APC = C/Y).

Average propensity to save (APS): The proportion of total income that is saved. (APS = S/Y).

Average revenue (AR): Total revenue divided by the number of units sold.

Average total cost (ATC): See average cost.

Average variable cost (AVC): Total variable cost divided by the number of units produced.

B

Backward-bending labour supply curve: Illustrates that higher wages may result in a decrease in the number of hours worked.

Bad money: Money whose face value is less than the value of the commodity from which it is made.

Balance of merchandise (visible) trade: Total goods exported minus total goods imported.

Balance of payments: A record of a country's economic transactions with the rest of the world.

Balance of trade: The difference between the value of a country's exports and the value of its imports.

Balance of trade deficit: The excess of imports over exports.

Balance of trade surplus: The excess of exports over imports.

Balance sheet: A statement of assets, liabilities, and owners' equity.

Balanced budget: A situation in which government spending equals tax receipts.

Balanced budget change in spending: A situation involving an equivalent change in government spending and taxes.

Balanced budget multiplier: The number which, when multiplied by the change in government spending, yields the change in equilibrium income when G = T.

Balanced budget theorem: The hypothesis that, in the simple Keynesian model, the balanced budget multiplier equals 1.

Bank Act: Federal legislation that governs the chartered banks.

Bank of Canada Act: Federal legislation enacted in 1934 to establish the Bank of Canada.

Bank rate: The rate of interest the central bank charges on loans to members of the Canadian Payments Association.

Banking system: The network of the central bank and chartered banks.

Barriers to entry: Obstacles preventing firms from entering an industry.

Barter: The direct exchange of goods and services for other goods and services (without the use of money).

Base year: A year chosen as a reference point when comparing price level changes from period to period. Current values are expressed as constant values with reference to a base year.

Basic economic problem: The scarcity of resources relative to wants.

Basic sectors of the economy: Household sector, producing sector, and government sector.

Beggar-thy-neighbour policy: A policy of trade protectionism that restricts the flow of imports.

Benefit principle (of taxation): The idea that people should be taxed in proportion to the benefits received from goods and services provided by the government.

Better measure of economic well-being (BMEW): GDP plus non-marketed goods and services plus under-the-table transactions minus environmental damage.

Black market: A market in which goods and services are sold illegally above the legal maximum price.

Bond: A written evidence of debt issued by a borrower, which pays interest to the lender for a specified period and the principal when the loan matures.

Boycott: An effort to persuade consumers not to purchase certain goods and/or services, or not to deal with certain firms.

Branch banking system: A banking system having few banks with many branches.

Break-even level of income: The level of income at which consumption equals income.

Break-even level of output: That output level at which the firm's total cost is equal to its total revenue.

Break-even point: The output level at which total revenue equals total cost; profits are 0.

Budget deficit: The excess of government spending over government revenue.

Budget deficit theory of inflation: Theory that government deficit spending causes inflation.

Budget philosophy: A general view concerning budget policies.

Budget surplus: The excess of government revenue over government spending.

Built-in stabilizers: See automatic fiscal policy.

Business cycles: Alternating periods of ups and downs in economic activity.

Business sector: See firm.

C

Caisse populaire: See credit union.

Canada Deposit Insurance Corporation (CDIC): Government agency that insures deposits in chartered banks, trust companies, and loan companies up to a maximum of $60 000 per depositor.

Canadian International Development Agency (CIDA): Government agency that dispenses foreign aid to less-developed countries.

Canadian Payments Association (CPA): An industry association that facilitates transfers between financial institutions.

Capital: The productive factor defined as all man-made means of production. It includes the stock of machinery, equipment, buildings, etc.

Capital account: The part of the balance of payments that contains long-term and short-term capital flows.

Capital consumption allowance: The allowance made for the depreciation of capital stock during production.

Capital flows: Movement of capital, usually between international economic entities.

Capital-output ratio: The ratio of the value of capital stock to the value of annual output.

Capitalism: An economic system characterized by free enterprise and which emphasizes private ownership of resources.

Cartel: An organization of firms whose objective is to act jointly to control price and output in the market for a particular product.

Cash reserve ratio: The ratio of a bank's cash to its deposits.

Central bank: An institution whose function is to act as banker to the commercial banks and the government, and to ensure the efficient working of the country's monetary system.

Central planning: The mechanism whereby decisions about what to produce, how to produce it, and for whom to produce are made by central authorities in a command economy.

Ceteris paribus: A Latin phrase meaning "other things being equal."

Chartered bank: A financial institution operating under federal charter. It accepts deposits, including those transferable by cheques, and makes loans and investments. Also called commercial bank.

Choice: The need to choose between one thing and another when the means to obtain both is not available.

Circular flow: The flow of income, resources, goods, and services between economic sectors.

Classical economics: The body of pre-Keynesian economic knowledge based on the assumption of flexible wages and prices, and leading to the conclusion of automatic full employment.

Classical range: The vertical range of an AS curve, in which output is at a maximum.

Clearing house system: The mechanism through which the net indebtedness between financial institutions is determined.

Closed economy: An economy that does not engage in foreign trade.

Closed shop: An arrangement in which jobs are given only to union members.

Coefficient of elasticity: The number derived from the calculation of the elasticity measure.

Coincidental indicators: Indicators that coincide exactly with the business cycle.

COLA clause: Cost-of-living-adjustment clause often found in labour agreements.

Collective bargaining: The process by which wages and other working conditions are negotiated between a union and an employer.

Collusion: An agreement among firms not to compete against one another.

Command economy: An economy in which economic decisions are made mainly by central authorities.

Commercial bank: See chartered bank.

Commodities: Goods and services that satisfy wants.

Common market: An arrangement between nations to allow the free movement of goods and factors between them.

Comparative advantage: If a country is more efficient than another country in the production of two commodities, but its efficiency is greater in the production of one commodity, then it has a comparative advantage in the production of that commodity.

Competitive capitalism: The free enterprise economic system.

Complementary goods: Goods that are consumed together. Examples are tennis racquets and tennis balls, and coffee and cream.

Compound tariff: A combination of specific and ad valorem tariffs.

Compulsory arbitration: An arrangement whereby the parties to a dispute are forced to submit their dispute to an arbitrator, whose decision is binding.

Concentration ratio: The proportion of the total market output produced by a few (usually four or eight) of the largest firms in an industry.

Conciliation: The process of submitting a dispute to a mediator for suggestions for settlement.

Constant: Anything that does not vary.

Constant-cost industry: Costs remain unchanged as the industry expands.

Constant prices: Values expressed in terms of the prices existing in a given (base) year.

Constant returns (to scale): A situation in which output increases in proportion to the increase in all inputs.

Consumer durables: Consumer goods intended to last for a long period of time (arbitrarily, more than a year).

Consumer price index (CPI): An index that measures the changes in the prices of consumer goods and services over time.

Consumer sovereignty: The notion that consumers have the power to decide, by their expenditures, what goods and services will be produced.

Consumer surplus: The difference between what consumers would be willing to pay and what they actually pay.

Consumption: The use (or purchase) of consumer goods and services to satisfy wants.

Consumption curve: A curve that illustrates a consumption schedule of current income and consumption.

Consumption function: The functional relation between consumption expenditure and its determinants. Often, a relation between consumption and income.

Consumption schedule: Relates total income and total consumption.

Consumption tax: Taxes on goods and/or services, such as sales tax and excise tax.

Contestable markets: Markets characterized by easy entry.

Contractionary fiscal policy: Any change in government spending and/or taxes designed to reduce total spending.

Cooperative: A special type of corporation in which benefits are distributed according to member patronage. Each member has only one vote, regardless of the number of shares owned.

Corporate income tax: A tax on the profits of corporations.

Corporation: A form of business organization that is a legal entity apart from its owners, and enjoys limited liability.

Correlation: A relationship between variables. Variables are correlated if they change together.

Cost function: The relation between cost and output.

Cost-push inflation: Inflation resulting from increases in wages and the cost of other factor inputs.

Cost-plus (mark-up) pricing: Price equals cost plus a percent mark-up.

Craft union: A union whose membership consists of workers in a single occupation. Also called trade union.

Credit union: A financial institution organized on the principle of the cooperative. Also called a caisse populaire.

Creeping inflation: inflation that creeps at a rate lower than 10%.

Cross elasticity of demand: A measure of the degree of responsiveness of the quantity of a commodity purchased to a change in the price of some other commodity.

Crowding-out effect: The concept that increases in government spending lead to a reduction in private sector spending.

Crown corporation: A corporation owned by the government.

Currency: The notes and coins which serve as a country's medium of exchange.

Current account: The section of the balance of payments that contains exports and imports of goods and services, investment income, and transfers.

Current account balance: Total current receipts from foreigners minus total current payments to foreigners.

Current GDP: Gross domestic product measured in current (as opposed to constant) dollars.

Current income hypothesis: The proposition that consumption depends on current income.

Customs union: An arrangement between nations to eliminate tariffs on goods traded between them, and to maintain a common tariff with the rest of the world.

Cyclical unemployment: Unemployment that results from cyclical fluctuations in economic activity.

D

Debentures: Bonds secured by the credit-worthiness of the borrower rather than by specific assets.

Debit (payment) cards: Similar to a credit card, except the money is transferred from the consumer's bank account to the merchant's account immediately.

Debt capital: Capital (funds) raised by selling bonds or by using bank credit.

Decision lag: The time that elapses from the recognition of a problem to the implementation of a policy to deal with the problem.

Decreasing returns (to scale): A situation in which output increases less than in proportion to the increase in all inputs.

Deficiency payments: A subsidy to farmers given at a certain amount per unit.

Deficit: Occurs when spending exceeds income.

Deficit financing: The methods used to finance a budget deficit.

Definitions: Identify the variables of the model so that measurement can be facilitated.

Deflationary gap: The amount by which aggregate expenditure falls short of aggregate output at full employment. Also called recessionary gap.

Demand: The various quantities of a good or service that people are willing to buy at various prices.

Demand curve: The curve showing the relation between price and quantity demanded.

Demand deposit: A bank deposit that can be withdrawn on demand and is transferable by cheque.

Demand-pull inflation: Inflation resulting from excess aggregate demand. Also called excess demand inflation.

Demand schedule: A table showing the relation between quantity demanded and price.

Demand shifters: Non-price determinants of quantity demanded that cause the demand curve to shift.

Dependent variable: The variable to be explained.

Deposit switching (drawdowns and redeposits): Switching of federal government deposits between the central bank and the chartered banks.

Depreciation (in national income accounting): The wear and tear of the capital stock during production. Also called capital consumption.

Depreciation (of exchange rate): A market-determined decrease in the value of a country's currency in terms of another country's currency.

Depression: A period characterized by low economic activity and high unemployment.

Derived demand: The demand for a productive factor that exists because of the demand for the output produced by the factor.

Devaluation (of exchange rate): The lowering of the value of a country's currency in terms of another country's currency.

Differentiated oligopoly: A market with few firms selling differentiated products.

Differentiated products: Products that are similar in many respects yet sufficiently different that the sellers are able to charge prices different from those charged by their competitors.

Diminishing marginal utility: The decrease in satisfaction experienced as additional units of a commodity are consumed.

Diminishing returns: A situation in which output increases less than the increase in the variable factor when at least one factor remains constant.

Direct demand: The demand for final goods and services as opposed to the demand for inputs.

Direct foreign investment: Investment in a foreign country that involves ownership or control of a firm.

Direct relation: The relation that exists between variables that increase or decrease together.

Dirty float: See managed flexible exchange rate.

Discomfort index: The rate of inflation plus the rate of unemployment.

Discouraged workers: Workers who have given up looking for work because they think there is none.

Discretionary fiscal policy: Deliberate changes in government spending and taxes in an effort to promote economic stability. **Diseconomies of scale:** A situation in which long-run cost rises as output increases.

Disposable income: After-tax income available to households to spend or save or both.

Dissaving: Negative saving. A situation where current consumption exceeds current income.

Dividends: Payments made to shareholders of corporations. The reward for capital.

Division of labour: A situation in which a task is broken up into a number of operations, each of which is performed by a different worker.

Double coincidence of wants: Required for successful bartering: each party wants what the other can provide.

Double counting: Counting an item more than once when calculating the GDP.

Drawdown: See deposit switching.

Dual economy: The coexistence of an advanced sector and an underdeveloped sector in the same economy. Found in many less-developed countries.

Dumping: The act of selling a good in the export market at a price below the domestic price.

Duopoly: An industry consisting of only two firms.

Durable good: A good that is intended to last for a long period of time (arbitrarily, more than a year).

E

EB curve: Curve showing equilibrium in the foreign exchange market.

Econometrics: The branch of economics that uses statistics to test economic theories.

Economic cooperation: An arrangement between two or more countries to reduce certain forms of trade discrimination among them.

Economic discrimination: A situation in which certain groups are treated differently in the labour market.

Economic efficiency: A situation in which the least costly method of production is attained.

Economic efficiency ratio: The value of output divided by the cost of the input.

Economic externality: The social costs or benefits of an economic decision.

Economic forecast: A statement giving specific values predicted for particular variables.

Economic growth: An increase in real per capita output.

Economic integration: An arrangement between two or more countries to abolish certain trade-discriminatory practices among them.

Economic policy: A course of action designed to achieve some economic objective.

Economic prediction: A conditional statement about the general direction of economic events or situations.

Economic profits: The difference between total revenue and the opportunity cost of the factor inputs.

Economic rent: A payment to a factor input in excess of what is required to supply the factor.

Economic system: A set of mechanisms by which a society accomplishes the task of producing goods and services to satisfy its wants.

Economic union: An arrangement between two or more countries to abolish restrictions on the free movement of goods and factor inputs and to harmonize economic policies.

Economies of scale: A situation in which long-run average cost decreases as output increases.

Economies of scope: Cost reduction derived from producing products together rather than producing each separately.

Economy: An entity within which production, consumption, and exchange take place.

Effluent charge (fee): A fee imposed on a producer for polluting the environment.

Elasticity: A measure of the degree of responsiveness of quantity to changes in some variable.

Electronic funds transfer system (EFTS): Transfers funds instantly between bank accounts.

Empirical: Descriptive; as in observed, measured, and recorded.

Endogenous variable: A variable whose value is determined within a model.

Engel's Law: As income rises, the percentage spent on food will diminish.

Entrepreneurship (entrepreneurial services): The services provided by the organizer of land, labour, and capital in the process of production.

Envelope curve: See long-run average cost curve.

Equalization payments: Transfer payments from the federal government to the provinces to reduce economic inequality among the provinces.

Equation of exchange: The quantity of money times the velocity at which it turns over is equal to the quantity of output produced times the average price per unit ($MV = PQ$, where M is the money supply, V is the velocity of circulation, P is price level, and Q is the quantity of output).

Equilibrium: A situation in which change is unlikely to occur. A state of balance.

Equilibrium income: Income is at its equilibrium level when aggregate expenditure equals aggregate output.

Equilibrium price: The price at which quantity demanded equals quantity supplied.

Equilibrium quantity: The quantity traded at the equilibrium price.

Equimarginal principle: Equates marginal values to maximize or minimize a variable.

Equity capital: Funds raised by selling stocks (shares).

Escalator clause: A stipulation in a labour contract that future wages and salaries will be adjusted to reflect changes in the price level.

Ex ante, ex post: Before the fact, after the fact.

Excess capacity theorem: The hypothesis that firms in monopolistic competition will have excess capacity when they are in equilibrium.

Excess demand inflation: See demand-pull inflation.

Excess quantity demanded: The amount by which quantity demanded, at a given price, exceeds quantity supplied at that price. Also called shortage.

Excess quantity supplied: The amount by which quantity supplied, at a given price, exceeds quantity demanded at that price. Also called surplus.

Excess reserves: Any reserves in excess of desired reserves.

Exchange rate: The value of a country's currency in terms of another country's currency.

Excise tax: A tax imposed on a specific commodity.

Exogenous variable: A variable whose value is determined by factors outside the model being considered, but which affects the variables in the model.

Expansion: The phase of the business cycle characterized by an increase in employment, income, and economic activity in general. Also called recovery.

Expansionary fiscal policy: Changes in government spending and taxes designed to increase total spending.

Expectational inflation: Inflation believed to be caused by the behaviour of buyers and sellers responding to expectations of inflation.

Expenditure approach: Measures the total amount spent on the total output.

Explicit costs: Payments to parties that are external to the producer. Examples are wages, rent, and utility bills.

Export subsidies: Assistance offered to exporters by the government to help them compete in world markets.

Exports: Goods and services sold to foreign countries.

External balance: Equilibrium in the foreign exchange market.

External debt: A debt owed to a foreign entity.

Externalities: Costs or benefits that accrue to persons not directly involved in the production or consumption of a commodity.

F

Factor market: A market in which factors of production are sold.

Factors of production: Resources used to produce goods and services.

Fallacy of composition: The assumption that what is true of the part is also true of the whole.

Featherbedding: Providing workers with unnecessary work in order to keep them on the payroll.

Federation (of unions): An association of national unions.

Fiat money: Legal tender money that is not backed by gold or any other precious metal.

Final products: Products intended for final use and not to be subjected to further processing.

Financial market: The market in which funds are lent and borrowed.

Fine tuning: Controlling some of the ups and downs of the economy by minor adjustments in government spending and/or taxes.

Firm: The economic unit within which production takes place. The firm buys inputs and converts them into output.

Fiscal drag: Automatic stabilization that prevents the economy from recovering from a recession.

Fiscal policy: Changes in government spending and taxes designed to promote economic stability.

Fixed costs: Costs that do not vary with the volume of output; they exist even when output is zero.

Fixed exchange rate: An exchange rate that is fixed by the government at some specified level.

Fixed factor: A factor of production whose quantity does not vary with the volume of output.

Flexible exchange rate: An exchange rate determined by market forces.

Flow variables: Income, consumption, and interest earned.

Fractional reserve banking system: A banking system in which banks are required to hold only a fraction of their deposit liabilities as cash reserves.

Franchise: An exclusive right given to a firm to provide a good or service in a certain area.

Free enterprise system: See capitalism.

Free good: A good that is so plentiful that even at a price of zero, the quantity available exceeds the quantity demanded.

Free trade: Trade between countries that is unimpeded by tariffs or other trade restrictions.

Free trade area: An arrangement between two or more countries to eliminate tariffs between them. Each member, however, maintains its own tariffs on goods from non-member countries.

Frictional unemployment: The unemployment of people who are between jobs or are new entrants into the labour market.

Full-employment budget: The position of the budget if the economy were at full employment.

Full-employment surplus: The difference between government revenues and expenditures at the full-employment level of income.

Function: The expression of a relation between two variables.

Functional distribution of income: Income distribution according to the ownership of the factors of production.

Functional finance: Using government spending and taxes as a tool of economic stability.

Functional notation: A mathematical tool that uses functions to show relations between variables.

Functional relationships: Cause-effect relationships among variables.

Fundamental psychological law: People increase consumption as their income increases, but by less than the increase in income.

G

Galloping inflation: Inflation that gallops at a rate between about 10% and 1000%.

GDP per capita: The GDP divided by the population.

General equilibrium analysis: A method of analysis that studies the effects of a variable in different markets.

Generalized multiplier: The multiplier that results from considering all withdrawals. It is the reciprocal of the marginal propensity to withdraw.

Gentlemen's agreement: Informal business agreement, often concluded with a handshake.

Geographical determinism: The theory that comparative advantage is determined by natural endowments.

Gini coefficient: A ratio that measures the degree of inequality in income distribution.

Good: Anything that is tangible and satisfies a want.

Good money: The face value of good money is equal to the value of the commodity it is made from.

Goods and Services Tax (GST): A consumption tax imposed on the final sale of goods and services.

Government sector: [definition to come—two lines left]

Government spending multiplier: The ratio of the change in income to the change in government spending that causes it.

Government transfer payments: Payments that do not represent payments for production.

Graph: A geometric (diagrammatic) representation of information.

Great Depression: A period in the 1930s during which many people were unemployed. Economists had to revise their thinking.

Greenhouse effect: Greenhouse gases maintaining the earth's temperature at comfortable levels.

Green revolution: The tremendous increases in agricultural yields.

Gresham's Law: The proposition that bad money will drive good money out of circulation.

Gross domestic product: The market value of all final goods and services produced within the borders of a country during a period of time.

Gross domestic product (GDP) deflator: The price index used to deflate the gross domestic product (to express current or nominal GDP as real GDP). Also called the implicit price deflator.

Gross investment: The total expenditure on investment goods. The sum of net investment and replacement investment.

Gross national product (GNP): The market value of all final goods and services produced by a country's nationals and their resources during a period of time.

Growth rate: The rate of change of a variable.

H

Homogeneous product: Products that are so similar that no one firm can profitably charge a different price from that charged by other sellers.

Household sector: The unit that makes decisions about the sale of factor services and the purchase of consumer goods and services.

Human capital: The education, training, skills, and health possessed by individuals.

Hyperinflation: An excessively high rate of inflation.

Hypothesis: An expression of the relation among variables.

I

IB curve: Curve showing equilibrium in the domestic economy.

Impact lag: The time required for decisions to take effect.

Imperfect competition: A market structure other than pure or perfect competition, particularly monopolistic competition and oligopoly.

Implementation lag: The time required for decisions to be implemented.

Implicit cost: The opportunity cost of using factors already owned by the producer. Also called imputed cost.

Implicit price deflator: See gross domestic product deflator.

Import quotas: Restrictions on the quantity of a good that may be imported.

Imported inflation: Inflation caused by increases in the prices of imported inputs.

Imports: Goods and services bought from foreign countries.

Imputed cost: See implicit cost.

Incidence of poverty: The probability of being poor.

Incidence of tax: The burden of the tax.

Income approach: Measures the total income of those involved in production.

Income effect: The effect on real income or purchasing power of a change in price.

Income elasticity of demand: A measure of the degree of responsiveness of quantity demanded to changes in income.

Income (output) gap: The difference between full-employment output and actual output.

Income statement: A statement showing revenues and expenses.

Incomes policies: A whole set of policies ranging from wage-price guidelines to wage and price controls designed to curb inflation.

Increasing-cost industry: Costs increase as the industry expands.

Increasing returns (to scale): A situation in which output increases more than in proportion to the increase in all inputs.

Independent good: Goods for which the demands are not related.

Independent variable: The variable that explains the dependent variable.

Index numbers: Numbers that measure changes in variables from one time period to another.

Indexation clause: In a labour contract, adjusts wages as prices rise.

Indirect business taxes: Taxes other than income tax, imposed on businesses, such as property taxes and sales taxes.

Induced investment: Investment that depends on changes in income.

Industrial union: A union whose membership comprises workers in a given industry.

Industry: A group of firms producing similar products.

Industry equilibrium: A situation in which all firms in the industry are in equilibrium. Industry output remains stable.

Inertial inflation: See expectational inflation.

Infant industry argument (for tariffs): The notion that new domestic industries need protection from foreign competition so that they can develop their potential.

Inflation: A sustained increase in the average level of prices over time.

Inflationary gap: The amount by which desired aggregate expenditure exceeds full-employment income or output.

Inheritance (bequest) saving: Saving motivated by the desire to leave an inheritance to children or grandchildren.

Injections: Any income injected into the income-expenditure stream.

Innovation: The introduction of new techniques of production.

Input: Anything used in the process of production.

Institution of private property: The right of individuals to own things.

Interest: The reward for capital; the payment for borrowed money.

Interest rate: The ratio of the interest to the amount borrowed.

Intermediate product: An output of one firm that is to be used as an input of another firm.

Intermediate range: The upward sloping range of an AS curve, in which real output and price level are related.

Internal balance: A situation in which aggregate expenditure equals aggregate output at full employment.

Internal debt: A debt that a nation owes to its citizens.

Internalize: To take a previously external effect into account.

International economy: The economy viewed from a global or international perspective.

International trade: The exchange of goods and services between nations.

International union: A union whose membership consists of local unions in different countries.

Inventories: Stocks of finished and semi-finished goods and raw materials kept by a firm.

Inventory cycles: Economic fluctuations caused by changes in inventory.

Inverse relation: As one variable increases, a related variable decreases.

Investment: Expenditure on capital goods.

Investment function: The relation between investment spending and its determining factors.

Invisible hand: The term given by Adam Smith to the market mechanism.

J

Joint products: Complements in production, produced together. One may be a byproduct of the other.

K

Keynesian cross: The 45-degree diagram showing aggregate expenditure and aggregate output.

Keynesian economics: Economics based on the premise that total output is determined by total spending. The demand side of the economy is emphasized.

Keynesian model: A model of the economy that emphasizes demand-side factors as determinants of output and employment, and the importance of fiscal policy as a means of stimulating the economy.

Keynesian range: The horizontal section of an AS curve that represents high unemployment.

Kinked demand curve: A demand curve with a kink, used to explain price rigidity in oligopoly markets. The upper portion of the curve is relatively flat while the lower portion is relatively steep.

L

Labour force: The number of people employed plus the number unemployed.

Labour: The factor of production defined as human effort.

Labour force participation rate: The labour force as a percentage of the adult population.

Labour market: The market in which labour is traded.

Labour mobility program: Program designed to reduce unemployment by encouraging movement of labour.

Labour union: See union.

Laffer curve: A graph showing that revenues increase as the tax rate rises, but after a while, further increases in the tax rate cause revenues to fall.

Lagging indicators: Indicators that turn downward after the cycle peaks and upward after the trough.

Land: The factor of production defined to include all natural resources.

Law of demand: The hypothesis that the higher the price of a commodity, the smaller the quantity demanded, other things being equal.

Law of diminishing marginal utility: The hypothesis that, as more and more of a commodity is consumed, extra satisfaction diminishes.

Law of diminishing returns: The hypothesis that as increasing quantities of a variable factor are added to a fixed factor, after a point, the increase in the total product will diminish.

Law of supply: The price of a product and the quantity offered for sale are directly related, all other things being equal.

Law of variable proportions: See the law of diminishing returns.

Leading indicators: Indicators that turn downward before the cycle peaks and upward before the trough.

Leakage: See withdrawal.

Legal tender (money): Anything that must, by law, be accepted as payment for goods and services or in settlement of a debt.

Lender of last resort: The central bank's function of advancing loans to financial institutions.

Less-developed country (LDC): A country with a relatively low per capita income.

Liability: Debt. The amount owed to a creditor.

Life-cycle saving: Saving that is motivated by the desire to maintain a certain level of consumption during retirement.

Limit pricing: A strategy of setting price low enough to prevent entry of new firms into the industry. Also called predatory pricing.

Limited liability: Liability limited to the amount of money invested in a business.

Limited partnership: A partnership in which one or more partners have limited liability. There must be at least one partner without limited liability.

Liquidity: The ease with which an asset can be converted into cash without much loss.

Liquidity preference: The total demand for money.

Liquidity preference schedule: A schedule showing the relation between the quantity of money demanded and the rate of interest.

Liquidity trap: A situation in which the liquidity preference curve becomes perfectly flat so that increases in the money supply have no effect on the rate of interest.

Loanable funds theory of interest: The interest rate is determined by the demand for and supply of loanable funds.

Local union: The lowest level of a union, to which a worker belongs directly.

Lockout: A temporary closing of a plant by the employer, in order to win or end a dispute.

Long run: A situation in which the firm is able to vary all its factors of production.

Long-run average cost curve: The curve showing the minimum average cost of producing each level of output in a situation where all inputs are variable.

Long-run supply curve: Curve showing supply conditions after the economy has adjusted to change.

Lorenz curve: A curve showing the degree of inequality that exists in the distribution of income.

Low-income cut-off: See poverty line.

Lump-sum tax: A fixed tax, independent of income level.

M

M1: A measure of the money supply consisting of currency and demand deposits.

M1A: A measure of the money supply consisting of M1 plus daily interest chequable and non-personal notice deposits.

M2: A measure of the money supply consisting of M1A, other notice deposits, and personal term deposits.

M2+: A measure of the money supply consisting of M2, deposits at trust and mortgage loan companies, credit unions and caisses populaires; life insurance company individual annuities; personal deposits at government-owned savings institutions; and money market mutual funds.

M3: A measure of the money supply consisting of M2, other non-personal fixed-term deposits, and foreign currency deposits of residents of Canada.

Macroeconomic policy: Deliberate government action taken to achieve certain economic objectives.

Macroeconomics: The branch of economics that studies the behaviour of aggregate economic variables such as national income, employment, and the price level. Also referred to as income and employment theory.

Managed flexible exchange rate: An exchange rate that is neither fixed nor flexible. Also called dirty float.

Marginal cost: The extra cost incurred in producing an additional unit of output.

Marginal cost pricing: A pricing strategy that involves setting price equal to marginal cost.

Marginal efficiency of investment (MEI) schedule: The schedule showing the relation between the rate of interest and the level of investment.

Marginal (physical) product (MPP or MP): The extra output produced by employing one more unit of a variable factor.

Marginal product (MP): See marginal physical product.

Marginal productivity theory (of wages): The notion that the employment of labour should be carried to the point where the marginal revenue product equals the wage rate.

Marginal propensity to consume (MPC): The change in consumption resulting from a change in income. (MPC = C/Y). Mathematically, it is the slope of the consumption function.

Marginal propensity to save (MPS): The change in saving resulting from a change in income. (MPS = S/Y). Mathematically, it is the slope of the saving function.

Marginal propensity to withdraw (MPW): The change in total withdrawals resulting from a change in income.

Marginal revenue: The extra revenue received from selling an additional unit of output.

Marginal revenue product: The additional revenue contributed by the last unit of a variable factor.

Marginal tax rate: The fraction of extra income that is paid in taxes. (MTR = T/Y).

Marginal utility: The extra satisfaction derived from consuming an additional unit of a commodity.

Market: A point of contact between buyers and sellers.

Market economy: An economy in which the market forces of demand and supply play a prominent role.

Market failure: The inability of the price system to achieve an efficient allocation of resources because of externalities or market imperfections.

Market mechanism: The complicated network of markets and prices found in most western countries.

Market period: A situation in which supply is perfectly inelastic.

Market power: The extent to which a firm or a group of firms can influence the price of a product.

Market quotas: Limits placed upon the amount of a product that producers may market.

Market share: The fraction of the total output of goods accounted for by a firm or a group of firms.

Market size effect: Demand increases when the market size increases.

Market structure: Market features that affect pricing and output decisions: pure competition, monopoly, monopolistic competition, and oligopoly.

Maturity: The date at which a loan becomes due.

Medium of exchange: Anything that is generally accepted as payment for goods and services.

Menu costs: Costs incurred when changing prices, such as updating catalogues and labels.

Merit goods: Goods determined by the government to be good for people, regardless of people's evaluation of these goods.

Microeconomics: The branch of economics that deals with the behaviour of the individual units of the economy, allocation of resources, and price and output determination of individual commodities. Also called price theory.

Minimum efficient scale: The level of output at which economies of scale end and constant returns to scale begin.

Misery index: See discomfort index.

Mixed economy: An economy in which there is a mixture of free enterprise and central decision-making.

Mixed private enterprise economy: A free enterprise economic system with some government intervention.

Model: A simplified version of a more complex system of relationships. See theory.

Monetarism: The school of thought that claims that changes in the money supply are the major cause of economic fluctuations, and that macroeconomic stability can be achieved by a steady increase in the money supply.

Monetary policy: Action taken by the central bank to change the money supply and the rate of interest in order to achieve a high level of employment and relative price stability.

Monetary theory: The study of the demand for and supply of money and their effects on the economy.

Monetary theory of inflation: The proposition that inflation is caused by increases in the money supply.

Money: Anything that is generally accepted as payment for goods and services.

Money (deposit) expansion multiplier (bank multiplier): Reciprocal of the reserve ratio.

Money multiplier: The number that, when multiplied by a change in reserves, gives the potential change in the money supply.

Money supply: The total quantity of money.

Monopolistic competition: A market structure characterized by a large number of firms selling a differentiated product.

Monopolized market: A market in which sellers have significant control over price or output.

Monopoly: A market structure in which there is only one seller of a commodity that has no close substitutes.

Monopoly power: The ability to control price or output, but not both, in an industry.

Moral suasion: An appeal by the central bank for the support of the commercial banks in achieving certain economic objectives.

Multiplier: The ratio of the change in income to the change in autonomous spending which generates the change in income.

Multiplier effect: The result that the ultimate change is greater than the initial change by some multiple.

N

National debt: The amount the government owes its creditors. Also called the public debt.

National energy policy: The federal government's program for energy self-sufficiency.

National income: The total income earned for factor services by the owners of the factors of production.

National income accounting: The process of measuring and recording various economic aggregates which describe the economic health of a country over time.

National union: A national association of local unions, which usually sets policy and does the bargaining for the associated unions.

Natural monopoly: A situation in which one firm can supply the entire market most efficiently.

Natural rate of unemployment: The rate of unemployment that is consistent with price stability.

Near bank: A financial institution such as a credit union, trust company, or mortgage loan company.

Near money: Assets that can be easily converted into the medium of exchange without any appreciable loss of value.

Negative income tax: A system whereby payments are made by the government to persons whose incomes are below the taxable level.

Negative slope: The slope of a declining curve.

Net capital formation (net investment): The difference between total (gross) investment and replacement investment. Net investment increases the capital stock.

Net domestic income at factor cost: The total income earned by the factors of production.

Net income: Revenue minus expenses.

Net investment: The difference between gross investment and depreciation; investment that increases the capital stock.

Net national income at factor cost: The total income earned by a country's factors of production.

Net national product (NNP): Gross national product minus depreciation.

New classical economists: Economists who emphasize rapid macroeconomic adjustment.

New Keynesian economists: Economists who hold that there are factors that prevent the economy from adjusting rapidly to full employment equilibrium.

Nominal income: Income expressed in current dollars.

Non-merchandise transactions (invisibles): Services, investments, and transfers, as noted on the current account.

Normal profit: Income that is just sufficient to make production worthwhile to the entrepreneur.

Normative economics: The study of what the economic situation ought to be.

Normative statement: A statement that expresses what ought to be as opposed to what is.

Notice deposits: Interest-earning deposits subject to notice before withdrawal.

O

Offers to purchase: See price supports.

Official Development Assistance (ODA): Foreign developmental aid channelled through CIDA.

Official reserves: Reserves held by a central bank to make international payments.

Okun's law: The observation that for a given percentage rise in unemployment, output falls by a greater percentage.

Oligopoly: A market structure in which there are only a few sellers. They recognize their interdependence.

Open economy: An economy that engages in international trade.

Open-market operations: The buying and selling of securities (bonds) by the central bank.

Open shop: An arrangement in a work situation whereby union membership is not a prerequisite for employment.

Opportunity cost: The alternative that is sacrificed in order to obtain something else.

Optimal labour force: The labour force that produces maximum real output per worker.

Optimum tariff: The tariff that maximizes the country's welfare.

Optimum tax rate: For a revenue tax, the rate that maximizes tax revenue.

Origin: The intersection of the x-axis and the y-axis, (0,0), on a graph.

Output (income) gap: The potential GDP minus the actual output.

Outputs: The goods and services produced by the factors of production.

Overall balance: This is achieved where the IB and EB curves intersect.

P

Paradox of thrift (saving): The apparent contradiction in the fact that an increase in intended aggregate saving results in a decrease in actual saving.

Paradox of value: The apparent contradiction in the fact that an absolute necessity like water has a lower value than a luxury item such as diamonds. Also called the water-diamond paradox.

Pareto optimality: A situation in which it is impossible to make someone better off without at the same time making someone else worse off. Also called Pareto efficiency.

Partial equilibrium analysis: A method of analysis that studies the behaviour of variables in individual markets in isolation from other markets.

Participation rate: The labour force expressed as a percentage of the adult population.

Partnership: A nonincorporated business formed by two or more partners.

Patent: A legal right given to a producer to produce a good or service and not extended to any other producer for the duration of the patent. It is therefore a barrier to entry.

Payments system: The mechanism by which exchange of goods and services is effected in non-barter situations.

Peak: The phase of the business cycle when economic activity has reached its highest point.

Per capita income: Total income divided by total population.

Perfect competition: A market structure characterized by a large number of firms selling an identical product. None of the firms has the ability to influence the price of the product it sells, and there is freedom of entry and exit. Also called pure competition.

Permanent income hypothesis: The hypothesis that current consumption depends significantly on permanent (average longterm) income.

Personal disposable income: Personal income minus personal taxes and personal transfers to the government.

Personal income: Total income of an individual before personal income taxes are paid.

Personal income tax: Taxes, based on income, paid by individuals to federal and provincial governments.

Personal saving: The part of the disposable income not spent on consumer goods and services.

Phillips curve: The curve showing the trade-off between inflation and unemployment.

Political business cycle: Economic fluctuations caused by government spending policies timed to create a favourable economic climate prior to an election.

Population explosion: Rapid population growth.

Portfolio investment: The purchase of securities whose term to maturity is more than one year.

Positive economics: The descriptive study of the behaviour of economic units and the operation of the economic system.

Positive slope: The slope of a rising curve.

Positive statement: A statement about what is. It can be verified by looking at the facts.

Post hoc, ergo propter hoc fallacy: The common error in thinking that A causes B just because A precedes B.

Potential gross domestic product: The level of gross domestic product that an economy could produce if full employment existed. Also called full-employment income or full-employment gross domestic product.

Poverty line: The level of income below which a family is considered to be poor.

Precautionary demand for money: The desire to hold money for unexpected contingencies.

Precautionary saving motive: The notion that people save in order to provide for illness and emergencies.

Predatory pricing: See limit pricing.

Price: Value expressed in terms of money. The amount of money paid for a unit of a commodity.

Price ceiling: A maximum price at which a commodity may be sold.

Price discrimination: The sale of a commodity at different prices to different customers for reasons unrelated to cost differentials.

Price elasticity of demand: The percentage change in quantity demanded as a result of a small change in price.

Price elasticity of supply: The percentage change in quantity supplied as a result of a small change in price.

Price floor: A minimum price at which a commodity may be sold.

Price indexes: Numbers that show changes in prices over a period of time.

Price leadership: A situation in which one firm (the leader) sets the price, and the other firms (the followers) simply follow.

Price level: The average level of prices as measured by an appropriate price index.

Price line: See budget line.

Price supports: A system established by government to prevent the prices of certain farm products from falling below a certain level.

Price system: A system of markets and prices that determines what to produce, how to produce, and for whom to produce.

Price taker: A firm that cannot, by itself, affect the market price of its product by varying its production. A firm in pure competition is a price taker.

Price theory: See microeconomics.

Primary reserves: Cash reserves held by banks.

Prime (lending) rate: The rate of interest that banks charge their most credit-worthy customers.

Principal: The amount lent (or borrowed) upon which interest is normally paid.

Principle of substitution: The hypothesis that a firm will use less of a more-expensive factor and more of a less-expensive factor.

Private costs: Costs that are borne solely by the individuals or firms making the decision.

Private debt: A debt owed by households or firms to other households or firms.

Private sector: The household sector and the private business sector. The non-public sector.

Private transfer payments: Payments by individuals and firms that do not represent payments for production.

Producer: See firm.

Producer sovereignty: The concept that producers decide what to produce and then convince consumers to buy it.

Product differentiation: A situation in which the firms in an industry sell similar but not identical products.

Product market: A market in which firms sell their products.

Production: The process of converting or transforming inputs into outputs.

Production function: The relation between a firm's inputs and its output.

Production possibility curve: A curve showing the various combinations of commodities that can be produced if all resources are fully employed and technology is constant.

Production possibility point: A combination of goods or services that an economy can produce.

Production possibility schedule: A table showing the different combinations of goods that an economy can produce if it uses all its resources.

Profit: The difference between total revenue and total cost. The reward for risk taking.

Progressive tax system: A system in which the tax rate increases as income increases.

Property tax: A tax levied on property, usually on real estate.

Proportional tax system: A system in which the tax rate remains constant as income increases.

Protective tariff: A tariff whose main objective is to protect domestic producers.

Psychic income: Non-monetary rewards, such as satisfaction, derived from a job.

Public debt: See national debt.

Public finance: The study of the microeconomic aspects of government spending and taxing.

Public good: A good or service for which the consumption by one person does not diminish the amount available to others. Once the good or service is produced, it is often impossible to prevent anyone from consuming it. An example is national defence.

Public investment: The purchase of new capital or the production of capital goods by the government.

Public sector: The sector of the economy where production decisions are made by government or government agencies. Also called the government sector.

Pure competition: See perfect competition.

Pure economic rent: The income earned from a factor of production whose supply is completely price inelastic.

Q

Quality competition: Competition by a firm attempting to make its products superior to the competitors'.

Quantity demanded: The amount of a commodity that households are willing to buy at some given price.

Quantity supplied: The amount of a commodity that firms are willing to sell at some given price.

Quantity theory of money: The theory that states that the money supply is directly proportional to the price level. A modified version states that the money supply is directly proportional to nominal income.

Quasi rent: The income from a factor whose supply is fixed only in the short run.

R

Rand Formula: Legislation that made it compulsory for a worker to pay union dues even if not a union member.

Rational expectations: The theory that people are aware of all the factors that determine a given event and that they base their expectations on this knowledge.

Real business cycle: The theory that the main causes of business cycles are shifts in the aggregate supply curve.

Real capital: Capital items such as buildings, tools, and equipment.

Real gross domestic product: Gross domestic product adjusted for price level changes.

Real income (constant prices): Income expressed in constant dollars.

Real output per capita: Real GDP divided by the population.

Real rate of interest: The rate of interest adjusted for inflation.

Recession: A phase of the business cycle characterized by a general downswing in economic activity.

Recessionary gap: See deflationary gap.

Recognition lag: The time required to recognize a problem.

Recovery: See expansion.

Redeposit: See deposit switching.

Regional specialization: A situation in which different' regions of a country concentrate on the economic activity in which they have an advantage.

Regressive tax system: A system in which the tax rate decreases as income increases.

Regulated monopoly: Monopolies controlled by government legislation.

Relative price: The ratio of two absolute prices. The price of one good expressed in terms of the price of another good.

Rent: Payment for the services of land.

Reservation price: The lowest price a seller is willing to accept for a good or service.

Reserve requirement: The amount the commercial banks were legally obliged to keep in cash or as deposits at the central bank. No longer in effect.

Resources: See factors of production.

Retained earnings: Profits of a firm that are not distributed to shareholders. Also called undistributed profits.

Revaluation (of exchange rates): The raising of the value of a country's currency in terms of another country's currency.

Revenue tariff: A tariff with the main objective of raising revenue for the government.

Risk premium: An extra charge that reflects the degree of risk involved in a transaction.

Robin Hood effect: The redistribution of income from high-income earners to low-income earners, thereby increasing consumer spending.

Rule of 70: A formula that allows quick calculation of the time required for the price level to double, given the rate of inflation. The time required is 70 divided by the rate of inflation.

S

Sales tax: A percentage tax imposed on the selling price of a wide range of commodities.

Saving: That part of disposable income that is not spent on consumer goods and services.

Say's Law: The proposition that the very act of production indicates the presence of an equivalent demand: that is, supply creates its own demand.

Scarcity: Limited resources in the face of unlimited wants.

Schedule A banks: Canadian-owned banks.

Schedule B banks: Foreign-owned banks.

Scientific method: A method of inquiry stressing the formulation and testing of hypotheses.

Seasonal unemployment: Unemployment caused by seasonal variations.

Secondary reserves: Excess cash reserves, treasury bills, and day-to-day loans held by banks.

Selective controls: Controls that affect certain industries or sectors of the economy, but not the whole economy directly.

Sellers' inflation: Inflation caused by price increases by firms due to increases in production costs. See cost-push inflation.

Services: Intangible things that satisfy a want. Examples are banking services and transportation services.

Short run: A situation in which the firm is unable to vary all its inputs.

Short-run shutdown point: The price-output combination at which price just equals average variable cost.

Short-run supply curve: That portion of the MC curve that lies above the AVC curve.

Short-term capital flows: Movements of financial assets whose term to maturity is less than one year.

Shortage (excess quantity demanded): Quantity demanded exceeds quantity supplied at a given price.

Single proprietorship: A form of business organization in which there is a single owner who is responsible for all actions taken by the firm. A single proprietor does not enjoy limited liability.

Size distribution of income: The distribution of income according to households in various income groups.

Slope of a linear curve: The slope is constant.

Slope of a non-linear curve: The slope at any point on the curve is the tangent to that point; the slope varies from point to point on the curve.

Social cost: The total cost to society as a whole of decisions made, and actions taken, by individuals and firms.

Social science: The study of aspects of behaviour of human society.

Socialism: The state owns and controls the economy's resources.

Socialistic system: See command economy.

Sole proprietorship: See single proprietorship.

Specialization: Concentration on a particular occupation or task to become proficient at that task.

Specific tariff: A tariff expressed as a certain amount per unit of the imported item.

Speculative demand for money: The desire to hold money in anticipation of the movement of the prices of financial assets.

Stabilization policies: Actions taken to promote economic stability.

Stagflation: The simultaneous occurrence of high rates of inflation and high rates of unemployment.

Stock variable: The amount existing at a point in time.

Stocks (shares): Evidence of ownership in a company.

Store of value: Money or other valuables put away for future use.

Strike: Work stoppage by a union in an attempt to put pressure on the employer.

Structural unemployment: Unemployment that results when workers do not possess the skills required for various job opportunities.

Substitutes: Goods that can be used in place of other goods. Examples are tea and coffee, pens and pencils.

Substitution effect: The effect on the demand for a product when the price of a substitute changes.

Supply: The various quantities of a commodity that will be offered for sale at various possible prices.

Supply curve: The curve showing the relation between price and quantity supplied.

Supply schedule: A table showing the relation between price and quantity supplied.

Supply shifters: Factors that cause the supply curve to shift.

Supply side: the production side of the economy.

Supply-side economics: An approach to economics that stresses supply factors such as incentives to work, save, and invest.

Surplus: See excess quantity supplied.

T

Target saving: Saving for a specific purpose, such as the purchase of a car or house.

Tariff: A tax imposed on imported goods.

Tariff evasion: Avoiding tariffs by rerouting goods through other countries.

Tax: A compulsory payment imposed by a government.

Tax-based incomes policies (TIPS): The use of tax incentives to encourage compliance with wage and price controls.

Taxable income: The portion of income on which income tax payable is calculated.

Technological efficiency: Efficiency measured in terms of the use of inputs in physical terms. Also called technical efficiency.

Technological unemployment: A type of structural employment caused by the introduction of labour-saving equipment or methods.

Terms of trade: The rate at which a country's exports exchange for its imports.

Theory: A testable hypothesis about the way in which variables are related.

Total cost (TC): The sum of all costs incurred in producing a given output of goods or services. The sum of total fixed cost and total variable cost.

Total product (TP): The total output of goods and services produced during a period of time.

Total revenue (TR): The total amount received from the sale of goods and services. It equals the product of price and quantity sold.

Total utility: The total satisfaction derived from consuming a commodity.

Trade creation: A situation in which economic integration leads to a change in the direction of trade from a higher cost supplier to a lower cost supplier.

Trade deficit: See balance of trade deficit.

Trade diversion: A situation in which economic integration leads to a change in the direction of trade from a lower cost supplier to a higher cost supplier.

Trade surplus: See balance of trade surplus.

Trade union: See craft union.

Transactions demand for money: The desire to hold money for transactions purposes.

Transfer earnings: The minimum payment required to attract resources away from other uses.

Transfer payments (transfers): Payments that do not represent a reward for productive services.

Treasury bill (T-bill): A security sold by the government with a promise to pay a certain amount within a short time, usually from 30 to 90 days.

Trough: The phase of the business cycle when economic activity is at its lowest level for that cycle.

20% Club: organizations which aim to reduce local greenhouse gas emissions by 20% from 1990 levels.

U

Underground economy: Includes all economic activities and transactions that are not recorded by national income statisticians and on which no taxes are paid.

Undistributed profits: See retained earnings.

Unemployment: A situation in which people are unable to find jobs.

Unemployment rate: The number of people unemployed expressed as a percentage of the labour force.

Union: An association of workers organized to negotiate the terms and conditions of their employment with their employer.

Union shop: An arrangement whereby workers who are not union members may be hired provided that they become union members within a specified period of time.

Unit banking system: A banking system with many independent banks.

Unit of account (measure of value): The unit for expressing the value of goods and services; in Canada, the dollar is the usual unit of account.

Util: The unit of satisfaction derived from consuming goods and services.

Utility: Satisfaction derived from consuming goods and services.

V

Value-added: The difference between the value of a firm's output and the value of its inputs purchased from other firms.

Variable: Anything that can assume different values.

Variable cost: Any cost that varies with the level of output.

Variable factor: Any factor whose quantity can be varied in the short run.

Velocity of circulation (of money): The number of times, on average, that a unit of money is spent during a period of time.

Very short period (market period): A situation in which sellers are unable to vary their output.

Voluntary arbitration: Each party in a labour dispute submits its case to an arbitrator and agrees to abide by the decision.

Voluntary restrictions: One government may ask another to restrict its exports to that country.

W

Wage and price controls (incomes policies): Imposed by the government to limit increases in both wages and prices.

Wage-price spiral: Increases in wages followed by increases in prices followed by increases in wages and so on.

Wage rate: The price of labour per unit of time.

Wage transfer mechanism: The process by which wage changes in one industry are transmitted to other industries.

Wages: Payment for labour services.

Wagner's Law: The statement that government spending will grow at a faster rate than the rate of increase in output.

Water-diamond paradox: See paradox of value.

Water pollution: Toxic waste, chemical spills, chemical production, municipal waste and acid rain.

Wealth: The value of one's assets.

Wholesale price index: A price index that measures price changes in primary goods.

Withdrawal: Any income taken out of the income-expenditure stream, including savings, taxes, and imports.

Workable competition: Under workable competition, an industry is competitive enough to maintain output and keep profits at reasonable levels.

X

X-inefficiency: Failure to use resources in a manner that results in the lowest cost of producing any given level of output.

INDEX